Everything used in this book
is from public sources.
The stuff that's available publicly
is far more frightening
than a lot of people realize.

TOM CLANCY

McWilliams marshals a vast army of anecdotes, quotes, statistics and assertions to argue that America would be a lot better off if we stopped using the force of law to save each other from drugs, alcohol, gambling, pornography, suicide and sex in its more exotic flavors.

Peter McWilliams has come up with a "reinvention" of government that would bring us closer to the ideals of the Founding Fathers, increase our personal liberties and save an impressive amount of money in the process.

There's a huge difference between crime and sin—and the government has no business making the former out of the latter. At least, not in America.

It might inspire a song if I can match your mix of humor and seriousness. Brilliant!

The forces arrayed against McWilliams are many and powerful, from the legions of the religious right to the political establishment. McWilliams' book brims with facts delivered with a gentle sense of humor and spiced with pithy quotations from sources as diverse as Thomas Jefferson and Joni Mitchell.

Here is a controversial book that contains so much logical thought, it is destined to be roundly ignored by policy makers.

Just as bootleggers were forced out of business in 1933 when Prohibition was repealed, making the sale of liquor legal (thus eliminating racketeering), the legalization of drugs would put drug dealers out of business. It would also guarantee government-approved quality, and the tax on drugs would provide an ongoing source of revenue for drug-education programs. An added plus: there would be far less crowding in our prisons due to drug-related crimes. It's something to consider.

Abigail Van Buren

Recently there crossed my desk (delicate way of saying "free") a book sufficiently intriguing that, breaking the habits of a lifetime, I bought another copy. The book is *Ain't Nobody's Business If You Do* by Peter McWilliams.

Newhouse News Service

Don't miss the point: In our "free country" over 750,000 people are now in jail for consensual crimes. You should also know that another 2 million are now on parole or probation; over 4 million more will be arrested this year; we will spend $50 billion this year punishing people who have been convicted of consensual crimes; and we will lose $150 billion this year in tax revenue. It's your money. You're paying for it.

Phil Donahue

If you want to stop this madness, you may want to begin by reading Peter McWilliams' book. A highly readable and entertaining work, *"Ain't Nobody's Business If You Do."*

Hugh Downs

Why don't we reconsider the criminalization of consensual activities by adults? Why is the option considered so far beyond the pale that hundreds of timid elected officials who know all this and privately agree are convinced that to question consensual crimes is political suicide?

Orange County Register

Using his trademark clear logic and simple language, McWilliams points out that freeing the police, courts and prisons from prosecuting consensual criminals will make available whole armies of fighters against consumer fraud, terrorism, murder and rape.

Dayton Ohio News

What's the difference between a crime that hurts a fellow citizen and a crime that only hurts the fool who commits it? All the difference in the world, according to Peter McWilliams.

Rocky Mountain News

In witty, well-researched pages, McWilliams gives a series of compelling arguments to back up his contention that it's morally wrong to prosecute people for victimless crimes against morality.

Detroit News

One more reason to buy this book is for the boxed quotes on almost every page. One of the greatest collections of funny, hilarious, unusual and trenchant remarks ever.

Liz Smith

So you have your rapist, your strong-arm robber, your mugger being released early to make room for somebody who took money for sex or smoked dope in what he thought was private, but turned out to be not quite. That doesn't look like much of a trade from here. However much you're repelled by, say, prostitution, wouldn't you rather meet a hooker than a mugger coming down an alley?

Reno Gazette–Journal

McWilliams is a *New York Times* best-selling author. Since 1967, he has published more than 30 books. He is a man well acquainted with controversy and shows no fear in rushing in where angels fear to tread. Well-written and fabulously interesting.

Tulsa World

McWilliams makes a strong argument for the elimination of such crimes, providing a history of consensual crimes and their absurdity. The blend of first-person observation, research, and argument makes for a fine and revealing title.

Bookwatch

I don't expect anyone to agree with all of McWilliams' assertions. Even he admits that. But there is one point you should not overlook. What starts with control of narcotics and sexual activity can spread wherever a majority (or powerful minority), often powered by religious zeal, decide it knows what's best for you.

Philadelphia News Gleaner

How truly revolutionary, libertarian, frightening and funny this book is. Grand in scope and scale. The book is interesting and meticulously researched.

Little Rock Free Press

Peter McWilliams has written a book for our times—the quintessential book on the subject of consensual crimes. With public sympathy geared toward harsher sentences for those who commit felonies, McWilliams demonstrates the absurdity of prosecuting those guilty of "victimless" crimes.

Newport News Press

Imposing criminal sanctions on human conduct which is wholly consensual and does not harm another person or his or her property is a misplaced and counterproductive act . . . we violate the premise upon which America was founded.

New Orleans Times—Picayune

Ain't Nobody's Business If You Do **was nominated for the H. L. Mencken Award.**

There is no need to read this entire book.

> *While this book is relatively heavy to lift, it isn't heavy reading. It's broken into dozens of short chapters and is more suited to browsing than to reading cover-to-cover.*
>
> —*Seattle Times*

This book is about a single idea—consenting adults should not be put in jail unless they physically harm the person or property of a nonconsenting other.

This idea is explored in the chapter "An Overview," which begins on page 3. After reading "An Overview," please feel free to skip around, reading what you find interesting, ignoring what you don't. It is my fond hope, of course, that you will eventually find your way to Part V, "What to Do?"

If nothing else, the boxed quotes on each page (the part of the book written by other people) are worth turning the page for. (By the way, the most controversial quote—but an absolutely accurate one—is found in the box on page 9.)

Thank you for reading.

Peter McWilliams

*I never hurt nobody but myself
and that's nobody business
but by own.*

BILLIE HOLIDAY

CONTENTS

CONTENTS

CONTENTS

CONTENTS

CONTENTS

Your book is dedicated
by the soundest reason.
You had better get out of France
as quickly as you can.

VOLTAIRE
1758

This book is dedicated
with deep appreciation

to

Steven, Jadwiga, Emily, and Thomas (aka Sushi) Markoff

and

Michael, Maryanne, Danielle, and Rebecca Hesse

Thank you

It rankles me when somebody
tries to force somebody
to do something.

JOHN WAYNE

Ain't Nobody's Business If You Do

The Absurdity of Consensual Crimes in Our Free Country

Peter McWilliams

Prelude Press
8159 Santa Monica Boulevard
Los Angeles, California 90046
1-800-LIFE-101

The complete texts of this book and other books by Peter McWilliams are available for free browsing, downloading, or burning on the Internet.
http://www.mcwilliams.com

ISBN: 0-931580-58-7

Editor: Jean Sedillos
Research: Chris GeRue
Chart design: Scott Ford, David Goldman
Desktop publishing: Jean Bolt

*Perhaps the sentiments
contained in the following pages,
are not yet sufficiently fashionable
to procure them general favor;
a long habit of
not thinking a thing wrong,
gives it a superficial appearance
of being right,
and raises at first
a formidable outcry
in defence of custom.
But the tumult soon subsides.*

THOMAS PAINE

Common Sense

January 1776

Author's Notes

> *Nobody can be*
> *so amusingly arrogant*
> *as a young man*
> *who has just discovered*
> *an old idea*
> *and thinks it is his own.*
>
> SYDNEY J. HARRIS

I'VE BEEN WAITING YEARS for someone to write this book. If someone had, I wouldn't have had to.

I have simply never understood why people should be jailed for actions that do not physically harm the person or property of others.

I have thus always been distinctly in the minority. People I admired and people I abhorred all seemed to agree: on this point I was wrong. I filed my conviction away under "something I'll understand when I'm older." Now I am older. It makes even less sense than it ever did.

From the mid-sixties to the early eighties, although the subject of consensual crimes (mostly referred to as "victimless crimes") was occasionally discussed and a number of scholarly tomes were published (some of them quite good), a comprehensive view of the subject for "just folks" like me never appeared.

Once the "War on Drugs" was declared, however, all discussion stopped. One might as well have tried saying something good about Emperor Hirohito in 1942. ("Nice uniform!")

The image that outraged me into putting my childish notion on the front burner was the cover of a news magazine from the mid-1980s. Workers in a cocaine field were piled like firewood, their white peasant clothing red with blood. They had been gunned down in cold blood by American troops. The workers didn't own the field—they were brought in for the harvest, paid subsistence wages.

But was this cover an exposé on the dangers of prohibition? A warning about what happens when rhetoric and prejudice be-

> I haven't voted since 1964,
> when I voted for Lyndon Johnson,
> the peace candidate.
>
> GORE VIDAL

come more important in setting national policy than logic and reason? A bold illustration of why "military solution" is the most destructive oxymoron of all?

No. The headline blared: WINNING THE WAR ON DRUGS. Inside, the war on drugs was touted as though the magazine were covering the landing at Normandy. Page after page, article after article, arrest photo after arrest photo, diagrams, maps, bar graphs, pie charts—today they probably would have included a CD-ROM.

Like the one-sided reports about Vietnam two decades before, in this editorial orgy of support, not one word was written to defend the rights of those who wanted to take drugs. Not one voice was quoted crying in the wilderness, "So they want to take drugs. So what?"

I began researching the topic of this book, hoping desperately it had already been written. (Spending several weeks reading Supreme Court decisions is not my idea of a good time. And then there are those brilliantly written government reports— books, actually—with names such as *Federal Recidivism Rates 1989–1990* or my bedtime favorite, *Statistical Abstract of the United States, 1994.*) Alas, I couldn't find a book such as the one you hold in your hands, so I had to write it.

I explored every argument I could find opposing the legalization of consensual crimes. Not one of them held up to logical analysis; not one was supported by history; every solution was worse than the "problem" it was trying to solve.

Then came the dark part of the research—the terrible fact that laws against consensual activities were destroying lives, our society, our freedom, our safety, and our country.

The more I discovered, the more I was reminded of Rémy de Gourmont's comment, "The terrible thing about the quest for truth is that you find it."

I hope this new edition of the book causes the sort of controversy caused by asking in 1773, "Why don't we break from England and start our own country?" or, in 1833, "Aren't slaves human beings and therefore entitled to their freedom?" or in 1963, "Shouldn't Vietnam have the right to determine its own form of government?"

> *Ye shall know the truth,*
> *and the truth*
> *shall make you mad.*
>
> ALDOUS HUXLEY

It's all a variation of "Why isn't the emperor wearing any clothes?"

As Bertrand Russell observed, "*Change* is scientific, *progress* is ethical; change is indubitable, whereas progress is a matter of controversy." Throughout the controversy caused by the hardcover edition, I was buoyed by this from Herb Lock: "You say what you think needs to be said; if it needs to be said, there are going to be a lot of people who will disagree with it or it wouldn't need to be said."

⚖️ ⚖️ ⚖️

One of the fears about discussing consensual activities is that if you defend a certain practice, you're often accused of being or doing that. Well, if you're wondering about me, why not assume that I do it all? Yes, you can safely presume that I am a drug-selling homosexual prostitute gambler who drunkenly loiters all day with my six wives and fourteen husbands, making and watching pornography while being treated by strange medical practices.

You can also assume my motives to be the darkest, most selfish, and pernicious you can imagine: I'm doing it for the money; I have a pathological need for attention; my mother didn't love me enough when I was three. No matter how many times I say that I'm not advocating any of the consensual crimes,

> *Until you've lost your reputation, you never realize what a burden it was or what freedom really is.*
>
> MARGARET MITCHELL

someone will, of course, accuse me of "recruiting" for them all.*

Although the subject is serious, this book is occasionally funny. I know if I lose my sense of humor about a subject, I am truly lost.

Call it a quirk in my personality, call it a defense mechanism, but in my mind things go from bad to worse to appalling to absurd to funny. Then they start all over again. This, for example, from the *1993 World Almanac and Book of Facts:*

> Dorothy Ries filed a $40 million lawsuit against Texas evangelist Robert Tilton, saying he continues to send solicitation letters to her dead husband, promising that God will restore his health.

Or take the Reverend Jimmy Swaggart.** Every time he slammed his Bible on the pulpit, I knew a thousand more consensual "criminals" were going to prison. When he was caught with a prostitute, he insisted it was the devil's work and asked his congregation to forgive him. Pretty standard Christian-hand-in-the-cookie-jar response. Not very funny. When he was caught a *second* time, however, he told his congregation, "The Lord told me it's flat none of your business!" Amen, Brother Swaggart! I look forward to the day when I can be similarly amused by Pat Robertson and Jerry Falwell.

If one could only remind Reverend Swaggart of Hyman Rickover's advice, "If you are going to sin, sin against God, not the

---

*It's a classic example of projection: the religions that believe most in vigorous proselytizing are the same ones that accuse others of recruiting. What they call "witnessing" and "testifying" becomes "recruitment" and "brainwashing" when used by others.

**As Henny Youngman might add, "Please!"

bureaucracy. God will forgive you but the bureauc-
racy won't."

That's the trouble, of
course: we have taken sins
out of God's domain,
where they can be forgiven,
and put them in the do-
main of law, where they
can only be plea-bargained.

Not only do we attempt
to drag personal morality

> *When we start
> deceiving ourselves into thinking
> not that we want something
> or need something,
> not that it is a pragmatic
> necessity for us to have it,
> but that it is a <u>moral imperative</u>
> that we have it,
> then is when we join
> the fashionable madmen.*
>
> JOAN DIDION

into the public arena; we put it into the hands of the least
efficient organization on earth: government bureaucracy. "The
only thing that saves us from the bureaucracy is inefficiency,"
Eugene McCarthy pointed out, "An efficient bureaucracy is the
greatest threat to liberty."

How inefficient is the bureaucracy? Well, in sunny California
the government spent four years and $600,000 to produce
twenty-five drafts of a "wellness guide." Some bureaucratic suggestions for wellness? "Don't buy something you can't afford"
and "Don't beat, starve, or lock up your kids." Or this letter, sent
from the South Carolina Department of Social Services:

> Your food stamps will be stopped effective March, 1992,
> because we received notice that you passed away. May
> God bless you. You may reapply if there is a change in
> your circumstances.

Increasingly, in utter desperation of a war lost, the enforcement of laws against consensual activities is being turned over to
the military. You may recall then–Air Force Chief of Staff Curtis
LeMay's 1965 comment:

> My solution to the problem would be to tell [the North
> Vietnamese] they've got to draw in their horns and stop
> their aggression or we're going to bomb them into the
> Stone Age.

The problem with declaring war on personal behavior that
does not harm the person or property of another is that the

> *I don't make jokes—*
> *I just watch the government*
> *and report the facts.*
>
> WILL ROGERS

military is not just a bureaucracy; it's a *heavily armed* bureaucracy. The lighter side of the dilemma is illustrated by this news item:

When the army tested a new air-defense gun called the Sergeant York, which was designed to home in on the whirling blades of helicopters and propeller-driven aircraft, it ignored the chopper targets. Instead, the weapon demolished a ventilating fan on a nearby latrine.

In war, the first fatality is the truth. The second and parallel fatality is the civil rights of all "dissidents." How much farther can my jaw drop than it did as I listened to then–Los Angeles Police Chief Daryl Gates testify before Congress that casual drug users should not be arrested, but *taken out and shot?* His reasoning? The country is at war, and all who use drugs are traitors. A good number of people agreed with Chief Gates.

The price of freedom is eternal—and internal—vigilance.

And an occasional laugh.

Peter McWilliams

Ain't Nobody's Business
If You Do

PART I

THE BASIC PREMISE

An Overview

> *Why doesn't everybody
> leave everybody else
> the hell alone?*
>
> JIMMY DURANTE

THIS BOOK IS BASED on a single idea: *You should be allowed to do whatever you want with your own person and property, as long as you don't physically harm the person or property of a nonconsenting other.*

Simple. Seemingly guaranteed to us by that remarkable document known as the United States Constitution and its even more remarkable Bill of Rights. And yet, it's not the way things are.

Roughly half of the arrests and court cases in the United States each year involve consensual crimes—actions that are against the law, but directly harm no one's person or property except, possibly, the "criminal's."

More than 750,000 people are in jail *right now* because of something they did, something that did not physically harm the person or property of another. In addition, more than 3,000,000 people are on parole or probation for consensual crimes. Further, more than 4,000,000 people are arrested each year for doing something that hurts no one but, potentially, themselves.

The injustice doesn't end there, of course. Throwing people in jail is the extreme. If you can throw people in jail for something, you can fire them for the same reason. You can evict them from their apartments. You can deny them credit. You can expel them from schools. You can strip away their civil rights, confiscate their property, and destroy their lives—just because they're different.

At what point does behavior become so unacceptable that we should tell our government to lock people up? The answer, as

> *No loss by flood and lightning,*
> *no destruction of cities and temples*
> *by hostile forces of nature,*
> *has deprived man*
> *of so many noble lives and impulses*
> *as those which his intolerance*
> *has destroyed.*
>
> HELEN KELLER

explored in this book: We lock people up only when they physically harm the person or property of a nonconsenting other.

Contained in this answer is an important assumption: after a certain age, our persons and property belong to us.

Yes, if we harm ourselves it may *emotionally* harm others. That's unfortunate, but not grounds for putting us in jail. If it were, every time we stopped dating person A in order to date person B, we would run the risk of going to jail for hurting person A. If person B were hurt by our being put in jail, person A could be put in jail for hurting person B. This would, of course, hurt person A's mother, who would see to it that person B would go to jail. Eventually, we'd all be in jail.

As silly as that situation sounds, it is precisely the logic used by some to protect the idea of consensual crimes.

Arguments in favor of laws against any consensual activity are usually variations of "It's not *moral!*" And where does the objector's sense of morality come from? For the most part, his or her religion. Some claim "cultural values" as the basis of morality, but where does this set of cultural values come from? The sharing of a similar religion.*

To a large degree, we have created a legal system that is, to quote Alan Watts, "clergymen with billy clubs."** Says Watts:

> The police have enough work to keep them busy regulating automobile traffic, preventing robberies and crimes of violence and helping lost children and little old ladies

*Laws that are primarily based on the rules of society and not the rules of religion are discussed in the chapter, "Separation of Society and State."

**Watts was British. In the United States, it is clergymen with .38 caliber revolvers, magnums, machine guns, helicopters, and tanks.

find their way home. As long as the police confine themselves to such activities they are respected friends of the public. But as soon as they begin inquiring into people's private morals, they become nothing more than armed clergymen.

> *That which we call sin in others is experiment for us.*
>
> RALPH WALDO EMERSON

Please don't think I'm against religion. I'm not. *Individual* morality based on religious or spiritual beliefs can be invaluable. It can be an excellent guide for *one's own life*. But religious belief—especially someone else's—is a terrible foundation for deciding who does and does not go to jail.

If people physically harm someone else's person or property, they go to jail. If not, they don't. Every other behavior we would like them to follow (for their own good or our own comfort) must be achieved through education or persuasion—not force of law.

In exchange for extending this tolerance to others, we know that unless we physically harm another's person or property, we will not be put in jail. This assurance gives us the boundaries within which we can live our lives. It allows us to explore, to take risks, and—as long as we risk only our own person and property—we know that at least one risk we won't be taking is the risk of being thrown in jail.

With such freedom, of course, comes responsibility. As we take risks, bad things will occasionally happen—that's why they're called risks. At that point, we must learn to shrug and say, "That's life," not, "Why isn't there a law against this? Why isn't the government protecting me from every possible negative occurrence I might get myself into?" When we, as adults, consent to do something—unless we are deceived—we become responsible for the outcome.

> *It has been my experience that folks who have no vices have very few virtues.*
>
> ABRAHAM LINCOLN

We must become involved, educated, aware consumers—and teach our children to be the same. Just because some activity is available, and just because we won't be thrown in jail for doing it, doesn't mean it is necessarily harmless.

If it's not the government's job to protect us from our own actions (and whoever said the government is equipped to do so when the government can't seem to buy a toilet seat for less than $600?), then the job returns to where it always has been: with us.

Consensual crimes are sometimes known as *victimless crimes* because it's hard to find a clear-cut victim. The term *victimless crimes,* however, has been so thoroughly misused in recent years that it has become almost meaningless. One criminal after another has claimed that his or hers was a victimless crime, while one self-appointed moralist after another has claimed that truly victimless crimes do, indeed, have victims. It seems easier to use the lesser-known phrase *consensual crimes* than to rehabilitate the better-known phrase *victimless crimes.*

Please keep in mind that I am not advocating any of the consensual crimes. Some of them are harmful to the person doing them. Others are only potentially harmful to the doer. Still others are genetic orientations, while others are simply lifestyle choices.

No matter how harmful doing them may be to the doer, however, it makes no sense to put people in jail for doing things that do not physically harm the person or property of another. Further, the government has no right to put people in jail unless they do harm the person or property of another. The United States Constitution and its Bill of Rights—the "supreme law of the land"—prohibit it.*

AIN'T NOBODY'S BUSINESS IF YOU DO

People often use the word *legal* too loosely. They fail to give sufficient thought as to what *legal* and *illegal* really mean. When we say a given activity should be illegal, what we're saying is that if someone takes part in that activity, we should put that person in jail. When it comes to consensual crimes, however, when people say, "It should be illegal," what they usually mean is, "That's not right," "That's not a good idea," or "That's immoral." When using the word *illegal,* it's important to remember how forceful the force of law truly is. We are all entitled, of course, to our opinions about certain activities, but do we really want to lock up people who don't go along with our opinions?

> *My definition of a free society is a society where it is safe to be unpopular.*
>
> ADLAI E. STEVENSON

We all have the right to be different. The laws against consensual activities take away that right. If we let anyone lose his or her freedom without just cause, we have all lost our freedom.

With this thought in mind, here are the most popular consensual crimes: gambling, recreational drug use, religious and psychologically therapeutic drug use, prostitution, pornography and obscenity, violations of marriage (adultery, fornication, cohabitation, sodomy, bigamy, polygamy), homosexuality, regenerative drug use, unorthodox medical practices ("Quacks!"), unconventional religious practices ("Cults!"), unpopular political views ("Commies!"), suicide and assisted suicide, transvestism, not using safety devices (such as motorcycle helmets and seat belts), public drunkenness, jaywalking, and loitering and vagrancy (as long as they don't become trespassing or disturbing the peace).

**If you are a citizen of a country other than the United States, this book still applies. Your country is almost certainly a signatory of the United Nations Declaration of Human Rights, which also guarantees the freedom of individual expression.

Even if you don't want to take part in any of the consensual crimes, working to remove the consensual crimes from the books has a trickle-down effect of tolerance, acceptance, and freedom for the things you do want to do. (This may be one trickle-down theory that actually works.)

While exploring the extremes of social prejudice, we can explore our personal prejudices as well. I suggest that, when we want to put people in jail for what they do to their own person or property, our individual tolerance and compassion probably need a little exercise.

But this isn't just my idea. Here's how another person—a carpenter by training—put it:

> Why do you look at the speck of sawdust in your brother's eye and pay no attention to the plank in your own eye? How can you say to your brother, "Brother, let me take the speck out of your eye," when you yourself fail to see the plank in your own eye? You hypocrite, first take the plank out of your eye, and then you will see clearly to remove the speck from your brother's eye.

That, of course, was said by Jesus of Nazareth, that dear misunderstood man many people use as the authority to "lock the bastards up."*

The fact that we would find his idea so controversial 2,000 years later, and more than 200 years after we formed a government based on "life, liberty and the pursuit of happiness," shows how much work we have to do.

⚖️ ⚖️ ⚖️

---

*Those who have their Bibles handy can read all about it in Matthew 7:3–5 and Luke 6:41–42. More on people's misrepresentation of Jesus in the chapter, "What Jesus Really Said about Consensual Crimes."

Here's the condensed list of reasons why having laws against consensual activities is not a good idea (each point has a chapter of its own later in the book):

It's un-American. America is based on personal freedom and on the strength of diversity, not on unnecessary limitation and slavish conformity. The American dream is that we

> *The government of the United States is not, in any sense, founded on the Christian religion.*
>
> GEORGE WASHINGTON
> Treaty of Tripoli
> 1796

are all free to live our lives as we see fit, providing we do not physically harm the person or property of another.

It's unconstitutional. The United States Constitution and its Bill of Rights clearly give us the right to pursue our lives without the forced intervention of moralists, do-gooders, and busy-bodies.

Laws against consensual activities violate the separation of church and state. The Constitution guarantees that not only can we freely practice the religion of our choice, but also that the government will not impose religion upon us. Almost all the arguments in favor of maintaining laws against consensual activities have a religious foundation. The government is then asked to enforce these religious beliefs by arresting the nonbelievers and putting them in jail.

Laws against consensual activities are opposed to the principles of private property, free enterprise, capitalism, and the open market. If everything thus far has sounded hopelessly liberal, here's a nice conservative argument: Our economic system is based on the sanctity of private property. What you own is your own business; you can give it away, trade it, or sell it for a profit or a loss—none of which is the government's business. This is the system known as capitalism. We recently fought (and won) a forty-five-year cold-and-hot war against communism to maintain it. For the government to say that certain things cannot be owned, bought, given away, traded, or sold is a direct violation of both the sanctity of private property and the fundamental principles of capitalism.

It's expensive. We're spending more than fifty *billion* dollars per year catching and jailing consensual "criminals." In addition, we're losing at least an additional $150 billion in potential tax revenues. In other words, each man, woman, and child in this country is paying $800 per year to destroy the lives of 5,000,000 fellow citizens. If we did nothing else but declare consensual crimes legal, the $200,000,000,000 we'd save each year could wipe out the national debt in twenty years, or we could reduce personal income tax by one-third. Another economic high point: moving the underground economy of consensual crimes aboveground would create 6,000,000 tax-paying jobs. And then there's the matter of interest. The $50 billion we spend jailing consensual "criminals" is not just spent; it's *borrowed*. The national debt grows larger. Six percent interest compounded over thirty years adds $250 billion to that $50 billion figure—a dandy legacy for our progeny.

Lives are destroyed. Yes, by taking part in consensual crimes, people may destroy their own lives. This is unfortunate, but that's their business. The problem with making consensual activities crimes, however, is that the government moves in and by force destroys the life of the consensual "criminal." A single arrest and conviction, even without a jail sentence, can permanently affect one's ability to get employment, housing, credit, education, and insurance. In addition, there is the emotional, financial, and physical trauma of arrest, trial, and conviction. If any significant amount of jail time is added to this governmental torture, an individual's life is almost certainly ruined.

Consensual crimes encourage real crimes. Because consensual crimes are against the law, taking part in them costs significantly more than is necessary. In order to pay these artificially inflated prices, some of those who take part in consensual crimes go out and commit real crimes: mugging, robbery, burglary, forgery, embezzlement, and fraud. If the consensual activities were cheap, real crimes would decrease significantly. In addition, to someone who is regularly breaking a law against a consensual activity, all laws may start to seem unimportant.

> *All men are frauds. The only difference between them is that some admit it. I myself deny it.*
>
> H. L. MENCKEN

Consensual crimes corrupt law enforcement. The law enforcement system is based on a perpetrator and a victim. With consensual crimes, perpetrator and victim are the same person. Whom are the police supposed to protect? Theoretically, they arrest the perpetrator to protect the victim. With a consensual crime, when the perpetrator goes to jail, the victim goes too. It's a sham that demoralizes police, promotes disrespect for the law, and makes arresting real criminals more difficult. Asking the police to enforce a crime that does not have a clear-cut victim makes a travesty of law enforcement. It's sad that the laws against consensual activities have turned one of the true heroes of our society, the honest cop, into an endangered species.

The cops can't catch 'em; the courts can't handle 'em; the prisons can't hold 'em. As it is, the police are catching less than 20% of the real criminals—those who do harm the person or property of others. There is simply no way that the police can even make a dent in the practice of consensual crimes. Even if the police could catch all the consensual criminals, the courts couldn't possibly process them. The courts, already swamped with consensual crime cases, can't handle any more. Real criminals walk free every day to rape, rob, and murder again because the courts are so busy finding consensual criminals guilty of hurting no one but themselves. And even if the courts could

> *The first thing to learn*
> *in intercourse with others*
> *is non-interference with their own*
> *particular ways of being happy,*
> *provided those ways do not assume*
> *to interfere by violence with ours.*
>
> WILLIAM JAMES

process them, the prisons are already full; most are operating at more than 100% capacity. To free cells for consensual criminals, real criminals are put on the street every day.

Consensual crimes promote organized crime. Organized crime in America grew directly out of an earlier unsuccessful attempt to legislate morality: Prohibition. Whenever something is desired by tens of millions of people each day, there will be an organization to meet that desire. If fulfilling that desire is a crime, that organization will be organized crime. Operating outside the law as organized criminals do, they don't differentiate much between crimes with victims and crimes without victims. Further, the enormous amount of money at their disposal allows them to obtain volume discounts when buying police, prosecutors, witnesses, judges, juries, journalists, and politicians. And guess who finances some of those let's-get-tough-on-consensual-crime campaigns? You guessed it. Once consensual crimes are no longer crimes, organized crime is out of business.

Consensual crimes corrupt the freedom of the press. Reporting on consensual crimes has turned a good portion of the media into gossips, busybodies, and tattletales (The Hugh Grant Syndrome). With so much important investigation and reporting to be done concerning issues directly affecting the lives of individuals, the nation, and the world, should we be asking one of our most powerful assets—the free press—to report who's doing what, when, where, how, and how often with other consenting whom's?

Laws against consensual activities teach irresponsibility. If we maintain that it is the government's job to keep illegal anything that might do us harm, it implies that anything not illegal is harmless. This is certainly not the case.

Laws against consensual activities are too randomly enforced to be either a deterrent or fair. The laws against consensual activities provide almost no deterrent whatsoever. If the chances of being caught at something are only, say, one in ten million, that's hardly a deterrent. In fact, their very illegality sometimes makes consensual crimes fascinating, glamorous, and irresistible.

> There were seven times as many black women in prison as white women in 1994, and the proportion of black men incarcerated was eight times higher than that of white men. Almost 7% of all black men were incarcerated in 1994, compared with less than 1% of white men. Drug crimes played a major role in the prison population increase.
>
> *LOS ANGELES TIMES*
> December 4, 1995

Laws against consensual activities discriminate against minorities and the poor. In selecting which consensual activities should and should not be crimes, the views of the poor and minorities are seldom considered. Therefore, many consensual activities that the mostly white, male, heterosexual, affluent, Christian lawmakers have deemed illegal do not necessarily reflect the preferences or experiences of minority groups. Further, the laws against consensual activities are not uniformly enforced—the poor and minorities, for a variety of reasons, tend to receive the brief end of the stick.

Problems sometimes associated with consensual activities cannot be solved while they're crimes. Some people take part in consensual crimes as a symptom of, or escape from, deeper problems. These problems are not easily addressed until we dispense with the irrational, illogical, and transparently inaccurate myth that participation in the currently illegal consensual activities is always wrong. It wasn't until after Prohibition, for example, that those who had real drinking problems could see, admit to, and do something about them. Maintaining the fallacy that participation in illegal consensual activities is always wrong keeps those for whom it *is* wrong from doing something constructive about it.

We have more important things to worry about. The short list of national and global problems more deserving of our pre-

> *Truth resides in every human heart,*
> *and one has to search for it there,*
> *and to be guided by truth*
> *as one sees it.*
> *But no one has a right*
> *to coerce others to act according*
> *to his own view of truth.*
>
> MOHANDAS K. GANDHI

cious resources includes: real crime (robbery, rape, murder—the chances are one in four that you or someone in your household will be "touched," as they say, by a violent crime this year), abducted children (more than 400,000 abducted children each year), insurance fraud (a $100-billion-per-year problem that adds from 10% to 30% to all insurance premiums), illiteracy (one in seven American adults is functionally illiterate; one in twenty cannot fill out a job application), poverty (14.2% of the population—35.7 million people—live below the poverty level; a good number of these are children), pollution (all the pending environmental disasters cannot be summed up in a single parenthesis), our addiction to foreign oil (the Gulf War should have been called the Gulf-Standard-Mobil War), terrorism (the bombing of the World Trade Center was, in reality, a terrorist warning: the next time it might be an *atomic* bomb), AIDS (by the year 2000, the largest number of newly HIV-infected people will be heterosexual women), supposedly government-regulated but not-really-regulated industries (the $100 billion savings and loan bailout is an obvious example), and last, but certainly not least, the national debt ($5 trillion, and growing faster than almost anything in this country other than intolerance).

It's hypocritical. To give but one obvious example: Cigarettes do more damage and cause roughly one hundred times the deaths of all of the consensual crimes combined. Each year, 500,000 people die as a direct result of smoking. And yet, cigarettes are perfectly legal, available everywhere, and heavily advertised; tobacco growers are government subsidized; and cigarette companies are free to use their influence on both politicians and the media (and, boy, do they ever). How can we tolerate such contradictions in this country? We are, as Thomas Wolfe pointed out, "making the world safe for hypocrisy."

Laws against consensual activities create a society of fear, hatred, bigotry, oppression, and conformity; a culture opposed to personal expression, diversity, freedom, choice, and growth. The prosecution of consensual crimes "trickles down" into ostracizing, humiliating, and scorning people who do things that are not quite against the law—but probably should be. "They're different; therefore, they're bad" seems to be the motto for a large segment of our society. We are addicted to normalcy; even if it means we must lop off significant portions of ourselves, we must conform.

> *The legitimate powers*
> *of government*
> *extend to such acts*
> *as are only injurious to others.*
>
> THOMAS JEFFERSON

⚖️ ⚖️ ⚖️

There's no need to accept the validity of all these arguments; the validity of any one is sufficient reason to wipe away all the laws against consensual activities.

In this book, we will explore each of the consensual crimes, asking not, "Is it good?" but, "Is it worth throwing someone in jail for?" We'll explore the prejudice about consensual crimes—the prejudices we have been conditioned to believe. You'll find that the number of lies within lies within lies is amazing.

Responsibility is the price of freedom. So is tolerance.

⚖️ ⚖️ ⚖️

In the time it took you to read this overview, 342 persons were arrested for consensual crimes in the United States.

What Are Consensual Crimes?

A CONSENSUAL CRIME IS any activity—currently illegal—in which we, as adults, choose to participate that does not physically harm the person or property of a nonconsenting other.

Does this mean that consensual crimes are without risk? No. Nothing in life is without risk. The fact is, we're all going to die. Life is a sexually transmitted terminal illness.

Consensual crimes are sometimes referred to as "victimless crimes." Alas, every scoundrel committing a real crime of extortion, fraud, or embezzlement declared it a victimless crime, attempting to argue that a crime without physical violence is also a crime without a victim. Everyone who has been robbed with a fountain pen—or computer terminal—rather than a gun knows that's not true. Another group claiming protection under the victimless crime umbrella are those, such as drunk drivers, who recklessly endanger innocent (nonconsenting) others. Just because no one actually got hit, it was okay to go seventy miles an hour through a school zone. Not so.

Meanwhile, all the intolerance mongers, attacking a bona fide consensual crime, maintain the crime *does so* have a victim. ("We're *all* victims!" is one of their favorite phrases.)

It's hard to find any activity in life that does not, potentially, have a victim. People who live in Florida may become victims of hurricanes; drivers of cars may become victims of traffic accidents; and each time we fall in love we may become the victim of someone tearing the still-beating heart from our chest and stomping it into the dust of indifference. (Sorry, it's been a hard month.)

Does this mean we should outlaw Florida, automobiles, or falling in love? Of course not. It isn't whether we could be victims that puts such activities outside the realm of criminal law enforcement, but that we, as adults and knowing the risks, *consented* to take part in them. "Please know that I am aware of the hazards," Amelia Earhart wrote her husband before her last flight; "I want to do it because I want to do it."

> *A civilized society is one which tolerates eccentricity to the point of doubtful sanity.*
>
> ROBERT FROST

Consent is one of the most precious rights we have. It is central to self-determination. It allows us to enter into agreements and contracts. It gives us the ability to choose. Being an adult, in fact, can be defined as having reached the "age of consent"—we become responsible for our choices, our actions, our behaviors. (Nothing in this book refers to children. Children have not yet reached the age of consent. This book discusses only activities between consenting adults.)

Sometimes we land on the sunny side of risk and get the reward. Sometimes we land on the dark side of risk and get the consequences. Either way, as responsible adults, we accept the results (sometimes kicking and screaming, but we accept them nonetheless).

Our governmental elders have decided, however, that some activities are just *too* risky, and that people who consent to take part in them should be put in jail (where, presumably, these people will be safe).

Ironically, many activities far more risky than the officially forbidden activities are not crimes. Why should cocaine be illegal and Drāno not? Whether snorted, swallowed, or injected, Drāno is far more harmful than cocaine. And yet Drāno is available in every supermarket. Children can buy Drāno. No one asks, "What

> *Freedom is the right to choose:*
> *the right to create for oneself*
> *the alternatives of choice.*
> *Without the possibility of choice*
> *and the exercise of choice*
> *a man is not a man*
> *but a member, an instrument,*
> *a thing.*
>
> ARCHIBALD MACLEISH

are you doing with this Drāno? You're not going to snort it, are you?") There is also no "Drāno law" that prohibits us from ingesting Drāno nor a Drāno Enforcement Agency (DEA) to enforce the law. Nor is there an Omnibus Drāno Act designed to reduce the international use and trafficking of Drāno.*

All the consensual activities the government makes illegal must have *some* up-side. People don't bother with things that have only a down-side. (In this way, consensual crimes are the government's way of writing a handbook for rebels, saying, in effect, "This is the latest thing we think should be illegal. Try it today.")

Another way of defining consensual activities is this from Hugo Adam Bedau:

> Government should allow persons to engage in whatever conduct they want to, no matter how deviant or abnormal it may be, so long as (a) they know what they are doing, (b) they consent to it, and (c) no one—at least no one other than the participants—is harmed by it.

♎ ♎ ♎

---

*If you think this is some sort of far-out example, allow me to quote Colin Campbell in the March 10, 1993, edition of the *Atlanta Journal and Constitution:* "Plaza Drugs never closes. But I was disturbed to hear how some of the homeless veterans who live in the jungle not far away buy Lysol there so they can cut it and ingest it in ways that make them very high and radically unhealthy." Lysol! My God! When Lenny Bruce appeared on *The Steve Allen Show* in the late 1950s and did a routine about children sniffing airplane glue, the audience's response was, "What an exaggerated concept, but we'll go along with it so we can enjoy the routine." What Lenny said about glue was true.

Why are some consensual activities considered crimes while others are not? The short answer is *religious beliefs*. Almost all of the consensual crimes find the basis of their restrictions and prohibitions in religion. Even the idea that one should take good care of oneself has a religious base. ("The body is the temple of the soul.")*

> *Liberty exists in proportion to wholesome restraint; the more restraint on others to keep off from us, the more liberty we have.*
>
> DANIEL WEBSTER
> 1847

Prudent participation in consensual crimes, however, is not necessarily anti-God, anti-religion, or even anti-biblical. The prohibitions against certain consensual activities grew from a misinterpretation and misapplication of biblical teachings. (This is discussed in the chapter, "What Jesus and the Bible Really Said about Consensual Crimes.")

The fact is, however, that religious beliefs (or misbeliefs) are what most people use when choosing what is right or what is wrong *for themselves*. This is fine. It's when they try to bestow that system of right and wrong on others—by force—that consensual *crimes* are born.

⚖ ⚖ ⚖

The argument that society prohibits certain consensual acts to protect itself is almost instantly transparent. Any number of things that are far more damaging both to individuals and to society are perfectly legal. (These are discussed in detail in the chapters, "Putting the 'Problem' in Perspective" and "Hypocrites.") Besides, society can protect itself just fine—it doesn't

---

*As Paul put it, "Do you not know that your body is a temple of the Holy Spirit, who is in you, whom you have received from God? You are not your own; you were bought at a price [the Crucifixion]. Therefore honor God with your body" (1 Corinthians 6:19–20).

> *In framing a government,*
> *which is to be administered*
> *by men over men,*
> *the great difficulty lies in this:*
> *you must first enable the*
> *government to control the governed,*
> *and in the next place,*
> *oblige it to control itself.*
>
> JAMES MADISON

need the government's help. (Please see the chapter, "Separation of Society and State.")

Let us assume just for a moment, however, that it is the job of the government to protect people from themselves and to protect innocent wives and husbands from being emotionally hurt by the self-destructive behavior of their spouses. Let's assume we are our brothers' keeper—whether our brothers like it or not. Is the best way to protect a wayward brother by seizing all his property and putting him in jail? Is this helping either the "criminal" or the people who love him? Would a wife really feel more secure knowing that her husband is safe in jail and not running around with gamblers? Would a husband truly be happier living on the street, penniless, because the state accused his wife of selling marijuana and tossed her in jail after seizing the house, car, and all their joint* assets?

"But what about the children?" some lament. "The children are the victims!"** Children are too young to give their knowing consent; that, by definition, is why they are children. If children are genuinely being harmed, it is the job of the government to remove them from the harmful environment.

To put parents in jail, however, for things that they consent to do with other consenting adults, activities that do not directly

---

*Sorry.

**Whenever people bring children into the argument of consensual crime between adults, I know that these people have exhausted all logical arguments and are reduced to knee-jerk emotional pleas. As George M. Cohan once said, "Many a bum show has been saved by waving the flag." Many a bum argument has been won by appealing to a person's natural tendency to protect the young. In discussing activities of consenting adults that do not directly involve children, the plea is a cheap shot.

AIN'T NOBODY'S BUSINESS IF YOU DO

involve children—their own or others—is counter-productive. Is a parent's possible "bad example" worse for the children than throwing the parents in jail, confiscating their money and property, and making their children wards of the state?

Prenatal care in this country is a national shame; twenty-two other countries have lower infant mortality rates than the United States.* Every day, children in this country die of malnutrition and preventable diseases.

These are enormous problems. Pretending that the enforcement of laws against consensual activities is making these problems any better, when it is only making them worse, is tragic.

The United States ranks 13th on the Human Freedom Index. Twelve other countries are freer than the United States.

UNITED NATIONS

⚖️ ⚖️ ⚖️

Just because certain acts do not involve violence does not make them legal. The act of taking something that belongs to another—whether done with a knife or a deceptive smile—is a crime.

To avoid committing crimes, then, all we need to remember is what we were probably told when we were five: "If it's not yours, leave it alone."

Central to all this discussion of crimes and victims is the

---

*The environment some parents provide for their children is appalling. Those who try to argue that more children die due to America's "drug problem" might take note of the fact that the Netherlands has almost no drug restrictions and yet it has a higher percentage of children who live to be one year old than the United States. In fact, the punishment for drug crimes is more severe in the United States than in any of the twenty-two countries that have a lower infant mortality rate than the U.S.

> *Do what's right for you,*
> *as long as it don't hurt no one.*
>
> ELVIS PRESLEY

matter of innocence. Here I mean innocence in the sense of "not consenting" rather than "not guilty."

If you are walking down the street and get hit by a baseball that someone intentionally dropped from a tall building, you are innocent. The person who dropped the ball is guilty of a crime and is responsible for all damage. He or she may not have intended to hit you, but intentionally dropping a baseball from a tall building includes the possibility (in fact, the high probability) that the ball will physically harm the person or property of another. If you are playing second base, however, and get hit by a baseball, you are responsible, not the batter. When you consent to play second base, the possibility you might be hit by a baseball comes with the territory.

Batters do not hit balls with the intention of striking players. In fact, batters try to hit balls as far away from opposing team members as possible. Although being hit by a baseball while playing second base is unfortunate, you are at best (worst?) only a victim of Newton's First Law of Physics: "If a body is moving at a constant speed in a straight line, it will keep moving in a straight line at a constant speed unless . . . *ouch!*" The batter may feel very bad about it, but the batter has committed no crime.

Although the physical harm done is the same with either a dropped ball or a batted ball, in one situation you were innocent and another person was guilty of a crime; in the other situation, you were responsible because *you gave your consent.* (No, you didn't give the batter consent to hit you, but you consented to the risks of baseball.)

It is the law's job to protect innocent people from likely harm to their person or property. It is not the law's job to protect adults from the risks of their own consensual acts.

It is the law's job, for example, to reasonably insure that the food and drugs we purchase are pure and that the measurements are accurate. It is not the law's job to tell us when, where, how, why, or how much of this food or drug we can and cannot consume. It is the law's job to see that the gambling it regulates— from casinos to the stock market—is fair and that all players have an equal chance. It is not the law's job to determine how much we can bet, how skilled we are, or how much we can afford to lose.

> *Heterosexuals don't practice sodomy.*
>
> SENATOR STROM THURMOND
> May 8, 1993

As Arthur Hoppe wrote in the *San Francisco Chronicle,* September 2, 1992:

> In a series of dramatic raids last week, police rounded up a number of hardened jaywalkers.* They will undoubtedly claim they've broken the back of San Francisco's notorious jaywalking ring. . . .

> Just as you might suspect. It's another case of creeping government paternalism. Even we most notorious jaywalkers endanger no one but ourselves. Once again, the government is out to protect me from me.

> This isn't the function of government. The government is a fictitious entity created by us individuals to protect ourselves from each other. I agree not to murder them in return for their agreeing not to murder me. Fair enough. But if I want to kill myself, that's my business.

> Unfortunately, this fictitious entity we created more and more takes on a life of its own. It pokes its nose into everything. . . . It tells me I'm too stupid to wear a seat belt and too careless to wear a motorcycle helmet. If I

*When jaywalking becomes *obstructing traffic*, then it becomes a crime. Until then, it's not.

> *Liberty is the only thing*
> *you cannot have*
> *unless you are willing*
> *to give it to others.*
>
> WILLIAM ALLEN WHITE

don't, it says, wagging its finger, I will be sent to bed without any supper . . .

The function of government is to protect me from others. It's up to me, thank you, to protect me from me.

⚖ ⚖ ⚖

It may seem that if people were running around doing what they wanted, society would run amok. Wouldn't this lead to all sorts of immorality? No. The need to be social, to *interact*—to be part of a society—takes care of that.

Separation of Society and State

> *All that is good*
> *is not embodied in the law;*
> *and all that is evil*
> *is not proscribed by the law.*
> *A well-disciplined society*
> *needs few laws;*
> *but it needs strong mores.*
>
> WILLIAM F. BUCKLEY, JR.

IN DEFENDING THE LAWS against consensual activities, some ask, "Shouldn't the laws of the state describe—or at least reflect—what is acceptable and not acceptable to a broad segment of society?" Absolutely not.

The government—which makes and administers the laws—is there to keep physical violence from being inflicted on its citizens, whether that violence comes from foreign governments, groups of citizens, or individuals. A government that provides a level playing field for commerce and keeps everyone's person and property relatively safe from the physical harm of others is doing a good job. As Thomas Paine wrote in his 1776 pamphlet, *Common Sense,*

> Society in every state is a blessing, but Government, even in its best state, is but a necessary evil; in its worst state, an intolerable one.

Society, on the other hand, determines acceptable and unacceptable social behavior. Many of society's rules are so thoroughly accepted we don't even think about them. That we speak primarily English in the United States is purely a matter of custom. That we eat certain animals and don't eat others (horse is very popular in France), sleep in a bed (the Japanese do not understand why we need a bed*room),* bury our dead (cremation is the tradition in India), and so much more, are all purely matters of social custom. Although in this country one can speak

> *It is hard to fight an enemy*
> *who has outposts*
> *in your head.*
>
> SALLY KEMPTON

Croatian, eat horse, sleep on a futon, and be cremated, the vast majority of people choose not to.

The reason? Our conditioning. "Society attacks early," B. F. Skinner pointed out, "when the individual is helpless." We do some things, don't do other things, and behave in certain ways because that's how we were trained. Much of the time we do what we do because (a) it's the only thing we know (are you fluent in any language other than English?), (b) it's what we're comfortable with (would you feel comfortable eating a horseburger?), or (c) we have to get along in society.

That last one—getting along in society—is what keeps us in place when cultural conditioning fails. Even as rebellious a rascal as George Bernard Shaw acknowledged the need for society—and its power:

> Nobody can live in society without conventions. The reason why sensible people are as conventional as they can bear to be is that conventionality saves so much time and thought and trouble and social friction of one sort or another that it leaves them much more leisure time for freedom than unconventionality does.

The more we pull away from society's norms, the more society pulls away from us. We can, quite legally, be total renegades. The cost (or punishment, if you will) is that we become social outcasts. If we wore aluminum-foil clothing, never washed, communicated only with grunts and squeaks, walked backwards, and lived off live grasshoppers, we might occasionally find ourselves as a guest on daytime talk shows, but we would never be a guest at a dinner party, be rented an apartment, or offered much work (except, perhaps, for organic pest control during grasshopper infestations). If our behavior is sufficiently eccentric, society punishes without any help from the law.

Prior to complete isolation, however, any number of punitive societal responses keep us in line—sometimes literally. It is not, for example, illegal to cut in front of someone at an automated teller machine. And yet, very few people take cuts. Some wait their turn because they believe in fair play; others because they're afraid of disapproval. (In Los Angeles, we wait because we're afraid someone else in line might be carrying a gun.) The reason there are no laws against taking cuts is that most people understand the fairness of lines and agree to cooperate. Most of those who don't believe in fairness do believe in avoiding barrages of negative comments. The very small minority who do take cuts do not cause enough of a problem to warrant legal regulation.

> *Never speak disrespectfully*
> *of Society, Algernon.*
> *Only people who can't get into it*
> *do that.*
>
> OSCAR WILDE
> *The Importance of Being Earnest*

Most of us want to fit into society. A cartoon appearing in *The Realist* many years ago showed a line of sack-clothed bearded men—one looking just like another—holding identical signs reading, "We protest the rising tide of conformity." Even the rebels follow certain counter-social mores in order to be accepted in the counterculture society. To get (or keep) a job, living arrangement, or lover, we will conform to any number of standards—without a police officer or legislature in sight.

Society has the means to change itself without anyone changing a single governmental law. Thirty years ago, for example, an earring on a man would mean that he was (a) a transvestite, (b) a pirate, or (c) Mr. Clean. Today, earrings are *de rigueur* as proof of machismo among certain groups of men. No one had to write a law, enforce a law, or repeal a law regarding earrings on men. As Lewis Thomas explained,

> *Justice is: JUST US*
>
> RICHARD PRYOR
>
> *Is Justice JUST ICE?*
>
> JONI MITCHELL

We pass the word around; we ponder how the case is put by different people; we read the poetry; we meditate over the literature; we play the music; we change our minds; we reach an understanding. Society evolves this way, not by shouting each other down, but by the unique capacity of unique, individual human beings to comprehend each other.

Imagine if every rule we have in society required a law, law enforcement, court time, and jail space. Several laws, for example, have been proposed to make English the national language of the United States. These laws have been dismissed, for the most part, because they were unnecessary. Not only were they unnecessary; they were unenforceable. Although the proposals sparked interesting debates (one congressman said, "Jesus spoke English, and that's good enough for me"), people realized such laws were futile. Why don't people come to the same conclusion about consensual crimes?

Not only is the law's help inappropriate; society doesn't need the law's help—society does just fine on its own. In fact, society has far more power over the individual than law enforcement does. "Order is not pressure which is imposed on society from without," José Ortega y Gasset wrote in 1927, "but an equilibrium which is set up from within."

Society, in fact, does not mind that some people flout its regulations: some people must be outside society in order for those inside society to know they're inside. If everybody were "in," then nobody would be "in." The very fact that some people are "out" makes being "in" worthwhile. Only certain religions live under the misguided notion that everyone must or should be "good."

AIN'T NOBODY'S BUSINESS IF YOU DO

From the government's point of view, which drug one uses recreationally should make no more difference than, say, whether or not one wears an earring. Both are primarily a matter of fad and fashion that the government has no business becoming involved in. The government has far more important issues to consider than the prevailing currents on earrings or drug choices.

> *He who is unable to live in society, or who has no need because he is sufficient for himself, must be either a beast or a god.*
>
> ARISTOTLE

This means not just a separation of church and state, but a separation of society and state. (Whether there should be a separation between church and society is for church and society to work out between themselves. This is a book about government intervention in private lives.) The government has no more business being the enforcer of social policy than it has being the enforcer of religious belief.

Both the church and society have lasted longer than any government. The *people* need the government to keep forced intrusions of both religion *and* society out of their lives.

As usual, Thomas Jefferson said it best. At the age of seventy-seven, he wrote,

> I know no safe depository of the ultimate powers of the society but the people themselves; and if we think them not enlightened enough to exercise their control with a wholesome discretion, the remedy is not to take it from them, but to inform their discretion.

Personal Morality
Versus
Governmental Morality

> *Whether or not legislation*
> *is truly moral*
> *is often a question*
> *of who has the power*
> *to define morality.*
>
> JEROME H. SKOLNICK

SOME PEOPLE BELIEVE that consensual crimes should remain crimes because they are "immoral." It's too easy to respond, "No, they're not immoral!" To the people who find them immoral, they are and may always be immoral. That is their *personal* morality. This is all well and good. The trouble arises when people confuse personal morality with governmental morality.

Personal morality is what we personally believe will make us happier, safer, healthier, more productive, and all-around better human beings. It includes all the personal "rights" and "wrongs" we choose to believe. It is everything we think will help us toward "life, liberty, and the pursuit of happiness." In a free country, we should be free to explore, experiment with, discard, or adopt any belief or activity that might enhance our lives, *unless* we violate governmental morality.

Governmental morality is seeing to it that citizens are safe from physical harm.

Our personal morality comes from many sources—religion, philosophy, good advice, family, culture, society, ancient wisdom, modern scientific thought, and, of course, personal experience. From the many beliefs about how to live, we choose the ones we apply to our lives.

Sometimes we choose consciously—we read a book, like one

of its ideas, try it, find that it works, and choose to make it part of our lives. Other times, we choose by default. Our family (church, club, tribe, school, gym, or whatever) has always done a thing a certain way and we continue doing it that way without any further exploration, investigation, or thought.

> *Moral indignation is
> in most cases
> 2% moral,
> 48% indignation
> and 50% envy.*
>
> VITTORIO DE SICA

Our culture conditions us to be "good," and we either go along with that programming or we challenge it and adopt other behavior that we personally find better. This collection of beliefs and practices forms our morality—our personal morality.

When individuals come together to form a government, however, there must be a way of deciding what is "right" and "wrong" within that society.

In a *dictatorship* or *monarchy,* the dictator, king, or queen decides what's what. The ruler's personal morality becomes the governmental morality. Hitler didn't like Jews and homosexuals? Get rid of them. King Henry VIII didn't like the way the pope treated him? Ban Catholicism and form the Church of England.

In a *totalitarian state,* a committee or ruling body decides what's best for everybody. The populace seldom, if ever, has a chance to decide who is part of that committee. The collective personal moralities of the committee members become the governmental morality. The result is very much like a dictatorship, except blander. ("A committee is a group of individuals who all put in a perfectly good color," Alan Sherman pointed out, "and it comes out gray.") In a totalitarian state, there is no one to blame—everything is done "by committee." To whom can one complain? Oh, there's probably a form to fill out, a line to stand in, or a government building to write to. Totalitarianism becomes tyranny by bureaucracy.

Some governments are based on religious or spiritual beliefs.

> *Give me chastity*
> *and self-restraint,*
> *but do not give it yet.*
>
> SAINT AUGUSTINE

The person or group the society deems to be most in touch with God, spirit, nature (or whatever represents the highest collective belief) is put in charge.

In a *democracy* each person has one vote to cast and, hence, each person has an equal say in the way things are run. In the Declaration of Independence,* however, there is a catch to the democratic process: each person is endowed with certain "unalienable Rights, that among these are Life, Liberty, and the pursuit of Happiness." In other words, the right to life, liberty, and the pursuit of happiness cannot be taken away (alienated) from an individual *even* by the democratic process. So, if 250,000,000 people agree that chartreuse is not the "right" color for hair, our form of democracy, nonetheless, guarantees the one individual who chooses chartreuse hair the freedom to go green. In this way, the collective personal moralities of even a majority of the people cannot dictate the personal moralities of the minority of people.

But where are the limits? If we say, "Hitting innocent people with a stick is an expression of our liberty to wave a stick around," or "Joy riding in other people's cars makes us happy," then we obviously have a conflict. Where does our right to life, liberty, and the pursuit of happiness end?

As the old saying goes, "Your freedom to swing your fist ends where my nose begins."

Another basic element of our government is the right to private property. Under *communism,* everything is communally owned. Under *socialism,* certain things are owned by the government and other things are not. Under *capitalism,* you own what you own until you sell it or give it away, at which point it is

---

*And made the "supreme law of the land" by the Constitution.

owned by someone else. Our property, then, becomes an extension of ourselves.

Property represents a certain amount of energy we invested in something, or a certain degree of good fortune we may have had. The energy is ours, the good fortune is ours, and the symbol of that energy or good fortune is our property.

> *In a free society, standards of public morality can be measured only by whether physical coercion— violence against persons or property—occurs. There is no right not to be offended by words, actions or symbols.*
>
> RICHARD E. SINCERE, JR.

So, to paraphrase the above maxim, your right to swing your fist ends where my window (television, house boat, model airplane collection) begins.

Something else we own is our *person,* that is, our body and all things associated with it. One of the foundations of our form of government is that, after a certain age, your body becomes your own. Yes, your parents created it, fed it, clothed it, and educated it, but, after a certain age, you are not legally bound by the wishes of your parents. This idea is radically different from the beliefs of those cultures which hold that children are the property of their parents.

⚖ ⚖ ⚖

So, we own our bodies and we own our property, and what we do with them is our own business, as long as we don't physically harm the person or property of another. In exchange, we allow others the freedom to do with their person and property whatever they choose, as long as they do not physically harm our person or property. This is the fundamental agreement (government) under which everyone is guaranteed maximum freedom and maximum protection.

To determine, then, whether or not something is moral on a governmental level, we need only ask, "Is it physically harming

> *Without doubt the greatest
> injury of all was done
> by basing morals on myth.
> For, sooner or later,
> myth is recognized for what it is,
> and disappears.
> Then morality loses the foundation
> on which it has been built.*
>
> LORD HERBERT LOUIS SAMUEL

the person or property of another?" If the answer is no, it's moral. If the answer is yes, it's immoral.

On the personal level, however, we must ask of ourselves an even more intimate question: "Will this action harm *my own* person or property?" Answering this question—and then attempting to act accordingly—will keep us so busy we won't have time to worry about what other people (especially strangers) are doing with and about their personal morality.

As Hank Williams sang, "If you mind your own business, you won't be minding mine," or as Fats Waller wrote, "You run your mouth; I'll run my business."

Although at times we may seem to be physically harming ourselves, we know, in fact, we are simply sacrificing momentary happiness for future gain. People jogging, for example, usually appear to be in pain. A compassionate person, not familiar with the jogger's greater goal, might stop and offer the jogger a ride—perhaps to the hospital. A person seeing a jogger might report to friends, "I saw this poor person running down the road wearing only shorts. There must have been some terrible accident."

Some caring souls, with the sincere goal of putting an end to pain, might suggest that jogging be outlawed. This group might show pictures of George Bush and Bill Clinton looking extremely unhappy jogging and compare them to pictures of a contented Eisenhower in a golf cart or a happy Reagan on a horse. As seemingly conclusive proof, the Anti-Jogging League could point out that the man who started it all, Jim Fixx, author of *The Complete Book of Running,* died at fifty-two *while running.* Jogging, obviously, is immoral.

Joggers, however, know that jogging, for them, is perfectly moral. They believe they are trading present pain for future gain.

AIN'T NOBODY'S BUSINESS IF YOU DO

While they may never convince the non-joggers of jogging's benefits (although, God knows, they try, they try), they're glad to live in a free country where their idiosyncrasy is tolerated. Although their scantily clad bodies and expensively shod feet are an annoyance to some, joggers take their freedom and allow others the freedom to sit in doughnut shops and consume their daily dozen.

> *The happiness and prosperity of our citizens is the only legitimate object of government.*
>
> THOMAS JEFFERSON
> 1811

The problem of postponing immediate pleasure to attain eventual satisfaction becomes even more pronounced when we enter the world of religion. People may routinely and systematically deny themselves earthly delights in order to gain eternal paradise. If this is the belief of certain people, should the government step in and insist they enjoy themselves more often? Conversely, if the believers become popular enough or powerful enough, should they be able to, by law, prohibit everyone from doing whatever the believers consider too (that is, sinfully) pleasurable? In order to preserve the rights of both the heathen and the holy, the answer to both questions must be "No."

I'm not asking that any new system of government be adopted; I'm merely suggesting that we try the system we already have. As United States Supreme Court Justice Robert H. Jackson explained:

> The very purpose of a Bill of Rights was to withdraw certain subjects from the vicissitudes of political controversy, to place them beyond the reach of majorities and officials and to establish them as legal principles to be applied by the courts. One's right to life, liberty, and property, to free speech, a free press, freedom of worship and assembly, and other fundamental rights may not be submitted to vote; they depend on the outcome of no elections.

Relationship

WHEN WE USE THE word *relationship,* we generally use it to describe how we relate to other people. When we want to really single someone out as special, we say, "We are in a relationship." That's the one that usually starts with "Some Enchanted Evening," and too often ends, "Another One Bites the Dust."

I'd like, however, to use the word *relationship* in the broadest possible sense: how we *relate* to everyone and everything—mentally, emotionally, or physically.

With some things, we have good relationships; with others, we have bad relationships. When most of our relationships are going well, we say life is good; when most of our relationships are going poorly, we say life is bad. Most things are neither good nor bad *in themselves,* but get a reputation for being good or bad based on how most human beings relate to them. Individually, we can have a good relationship with "dreadful" things, and we can have a bad relationship with "wonderful" things.

Iodine, for example, is neither good nor bad in itself. Taken in small quantities, iodine is an essential nutrient. Taken in larger quantities, iodine is a lethal poison. One could say people were in a good relationship with iodine if they had just enough but not too much; and one could say people were in a bad relationship with iodine if they had so little they had an iodine deficiency, or so much they had iodine poisoning.

We could have bad relationships with things that almost everyone agrees are good. Food, for example. Food is not only good, it's essential. Some people are in a good relationship with food: they eat enough to keep alive, but not so much that it endangers their health. Other people have a bad relationship with food: they eat so little, so much, or so much of the wrong foods, that it negatively affects their lives.

Our lives are made up of both good and bad relationships: we may have a good relationship with our

> *I like white trash cooking.*
> *Cheeseburgers.*
> *The greasier the better.*
> *Mashed potatoes served in a scoop,*
> *a little dent in the top for the gravy.*
> *Drake's Devil Dogs for dessert.*
> *Pure pleasure;*
> *no known nutrient.*
>
> ORSON BEAN

dog, a bad relationship with money, a good relationship with our health, a bad relationship with programming our VCR. There may be some things you have a good relationship with that most people have a bad relationship with (speaking in public, the IRS, airline food); and you may have a bad relationship with things that most people have a good relationship with (movies edited for television, lite beer, Nutra Sweet).

The idea behind laws against consensual activities is that if some people are in a bad relationship with something, then that thing should be banned. The problem is, that solution doesn't solve anything: the problem doesn't lie with the thing itself, but with some people's relationship to it.

Yes, there are some things with which it is easier to be in a bad relationship than others. Cigarettes practically beg for a bad relationship. But then, they were designed that way. For the several centuries prior to the Civil War, tobacco's use was primarily recreational: people would inhale it, choke, get dizzy, fall on the floor, roll around—typical Saturday night recreation. For the most part, people used tobacco (a botanical relative of deadly nightshade, by the way) once or twice a week and that was it.

After the Civil War, the South needed a cash crop less labor intensive than cotton. A special strain of tobacco was developed that allowed people to inhale deeply without coughing. This let people smoke almost continuously, if they liked. It also resulted in almost immediate addiction.

> *I have every sympathy with the American who was so horrified by what he had read of the effects of smoking that he gave up reading.*
>
> LORD CONESFORD

Almost everyone who smokes is addicted to tobacco. While there are many "social drinkers," there is almost no such thing as the "social smoker."* Smokers begin smoking from the time they wake up in the morning and continue smoking regularly throughout the day until they go to sleep.

Addiction is a sure sign of a bad relationship. At first, the addictive substance (or activity) makes us "high." After a while, however, the body builds up an immunity to the substance (or activity), and more and more is needed to achieve the same euphoric effect. Unfortunately, the toxic effects of the substance (or activity) eventually counteract the elation. At that point, we take the substance (or partake in the activity) more to get by than to get high.

A perfect example is caffeine. At first, caffeine produces extra energy, alertness, and a sense of well-being. The body, however, becomes immune to caffeine faster than almost any substance. Soon people are drinking coffee or Coca-Cola or eating chocolate (an eight-ounce bar of chocolate has as much caffeine as a half a cup of coffee) to get them back to "normal." ("You *know* I'm not myself until I've had my morning coffee.")

People can become addicted to (that is, form bad relationships with) many of the things we usually think of as "good." Some people become addicted to romance—not love, but the initial rush of "falling in love." So many people become addicted to otherwise productive work that psychologists have coined the term *workaholics.* Even the highest forms of attainment and attunement are not immune to the dangers of addiction, as Father

---

*This is why Americans spend more each year on tobacco than they do on shoes, furniture, household appliances, prescription drugs, dentists, health insurance, higher education, air travel, or car insurance, and more than four times as much as they spend on flowers, funerals, or books.

Leo Booth explains in his book, *When God Becomes a Drug:*

> When, in the name of God, people hold black-and-white beliefs that cut them off from other human beings; when, in the name of God, they give up their own sense of right and wrong; when, in the name of God, they suffer financial deprivation; then, they are suffering from religious addiction.

> *Tolerance is the positive and cordial effort to understand another's beliefs, practices, and habits without necessarily sharing or accepting them.*
>
> JOSHUA LIEBMAN

No matter how good something is, it can become bad through a bad relationship. Conversely, no matter how bad most people think something is, some people can have a good relationship with it—without physically harming themselves or the person or property of others.

Many people would be surprised to learn that some prostitutes actually enjoy their work, consider the service they provide as valuable as that of any other professional, and are physically and emotionally healthier than some who claim, "All prostitutes are sick and spend their time spreading their sickness to others."

Cocaine is considered by many to be instantly and irreparably demoralizing, demeaning, and destructive. And yet, there are thousands upon thousands of people who have used cocaine regularly*—albeit recreationally—for years (in some cases, decades) and have managed to create great art, business empires, and, yes, even grow healthy children.

Most people think heroin is the most addictive and destructive of drugs. It is addictive (although, according to former Sur-

---

*What is regular for one person is not regular for another; again, it depends on one's relationship to the drug. As with indulging in anything—exercise, sex, television, prayer—the time between indulgences is just as important to a healthy relationship as the indulgences themselves.

> *It is not heroin or cocaine that makes one an addict, it is the need to escape from a harsh reality. There are more television addicts, more baseball and football addicts, more movie addicts, and certainly more alcohol addicts in this country than there are narcotics addicts.*
>
> REP. SHIRLEY CHISHOLM
> September 17, 1969
> to House Select Committee on Crime

geon General C. Everett Koop, not as addictive as cigarettes) and bad relationships with heroin have destroyed lives, but a good relationship with heroin or its less potent brother, morphine, is not impossible. Dr. William Stewart Halsted, the father of modern surgery and one of the four doctors who founded the Johns Hopkins Medical Center—a responsible, productive, well-respected physician and educator—took morphine daily for almost his entire professional life. Forty-seven years after he died, his secret came out. The only thing that made his relationship with morphine potentially unhealthy was the fact he had to keep it so hidden. This is not a rare story in the medical community.

And adultery is always wrong, right? Certainly no one in a position of social or political leadership—the one who sets an example for an entire people—should commit adultery. Right? Well, if history is anything to go on, that's not necessarily true. Accusations have been made, and some well documented by noted historians, that every United States president since FDR—with the possible exceptions of Harry S. Truman, Jimmy Carter, Richard Nixon, and Gerald Ford—have strayed from the sanctity of their marriage vows. Of the exceptions, Carter was doing it in his heart, Nixon was doing it to the country, and Truman was too busy playing either piano or poker.*

---

*In his autobiography, Clark Clifford revealed that one of his jobs in the Truman White House was arranging regular poker games. They included top government officials as well as visiting heads of state. One game was with Churchill. Truman ordered that he lose, but not lose big. Churchill lost $250. That's the equivalent of about $2,500 today. This gives an idea of the stakes at these poker games. Although discussed in the book in a wink-wink, those-were-the-good-old-days manner, the president of the United States regularly committed felonies with the heads of our own and

Kennedy's pre- and in-office escapades must be some kind of record. He had more skeletons in the closet than the gay catacombs. According to FBI files, in 1942 he had a torrid affair with Inga Arvad, generally believed to be a Nazi spy. The FBI bugging of their trysts revealed no spying, but a good deal of "sexual intercourse."

> *The good that*
> *Martin Luther King, Jr. did*
> *remains undiminished.*
> *He was great precisely because,*
> *like other heroes,*
> *he did not allow human weakness*
> *to deter him from*
> *doing great works.*
>
> CARL McCLENDON

(That's an FBI technical term.) FBI files also reveal that Kennedy was married briefly when he was twenty-two. His father, Joseph P. Kennedy, put pressure on two successive New Jersey governors (the state in which the wedding had taken place) to have the marriage removed from the records. He was successful.* Cardinal Spellman, a family friend, arranged for an annulment in 1952. The following year, Spellman officiated at the wedding ceremony of Kennedy to Jacqueline Bouvier. Over the years, Kennedy was linked (so to speak) with Gene Tierney, Angie Dickenson, Jayne Mansfield (I am *not* making this up) and, of course, Marilyn Monroe. As Edie Adams wrote in her autobiography, "I may be the only shapely, blonde female then between the ages of fifteen and forty-five who said no to JFK, but it wasn't because I wasn't asked." The story about Kennedy's affair with Marilyn Monroe while he was in the White House is now famous. When she became too demanding and threatened to become a political liability, Kennedy, like all good presidents, turned the "matter"

of foreign governments. Can you imagine the president, the prime minister of England, and five other top-ranking government officials all arrested and jailed for gambling? Nonetheless, gambling arrests were common in the United States in those days, as they continue to be to this day.

*Kennedy Senior once cabled his son on the election trail, "Spend as much as you need to, but don't get carried away. I'll be damned if I'll buy you a landslide!"

> *If we cannot end our differences,*
> *at least we can help*
> *make the world*
> *safe for diversity.*
>
> JOHN F. KENNEDY

over to his attorney general, Robert Kennedy, who filled his brother's, um, who took his brother's place. The stories of JFK's infidelities became such common knowledge that Bette Midler said in her act, "Guess what? *I* slept with Jack Kennedy! Guess what else?" she would ask, gesturing to her back-up singers, the Harlettes, *"They* slept with Jack Kennedy." Few people in the audience needed to have the joke explained. It is also rumored that Kennedy was visited in the White House by Dr. Max Jacobson, who was later labeled by the tabloids "Dr. Feelgood" due to his propensity for giving his patients injections of amphetamines and other mood-elevating substances to cure anything from a cold to a divorce. After an investigation, he lost his medical license.* Who knows how many of Kennedy's staff were also "treated" by Dr. Jacobson while at the White House. Can you imagine? For three years, the trembling hand of an intravenous speed-freak might have been hovering over the great nuclear Button.

President Clinton had not one, but two scandals revealed during his campaign, but he was elected anyway. This demonstrates either the maturing of the American electorate or the country's utter frustration with Bush. (I like to think the former, but I fear it's the latter.) It turned out that Clinton smoked marijuana and may have had an affair with a woman named Gennifer Flowers (not necessarily, but not necessarily not at the same time). People, for the most part, shrugged and repeated the phrase from the 1960s, "So what if he's smoking flowers?" Happily, the electorate decided that Clinton's behavior in the State

---

*Dr. Jacobson told Alan Jay Lerner about the Kennedy White House visits. Perhaps it is ironic—or perhaps not—that Alan Jay Lerner wrote the lyrics to the song most often associated with the Kennedy years, "Camelot," while speeding along under Dr. Jacobson's care.

House was more important than his behavior in his own house, and he was elected by a broad margin.

> *If you say a modern celebrity*
> *is an adulterer,*
> *a pervert,*
> *and a drug addict,*
> *all it means is that*
> *you've read his autobiography.*
>
> P. J. O'ROURKE

The wave of "tell all" biographies (and autobiographies) so popular in the last two decades has clearly shown that everybody's got a bad relationship with something. No matter how great, accomplished, successful, or magnificent a person may be in one area of life, there always seems to be that little dark corner he or she tries so desperately to keep hidden.

At first, these revelations about the heroes of our time seem as though they were written by editors of supermarket tabloids. "LORD LAURENCE OLIVIER AND DANNY KAYE WERE LOVERS!" After the initial shock and laughter die down, a surprisingly large number of these revelations turn out to be true. In his meticulously researched biography, *Laurence Olivier,* Donald Spoto revealed what Hollywood insiders had known for years: that for the entire decade of the 1950s, Kaye provided the nurturing, encouragement, and emotional support Olivier was no longer receiving from Vivien Leigh. (From 1939 to 1950, Scarlett O'Hara had become Blanche du Bois.) Did their indulgence in this "crime"* negatively affect their careers? No. All indications are that their careers were mutually enhanced by it.

What if their "crime" had become public knowledge? *That* would have destroyed their careers—and just about every other part of their lives. Danny Kaye would never have had his TV series, which ran for four years in the early 1960s, nor would his exemplary work with the United Nations Children's Fund have been permitted. ("A *homosexual* with our *children?!*") Olivier's bril-

---

*At that time, homosexual acts between consenting adults—even between consenting *actors*—were illegal in all the places where the affair took place: England, New York, and California.

> *I am an actor.*
> *Of <u>course</u>*
> *I can play a heterosexual!*
>
> SIR JOHN GIELGUD

liant work in the last three decades of his life probably never would have happened; he never would have been made director of the National Theater, thus, it probably never would have gotten off the ground; he certainly wouldn't have been elected to the House of Lords. (Although there are certainly homosexuals in that august body, when the more-open-about-his-sexuality Sir John Gielgud was suggested for lordship, one person commented, "England already *has* a queen.") Spoto's book portrays Kaye as a deeply devoted admirer of Olivier and Olivier as, well, an *actor*. Like most performers, Lord Olivier's weakness was praise, which just happened to be Kaye's strength.

Even the silly books, where rumor is reported as fact (Kitty Kelley with her "Kitty Litter" being the reigning queen of that genre), also lead to a monumental "So what?" and a bit of tolerance for the variety of relationships of which human beings are capable. So what if Ron and Nancy smoked pot in the governor's mansion? Did Sinatra do it "his way" with Nancy in the White House? If so, so what?

The point is that people can have a bad relationship with some parts of their life (marital fidelity, for example) and still have a good relationship with other parts of their life (career, public service, and so on).

William F. Buckley, Jr., has taken daily, for thirty years, a psychoactive prescription drug known as Ritalin. Ritalin is prescribed for hyperactive children and lethargic adults. (It seems to calm kids down and pick adults up.) Mr. Buckley apparently has a good relationship with this drug. Anyone who knows him will tell you he has never, *ever,* experienced either of Ritalin's most common side effects: weight loss and irritability. Mr. Buckley, in his usual candor, freely admitted to his decades of daily usage. As

Ritalin has for some people amphetamine-like effects, rumor got out that Buckley "took speed" every day. This is, of course, an exaggeration and oversimplification. When I asked him about this, Buckley wrote me:

> I hope you will have a chance to mention that what the doc said, after I had fainted (first and last time) was that my blood pressure is so low that I should either take a quarter pound of chocolate in mid afternoon, or a Ritalin. Big deal! I doubt, by the way, that a doctor would nowadays say that because some people are affected adversely by Ritalin. But after 30 years, nobody has detected any change in me, haahaaaahaaha-hahhhaaaaaaa, eeeeeeee, oooooo-ooooooooo oooooo! Now I'm feeling uiqte [sic] fine, as you can see.

Our relations with a good joke are direct and even divine relations.

G. K. CHESTERTON

Good relationships with drugs are possible without a doctor's prescription, and—as any doctor will tell you—bad relationships with drugs are possible even with a doctor's prescription. The point again: it is not the substance, but the relationship to the substance that causes problems.

Attempting to control the substance in no way helps control the problem—in fact, it only makes the problem worse.

If someone is in a bad relationship with a substance and you take the substance away, the person will find a new substance and enter into a bad relationship with it. There seems to be something in people who are in a bad relationship that requires—nay, *demands*—some sort of bad relationship. The substance is secondary—almost incidental—to the desire for the bad relationship. This transference of addiction can occur even when a substance is given up by choice. People who stop smoking, for example, will sometimes put on weight. They simply

> *Tolerance comes of age.*
> *I see no fault committed*
> *that I myself*
> *could not have committed*
> *at some time or other.*
>
> GOETHE

transfer their bad relationship with tobacco to a bad relationship with food. If you eliminate people's bookies, they'll take up with stockbrokers. Deprive people of coffee, and they'll turn to Diet Coke.

Certain people with addictive personalities are giving some poor, innocent substances (and activities) a bad name.

Most people who condemn currently illegal consensual activities know little or nothing about them. All they know are the sensationalized media accounts designed not to educate, but titillate. Unless they take part in the activities themselves—or have close friends who do—most people have bad relationships with the mere existence of these consensual activities. The primary emotions seem to be revulsion and fear, born of ignorance. Revulsion and fear keep one from investigating and learning that there is nothing much to be repulsed by or afraid of. It is a closed loop of ignorance (ignore-ance).

The unwillingness to see that "It is my judgment, based on my ignorance, that is causing the problem" *is* the problem. Bad relationships promote worse relationships. Worse relationships promote impossible relationships. Impossible relationships promote laws against consensual activities.

Most people, of course, do not intentionally set out to create a bad relationship. Most relationships initially start out good, and gradually—often imperceptibly—become bad. If, however, a formerly good relationship has turned bad and we don't realize it yet, no one has the right to throw us in jail for our lack of perception. If we do realize the relationship has become bad and we choose to continue with it for whatever reason, no one has the right to arrest us for our poor choices. As long as our relationships don't physically harm the person or property of another, we are free to choose what we relate to and how we relate to it.

⚖️ ⚖️ ⚖️

People use all kinds of things for their corruption, but nothing corrupts everybody. Successful change takes place by changing the individual, not prohibiting activities or substances.

Fanaticism consists in redoubling your effort when you have forgotten your aim.

GEORGE SANTAYANA

PART II

WHY LAWS AGAINST CONSENSUAL ACTIVITIES ARE NOT A GOOD IDEA

THE NEXT SEVERAL CHAPTERS elaborate on why laws against consensual activities are not a good idea. Please keep in mind as you read these chapters that you don't have to agree with all of the points or all of the objections—any one is sufficient reason to stop putting people in jail for activities that do not harm the person or property of nonconsenting others.

It's Un-American

> *Every effort to confine
> Americanism to a single pattern,
> to constrain it to a single formula,
> is disloyalty to everything that
> is valid in Americanism.*
>
> HENRY STEELE COMMAGER

THE UNITED STATES IS the most diverse country on earth. Nowhere else do so many people with differing ethnic, religious, racial, and cultural backgrounds live side by side in relative peace and harmony. The "melting pot" did not melt us into one, uniform people, but melted away a good portion of the intolerance, prejudice, and the notion that one group or another "shouldn't be here."

It happened over time. The prejudice of one generation became the toleration of the next generation, which became the fascination of the next generation and the norm of the next.

Drawn by the concept of a "new world" and, later, "the land of the free," settlers eventually realized that, in order to get the freedom they sought, they would have to give others freedom as well. This realization sometimes came through rational thought, but more often came as a compromise in settling bloody disputes.

The Europeans who first arrived in America fell into roughly three categories: (1) those seeking religious freedom, (2) those seeking fame and fortune, and (3) criminals.* These three elements were at odds, and within each element was discord.

---

*England did not have prisons as we know them for its common classes—only the aristocracy got to spend years "in The Tower"—and they had to pay the Crown room and board for the privilege. For the average British citizen, small crimes were punished by fines, flogging, or torture. Sentences for greater crimes were served on prison ships or by exile to a distant land, often for life. America was the favorite choice from the mid-1600s through 1776. From 1776 on, Australia picked up the slack.

> *I hate people*
> *who are intolerant.*
>
> LAURENCE J. PETER

On the religious front, the Catholics and the Protestants hated each other, and both despised the Jews. Protestants divided along the lines of those who were happy with the Church of England (the Anglicans) and those who wanted major reforms (the Puritans).

Those seeking fame and fortune vied for land, trading rights, transport routes, reserved parking places, and all the other material goodies entrepreneurs squabble over.

The criminals were anything from political dissidents and recalcitrant serfs to thieves and murderers. They had little in common except that they had broken England's common law or had offended someone in power.

The religious, ambitious, and malicious Europeans—all hating each other and made up of splinter groups that didn't get along—also had to contend with the Native Americans (and vice versa). When the Europeans arrived, there were as many as 4,000,000 Native Americans on the land now known as the United States. The natives who were, at first, friendly, or, at worst, had a live-and-let-live attitude toward the immigrants, eventually turned hostile. Spain, starting with Christopher Columbus's shipping natives back to Spain as slaves, had created a policy (by then over a century old and, therefore, a *tradition)* of enslaving, exploiting, and abusing the natives. The native North Americans would have none of this. Here began the most dramatic—and the most tragic—failure of the melting pot. As many differences as the European settlers had among themselves, they had more in common with each other than they did with "the redskins." The Native Americans were never officially included in the melting pot—even those who converted to Christianity, learned English, applied for statehood under the system prescribed by the newly formed federal government, and attempted to fit into the white man's ways. (The Native Americans' application for statehood was summarily denied.)

Within the colonies, changes started when some of the children of the Puritans turned out to be not quite as religious as their parents. Conversely, the children of some of the criminals were more religious than Ma and Pa. In both cases, the older generation shook their heads and moaned, "What's the younger generation coming to?" When the slightly less religious children of the Puritans and the slightly more religious children of the criminals married (in wedding chapels set up by the entrepreneurs), the Puritan parents and the criminal parents discovered they had something in common after all: children who were *positively out of their minds!* Some children married Native Americans; others married new immigrants. They had children, and the first generation of Americans was born.

> *He who passively accepts evil is as much involved in it as he who helps to perpetuate it.*
>
> MARTIN LUTHER KING, JR.

Soon, another group was added: slaves from Africa. They, as the Constitution euphemistically puts it, "migrated" to America—but much against their will. They weren't even included in the melting pot until after the 1860s, and significant melting did not take place until the 1960s.

After the Revolutionary War and the formation of "a new nation conceived in liberty and dedicated to the proposition that all men are created equal," people seeking freedom of all kinds began flocking to America.

The French, who were our allies in the Revolutionary War, were welcome, but "spoke funny." The Chinese, imported as cheap labor to build the railroads, were despised, abused, but eventually accepted. The Irish, who came to escape the devastation of the potato famine and the tyranny of England, arrived at roughly the same time as the Italians. These two took an instant

> *It gives me great pleasure indeed
> to see the stubbornness
> of an incorrigible nonconformist
> warmly acclaimed.*
>
> ALBERT EINSTEIN

dislike to one another. It was nearly a century before the animosity dissolved. The Jews came from many countries, primarily Russia and eastern Europe. One pogrom after another forced them to try the religious freedom promised by the Constitution. They did not immediately find it. Strong antisemitism and "restricted" hotels, clubs, restaurants, and neighborhoods caused the sort of ghettoizing the Jews had unfortunately become accustomed to in their native lands. This discrimination would not decrease until after World War II, when Hitler demonstrated to the world the ultimate result of intolerance. Six million concentration camp deaths later, America finally woke up in the late 1940s and began to refer proudly to its "Judeo-Christian" heritage.

The philosophy that made the melting pot work was a belief both high-mindedly enlightened and street-wise practical: "You allow me my diversity and I'll allow you yours." It's an ongoing process—ever changing, ever growing, ever looking for the balance between the extremes.

⚖️ ⚖️ ⚖️

Defenders of the status quo have always tried to keep their status, well, quo. "The way it is is the way it's meant to be, the way God wants it to be, and if you don't like it here, you can go back where you came from." Recently, for example, we have seen an influx of immigrants from "non-Christian nations" (India, other parts of Asia, and the Middle East), which has struck fear into the hearts of those who feel it their "duty" to protect "traditional American values"—their values. That these Hindus, Buddhists, and Muslims are turning out to be perfectly good citizens is even more disturbing. ("They must be up to something.")

So, a movement is afoot to declare the United States a "Christian nation." The plan is that, when all naturalized citizens swear allegiance to the flag, they will also swear allegiance to the specific interpretation of Christianity popularized by, among others, St. Patrick Robertson and St. Jerome Falwell. The new immigrants will have to abandon their native religions just as they must abandon allegiance to the country of their birth.

> *So Mainline Christians allow the television preachers to manipulate their audiences, most times to their own financial gain, by making the most absurd biblical claims without their being called to accountability in the name of truth.*
>
> BISHOP JOHN SHELBY SPONG

Ruling by religion, however, was tried in this country and it failed—miserably. Here, for example, is an early colonial law:

> If any man have a stubborn or rebellious Son, of sufficient understanding and years, *viz. fifteen years of age,* which will not obey the voice of his Father, or the voice of his Mother, and that when they have chastened him, will not hearken unto them; then shall his Father or Mother, being his natural Parents, lay hold on him, and bring him to the Magistrates assembled in Court, and testify unto them, that their Son is Stubborn and Rebellious, and will not obey their voice and chastisement, but lives in sundry notorious Crimes, such a son shall be put to death.

The law then states the specific biblical chapter and verse on which the law was based (Deuteronomy 21:18–21).

> If a man have a stubborn and rebellious son, which will not obey the voice of his father, or the voice of his mother, and *that,* when they have chastened him, will not hearken unto them: Then shall his father and his mother lay hold on him, and bring him out unto the elders of his city, and unto the gate of his place; And they shall say unto the elders of his city, This our son *is* stubborn and rebellious, he will not obey our voice; *he is* a glutton,* and

a drunkard. And all the men of his city shall stone him with stones, that he die.

How many of us would be alive today if that law were still on the books? The founding fathers realized ruling by religion wouldn't work, and, wisely, prevented it. The United States opted for a government not dictated by any person's or group's interpretation of any religious text. (More on this in the chapter, "Laws against Consensual Activities Violate the Separation of Church and State, Threatening the Freedom of and from Religion.")

Diversity, not conformity, is America's true strength.

> The ugliness of bigotry stands in direct contradiction to the very meaning of America.
>
> HUBERT H. HUMPHREY

𓏤 𓏤 𓏤

In nature, purebreds excel in certain characteristics, but at the expense of others: they may be beautiful, but stupid; gentle, but sickly; ferocious, but unpredictable. It's the crossbreeds that have the strength, flexibility, and multileveled instincts not only to survive, but to thrive in a broad range of conditions.

The United States is not just a crossbred; it's a mongrel—the most mongrel nation on earth. It's what gives us our strength,

---

**Far be it from *me* to cast the first stone, but . . . have you seen Jerry Falwell lately? Hasn't anyone told him that gluttony is one of the Seven Deadly Sins? Hasn't anyone warned him what would happen to him if his cry for "God's law to become man's law" should include Deuteronomy 21:18–21, or Proverbs 23:2 ("put a knife to your throat if you are given to gluttony")? Proverbs 28:7 says that Jerry shames his whole congregation (and their fathers) ("a companion of gluttons disgraces his father"). As Orson Welles pointed out: "Gluttony is not a secret vice." Frankly, I don't care if Jerry consumes more than several third-world nations. I just wish he wouldn't do it in public where it frightens the children. (THIS JUST IN: Rush Limbaugh has agreed to be Jerry Falwell's personal trainer. Film at eleven.)

sensitivity, tenacity, flexibility, common sense, and spunk. ("You have spunk, don't you?" Lou Grant asked Mary Richards at their first meeting. Mary nodded proudly. Lou glared: "I *hate* spunk.")

> *That at any rate is the theory*
> *of our Constitution.*
> *It is an experiment,*
> *as all life is an experiment.*
>
> JUSTICE OLIVER WENDELL HOLMES, JR.

Many citizens of the United States have stopped even trying to trace their national roots. When asked, "What nationality are you?" they respond, "American." And rightly so.

I have flowing in my veins Irish, Italian, a little Cherokee, and God knows what-all. I'm an American. The struggle between the Irish and the Italians came to an end with me and hundreds of thousands like me. How could the Italians hate me? I'm part Italian. How could the Irish hate me? I'm part Irish. How can I side with the settlers? I'm part Native American. How can I side with the Native Americans? I'm mostly settler. I have compassion for many sides. And I am one of millions who have the blood of many nations flowing through our veins: the wealth of many cultures, the wisdom of many generations—and many, many ways to love God.

As Bishop Fulton J. Sheen explained,

> Democracy cannot survive where there is such uniformity that everyone wears exactly the same intellectual uniform or point of view. Democracy implies diversity of outlook, a variety of points of view on politics, economics, and world affairs.
>
> Hence the educational ideal is not uniformity but unity, for unity allows diversity of points of view regarding the good means to a good end.

"If there is any fixed star in our constitutional constellation," said Supreme Court Justice Robert H. Jackson, "It is that no official, high or petty, can prescribe what shall be orthodox in

> *I am determined*
> *my children shall be brought up*
> *in their father's religion,*
> *if they can find out what it is.*
>
> CHARLES LAMB

politics, nationalism, religion, or other matters of opinion or force citizens to confess by word or act their faith therein."

America is a bold, dynamic, audacious, enthralling, and ongoing experiment. There have been many risks, many embarrassments (Richard Speck, John Hinckley, Jeffrey Dahmer) and many glories (Luther Burbank, Helen Keller, Thomas Edison,* Liberace**).

Where else but in America could we read this news item?

> A De Kalb County, Georgia, Superior court ruled that Gary Eugene Duda, 35, could change his first name to "Zippidy." Duda said that he had already been called "Zippidy" by friends for most of his life.

The American experiment has seen its tragedies (the executions of Sacco and Vanzenti; the imprisonment of 110,000 Japanese Americans during World War II; the cold war with its nuclear arms race) and its triumphs (Lindbergh's flight to Paris, putting a man on the moon, the Human Genome Project).

The experiment continues.

There are some who want to call the experiment off, who

---

*Imagine: one man invented the electric light, the phonograph, the motion picture, the ticker tape, and the improved telephone. Edison knew the value of experimentation.

**Another man who knew the value of experimentation. What other culture could create Liberace? (All right, maybe Spain—but he would have been a bullfighter.) Flamboyance and eccentricity are certainly a part of our national character—essential and valued parts. And who was more flamboyantly, eccentrically himself than Liberace? When told by a concerned fan, "You wouldn't smile so much, Mr. Liberace, if you heard the things people said about you," Liberace smiled, "I heard 'em. You know what else?" Liberace smiled broader, "I started 'em."

want to roll back America to those happy, carefree, God-fearing pre-Constitutional times. Then, *their* God would rule. By force of law.

Let's not let them.

> *Restriction of free thought*
> *and free speech*
> *is the most dangerous*
> *of all subversions.*
> *It is the one un-American act*
> *that could most easily defeat us.*
>
> JUSTICE WILLIAM O. DOUGLAS

Laws against Consensual Activities
Are Unconstitutional

> *Our Constitution is
> in actual operation;
> everything appears to promise
> that it will last;
> but in this world
> nothing is certain
> but death and taxes.*
>
> BENJAMIN FRANKLIN

ALTHOUGH THE Declaration of Independence is not, like the Constitution, the "law of the land," it is certainly the spirit of the land. In the words of Abraham Lincoln,

I have never had a feeling, politically, that did not spring from . . . the Declaration of Independence . . . that all should have an equal chance. This is the sentiment embodied in the Declaration of Independence . . . I would rather be assassinated on this spot than surrender it.

The Declaration of Independence was not about just independence from England or even Europe—it was a declaration of independence from ignorance, religious intolerance, and political tyranny.

What we call the "Declaration of Independence" is officially "The Unanimous Declaration of the Thirteen United States of America." There is, by the way, no signed Declaration of Independence from July 4, 1776. The Declaration of Independence was approved by voice vote on July 2, 1776, and the parchment copy was signed by the first delegates on August 2, 1776. Other signatures rolled in throughout the year. (Thomas McKean did not sign until 1781.) The only reason we celebrate the Fourth of July is that both Thomas Jefferson and John Adams remembered it as the date of the signing. There is, however, no congressional record of a signing on that date. Were it not for Adams and

Jefferson remembering its being on the fourth, the Fourth of July would either be the Second of July or the Second of August.

That both men—first comrades, then political enemies, and finally friends—should misremember the day is part of one of those truth-is-stranger-than-fiction stories. In the early morning of July 4, 1826, Thomas Jefferson awoke and asked, "Is it the Fourth yet?" Told that it was, he quietly died. Five hours later, John Adams, not knowing of Jefferson's death, declared, "Thomas Jefferson still survives!" and died.

Nature intended me for the tranquil pursuits of science, by rendering them my supreme delight. But the enormities of the times in which I have lived have forced me to commit myself on the boisterous ocean of political passions.

THOMAS JEFFERSON

July 4, 1826, marked the fiftieth anniversary of July 4, 1776.

In his last letter, written ten days before his death, Jefferson gave his final thoughts on the Declaration of Independence:

> May it be to the world, what I believe it will be (to some parts sooner, to others later, but finally to all), the signal of arousing men to burst the chains under which monkish ignorance and superstition had persuaded them to bind themselves, and to assume the blessings and security of self-government. That form which we have substituted, restores the free right to the unbounded exercise of reason and freedom of opinion. All eyes are opened, or opening, to the rights of man.

> The general spread of the light of science has already laid open to every view the palpable truth, that the mass of mankind has not been born with saddles on their backs, nor a favored few booted and spurred, ready to ride them legitimately, by the grace of God. These are grounds of hope for others. For ourselves, let the annual return of this day forever refresh our recollections of these rights, and an undiminished devotion to them.

> *The natural progress of things
> is for liberty to yield
> and governments to gain ground.*
>
> THOMAS JEFFERSON

Jefferson wrote into the Declaration of Independence one of the most brilliant definitions of freedom in history:

We hold these truths to be self-evident, that all men are created equal, that they are endowed by their Creator with certain unalienable Rights, that among these are Life, Liberty, and the pursuit of Happiness.

We don't use the terms *inalienable* or *unalienable** much today, but in the eighteenth century they were well known and often used.

Alienable is a form of the word *alienate:* to take away from, to separate. An alienable right is a right that can be taken from you or a right that you can transfer to another. For example, owning a car is an alienable right. Selling the car and transferring the title to another *alienates* your right to own and drive that car—you have alienated yourself from the possession and use of the car. If you have an alienable right to something, the government can—with just cause—take it from you. In time of war, or build-

---

*There is no real difference between *unalienable* and *inalienable.* The best guess as to how *inalienable* became *unalienable* is that the "u" replacing the "i" was simply a typographical error. It was probably not changed because the founding fathers were in a hurry. This Declaration was a hot document. The Declaration of Independence called for the violent overthrow of the British government in what was then known as British America. This was high treason and punishable by death. The signers of the Declaration of Independence were not exaggerating when they included in the document, "For the support of this Declaration . . . we mutually pledge to each other our Lives, our Fortunes, and our sacred Honour." It's little wonder, then, that the difference between *inalienable* and *unalienable* would not be challenged.

ing a new freeway, the government can take your house, for which you would be paid the fair market value.

Inalienable rights, on the other hand, are rights that cannot be taken from you or transferred to another *no matter what*. These are the basic rights guaranteed to every citizen of the republic. What did our founding fathers consider to be our basic, inalienable rights? "Among these are Life, Liberty, and the pursuit of Happiness."

> *The self-evident truths announced in the Declaration of Independence are not truths at all, if taken literally; and the practical conclusions contained in the same passage of that Declaration prove that they were never designed to be so received.*
>
> WILLIAM PINKNEY

Wrote Samuel Eliot Morison in *The Oxford History of the American People* (1965),

> These words are more revolutionary than anything written by Robespierre, Marx, or Lenin, more explosive than the atom, a continual challenge to ourselves as well as an inspiration to the oppressed of all the world.

Life, liberty, and the pursuit of happiness cannot be taken from us; they are inalienable. Note that inalienable rights are not limited to life, liberty, and the pursuit of happiness: *"among these* are Life, Liberty, and the pursuit of Happiness" (emphasis added).

Life is obvious; it is our physical life. *Liberty* is the freedom to live that life the way we choose. The phrase *the pursuit of happiness* is so vague, so broad, and so far-reaching that it is revolutionary even today—perhaps especially today. It, of course, does not guarantee happiness; but it does give us the right to pursue happiness—whatever we think that may be, in whatever way we think will get us there.

Naturally, there are limits. My pursuit of happiness might include your new car. Does that mean that I, as a citizen, have a right to take your car? Of course not. Where should the limit be? As you already know, I propose the limits are the physical harming of another's person or property. As I'll attempt to show here

> *I think your slogan*
> *"Liberty or Death"*
> *is splendid*
> *and whichever one you decide on*
> *will be all right with me.*
>
> ALEXANDER WOOLLCOTT

and in other chapters, this is precisely the same limit that the founding fathers had in mind when they created our government.

⚖ ⚖ ⚖

Before forming the government, however, there was a little business of a revolutionary war. King George III of England did not, after reading the Declaration of Independence, say, "Oh, they'd like their independence; I hope they enjoy it." No. England is not famous for letting her people go. Only Princess Di got away from the British crown without a fight.

Soon after the Declaration of Independence, the thirteen colonies of British America gathered together under the loosely stated Articles of Confederation—a document designed to last the duration of the war. All power was put in the hands of a Continental Congress. The Continental Congress had the dual disadvantage of being (a) a committee and (b) unable to tax. They had the power to "request" money from state legislatures, but, as you can imagine, such requests often went unheeded.* Two important lessons were learned from the Continental Congress: (a) committees do not govern well, and (b) a government is no government without the power of taxation (or some other way to raise funds).

After the war, in the summer of 1787, a group of elected representatives was given the task of adapting the Articles of Confederation into a permanent document outlining an ongoing

---

*It got so bad at one point that the standing army—who had not been paid in months—marched on the Continental Congress. The army asked George Washington to lead them and become the first king of America. (We came perilously close to trading England's King George III for our own King George I.) Washington turned down the idea and severely rebuked the troops for their actions. The troops, nonetheless, got paid.

AIN'T NOBODY'S BUSINESS IF YOU DO

government for the Con-
federated States of Amer-
ica. This group of fifty-five
delegates took to their task
with rare enthusiasm.
Some historians say they
ignored their mandate en-
tirely. (Jefferson, who was
in France at the time, expressed concern that they
"met in secret session.")
The delegates threw out
the Articles of Confedera-

*There can be no prescription
old enough to supersede
the Law of Nature
and the grant of God Almighty,
who has given to all men
a natural right to be free, and they
have it ordinarily in their power
to make themselves so,
if they please.*

JAMES OTIS

tion entirely and began work on a new document, the Constitution of the United States of America. From that point on, the
gathering of those fifty-five delegates was known as the Constitutional Convention.

Although Jefferson was absent, many great men were in attendance. Jefferson called them an "assembly of demigods."*
Benjamin Franklin arrived each morning in a sedan chair carried
through the streets of Philadelphia by convicts—he was eighty-
one and suffered gout. Also present were future presidents John
Adams and James Madison, as well as Alexander Hamilton who
later, with Madison, "sold" the Constitution—and the concept of
a strong federal government**—to the citizenry in a series of
eighty-five newspaper articles known as *The Federalist*. George

*Thomas Jefferson would later regret this endorsement of one of the dele-
gates, Alexander Hamilton. Hamilton and Jefferson, who both served in
George Washington's first presidential cabinet, were such bitter enemies
and political rivals, yet each so powerful and persuasive, that they began
the two-party system.

**The concept for a federal government was taken from the confederation
of five Native American tribes—the Mohawk, Oneida, Onondaga, Cayuga,
and Seneca—known collectively as the Iroquois Federation. Hiawatha,
paddling between the tribes in his white canoe, persuaded them to form a
con*federation,* from which the word *federalist* comes. The Iroquois Federation had a common council (congress) to which each tribe had a fixed number of delegates.

> *The American Constitution,*
> *one of the few modern political*
> *documents drawn up by men*
> *who were forced by the sternest*
> *circumstances to think out*
> *what they really had to face,*
> *instead of chopping logic*
> *in a university classroom.*
>
> GEORGE BERNARD SHAW

Washington prepared for his role as the nation's first president by presiding over the convention.

The major question facing the convention—and American politics at large—was how much power would remain at the state level, and how much would go to the federal government.

The federalists believed in a strong federal—that is, national—government. Without it, they argued, the thirteen colonies would become like the countries of Europe—eternally caught in the ritual of alliances, betrayals, intrigues, and hostilities that had marked the history of Europe for more than a thousand years. Further, Federalists argued, without a strong central government, each state would be ripe for individual plucking by the then-aggressively imperial powers of France, Spain, Russia, or a return engagement from Great Britain. Moreover, the federalists claimed, all the people of the colonies had pulled together and won a rousing victory for life, liberty, and the pursuit of happiness. These courageous souls were now one people; members of one country, a country that—united—defeated the strongest military power on earth. These people of one nation did not want to return to being citizens of individual states, states that—if history were any indicator—would be at each other's throats over borders, territorial rights, and tariffs within a matter of years. And if one state went to war against another, did one really want to fight brother against brother?

The anti-federalists held that states' rights were sovereign. Each state already had a constitution—or was busy working on one—which was to be the supreme law of the people within that state. Why couldn't the Confederated States get along as well as the Nordic countries, which were independently sovereign, lived together in peace, and banded together in time of war? This, the anti-federalists claimed, was what the Articles of Confederation were intended to do: form an alliance against Great Britain and nothing more. Once victorious, the states would return to the status quo. Oh, it might be nice, the anti-federalists acknowledged, to have some sort of central government, but it should be more a voluntary alliance, a forum in which sovereign states could meet and discuss treaties, national defense, trade, and the like. In this, the anti-federalists wanted something more along the lines of the current United Nations than the United States.

> *In a democracy, the opposition is not only tolerated as constitutional, but must be maintained because it is indispensable.*
>
> WALTER LIPPMANN

The federalists demanded a strong chief executive with sweeping powers. He (women were not allowed to vote, much less run for office) would be something of an emperor, but one chosen by the people in regular but widely spaced elections.

The anti-federalists thought that a simple amendment to the Articles of Confederation—something along the lines of "Resolved, that this document is null and void unless some country declares war on one of the states"—was all that was necessary. ("And can't we all go home now? It's Philadelphia and it's summer and it's *hot*.")

As in all politics, the final document was a compromise: there would be a strong federal government, but the power would be held jointly between three equal branches—the executive, the legislative, and the judicial. The Constitution, however, would be "the supreme law of the land," superseding all state constitutions and laws on certain specific points, but leaving the states free to legislate on matters not given to the federal government.

Overall, the Constitution of the United States is a federalist document. The federalist nature is evident in the first line. The original draft read, "We the people of the states of . . ." and then

> *We may be tossed*
> *upon an ocean*
> *where we can see no land—*
> *nor, perhaps, the sun or stars.*
> *But there is a chart and*
> *a compass for us to study,*
> *to consult, and to obey.*
> *That chart is*
> *the Constitution.*
>
> DANIEL WEBSTER

listed each state. The revised document, the one we know today, begins, "We the People of the United States. . . ."

One people. One nation. One supreme law.

⚖ ⚖ ⚖

Allow me to highlight certain portions of the Constitution that apply most directly to our discussion of consensual crimes.

The Constitution begins with the famous preamble, which lays out the purpose of the Constitution:

> We the People of the United States, in Order to form a more perfect Union, establish Justice, insure domestic Tranquillity, provide for the common defense, promote the general Welfare, and secure the Blessings of Liberty to ourselves and our Posterity, do ordain and establish this Constitution for the United States of America.

We the People . . . Here, it's we the people; not we the Protestants, we the Catholics, or we the atheists, but we the people— all the people.

Compare this simple, direct, all-inclusive opening with a typical formal governmental document from the days of monarchy. The documents were always in the name of the monarch who ruled by the grace of God, and usually granted a privilege to some Special Class of Human Beings, or took some privilege away from one Special Class of Human Beings and gave it to an Even More Special Class of Human Beings. Take, for example, the opening of the Magna Carta:

> John, by the grace of God, King of England, Lord of Ireland, Duke of Normandy and Acquitaine, and Count of Anjou, to the archbishops, bishops, abbots, earls, barons, justiciars, foresters, sheriffs, provosts, officers, and all his bailiffs and faithful people, Greeting. Know that by the in-

spiration of God and for the salvation of our soul and those of all our ancestors and successors, to the honor of God and the exaltation of the Holy Church, and the improvement of our kingdom . . .

Note the delineation of power—the holy royal pecking order. We knew who was on first (God),

> *I love my country.*
> *I fear my government.*
>
> BUMPER STICKER

who was on second (the king), who was on third (the archbishops). Somehow you knew that in a disagreement between, say, an archbishop and one of the "faithful people" (way, way down the list), the archbishop would win.

None of this nonsense opens the Constitution. In a government document at that time, it was radical not to mention the ruling monarch and downright revolutionary not to mention God. Even the individual states don't get special recognition. From the outset, it was a document without classes of people, with no highs, no lows, no one better or worse—it is a document of "We the People."*

In Order to form a more perfect Union . . . The intent was to form a union (a government) "more perfect" than had ever existed before. The imperfections (injustices) of other governments were well known and eloquently documented. The most obvious example of an imperfect union was the Inquisition. Like the Spanish flu, it was not limited to Spain. The Inquisition had been alternately smoldering and flaring since the late 1400s. Not only were heretics tortured and burned at the stake, but, when taken over by the government (as it soon was), the Inquisition was a tool of terror and oppression against anyone's actions, values, or

---

*In 1787, this did not include women, Native Americans, or blacks. Subsequent amendments did include them. The Constitution, as it stands today—and as it has stood since 1920—excludes no individual or group of United States citizens from the phrase, "We the People."

> *If there is any principle
> of the Constitution
> that more imperatively calls
> for attachment than any other
> it is the principle of free thought—
> not free thought for those
> who agree with us
> but freedom for the thought
> that we hate.*
>
> JUSTICE OLIVER WENDELL HOLMES, JR.

ideas that irritated the rulers. (They still did all this, of course, in the name of God.)

Galileo, for example, was summoned before the Inquisition in 1633 at the age of sixty-nine and forced to publicly admit he was wrong when he said the earth was not the center of the universe and that the earth revolved around the sun. According to the prevailing interpretation of the Bible, the universe revolved around a God-created stationary earth. To say otherwise was heresy. (The apocryphal story has Galileo saying under his breath as he listened to the pronouncement of the Inquisition, "It moves just the same.") Because Galileo recanted, he was spared the stake and was instead placed under house arrest for the remaining nine years of his life.

The great thinkers of the Enlightenment—who adored scientific advancement—found the persecution of Galileo particularly appalling. They used it again and again as an example of what governments should not do.

The "more perfect Union of the United States," then, would be one not based on intolerance, injustice, prejudice, religious beliefs, or the whims of the ruling class. It was based on "Life, Liberty, and the pursuit of Happiness."

Establish Justice . . . Justice—a fundamental fairness in the government's interactions with its people—was notably lacking in 1787. Throughout the world one was generally presumed guilty when accused and had a few frantic moments in which to prove one's innocence while one's method of punishment (often execution) was being prepared. Those afforded a trial of any kind—a luxury in itself—were often given such treatment as "trial by fire," in which the accused carried a glowing-hot bar of iron up three stairs and then dropped it (if you had blisters on your hands three days later, you were guilty), or "trial by water," in which you were thrown into a body of water and, if you sank and didn't re-surface (something human bodies seldom do when thrown into water), you were presumed innocent and were set free (providing, of course, you didn't drown before they fished you out). For the common person, trial before a jury of one's peers was almost

> *I believe in only one thing: liberty; but I do not believe in liberty enough to want to force it upon anyone.*
>
> H. L. MENCKEN

unheard of. Generally, the most one got was a trial before a magistrate or bailiff who was constable, judge, jury, and executioner all in one.

The idea that there would be justice—fair laws equally applied to all—was again revolutionary. The vast majority of injustices discussed by the great writers of the Enlightenment consisted of punishing "crimes" that had no innocent victims. No one complained when a highwayman was hung; it was the hanging of heretics (after torturing them so that "the devil" would leave their bodies) that incensed these writers. If one was killed while physically attacking a king, well, *c'est la politique*. What infuriated our founding fathers was that people were condemned for high treason and beheaded because they, oh, refused to acknowledge the monarch's right to dump his current wife (again) and marry another.*

To the framers of the Constitution, such excesses of the ruler's power—supported by, demanded by, or excused by the ruler's religion—were not justice. Each citizen was entitled to justice without being aligned and in slavish agreement with the ruling powers.

---

*This was the fate of Sir Thomas More, who never actually criticized the marriage of King Henry VIII and Anne Boleyn, but committed the capital offense—so offensive to the king—of keeping silent about it. If this was the treatment received by the chancellor of England, second in power only to the king, imagine the injustices heaped upon less lofty subjects.

> *The Constitution is not neutral.*
> *It was designed*
> *to take the government*
> *off the backs of people.*
>
> JUSTICE WILLIAM O. DOUGLAS

Moreover, it was the government's job to *guarantee* justice to any citizen whose liberty was being threatened—to defend anyone from being forcefully put upon by others—including religious groups or the government itself. This is what the founding fathers meant by "establish Justice."

Ensure domestic Tranquillity . . . It's hard to imagine that the domestic tranquility our founding fathers wanted to preserve was the tranquillity of the self-righteous—no matter how vocal or how many. On the contrary, they seemed to enjoy tweaking the righteousness of the mighty—promoting anything but tranquility in the domiciles of authority. The sort of don't-rock-the-boat-leave-well-enough-alone complacency ("If we legalize all the consensual crimes, think of all the *trouble* it will cause") was clearly not the domestic tranquility the founding fathers intended to promote. They advocated—and succeeded at—a violent revolution against a centuries-old religious belief (that the king of England ruled by "divine right") and a government (Great Britain's) that had done little more than impose on British Americans minor taxes. However upsetting the results might be to some, "domestic Tranquility" meant freedom—not conformity for the sake of "smoothing things over."

Promote the general Welfare . . . The general welfare the framers of the Constitution were trying to promote was a government in which all people had sufficient individual freedom to explore ideas, themselves, and life itself, and to do with that life what they thought best. The general welfare was a government of freedom of thought and action for which our forebears risked everything.

AIN'T NOBODY'S BUSINESS IF YOU DO

Secure the Blessings of Liberty to ourselves and our Posterity . . . That's us: Posterity. The Blessings of Liberty? I'm sure you know my definition of that.

⚖️ ⚖️ ⚖️

Article I of the Constitution discusses the various qualifications for holding office. The only require-

> *One of the things that really bothers me is that Americans don't have any sense of history. The majority of Americans don't have any idea of where we've come from, so they naturally succumb to the kind of cliché version that Ronald Reagan represented.*
>
> ROBERT MASSIE
> Pulitzer Prize–winning historian

ments are age, citizenship, and residency. It's more important to note the qualifications that are not given. There was no need to espouse religious, political, or moral beliefs, sexual preference, or anything else to be eligible to hold office. As we will discuss in the next chapter on separation of church and state, most states at that time had religious restriction for those holding office—a belief in the Christian religion, a belief in the Trinity, to be a practicing Protestant. These restrictions were swept aside by the Constitution.

As we shall see when we discuss the Tenth Amendment, what the Constitution doesn't say is just as important as what it does say. Essentially, all rights not taken by the Constitution for the federal government remain those of the states or the people. But just so there would be absolutely no doubt about the framers' intent, Article VI of the Constitution reiterates,

> . . . no religious Test shall ever be required as a Qualification to any Office or public Trust under the United States.*

Article I, Section 8 lists what the Congress—and, hence, the government of the United States—has the power to do. This section is known as the *Enumeration of Powers.* It lists, quite

---

*Although eleven of the thirteen colonies had some religious test of office, this article was unanimously passed by the Constitutional Convention. It would be used as ammunition by those who opposed the Constitution, claiming it was a Godless document, worthy only of a Godless people.

> *Outside of the Constitution*
> *we have no legal authority*
> *more than private citizens,*
> *and within it we have*
> *only so much*
> *as that instrument gives us.*
> *This broad principle*
> *limits all our functions*
> *and applies to all subjects.*
>
> ANDREW JOHNSON

clearly, what the federal government can do: collect taxes, borrow money, regulate commerce, standardize bankruptcy laws, coin money, punish counterfeiters, establish a post office, assign patents and copyrights, set up courts, punish pirates, declare wars, raise armies, maintain a navy—the practical running of a lean, mind-your-own-business government. Basically, it provides for a strong national defense, maintains a level playing field for those who wish to try their skill at commerce (it will even keep pirates at bay), creates an impartial court system for the settlement of disputes (which usually arise during acts of commerce), keeps ideas and things moving (with a post office, toll roads, copyrights, and patents), and that's about it. No, that's not about it—*that's it!*

Nowhere in the Enumeration of Powers is there anything remotely resembling "regulation of personal or public morality," "making sure no citizens hurt themselves by experimental, reckless, or even downright foolhardy behavior," or "bringing God's laws to Earth as God's laws are interpreted by whichever religious group gathers enough political power." The Enumeration of Powers gives the government the power to *run the government,* not the personal or religious lives of the people.

The last paragraph of Article II, Section 1 begins,

> Before [the president] shall enter on the Execution of his
> Office, he shall take the following Oath or Affirmation:—
> "I do solemnly swear (or affirm) . . ."

The use of the words *affirmation* and *affirm* is significant. In the eighteenth century it was clearly understood that an *oath* was something taken before God; an *affirmation* was something taken on one's personal integrity, without having to acknowledge there even was a God. One would either be "sworn in" before God, or one would make an affirmation, personally promising to tell the truth, uphold an office, or whatever one was about to do.

In England at the time, you could only take an oath—an oath to a *Christian* God; you could not make an affirmation. Before giving testimony in a court of law, one had to claim allegiance to the Christian faith and then swear to God to tell the truth. If one failed to take an oath, one could not provide testimony. The ramifications of the law were far reaching. If, for example, someone robbed you, and, if only you and the robber were present, it was not your word against his: if the robber agreed to take an oath and you did not, only the robber's evidence would be admissible in court. This put all non-Christians at a great disadvantage. The courts of law (as well as the sheriffs, magistrates, bailiffs, and other officials) were, for the most part, unavailable to them. The same was true if one were accused of a crime: unless one claimed allegiance to the Christian religion, one could not testify in one's own defense. This law remained in effect in England until 1879. (The antisemitic ramifications of this law are obvious.)

To add the words *affirmation* and *affirm* (and to repeat them in Article VI) is a clear and intentional separation of church and state. The existence of this separation, when discussing consensual crimes, is critical, and will be explored in detail in the chapter, "Laws against Consensual Activities Violate the Separation of Church and State, Threatening the Freedom of and from Religion"* and the chapter, "What Jesus and the Bible Really Said about Consensual Crimes."

> *Can it be*
> *I am the only Jew*
> *residing in Danville, Kentucky,*
> *looking for a matzo*
> *in the Safeway and the A&P?*
>
> MAXINE KUMIN

---

*Two small indicators of how far we've come from the constitutional separation of church and state: (a) The president's swearing in is always re-

> *When we lose*
> *the right to be different,*
> *we lose*
> *the privilege to be free.*
>
> CHARLES EVANS HUGHES

Article III, Section 3 of the Constitution states the limitation of what would be considered treason:

Treason against the United States, shall consist only in levying War against them, or in adhering to their Enemies, giving them Aid and Comfort. No Person shall be convicted of Treason unless on the Testimony of two Witnesses to the same overt Act, or on Confession in open Court.

This is a major statement affirming freedom of expression. For us, living in an age when the royal family of England has more trashy tabloid coverage than Madonna, Brad Pitt, and aliens from outer space combined, it's hard to imagine what a significant statement this was.

In eighteenth-century England—and in most of the world for that matter—saying, for example, "The king is a tyrant," could have gotten you beheaded. Further, if someone *said* that you said the king was a tyrant, that would probably have been enough to ensure your execution. King Henry VIII had Anne Boleyn beheaded for high treason. The grounds? Infidelity. All it took was one person to admit—under torture—that he "loved" Boleyn, and Boleyn went to the block. Can you imagine the blood bath in the royal family if the same rules applied today?

Back then it was treason merely to say something the monarch did not like. The preferences of the monarch, from religion to fashion, were well known—sometimes laws—and to flout

ferred to as the "Oath of Office," never the "Affirmation of Office." (b) The last phrase, "so help me God," which has become a standard part of the inauguration, is not part of the Constitution. All the Constitution requires is that the president swear or affirm to "faithfully execute the Office of the President of the United States, and will to the best of my Ability, preserve, protect and defend the Constitution of the United States."

AIN'T NOBODY'S BUSINESS IF YOU DO

convention might upset the monarch, which was treason. (Actually, upsetting a duke, earl, or baron was treason; upsetting the king or queen was high treason. Upsetting a bishop, archbishop, or cardinal was heresy, often punished by death and carried out— with the state's blessing— by the church's armed enforcers, who were often

> *You hear about*
> *constitutional rights,*
> *free speech and the free press.*
> *Every time I hear these words*
> *I say to myself,*
> *"That man is a Red!"*
> *You never hear a <u>real</u> American*
> *talk like that!*
>
> MAYOR FRANK HAGUE

more numerous than the crown's.) "That the king can do no wrong," wrote Sir William Blackstone in 1769, "is a necessary and fundamental principle of the English constitution."

The founding fathers basically said, "Enough!" To insult, affront, or even seriously disturb the ruler was no longer grounds for punishment.

The founding fathers asked themselves, "What is the purpose of laws against treason," just as they asked themselves, "What is the purpose of all law?" The purpose of laws against treason was to defend the United States against acts of physical violence— "levying War against" it, or giving "Aid and Comfort" to those who were physically warring against the United States. Here, the principle that every crime needs a victim is re-established.

In defending this principle, the founding fathers opened themselves to all sorts of personal discomfort. Some of them knew they would serve in some public capacity and, by making war the only basis for treason, they were giving the people and the press free reign to attack them in any way other than physically.

The second point, involving "two Witnesses to the same overt* Act" or "Confession in open Court," prohibited people

---

*Note the use of the word *overt*. One can't just be *thinking* about doing something; one actually has to *do* it. This, again, supports the notion that it is an act of *physical* harm (in this case, war) that constitutes a crime.

from manipulating others by threatening to accuse them of treason. Just as today threats of exposing or prosecuting consensual crimes are often used to blackmail and to extort information and behavior from an unwilling party, so too the laws of treason were used for similar underhanded manipulation. Requiring that there be two witnesses to an overt act makes it much more difficult to falsify charges.*

Article IV, Section 2 begins, "The Citizens of each State shall be entitled to all Privileges and Immunities of Citizens in the several States." This, once again, affirms that the Constitution is the supreme law of the land and that no state can take away the "Privileges" or "Immunities" (protections) given by the Constitution and the federal government. (This protection would be strengthened and deepened by the Fourteenth Amendment.)

At the close of the main body of the Constitution—desperate to find God in there somewhere—some people will point to the words "the Seventeenth Day of September in the Year of our Lord one thousand seven hundred and Eighty seven." They say, "You see, they claim that Jesus is their Lord."

"The Year of our Lord" is, of course, a legal term commonly used in the eighteenth century. It no more acknowledges that Jesus is Lord than writing, "It happened in 436 B.C." acknowledges that Jesus was the Christ. It's an agreed-upon way of counting days that happened to be invented by some Christian

---

*If all crimes have clear-cut victims, it's much more difficult to falsify testimony. For example, "He offered to sell me drugs," is much easier to falsify than, "He threw a brick through my window." To prove the latter, one would need to provide a brick and a shattered window. To prove the former, one needs only an imagination.

monks.* The Gregorian Calendar—the one that's been
in use since 1582—re-
quired the papal decree of
Pope Gregory XIII for its
adoption. (Science did not
determine things then; the
pope did.) Although the
current calendar is a "religious document" issued by a
papal bull, to say that each
time we refer to the calendar it is an act of Catholi-

> *Fear of serious injury
> cannot alone justify suppression
> of free speech and assembly.
> Men feared witches
> and burned women.
> It is the function of speech
> to free men from the bondage
> of irrational fears.*
>
> JUSTICE LOUIS D. BRANDEIS

cism, Christianity, or religion of any kind is absurd. Besides, at
least three signers of the Constitution—George Washington,
John Adams, and Benjamin Franklin (and almost certainly James
Monroe)—were not Christians at all. They were Deists. (More on
this in the next chapter.)

⚖ ⚖ ⚖

The Bill of Rights

Once it was decided that there would be a strong, central
(federal) government, many people—most notably, Thomas Jefferson, James Madison, and, later, John Adams—wanted to make
sure that the power of that government was severely limited—
especially where the rights of the individual were concerned.

*If you think I'm getting a little paranoid here in suggesting that anyone in
his or her right mind would use the single phrase, "in The Year of our
Lord," to ignore all the constitutional guarantees of separation of church
and state, allow me to quote the once (and probably future) presidential
hopeful, founder and chairman of the Christian Broadcasting Network, described by his publisher as "America's best known and most listened to
Christian leader" (Jerry Falwell, eat your heart out), Pat Robertson, from his
book *The New Millennium:* "When George Washington signed our Constitution, he dated it 'In the year of our Lord, 1787.' There was only one Lord
whose birthday dated back 1787 years: Jesus Christ. The founding document of the United States of America acknowledges the Lordship of Jesus
Christ, because we were a Christian nation."

> *A bill of rights is what*
> *the people are entitled to*
> *against every government on earth,*
> *general or particular,*
> *and what no just government*
> *should refuse to rest on inference.*
>
> THOMAS JEFFERSON
> Letter to James Madison
> December 20, 1787

They wanted to be certain that the government did what it needed to do, and nothing more. Other than defending the borders, establishing treaties, settling disputes, keeping a level playing field for commerce, and ensuring the free flow of goods and ideas, they wanted to make sure the government left the people blessedly alone. "I am for a government rigorously frugal and simple," wrote Jefferson. "Were we directed from Washington when to sow, when to reap, we should soon want bread."

Jefferson and the others called for a Bill of Rights, a series of amendments to the Constitution which clearly delineated what the government could and, more importantly, could not do to regulate individual thought and behavior.

Those who favored the Constitution without a Bill of Rights were not against the *ideas* propounded in the Bill of Rights, but only argued that such guarantees were unnecessary because they already were contained within the main body of the Constitution. The Enumeration of Powers, they claimed, limited the government to basic functions. None of these enumerated powers infringed on the individual unless that individual harmed the person or property of another. The government could not take on additional powers—such as regulating speech, religion, the press, or anything else—without adding a constitutional amendment. In other words, if the Constitution didn't say that the government specifically *could* do something, it couldn't. As Alexander Hamilton explained,

> For why declare that things shall not be done which there
> is no power to do? Why, for instance, should it be said
> that the liberty of the press shall not be restrained, when
> no power is given by which restrictions may be imposed?

AIN'T NOBODY'S BUSINESS IF YOU DO

"No," said those in favor of a Bill of Rights, "we all understand that the intent of the government is not to restrict freedom, but we don't know what some nefarious people twenty, fifty, two hundred years from now might attempt to do with the Constitution. The Constitution is a contract between the government and the people. It is

> *It's easy for people to assume that the Bill of Rights will be, as somebody once called the Constitution, a machine that runs itself. I disagree. I think eternal vigilance is the price of keeping it in working order.*
>
> JUDGE LAWRENCE TRIBE

important to spell out clearly not only what the government can do, but what it cannot do as well."*

"But," argued those against a Bill of Rights, "if we specifically say that the federal government cannot do certain things, then the implication will be that it can do everything else. The list of what it can't do could go on forever. And what about those things it can't do that haven't been invented yet?"

Those in favor of a Bill of Rights responded, "We will make the limitations general enough to cover large areas of freedoms, but specific enough to give a clear indication of what we mean. The basic form of government in the world today is tyrannical and opposed to individual freedoms. We want the people of the United States, all the world, and all posterity to see clearly—without having to read between the lines—the freedoms we believe the government simply cannot take away."

The pro–Bill of Rights argument won the day. So those in favor of the Constitution as it was said, "Let's pass the Constitution as it is, and we'll immediately begin working on a Bill of Rights." It was this promise of a Bill of Rights that got the Constitution enough support to become the supreme law of the land. The basic Constitution was submitted to the states for ratifica-

---

*"In questions of power," Thomas Jefferson wrote, "let no more be heard of confidence in man, but bind him down from mischief by the chains of the Constitution."

tion in 1787, and ratified in 1788. In 1789, at the first session of Congress, the Bill of Rights was proposed, and its adoption was certified on December 15, 1791. (The three states that failed to ratify the Bill of Rights—Massachusetts, Georgia, and Connecticut—eventually did so. In 1939.)

Let's look at the Bill of Rights in David Letterman order—from ten to one. To the average citizen, the First Amendment—guaranteeing freedom of speech, the press, assembly, petition, and freedom of and from religion—seems the most important. From a legal point of view (many of the founding fathers were lawyers, and the judges in the courts interpreting the Constitution today are all lawyers) number ten is the most significant.

The Tenth Amendment reads,

> The powers not delegated to the United States by the Constitution, nor prohibited by it to the States, are reserved to the States respectively, or to the people.

This affirms what the founding fathers unanimously agreed on at the time—that if the Constitution didn't specifically take away a power (that is, a right or a freedom) from the people, the people kept it. This settled once and for all, the fundamental question, "Does the government inherently have all the power and then dole out rights to the people, or do the people inherently have all the power and—in exchange for certain benefits—surrender specific powers to the government?" Concerning the government of the United States, the answer is clear: the people inherently have the power and turn specific powers over to the government in exchange for certain benefits. These powers were detailed in the Constitution (the Enumeration of Powers), and all other powers belong to the people.

The Ninth Amendment says,

> The enumeration in the Constitution, of certain rights, shall not be construed to deny or disparage others retained by the people.

Just because the Constitution says you have certain rights does not mean that you don't also have

> *The layman's constitutional view is that what he likes is constitutional and that which he doesn't like is unconstitutional.*
>
> JUSTICE HUGO BLACK

other rights which the Constitution didn't bother to enumerate. This amendment was designed to counter the argument, "If we list certain rights, then it might be supposed that those are the only rights the people have." As in the Tenth Amendment, the people clearly hold all the rights, and just because some of those basic rights are listed in the Constitution does not in any way mean to limit the rights not mentioned.

The Eighth Amendment reads,

> Excessive bail shall not be required, nor excessive fines imposed, nor cruel and unusual punishments inflicted.

To me it seems both cruel and unusual to punish people for doing something that potentially could harm only themselves. This is especially true when the punishment is almost always worse than the damage they might do to themselves. Such punishment is, however, so usual we've become numb to its cruelty.

The Seventh Amendment guarantees a jury in civil matters. While the government is there to protect us from harm, it cannot protect us from all possible harm, nor can it lock up everyone we feel has harmed us. The government can, however, guarantee a fair system by which disputes between individuals (*civil* matters) can be settled. This system is a trial by jury.

We can't make everything a *criminal* matter, the Constitution is saying: we can't lock up every citizen who displeases another citizen. Citizens do, however, harm each other in ways not pro-

> *An individual,*
> *thinking himself injured,*
> *makes more noise*
> *than a State.*
>
> THOMAS JEFFERSON
> 1785

hibited by criminal law, and there should be a system for rectifying the harm.

If, for example, I borrow ten dollars from you and do not pay it back when promised, I have physically harmed you (by not returning your property). I have not, however, stolen from you in a criminal way: you did, after all, consent to loan it to me. Implied in the consent to loan is the risk you won't get it back. (A victim of criminal thievery never consents at any point.) Nonetheless, the ten dollars is rightfully yours. While you cannot put me in jail, you can take me to court, and the government's job is to (a) make sure the rules of the court are fair and equally applied to us both, and (b) use force, if necessary, to carry out the judgment of the court. If the court finds in your favor and orders me to pay the money but even then I refuse to pay it (never loan money to a writer), the court can send law enforcement agents to seize my property, sell it, and pay you your ten dollars from the proceeds. It cannot, however, throw me in jail until I pay up.

This amendment acknowledges that not every physical harm one person does another is a criminal offense. How much less a criminal offense it must be, then, when people only potentially harm themselves. Not only does the Constitution have no authority to regulate personal morality; it offers no system by which to do so.

This amendment also gives moralists a system by which they can protect themselves without using the full force of the criminal justice system. The moralist groups can take those who offend them to civil court. Let a jury decide. The reason most moral groups don't do this is (a) most of their cases would be thrown out of court for lack of sufficient grounds and (b) most cases that went before a jury would lose.

Instead, moralist groups threaten—or have elected—legislators, badger police, intimidate the media, and frighten the public into using the criminal arm of the law to punish the very same actions they could not hope to control in civil court. For example, if there were no laws against drug use, can you imagine Pat Robertson taking me to civil court and getting a court order prohibiting me from smoking pot in my own home? Jerry Falwell believes drinking alcohol is a sin. Can you imagine how few liquor stores he could close through the civil courts? (His political-spiritual ancestors, however, closed down all the liquor stores during Prohibition by making possession of liquor a criminal offense.)

> *Anyone who does anything*
> *for pleasure*
> *to indulge his selfish soul*
> *will surely burn in Hell.*
>
> LENNY BRUCE

The Constitution made provisions for the settlement of civil disputes so that the government could use its criminal enforcement arm for only the most clearly criminal acts. The acts of civil misconduct—even many that do cause physical harm to others—the Constitution left to the civil courts.

The Sixth Amendment lists one's rights in criminal prosecution. This amendment guarantees "the right to a speedy and public trial, by an impartial jury."* One of the requirements for this jury trial in criminal prosecutions is for the accused "to be confronted with the witnesses against him." In a trial for a consensual crime, who are the witnesses against the person accused? In a genuine crime (except murder, of course) the victim can come forth and testify against the accused. If someone

---

*In 1995, the chief prosecutor of Los Angeles County, James Hahn, admitted that the courts were clogged with criminal cases and things were only going to get worse. His solution? Among other notions, he recommended eliminating the right to a jury trial for "drug offenders." Was there any sort of outcry against his clearly unconstitutional proposal? No.

> *[The Bill of Rights is] designed to protect individuals and minorities against the tyranny of the majority, but it's also designed to protect the people against bureaucracy, against the government.*
>
> JUDGE LAWRENCE TRIBE

pushes you down and takes your money, you can go to court and testify against the person who did it.

But if there is no clear-cut victim, who is there to testify "against" you? In trials involving consensual crimes, the witnesses are generally the police ("I broke down the door and after a diligent search of the premises found a small bag containing two grams of white powder which I believed to be an illicit substance"), friends of the accused who testify against the accused in order to avoid prosecution for the same consensual crime (this is called "turning state's evidence" as well as "turning on your friends"), police lab technicians who proclaim, "Yes, this is pot," and state social workers who proclaim, "Yes, this is a prostitute." None of these people was harmed by the accused. In fact, all of them are being paid by the government in some way to testify.

The intent of the Sixth Amendment was that before the government can punish a citizen, the person or persons harmed by that citizen must stand in public court and tell a jury what harm was done to them and how the accused did it. In cases involving consensual crimes, unharmed, government-paid (or government-coerced) witnesses testify against Accused A, who could just as easily be Accused B, C, or D. This system, to which we have become painfully accustomed (it's used for roughly half the court cases in the country), is an obvious perversion of the intent behind the Sixth Amendment's requirement that the accused "be confronted with the witnesses against him."

The *Fifth Amendment* is most famous for the provision that one does not have to testify against oneself in a criminal case—to "take the Fifth." If you were made to testify against yourself, you would often be torn between self-incrimination and perjury. This amendment, too, offers protection against prosecution for consensual activities: since the only clear-cut victim in a consensual crime is the person involved in the crime, and the person involved in the crime is the one who would be accused, the Fifth Amendment says that you don't have to give any information about the crime. Hence, a lot of consensual crimes have— thanks to the Constitu-

> *The privilege against self-incrimination is one of the great landmarks in man's struggle to make himself civilized. . . . The Fifth is a lone sure rock in time of storm . . . a symbol of the ultimate moral sense of the community, upholding the best in us.*
>
> ERWIN GRISWOLD
> former dean of Harvard Law School

tion—not been prosecuted as vigorously as they might. Courts can prove possession of drugs, but not necessarily drug use; prostitutes can be convicted for soliciting, but not necessarily having sex; gamblers can be convicted for being where gambling is taking place, but not actually gambling.

Another important guarantee of the Fifth Amendment reads, "Nor shall private property be taken for public use without just compensation." This affirms the sanctity of private property. The government does not own or control our property; we do. If the government takes it "for public use," the government must provide "just compensation." In other words, even if the public—the *people*—have a pressing need for your private property, they can't have it unless they justly compensate you. This is a clear statement that the government will protect the individual against the majority and even protect the individual against the government itself. As we will explore more fully in the chapter, "Laws against Consensual Activities Are Opposed to the Principles of Private Property, Free Enterprise, Capitalism, and the Open Market," the idea of private property encompasses the idea that we can do with our property as we see fit—use it, sell it, trade it, give it, and, yes, even destroy it. As long as it doesn't infringe on the person or property of another, it ain't no government's business if we do.

The Fourth Amendment begins,

> *The 4th Amendment*
> *and the personal rights it secures*
> *have a long history.*
> *At the very core stands*
> *the right of a man*
> *to retreat into his own home*
> *and there be free*
> *from unreasonable*
> *governmental intrusion.*

JUSTICE POTTER STEWART

The right of the people to be secure in their persons, houses, papers, and effects, against unreasonable searches and seizures, shall not be violated . . .

Again, we have a clear directive that the government should stay out of our private property, unless it has a specific search warrant (described in the rest of the amendment).*

The Third Amendment reads,

No Soldier shall, in time of peace be quartered in any house, without the consent of the Owner, nor in time of war, but in a manner to be prescribed by law.

Once again, the Constitution affirms the absolute sanctity of private property. Even a soldier—who may someday risk his or her life to defend your life and property—cannot spend a night

---

*Consensual crimes have been used to make "unreasonable" search and seizure seem more reasonable. For example, a car is considered an extension of one's person, house, papers, and effects, and a police officer cannot search a car without a warrant. The courts have added, however, that if police officers can easily sense "probable cause" to believe a crime has been committed, they have the right to search the car on the spot without a warrant. (An example of probable cause is a large amount of what appears to be fresh blood on the back seat.) If, in their "probable cause" search for one thing, they find another (or if they merely destroy the car in the process), it is an acceptable search and seizure. If, when stopping a car, the police claim to "smell marijuana," many courts have upheld this as probable cause. Obviously certain less-than-ethical police officers can claim to "smell marijuana" to justify overriding the Constitution whenever they wish. The public concern over the increase in crime (caused almost entirely by the war on drugs) has allowed legislators to give police even more opportunities to break into our homes. Less and less is a court order necessary; more and more it is left to "police discretion." Aren't people aware that with enough police discretion, our country will become a police state?

in your house without your permission. Second, the amendment shows that, in time of war, things change. In time of war, it is understood that certain sacrifices must be made, but even then a soldier can't stay in a private house unless a law is passed allowing him or her to do so. In other words, the legislature must pass a bill, the president

> *This provision speaks for itself. Its plain object is to secure the perfect enjoyment of that great right of the common law, that a man's house shall be his own castle, privileged against all civil and military intrusion.*
>
> JUSTICE JOSEPH STORY
> 1833

must sign it (or be overriden by a veto), and the courts are available for recourse if someone considers the law unfair. This is one of many safeguards in the Constitution against a police state, against a military body that decides its needs are more important than those of a citizen and takes what it wants by force. In order for this to happen, according to the Constitution, the Congress must first declare war and then, in addition to declaring war, pass a law stating that, for the duration of the war, soldiers may stay in private houses without the owners' permission and (going back to the Fifth Amendment) stating what sort of compensation the owners of the houses shall receive.

The Second Amendment affirms "The right of the people to keep and bear Arms." Here is the constitutional basis of what some—mostly liberals—call the paranoia of people who feel the need to arm themselves.

The reasoning behind this amendment turns out to be not the paranoia of a few gun-stockpiling kooks, but the hard-edged pragmatism of the founding fathers; a pragmatism based firmly on historical precedent. People who are not permitted to individually keep and bear arms are relatively easy to conquer and subdue by even a small well-armed group. In taking control of an innocent group of people, a tyrant almost invariably first deprives them of their right to bear arms, making it easier to later deprive them of liberty and life.

> *Power may be at the end of a gun,*
> *but sometimes it's also*
> *at the end of the shadow*
> *or the image of a gun.*
>
> JEAN GENET

Quite often the well-armed populace does not need to defend itself from a door-to-door attack because, frankly, a well-armed populace is such a deterrent that tyrants often spread their tyranny among the lambs and avoid significant interaction with the lions.

Imagine for a moment that you are a tyrant. Town A (Lambsville) has $10,000,000 in wealth spread among an unarmed populace of 10,000. Town B (Lionsburg) has $10,000,000 in wealth spread among 5,000 well-armed, well-trained citizens. Which town would you plunder first? As has been clear to tyrants throughout time, Lambsville will get shorn while Lionsburg sleeps peacefully in the sun.

Even our own government (and I'm not going to speculate on its position on the benevolent-to-tyrannical scale) pursues unarmed consensual crime quarries far more often than heavily armed ones. If the Branch Davidian compound at Waco had been your ordinary, unarmed weirdo cult, do you think any of us would have heard about what would have been a very uneventful raid? Although it would have made the front page in Waco, the swift round-up and eventual release of a band of odd believers would have been buried in the second section of the Dallas papers and probably never mentioned by *Time, Newsweek,* the *Los Angeles Times,* or the *New York Times*. And although the Branch Davidians died in the mystery inferno, they certainly made their point; I doubt very much if a branch of the federal government will be attacking an armed cult again in the near future.

On local levels, it is well known that individual drug users or casual drug sellers are arrested more often than residents of heavily fortified crack houses or well-armed drug-lord lairs. Most law enforcement officials just hate being shot at.

⚖️ ⚖️ ⚖️

It is in this space be-
tween the Second and the
First Amendments that liberals and conservatives
have their greatest split:
liberals love the First
Amendment; conservatives
love the Second. This is
also the space where liberals and conservatives show

> *I'm a card-carrying member*
> *of the ACLU and the NRA.*
>
> DAVID MAMET

their greatest similarities: each uses the same reasoning in attempting to deny the other group rights guaranteed by the Constitution.

Both say, "Yes, it's in the Constitution, *but . . .*" and then give
a variety of reasons why the supreme law of the land should be
suspended in this particular case. The arguments for banning
guns sound perfectly reasonable to liberals, and the arguments
for banning pornography (for example) sound perfectly reasonable to conservatives. To the celebration and consternation of
both sides, the Constitution guarantees both the right to bear
arms and to bare arms (and anything else one chooses to bare).

Like it or not, the Constitution is the rules of the game. The
rules cannot be changed by argument; they can only be changed
by *amendment.*

⚖️ ⚖️ ⚖️

Many will consider this book a liberal tome. It's not.* It may
seem to be a liberal tome only because the conservatives have
been more successful in keeping the constitutional rights most
important to them intact—as much as liberals might like it to be,
gun ownership is not, for the most part, a crime.

---

*This book, in fact, espouses Libertarianism—or at least what most Liber-
tarians believe about government and crime. I am not a spokesperson for
the Libertarian Party, not even a member. But I think I'll join. The Libertarian Party can be reached at 202–333–0008.

> *After a shooting spree,*
> *they always want to take the guns*
> *away from the people*
> *who <u>didn't</u> do it.*
> *I sure as hell*
> *wouldn't want to live in a society*
> *where the only people*
> *allowed guns*
> *are the police and the military.*
>
> WILLIAM BURROUGHS
> 1992

The conservatives are to be congratulated for this. If the conservatives hadn't done as good a job, and gun ownership were illegal, it would be on the list of consensual crimes. As the NRA puts it, "Guns don't kill people. People kill people." Amen.

The press is astonishingly biased when it comes to reporting acts of violence performed by individuals using guns. My favorite is the almost universal use of the term *assault weapons*. In fact, these semi-automatic Gatling guns could be just as accurately called "family and children protection devices." Who is to say that one of those portable bullet-spewing contraptions won't be used to defend innocent would-be victims from the deranged attack of a lunatic armed with merely a .457 magnum?

Further, those who argue for an unarmed populace do so based on the fantasy that the government can protect us from physical harm. If a burglar is breaking down your door, do you think the police will protect you? The burglar would be in and you'd be out cold before you could get 911 to answer. But if you have a gun, there's no need to wait. Protection is—literally—at hand.

We look at the number of hand gun deaths in this country (which is appalling), but who is to say how many crimes of violence were prevented by the potential victim's judicious production of a gun or by a criminal saying, "Let's not mess with him; he keeps a gun." One study showed that for each crime committed with a gun, 67 crimes were prevented with one.

The inordinate amount of Americans killing each other is caused not by guns, but by the ongoing psychotic breakdown in our culture. Picking up a gun does not instill in one the urge to kill; people have the urge to kill and then pick up guns. If there weren't a single firearm—antique or automatic—in this country,

AIN'T NOBODY'S BUSINESS IF YOU DO

we would still be murdering each other in astonishing numbers. We would just be offing each other with kitchen knives, poison, bombs, and a few hundred other devices.

Does this mean we should stop the murderers by banning kitchen utensils, household cleaners, and all the rest? I am told that you can effectively do

> *Television has brought back murder into the home —where it belongs.*
>
> ALFRED HITCHCOCK

someone in by slipping ground glass into his or her Lean Cuisine. Do we ban glass? Then there are blunt instruments, high places, bathtubs, electricity, and a whole series of potentially lethal "weapons" that can be put to use by even remedially creative humans bent on the destruction of others.*

As with drugs, prostitution, gambling, consensual sex, and all the rest, it's not the item or act that causes misery, but human misuse of same.

The liberal agenda to ban private ownership of guns is as much a constitutional violation as the conservative agenda to continue the ban on prostitution, pornography, or other currently illegal consensual activities. (The war on drugs now cuts across conservative/liberal lines, although, as we shall see, it started as a conservative notion.) Rather than take away the conservatives' constitutional rights with the same logic that the conservatives use to keep the laws against certain consensual activities on the books ("It *hurts* people!"), the liberals might be better off using some of the conservatives' tactics in pursuing their own not-fully-realized constitutional guarantees. (The NRA is powerful, but the ACLU is no slouch.)

---

*In Alfred Hitchcock's favorite episode of *Alfred Hitchcock Presents,* a wife beats her husband to death with a frozen leg of lamb, thaws it, and blithely serves it for dinner to the police inspector, who does not arrest her because he can not find the murder weapon.

> *History teaches us*
> *that men and nations*
> *only behave wisely*
> *once they have exhausted*
> *all other alternatives.*
>
> ABBA EBAN

To continue to live together under the Constitution, liberals must learn to give the conservatives their constitutional "favorites," (gun ownership, private property, strong militia), and conservatives must bite the bullet and give the liberals their favorites (freedom of press, freedom of and from religion, personal privacy).

Until the Second Amendment is repealed, people have a right to own guns. Until the First Amendment is repealed, people have the right to free speech, press, and religious choice. That's politics. That's tolerance. That's compromise. That's cooperation. That's the Constitution.

⚖️ ⚖️ ⚖️

There. Now that I've got *everybody* mad, let's move on to the greatest friend of the currently illegal consensual activities, the First Amendment.

The *First Amendment.* Ah, the best for last. The First Amendment, forty-five words that spell "freedom." Here it is in its full glory:

> Congress shall make no law respecting an establishment
> of religion, or prohibiting the free exercise thereof; or
> abridging the freedom of speech, or of the press; or the
> right of the people peaceably to assemble, and to peti-
> tion the Government for a redress of grievances.

Allow me to emphasize one portion of the First Amendment: "Congress shall make *no law*"—allow me to emphasize that again:

NO
LAW

—allow me to emphasize that once again:

NO

LAW

> *I am for the First Amendment from the first word to the last. I believe it means what it says.*
>
> JUSTICE HUGO BLACK

—"respecting an establishment of religion, or prohibiting the free exercise thereof; or abridging the freedom of speech, or of the press; or the right of the people peaceably to assemble, and to petition the Government for a redress of grievances." (Emphasis added.)

Considering these forty-five words, by what authority does Congress *dare* make laws based on limiting assembly, speech, and religion? The Enumeration of Powers, as we have seen, does not give the government this authority—and even if it did, the First Amendment would take away.

The freedom of religion is guaranteed to us twice: the freedom *from* religion and the freedom *of* religion. Most laws against consensual activities are based on religious beliefs.

With the implementation of the Constitution, the United States government broke from almost every other government in the world by not establishing an official state religion ("Congress shall make no law respecting an establishment of religion . . ."). In the 1700s, Virginia (the home state of Thomas Jefferson and George Washington) used tax dollars to support the Anglican church. Both Jefferson and Washington saw firsthand how unfree, unfair, and downright unworkable it was. In the next chapter, on the separation of church and state, we'll explore the restriction of freedom, not just by the established state religion, but by the battles fought over which religion would become The One.

The second clause of the First Amendment prohibits Congress from making any law "prohibiting the free exercise" of religion. *If the Constitution guaranteed no other freedom than this one, it would be enough to immediately abolish all consensual crimes.* Who is to say the practice of my religion should not include any activity currently on the list of consensual crimes (as long as it does not physically harm ... etc.)? More on this in the next chapter.

Congress shall also make no law "abridging the freedom of speech, or of the press." Well, there go all the censorship arguments. Period. "No law" is *no law*. I don't know how anything could be any clearer than that—and yet, and yet . . .

> *The First Amendment makes confidence in the common sense of our people and in the maturity of their judgment the great postulate of our democracy.*
>
> JUSTICE WILLIAM O. DOUGLAS

As Frank Zappa explained,

> Asked random questions about the First Amendment and how they would like to have it applied, if you believe in polls at all, the average American wants no part of it. But if you ask, "What if we threw the Constitution away tomorrow?" the answer is "No, that would be bad!" But living under the Constitution is another story altogether.

Also guaranteed in the First Amendment is "the right of the people peaceably to assemble." This constitutional guarantee is often set aside in hysteria over consensual crimes. Law enforcement agencies must merely claim that the people peaceably assembling are primarily homosexuals (or prostitutes, or drug dealers, or bookies, or indigents), declare the assembly to be "loitering," and the assembly is "legally" disassembled. Even private gatherings have a long history of being raided. This clearly goes against the freedom of peaceable assembly clause, but as with so many constitutional violations, it's been going on for so long people forget to notice.

The final guarantee of the First Amendment is the right of the people to "petition the government for a redress of grievances." Have I suggested yet that you write a letter to all of your elected representatives suggesting the elimination of all laws against consensual activities? No? I will.

⚖ ⚖ ⚖

Over the years, other amendments have been added to the Constitution which either directly or indirectly affect consensual crimes. None of them gives the government the right to control crimes without clear-cut victims—except the Eighteenth Amendment (Prohibition), which was so blatantly unsuccessful it was repealed by the Twenty-first Amendment thirteen years later. But even Prohibition proves the point: if you want to regulate an activity that does not have a clear victim, it takes a *constitutional amendment* to do so.

No state or federal law has the power to override the individual freedoms guaranteed each of us in the Constitution and the Bill of Rights.

Let's look at a few of the amendments which have been passed since the Bill of Rights.

The Fourteenth Amendment—hard won by the Civil War—guaranteed that a state could not take away the freedoms granted by the Constitution.

> . . . No State shall make or enforce any law which shall abridge the privileges or immunities of citizens of the United States; nor shall any State deprive any person of life, liberty, or property, without due process of law; nor deny to any person within its jurisdiction the equal protection of the laws. . . .

This amendment affirmed once again that the Constitution and the Bill of Rights were the *supreme* law of the land and the rights guaranteed by the Constitution could not be taken away by any state under the guise of "state's rights."

It also guarantees that a state cannot "deprive any person of life, liberty, or property, without due process of law." This affirms, once again, that we are innocent until proven guilty in a court of law, and that no group—even a majority—has the right to deprive "any person" of his or her "life, liberty, or property" just because the majority doesn't like the way that person is living. The Fourteenth Amendment is our greatest protection against a police state and against the rule by the iron whim of either the majority or a highly vocal minority.

It was we, the people;
not we, the white male citizens;
nor yet we, the male citizens;
but we, the whole people,
who formed the Union.

SUSAN B. ANTHONY

The Sixteenth Amendment, passed in 1913, gives the federal government the authority to "collect taxes on income." This reaffirms that the Constitution can only be changed by amendment. Although taxing people's incomes removes a great deal of power from the people, there is something that removes even more power from them: jailing them.

The Eighteenth Amendment. The day this amendment was ratified was a dark day in the history of freedom. One has to give the Prohibitionists credit, however, for at least doing it right. If the government is going to take away basic freedoms, the only way it can do so is through a constitutional amendment. Period. All lesser laws must fall before the "supreme law of the land" and the supreme law of the land sides with individual freedom.

The Nineteenth Amendment gave women the right to vote. It's hard to believe that in this country women did not have the right to vote until 1920. (Women didn't get the right to vote in Canada until 1948!) The outrageousness of this is another issue. Although the Constitution could have been reinterpreted to include women, it was not. This amendment is another example of change—in this case giving rights rather than taking them away—requiring a constitutional amendment.

> *There is as much chance
> of repealing the 18th Amendment
> as there is for a humming-bird
> to fly to the planet Mars
> with the Washington Monument
> tied to its tail.*
>
> MORRIS SHEPPARD

Section 1 of the *Twenty-first Amendment,* ratified in 1933, repealed the Eighteenth Amendment. Section 2 of the Twenty-first Amendment is also significant:

The transportation or importation into any State, territory, or possession of the United States for delivery or use therein of intoxicating liquors, in violation of the laws thereof, is hereby prohibited.

This was a compromise tossed to the Prohibitionists (still powerful in 1933) which allowed individual states to continue Prohibition if they so chose. Note that the control of "intoxicating liquors" had to be *constitutionally given* from the federal government to the state governments. The implication here is that other consensual activities—such as the use of drugs other than alcohol—are not within the province of the states to regulate. If people feel so strongly about the war on drugs (or warring on any other consensual activities), why don't they do the right thing by America, freedom, and the Constitution and propose an amendment?

The Twenty-seventh Amendment is mentioned here primarily for its entertainment value. It limits the number of pay raises Congress can vote itself. (Not the amount of the raise; just the number of raises.) Proposed in 1789 by James Madison, it was finally ratified by Congress—in 1992.

⚖️ ⚖️ ⚖️

So what happened? If the Constitution is so clear about our personal freedoms—as it obviously is—how did we lose them?

We never lost them because we never had them.

As constitutional scholar Professor Robert Allen Rutland explained,

> For almost 150 years, in fact, the Bill of Rights was paid lip service in patriotic orations and ignored in the marketplace. It wasn't until after World War I that the Supreme Court began the process of giving real meaning to the Bill of Rights.

> *For most Americans the Constitution had become a hazy document, cited like the Bible on ceremonial occasions but forgotten in the daily transactions of life.*
>
> ARTHUR M. SCHLESINGER, JR.

After the Bill of Rights was passed, it was pretty much forgotten. In an 1818 letter to Thomas Jefferson, John Adams wrote,

> When people talk of the freedom of writing, speaking, or thinking, I cannot choose but laugh. No such thing ever existed. No such thing now exists; but I hope it will exist. But it must be hundreds of years after you and I shall write and speak no more.

When it came to guaranteeing personal freedoms (usually known today as *civil rights), the federal government was lackluster at best. When it came to using the Constitution to raise money or wage war, however, the government was in top form.*

In 1794, the first major challenge between federal rights and states' rights took place. In 1791, Secretary of the Treasury Alexander Hamilton passed a tax on, among other things, liquor, to help pay off the revolutionary war debt (which was, in relative terms, greater than our national debt today). A group of Pennsylvania farmers decided they shouldn't have to pay a tax on their homemade whiskey, but the federal revenue collectors (the "revenuers") did not agree. The federal authorities applied pressure on the Pennsylvanians, and the chief revenuer's house was torched by the rebellious farmers. President George Washington personally led thirteen thousand troops to quell what the revenuers had told him was a mass rebellion. The troops found no

> *America was born of revolt,*
> *flourished on dissent,*
> *became great*
> *through experimentation.*
>
> HENRY STEELE COMMAGER

rebellion. Several arrests were made, there were two convictions (later pardoned by Washington), and the Whiskey Rebellion was over.

Many, including Thomas Jefferson, expressed concern that the federal government should so violently overreact. The point, nonetheless, had been made: Don't mess with the federal government when it comes to paying your federal taxes.

From the passage of the Bill of Rights in 1791 until the Civil War, states were generally allowed to violate an individual's constitutional rights as they pleased, as long as the federal government got its taxes and its troops.

The Civil War was not, as most people think, fought for the civil rights of the slaves. It was, in fact, an extension of the Whiskey Rebellion. The federal government said, "You do it our way," and the southern states said, "No, we're going to do it our way." Slavery was only one of the issues on which North and South disagreed. The primary disagreements were over (1) money and (2) men and equipment for war—which is a variation of (1).

The judicial view of slavery was made painfully clear in the Supreme Court's 1857 Dred Scott Decision. It proclaimed that slaves were not human beings but "articles of merchandise," that slaves "had no rights which the white man was bound to respect," and that slaves were never entitled to become citizens of the United States. (If you ever want to question the fallibility of the Supreme Court, look no further than this.)

When elected to office in 1860, Abraham Lincoln stated he did not like slavery personally, but he was willing to endure it for the sake of peace and national unity. Lincoln firmly proclaimed, however, that, although he was flexible on almost all other issues, he would have a Union and he would do whatever was necessary to preserve that Union.

Shortly after his inauguration in 1861, seven southern states decided to rebel against what they viewed as his too-paternal attitude and seceded from the Union. Had Lincoln acknowledged their right to secede, there probably

> *[The South] has too much common sense and good temper to break up [the Union].*
>
> ABRAHAM LINCOLN
> August 1860

would have been no war. Instead, Lincoln blockaded the southern seaports (essential for trade and Southern survival), the Confederates fired in retaliation on Fort Sumpter, and the war was on. In 1862, Simon Cameron, U.S. Secretary of War, wrote,

> President Lincoln desires the right to hold slaves to be fully recognized. The war is prosecuted for the Union, hence no question concerning slavery will arise.

It wasn't until 1863 that Lincoln issued the Emancipation Proclamation as a political move to get the Northern Abolitionists on his side after two years of bloody fighting and few victories.

What was later portrayed as a holy war against slavery was, in fact, the federal government putting its foot down firmly and finally: the United States Constitution (not any state constitution) was the supreme law of the land, and that was that.

Shortly after the North won the Civil War, the Thirteenth Amendment abolished slavery "within the United States, or any place subject to their jurisdiction." Although the slaves were technically free, they were not recognized as citizens. Denied all civil liberties, many of them continued working only for food and shelter—what became known as "slave wages."

The Fourteenth Amendment, ratified in 1868, gave full and equal citizenship to all slaves and an equal vote to all black men over the age of twenty-one. The Fourteenth Amendment also

> *The illegal we do immediately.*
> *The unconstitutional*
> *takes a little longer.*
>
> HENRY KISSINGER

applied the personal freedoms guaranteed in the federal Constitution to the citizens of all states, and prohibited states from making laws restricting any of these rights.

And then everything was quiet again.

It was not until 1925 that the Supreme Court ruled the Fourteenth Amendment (1868) applied the Bill of Rights (1791) to all citizens of all states. U.S. Supreme Court Justice Edward T. Sanford wrote for the majority in 1925,

> Freedom of speech and of the press—which are protected by the First Amendment from abridgment by Congress—are among the fundamental personal rights and "liberties" protected by the due process clause of the Fourteenth Amendment from impairment by the States.

Over time, the Supreme Court—and even occasionally Congress and the president—have reluctantly "given" us some of the rights the Bill of Rights proclaimed for all citizens more than two hundred years ago. In fact, all the civil rights obtained have been taken, not given. Each and every fragment of freedom had to be won—hard won.

No one is ever given freedom. Power is never given away freely—either by tyrant or bureaucracy. Rights—even inalienable rights—must be claimed, and often fought for.

In 1912, Woodrow Wilson set the stage for people insisting on their natural and constitutional rights:

> Liberty has never come from the government. Liberty has always come from the subjects of government. The history of liberty is the history of resistance. The history of liberty is a history of the limitation of governmental power, not the increase of it.

That's what this book is about: getting some of the rights we've had available to us since 1788, rights we never took the time or trouble to claim.

> *They said it couldn't be done*
> *but sometimes*
> *it doesn't work out that way.*
>
> CASEY STENGEL

Laws against Consensual Activities Violate the Separation of Church and State, Threatening the Freedom of and from Religion

> *The government*
> *of the United States*
> *is not, in any sense,*
> *founded on the Christian religion.*
>
> GEORGE WASHINGTON
> Treaty of Tripoli
> 1796

IN 1982, ON THE CELEBRATION of his ninetieth birthday, Dumas Malone, noted historian and Thomas Jefferson biographer, was asked, "What is the most fortunate aspect of American history?" Malone replied,

The fact that we became a nation and immediately separated church and state—it has saved us from all the misery that has beset mankind with inquisitions, internecine and civil wars, and other assorted ills.

True, but there is little doubt that America was founded on the passionate pursuit of the Almighty—Almighty God and the Almighty Dollar.

Less than seven weeks after arriving in the New World, Columbus wrote in his journal,

And I say that Your Highnesses ought not to consent that any foreigner does business or sets foot here, except Christian Catholics, since this was the end and the beginning of the enterprise, that it should be for the enhancement and glory of the Christian religion, nor should anyone who is not a good Christian come to these parts.

> *What a pity,*
> *when Christopher Columbus*
> *discovered America,*
> *that he ever mentioned it.*
>
> MARGOT ASQUITH

From the start, commerce and religion; religion and commerce. Thus began—from the Christian European view of world history—the American dream.

A little over a hundred years after Columbus's 1492 holy business expedition, those who spoke English and worshiped the Almighty Pound began arriving in the New World. Virginia was settled by Sir Walter Raleigh more for his personal gain and financial enhancement than for the glory of God (he never set foot in the colony himself). The original settlers of the colony had the idea that the Indians would do all the work and the white man had only to provide ideas and direction. But somehow the native tribes in Virginia—those savages!—failed to cooperate. The intrinsic intellectual superiority of the white man somehow escaped these Native Americans. Eventually, the colonists were asked by their leaders to work. Each man, woman, and child in the settlement was given a military rank. The duties of each rank were spelled out to the smallest detail. Penalties were harsh—whipping for a second offense and a year on a British prison ship for a third offense. Complaining was not permitted, and there was no going back to England—this is your life, Virginia.*

All of this oppression was done, of course, in the name of God. What God wanted—and was kind enough to communicate

---

*The descendants of this group eventually got all the "servants" they could use. By 1670, there were 2,000 African slaves in Virginia; by 1715, there were 23,000; and in the glorious year of independence—for white American males, at least—1776, there were 150,000 slaves, some of them owned by George Washington and Thomas Jefferson. By that time, the Native Americans had been, uh, displaced.

> *Perhaps, after all,*
> *America never*
> *has been discovered.*
> *I myself would say that*
> *it had merely been detected.*
>
> OSCAR WILDE

to the settlers by way of the British crown—was tobacco. A powerful strain of Virginia tobacco was popular in Great Britain. God wanted the people of England to have their tobacco (making the first cash crop from America a drug). In addition, God wanted the investors in the Virginia Company to turn a profit on their investments and, by God, if it took a police state to bring about God's will, so be it.

⚖ ⚖ ⚖

IN The Name of God, Amen . . . Having undertaken for the Glory of God, and Advancement of the Christian Faith, and the honour of our King and Country, a voyage to plant the first colony in the northern parts of Virginia. . . .

So began the Mayflower Compact of 1620. No secular voyage this. On board the *Mayflower*, the other passengers referred to a third of the passengers as "pilgrims" because they were on a religious quest. They were journeying to the New World to found the City on the Hill, the New Jerusalem. It was to be a shining beacon for the entire world; proof not only that Christianity was the One True Way, but that their specific interpretation of Christianity was the One True Interpretation.

Besides, England had had enough of them. They were known as the Puritans, and, goodness, were they pure. Protestants protested against Catholicism and Puritans protested against Protestants. Even though the Protestants had overthrown the Catholic church in England—a monumental undertaking—the Puritans wanted to purify Protestantism even further. By the early 1600s, England had been through decades of religious wars and was temporarily tired of it all.

In 1534, King Henry VIII separated from the Catholic church ("the Church of Rome") and established Protestantism as the official state religion—the Church of England. Although a major advance for Protestantism, the new religion still didn't please the Puritans. It was, they thought, the same old Catholic hierarchy and form of worship under a new name. When Queen Mary ascended the throne in 1553, Roman Catholicism returned to England; a great many Protestants—especially Puritans—were executed or exiled. In 1558, with the ascension of Elizabeth I, Protestantism returned. Although Protestant, Elizabeth still wasn't pure enough for the Puritans. They continued to protest and, of course, were repressed.

> *The Revolution was effected before the War commenced. The Revolution was in the minds and hearts of the people; a change in their religious sentiments of their duties and obligations . . . This radical change in the principles, opinions, sentiments, and affections of the people, was the real American Revolution.*
>
> JOHN ADAMS
> February 13, 1818

The Puritans spent the next forty-five years being pure anyway. Like the Pharisees of old, they established elaborate customs to separate themselves—the chosen elite—from the heathen, condemned-to-perdition, mainstream Protestants and the completely-lost-from-all-hope-of-salvation Catholics. Nearly every aspect of Puritan life was set, regulated, and ordered. The smallest detail of lifestyle became a religious function which either glorified God or condemned one to hellfire.

In 1603, the Puritans had their last, best hope when King James IV of Scotland became James I of England. King James was a Calvinist and the Puritans thought of themselves as Calvinists (although after the death of John Calvin in 1564, the Puritans' form of Calvinism had become more severe than even Calvin prescribed). The Puritans presented their many grievances to King James I in 1604, but, as the Puritans were not part of the power structure, they were dismissed. "No bishop, no king," James told them. So, the Puritans set their sights on the New World.

> *A puritan is a person who pours righteous indignation into the wrong things.*
>
> G. K. CHESTERTON

The Puritans were well-educated, hard-working (the "Puritan work ethic" lives today) and influenced the educational and business communities of England. They decided to demonstrate to the world how Puritanism (which, of course, they thought of as the true Christianity) could flourish when not repressed by Catholics and quasi-Catholics (Protestants). It would be a community of such spiritual integrity, moral purity, and economic productivity that all the people of the world would herald it a success; the scales would fall from their eyes; they would drop their chains of religious oppression; and the world would be Puritan Calvinistic Christian for ever and ever, amen.

By 1620 these pilgrims were ready to go. They sailed for the New World, the spiritual destiny of humankind resting on their shoulders. Their goal was Virginia, but God apparently had more northerly plans. The ship was blown off course. Considerably off course. They landed in Massachusetts.

Hmmm. This meant they were no longer bound by the agreements they had made with the Virginia Company. While still on the Mayflower, they made their own Compact. Unshackled from the economic bonds of the Virginia Company, they were now free—to freeze to death. It was colder than anyone imagined. (Massachusetts is like that.) As Ulysses S. Grant later explained, "The Pilgrim Fathers fell upon an ungenial climate, where there were nine months of winter and three months of cold weather."

Due almost entirely to the compassion, openness, and generosity of the Native Americans (whose behavior was downright Christian), more than half of the Puritans survived their first winter in what is now Plymouth, Massachusetts. The Native Americans taught the pilgrims how to hunt, fish, and grow crops;

showed them which plants were nutritional, which were medicinal, and which were purely recreational.

The pilgrims learned quickly, applied what they learned with diligence, and made a success of things. Everything went along fine until the next generation grew up. Those pesky youngsters! The pilgrims soon learned what a brief study of history could have taught them—religious belief is not always hereditary.

> *My ancestors were Puritans*
> *from England.*
> *They arrived here in 1648*
> *in the hope of finding*
> *greater restrictions*
> *than were permissible*
> *under English law*
> *at that time.*
>
> GARRISON KEILLOR

Those who toed the line of Puritan orthodoxy were part of a group, a community, an extended family where life was congenial and everyone helped each other. Those who strayed from the fold (by being either less devout or, in rare cases, more devout than the elders considered proper) were punished. If punishment didn't bring them into line, they were banished. Connecticut and Rhode Island were founded by improper Puritans.*

And then there were the French. Good God, the French! Some had no religion at all, and those who did were what only could be called Bastard Catholics. The French weren't after religious freedom; they were after beaver pelts. And stories were circulating that the trappers were having more than social intercourse with the Indians.

This, as it turned out, was quite true. Some members of the Native American tribes admired the white man and offered their women to him; the offspring were proudly raised within the tribe. News of this flexible, casual, experimental quality of the Native Americans was brought back to Europe by the French

---

*Rhode Island was founded by Roger Williams, whose most unpopular thought was that good Christians should not occupy Indian land without paying the Indians. Well, what can you do with such a radical? Such anti-God thinking had to be x'ed out with exile, excommunication, or execution.

> *America's one
> of the finest countries
> anyone ever stole.*
>
> BOBCAT GOLDTHWAITE

trappers. This influenced the French philosophers—particularly Rousseau—who found it a perfect example of man living in nature, enjoying his inherent natural rights. This philosophy was brought back across the Atlantic in the works of Rousseau, Voltaire, and John Locke. It inspired Franklin, Jefferson, Paine, and others in shaping their political philosophies.

⚖ ⚖ ⚖

The Puritan adventure was but one example of religion motivating migration. Lord Baltimore settled Maryland in the hope of establishing a haven for Roman Catholics. Although most of the settlers were Protestants, the land was owned by Catholics. (Not unlike New York City today.) The fastest method of advancement in the colony was to "see the light" and convert to Catholicism.

The Dutch settled New Netherlands for purely economic reasons. Peter Stuyvesant took what he learned about authoritarianism, control, and domination from his Calvinist minister father and applied it to the practice of making money for the Dutch West India Company. When the English captured the colony in 1664, it became New York, named after the Duke of York. When the Duke of York became King of England in 1685, New York became an official crown colony.

North and South Carolina, it was thought, would be ideal places to produce silk. (They were not.)

Georgia was settled so that the inhabitants of Britain's overcrowded debtors' prisons could start a new life. The restrictions were harsh; the limitations economic, not religious.

William Penn knew well the dangers of following an unpopular religion. Penn was a member of the Society of Friends—the

AIN'T NOBODY'S BUSINESS IF YOU DO

Quakers. In England, he was fined and ultimately dismissed from Oxford for refusing to attend chapel. He was imprisoned four times for writing or speaking his religious beliefs.* He intended his Pennsylvania (the woodlands of Penn) to be a haven for all religious minorities, not just Quakers. Most of his time was spent persuading the British government to allow his "holy experiment" to continue. This kept him in England and, consequently, Penn only spent two two-year periods in the colony that bore his name. It was because Penn not only tolerated but welcomed diversity that Pennsylvania became the most diverse, dynamic, and prosperous of the original thirteen colonies. This provided fertile ground for free and, later, radical, and later still, revolutionary thinking.** By 1776, Philadelphia was the largest city in the thirteen colonies, with a population of 40,000. This was larger than Boston and New York combined (24,000).

> *I'm really a timid person— I was beaten up by Quakers.*
>
> WOODY ALLEN

⚖️ ⚖️ ⚖️

By 1770, the British American Colonies had become a billion-pound enterprise, importing more than £1 billion of goods from England and exporting nearly £2 billion. The effects of religion were still felt—even the centers of higher learning (Harvard, Yale, Princeton) began as religious institutions. For the most

*What can one do with a man who says things like, "It is a reproach to religion and government to suffer so much poverty and excess," or "The public must and will be served." Heavens!

**Benjamin Franklin, at twenty, chose Philadelphia as his permanent home over New York and his native Boston. (His relocation may have had something to do with his meeting his wife-to-be on his first day in Philadelphia.)

part, however, by the early 1770s, currency was king in the colonies.

Trying to re-establish their influence, churches with once-rigid restrictions on membership opened their doors to all. "Harvests," they were called. God, not man, chose who would and would not find salvation. With some good ol' hellfire and brimstone preaching, the fear of damnation, and the knowledge that only God could save them from the eternal flaming pit, the congregates had experiences we would now call "born again." The time was known as the Great Awakening. While still high on the ecstasy of deliverance, the new converts were convinced that the rules and regulations of that particular variation of Christianity were what God desired—in fact, demanded—if one wanted to be truly and permanently saved. The ecstasy of the Awakening was just a taste of what one could look forward to in paradise—provided one followed God's laws here on earth without deviation or question. The alternative? An eternal afterlife of bubbling sulfur.

On the cooler end of the spectrum were the great thinkers of the Enlightenment. Deism was the religion of the age of Enlightenment. If reason could be applied to government, science, and philosophy, surely (they reasoned) it could also be applied to religion. That there was a God, in the form of a creator, was reasonable; something had to create this incredible universe—the wonders of which were, through travel, telescope, and microscope, being revealed daily—and something had to account for the miracle of life itself.

"An overruling Providence," Jefferson called it, "which by all its dispensations proves that it delights in the happiness of man here and his greater happiness hereafter." Jefferson also referred to the creator as "that Infinite Power which rules the destinies of the universe." Neither of these statements was privately written by Jefferson and communicated to a select group of friends; both came from his first inaugural address.

Washington, in his first inaugural address, referred to this power as "the Great Arbiter of the Universe." Deists called this power "God" or "the Creator."

> *The legitimate powers of government extend to such acts only as are injurious to others. But it does me no injury for my neighbor to say there are twenty gods, or no God. It neither picks my pocket nor breaks my leg.*
>
> THOMAS JEFFERSON

The Deists were not Christians. This comes as something of a shock to the religious right, who decorate their homes with Early American furniture, or the conservative Daughters of the American Revolution* who make almost religious pilgrimages to Mount Vernon and Monticello. It is, nonetheless, true that our first three presidents—Washington, Adams, and Jefferson—(as well as Benjamin Franklin) were Deists, not Christians.**

The Deists admired, even loved, Jesus as a teacher and an example ("Imitate Jesus," Franklin reminded himself), but Deists had little use for the portion of the New Testament that did not deal directly with the life and words of Jesus. They did not believe in "the revealed word"—Peter, Paul, John, the prophets, Moses, it didn't matter. If God wants to reveal something to me, a Deist reasons, He certainly has the power to reveal it to me Himself. What Jesus did and actually said while on earth was studied and deeply appreciated. Studied too, according to founding father Samuel Adams, were "Confucius, Zoroaster, Socrates, Mahomet [*sic*]" and other teachers and sources of wisdom.

---

*My forefather, Patrick McWilliams, arrived on these shores in 1774, which I suppose makes me a Daughter of the American Revolution. On my mother's side of the family, on the other hand, I am a Son of Ellis Island.

**The fourth president of the United States, James Madison, was almost certainly a Deist as well.

It was not so much who said or wrote something, but whether or not what was said or written rang a bell of truth within the reader. This indicator of truth within the reader, it was believed, was put there by the Divine as a way of divining truth from falsehood. Whatever a Deists would read—be it Bible, book, or almanac—they would listen for the bell.

Deists therefore found something of value in all religious practices: for example, the Quaker custom of sitting quietly and listening for revelations was much admired.

Deists did not believe in damnation. They believed that God only wanted what was good for humanity, and hell was not reasonable from one who wanted only good. Deists believed in repentance: if they wronged another person, they made it up *to that person*. God, being God, did not need to be apologized to.

Deists believed that God—like all good creators—after creating Creation, went off to create something else. One can see, admire, and even stand in awe of Michelangelo's *David* and not expect to see Michelangelo nearby answering questions, accepting praise, or fulfilling requests. Nietzsche's idea that "God is dead" seemed in 1890 to be the height of blasphemy, heresy, and bad taste. The Deists, however, would have no trouble with this concept. They might be momentarily saddened to hear of Michelangelo's passing, but it would not interfere with their enjoyment of Michelangelo's creations.

Deists did not pray. They may have given praise, as in "Lord, what a beautiful morning," or "Lord, what a beautiful painting," but they did not pray to make requests. They believed that, as part of the creation, God created logically discoverable methods by which needs, desires, and wants could be fulfilled; and by discovering and practicing these techniques, one could fulfill one's desires. God may have set up the system, but was not necessary for the delivery any more than Benjamin Franklin, who created the postal system, needed to deliver each letter personally.

"I simply haven't the nerve to imagine a being, a force, a cause which keeps the planets revolving in their orbits," said Quentin Crisp, "and then suddenly stops in order to give me a bicycle with three speeds." If you wanted a bicycle with three speeds, the Deists believed, you did what was necessary to get the money and then went to the bicycle shop and bought one. Knowledge, planning, and work were required, not prayer.

> *It is much to be lamented that a man of Dr. Franklin's general good character and great influence, should have been an unbeliever in Christianity, and also have done so much as he did to make others unbelievers.*
>
> DR. JOSEPH PRIESTLEY

Deists didn't believe in the sole divinity of Jesus (they took seriously Jesus' statement, "Anyone who has faith in me will do what I have been doing. He will do even greater things than these" [John 14:12]). Because of this, and because Deists did not believe in hell or eternal damnation, most Christians disapproved of Deists. Christians denounced the Deists as heretics who were too cowardly to say what they really were: *atheists.*

Not suffering the condemnations of Christians gladly, Deists accused Christians of turning God into a tyrant for their own selfish ends. It was an unfriendly stalemate at best. From the *Encyclopedia Britannica:*

> The Deists were particularly vehement against any manifestation of religious fanaticism and enthusiasm. . . . Any description of God that depicted his impending vengeance, vindictiveness, jealousy, and destructive cruelty was blasphemous. . . . The Deist God, ever gentle, loving, and benevolent, intended men to behave toward one another in the same kindly and tolerant fashion.

As Deism became increasingly refined, it eventually evaporated by the mid-1800s, a victim of its own refinement. It was a little too cool for those who wanted a religion with history such as Roman Catholicism, with popes going back to St. Peter, and, hence, to Christ; or one of the evangelical religions in which one experienced— even if only for a moment—the promised bliss of salvation.

⚖ ⚖ ⚖

There is little doubt that the separation of church and state was a major theme of the American Revolution.

The resolution of the first Continental Congress issued in October 1774 listed among the "infringements and violations of the rights of the colonists" the fact that the British Parliament had established as the official state religion the "Roman Catholic religion in the province of Quebec" which, the Continental Congress claimed, had the effect of "erecting a tyranny there to the great danger . . . of the neighboring British colonies." The members of the first Continental Congress were not specifically anti-Catholic (although it's certainly true that most of them were either Protestants or Deists, and also true that Protestants and Catholics were not on the best of terms back then). The founding fathers were complaining of the "tyranny" of *any* state-authorized religion.

In January 1776, Thomas Paine published *Common Sense*. This pamphlet, more than anything else, moved popular opinion from merely protesting against British rule to openly rebelling against it. Without *Common Sense* paving the way, it is doubtful that the Declaration of Independence would have been issued in July of that year—if at all. Here are some common sense ideas Thomas Paine had about the freedom of religion:

> *I consider the government of the U.S. as interdicted by the Constitution from intermeddling with religious institutions, their doctrines, discipline, or exercises . . . civil powers alone have been given to the President of the U.S. and no authority to direct the religious exercises of his constituents.*
>
> THOMAS JEFFERSON

> This new world hath been the asylum for the persecuted lovers of civil and religious liberty from every Part of Europe. Hither have they fled, not from the tender embraces of the mother, but from the cruelty of the monster . . .

> As to religion, I hold it to be the indispensable duty of all government, to protect all conscientious professors thereof, and I know of no other business which government hath to do therewith. . . .

> For myself I fully and conscientiously believe, that it is the will of the Almighty, that there should be a diversity of religious opinions among us. . . .

Paine argued that "above all things the free exercise of religion" was essential to freedom.

Declaring independence from the king of England in 1776 was the first taste of religious freedom that most Americans had. Calling the king a tyrant and breaking all ties with him may today seem a purely political move, but it was not viewed so in 1776. The king, it was believed, was the direct representative of God on earth, crowned by the highest church authority. Just as people owed God allegiance, so, too, they owed the king allegiance. Obeying the king was the same as obeying God; disobeying the king was the same as disobeying God.

When the revolutionary war was not going well, many moaned, "This is what we get for offending the king. God is not on our side." When, however, the war was won in 1781, Americans finally started believing that life without a God-anointed king was possible. They also started thinking that, perhaps, life

> *The First Amendment has erected a wall between church and state. That wall must be kept high and impregnable. We could not approve the slightest breach.*
>
> JUSTICE HUGO BLACK

with God but without a state-mandated religion was possible as well.

In Virginia, a state rich in religious tradition, Thomas Jefferson tried for more than a decade to have the principles of religious freedom incorporated as part of Virginia's bylaws. In January of 1786, with the help of James Madison, he finally succeeded. It was a testament not only to Jefferson's persuasive ability and persistence, but also to the gradual awakening of the American public. His Virginia Statute of Religious Liberty stands as a lighthouse of religious freedom. It would probably have as much trouble passing through any legislative body today as it did back in the late 1700s.

The Virginia Statute of Religious Liberty begins by stating that "Almighty God hath created the mind free," and any attempts to influence others in religious matters by using the force of government "tend only to beget habits of hypocrisy and meanness." Further, claimed Jefferson, laws based on religious beliefs are not just a civil injustice, but "a departure from the plan of the Holy author of our religion." After all, if God wanted to physically punish people for not obeying the precepts of a certain religion, he could, because it "was in his Almighty power to do."

> Our civil rights have no dependence on our religious opinions, any more than our opinions in physics or geometry.

Jefferson went on to point out that whenever one asks "the civil magistrate to intrude his powers into the field of opinion" and stop the spread of one thought or another "on the supposition of their ill tendency," the government is caught in "a dangerous fallacy, which at once destroys all religious liberty" because the magistrate will simply "approve or condemn the sentiments of others only as they shall square with or differ from his own."

Jefferson maintains that the civil government has plenty to do; there is barely "time enough for the rightful purposes of civil government," and the government should only instruct "its officers to interfere when principles break out into overt acts against peace and good order."

> Let us revise our views and work from the premise that all laws should be for the welfare of society as a whole and not directed at the punishment of sins.
>
> JOHN BIGGS, JR.

Jefferson continues, stating that "truth is great and will prevail if left to herself." Truth "has nothing to fear from the conflict" unless truth, by human intervention, is "disarmed of her natural weapons, free argument and debate."

> All men shall be free to profess, and by argument to maintain their opinion in matters of religion, and that the same shall in no wise diminish, enlarge or affect their civil capacities.

⚖ ⚖ ⚖

When our founding fathers gathered in 1787 to write a Constitution, the thirteen colonies were a crazy quilt of religious beliefs, philosophies, and practices. Eleven of the thirteen colonies had religious requirements to be met before one could serve in the state legislature. Some of the state constitutions embraced the church; others kept the church at arm's length. Some gave preference to one religious denomination, some to another. All were noticeably antisemitic.

The range of attitudes written into state constitutions and laws was quite remarkable. Massachusetts and Virginia represented two extremes.

> *Moral indignation:*
> *jealousy with a halo.*
>
> H. G. WELLS

Massachusetts, inspired by the Puritans and the total intermingling of church and state, thought that church and state should not only embrace each other, but live together—after a proper marriage, of course. Here is an excerpt from its constitution, passed in 1780:

As the happiness of a people, and the good order and preservation of a civil government, essentially depend upon piety, religion, and morality; and as these cannot be generally diffused through a community, but by the institution of the public worship of GOD, and of public instructions in piety, religion, and morality; Therefore, to promote their happiness and to secure the good order and preservation of their government, the people of this Commonwealth have a right to invest their legislature with power to authorize and require . . . the institution of the public worship of GOD, and for the support and maintenance of public Protestant teachers of piety, religion and morality.

Virginia, on the other hand—inspired by the works of Thomas Jefferson, James Madison, George Washington, and a truly unhappy experience with state mandated and supported religion—made a clear separation of church and state in its constitution, passed in 1776:

No man shall be compelled to frequent or support any religious worship, place or ministry whatsoever; nor shall any man be forced, restrained, molested or burdened in his body or goods, or otherwise suffer, on account of his religious opinions or belief; but all men shall be free to profess, and by argument to maintain, their opinions in matters of religion, and the same shall in no wise affect, diminish, or enlarge their civil capacities. And the legisla-

AIN'T NOBODY'S BUSINESS IF YOU DO

ture shall not prescribe any religious test whatever; nor confer any particular privileges or advantages on any one sect or denomination; nor pass any law requiring or authorizing any religious society, or the people of any district within this commonwealth, to levy on themselves or others

> *The day that this country ceases to be free for irreligion, it will cease to be free for religion.*
>
> JUSTICE ROBERT H. JACKSON

any tax for the erection or repair of any house for public worship, or for the support of any church or ministry; but it shall be left free to every person to select his religious instructor, and make for his support such private contract as he shall please.

In some states, as it had been in Virginia, a single church was established. Others restricted public office to Protestants. Some required belief in specific doctrines of the Christian religion, such as the divinity of Jesus, the Trinity, or immortality. The constitution of North Carolina is an example:

> No person who shall deny the being of God, or the truth of the Christian religion, or the divine authority of the Old or New Testament, or who shall hold religious principles incompatible with the freedom or safety of the state, shall be capable of holding any office or place of trust in the civil department within this state.

The founding fathers looked at the world beyond the thirteen colonies and they looked at history. There, church and state were so permanently, continuously, and unabashedly intermingled that the study of one automatically included the study of the other. Like television and commercials, religion and politics were, until the Constitution and its Bill of Rights, inseparable. Senator Sam J. Ervin, Jr., offers this account of two millennia of religious belief influencing government policy:

> *Lord, there's danger*
> *in this land.*
> *You get witch-hunts and wars*
> *when church and state*
> *hold hands.*
>
> JONI MITCHELL

The ugliest chapters in history are those that recount the religious intolerance of the civil and ecclesiastical rulers of the Old World and their puppets during the generations preceding the framing and ratifying of the First Amendment.

These chapters of history reveal the casting of the Christians to the lions in the Coliseum at Rome; the bloody Crusades of the Christians against the Saracens for the possession of the shrines hallowed by the footsteps of the Prince of Peace; the use by the papacy of the dungeon and the rack to coerce conformity and of the fiery faggot to exterminate heresy; the unspeakable cruelties of the Spanish Inquisition; the slaughter of the Waldenses in Alpine Italy; the jailing and hanging by Protestant kings of English Catholics for abiding with the faith of their fathers; the jailing and hanging by a Catholic queen of English Protestants for reading English Scriptures and praying Protestant prayers; the hunting down and slaying of the Covenanters upon the crags and moors of Scotland for worshiping God according to the dictates of their own consciences; the decimating of the people of the German states in the Thirty Years War between Catholics and Protestants; the massacre of the Huguenots in France; the pogroms and persecutions of the Jews in many lands; the banishing of Baptists and other dissenters by Puritan Massachusetts; the persecution and imprisonment of Quakers by England for refusing to pay tithes to the established church and to take the oaths of supremacy and allegiance; the banishing, branding, imprisoning, and whipping of Quakers, and the hanging of the alleged witches at Salem by Puritan Massachusetts;

and the hundreds of other atrocities perpetrated in the name of religion.

It is not surprising that Blaise Pascal, the French mathematician and philosopher, was moved more than three hundred years ago to proclaim this tragic truth: "Men never do evil so completely and cheerfully as when they do it from religious conviction."

> *In our country are evangelists and zealots of many different political, economic and religious persuasions whose fanatical conviction is that all thought is divinely classified into two kinds—that which is their own and that which is false and dangerous.*
>
> JUSTICE ROBERT H. JACKSON

And let's remember that religious intolerance involving Christians began with Christ himself, who, although put to death by Rome, was convicted of "blasphemy" by the ruling religious body of the day, the Sanhedrin.

From the pharaohs of ancient Egypt to the republics of ancient Greece and Rome, up to and including King George III and King Louis XVI, the rulers either were gods or held their positions through the direct mandate of God.

Just as we today generally think that a rich person (especially a self-made rich person) must know something that the rest of us don't, so too it was assumed that people with political power had some kind of connection to God the average person did not. God was the giver of life; God was the giver of power; and God obviously gave more power to a king than to a serf.

For every ruler whose belief in God made him or her just, compassionate, caring, and giving, there was a ruler who used the name of God to suppress, exploit, terrorize, and intimidate. Usually it is the tyrants who have their names writ large in history, but there were many rulers who genuinely believed in the more benevolent aspects of religion and sincerely (and, in some cases, successfully) administered a state with the kindness, encouragement, and fairness of a good parent.

What bothered the founding fathers about the intermingling of church and state was not that it never worked, but that it

> *We must respect*
> *the other fellow's religion,*
> *but only in the sense*
> *and to the extent that*
> *we respect his theory*
> *that his wife is beautiful*
> *and his children smart.*
>
> H. L. MENCKEN

worked intermittently. Like good monarchs and bad monarchs, the good and bad were too random, too illogical, too unreasonable a system on which to base an ongoing government.

So, even if there had been a single religion happily practiced by all the citizens of the thirteen colonies (which there was not), the intermingling of church and state would still have been unacceptable because no one knew how severely future despots might distort or manipulate that religion for their own selfish use.

The solution, then, was to separate church and state, to build a "wall of separation" between them, as Jefferson wrote:

> Believing with you that religion is a matter which lies solely between man and his God, I contemplate with solemn reverence that act of the whole American people which declared that their legislature should "make no law respecting an establishment of religion or prohibiting the free exercise thereof" thus building a wall of separation between Church and State.

Although it was highly experimental and relatively untried, the concept of separation fit perfectly with the founding fathers' needs and intentions:

1. The separation of church and state allowed the founding fathers to avoid the debate on which of the many diverse—and often contradictory—religious beliefs then practiced in the thirteen colonies should be the official state religion. This debate almost certainly would have destroyed the Constitutional Convention, and the states might never have united.

2. Although the separation of church and state may not have allowed for those elevated periods of spiritual benevolence that took place when government and grace combined, it would pro-

tect against the extrava-
gantly wasteful and down-
right terrifying religious-
political endeavors such as
the Great Crusades, the Inquisition, and the home-
grown Salem witch hunts.

3. Being able to choose
and practice one's own religion without government
intervention, pressure, or
control was completely har-
monious with the concept

> *Being an Episcopalian*
> *interferes neither*
> *with my business*
> *nor my religion.*
>
> JOHN KENDRICK BANGS
> 1862

that all rights naturally belonged to the individual, who voluntarily surrendered specific rights in exchange for the benefits and
protection of government. Taking a fresh look at it, why should
people give up their natural right to choose and practice a religion? And why should the government, as part of its service to
the people, choose, support, and enforce by law one particular
religious belief over all others? The answer to these questions
leaned overwhelmingly in the direction of leaving religious freedom where God originally put it—in the hands of the individual.

As James Madison wrote,

> We hold it for a fundamental and undeniable truth, that
> religion, or the duty we owe our Creator and the manner
> of discharging it, can be directed only by reason and con-
> viction, not by force or violence. The religion then of
> every man must be left to the conviction and conscience
> of every man; and it is the right of every man to exercise
> it as these may dictate. This right is in its nature an unal-
> ienable right.

And so the Constitution of the United States of America was
written without a single mention or reference to God.* If the

---

*The Declaration of Independence mentioned only the Deistic form of
God—which is not surprising considering that Jefferson and the two other
members of the committee to draft the Declaration of Independence were
Deists. These references were "the Laws of Nature and of Nature's God,"

various indicators of separation of church and state in the main body of the Constitution—discussed in the previous chapter—were not enough, the freedom *from* state-imposed religion and the freedom *of* religious practice were both guaranteed by the First Amendment. Had this not been enough, the Fourteenth Amendment made sure each state paid attention to the First Amendment.

⚖ ⚖ ⚖

And so there it was, and is, a shining example—clear, bright, and unambiguous—as to the religious rights retained by all citizens of the United States of America:

Congress shall make no law respecting an establishment of religion, or prohibiting the free exercise thereof. . . .

No qualifications. No excuses. No exceptions. No apologies.

The first part, "Congress shall make no law respecting an establishment of religion . . ." means that the government cannot dictate a religious belief to be practiced by all people. Further, it means that the individual beliefs of certain religions cannot be written into law simply because a number of people—even a majority of people—believe them to be so.

This application of the First Amendment is central to the discussion of consensual crimes. In listening to the reasons why laws against consensual activities are enacted, or why laws against consensual activities should not be eliminated, one begins to peel away layers, the core of which is almost invariably a religious belief. The progression often goes:

"It's not right."

"Creator," "the Supreme Judge of the World," and "Divine Providence."

"Why is it not right?"

"Because it's not moral."

"Why is it not moral?"

"Because God says so."

And this is usually followed by some reference—sometimes specific, but usually vague—to the Bible, a sermon, a televangelist, or a story remembered from Sunday School (or was it Cecil B. deMille?).

Knowing about that pesky separation of church and state rule (honored more in the breach, it seems, than in the observance), some politicians and commentators do their best to cloud the fact that criminalizing consensual activities is a religious issue. "The people of this country don't want this. The people of this country think it's wrong." Nine times out of ten, the people believe what they believe based on what they heard in church, through televangelism, or by simply accepting the opinion of other highly convinced people who got their opinions through church or televangelism.

Even if the first half of the First Amendment's religious guarantees were not there, the second half would be enough to permit all consensual activities:

> . . . or prohibiting the free exercise thereof . . .

"Thereof" refers, of course, to religion. Congress, then, can make no law prohibiting the free exercise of religion. There go all the laws against consensual activities.

All one must do is claim that the practice of a consensual activity is a "sacrament" in one's "church" and any of the consensual crimes can then be practiced under the protection of the law. Naturally, there must be some restrictions—not harming the person or property of another comes to mind for some reason.

When it comes to civil rights, however, saying, "It's my religion; therefore I'm protected by the First Amendment," is not a

> *But how shall we educate men to goodness, to a sense of one another, to a love of truth? And more urgently, how shall we do this in a bad time?*
>
> DANIEL BERRIGAN

> *It is useless for the sheep*
> *to pass resolutions*
> *in favor of vegetarianism*
> *while the wolf*
> *remains of a different opinion.*
>
> WILLIAM RALPH INGE

sufficient argument. It's an accurate argument, and even a workable argument, but it potentially adds a layer of pretense and hypocrisy to an individual's life, freedom, and religion. One should be able to participate in consensual activities without having to explain: "I do this because it's part of my religion." One should only have to say, "I'm entitled to do this because it does not physically harm the person or property of another. I never gave the regulation of my personal life over to the government."

There should be no need for prostitutes (the Rahabites) to harken back to Rahab, the prostitute whom God personally saved when Jericho fell; for gays (the Beloveds) to interpret Scripture to show that Jesus and his disciples were all lovers; for drug users (the Learyans) to say they're using chemicals for mystical and religious experiences—the wine at the last supper and the changing of water to wine at the wedding feast at Cana being just two scriptural examples; for gamblers (the Holy Rollers or Vegasites) to point out that the apostles cast lots to choose a replacement for Judas; for pornographers (the Lovelacians) to claim that God created Adam and Eve without clothing, and that we each came into this world without clothing, so lack of clothing is what God wants; and on and on.

⚖️ ⚖️ ⚖️

What we have today is a contemporary Inquisition in which 4,000,000 people are arrested each year and 750,000 people are currently in prison for "crimes" that offend the sensibility of highly vocal "religious" people. This situation directly violates the separation of church and state and the religious freedoms guaranteed by the United States Constitution.

The people who want to maintain laws based on their religious beliefs are taking their constitutionally guaranteed right of religious freedom too far—they are physically harming the persons and property of others and using the peace officers of this country to enforce their excessive exercise of a sacred constitutional right.

> *One day I sat thinking,*
> *almost in despair;*
> *a hand fell on my shoulder*
> *and a voice said reassuringly:*
> *"Cheer up, things could get worse."*
> *So I cheered up and, sure enough,*
> *things got worse.*
>
> JAMES HAGGERTY

Laws against Consensual Activities Are Opposed to the Principles of Private Property, Free Enterprise, Capitalism, and the Open Market

> *Don't I have the right
> to do what I want
> with my own money?*
>
> MATTHEW 20:15

THERE ARE FEW CERTAINTIES in American history—even recent American history. Did FDR know about Pearl Harbor in advance? Who killed JFK? Whither Whitewater?

Often, what we firmly believe is true later turns out to be false. In the war against Iraq, we prided ourselves on the precision of the missiles and the "pinpoint" bombing. Later, we found out that more than half the missiles and bombs did not hit their targets. (All, however, *did* hit something.)

Things change, or, as Arthur Miller put it, time bends.

There is one fact of American history, however, that no one doubts: our founding fathers believed deeply in the principle of private property. As Adam Smith (the original) wrote in his *Wealth of Nations,* published in 1776,

> Every man, as long as he does not violate the laws of justice, is left perfectly free to pursue his own interest his own way, and to bring both his industry and capital into competition with those of any other man or order of men.

Among a wealth of other qualities, the founding fathers were *rich.*

One of the signers of the Declaration of Independence, Robert Morris, was rich enough to *become* the treasury during the revolutionary war: his personal credit line saved the United States from bankruptcy. Benjamin Franklin made a fortune from his inventions and publications. Thomas Jefferson was born well-off and later assumed control of his wife's even more considerable land and fortune. And, at the time of the Constitutional Convention, George Washington was the richest man in America. (John Hancock ran a close second.)

> *The United States is a great country and rich in itself— capable and promising to be as prosperous and as happy as any.*
>
> GEORGE WASHINGTON

It wasn't that poor people were excluded from the Continental Congress, where the Declaration of Independence was drafted, or from the Constitutional Convention, where the Articles of Confederation became the United States Constitution; it was just that who but an independently wealthy person could volunteer to go to Philadelphia, unpaid, at the height of the growing season, for an indefinite period of time?

Not that they all came for purely selfless, patriotic reasons— each had his own agenda; many of which were financial. Most of the complaints against the British crown that caused the Revolution concerned monetary policies: taxes on tea, import duties, interference of trade, and so on. The British soldiers were not raping the women, selling the men into slavery, or randomly plundering the countryside. No. The colonists were furious when, for example, a law was passed saying that, if no other accommodations were available, British soldiers were allowed to be temporarily quartered in the colonists' *barns*. In the history of occupation and imperial domination, the North American colonies received benign, almost deferential treatment from the British crown.

This is because America, for the British, was an economic enterprise. It was a market for British goods; a supplier of its needs; and a good place to send its religious fanatics, political dissidents, and criminals. This kept England both thriving and tidy. England liked the fact that the British Americas were flourishing and only wanted to "wet its beak."

Britain wanted its beak a little too wet, thought the founding fathers. Even though the taxes England levied on the English were fifty times greater than the taxes it levied on the colonists, the colonists protested. It was an economic hardship up with which they would not put.* The taxes were not so much levied against the consumers as against the merchants—the importers and exporters. The taxes cut into their profits and they didn't like it.

But it was more than just the taxes; it was the way in which England was meddling with the commerce of the country in general.** Any sort of change required endless dealings with the bureaucracy that was England and the American entrepreneurs were tired of it. The freedom they wanted was freedom to de-

---

*Someone once wrote Sir Winston Churchill to complain that he had ended a sentence with a preposition. He wrote back agreeing that such unforgivable grammatical errors were among the things up with which he would not put.

**For example, the Proclamation of 1763 ordered that all "Anglo-Americans" remain east of the Allegheny Mountains and that any dealing with the Native Americans, for either lands or goods, must take place through London-appointed commissioners. The Native Americans no more respected the authority of these commissioners than did the colonists. But the commissioners were, by law, in the middle of every trade, treaty, or barter between the Native and the Anglo-Americans.

velop the country's re-
sources without the med-
dling, red tape, commis-
sions, and second-guessing
of British bureaucrats.

And so the colonists
had a revolution, and, by
making economic alliances
with France and Spain—the
second and third greatest
military powers of the
day—the colonists won.

Although victorious in

> *Next to the right of liberty,*
> *the right of property*
> *is the most important individual right*
> *guaranteed by the Constitution*
> *and the one which,*
> *united with that of personal liberty,*
> *has contributed more to*
> *the growth of civilization*
> *than any other institution*
> *established by the human race.*
>
> PRESIDENT WILLIAM H. TAFT

war, by 1786 the United States was an economic mess. Its primary trading partner, Britain, wanted nothing to do with the
rebellious upstarts; France and Spain were helping themselves to
the portions of North America they wanted; and the war had
plunged the country $60 million into debt—an amount, rela-
tively speaking, larger and more burdensome than our current
national deficit.

The gathering in Philadelphia in the summer of 1787 was
more an economic conference than a political one—although the
two, then as now, were intimately connected. Politically, various
founding fathers wanted forms of government from a monarchy
to a strong federal government; from no state government to
all-powerful state government. Economically, however, no one
even thought of proposing a system other than individual ownership of private property. The only questions were (a) how do I
most effectively trade my private property with others? and (b)
how do I get more of it? Harking back to John Locke, "Government has no other end than the preservation of property."
(Please see the chapter, "The Enlightenment.")

What the founding fathers wanted—and what they wrote
into the Constitution was for Congress to provide an environment in which commerce could thrive. Every one of the seventeen enumerated powers given to Congress by the Constitution
provided for a level field with fertile soil on which to do business: secure borders by developing and regulating armed forces

> *Private property was
> the original source of freedom.
> It still is its main bulwark.*
>
> WALTER LIPPMANN

(six of the powers relate to this), borrow money, regulate commerce, control immigration and establish uniform laws for bankruptcy, establish a common legal tender and coin money, punish counterfeiters, establish post offices and build post (toll) roads, issue patents and copyrights, settle disputes, and keep the sea lanes free of pirates. Powers 1 and 17—to collect taxes and to govern the nation's capital—gave the federal government the means to carry out powers 2–16. In addition, the Constitution prohibited the individual states from doing most of these things so that the United States would have one single, strong, central, uniform economic system.

All of the individual rights in the Constitution and the Bill of Rights were added not just because they were the "sacred rights of man" and made for good government; they also made for good business. To have the government involved in regulating religion, morality, and personal behavior was not only costly, it would distract the government from its primary task: keeping the world safe for American commerce.

⚖️ ⚖️ ⚖️

The essence of private property is that what's yours is yours, and it remains yours until you give it, trade it, or sell it. While it is yours, the government will protect—by force if necessary—your right to keep and use ("enjoy") it. Once you give it, trade it, or sell it, however, you have lost all title to it, and the government will now protect whomever you gave, traded, or sold it to.

What you do with property while it is yours is entirely your business. If you abuse it, misuse it, or even destroy it, the government cannot step in and stop you. If you have a table and put it under a leak in the roof, the government cannot step in and insist that you either move the table or fix the roof. It's your table, your roof, your leak, and your life.*

The limit of doing what you want with your property, of course, is when you begin to interfere with the property of others. Just because you own a hammer

> *Freedom and the power to choose should not be the privilege of wealth. They are the birthright of every American.*
>
> PRESIDENT GEORGE BUSH

doesn't mean you get to hit anything you want with it—just the things you own or have the owner's consent to hit.

You have the freedom to give, trade, or sell your private property. You can either make or lose money on a transaction and it's not the government's business—except where taxation comes in. As long as the government gets its due, however, you can do what you want. The government will not prevent you from being a foolish businessperson and it will not reward you for being a great one. As long as there is a free-will exchange without undue coercion or fraud, all interactions and exchanges of private property are the nongovernmental concerns of the people involved.

This right of private property certainly extends to our bodies. Whether we choose to be fit or fat, have a Cover Girl complexion or put tattoos on every inch of our body, shave our head or let

---

*This principle has been sorely contested at times. When a Japanese businessman who spent more than $100 million on two Van Goghs said he wanted to be buried with the paintings, it didn't cause much stir because it was assumed that the family would, sooner or later, dig him up and reclaim the paintings. When it was discovered, however, that he wanted to be *cremated* with the paintings, it caused an international furor that made even the front page of the *Wall Street Journal*. The debate over the extent and absoluteness of private property was cut short by the businessman's announcement that he would not, after all, take the Van Goghs with him. Why? The controversy was beginning to hurt his business.

our hair grow long, work for $1 a year or $100,000 a year, is simply not the government's business.

I'm not going to argue the pros and cons of private ownership, free enterprise, capitalism, and the free market system. That's another discussion. It is, however, indisputably true that *this is the economic system we have;* it is the economic system we have had since the ratification of the Constitution in 1788. It is precisely the system that the anti-Communists have worked so hard for so long to keep firmly in place. They have succeeded. Firmly in place it is.

And, our economic system is one of the best arguments against criminalizing consensual activities.

Laws against consensual activities are a restriction of trade. If I want to buy a farm, grow grapes, and make wine—as long as I meet all permit and licensing requirements—I am free to decide whom to hire to help me make the wine, how much to charge per bottle, and whether to use plastic corks or cork corks. If the enterprise is successful, I become an honored taxpayer, employer, wine maker, and citizen.

If, on the other hand, I choose to buy a farm and grow marijuana with the intent of selling it for profit, I would be a felon, a criminal, a drug lord, and a disgrace. Under current federal law, I could be put to death.

Going through a list of consensual crimes, it's easy to see that our right to give, trade, rent, or sell our person or property to another is severely hampered.

Of course, people are making money—and lots of it—from the false scarcity created by making consensual activities crimes. To coin a bumper sticker: WHEN DOING BUSINESS IS A CRIME, ONLY CRIMINALS ARE IN BUSINESS. Organized crime in this country is directly traceable to Prohibition. (Please see the chapter, "Prohibition.") When Prohibition went away, organized crime did not—it switched products and kept selling. That's because the government kept prohibiting things people wanted to buy.

When the government pretends that certain businesses are not going on, all the government regulations, inspections, and licensing that keep products uniform and relatively safe are impossible. When we drink a beer or a glass of wine, we know the approximate alcohol content and can regulate our intake and activities accordingly. We know the alcohol content because it is established and regulated by law. When we take an illegal drug, we have no idea of its strength, and consequently are unable to regulate either dosage or behavior.

> *Cherish the system*
> *of Free Enterprise*
> *which made America great.*
>
> PHILIP D. REED

From healthcare workers to restaurant employees, there are certain required procedures and practices to further their own and their clients' health and safety. No such restrictions apply to consensual crimes—and the lack of same is killing people.

When business is open and aboveboard, both businesses and consumers can be protected against real crime such as fraud, violence, and theft. As it is now, when indulging in any of the consensual crimes it's the law of the Old West—and often the law of the jungle.

Another legitimate aspect of regulation—impossible as long as the government holds certain transactions illegal—is discouraging minors from patronizing certain businesses. No liquor store owner in his or her right mind would knowingly sell to a minor. Do you think the same is true of drug dealers? The artificially high prices created by the criminalization of certain activities make opening new territories—such as schoolyards—profitable. One hears about drug dealers giving out samples of certain substances to school children. Have you ever heard of a liquor

> *Money, which represents*
> *the prose of life,*
> *and which is hardly spoken of*
> *in parlors without an apology,*
> *is, in its effects and laws,*
> *as beautiful as roses.*
>
> RALPH WALDO EMERSON

retailer handing out samples of alcohol on the playground? ("Hey, kid! Over here. Just got a new shipment of Stoli. One hundred proof. Check it out.") If drugs were available at a fair market price (plus, of course, an exorbitant tax) and sold in licensed and regulated retail outlets, the "marketing" to minors would dramatically decrease. This is true for all consensual crimes in which minors are currently encouraged to take part.

Which brings us to another far-from-insignificant point: taxation. Yes, taxes; everyone's favorite five-letter four-letter word. All those billions and billions and billions of dollars that change hands annually through the businesses created by consensual crimes are completely untaxed. No income tax. No sales tax. No capital gains. Nothing. We'll explore the financial ramifications of that in the next chapter. In this chapter, however, I'll only note that having massive industries—the consensual crimes—completely untaxed puts the businesses that are taxed under an enormous burden. All the tax money that goes toward maintaining a healthy business environment, enjoyed by both licit and illicit businesses, is paid entirely by the legitimate business world.

Aboveground businesspersons must abide by certain rules, restrictions, and professional standards designed to create fairness in the marketplace. Illicit business people have no such rules, regulations, or standards for professional conduct. They do whatever they can get away with—which, obviously, is quite a lot.

The artificially inflated prices caused by criminalizing certain acts of commerce take a large amount of money out of the legitimate loop of business and place it in the underworld. Protection money, pay-offs, kickbacks, bribes, legal fees, and all the other expensive but necessary costs of doing business in the consensual crime trade consume huge amounts of money that might otherwise go to aboveground businesses.

Let's say an honest, hard-working citizen has $50 set aside each week under the general category of "recreation." Let's say that $40 of this goes for recreational chemicals that, were they not against the law, would cost, even with an exorbitant tax, $4. This extra $36 per week—72% of this person's total recreational budget—goes directly into the hands of the economic underworld. With this $36, our citizen might have chosen to go out and do something else, thus spreading money into the general aboveground economy, rather than stay home and watch television. When reading about the billions of dollars spent each year by consumers taking part in consensual crimes, please keep in mind that (a) those dollar amounts are outrageously inflated only because these activities have been deemed illegal, and (b) all that money is being taken directly from the general aboveground economy and put in an underground economy where it is neither regulated, controlled, nor taxed. (And a good deal of it ends up abroad.) Imagine what an incredible boost to the U.S. economy the reintroduction of these lost billions would be.

As Jeff Riggenbach wrote in *U.S.A. Today,*

> As long as no children are involved, these "crimes" are merely what Harvard philosopher Robert Nozick calls "capitalist acts between consenting adults." In a free society, capitalist acts between consenting adults are not illegal, regardless of how many bluenoses might disapprove of them.

> *The instinct of ownership is fundamental in man's nature.*
>
> WILLIAM JAMES
> *The Variety of Religious Experience*
> 1902

⚖ ⚖ ⚖

Setting aside all thoughts of commerce, business, and exchange, however, there still is the question of personal property. Are we allowed to own whatever we want, providing it does not physically harm the person or property of another? The Constitution both implies and clearly states, yes. So, what are all these laws about *possession?* If you are caught possessing (not using, not selling) a certain amount of drugs, you could spend the rest of your life in prison, or—with the enactment of the 1995 Omnibus Crime Bill—be put to death. This is the extreme, but lesser penalties apply for possessing the products or paraphernalia associated with certain consensual crimes.

How the mere possession of something—be it drugs, equipment, or gambling paraphernalia—harms anyone, anywhere, any time, including the person possessing it, is completely beyond me. Criminalizing possession is an example of how far from the Constitution—and all logic and reason—the matter of consensual crimes has gone. You can be arrested for possessing something that, even if you used it, would not physically harm the person or property of a nonconsenting other.

⚖ ⚖ ⚖

The Nobel Prize–winning economist Milton Friedman is the ultimate guru of the free-market system. As Professor Friedman wrote in his 1962 book, *Capitalism and Freedom,*

> Freedom in economic arrangements is itself a component of freedom broadly understood, so economic freedom is an end in itself . . . . Economic freedom is also an indispensable means toward the achievement of political freedom.

In 1986, as rhetoric was fanning the fires of the war on drugs into an inferno, Professor Friedman (then one of Reagan's economic advisors) calmly stated his views:

> I'm in favor of legalizing drugs. According to my value system, if people want to kill themselves, they have every right to do so. Most of the harm that comes from drugs is because they are illegal.

If only Reagan had listened to his learned advisor.

> *Government is not the solution to our problem. Government is the problem.*
>
> RONALD REAGAN
> First Inaugural Address
> January 20, 1981

Enforcing Laws against Consensual Activities Is Very Expensive

> *We don't seem to be able*
> *to check crime,*
> *so why not legalize it*
> *and then*
> *tax it out of business?*
>
> WILL ROGERS

THIS IS A CHAPTER ABOUT money—what it costs us in good old Yankee dollars to enforce laws against consensual activities. We will not be exploring the cost in human suffering, the cost to our civil rights, the cost of our religious freedom, the cost to our moral character, the cost to our personal safety, or the cost to our human resources. This is a chapter about dollars and lack of sense.

We will explore not only what we spend each year enforcing laws against consensual activities, but also what we might gain if we brought the underground economy of consensual activities aboveground.*

Let's start with what we spend on enforcing laws against consensual activities, and let's start with the easy figures. Because there's a war going on, we get wartime reporting (that is, lots of reporting) on drugs. Tens of millions of dollars are spent each year gathering, compiling, analyzing, and publishing drug statistics. The Department of Justice even has a toll-free number (800–666–3332). At taxpayers' expense, you can have all your

---

*Except where noted, all the statistics in this chapter come from the Bureau of Justice Statistics; Drug Enforcement Administration; Bureau of Census; Bureau of Customs; Coast Guard; Bureau of Alcohol, Tobacco and Firearms; Border Patrol; Internal Revenue Service; or from "experts" who have testified before congressional subcommittees.

questions answered about drug busts, drug laws, and the war on drugs' battle plan. Consequently, what we are spending on the consensual crime of drug use is easy to discover—sort of.

The obvious figures are: each year we spend $13 billion* at the federal level and $16 billion at the state and local levels to catch and incarcerate (and, to a far smaller degree, educate) drug possessors, users, manufacturers, and traffickers. That comes to $29 billion a year.**

> *If you started a business when Christ was born and lost $1 million a day, it would still take another 700 years before you lost $1 trillion.*
>
> REPRESENTATIVE PHIL CRANE

Although this is a staggering sum of money, it is only the amount spent by the Justice Department, law enforcement, courts, and correctional institutions—the nail 'em, impale 'em, and jail 'em people. What about the other governmental divisions?

Here the figures get murkier. Government bureaucrats don't like taxpayers calling up and asking such bothersome questions as, "Where does the money go?" Getting information, therefore, has not been easy. The agencies don't have it; don't know who has it; don't know where to get it; and why do you want it, anyway?

---

*A million dollars is a stack of $100 bills three feet high; a billion dollars is a stack of $100 bills twice as high as the Empire State Building; and a trillion dollars is a stack of $100 bills 570 miles high.

**I hope you don't mind if I round off some of these numbers to the nearest billion. (If only I could make that statement when discussing my checking account.) I also hope you don't mind that, in this chapter, I avoid such modifiers as *approximately, more than, almost, nearly,* and so on. If I say, "State and local governments spent $16 billion in 1991 on drug enforcement," know that I've rounded it off. If I say, "State and local governments spent $15,888,665 on drug enforcement," you'll know that I'm being precise. Assume that if you don't see lots of digits, I've rounded them off.

> *Stop wasting jail space on prostitutes, drug users and other victimless criminals. Even if we find it morally acceptable to imprison these people for choices they make regarding their bodies, we must realize that we simply cannot afford to continue clogging the court system and the prison system with these harmless "criminals."*
>
> EDWARD B. WAGNER

For example, how much of the $21 billion we spend each year on foreign aid, international financial programs, and diplomacy is used to "persuade" other countries to stop growing, manufacturing, and exporting drugs to the United States? Hint: almost all foreign aid to countries that even might produce drugs is tied directly to those countries' pledges to eradicate the drug menace within their borders. Shall we conservatively say $3 billion?

How much of the $4 billion Coast Guard budget is spent on intercepting drug-running boats? The Coast Guard claims about one quarter of that. Shall we take their word for it? Okay. Here's another $1 billion.

And then we have that great Black Hole of money, information, and proportion: the Defense Department. How much do the Army, Navy, Air Force, and Marines spend keeping America drug free? We know they're going to spend $260 billion this year on something, but how much of it will be fighting the war on drugs?

A clue comes from the 1993 Department of Justice publication *Drugs, Crime, and the Justice System:*

> The Posse Comitatus Act of 1876, which prohibited military involvement in law enforcement, was amended in 1982 to allow State and local law enforcement officials to draw on military assistance for training, intelligence gathering, and investigation of drug violations. The amendment provided for the use of military equipment by civilian agencies to enforce drug laws.

> In 1989, Congress enacted a law designating the Department of Defense as the lead agency for detecting and monitoring aerial and maritime transit of illegal drugs.

In Thailand, for example, the U.S. military supplies the Thai government with planes, reconnaissance equipment (for the airplanes), computers (to analyze the reconnaissance), and training (how to operate the computers that analyze the reconnaissance gathered from the equipment flown in the airplanes). What are they looking for? Poppy fields, the source of opium, the source of heroin.* This scenario is repeated in country after country.

> *We have to pursue this subject of fun very seriously if we want to say competitive in the twenty-first century.*
>
> SINGAPORE MINISTER OF STATE

In the United States, military helicopters are engaged in low-flying surveillance looking for marijuana growing in backyards. Once the plants are discovered, ground-based law enforcement personnel arrest the owner, confiscate the owner's property, and practice the now-standard scorched-earth policy.

And then there's the military's war on drugs within the military. If, as reported by the Pentagon, the military spent half a billion dollars from 1980 to 1990 ferreting out homosexuals in its ranks (and we can add that $500,000,000 to the cost of consensual crime enforcement), imagine how much they spend eradicating the far more prevalent consensual activity of drug use. (The Defense Department's budget for military police, courts, and jails is separate from the Bureau of Justice's expenditures.)

---

*Remember in *The Wizard of Oz* when the witch wanted to keep Dorothy, Scarecrow, Tin Man, and Lion from reaching the Emerald City? She placed a field of poppies between them and the city gates. "Poppies, poppies," she crooned, caressing her crystal ball, "poppies will put them to sleep." And what does Glinda, the good witch, send to wake them up? Snow—a popular slang term in the thirties for amphetamines—particularly cocaine. The screenwriters, of course, had no knowledge of drugs, and these two occurrences are absolutely coincidental.

So, all together, what portion of its $260 billion does the Defense Department spend fighting the war on drugs? Let's say a very conservative $7 billion.

The war on drugs alone, then, is costing $40 billion per year. What about the rest of the consensual crimes? Here the statistics are not so readily available.

In some cases, information is simply not available. In the arrest statistics for consensual crimes, for example, only drug abuse, gambling, prostitution, drunkenness, disorderly conduct, and vagrancy are separated out. Homosexuality, adultery, bigamy, and polygamy are put into a category called "sex offenses" which includes arrests for any number of nonconsensual sexual activities. Further, consensual crimes are often hidden in other categories. For example, when two people agree to perform a consensual activity, they are sometimes charged with "conspiracy to commit a felony." By charging people with conspiracy, the police don't have to prove the people actually did something, only that they conspired to do it. The word *conspiracy* has some fairly evil connotations. It simply means, however, agreeing to do something. So, if you agree with another person to engage in drug use, prostitution, sodomy, adultery, gambling, or anything else illegal, you can be arrested for conspiracy. You can also be arrested for conspiring to blow up a building, murder someone, or kidnap a four-year-old. It all goes under the general category of "conspiracy to commit a felony." There are other terms that hide consensual crimes. *Pandering* (the charge Heidi Fleiss was arrested for) and *racketeering* are two favorites.

Then there's the category called "All Other Offenses." Dumped into this category are 3,743,200 arrests—22% of the total arrests in 1994. What's in *that* category? After dozens of phone calls, I discovered the answer: nobody knows. It's a catch-all where violations of all local, state, and federal ordinances that don't fit into the Department of Justice's clear-cut categories are put. How many of those are consensual crimes—and what it cost to enforce them—is anybody's guess.

Those who study such things and make professional guesses ("expert opinions") estimate that

> *No government ever voluntarily reduces itself in size. Government programs, once launched, never disappear. Actually, a government bureau is the nearest thing to eternal life we'll ever see on this earth!*
>
> RONALD REAGAN

between 4 and 6 million of the 15 million arrests each year are for consensual activities. Let's take the lower end of that range and call it 4 million.

We know that in 1994, 1,350,000 of these 4 million arrests were for "drug offenses." We also know that the government spent $29 billion on those 1.35 million drug arrests. Therefore, we can conservatively estimate that it spends at least another $10 billion a year on the other million consensual crime arrests, trials, and incarcerations.

Adding the $3 billion of foreign aid and the $8 billion spent by the Coast Guard and the military on consensual crimes, it's fair to say that we spend $50 billion a year on prohibiting consensual crimes. In fact, it's almost certainly an understatement.

There are innumerable financial costs I'm not including in that $50 billion. Each year, for example, $10 billion in personal property is stolen and never recovered. As we shall see in the chapter, "Consensual Crimes Encourage Real Crime," most of these thefts are committed by addicts to pay for the artificially inflated price of their drugs. Many of these thefts involve violence. According to the American Association for Public Health, violence in this country "costs nearly $500 billion in medical care and lost productivity."

⚖ ⚖ ⚖

> *He uses statistics*
> *as a drunken man*
> *uses lamp-posts*
> *—for support*
> *rather than illumination.*
>
> ANDREW LANG

"There are two kinds of statistics," wrote Rex Stout, "the kind you look up and the kind you make up." When we want to explore how much money the American economy loses each year by keeping the traffic of consensual crimes underground, you can make up as many statistics as I—or any "expert"—can invent. Surveys asking people to admit to criminal activity are notoriously inaccurate, and "statistics" given about some future event aren't really statistics, but projections, guesstimates, crystal-ball gazing, and blue-skying. Whether you see "Blue Skies" or "Stormy Weather," it's still a weather forecast and, as Gordy, the weatherman on *The Mary Tyler Moore Show*, defensively asked, "What do you think I can do? Predict the future?"

Determining how much money is lost to the U.S. economy due to laws against consensual activities requires knowing two things: (a) How big is the underground of consensual crimes? and (b) How much bigger or smaller would this economy become if it were legalized?

Determining the size of the underground economy depends on law enforcement estimates and surveys. This is a problem. Law enforcement estimates go up and down depending on what law enforcement wants the estimates to show. When law enforcement wants more money, it gives estimates of crime so severe it would seem that, for the protection of all citizens, leaving one's house should be made illegal. On the other hand, when law enforcement wants to show what a stellar job it is doing, the crime wave of April becomes the pastoral of May.

The other way to determine the level of consensual crime activity is through surveys conducted either over the phone, in writing, or in person. Even when surveys are conducted "anonymously," the person being surveyed hardly feels anonymous. An organization, after all, had to call or write you. It has your phone number or address. When you go in person to take part in an "anonymous" survey, you can hardly walk into the interview wearing a ski mask. (As these surveys sometimes take place in federal buildings, you had better not walk in wearing a ski mask.) Whether taking the

> *As society has become less tolerant of drugs, people have become less willing to report drug use, even in anonymous surveys.*
>
> NATIONAL INSTITUTE OF JUSTICE

survey by phone, by mail, or in person, the participant has every reason to believe that his or her identity is not entirely secret. Therefore, when one's responses could have criminal consequences, one tends to revert to self-protection and, quite simply, lie. Studies that asked about recent drug usage, for example, backed up by urine samples, revealed that only about half the people who had taken drugs (as revealed in the urine samples) admitted in the survey to having taken them.

What does all this mean? It means we don't know how big the underground economy in consensual crime is. Looking at a number of studies, one begins to get an idea of at least a range of underground commerce. I cannot, however, in good conscience say, "Because of this statistic, this study, this report, and this expert's opinion, we know the underground economy is . . ." How can one make a prediction without accurate data? And how can we predict the future when we still disagree about the past?

For example, although most historians agree that alcohol consumption increased during Prohibition, there is a school of thought that says alcohol consumption decreased during Prohibition, and took quite some time after Prohibition to build up to pre-Prohibition levels. Therefore, to people who believe this claim, Prohibition was a success. This reconstruction of history seems to have been circulated by William Bennett while he was drug czar, as justification for (a) the drug war and (b) his czarship. Others who find it too inconvenient, uncomfortable, or

> *Carlye said,*
> *"A lie cannot live";*
> *it shows he did not know*
> *how to tell them.*
>
> MARK TWAIN

time-consuming to re-evaluate their stance on drugs also bandy about the Prohibition-as-a-success argument.

This view of history relies on official government statistics on the consumption of alcohol before, during, and after Prohibition. These figures, for the most part, did not track home brewing, bootlegging, allowing grape juice to ferment into wine *("Bad, grape juice, bad!")*, using industrial alcohol for personal consumption, and "importing" alcohol from Canada, Mexico, and beyond the three-mile limit. About the only alcohol the government officially tracked during Prohibition was alcohol produced for medicinal purposes. While this was used for recreational purposes as well, it certainly did not reflect alcohol's complete recreational use. Prohibition ended as America was in the depths of the depression. Many people couldn't afford food, so it's not surprising they couldn't afford alcohol. The depression led directly to World War II, where sacrifices and shortages were commonplace, and a good deal of the drinking population (the young men) were shipped overseas where they did their drinking (or at least wanted to). Declaring that Prohibition "worked" is an example of using official—but drastically incomplete—figures to support a convenient point of view.[*]

So, guess along with me as we try to determine what the underground economy in consensual crimes might currently be, what it might become if it were allowed to rise aboveground,

---

[*]It's interesting to note that none of the people who claim Prohibition was successful is calling for a return of Prohibition. If it was so successful, why not bring it back? The answer is obvious: it would cause a hue and cry in this country that has seldom been huen or cried. Prohibition didn't work then for the same reasons it wouldn't work now—and isn't working to control other substances and activities.

and how much we can tax it (without driving it back underground again).

We know more about the size of the underground of drugs than any other consensual crime. Experts testifying before congressional committees say that $1 trillion in drug money is laundered worldwide each year. It is estimated that 40%, or $400 billion, of this is laundered in the United States. The remaining $600 billion is laundered outside of the United States, but much of that $600 billion either could have originated in the United States, or could have been used by a middleman to purchase drugs bound for the United States. (The U.S. is the #1 licit and illicit drug market in the world.)

> *3,699 metric tons of opium, 14,407 metric tons of marijuana, and 271,700 metric tons of coca leaves were produced worldwide in 1993.*
>
> U.S. DEPARTMENT OF STATE

That's just the amount laundered. Drug money doesn't have to be laundered until some of the big guys want to spend the money in big ways on big things. Smaller amounts of "dirty" money pass between smaller players all the time. All these cash transactions are not included in the $1 trillion figure of laundered money.

Another indication of the plenitude of drugs and the volume of sales is that each time law enforcement announces a new record drug bust in which tons and tons of some illicit substance worth billions of dollars were seized—usually with a comment such as, "At least this poison won't find its way into the schoolyards of America"—the street price for that particular drug does not alter *one cent.**

---

*Which makes one question the ruthlessness—or at least business sense—of drug dealers. They easily could raise their prices by, oh, 10%, explaining, "You read about that big bust in the paper, didn't you? Goods are scarce." The oil companies did it during the oil shortage in the 1970s. The price of gasoline went up. It must have been one hell of a shortage, because prices have yet to come back down.

> *I believe in*
> *getting into hot water;*
> *it keeps you clean.*
>
> G. K. CHESTERTON

Another way to estimate the size of the underground drug market would be to look at the value per pound of drugs seized and multiply that by the amount of drugs most experts claim is never detected. We would still get an astronomical figure. We can't pretend, however, that this would be the figure for drug sales if drugs were legal. The only thing that keeps drug prices high is that drugs are illegal. When legal, the marketplace will soon dictate the proper price. That people have been willing to pay outrageously inflated prices for drugs indicates they would also be willing to pay outrageously inflated taxes on drugs.

Yes, some people will abuse drugs (as they already do), and drug abuse will have its costs to society (as it already does). Drugs, however, unlike cigarettes, will be able to pay their way—and create a significant amount of government revenue besides.* What pot smoker, for example, would not pay $5.00 for a pack of twenty neatly rolled joints, even if $3.50 of that went for taxes?

Currently, legalized gambling is a $300 billion industry. In terms of illegal gambling, the amount gambled on sports alone is estimated at more than $300 billion—$5 billion just on the Super Bowl. One can imagine the increase in aboveground gambling if there were casinos in all major cities, slot machines in bars, and video poker games at 7-Elevens. If gambling were legal, placing a bet on almost anything you wanted could be done over the phone, using your Visa or MasterCard. In New York, right now, you can make a phone call and bet on the horses using the

---

*For cigarettes to pay their way, they would have to be taxed at $2.17 per pack—the amount lost to cigarette-related disease and death when divided by the number of packs sold. State and federal taxes combined— even in the highest taxing states—are less than $1.00 per pack. For each pack sold, society loses at least $1.17.

charge card of your choice. All these activities are—like state lotteries and the stock market—above ground and taxable.

Illegal gambling winnings traditionally go unreported and therefore untaxed. If all gambling were legal, honest people who win private wagers could remain in the good graces of their government by sending in a small donation from time to time.*

> *I'll tell you, it's Big Business.*
> *If there is one word*
> *to describe Atlantic City,*
> *it's Big Business.*
> *Or two words—Big Business.*
>
> DONALD TRUMP

Prostitution. Hmmmm. That's an interesting one. No one seems to even guess at the number of prostitutes, much less acts of prostitution by amateurs. The only state in the United States in which prostitution is even partially legal, Nevada,** is very closed-mouthed about how much money prostitution takes in. It has a Brothel Association, and the man who is the head of it will

---

*Okay. It's late. I'm hallucinating. However, by law, if you live in New York City and purchase something outside New York City and bring it into New York City for use there, you must pay the New York City sales tax. So, if you buy a VCR in New Jersey and bring it into New York City, you owe New York City sales tax. There is a form to fill out which should accompany your check for this sales tax. Twenty-five of these forms were printed in 1953 when the law was passed. Twenty of these forms still remain. One form was used by a member of a religious group who believes avoiding tax is a sin. (One of those weird cults.) One form was used by someone who mistakenly thought you had to fill it out if you were a New York City resident marrying someone from New Jersey. Another was taken by a collector who owns one of every form the government has printed since 1924. (His collection is stored in the airplane hangar that formerly housed the *Spruce Goose*.) One was used by a clerk in the forms department to write down a phone number when no other paper was readily available. And one form is unaccounted for because, after all, the forms have been in the hands of a bureaucracy for forty years.

**Prostitution is legal in the unincorporated areas of seven counties in Nevada, plus seven towns in those counties.

> *What it comes down to is this:*
> *the grocer, the butcher, the baker,*
> *the merchant, the landlord,*
> *the druggist, the liquor dealer,*
> *the policeman, the doctor,*
> *the city father and the politician—*
> *these are the people who make money*
> *out of prostitution.*
>
> POLLY ADLER
> *A House Is Not a Home*

talk to you (nice fellow), but how much the bordellos take in and how much they pay in taxes is treated as some sort of state secret. (Which, apparently, it is.)

To determine the national prostitution economy, we could take the number of arrests and multiply it by the number of clients the average prostitute sees between arrests, and multiply that figure by the average amount the average client contributes (financially, that is), and that would give us a figure. The problem is, most prostitutes I've talked with don't get arrested even once in a given year—most haven't been arrested at all. The number of clients between arrests, then, would be difficult to determine.

So what I thought I'd do is compare prostitution to an already aboveground industry that is similar to prostitution. We need to find an industry that projects a friendly image, satisfies a real need at a fair price, is conveniently located, and is designed for rapid turnover. The obvious answer: fast food.* McDonald's alone pulls in $21 billion a year; Burger King, $6.4 billion. Even the slogans fit: "We do it all for you" and "Have it your way." Then there's Wendy's (sounds like a bordello, doesn't it?) and Jack-in-the-Box. (I'm not saying a word—and I'm not even going to *mention* In-N-Out Burger.) Some innovative bordellos might, like the burger chains, offer drive-through service: pick what you want from a large illustrated menu, pay at window #1, pick up your order at window #2.

Of course, not everyone wants fast food. So, there are dining places from Big Boy's to Lutece that could be the inspiration for

---

*I certainly hope the prostitutes of America don't mind being compared with an industry that raises environmentally inefficient animals, kills them, grinds them up and serves them with a smile. If any do mind, I apologize.

more substantial bordellos. There could even be a theme park, Bordelloland. (Disney's theme parks rake in $3.3 billion per year.) Also known as the Magic Fingers Kingdom, it could feature such attractions as Wenches of the Caribbean, The Haunted Whore House, The Gay Nineties Dance Hall, Chip and Dale's Chippendale Review, and the

> *That place [Disneyland] is my baby, and I would prostitute myself for it.*
>
> WALT DISNEY

Mayflower Madam River Cruise. (I bet you thought this was gonna be some boring chapter full of numbers and statistics. I was going to do a whole thing here on Mickey and his dog Pimpo and Minnie Madam, but I think we've had enough silly puns for this chapter. Let's get on with it.*)

Unlike drug prices, prostitution rates will probably not lower significantly with legalization. Illegality does not significantly increase the price of prostitution—just the risk to both prostitute and client. Also, if prostitution ever became acceptable, the amount spent on flowers, candy, and greeting cards would probably drop. The loss to these industries would have to be deducted from the increase to the aboveground economy caused by legalizing prostitution. Nevertheless, the economy, overall, would be ahead.

Drugs, gambling, and prostitution are the Big Three underground "moneymakers" in consensual crime. There would be, however, significant boosts to the economy if the stigma attached to the other consensual crimes were eliminated through legalization.

Removing the laws against and, over time, the stigma of homosexuality would cause more and more gays to come out—come out and *spend their money*. Cities with large gay populations

---

*"Let's Get on with It" is a ride at Magic Mountains, Bordelloland's chief competitor.

> *I do not think*
> *Cary Grant was a*
> *homosexual or bisexual.*
> *He just got carried away*
> *at those orgies.*
>
> REPRESENTATIVE BOB DORNAN
> on the House floor

such as New York, San Francisco, and Los Angeles don't just have gay bars, but gay restaurants, gay bookstores, gay mini-malls, gay clothing stores (which carry clothing that looks very much like the clothing the GAP will be selling six months later), gay gyms, gay coffee shops, gay video stores, gay supermarkets, and just about every other human gathering place you can name. West Hollywood, California, with a 30% gay population, has a gay hardware store and a gay Mrs. Field's Cookies.

If gay marriages were legalized and bigamy and polygamy took off among heterosexuals (or gays), consider the boon to the wedding industry, already a $32 billion empire.

If we legalize—even encourage—transvestism, some people would be buying an entire second wardrobe. What a shot in the arm for the clothing industry. And *shoes.* Let's not forget shoes. Somewhere out there in America are any number of men, who, deep in their heart, want to be Imelda Marcos. And who knows how many women have Donald Trump's taste in suits? (His suits may not look good, but they're very expensive.)

And so on down the list of consensual crimes.

♎ ♎ ♎

Another great advantage of moving an underground economy aboveground is that for every $50,000 you move aboveground, you create a new aboveground job (or move someone who is currently working in a non–tax-paying underground job into a tax-paying aboveground job). Removing the laws against consensual activities would create at least 6,000,000 new jobs (or turn 6,000,000 underground employees into tax-paying citizens).

AIN'T NOBODY'S BUSINESS IF YOU DO

In all (with high taxes on drugs, the spur to the economy, the 6,000,000 more taxpayers, and all the other factors discussed), my "expert" conclusion is that legalizing consensual crimes would add $150 billion in tax revenue to the government treasury. When we eliminate the $50 billion we are currently spending to enforce the laws against consensual activities, we're looking at $200 billion per year in increased revenue.

> *In 1950,*
> *the average family of four*
> *paid 2% of its earnings*
> *to federal taxes.*
> *Today it pays 24%.*
>
> WILLIAM R. MATTOX, JR.

⚖ ⚖ ⚖

And now for the bad news.

Much of the $50 billion we're spending to prosecute consensual crimes each year we are, in fact, not just spending but borrowing. The $50 billion gets tossed into our national debt. Since it's already topping $5 trillion, $50 billion more hardly gets noticed.

But, noticed or not, the national debt does command our interest—6% interest to be exact. To finance the annual persecution of 4,000,000 Americans and the incarceration 750,000 more, the government sells treasury bills, which pay, as of early 1996, 6% interest per year. Fifty billion borrowed for 30 years at 6% compound interest comes to $250 billion in interest—providing we pay it off in 30 years, of which there is no guarantee.

Those who bemoan the harm consensual crimes might do to their children should take a good look at the very real harm that will befall their children when the interest on financing this year's Inquisition comes due somewhere down the pike. For every year we spend $50 billion enforcing laws against consensual activities, we're adding an additional $250 billion to the next generation's pile of inherited woes. That's if interest rates

> *The blame for [the national debt] lies with the Congress and the President, with Democrats and Republicans alike, most all of whom have been unwilling to make the hard choices or to explain to the American people that there is no such thing as a free lunch.*
>
> SENATOR WARREN RUDMAN

stay at 6%. Every percentage point they go up adds $67 billion to the total bill.

None of this, by the way, takes into account how much we're spending to borrow the $150 billion we could be collecting in yearly tax revenues.

⚖️ ⚖️ ⚖️

So, our yearly grand total for enforcing the laws against consensual activities is $450 billion. If interest rates climb from 6% to 7%, it will come to an even half-a-trillion dollars a year.

That amount could be used in any of the following ways:

- Pay off the national debt in less than ten years.
- Reduce personal income taxes by more than 75 percent.
- Allow the Pentagon to purchase 23 wrenches, 16 office chairs, and 243 paper clips.
- Send every man, woman, and child in the United States a check for $2,000 each year.
- Finance three rounds of congressional pay raises.
- Pay everyone's doctor, dentist, phone, and utility bills, as well as pay for gasoline and repair of every car in the United States.
- Send a check for $217,000 to every high school graduate for furthering his or her education or for starting real life.
- Spend sixteen times more money on education than we currently do.

- Send every person over 85 years old a check for $165,000 with a note saying, "Hey, congratulations!"

Rather than spinning our wheels asking what we can do to stop consensual crimes, why not direct all that creative energy toward how we can best spend that $450 billion?

> *For seven and a half years*
> *I've worked alongside*
> *President Reagan.*
> *We've had triumphs.*
> *Made some mistakes.*
> *We've had some*
> *sex . . . uh . . . setbacks.*
>
> PRESIDENT GEORGE BUSH

⚖ ⚖ ⚖

Finally, consider that almost every consensual criminal who goes through the criminal justice system and is incarcerated for, say, a year, becomes a permanent *negative economic unit*. Most people in society are positive economic units—that is, they produce more in goods, services, or ideas than they consume. Negative economic units, however, are a drain on society, the economy, and the nation. An ex-con is essentially unemployable—especially during times of high unemployment. This forces the ex-con—in order to physically survive—to go on welfare, turn to crime, or both.

Eventually, enough of these negative economic units become an economic black hole that, unseen, sucks the lifeblood from even the most productive economy. By turning ordinary consenting adults into criminals, we are creating millions of economic vampires.

We must be very careful that we do not unnecessarily create negative economic units. There will always be the criminals—those who go about physically harming the person and property of others—and they will need to be put away. Paying for this is part of the cost of living in a safe country. Each life destroyed, however, by the arrest, trial, and incarceration of a consensual criminal is an unnecessary permanent liability on our country and our economy. These people simply don't believe in the

> *We are not to expect*
> *to be translated*
> *from despotism to liberty*
> *in a feather bed.*
>
> THOMAS JEFFERSON

American dream anymore, know the American system is not fair, and are quite convinced that the entire system doesn't work.

And why should they believe in the system? Each time, as a child or an adult, they pledge allegiance to the flag, they are promised "liberty and justice for all." They used that liberty, and what did they get? Injustice. So much for the republic for which it stands. This psychic drain can be even more devastating than the economic drain, destroying the optimism, enthusiasm, and well-being of a nation.

The laws against consensual activities, then, hurt us all. Each life destroyed due to the enforcement of these laws is like a piranha. Alone, piranhas are relatively harmless. When enough of them combine, however, they can turn a cow into a skeleton within minutes. Imagine what they can do to the goose that laid the American Golden Egg.

Enforcing Laws against Consensual Activities Destroys People's Lives

> *Show me the prison,*
> *Show me the jail,*
> *Show me the prisoner*
> *whose life has gone stale.*
> *And I'll show you a young man*
> *with so many reasons why*
> *And there, but for fortune,*
> *go you or I.*
>
> PHIL OCHS

WHAT THE ENFORCE-MENT of laws against consensual activities does to individuals is nothing short of criminal. The government is destroying the very lives of the people it is supposedly saving.

A single arrest, even without a conviction, is, in many cases, enough to ruin a life; a conviction and a year in jail are almost guaranteed to. All this, of course, is "for their own good." As the Horace of Spain (1559–1619) wrote, "No pain equals that of an injury inflicted under the pretense of a just punishment."

Let's take a look at the process of arrest, trial, conviction, and jail. Please don't think of this as something happening to some "criminal" who "deserves it." Think of it as something happening to you or one of your friends or relatives. If you have ever taken part in any consensual crime, it was luck alone that kept at least some of these things from happening to you.

As the song goes: there, but for fortune, go you or I.

When you are arrested, you are thrown into a world of violent criminals handled by individuals who are well-trained in treating people like violent criminals. Don't expect that you will be treated any differently. (A friend of our family used to regale us with both horror and laughter at the treatment he received during a consensual crime arrest. After recounting an indignity

> *Once the law starts
> asking questions,
> there's no stopping them.*
>
> WILLIAM S. BURROUGHS

or personal violation, he would lift his hands to heaven and say, "Who was I gonna call? The police? They were already there!")

Prior to—or simultaneously with—the arrest, comes the search.

You can be home one evening watching TV when you hear a knock at the door. "Who's there?" you ask, having seen some nicely uniformed police officer in a documentary on crime prevention recommend that you never open your door without knowing who is on the other side.

"Open the door. It's the police. We have a warrant to search your premises."* This is likely to be the only warning you get before your door is broken down (if a "no-knock" warrant is issued, you won't even get a first knock). The police automatically assume that you are (a) guilty and (b) hurriedly destroying evidence: flushing drugs, pornography, or prostitutes down the toilet. The door is opened (by you or by them) and, without a

---

*The Constitution guarantees that there will be no "unreasonable searches and seizures" and that a warrant must be issued by a judge only "upon probable cause." Unfortunately, the word "probable" has degenerated into "possible," also known as "Let's have a look." Sometimes search warrants are issued on anonymous tips, or on the word of a police officer who received an anonymous tip. Sometimes police officers ask for and judges issue warrants that they know, if the case were taken to a high enough court, would be thrown out on constitutional grounds ("unconstitutional search and seizure"). The warrant is issued anyway because, chances are, contraband of some kind will be found and the person will plea bargain and confess guilt to a lesser crime. "Justice" will be served and the Constitution, once again, will be dishonored. Even without an arrest or conviction, the trauma of a search itself is sometimes used by law enforcement agencies as a "warning." Legislation passed by Congress in 1995 would in many cases of consensual crime eliminate the judge from the process altogether.

moment's hesitation, three or four or five or ten uniformed and/or uninformed police begin going through everything you own.

Here a frightening question may cross your mind: how do you know whether these are really police? Answer: you don't. Even if they flash a badge, everyone knows fake badges are readily avail-

> *The [Supreme] Court during the past decade let police obtain search warrants on the strength of anonymous tips. It did away with the need for warrants when police want to search luggage, trash cans, car interiors, bus passengers, fenced private property and barns.*
>
> DAN BAUM

able. If you have the presence of mind to ask to use the telephone to call the station house to confirm that this is an authorized search, the request will almost certainly be denied.

So there you are, surrounded by a group of armed authority figures who are going through everything you own, putting "suspicious" articles into boxes or plastic bags, and you can only hope it's really the police and not some enterprising band of criminals. (On the other hand, maybe one should hope it is a band of criminals—stuff can be replaced; time in prison cannot.)

At about this point, you are "Mirandized." Amidst the hubbub of your fish tank being drained (who knows what you may be hiding under the sand), your toilet being dismantled (lots of room for contraband behind, in, or "down there"), and every container in your kitchen being emptied onto the counter ("This stuff in the oregano jar smells a lot like marijuana"), being read your constitutional rights sounds something like this: "*Mumble mumble* you have the right to remain silent *mumble mumble* right to an attorney *mumble mumble* can and will be used against you *mumble mumble* do you understand?" And then, amidst this atmosphere of physical, emotional, and psychological terror, the questioning begins. By this time, often, you will be handcuffed.

You are asked about people, incidents, and things going back as far as seven years (the statute of limitation on most felonies). You are asked to remember where you were, who you were with and what you were doing at a particular time, on a particular

> *The right*
> *to be let alone*
> *is indeed*
> *the beginning*
> *of all freedom.*
>
> JUSTICE WILLIAM O. DOUGLAS

date. If you're like most people, you don't remember what you had for dinner two weeks ago, much less what you did on a specific date two years ago, but "not remembering" is treated as a clear indication of "withholding evidence," "interfering with justice," being "uncooperative," and, of course, guilt. If you happen to remember something, anything, these comments will be carefully recorded, and, if you happen to have a more complete recollection later, it will be taken as a sign that "you truly don't have an accurate memory of the situation" or that you "lied to the police."

Once armed with a search warrant, anything the police recover of an "illegal nature" or even a "suspicious nature" is fair game. They can dismantle and destroy anything that might hold any illegal substance—and, considering how compact certain drugs are, this means that they can dismantle and destroy anything. They can take with them any "suspicious substances" for laboratory testing. This could include the entire contents of your medicine cabinet, kitchen pantry, and garage. Anything that might be used to "document" your criminal activity can be confiscated. This means all files, correspondence, notes, diaries, address books, phone bills, video tapes, audio tapes, and even your computer. If you do business from your home, a police search can put you out of business immediately.

Getting back your possessions can take weeks, months, and, in some cases, years. You may find yourself trying to reconstruct your personal and business records from scratch at a time when you need them most—while gathering evidence for your defense. Meanwhile, the police could well be calling all the people in your phone book or professional database, asking if they know you and, when they respond yes, asking them such questions as, "Do you know anything about this person's involvement with drugs (prostitution, homosexuality, gambling, etc.)?"

Anything that might indicate what "kind of person" you are can also be seized, even if it's not directly related to a crime. This includes books on certain subjects, magazines, newspapers, even what station your television or radio was tuned to—anything that might make you look unusual, peculiar, unconventional, or make a jury of twelve "normal" people think you're pretty weird overall and probably deserve to go to jail for either the crime you are being charged or for the many crimes you've gotten away with.

> *Under a government which imprisons any unjustly, the true place for a just man is also a prison . . . the only house in a slave State in which a free man can abide with honor.*
>
> HENRY DAVID THOREAU

Whether you're arrested or taken to the police station for "questioning" or on "suspicion," your property that hasn't either been destroyed by the police or taken with them is pretty much up for grabs. If the police broke down your door, they don't exactly call a carpenter and locksmith to make sure that everything is secure before they head off for their next round of searching and seizing. They may put some tape across the outside of your door, saying "POLICE LINES. DO NOT CROSS," which, to any burglar, means "LOOT INSIDE. OWNER SAFELY IN JAIL. WELCOME." One person who had been searched and seized told another who had gone through a similar experience, "After the police left, burglars came, ransacked my apartment and took everything of value," to which the other victim replied, "How could you tell?"

Sometimes you can't tell. If you're carted off before the police are finished searching and seizing, you may come home and not know the difference between vandalism, theft, and the work of professional law enforcement. If you can't get bail together quickly—or are held in jail for two, three, four days before bail is even set—you may never see any of your property again. If the police suspect you were using your home, car, or any other pos-

> *If England treats her criminals*
> *the way she has treated me,*
> *she doesn't deserve to have any.*
>
> OSCAR WILDE

sessions for drug selling, they too will be immediately seized, and you may never see them again either.* But, we're getting slightly ahead of our story.

When you are taken downtown ("downtown" does seem to be the favorite euphemism for a police station; even if you live downtown, you will still be taken downtown), you will probably be put in some sort of holding cell (or, as they call it, a holding tank) for an indefinite period of time. (The Supreme Court says that you can be held for forty-eight hours without even being charged.) If you are lucky, you will be alone in such a cell. Most likely, however, what with jails at 101% capacity thanks to the rigorous enforcement of laws against consensual activities, you will probably find yourself in a much larger cell with some real criminals who have also been recently arrested—some yelling, some moaning, some covered in blood (their own or others'), some vomiting, and some with little or no control of other orifices.

Once there, you are a criminal. Period. No distinction is made between criminals whose crimes have innocent victims and criminals whose crimes do not. Even if you are not harassed, molested, abused, exposed to a contagious illness, or raped, the

---

*If your car, house, property, money, bank balance, stocks, or anything else is seized, you must prove that it was not used for the sale of drugs. In other words, it is not up to the government to prove that you did use it to sell drugs—the burden of proof is on you. This is a complete reversal of the fundamental tenet of law, "innocent until proven guilty." So, in addition to proving your own innocence and keeping yourself out of jail, you must also prove the innocence of your car, house, property, etc., in order to get them back. Often the property will be sold and the money given to the law enforcement agencies that took it before you have a chance to make your case.

sights, smells, and sounds are hideous. The odor of one person vomiting, for example, can cause a chain reaction of retching to which few are immune.

Seldom do holding tanks have anything soft in them, such as mattresses, pillows, or blankets. Concrete, wooden, or metal slabs are the most that one can hope for, and even on

> *The Supreme Court is steadily eroding the protections against police excess promised by the Fourth, Fifth, Sixth, Eighth and Fourteenth Amendments to the Constitution.*
>
> DAN BAUM
> *The Nation*
> June 29, 1992

these unforgiving surfaces—due to overcrowding—there is seldom room to actually lie down. If you are not physically strong enough to stake out your own territory you may end up sitting on the floor or standing until the police get around to questioning you, which might not be until some time the next day, or the next. (Suspects are sometimes intentionally put in the worst holding cells to "soften them up" for questioning.)

Then there is the questioning. Questioning is designed to be traumatic. Whether they use subtle psychological manipulation, hellfire and brimstone histrionics, or a combination of the two in the classic "good cop, bad cop" technique, questioning is designed to make you feel guilty about everything so that you'll confess your guilt about something. You'll be asked to explain pieces of your life pulled from the search and taken out of context: Polaroid pictures, journal entries, personal letters.

The courts have determined that, in order to get you to confess, police can confront you with evidence they have made up. They can show you drugs and claim to have found them in your house. They can show you affidavits signed by names taken from your address book accusing you of elaborate criminal conduct. The police will attempt to convince you that they have an airtight case against you on a greater charge so you'll plead guilty to a lesser charge.

Somewhere, you will be faced with yet another major choice. Could you—with one or two phone calls—contact a good, com-

> *Criminal lawyer.*
> *Or is that redundant?*
>
> WILL DURST

petent, honest criminal attorney? Few people know how to contact a criminal attorney because few people—including those who regularly take part in consensual crimes—think of themselves as criminals.

Eventually, the first wave of a very dark ocean known as The Truth About Lawyers reaches your beach. Criminal lawyers want retainers—that is, money up front of anywhere from $5,000 to $25,000. This is just the tip of the legal iceberg, which frequently runs into hundreds of thousands of dollars.

If you are arrested for a consensual crime involving drugs, it will be harder for you to obtain the services of an attorney than if you had been arrested for, say, murder. If an attorney takes your case for a drug charge and you are found guilty, the courts can force the attorney to give all the money he or she has made from your case to the law enforcement agency that arrested you. It's part of the assets forfeiture law. The courts have ruled that not only are your house, car, money, land, investments, bank accounts, and other tangible assets forfeitable, but everything you've paid your attorney as well. Consequently, criminal attorneys are hesitant to take on drug cases. Murderers, rapists, and robbers are getting better legal representation than pot smokers.

Many attorneys (un)scrupulously investigate the client's net worth and, lo, when the case is over, the final bill comes to within a few thousand dollars of this amount. If they can't justify charging all this money themselves, they call in any number of attorneys as "specialists" or "consultants." These same attorneys call your attorney in their cases to act as a "specialist" or "consultant."

The only alternative is to declare yourself too poor to hire an attorney, in which case you will be assigned a public defender who is overworked, underpaid, and sometimes not very good (which may be why he or she got a job as a public defender in the first place).

After you are arrested, questioned, and charged, you are arraigned. Basically, this is going before a judge who will set bail. Ah, bail. Let's say that your bail is set at a nice, low, reasonable $50,000. Can *you* put your hands on $50,000—in cash? From inside a jail?

> Government is like fire.
> If it is kept within bounds and
> under the control of the people,
> it contributes to the welfare of all.
> But if it gets out of place,
> if it gets too big and out of control,
> it destroys the happiness
> and even the lives of the people.
>
> HAROLD E. STASSEN

Can anyone you know (who would do it for you) immediately come up with $50,000 in cash? If the answer to these questions is "no," your choice is either (a) stay in jail until your trial (it might be months) or (b) visit the bail bondsman. Bail bondsmen take 10% of the bail in cash (they are kind enough, however, to accept Visa, MasterCard, and American Express). To put up a $50,000 bond, they take $5,000. Even if the charges are dropped the next day, they keep the $5,000. Still, if you can post bail in any form, you're one of the lucky ones: 51% of all those who go trial cannot afford bail and are jailed from the time of the arrest through the final verdict. If you're fortunate enough to have—or to have friends who will help you put up—the $5,000, you are then free to return to whatever is left of your previous life, much of which may have been confiscated under the assets forfeiture law.

You're also free to return to work. Ah, work. With the detention, questioning, arresting, arraigning, and gathering of bail money, you may have been in jail for several days, or several weeks. What do you tell your boss? In all likelihood, your boss already knows. The friendly detectives from the police department have already visited your boss, asking if you had behaved in any "unusual" ways which might indicate that you were involved in drugs (prostitution, gambling, sodomy, etc.).

You may be fired. If you argue (quite correctly) that you haven't been convicted of anything, and that one is, in our country,

> *Whenever the offence
> inspires less horror
> than the punishment,
> the rigour of penal law
> is obliged to give way
> to the common feelings
> of mankind.*
>
> EDWARD GIBBON
> (1737–1794)

innocent until proven guilty, the boss will probably vaguely refer to something such as, "Where there's smoke, there's fire," or "At our company, we can't even risk the hint of impropriety."

Finding another job will not be easy. An arrest, even if it ends in a dismissal or an acquittal in court, remains on your record. Many companies check for arrest records as a standard part of screening applicants. Banks, credit card companies, lending institutions, rental agencies, and others use it as an indication of credit worthiness. Even though it is blatantly unfair, and directly violates the tenet that you are innocent until proven guilty, many companies use a "record of arrests" as a reason not to hire you, rent you an apartment, or extend credit.

Ironically, the presupposition of guilt for consensual crimes is even higher than for violent crimes. If you are accused of, say, holding up a bank at gunpoint, even your boss might say, "Oh, I doubt it." If, however, you are accused of propositioning a hooker or smoking a joint, most people conclude, "Yeah, she probably did it," or "Why was he dumb enough to get caught?"

It is here that you go through the traumatic experience of finding out who your real friends are. Some might rally 'round with love, support, and material assistance. Others will practice the ancient wisdom, "A friend in need is a friend to be avoided."

Now, too, is the time when that church or religious group you've been supporting for so many years shows its true colors. If your alleged crime is one of the consensual crimes, chances are your church considers it a sin. Some clergy advise accepting the punishment for a consensual crime as an extension of God's punishment for having sinned and as a lesson not to do such a despicable-in-the-eyes-of-the-Lord thing again. Or they just avoid you and your calls altogether. In other words, don't expect a nun who looks like Susan Sarandon to appear and give you unlimited pastoral counseling.

And, of course, consensual crimes put an incredible strain on the family. If a significant other doesn't know about his or her partner's forays into consensual crimes, an arrest is a shocking way to find out (The Hugh Grant Syndrome, Part II). If the significant other does know and, perhaps, even takes part in the consensual crime with his or her partner, there is still lots of room for incrimination. "I *told* you not to bring that stuff in the house!"

> *Freedom does not*
> *always win.*
> *This is one*
> *of the bitterest lessons*
> *of history.*
>
> A. J. P. TAYLOR

A consensual crime arrest could cause parents to permanently lose custody of their children. In Oregon, for example, if you are arrested with even less than an ounce of marijuana, you can be charged with "endangerment"; your children can be taken from you and placed in the state's foster care system. Statistically, your child has, while in that foster care system, a 20% chance of being either physically or sexually abused. The children will also be exposed to kids who are, themselves, criminals. What innocent children might be forceably exposed to could destroy their entire lives.

If you're engaged or dating someone, how will he or she take it? We all like to think that our beloved will stand resolutely by our side. Yes, that's what we all like to think.

And what if it was one of your children, or one of your brothers or sisters, or even one of your parents who was arrested? How much of your time, energy, and, most importantly, financial resources could you commit to keeping him or her out of jail? Successfully defending a criminal prosecution can cost hundreds of thousands of dollars. Where would you have to draw the line? Your savings? Your home? Your credit limit? It's traumatic having to put a dollar amount on the people we love, but

> *Imprisonment,*
> *as it exists today,*
> *is a worse crime than*
> *any of those*
> *committed by its victims.*
>
> GEORGE BERNARD SHAW

when they're accused of a consensual crime, that is what we must do.

It's little wonder, then, that, at this point, most people accused of consensual crimes seriously contemplate suicide. Not only is one's own life in shambles—the loss of possessions, living space, savings, reputation, job, friends, future—but the fear of being a burden on the friends and family who are willing to help is a pressure some people cannot bear. All this despair, combined with the fear of prison, can make suicide seem not only the most logical, but the only solution. At the very least, one finds oneself in an ever-deepening and seemingly bottomless depression. (If this chapter is becoming too depressing, please remember that, unlike the consequences of being arrested for a consensual crime, this chapter does have an end.)

If you choose to stay alive (which, by the way, I recommend), now starts the seemingly endless round of hearings, motions, further questionings, preparation of defense, and waiting, waiting, waiting. One thing you will not have to wait for are your attorney's bills. These will come on time, and you will be expected to pay them on time.

Somewhere along the line, plea bargaining begins. Anyone who says that gambling is illegal in the United States needs only look at plea bargaining to know this is not the case. In plea bargaining, you are asked to gamble the rest of your money or the rest of your life on the verdict of your trial. Rather than go for an all-or-nothing, guilty-or-not-guilty, on the charge for which you are accused, you agree to plead guilty to a lesser charge with a preset lesser sentence. If you accept the "bargain," you will have a permanent criminal record—not just an arrest, but a conviction—and you may spend some time in jail, but less time than if you were found guilty of the original charge. The good news, however, is that the legal bills stop; the interminable waiting is over; and you can get on with what's left of your life. If you want to bet on The Trial, however, it means that the legal bills begin to escalate, and, if found guilty, you will almost certainly get a worse punishment than you would have if you had pled guilty to the lesser charge.

> *The highest patriotism is not a blind acceptance of official policy, but a love of one's country deep enough to call her to a higher standard.*
>
> GEORGE McGOVERN

(Prosecutors and some judges don't seem to like pushy people cluttering up the court systems looking for justice.)

A plea bargain may be the only economic alternative. It's hard to get a job when an employer discovers you are awaiting trial and may have to "go away" for, oh, five years at some point in the indefinite future.

Once the credit card companies find out about your arrest, they'll probably start canceling your cards. (If you use a credit card with the bail bondsman to get out of jail, that's a red flag to credit card companies.) People awaiting trial, you see, have this nasty habit of going bankrupt. Can you imagine why? Lawyers know this too, which is why they work very hard to be paid on a regular basis. (Bankruptcy attorneys want the full amount up front before they even touch a case.)

If you go to trial, you usually have the choice between a jury trial or a trial before a judge (a "bench trial"). When charged with a consensual crime, you are dealing not just with the facts of guilt or innocence; you are also dealing with individual prejudices. On hearing what you're accused of doing, will the prejudice of the jury be such that your guilt will be presumed and the trial merely a formality? Judges tend to be a bit more sophisticated, having dealt with real criminals who go around raping, robbing, and murdering, but judges have their prejudices too. They also have political pressure. During a "crackdown" or "war" on this or that consensual crime, a judge is more likely to find

> *Judge:*
> *a law student*
> *who marks his own papers.*
>
> H. L. MENCKEN

guilt and sentence heavily. Economics enter the picture once again: jury trials tend to last longer than bench trials, and legal fees during criminal trials often run $2,000 to $5,000 per day, per attorney. (If they don't have all your money yet, your attorneys will strongly recommend that you have at least two attorneys representing you at the trial. If you're rich, they'll suggest an entourage.)

Prosecutors hate to lose. If the trial seems to be going in your favor, you will be offered better and better plea-bargains. Your attorney doesn't want to lose either (it's very difficult to collect a final bill from a client who is in prison); so, if the case seems to be going against you, your attorney will recommend accepting poorer and poorer bargains.

Meanwhile, everyone is involved in the psychological guessing game of "reading the jury." Who's on our side? Who's not on our side? This process begins with the selection of the jury and continues throughout the trial. If you have money, your attorney can hire a professional who will, during the selection process, do on-the-spot instant psychological profiles of each potential juror along with a recommendation as to whether or not the juror would be favorable or unfavorable to your case. Once the juror is selected, investigative companies can give overnight reports as to the net worth, politics, religion, marital status, sexual preference, and spending habits of each juror. This overnight profile costs, oh, $5,000 to $15,000 per jury, and, if you can afford it, your attorney will claim it's "an invaluable tool" in helping to "shape" your defense.

A lot of invaluable tools are available, and the more valuable you are, the more invaluable they become. There is, for example, the expert witness. The expert witness is a professional who is paid an exorbitant amount of money to give the "expert opinion" that you are right and the state is wrong. A popular expert witness in consensual crime trials is the psychiatrist. For, $3,000 to $10,000 each (you'll want at least two), the psychiatrist will "examine" you and claim that you're not a criminal, you're just sick; you don't need jail, you need treatment. Why, with a year or two of therapy

> *A jury consists*
> *of twelve persons*
> *chosen to decide*
> *who has the better lawyer.*
>
> ROBERT FROST

you could once again be a productive member of society. (The only thing that made you an unproductive member of society, of course, was being arrested, but it's best not to mention that at this point in the trial.) Yes, if you were sentenced, that is, if the court referred you to five psychiatric sessions per week for a year, that would be much better for you and all of society than that same year in the Big House. And, if the court takes this suggestion, that's only another $25,000 to $50,000 out of your pocket.

When the case finally goes to the jury, the high-pressure waiting begins. Juries can deliberate for several minutes or several weeks. The plea bargaining can still continue. Until the jury actually announces its verdict, it isn't a verdict, and, if a bargain is struck, the judge can call in the jury, thank them for their efforts, and send them on their way.

If the verdict comes back not guilty, you do not get back your legal fees, the arrest remains on your record, you most likely won't get back your job, and you probably wouldn't want the friends, family, or fiancée who deserted you. You will get back the evidence that was seized during the initial search (it will have been gone through, categorized, labeled, disassembled, much of it will be missing—but you'll get it back). Even if you are found innocent, you still must go to court again to get back your house, car, and money—whatever was seized under asset forfeiture laws.

> JUDGE: *Are you trying to show contempt for this court?*
>
> MAE WEST: *I was doin' my best to hide it.*

If you are found guilty, the next wait begins: the wait for sentencing. During this time, you can choose whether or not to appeal your case. "An appeal," explained Finley Peter Dunne, "is when you ask one court to show its contempt for another court." If you thought the first round of legal fees was expensive, when you move into the world of appellate courts, legal fees go into hyperdrive.

You can appeal for a mistrial. Here, you are asking the appellate court to declare your original trial invalid because of a technical legal error made by the judge, jury, or prosecution. If you are successful in winning this appeal, your trial will be declared null and void—but that doesn't make you free: you have to start all over again with another trial, another jury, another round of legal fees.

You can also appeal on constitutional grounds. Your lawyer can claim—using some of the brilliant arguments given in the chapters, "Laws against Consensual Activities Are Unconstitutional" and "Laws against Consensual Activities Violate the Separation of Church and State, Threatening the Freedom of and from Religion"—that the very law violates your constitutional rights and that the court should overturn the law. Here, you are looking at cases going to state supreme courts and, perhaps, even the federal Supreme Court. You are also looking at legal fees, not in the hundreds of thousands, but in the millions. (Most cases involving individuals that reach the Supreme Court are paid for by organizations such as the ACLU, who are doing it not just for the individual, but to set a legal precedent that will affect others.)

While the case is on appeal, if you don't want to spend time in jail, there is a little matter of additional bail. You are now, in the eyes of the court, a convicted criminal; thus the new bail will probably be higher than the first. Not everyone can meet bail, of course. Most people can't afford anything other than accepting their sentence and doing their time.

Let's talk about doing time.*

If you've never visited a penitentiary, you might want to do so. The worst ones, however, are rarely, if ever, open for public inspection. The average citizen would be reluctant to send even a *real* criminal, much less a hooker or a pot smoker, to such a hideous place.

Here's what Jimmy Hoffa—who served time in and visited many prisons—had to say:

> I can tell you this on a stack of Bibles: prisons are archaic, brutal, unregenerative, overcrowded hell holes where the inmates are treated like animals with absolutely not one humane thought given to what they are going to do once they are released. You're an animal in a cage and you're treated like one.

Thanks entirely to the crackdown on various consensual crimes, prisons—never designed for comfort in the first place—are overcrowded. Cells designed for two inmates are holding three, sometimes four. Even spending, as we are, $5 billion per year on new prison construction, this overcrowding is likely to continue into the indefinite future.

*There is a legal distinction between jails and prisons. Jails are run by cities, municipalities, and counties and are for housing prisoners either awaiting trial or serving less than a one-year sentence. Prisons (penitentiaries) are run by the state or federal government and are usually for housing prisoners serving sentences of a year or longer. Due to the overcrowding of prisons, however, a small percentage of prisoners sentenced to more than a year are serving their time in county jails. The descriptions given here of the prison system are equally true of county jails; the only difference is that county jails tend to be worse.

> *They call it the Halls of Justice because the only place you get justice is in the halls.*
>
> LENNY BRUCE

> *[The prison guards are] capable of committing daily atrocities and obscenities, smiling the smile of the angels all the while.*
>
> JEAN HARRIS

The first two things you'll notice on entering a penitentiary* are the noise and the smell. The smell is body odor, cigarette smoke, unflushed or backing up toilets, diarrhea, vomit, and wafting through it all is the strange but clearly unpleasant aroma of the mysterious substances the prisoners are fed. The noise is a cacophony of televisions, radios—all tuned to different stations—boom boxes, and voices. Some of the voices are shouting. Some of the voices are babbling. Some of the voices are singing, chanting, or praying. Some of the voices are communicating. Because the person they are communicating with could be several cells away, to the untrained ear the conversation sounds like the rest of the yelling. (Sometimes twenty or thirty of these conversations are going on simultaneously.)

There is absolutely no privacy. A toilet (with no toilet seat) is bolted to the wall of each cell. It is usually only inches from the bottom bunk. If it becomes clogged and will not flush, it may take several days to get fixed, but the prisoners have to use it anyway.

There is little ventilation. This keeps the smells and any airborne bacteria or viruses carefully contained. Air conditioning? Hardly. It's sweltering in the summer and usually over- or underheated in the winter. It is a textbook breeding ground for misery and disease.

---

*Well, the first thing you'll probably notice is what it took Big Mike (Sid Caesar) on *Your Show of Shows* a little while to figure out: BIG MIKE: "While I was in solitary, I spent a lotta time thinkin'. I did a lot of thinkin'. I thought about the walls . . . the bars . . . the guards with the guns. You know what I figured out?" OTHER CON: "What?" BIG MIKE: "We're in prison."

There are few telephones. Needless to say, it's pay phones, collect calls only. Visitation days are once a week (in some prisons, once a month) and you usually see your friends or loved ones (those who are willing to travel the hundreds, sometimes thousands of miles) through a thick, plastic partition. No touching is permitted. In some prisons, you talk by telephone as the separation between the two of you is not only bullet-proof but sound-proof. These conversations may be monitored and recorded. The prisons that allow conjugal visits only do so only every few months.

> *Don't do drugs because if you do drugs you'll go to prison, and drugs are really expensive in prison.*
>
> JOHN HARDWICK

In most prisons, reading is limited to what's in the prison library. In many prisons, reading material must be sent directly from the publisher. Books, magazines, or newspapers sent by individuals are returned or destroyed. That means if you want to read a book that's out of print (which most books are) or is printed by a publisher that does not do direct mail order, you are out of luck.

Then there's a matter of money. Except for the absolute necessities, you must pay for everything: books, stationery, postage, cigarettes, cassette tapes, your television, everything. You can make this money at a prison job that pays approximately twenty cents per hour. If you are transferred from one prison to another—which can happen at any time and as often as the penal authorities dictate—you must leave all but the basic necessities behind and start over.

If you are marginally young, marginally attractive, or white (and heaven help you if you're all three), your chance of being raped is about as good as your chance of getting a cold or the flu. Even if you go to a prison that makes an attempt to separate "likely targets" from the rest of the prison population, rape

> *The solution to our drug problem is not in incarceration.*
>
> RETIRED GENERAL BARRY MCCAFFREY
>
> U.S. Drug Czar
> *Los Angeles Times,* March 6, 1996

doesn't take long—and who is to say rape is not going to take place within that separated population?

Rape in prison is something of a sport, like hunting. Devout heterosexuals, who would just as soon kill (and may have killed) a male who approached them with a sexual proposition, seem to become sexually ravenous as soon as the prison door slams behind them. Rape, of course, in any situation is not a sexual act; it is an act of violence, domination, control. The macho sport in prison is who-you-can-get-how-often-and-when. The only way to keep from becoming an open target and susceptible to gang rapes and individual hits at every possible opportunity is to become the "punk" of the most powerful hunter you can. He will then protect you from all the rest—although he may occasionally trade you or give you as a gift to one of the other hunters.*

By the way, if you report any of this to the authorities, you will be killed. It's that simple. Turning in a fellow prisoner will mark you, both in and out of prison, for the remainder of your life (which will not be a long one).

Although rape is excruciatingly painful, humiliating, and degrading, if you don't die of hemorrhaging, there's always AIDS. Due to the high incidence of intravenous drug use, both in and out of prison, and completely unprotected sexual activity inside

---

*This obviously depicts the scene in a male prison. A parallel form of violent and psychological dominance, although not as sexually charged, takes place in women's prisons. The ratio of men to women behind bars is 18:1. Only 5.8% of the prison population in 1991 was women. There is evidence, however, that women are more often mistreated by prison personnel. According to the 1990 Report of the Florida Supreme Court Gender Bias Study Commission, "Women are treated more harshly than similarly situated male offenders."

of prison, AIDS has reached epidemic proportion within the prison system. In 1991, 15% of all deaths in prison were AIDS-related. Condoms, of course, are not provided by most prisons. Prisoners are not supposed to be having sex; therefore, they're not; therefore, they don't need condoms. Even when condoms are available, rapists tend not to

> *Do you think someone who is about to rape you is going to stop and think about a condom?*
>
> ELI ADORNO
> quoted in the *New York Times*

use them even to potentially save their own lives—it just isn't very macho.

As a perpetrator of a consensual crime, you will probably end up at the bottom of the prison pecking order. Every one seems to know, even before you arrive, exactly what you're in for. In prison, consensual crimes are thought of as somewhat wimpy things, and since your crime did not involve violence against another person or another person's property, it will be assumed that you won't fight back. You will be taken advantage of at every opportunity. Your pillow, blanket, and even mattress may be "borrowed" by another cellmate. Your clean towel will be exchanged for a dirty one. Any food that is even marginally edible will be consumed by others. ("You don't want this, do you?") Your hunter, by the way, will not protect you from all this; he is only there to protect you from sexual attack. If you want additional protection, you will have to provide additional favors: money, cigarettes, running errands—little tokens of your appreciation.*

---

*All of this, of course, refers to American prisons, which are veritable summer camps compared to foreign prisons. There are 2,500 American citizens being held in foreign jails. Approximately half are being held on drug charges. Most countries have enacted strict anti-drug laws at the urging of the United States government. The more than 800 American citizens currently being held in Jamaican and Mexican prisons, for example, would probably be released tomorrow if America set an example of freedom and

> *Pretty soon,*
> *there will not be any*
> *debate in this city*
> *about overcrowded prisons.*
> *AIDS will take care of that.*
>
> DISTRICT ATTORNEY MARIO MEROLA

When you are sentenced to prison, you are enrolled in the Institute of Higher Criminal Learning, the world's foremost university of crime. Here, you make contacts and learn a new trade. It's obvious that, if you are unable to get a job while awaiting trial, you certainly aren't going to get one as an ex-con. At least not in the pristine nine-to-five world of American business. To make a living when you get out, you have two choices: become a professional writer or become a professional criminal. The professional writing game seems to be pretty full, what with Stephen King turning out a new book every three weeks and Norman Mailer no longer sponsoring former prisoners with literary aspirations. With writing unavailable, that leaves the alternative form of crime: crime.

As with the prison pecking order, having a conviction for *only* a consensual crime does not look very good on your criminal résumé. Fortunately, in prison you will have many opportunities to prove yourself worthy of recommendation to one of the outside criminal organizations. You could show your daring, for example, by distributing drugs within the prison. Doing this, you might even be able to put a few dollars aside over and above your weekly protection payment. Smuggling weapons, either into or around the prison, is always popular—and will get you points for courage. Even if you don't want to be a part of some of the more serious crimes for which those weapons are used, being a lookout while those crimes take place can get you high points for low risk.

What does the state give you on release? On what can you start a new life? It varies, but usually it's $100 and a new suit.

declared consensual crimes no longer crimes.

Meanwhile, whatever remnants of a life you had on the outside are now almost entirely gone. Loves find other loves. Friends find other friends. Apartments get rented to other tenants. People change and, more importantly, so do you.

Prison is a crash course in the darker side of life. Few survive it without be-

> *Crime is contagious.*
> *If the government*
> *becomes a law breaker,*
> *it breeds*
> *contempt for the law.*
>
> JUSTICE LOUIS D. BRANDEIS

coming a different person: more cynical, jaded, fearful, angry. It's hard to trust again, hard to believe, easy to hate a system that destroyed your life behind the pompous pretense of "saving you from yourself for your own good."

⚖ ⚖ ⚖

Even without police intervention, the laws against certain consensual activities make them far more dangerous than they need to be. Activities involving consensual crimes are completely unregulated—either by governmental or private consumer groups. It's not the law of the marketplace but the law of the jungle that prevails.

The list of these unnecessary risks is long indeed. Here are some obvious examples:

- The purity, dosage, and even type of drug are completely unregulated. The government reports that the purity of heroin sold on the street ranges from 32% to 90%. This is quite a range. It proves fatal thousands of times each year. (River Phoenix's death was one such fatality, as was John Belushi's.) Most of the slightly more than 6,000 drug overdoses each year could be prevented if drug users simply knew the dosage of the drug they were using.

> *When is conduct a crime,*
> *and when is a crime not a crime?*
> *When Somebody Up There—*
> *a monarch, a dictator,*
> *a Pope, a legislator—*
> *so decrees.*
>
> JESSICA MITFORD

- Low-grade marijuana is sometimes laced with the drug PCP to make the pot seem more potent. It's hard for users to know whether or not they've gotten great pot or PCP pot. Alas, PCP is far more damaging than even the most potent marijuana. Similarly, LSD is sometimes "enhanced" (without the buyer's knowledge) with strychnine, a lethal poison.

- When dosages are unknown, it is difficult for the user to moderate consumption. If marijuana were legal, for example, the THC (the psychoactive element in marijuana) level could be printed on each package. People could then intelligently moderate their usage. As it is, one joint could have twenty times more THC than another, and the user—short of trial and error—has no way of knowing. This becomes particularly dangerous when it comes to driving, operating machinery, or even cooking. With regulated, legal alcohol, one can moderate intake. The same is not true of uncontrolled substances.

- Gay bars, coffee houses, and bookstores are often forced into the less-than-savory parts of town. The higher crime of these areas is visited upon the gay visitors and makes preventing hate crimes such as gay-bashing more difficult.

- The real crime (violence, robbery, extortion) often associated with consensual crimes often takes place only because the consensual crimes are crimes. A customer robbing a prostitute or a prostitute robbing a customer would be far less likely to happen,

> *The first duty of government is to protect the citizen from assault. Unless it does this, all the civil rights and civil liberties in the world aren't worth a dime.*
>
> RICHARD A. VIGUERIE

for example, if both prostitutes and bordellos were licensed. In that case, either party could call the police if a nonconsensual crime took place.

- Because those who take part in illegal consensual activities do not have access to the civil courts to resolve differences, a great deal of vigilante violence takes place. Almost all gang violence, for example, is drug related—protecting turf, collecting debts, enforcing punishments.

- If gambling were legal, credit could be extended to gamblers based on the prevailing credit policies of the aboveground marketplace. ("Sorry, a $100 bet takes you over your Visa credit limit. Do you want to put part of this on your MasterCard?") As it is, credit is extended in a haphazard fashion and collection techniques are more intrusive and violent than even those practiced by DiscoverCard (although I know that's hard to believe).

⚖ ⚖ ⚖

By now, however, we are veering into the chapter, "Consensual Crimes Encourage Real Crimes." (This chapter is about ruining lives. Having your arm broken by the Mafia would probably

> *You've got to rattle your cage door.*
> *You've got to let them know*
> *that you're in there,*
> *and that you want out.*
> *Make noise. Cause trouble.*
> *You may not win right away,*
> *but you'll sure have*
> *a lot more fun.*
>
> FLORYNCE KENNEDY

not ruin your life. It may play havoc with your penmanship for a while, but your life would go on.)

At any rate, I'm tired. Do you need a break? I do. Thinking about the 4,000,000 arrested each year and the 750,000 currently in jail for consensual crimes is exhausting. "It's all so solemn," Pauline Kael observed, "like Joan Crawford when she's thinking."

Intermission
to Part II

> *And heaven knows*
> *I took the blows*
> *and did it my way.*
>
> FRANK SINATRA

IF WE MUST PUNISH people for consensual crimes, I suggest an alternate method.

Here's the idea, as reported in the 1993 edition of the *World Almanac and Book of Facts:*

Chicago teacher Bruce Janu deals with kids who are late to his class or talk out of turn by sentencing them to the Frank Sinatra Detention Club. Students are forced to listen to tapes of "My Way," "Love and Marriage," and other Sinatra classics. There is no talking and no homework.

The students "just hate it," Janu says. "I get a grimace, like, 'I can't believe I'm listening to this, something my parents and grandparents listened to.' I get a lot of rolls of the eyes." Janu says the kids can sing along, but no one has.

A senior got two "Franks" in a day—60 whole minutes of Sinatra. "I just got to where I couldn't stand it," he said.

Consensual Crimes
Encourage Real Crimes

> *[When a victimless criminal] is treated as an enemy of society, he almost necessarily becomes one. Forced into criminal acts, immersed in underworld-related supply networks, and ever-conscious of the need to evade the police, his outlooks as well as behavior become more and more anti-social.*
>
> EDWIN M. SCHUR
> *Victimless Crimes*

WE LIVE IN A SOCIETY of agreements; in fact, if these agreements (or, if you prefer, contracts) were not in place and voluntarily kept by most of the people most of the time, society as we know it would be impossible.

We agree, for example, to drive on the right side of the road. Why? It's a fairly arbitrary decision—half the world drives on the left side of the road. We, however, drive on the right side of the road. Even though no one asked our opinion as to which side of the road we would prefer to drive on (it was a decision made long before we were born), we still follow that agreement almost unthinkingly.

Can you imagine what driving would be like if even one-hundredth of one percent of the drivers refused to honor that agreement—if they tried to drive on the left side of the road at every possible opportunity? Can you imagine the chaos? The six-foot cement walls dividing even country lanes? The number of police it would take to *force* all cars to drive on the right side of the road?

During the 1992 Los Angeles riots, television showed us what happens when our tightly knit fabric of agreements begins to unravel. There was simply no way law enforcement could stop people from looting. The video images of this were astonishing: people would be seen carrying televisions, dishwashers, and VCRs out of appliance stores; a police car would pull up; people would set down whatever they were carrying, walk two feet away from it, stand there; the police car would drive off; people would put the loot in their cars and go back for more.

Watching an entire store picked clean in less than thirty minutes by an unorganized group of people struck fear in the hearts of Los Angeles residents: "What would happen if these people came to my house? What would stop them from coming into my apartment and taking everything I own in a matter of minutes?"

Answer: nothing.

Then something interesting happened. On television, one bit of video was played over and over. At first, it was humorous, but, with repeated viewings, it grew increasingly disturbing. The video showed someone who had put a looted television in the back of his pick-up truck. While he was caught in the traffic jam caused by other drive-in looters, two pedestrian looters picked up the television from the back of his pick-up truck and walked away with it. The original looter had a choice: his pick-up truck or the television. He chose his pick-up truck—and also avoided the confrontation of the superior two-against-one force.

Even people watching the scene it on freshly looted televisions began to realize that anyone with superior force could come in at any time and take the TV. The police could no more protect them than the police protected the store that owned the television set only hours before.

It wasn't the curfew or calling out the National Guard or a "show of strength" that brought an end to the riots. It was people voluntarily returning to the social contract of not harming other people's person or property. They did it out of fear—not fear of jail, but fear that, if most people did not voluntarily keep that contract most of the time, one's own possessions could never be considered secure—not ever, no matter what. People,

> *Thieves respect property.*
> *They merely wish the property*
> *to become their property*
> *that they may*
> *more perfectly respect it.*
>
> G. K. CHESTERTON

> *Members of society
> must obey the law
> because they personally believe
> that its commands
> are justified.*
>
> JUDGE DAVID BAZELON
> *Questioning Authority*

as they say, "returned to their senses," and the sense they returned to was common sense.

It is not police protection, it turns out, that keeps us safe. It is the social agreement not to harm each other's person and property. The police are there—and can only be there—for that small percentage of people who choose not to honor the agreement.

When government comes along, certain agreements become written down as laws. For the most part, the laws existed before we were born and the laws will exist after we're gone. Some of them are absolute ("Thou shalt not steal") and some of them are arbitrary ("Drive with your headlights on, not your parking lights"*). In Rome, for example, people drive at night with their parking lights on, but their headlights off. It works just as well and gives the city a quieter, softer glow.

Most people are willing to cooperate with both the absolute and the arbitrary laws of the government into which they were born, providing (a) the majority of people follow them, and (b) those agreements are fair: that they somehow make sense. "Don't harm other people's person or property and they won't harm yours" (a modern restating of "Do unto others as you would have them do unto you") makes sense. We will make personal allowances for others, knowing that others are making personal allowances for us. For those who don't choose to obey this fundamental agreement, there are police, courts, and jails.

When laws are irrational, however, people are less likely to sacrifice in order to obey them. A law against an activity which potentially can only hurt the person or property of the person committing the "crime" is far less likely to be honored than a law

*What on earth are parking lights *for,* anyway?

AIN'T NOBODY'S BUSINESS IF YOU DO

against an activity that does physical harm to the person or property of another.

Far, far, more consensual crimes take place than crimes with genuine victims. We hear more about crimes with genuine victims because these crimes tend to get reported. The victim calls the police and says, "Hey, there's been a crime here." With a consensual crime, who's going to call the police? Except for some busybodies, do-gooders, and police entrappers, no one's going to report a consensual crime. And, unless a celebrity is involved (The Hugh Grant Syndrome, Part III), most consensual crime arrests are not reported on the news.

> *What I'd like to see police do is deal with important issues and not these sorts of victimless crimes when society is riddled with problems.*
>
> ALDERMAN RODNEY BARKER

People take part in consensual crimes because the activities are appealing. A person discovers that he or she has broken the law, had a good time doing it, and reaped few, if any, negative consequences. This positive reinforcement makes it easy to commit the consensual crime again. And again. And again. Other consensual crimes are tried. Not bad. Although not yet caught, the person is, nonetheless, living outside the law and a criminal many times over.

Meanwhile, the leaders of government—the keepers of the rules—are going on and on about how bad drug use, homosexuality, prostitution, etc., are. Our leaders certainly seem more concerned about these than, say, shoplifting, insurance fraud, stealing from work, or other crimes with genuine victims. Our government certainly seems to be more concerned with combating hookers, homosexuals, and heroin than it is with combating sexism, racism, and air pollution.

This creates a truly subjective morality based on what the powerful do and do not like. It allows consensual sex among adults, for example, to be linked with muggings, bashing, rape, and murder. We hear condemnations of "sex and violence" as though they were some-how the same. They are, in fact, nearly polar opposites.

The lines blur between genuine right and wrong, moral and immoral, good and evil.

The transition from committing consensual crimes to committing crimes with genuine vic-tims can be an easy one. Once the fabric of obeying the rules is torn, it is very difficult to mend. The criterion for choosing a certain action is no longer "Is this right?" but "Will I get caught?" The person becomes an outcast in a world in which the police are the enemy and not the protector, in which every-one who appears to follow the rules of society is fair game, and in which one looks out for number one, no matter what the cost to others.

> *It is not the business of the law*
> *to make anyone*
> *good or reverent or moral*
> *or clean or upright.*
>
> MURRAY ROTHBARD

⚖ ⚖ ⚖

Declaring certain activities "criminal" has caused artificially inflated prices for the criminalized activities, thus guaranteeing real crime. If drugs were legalized and regulated, no drug user, even the most severely addicted, would have to spend more than $5 per day on drugs. As it is now, some people have $200, $300, $400 daily habits. To get $200 worth of drugs a day, one must be either (a) rich, (b) a doctor, (c) a thief, or (d) a drug dealer. Most end up, by default, at (c) and (d). In order to clear $200 a day, one must steal $2,000 a day in goods (fences pay about ten cents on the dollar) or directly rob enough people to accumulate $200 in cash.

According to Mark Moore of Harvard University, as reported by the National Institute of Justice,

> Very large proportions of those arrested for street crimes such as robbery, burglary, and larceny are drug users. The

addict's need for money to finance his habit and the mechanisms of addiction establish a link between drugs and crime. Insofar as drug use itself is illegal, society has linked drugs to crime directly. Any possession or use is, by definition, criminal conduct.

> *Petty laws*
> *breed great crimes.*
>
> OUIDA
> 1880

The result: each addicted drug user becomes a one-person crime wave. It's not the drug that causes the crime; it's the prohibition of the drug. Having to come up with $200 per day might turn any of us into criminals. Five dollars a day: that's easy. A drug user could get that panhandling. He or she might even get a part-time job.*

Some drug users make the money to pay the artificially inflated prices by selling drugs—in fairly large quantities. As I have pointed out before, these people are not too particular as to whom they sell: they can't afford to be. If children have the money, they sell to children. Because the drug underworld cannot depend on police protection or take disputes to civil courts, disagreements tend to be handled in an unpleasantly messy, highly criminal fashion.

Consensual crimes also encourage real crime by eroding public confidence in law enforcement. People are afraid to cooperate with police because it may allow the police to discover some little, hidden, private secret that would be best for the police not to know.

---

*Contrary to the popular stereotype, a great many regular drug users—including heroin addicts—live relatively normal, productive lives. Most of the dangers from heroin come from the fact that it is illegal. Even the National Institute on Drug Abuse admits, "Most medical problems are caused by the uncertain dosage level, use of unsterile needles and other paraphernalia, contamination of the drug, or combination of a narcotic with other drugs, rather than by the effects of heroin (or another narcotic) itself."

> *As a heterosexual
> ballet dancer,
> you develop a thick skin.*
>
> RONALD REAGAN, JR.

Time was when people cooperated with the police fully, openly, immediately. If the police inquired about a friend or relative, it was assumed that the friend or relative was the victim of a crime and the police were trying to help. Now there is the fear that the friend or relative might be involved in a consensual crime. Our frank and immediate cooperation with the authorities might just help put a friend or a relative in jail. Even though we may not personally approve of our friends' or relatives' extracurricular activities, and may even think it best that they didn't take part in them, we don't want them to go to jail, and we certainly don't want to help put them there.

As most people at one time or another have taken part in one consensual crime or another, the respect given law enforcement officers has seriously eroded. A Robin Hood mentality has people identifying more with the criminals than with the police—who seem to be acting increasingly like the Sheriff of Nottingham.

⚖️ ⚖️ ⚖️

Consensual crimes simply overburden an already groaning criminal justice system. With one serious, violent crime (murder, negligent manslaughter, forcible rape, robbery, aggravated assault, burglary, theft, motor vehicle theft, arson) taking place every two seconds in the United States, do we really want the precious time of law enforcement officials spent regulating the private lives of individuals? Stories such as this, from the June 13, 1991, edition of the *New York Times,* are increasingly common:

> The man charged with stabbing a former Rockette to
> death was indicted yesterday as prosecutors remained

under pressure to explain their handling of an earlier case against the defendant.

The Manhattan District Attorney's office has been criticized for allowing the defendant to plea bargain 15 months ago to a trespass charge after having been charged with attacking a woman

*Wherever a Knave
is not punished,
an honest Man
is laugh'd at.*

GEORGE SAVILE
(1633–1695)

with an ice pick. The defendant received a 45-day sentence and served 30 days. . . .

Mr. McKiever had been arrested three other times: in 1982 for trespassing, in 1982 for petty larceny and in 1978 for grand larceny. . . .

At a news conference announcing the indictment in the slaying, Robert M. Morgenthau, the District Attorney, defended his office's action last year. . . . "I don't blame the public for being upset. This is a tragedy, and I wish it could have been averted. There are a lot of potentially dangerous people running around on the streets, and we'd like to lock up every one of them, but we can't do it. . . ."

Some lawyers say Mr. Morgenthau and his prosecutors are often forced into difficult decisions by a system that is overburdened by too many criminals and not enough judges.

"People blame Mr. Morgenthau, but what really can he do?" said William E. Hellerstein, a professor at Brooklyn Law School. . . . "There is still a lot of time being devoted to victimless crimes, . . ." he said. "But meanwhile there are large chunks of activity, violent activity, that as a practical matter has become decriminalized because the system cannot cope."

> *The most efficacious method*
> *of dealing with deviancy*
> *is to ignore,*
> *to the furthest point*
> *of our tolerance,*
> *those items*
> *which we find offensive.*
>
> GILBERT GEIS

Here's how overworked law enforcement is in the United States: Only 21% of the people who commit murder and negligent manslaughter, forcible rape, robbery, aggravated assault, burglary, theft, motor vehicle theft, or arson are ever arrested; 79% of them—almost four out of five—get off scot-free.

The state of law enforcement is, in fact, worse than that. By the time the real criminals go through the court system, few of them spend any time in jail. According to the National Center for Policy Analysis,

> Only 17% of all murders lead to a prison sentence; only 5% of all rapes lead to a prison sentence; and a convicted felon goes to prison less than 3% of the time in cases of robbery, assault, burglary, and auto theft.

With people literally getting away with murder (one conviction in six), only 5% of the forcible rapes leading to prison, and nearly eight out of ten burglars getting off without so much as an arrest, is it sane, rational, or practical to ask law enforcement to enforce "morality"?

Consensual Crimes
Corrupt Law Enforcement

> *Few men have virtue
> to withstand the highest bidder.*
>
> GEORGE WASHINGTON

NO MATTER HOW loudly they may pontificate, the fact is most people in law enforcement do not consider consensual activities crimes. Each year since 1930, the United States Department of Justice and the Federal Bureau of Investigation have published the telephone book–sized *Uniform Crime Reports*. The advisory board for this report includes the International Association of Chiefs of Police and the National Sheriffs Association.

And what crime statistic do the U.S. Department of Justice, the Federal Bureau of Investigation, the International Association of Chiefs of Police, and the National Sheriffs Association think most important? They have two categories: *violent crime* and *property crime*. Under violent crime are murder and negligent manslaughter, forcible (as opposed to statutory) rape, robbery, and aggravated assault. Under property crime are burglary, larceny-theft, motor vehicle theft, and arson. The report says that these crimes, known collectively as the "Crime Index," are used "for gauging fluctuations in the overall volume and rate of crime."

According to the most recent report, in the late 1980s "law enforcement called for a thorough evaluative study that would modernize the UCR (Uniform Crime Reporting) program." After years of study, what was added to the report? Hate crime statistics and law enforcement officers killed and assaulted.

Not a single consensual crime in the lot.

> *The contempt for law*
> *and the contempt*
> *for the human consequences*
> *of lawbreaking*
> *go from the bottom*
> *to the top of American society.*
>
> MARGARET MEAD

Law enforcement is based on a very simple premise: there is a *perpetrator* and a *victim*. The police catch the accused perpetrator and put him or her in jail. The courts then decide the guilt or innocence of the accused and an appropriate punishment if guilty. This protects the victim and others from further victimization and keeps the perpetrator from further perpetrations.

A serious problem arises when the accused perpetrator and the victim are one and the same. Such is the case with consensual crimes. When the police put the accused in jail, they are putting the victim in jail too. How, then, can the police protect the victim? Law enforcement, thus perverted, begins to deteriorate.

With a real crime, the genuine victim goes to the police and reports it. The police then set about to catch the criminal. With consensual crime, who reports the crime? Obviously, no one directly involved. Everyone consented to it; they're not going to be complaining to the police. The police, then, must become spies, busybodies, and entrappers in order to catch consensual criminals victimizing themselves. Imagine how demoralizing and corrupting this entire procedure can be to both police and society.

As Jackson Eli Reynolds reported in *The Washington Post,*

> Drug offenses . . . may be regarded as the prototypes of non-victim crimes today. The private nature of the sale and use of these drugs has led the police to resort to methods of detection and surveillance that intrude upon our privacy, including illegal search, eavesdropping, and entrapment.

AIN'T NOBODY'S BUSINESS IF YOU DO

Indeed, the successful prosecution of such cases often requires police infringement of the constitutional protections that safeguard the privacy of individuals.

Why, then, don't law enforcement officials speak out against the enforcement of laws against consensual activities? It's not a popular position—not with the general public, not with religious leaders, not with organized crime, not with politicians (who use crackdown-on-consensual-crime rhetoric to get easy votes), and not with some law enforcement officials.

> *The police
> are not here
> to create disorder.
> The police are here
> to preserve disorder.*
>
> MAYOR RICHARD DALEY

⚖ ⚖ ⚖

Law enforcement officials who are against the legalization of consensual crimes tend to fall into three categories: the conservative, the concerned, and the corrupt.

The Conservative. Due to their personal convictions (often religious), they do not like one, some, or all of the consensual crimes. These officials usually discuss "morality," "the family," and "the values of decent Americans."

These law enforcement officials are sincerely misguided. They are in a better position than most to know that personal morality cannot be regulated by force of law. They are faced daily with genuine victims of preventable crimes, whose suffering could have been avoided if there were more police to patrol certain areas or investigate certain crimes. These officials watch violent criminals, who they know are guilty, go free because there aren't enough detectives to gather the evidence necessary for conviction. And yet, because these officials believe personally that consensual crimes are wrong, they believe that consensual "criminals" should be punished.

> *When you're a lawman
> and you're dealing with people,
> you do a whole lot better
> if you go not so much by the book
> but by the heart.*
>
> ANDY TAYLOR
> *The Andy Griffith Show*

The Concerned. These law enforcement officials know that the pursuit of consensual crimes is (a) hopeless, (b) a waste of time, and (c) counterproductive. Yet, when they consider the consequences of legalization, they become concerned. For example, drunk drivers kill more than 22,000 people each year. If drugs were legalized, wouldn't this rate be increased by "stoned" drivers? One doesn't need to see too many traffic accidents to realize that whatever we need to do to prevent even one more of these should be done. These officials are concerned, too, that a useful tool for investigating and gaining confessions to genuine crimes might be taken away. (In order to have a consensual crime charge dropped, some suspects "talk" and provide valuable information about real crimes.)

As to these people's concerns, I pray that a thoughtful reading of this book will ease many of them. We'll explore the genuine crime of operating a motor vehicle while incapacitated (for whatever reason) in the chapter, "Protective Technology." As to using consensual crimes as a tool for gathering information on genuine crimes, I can only suggest that loyal law enforcement officers were probably concerned when physical torture was officially removed from their arsenal of interrogation. As effective as using consensual crime violations to reveal information about real crimes may be, its potential for abuses far outweighs its advantages. For example, in order to get off, a suspect might give false evidence against someone, helping to convict an innocent person. As much as law enforcement officials want crimes solved, only corrupt law enforcement officials want those crimes "cleared" by the conviction of innocent parties. Which brings us to . . .

The Corrupt. These are the law enforcement officials who are getting something from consensual crimes remaining crimes. At the lower levels of corruption are police officers looking for easy collars. A *collar* is a police term meaning "arrest." Many police departments require a minimum number of collars per officer per month. As

> *Only in a police state is the job of a policeman easy.*
>
> ORSON WELLES

the month nears its end, police officers actively seek arrests to fulfill their quotas. What do you suppose are the easiest collars to make? People committing consensual crimes, of course. What could be easier than going where drug dealers and prostitutes ply their trades, or where gays and gamblers hang out, and then wait until something "illegal" is either offered or observed? Not only are these easy arrests; they also tend to be relatively risk-free. Consensual "criminals" (other than higher-level and gang-related drug dealers) are not famous for carrying weapons or resisting arrest.

At the next level of corruption are the officers who get "free samples" from drug dealers, prostitutes, and the like. At the next level up (down?) are the ones who get financial kickbacks for looking the other way.

Then there are those who get the collars and the cash. The famous "suitcases full of money" are very real, especially in drug dealing. (Prostitutes don't tend to carry suitcases full of money.) Who knows how much money is in a suitcase full of cash? (A million dollars in $100 bills fits comfortably into a mid-sized Samsonite.) From the time of the bust until the suitcase gets checked into evidence, the contents could be down by, oh, $50,000. With the outrageously inflated prices caused by the illegalization of drugs, $50,000's worth of cocaine or heroin could get sidetracked on the trip downtown and nobody would

> *Someday I want to be rich.*
> *Some people get so rich*
> *they lose all respect for humanity.*
> *That's how rich*
> *I want to be.*
>
> RITA RUDNER

notice. If somebody did notice, well, an arrangement could be made. ("Here. You take a bag, too.")

Sometimes otherwise honest cops go wrong simply because the amounts of money involved in consensual crimes are entirely too tempting. These are cops, not saints.

This "easy money" corruption goes right to the top. One example: When an accused consensual criminal's land, property, or money is seized under federal assets forfeiture laws, the income is split between federal and local law enforcement. According to the *Los Angeles Times* (April 13, 1993), however, the Los Angeles Sheriff's Department failed to turn over $60 million to the feds. A former sheriff's department sergeant was quoted as saying the sheriff's department "stole $60 million" from the feds in 1988 and 1989 drug busts, and the *Times* added, "he is convinced such practices continue."*

In addition to the opportunity for pilfering cash and drugs seized in raids, organized crime offers police large sums of money in exchange for information, participation, or cooperation. In multimillion dollar drug deals, a sizable amount is set aside for "security." Should consensual crimes go the way of alcohol prohibition, there would be very little for law enforcement personnel on the take to take.

There's not much to say about corrupt law enforcement officials. Even though their graft may have begun innocently enough—perhaps even accidentally—over time they become spoiled, complacent, and lazy. If you're getting $200,000 a year

---

*This doesn't surprise me; but I do have a procedural question: Whom do the feds call when the criminal is the Los Angeles County Sheriff's Department? The LAPD? The National Guard? The governor? ("Oh, governor: the Sheriff's Department has been naughty again!") Is this one of those things that has to go before the U.N.? Inquiring minds want to know.

AIN'T NOBODY'S BUSINESS IF YOU DO

for simply looking the other way, why would you want to go back to $38,000 a year looking for criminals? This laziness extends even into the milder forms of corruption, such as padding the collar quota with consensual crimes. Those on the easy "vice" details—entrapping prostitutes and gays or rounding up pornographers and gamblers—are not going to be pleased at the prospect of returning to the real world of cops and robbers.

> *If my business could be made legal I and women like me could make a big contribution to what Mayor Lindsay calls "Fun City," and the city and state could derive the money in taxes and licensing fees that I pay off to crooked cops and political figures.*
>
> XAVIERA HOLLANDER
> The Happy Hooker

And, in case you think the judicial system is keeping a watchful eye on police corruption, this news item should soothe:

> In Michigan, Alger County Circuit Court Judge Charles Stark sentenced convicted rapist David Caballero to pay $975 in court costs and $200 compensation to the victim and serve three years' probation, after which the conviction would be removed from his record. Stark explained he gave Caballero the lenient sentence because a conviction would have prevented the twenty-one-year-old college student, a criminal justice major, from achieving his goal of becoming a police officer.

⚖️ ⚖️ ⚖️

It's time we returned to respect and admiration for law enforcement, and made law enforcement, once again, a respectable and admirable profession. With the ambivalence many have about police, some who are naturally drawn to the field of law enforcement have mixed feelings about becoming police. This reluctance is unfortunate.

When we, as a society, stop forcing the police to be "clergymen with billy clubs," we will naturally appreciate them for the service they provide each day.

> *Stan Guffey,*
> *a high school basketball referee,*
> *was working a game*
> *in Oklahoma City*
> *when a policeman came*
> *onto the court and arrested him*
> *for not calling enough fouls*
> *during the game.*
>
> *1993 WORLD ALMANAC AND*
> *BOOK OF FACTS*

No one has mixed feelings about firefighters, for example. Firefighters are there when we need them and, when we don't, they are happy to play cards, watch television, and give lectures on fire prevention. If, however, we gave the firefighters the added responsibility of making sure that there were no "inappropriate" sexual fires blazing in the community, we would probably start to look on firefighters with a wary eye.

As absurd as this situation sounds, this is precisely the job we've given the police. It's an impossible job that invites corruption and dissipates respect. The police have been burdened with this job far too long. It's time to free the police to do their real job, which is catching real criminals—people who physically harm the person or property of others. That's all.

As Norval Morris and Gordon Hawkins explained in their book, *The Honest Politician's Guide to Crime Control,*

> The prime function of the criminal law is to protect our persons and our property; these purposes are now engulfed in a mass of other distracting, inefficiently performed, legislative duties. When the criminal law invades the spheres of private morality and social welfare, it exceeds its proper limits at the cost of neglecting its primary tasks. This unwarranted extension is expensive, ineffective, and criminogenic.

Personally, I have great respect for the police, not only because they have the courage to face muggers and murderers, but also because they have the courage to face all that paperwork. As P. J. O'Rourke pointed out,

> A modern arrest requires a stack of forms as thick as a Sunday New York Times "Arts and Leisure" section, and

filling them out is as complicated as buying something at Bloomingdale's with an out-of-state check. A modern conviction requires just as much effort and tedium in court. The average D.C. cop, for example, spends twenty days of his month testifying or waiting to do so.

> *Bureaucracy defends the status quo long past the time when the quo has lost its status.*
>
> LAURENCE J. PETER

Most of the police I've met are genuinely dedicated to peace, in the broadest sense of the term. They want people to feel safe in their homes, in their cars, in their businesses, and walking down the street. If the police keep in check the small percentage of the population that violates that peace, they consider their job well done.

I wholeheartedly support that job. If we removed the futile enforcement of laws against consensual activities from their job descriptions, policemen, policewomen, sheriffs, constables, G-men, G-women, and all the rest would once again become something they haven't been called in some time: peace officers.

The Cops Can't Catch 'Em;
the Courts Can't Handle 'Em;
the Prisons Can't Hold 'Em

> *There are not enough jails,*
> *not enough policemen,*
> *not enough courts to enforce a law*
> *not supported by the people.*
>
> HUBERT H. HUMPHREY

THE MORE THAN 4,000,000 arrests made each year for consensual crimes aren't even the tip of the iceberg; they're more like the ice cube of the tip of the iceberg.

When you consider the ubiquity of the drug trade, and all the prostitutes paid, bets made, illicit sex bade, loiterers in the shade, vagrants on parade, and transvestites in masquerade, it's easy to see that the cops can't catch 'em, the courts can't handle 'em, and the prisons can't hold 'em.

To give one obvious example: In 1994, fewer than 15 million people were arrested for all crimes in the United States. In that same year, according to the Department of Health and Human Services, almost 26 million people illegally used drugs. The criminal justice system was burdened beyond capacity with the 15 million arrests (1.35 million of which were drug arrests). Can you imagine what would have happened if they had added 25 million more drug arrests? And that's just drugs.

When it comes to consensual crimes, the term *criminal justice* is an oxymoron. There's no *justice* because they're not *criminals.* As we explored in the chapter, "Enforcing Laws against Consensual Activities Destroys People's Lives," putting consensual criminals into a system designed for real criminals has significant detrimental effects on the former.

It also has detrimental effects on the system itself. Avowed to treating all criminals alike (the woman holding the scales of justice is blindfolded), the courts, when they become over-crowded, treat all criminals a little bit easier.

The scales of justice are a delicate balance. We may be able to add more jail cells by spending more money, but an effective court takes more than just an additional wing on the courthouse. Good judges take decades of seasoning. Around each judge must be assembled a support system of court clerks, legal researchers, court reporters, bailiffs, and other individuals.

> Concepts of justice
> must have hands and feet
> or they remain sterile abstractions.
> The hands and feet we need
> are efficient means and methods
> to carry out justice in every case
> in the shortest possible time
> and at the lowest possible cost.
>
> JUSTICE WARREN E. BURGER

In our courts we seek the highest wisdom—the guidance of intelligence and maturity. Overcrowding the court system with consensual noncriminals keeps the bad judges in place, encourages incompetent lawyers to become judges, and prevents the truly good judges from doing their best.

As *Legal Times* accurately predicted in 1989,

> Before long the judiciary could become just another bu-
> reaucracy, with thousands of judges and magistrates
> processing dreary caseloads likely to attract only hacks
> and drones to the bench.

The courts can be corrupted at any of four levels: prosecutors, judges, juries, or witnesses. The techniques of corruption include threats of violence, blackmail, and bribery.

The sophisticated will, of course, remember this exchange from *The Addams Family:*

> GOMEZ ADDAMS: I've gone through the city ordinances, the Bill of Rights, and the seventeen volumes of assorted jurisprudence—and I've come to a conclusion.
>
> MORTICIA ADDAMS: What?

> *Judges . . . rule on the basis of law,*
> *not public opinion,*
> *and they should be totally*
> *indifferent to pressures*
> *of the times.*
>
> JUSTICE WARREN E. BURGER

GOMEZ: That we haven't got a leg to stand on.

UNCLE FESTER: Not even if we bribe the judge?

The jury is as susceptible as its twelve members. With enough investigation money (and the perpetrators of organized consensual crimes have plenty of that), the defense can know by the first day of the trial almost everything there is to know about each juror. Which would be most susceptible to a threat, a bribe, or a little blackmail? Except in rare cases, the jurors go home after court adjourns and can easily be contacted. One or two highly motivated jury members can often create enough reasonable doubts (and juries in criminal cases are instructed to reach their conclusion of guilt beyond a reasonable doubt) in the minds of the other jurors to bring in a verdict of not guilty. At worst, it only takes one member of a jury to withhold his or her guilty vote for there to be a hung jury. After a hung jury, the prosecutor is usually more than willing to enter into passionate plea bargaining: the concept of retrying the same case from scratch (which is what must happen with a hung jury) is, at best, disheartening. After a second or third hung jury, the case might be dropped entirely. Bribing or threatening jurors is such a common practice that it's known by the relatively trivial phrase *jury tampering,* which in no way conveys the seriousness or the significance of the crime.

Finally, there are witnesses. Far from the melodramatic courtroom myth, the last-minute "secret witness" almost never appears. (In courtroom dramas, whenever a surprise witness is introduced, the judge invariably proclaims, "This is highly irregular!") By law, the witnesses each side plans to call to the stand must be presented to the other side some time before the trial. Thus witnesses, like jurors, judges, and prosecutors, are open to pretrial persuasion. Many trials are never brought to court because someone "gets to" the main witness for the prosecution, who "suddenly remembers" a different set of facts.

And then there are witnesses who are paid to bear false witness. Their payment may be in the form of money, drugs, or favors; or they may simply be blackmailed. These people will claim that the defendant couldn't possibly have been at the scene of the crime because they were all spending the weekend together in Wyoming—fishing by day and reading the Bible aloud at night. False witnesses can also be used to impugn the credibility of otherwise credible witnesses.

> ALEX REIGER: *Louie, when you walk into that hearing room, you're going to be under oath. You know what that means?*
>
> LOUIE DE PALMA: *Yeah. It means they gotta believe you. I love this country.*
>
> *TAXI*

When you combine the delicate balance of the criminal justice system with the large amounts of money made by the peddlers of consensual crimes (especially drugs and gambling), the potential for corruption is high and all too often realized. The big players with the big money tend to get off, while the little players with little money tend to get big sentences. In this way, defenders of the criminal justice system can say, "See, we're doing *so much* about drugs (or whatever the consensual crime may be). Our conviction rate is up and the sentences are stiffer."

In courts that aren't corrupt, the massive overloading caused by the burden of processing consensual criminals as though they were real criminals creates, at best, a system with enough loopholes for plenty of real criminals (especially the ones who can afford the best lawyers) to go free.

This editorial from the *Los Angeles Times*, April 25, 1993:

> Two more senior federal judges recently joined a growing list of their colleagues nationwide in refusing to preside over drug cases as a protest to the extreme and counterproductive sentences they are required to impose in these cases. We are sympathetic with their distress.

> *Efforts to combat this tidal wave*
> *of [violent] crime*
> *are continually frustrated*
> *by a criminal justice system*
> *that is little more*
> *than a revolving door.*
>
> SENATOR ALFONSE D'AMATO

Tough, inflexible federal sentencing rules, once considered "the answer" to rising drug use and crime, threaten to make a mockery of our federal criminal justice system. . . .

A young offender convicted of first-time possession of $50 worth of drugs might be sentenced to a 20-year prison term or even a life term without the possibility of parole. . . .

Nearly 60% of all federal prisoners are now drug felons. Average prison terms for federal drug offenders have shot up 22% since 1986—while those of violent criminals fell by 30%. . . .*

Congress has been unwilling to amend the Draconian sentencing law for fear of seeming "soft on crime." But the protests of these respected judges, along with the private rumblings of hundreds more across the country, must signal Congress that the law is unfair and unworkable.**

The solution? Obviously, stop pretending that consensual activities are crimes. This would stop most organized crime—with its threats, blackmail, and bribery—overnight. Ending multi-prohibitions would immediately cut the workload of the criminal justice system in half. This would give the courts time to decide the guilt or innocence of people accused of crimes such as murder, rape, robbery, aggravated assault, burglary, larceny, theft, motor vehicle theft, arson, hate crimes, forgery, counterfeiting,

---

*All of the figures are worse now.

**Instead, Congress passed the Omnibus Crime Bill, which made matters far more intolerable and added the death penalty for drug possession.

fraud, embezzlement, buying and selling stolen property, vandalism, carrying concealed weapons, child molestation, and driving under the influence of alcohol or other intoxicating substances.

⚖ ⚖ ⚖

Prisons, as previously noted, are filled to capacity and beyond. In most areas an early-release program has been instituted, which, of course, does not differentiate between prisoners whose crimes had innocent victims and prisoners whose crimes did not. This puts truly dangerous criminals on the street sooner, giving them extra months—and in some cases years—to rape, rob, and plunder anew.

> *Of all the tasks of government, the most basic is to protect its citizens from violence.*
>
> JOHN FOSTER DULLES

Consensual Crimes
Promote Organized Crime

> *You can get much farther*
> *with a kind word and a gun*
> *than you can*
> *with a kind word alone.*
>
> AL CAPONE

MOST CRIMES WITH genuine victims are individual enterprises, small businesses at best. Murder, rape, robbery, assault, burglary, theft, arson, hate crimes, forgery, counterfeiting, fraud, embezzlement, buying and selling stolen property, vandalism, carrying concealed weapons, child molestation, and driving under the influence of alcohol or narcotics can usually be done by one, two, or, at most, a small band of people.

Supplying the needs of people who engage in consensual crimes, on the other hand, is big business. Drugs are the best example. Getting all that marijuana, hashish, cocaine, heroin, and other chemicals to the millions of eager users every day (many of whom receive home delivery) requires enormous planning, preparation, personnel, coordination—in short, organization. Because the moralists of our society have chosen to label the distribution of these obviously desired substances crimes, these big businesses are known as *organized crime.*

The big-business, international quality of organized crime today is evident even in the name it chooses to call itself. In the early days, crime organizations were called *families* because they were, in many cases, extended family units. As organized crime grew into a business at which anyone could play, it became known as a *syndicate.* Today it's known as a *cartel,* a word of international scope (the Germans spell it *Kartell,* the French *cartel,* and the Italians *cartello).*

Organized crime was first organized around a consensual crime during Prohibition. Making and distributing alcohol required breweries, distilleries, bottling plants, truck drivers, places to sell it (speakeasies), waiters, cooks, jazz musicians to entertain—it was a regular empire. When Prohibition ended in 1933, the empire

> *You can imagine my embarrassment when I killed the wrong guy.*
>
> JOE VALACHI

was firmly in place and, with a little retooling, it turned to the marketing of other consensual crimes: prostitution, gambling, loansharking, and drugs.

The organized crime of today is nothing like the organized crime of yesterday—it's much better organized, therefore much worse for the rest of us. Organized crime competes with IBM, GM, and Sears for law school and MBA graduates. (Based on results, IBM, GM, and Sears have not gotten the cream of the crop.) Organized crime's boats outrun the Coast Guard, their planes outfly the Air Force, their soldiers outshoot the Army, and their intelligence is smarter than the CIA's.

As Franklin D. Roosevelt observed,

> A man who has never gone to school may steal from a freight car, but if he has a university education he may steal the whole railroad.

In addition to police, judges, prosecutors, and politicians, organized crime also has on its payroll doctors, scientists, and journalists in all media whose job it is to predict and report how terrible life would be if consensual crimes were legalized. (Organized crime's very existence depends on consensual crimes remaining illegal.) The media people on the payroll are also to report that organized crime is on the decrease, that its influence is minimal, and that the government is doing an absolutely crackerjack job of rounding up the few minor hoodlums that remain.

> *I hate this "crime doesn't pay" stuff.*
> *Crime in the U.S. is perhaps*
> *one of the biggest businesses*
> *in the world today.*
>
> PAUL KIRK
> *Wall Street Journal*

("*No one* is beyond the reach of the federal authorities. Well, just look at Noriega.")

Unlike in the old days, organized crime is hardly homegrown. Consensual crimes (especially drugs) have international investors. Most of the ill-gotten gain leaves our shores, never to return. (Well, some of it returns—when the cartel buys an American bank, high-rise office building, or other legitimate business.)

The heavy-handed tactics and enforcement by violence continue, of course. Some things are traditional. Organized crime doesn't differentiate between crimes with genuine victims and crimes without. The well-oiled, well-run, well-connected machine runs just as well whether promoting a crooked investment scheme (bilking thousands out of retirement money) or importing cocaine (for obviously willing consumers). The criterion is never "Is it right?" only "Is it profitable?" The reason organized crime has stayed primarily with consensual crimes is that, due to the artificially inflated prices, consensual crimes are the most profitable.*

Thanks to the consensual crimes, the flow of money goes something like this: To pay the outrageously inflated price of their addiction, people steal things—from you and me. If what was stolen is not money, the item is taken to a fence, who pays about ten cents on the dollar (if the item is in new condition).

---

*Next to drugs, the most profitable activity of organized crime is loansharking, in which money is loaned without collateral. If you don't pay, however, you get a visitation from Big Louie, who will persuade you that borrowing money and not paying it back is a violation of the Eighth Commandment. Most loan shark customers, of course, borrow money to pay the artificially inflated prices of consensual crimes. If consensual crimes were made legal, most of the demand for loansharking would dry up.

The underworld resells the item at a profit. For every $100 of merchandise stolen, perhaps $30 goes into the cartel coffers. Then there are people who steal money. When people steal money to buy drugs, all of it goes into the underworld treasury. The money is then laundered by a trillion-dollar international scheme of money scrubbing, and the

> CRIMINAL: A person with predatory instincts who has not sufficient capital to form a corporation.
>
> HOWARD SCOTT

newly legitimized dollars are stored in Swiss bank accounts, off-shore banks, and other places outside the United States where they cannot be traced—or taxed.

Here we find another significant way in which organized crime hurts us: no taxation. Just about all the money is tax free. Organized crime learned well the lesson taught by Al Capone, who was sent away for eleven years not for racketeering, bootlegging, or murder, but for tax evasion. The lesson organized crime learned was not to pay more taxes, but to be a lot more careful at bookkeeping.

⚖ ⚖ ⚖

When illegal consensual activities are made legal, some of the underground will wallow about looking for new and better crimes to commit. Many—like the speakeasy operators who overnight became owners of successful nightclubs—will move aboveground (some by choice, some by necessity) and continue business as usual. For the first time in a long time these entrepreneurs will be able to focus on business and not on the business of protecting themselves from the police. The police will be able to find real criminals. The press will be able to report truth freely again, and we can all celebrate an unprecedented cycle of economic prosperity and decline in crime.

And have I told you about my plan to raise Atlantis?

Consensual Crimes Corrupt the Freedom of the Press

> *A free press*
> *is not a privilege*
> *but an organic necessity*
> *in a great society.*
>
> WALTER LIPPMANN

A FREE PRESS, WHICH leads to an informed populace, is essential to liberty. As Thomas Jefferson put it,

The basis of our government being the opinion of the people, the very first object should be to keep that right; and were it left to me to decide whether we should have a government without newspapers, or newspapers without a government, I should not hesitate for a moment to prefer the latter.

"The press" is an extremely broad term and includes all systems that make information available to people: newspapers, television, radio, books, lectures, movies, art, dance, telephone, cassettes, CDs, video discs, magazines, electronic bulletin boards, computer networks, billboards, video tapes, you name it. It's generally known as "the press" in our country because, when the founding fathers wrote freedom of the press into the Bill of Rights, the printing press was the most popular form of mass communication. Today we call it "the media."

All of the world's major religions, philosophies, schools of political thought, and systems of government were spread through writing. In fact, the spread of civilization, religion, and the written word occurred simultaneously, each dependent on the other. The written word inspired, and the inspiration was passed on to others through the written word. All of the great religions were based on a "book"—a collection of writings—

AIN'T NOBODY'S BUSINESS IF YOU DO

even before there were books. The Egyptians had the Book of the Dead; the Hindus had the Upanishads; the Jews had the Torah; Homer's *Iliad* and *Odyssey* told of the Greek gods; and the writings of Zoroaster, Lao-tzu, Confucius, Buddha, the Jewish prophets, and the Greek poets made the sixth century B.C. a remarkable century indeed. Without writing and the ability to circulate this writing (a "free press"), these traditions would have influenced very few and would probably be entirely forgotten today.

> *A man has only to murder a series of wives in a new way to become known to millions of people who have never heard of Homer.*
>
> ROBERT LYND

Christianity first spread due to the freedom-of-speech tradition of the Jewish synagogues: any adult Jewish male was free to have his say. Jesus (and, later, his disciples) used this freedom to spread his teachings.* Although Jesus never published a word,** selections of what he said were written down and circulated on scrolls. These "sayings" scrolls were very popular and, considering that each had to be copied by hand, they were what we would now call bestsellers—sort of a *Lord's Little Instruction Book.*

---

*There were certain risks involved in this, however. If others found what you were saying blasphemous, you could be stoned (which happened to Stephen), or, at the very least, run out of town (which happened to Jesus when he taught at the synagogue in his home town, Nazareth).

**The only mention of Jesus writing was while he was figuring out how to save the adulteress from being stoned—and figuring out how to save himself as well: "They were using this question as a trap, in order to have a basis for accusing him. But Jesus bent down and started to write on the ground with his finger. When they kept on questioning him, he straightened up and said to them, 'If any one of you is without sin, let him be the first to throw a stone at her.' Again he stooped down and wrote on the ground" (John 8:6–8). What he wrote, alas, is not recorded. I like to think it was some variation of "Ain't nobody's business if she do."

After the death of Jesus, the "quote books" continued to be popular and the letters (epistles) from various church fathers were copied, widely circulated, and studied. The surviving letters of Paul make up the majority of the New Testament. Thirty years or so after the death of Jesus, the sayings books were expanded by Matthew, Mark, Luke, and, later, John into the story of Jesus that we now know as the first four books of the New Testament. Four hundred years after the time of Christ, the Bible as we know it was compiled.

The Bible was to become the most banned book of all time. For centuries, reading the Bible was forbidden—it was said that the ordinary person could not handle the power conveyed by direct contact with God's holy word. In fact, banning the book allowed religious and political leaders to manipulate the populace into submission, threatening eternal damnation for disobedience.

Gutenberg's decision to use the Bible in 1455 as the first book printed on his new press is portrayed by many as an act of great faith—he was so much a man of God that he chose to print a holy book instead of a romance novel. It was, in fact, an act of rebellion—a major statement for freedom of the press.

Prior to Gutenberg, all Bibles were copied by hand by monks in monasteries. The Catholic church had a monopoly on the production and distribution of Bibles. Not only were they very expensive, but their distribution was carefully regulated. Buying a Bible was part of a package deal: you usually had to build a chapel to house it and hire a priest (one who could read and write) to interpret it. Like buying a computer in the 1950s, it was a major commitment only a handful could afford.

Gutenberg changed that. His Bible was relatively cheap (by Bible standards of the day), and available to anyone who could pay the price. For the first time, the word of God could be read and studied without the permission or interpretation of the holy mother church. Some say that this one act of freedom of the press was the greatest single factor behind the Reformation. The Bible, religion, Christianity, and the world would never be the same.

> *The ink of a scholar*
> *is more sacred*
> *than the blood*
> *of the martyr.*
>
> MOHAMMED

In our own country one book, more than any other single cause, was responsible for the revolutionary war: *Common Sense* by Tom Paine. This book (more a pamphlet, actually) was published in January 1776. The mood at that time in the British colonies was to continue negotiations with the mother country. A war against king and crown—the direct representatives of God on earth—was still, for many, unthinkable. *Common Sense* changed that. It sold more than 500,000 copies within a few months—that's one copy for every eight people living in the colonies.* Certainly everyone who could read back then read it. It changed people's attitudes from placation to rebellion almost overnight.

In July of 1776, the moment the Continental Congress approved the Declaration of Independence, it was "off to the press." Copies were printed and reprinted throughout the colonies. A good number of the colonists had read and studied it by the time the official signing took place in early August. The document was translated and widely circulated throughout Europe, where the mere possession of it in some countries was punishable by death. The Declaration fulfilled its intended purpose, and a nation prepared for war.

*This is the equivalent of a book selling more than 31 million copies today. The biggest bestsellers sell fewer than two million copies in the first few months.

> *Whenever people are
> well-informed
> they can be trusted
> with their own government.*
>
> THOMAS JEFFERSON

After the United States Constitution was written in 1787, it had to be "sold" to the electorate. This was done through a series of eighty-five articles—written primarily by James Madison and Alexander Hamilton—printed in newspapers throughout the country. The articles are now collectively known as *The Federalist* or *The Federalist Papers.* Without these, it is doubtful that the radical experiment known as the United States ever would have happened. Clearly seeing the power of the press, the founding fathers guaranteed its complete freedom in the very first amendment they added to that Constitution.

Probably the most influential book of the entire 1800s was a novel, Harriet Beecher Stowe's *Uncle Tom's Cabin.* (The alternate title was *Life Among the Lowly.*) Published in 1852, it portrayed slaves not as chattel or animals, but as human beings, and (gasp!) portrayed their white owner, Simon Legree, as the villain. Talk about your book burnings in the South! Of the 300,000 copies sold during the first year, who knows how many were purchased in the South specifically for burning. The book and its 1853 follow-up collection of factual documents, *The Key to Uncle Tom's Cabin,* swayed popular opinion in the North toward the abolition of slavery. Without these books, anti-slavery might never have been a major theme of the Civil War.

In 1906, a book by Upton Sinclair, *The Jungle,* took a hard look at the meat-packing industry in the United States. A novel filled with many frightening and disturbing facts, *The Jungle* changed the way all food products were processed and packaged in the United States, and made major strides toward the enactment of worker protection and child-labor laws.

Radio found its stride in the 1930s. Some say Franklin Delano Roosevelt literally talked the nation out of its depression. By the

AIN'T NOBODY'S BUSINESS IF YOU DO

late 1930s, while storm clouds gathered over Europe (as the more dramatic histories of the day like to put it), the mood of the American people was fiercely isolationist. "No more European wars!" was the battle cry. And yet, Americans were gently prodded into taking sides by what they heard on the radio. The major protago-

> *I am entirely persuaded that the American public is more reasonable, restrained and mature than most of the broadcast industry's planners believe. Their fear of controversy is not warranted by the evidence.*
>
> EDWARD R. MURROW

nists in the "European War" were England and Germany. What we heard from Germany were the unintelligible sounds of a ranting lunatic followed by the lock-stepping masses shouting, *"Sieg heil! Sieg heil! Sieg heil!"* England, on the other hand, had the warm, gentle, sometimes roaring, sometimes humorous voice of Winston Churchill. Surely it would be okay to lend this nice man a few boats and lease him a few airplanes. And so, lend-lease was born, and the United States was no longer neutral.

On CBS Radio, Edward R. Murrow reported firsthand the devastation of German bombings on London during the blitz. This further tilted American sympathies toward the underdog, England. His voice did more to fight Hitler than probably any other. In 1954, he was to use television to take on yet another monster, Senator Joseph McCarthy and his witch hunt. "We must not confuse dissent with disloyalty," said Murrow on that historic telecast. "We will not be driven by fear into an age of unreason if we remember that we are not descended from fearful men, not from men who feared to write, to speak, to associate and to defend causes which were, for the moment, unpopular." In both instances, he risked his life; in both instances, he won. (He lost the battle with cigarettes, however, dying of lung cancer in 1965.)

In our own time (well, I suppose that depends on when you were born, doesn't it?—in *my* own time, at any rate), we saw a president toppled by a couple of reporters, Woodward and Bernstein, who inspired thousands of young people to take up inves-

> *The media I've had a lot to do with is lazy.*
> *We fed them and they ate it every day.*
>
> MICHAEL DEAVER
> Former top aide to President Reagan

tigative journalism. Then, after Woodward and Bernstein were portrayed in the movies by Dustin Hoffman and Robert Redford, tens of thousands applied to journalism schools.

⚖ ⚖ ⚖

Through the media we learn about our world, our life, medical breakthroughs, scientific advances, toppling regimes, the truth about history, useful news, trivial news, useful trivial news, good news, bad news—*news.*

We rely on it, depend on its accuracy, and, if it turns out to be inaccurate, we expect another news organization to expose the exposé. Freedom of the press is a fundamental right, up there with freedom of speech and freedom of and from religion. A free press is not a luxury; it's a necessity.

How do consensual crimes corrupt our free press? Several ways.

First, since committing a consensual crime is breaking the law and since breaking the law is news, reporters are often sent out looking for video on drug busts, hookers, or stories on who is sleeping with whom and whether they're married to someone else. In the end, none of this has much to do with our lives (certainly not in the way that murderers, rapists, robbers, polluters, price-fixers, and bribe-takers do). So—like the police, courts, and prisons—the reporters' time and the media's space are overburdened with fluff. And not very interesting fluff at that. (You've seen one drug bust on TV, you've seen 'em all.)* There's plenty of international tension, domestic strife, real crime, corruption, and consumer activism to keep every reporter and his or her place of reporting busy, productive, highly rated, and of service to the

---

*"From the American newspapers," Lady Astor wrote, "you'd think America was populated solely by naked women and cinema stars."

AIN'T NOBODY'S BUSINESS IF YOU DO

community. There might even be a little time to dig up some good news.

Second, since consensual crimes are not based on hurting others but on religious interpretations by a handful of moralists, some journalists have been turned (some willingly, some not) into professional gossips and busybodies. Gossip is fine, gossip is entertaining, but it belongs on *Entertainment Tonight* and best-seller lists, not the network evening newscasts. "The things most people want to know about," wrote George Bernard Shaw, "are usually none of their business." Did Gary Hart really deserve to lose all of his political credibility because he took a boat ride with a young beauty? Mr. Hart's wife did not object; his ocean-going companion did not object; one must assume Mr. Hart himself did not object. To quote a television commercial of roughly that same time frame: "Where's the beef?"* Was this one seagoing sexual misadventure really sufficient grounds to completely ignore everything political about him, everything this man stood for, spent a lifetime building, and was doing a fairly good job bringing to the arena of public discussion? Gary Hart was sacrificed to a group of yapping moralists who claim that "an adulterer" is not fit to run for president. The yapping was served up by a "free" press bound by the chains of delivering late-breaking scandals with photos, video, and sound bites if at all possible. And what did the American people get in exchange? A truly dull

> *If a nation expects*
> *to be ignorant and free . . .*
> *it expects*
> *what never was*
> *and never will be.*
>
> THOMAS JEFFERSON
> 1816

---

*I *think* that commercial happened at about the same time as Gary Hart's aborted presidential campaign. I cannot be sure. History for me is broken into four phases: (1) before I was born, (2) from the time of my birth until now, (3) now, and (4) has it happened yet? I do know that both Gary Hart's being caught in adultery—not quite in the act, but at least in the yacht—and that dear lady asking "Where's the beef?" happened some time during Phase 2.

> *The media.*
> *It sounds like*
> *a convention*
> *of spiritualists.*
>
> TOM STOPPARD

campaign: Dukakis versus Reagan. Yawn. As Jay Leno observed, *"Dukakis is Greek for Mondale."*

Third, just as when cops need some easy collars and round up some consensual criminals, so too, reporters—when there's dead air to fill or an article to embellish—go out and round up some consensual crime stories. Need some quick video? Take a female reporter, put her in some fishnet stockings and a dress cut low enough to reveal her journalistic integrity, have her meander the sidewalk with the streetwalkers, and follow her with a hidden camera. (The camera can be hidden in a van marked ACTION NEWS with a little satellite dish on top and you'll still get good video—men are terribly unobservant of all but one thing when their testosterone is raging.) If you really want ratings, put a male reporter in the same costume and situation.

Finally, as with police, journalists should regain the respect they are entitled to. Reporting a lot of "trash for cash" has tarnished the good name of reportage. Remember when Walter Cronkite, as the anchor of an evening newscast, was considered "the most trusted man in America"? Why not return to those thrilling days of yesteryear? It wasn't just Walter Cronkite; Huntley and Brinkley were well respected. Brinkley's still at it, saying wonderfully honest things, such as "The one function that TV news performs very well is that when there is no news we give it to you with the same emphasis as if there were." There are, of course, other contemporary examples: Hugh Downs, Larry King, John Chancellor, and Bill Moyers.

The press not only cheapens itself by playing tattletale and reporting the consensual exploits of others; it also "eats its young" by reporting on the consensual activities of its own. An absurd example of the latter involves an attractive female "reporter" who invited Larry King up to her hotel room, which just happened to have more hidden cameras than Allen Funt's bathroom. Well, the tape went on and on and on, and Mr. King made nary an improper move. But, dull as it was, they showed the tape anyway. After all, Larry King is a star; there's air time to fill; and, even if he didn't

> *Newspapers have degenerated.*
> *They may now be*
> *absolutely relied upon.*
>
> OSCAR WILDE

do anything, it will make a great teaser: "Larry King follows our reporter up to her hotel room! What happens then? Tune in tonight and find out!" (Although I don't remember the name of the show, why do I have the sneaking suspicion it was on Fox?* "All the networks are struggling now with their desire to put on live executions, if they could, to get the ratings," said Gary David Goldberg; "I think the difference is that Fox would put on *naked* live executions.")

We're entitled to a free press, and the press is entitled to be free from rumor-mongering and reporting on the latest scandal from Gossip Central.

Later, in the chapter, "Pornography, Obscenity, Etc.," we'll explore how censorship even more directly corrupts the freedom of the press.

*I checked. It was Fox.

Laws against Consensual Activities
Teach Irresponsibility

> *If you want a Big Brother,*
> *you get all*
> *that comes with it.*
>
> ERICH FROMM
> *Escape from Freedom*

IRRESPONSIBILITY IS AS old as mankind—literally. When God asked Adam, "Have you eaten from the tree that I commanded you not to eat from?" Adam answered, "The woman you put here with me—she gave me some fruit from the tree, and I ate it." Note the dual layer of irresponsibility: Adam blames not only Eve, he also blames God for putting her with him.

Irresponsibility is as old as womankind, too. After God heard Adam's rational lies, he turned to Eve and asked, "What is this you have done?" And Eve responded, "The serpent deceived me, and I ate." (Modern translation: "The devil made me do it!") It seems that the buck never stops in Eden. It's amazing that the serpent didn't blame its upbringing, claim it was high on drugs, or simply plead insanity. At the very least, the serpent could have argued that it was only following its religious beliefs. But responsible or not, God punished them all, and so here we all are today.

Did you ever notice how disarming it is when people take responsibility and how irritating it is when they blame? If people spent half as much mental energy finding a way to keep an unfortunate occurrence from happening again as they spend on finding reasons why (a) what happened wasn't so bad, or (b) "It wasn't my fault," the world would be a lot better off.

Responsibility is often confused with blame. When someone asks, "Who's responsible for this?" people often hear, "Who's to blame for this? Who can we punish?" Responsibility simply means that we are willing to accept the *consequences* of the choices we make. The unwillingness—and for some it appears to be a congenital inability—to accept the consequences for our choices is the definition of immaturity.

When children make a bet and lose, they get out of it by saying, "I had my fingers crossed!" So many

> A man must pay the fiddler. In my case it so happened that a whole symphony orchestra often had to be subsidized.
>
> JOHN BARRYMORE

of the explanations adults give to justify their behavior sound just as silly.

No sooner was the term *victimless crime* coined than every scalawag, rascal, and down-and-dirty crook used it out of context to justify his or her genuinely criminal behavior. Michael Milken, for example, paid a public relations agency $150,000 per month to transform him in the public eye from criminal to victim. The goal, as James Stewart explains in his book, *Den of Thieves,* "was to turn public opinion from outrage to neutrality to acceptance, and finally to admiration." How did the PR people do this? By claiming Milken's legion of offenses, which caused plenty of innocent people to suffer, were victimless crimes. Because he didn't use a gun or a lead pipe, the PR firm did its best to convince the public that a crime without physical *violence* is also a crime without innocent *victims*. This, of course, is nonsense, but with $150,000 a month and a few gullible journalists, you can fool some of the people some of the time.

After the concept that Milken's transgressions were victimless crimes was swallowed by enough of the press and public, the PR agency made it look as though *he* was the victim. (No wonder some people hate the term *victimless crime*.) "The campaign was remarkably effective," reported Stewart, and the *Christian Science Monitor* lamented, "This episode demonstrates once more how modern public relations can manipulate public opinion. Some of the press, sadly, was sucked in by the blather."*

> *The real freedom of any individual*
> *can always be measured*
> *by the amount of responsibility*
> *which he must assume*
> *for his own welfare and security.*
>
> ROBERT WELCH

Responsibility also means the *ability* to *respond:* no matter what happens to us, there's always some response we can make. The response is sometimes external, sometimes internal, often both. Even when one's external options are severely limited, one can choose to respond to them internally in productive and even uplifting ways. In his book, *Man's Search for Meaning,* Viktor Frankl recounts his experiences in a Nazi concentration camp. Subjected to physical horrors beyond imagining, Frankl learned that although he was not responsible for where he was or what was happening around him, he was responsible for his *reaction* to the events around him. He discovered this was a personal freedom the Nazis could not take away.

> The last of the human freedoms—to choose one's attitude in any given set of circumstances, to choose one's own way.

But in our society, such courageous examples of responsibility and personal freedom are seldom discussed. We always seem to be on the lookout for *who's to blame?* Somehow, we think, if we can prove it's someone else's fault, it will make everything "all better." Somehow we believe that Life will comfort us in its arms, like a nurturing parent; if we can only prove we had noth-

---

**This from *Den of Thieves:* "The securities laws were implemented to help protect that process [of rewarding merit, enterprise, innovation, hard work, and intelligence], to guard the integrity of the markets and to encourage capital formation, by providing a level playing field on which everyone might pursue their fortunes. Violations of the securities laws are not victimless crimes. When insider traders gain windfall stock profits because they have bribed someone to leak confidential business secrets, when prices are manipulated and blocks of stock secretly accumulated, our confidence in the underlying fairness of the market is shattered."

ing to do with our injury, we will receive extra strokes. "The tree made me fall out of it."

"Did the tree push you out?"

"Yes. It pushed me!"

"Oh you poor thing. That bad tree. Shall we chop it down?"

"Yes! Let's chop down that bad tree!"

Although such com-

> *We have not passed that subtle line between childhood and adulthood until we move from the passive voice to the active voice—that is, until we have stopped saying, "It got lost," and say, "I lost it."*
>
> SYDNEY J. HARRIS

ments may be momentarily comforting, they do very little to teach us to climb trees better. We seem to be seeking from life a giant parental "Oh, you poor thing."

In eternally looking for someone or something outside ourselves to blame, we turn ourselves into victims. We begin to believe that we are powerless, ineffective, and helpless. "There was nothing I could do," people whine, as an affirmation of their powerlessness, rather than, "What could I have done?" or "What will I do differently next time?" This self-victimization erodes our character, our self-esteem, and our personal integrity. But we learn to whine about it so awfully well.

⚖️ ⚖️ ⚖️

The idea that certain consensual activities should be crimes helps create irresponsibility. The idea behind consensual crimes is that the government—like a great, caring parent—will protect us from the bogeyman, the wicked witch, and inhospitable trees. "We have thoroughly investigated everything," the government assures us, "and you will be safe as long as you don't do these things." To make sure we don't do those things, the government locks up everyone who attempts to lead us into temptation and, as an example, puts a few bad boys and girls away, too. (A multi-year version of "Go to your room!")

If we accept the view that government is the Great Protector, then it logically follows that whatever the government does not prohibit is okay. As we all know, this is not the case.

Each of us is unique. We have our own set of needs, wants, tolerances, reactions, strengths, weaknesses, and abilities. Some people are deathly allergic to wheat, while others can chew double-edged razor blades. (I saw it on a newsreel once. Eeeeee!) Few people fit within the "norm" on absolutely everything. To be perfectly normal is abnormal.

Government-set standards for personal behavior are based on the average. By making the norm the law, the government encourages us not to explore our own strengths and limitations, but to adapt and fit in as best we can to the norm. The strength and power of the diversity within us are never fully explored. Our depths are never plumbed and our heights are never scaled. We are not taught to learn from our mistakes, only to blame others for our failures. We don't discover what responses we are able to make; therefore, we never become responsible.

This limitation creates a double danger: we may avoid the currently illegal consensual activities that could be, for us, a component of our health, happiness, and well-being (non-FDA-approved medications, for example). On the other hand, we may blithely indulge in perfectly legal consensual activities that cause us great harm (smoking is the most obvious example). At the very least, this double jeopardy is unsatisfying. At worst, it's deadly.

Once we realize things aren't going so well, we either wake up and start exploring our response options (which can be difficult, because there's little in our cultural programming to support such action), or we decide we aren't playing society's game fully enough and try to find satisfaction by "toeing the mark" ever more vigorously.

Some people become professional victims. They complain and sue their way to riches. "I saw a little lawyer on the tube," sings Joni Mitchell, "He said, 'It's so easy now, anyone can sue. Let me show you how your petty aggravations can profit you.'" In Framingham, Massachusetts, a man stole a car from a parking lot and was killed in a subsequent traffic accident. His estate sued the parking lot owner, claiming he should have done more to keep cars from being stolen. Does one smell a RAT (Run-of-the-mill Attorney Transaction)?

> *The holier-than-thou activists who blame the population for not spending more money on their personal crusades are worse than aggravating. They encourage the repudiation of personal responsibility by spreading the lie that support of a government program fulfills individual moral duty.*
>
> PATRICK COX
> *USA Today*

If people leave your house drunk and become involved in an accident, you can be held responsible, even if they insisted on leaving. If people are drunk and leaving your house, what are you supposed to do? Tackle them? Mace them and grab their keys? Shoot them, for their own protection and the protection of others?

In his book, *A Nation of Victims,* Charles J. Sykes gives more examples:

> An FBI agent embezzles two thousand dollars from the government and then loses all of it in an afternoon of gambling in Atlantic City. He is fired but wins reinstatement after a court rules that his affinity for gambling with other people's money is a "handicap" and thus protected under federal law.

> Fired for consistently showing up late at work, a former school district employee sues his former employers, arguing that he is a victim of what his lawyer calls, "chronic lateness syndrome."

> *Include me out.*
>
> SAMUEL GOLDWYN

On the other extreme, another group of people use their well-honed victim-finding mechanism to help other (often unwilling) people discover how they are screwing up their lives. "The busybodies have begun to infect American society with a nasty intolerance—a zeal to police the private lives of others and hammer them into standard forms," wrote Lance Morrow in his *Time* essay, "A Nation of Finger Pointers." He continues,

> Zealotry of either kind—the puritan's need to regiment others or the victim's passion for blaming everyone except himself—tends to produce a depressing civic stupidity. Each trait has about it the immobility of addiction. Victims become addicted to being victims: they derive identity, innocence and a kind of devious power from sheer, defaulting helplessness. On the other side, the candlesnuffers of behavioral and political correctness enact their paradox, accomplishing intolerance in the name of tolerance, regimentation in the name of betterment.

The irony is not lost on our British brethren across the sea, from whom, two-hundred-and-some years ago, we broke in the name of liberty. "[There is] a decadent puritanism within America:" the *Economist* reports, "an odd combination of ducking responsibility and telling everyone else what to do." Britain—that suppresser of liberty—is, ironically, far freer with regard to consensual activities than the we're-going-to-have-a-revolution-for-freedom United States.

⚖️ ⚖️ ⚖️

Two of the basic common-sense rules of personal behavior are: (1) Make sufficient investigation before taking part in anything and (2) If you consent to do something, you are responsible for the outcome. Laws against consensual activities undermine both rules.

The situation is unfortunate but, hey, let's be responsible about it. We can't spend too much time blaming consensual crimes for irresponsible attitudes. "I'd be a responsible person if it weren't for consensual crimes!" That's irresponsible.* Whatever degree of irresponsibility we may have, let's be responsible for it.

The existence of consensual crimes is a problem to which we are able to respond. Let's work to change the laws, and, until then, in the words of Sergeant Esterhaus of *Hill Street Blues,* "Let's be careful out there."

> *Great spirits
> have always encountered
> violent opposition
> from mediocre minds.*
>
> ALBERT EINSTEIN

---

*How about a new TV show: *That's Irresponsible!* Each week people appear and tell their victim stories. The most irresponsible victim is named the winner (by some genuinely unfair process) and gets to choose from among three prizes. Whichever prize is chosen, the contestant gets a different one. The prize, of course, is shipped so that it arrives broken.

Laws against Consensual Activities
Are Too Randomly Enforced
to Be Either a Deterrent or Fair

> We simply do not catch
> a high enough percentage of
> users to make the law a real threat,
> although we do catch enough
> to seriously overburden
> our legal system.
>
> JACKSON ELI REYNOLDS
> *The Washington Post*

THE PERFECT LAW, when broken, is followed by immediate punishment. This punishment follows in all cases, in all situations, every time the law is broken, no matter what.

The best example of this is the law of gravity. Each time we violate the law of gravity, the consequences are immediate and consistent. If you drop something, it falls—every time. The law of gravity is not suspended for your birthday, religious holidays, or because you have friends in high places. What do we do when a law is so absolute and unrelentingly ruthless? We obey it and we forget about it. Even when something falls and breaks, we seldom blame gravity.

And so it is with crime laws. The more likely one is to get caught, the less likely one is to commit a crime.

There is, for example, a greater chance of being arrested and convicted for robbing a bank than for robbing a retail establishment, and a greater chance of getting caught robbing a retail establishment than a home. Criminals know this, which is why more homes are robbed than retail establishments, and more retail establishments are robbed than banks. But even house burglaries are kept in check because every burglary has a genuine victim—the owner of the house—and the crime usually gets reported to the police.

Consensual crimes, however, by definition, have no genuine victims. If you visit a prostitute or place a bet with a bookie, neither you nor the prostitute nor the bookie is going to call the police to report the "crime." Each time a person takes part in a consensual crime, there is only a miniscule chance that person will be caught.

> *The growth of drug-related crime is a far greater evil to society as a whole than drug taking. Even so, because we have been seduced by the idea that governments should legislate for our own good, very few people can see how dangerously absurd the present policy is.*
>
> JOHN CASEY

Thus, the deterrent factor in consensual crime is almost entirely missing.

For every consensual crime arrest, there are millions of undetected, unreported, and unpunished occurrences. Some say the answer is to beef up law enforcement, make more arrests, and put 'em all "behind bars where they belong." It is just such statements—bristling with ignorance and arrogance—that have gotten us into the mess we're in today. If every person who ever committed a consensual crime were put behind bars, there would be more people behind bars than in front of them.

"Make the punishments more severe! Set an example!" That doesn't work either. Historically, when consensual crimes were punished more severely than now—by flogging, dismemberment, burning at the stake—the incidence of consensual crimes was not abated, nor did harsh punishment "set an example" for the youth. It sometimes made the consensual crime irresistible. "If people risk *torture* for it," some concluded, "it must be pretty terrific."

Each time you get in a car, there is a statistical chance you will be injured, disabled, or killed. If you knew that you were going to be involved in an accident on a particular day, chances are you wouldn't drive that day. Not knowing on what day it will occur, however, you get in your car and drive off, thinking about where you're going and what to listen to along the way, not about death on the highway. Each time someone takes part in a

> The ultimate result
> of shielding men
> from the effects of folly
> is to fill the world with fools.
>
> HERBERT SPENCER

consensual crime, there is a chance—a statistically slim chance, but a chance—that he or she will be arrested, tried, and sentenced to prison. It is a such a small chance, however, most people don't even think about it.

If the chance of punishment is so slim, why even write this book? One of the reasons (the one being discussed in this chapter) is fairness to those who are unlucky enough to be in the wrong place at the wrong time.

The pain and suffering heaped on this random sampling, the 4,000,000 unfortunates each year who happen to be caught partaking in a consensual crime and, especially, the 750,000 currently in prison, can be eliminated overnight through legislation. We need only repeal the laws that put them in jail in the first place and grant a general amnesty for those who fell on the short side of the odds.

Laws against Consensual Activities Discriminate against the Poor, Minorities, and Women

IF YOU HAVE LOTS OF money, you can pretty much take part in consensual crimes with impunity. (Note that not even one of Heidi Fleiss's well-heeled clients was investigated, much less arrested. She—far less rich and powerful than they—is left to hold the outrageously heavy bag.) A middle-class person runs more risk than a rich person, and a poor person runs the greatest risk of all.

Rich people have drugs delivered by a reputable dealer who supplies "pure" drugs of uniform strength. Middle-class people go to the apartments of fairly reputable dealers, who sell drugs of varying degrees of purity and potency. Poor people go to crack houses or street corners; the dealer and potency are unknown; the impurity of the drug is guaranteed.

In addition, crack houses established for more than a week are well known to both police and crooks. The crooks know that everybody going there has money; the police know that everyone leaving has drugs. On your way in, the crooks ask for a small donation (oh, one hundred percent) of your drug money (and, if you have it on you, your rent money, food money, and season-tickets-to-the-Philharmonic money). On your way out, the police arrest you.*

***

*Police, in quest of their monthly quota of collars, have been known to wait outside crack houses and arrest, one after another, the customers as

> *He didn't know the right people.*
> *That's all a police record means*
> *in this rotten crime-ridden country.*
>
> RAYMOND CHANDLER

As it is with drugs, so it is with all the consensual crimes. With prostitution, the rich can afford expensive, exclusive escorts; the middle class deal with relatively safe call girls; and the poor take their chances with hookers on the streets. For legal gambling, the rich can fly to Atlantic City or Las Vegas. The middle class enjoy poker clubs or Las Vegas Nights at the local church; but the poor are stuck buying lottery tickets at the supermarket (which, as we shall see in the chapter on gambling, have worse odds than even the most crooked gambling casino).

Across the entire spectrum of consensual crimes, the poor have less selection, lower quality, more arrests, higher risks, and a far greater chance of being victims of genuine crimes.

As we explored in the last chapter, consensual crimes are sporadically enforced. This type of arrest pattern invites a law enforcement officer to act on his or her personal prejudices, especially cultural stereotypes. The prosecutor, judge, and jury will—sometimes subconsciously—go along. "Blacks and Hispanics use drugs." "Provocatively dressed women are prostitutes." "Effeminate men are homosexuals." And on and on.

All of this accounts for the outrageously disproportionate consensual crime arrest rates between rich and poor and between whites and blacks. According to the 1991 Uniform Crime Reports, 58% of the drug arrests were of whites versus 41% for blacks; 45% white arrests for gambling, and 47% black arrests for gambling. For prostitution, 60% white, 38% black. Vagrancy, 51% white, 47% black. This sounds evenly distributed until you con-

they exit. Like anteaters outside the opening of an anthill, they arrest their fill. Some police districts intentionally allow popular crack houses to remain in business because the customers are such easy pickings for officers who need to meet their collar quota.

sider that, in 1991, blacks composed only 12% of the U.S. population. Does this mean that blacks are more crime prone than whites? No. For a crime where there really is a victim, driving under the influence of drugs or alcohol, 89% of those arrested were white, only 9% black. This means that on a per capita basis, roughly the same number of blacks as whites were arrested for driving under the influence of alcohol or narcotics. On the other hand, also on a per capita basis, three times as many blacks were arrested for drug abuse than whites.

The ultimate measure of a man is not where he stands in moments of comfort and convenience, but where he stands at times of challenge and controversy.

MARTIN LUTHER KING, JR.

When focusing on a single drug, crack cocaine, the statistics are even more staggering. Here is an excerpt from a front-page story in the Sunday, May 21, 1995, issue of the *Los Angeles Times* (Keep in mind that the *Times* is one of the most anti-drug major newspapers in the country.):

War on Crack Targets
Minorities over Whites

■ **Cocaine: Records show federal officials almost solely prosecute nonwhites. U.S. attorney denies race is a factor.**

A growing chorus of scholars, civil rights advocates and clergy contend that the vast disparity in sentences between white and nonwhite crack dealers illustrates how the war on drugs has unfairly punished minorities.

Whites are more likely than any other racial group to use crack, according to surveys by the National Institute on Drug Abuse. But the U.S. Sentencing Commission reports that about 96% of the crack defendants in federal court are nonwhite. And, records show, the majority are low-level dealers, lookouts and couriers rather than

> *If we accept and acquiesce in the face of discrimination, we accept the responsibility ourselves.*
> *We should, therefore, protest openly everything . . . that smacks of discrimination or slander.*
>
> MARY McLEOD BETHUNE

drug kingpins.

A commission survey in 1992 showed that only minorities were prosecuted for crack offenses in more than half the federal court districts that handled crack cases across the country.

No whites were federally prosecuted in 17 states and many cities, including Boston, Denver, Chicago, Miami, Dallas and Los Angeles. Out of hundreds of cases, only one white was convicted in California, two in Texas, three in New York and two in Pennsylvania.

While defending themselves in court last year against accusations of discrimination, federal prosecutors in Los Angeles stated that they did not contest accusations that only minorities have been prosecuted federally for selling crack.

"Unfortunately, in this court's experience, those high in the chain of drug distribution are seldom caught and seldom prosecuted," said U.S. District Judge J. Spencer Letts in Los Angeles, as he gave a 10-year sentence to a young black man—a college graduate who had mailed a package containing crack.

In another Los Angeles case, U.S. District Judge Richard A. Gadbois lamented handing down a mandatory 10-year prison sentence to a welfare mother of four who was paid $52 to mail a package that, unbeknown to her, contained crack.

"This women doesn't belong in prison for 10 years for what I understand she did," Gadbois said. "That is just crazy."

This uneven enforcement tends to support the belief held by the poor and nonwhites that the police are there to protect the rich and the white from—and at the expense of—the poor and nonwhite. The uneven enforcement increases distrust and contempt for all law enforcement among the poor and nonwhites. In these racially troubled times, it is a rift that we can ill afford.

Edwin M. Schur observed in his landmark book, *Victimless Crimes,*

> The uneven impact of actual enforcement measures tends to mirror and reinforce more general patterns of discrimination (along socioeconomic, racial and ethnic, sexual, and perhaps generational lines) within the society. As a consequence, such enforcement (ineffective as it may be in producing conformity) almost certainly reinforces feelings of alienation already prevalent within major segments of the population.

> *Government is like a baby.*
> *An alimentary canal*
> *with a big appetite at one end*
> *and no sense of responsibility*
> *at the other.*
>
> PRESIDENT RONALD REAGAN

Alcohol is used by 17% more whites than blacks (all these figures are on a per capita basis), and alcohol, society says, is fine (and legal). Marijuana is used once a week or more by twice as many blacks as whites, and marijuana, we're told, is bad. Blacks use heroin four times more often than whites and, well, heroin is so bad (we've been told), we are not to even think about it.

On the other hand, hallucinogens are used by three times more whites than blacks, and we don't worry much about hallucinogens at all. How many peyote busts have you seen on *COPS*? Who was the last politician promising to "Get tough on mushrooms"? When was the last time you were warned that LSD would ruin your chromosomes? Whites use nonprescribed (illegal) tranquilizers 50% more often and stimulants twice as often as blacks, and we hear very little about these "dangers."

Wouldn't it be better for all classes of society—economic, ethnic, racial, sexual, and religious—to agree that physically harming the person or property of another is simply wrong,

> *Bear in mind this sacred principle, that though the will of the majority is in all cases to prevail, that will to be rightful must be reasonable; that the minority possess their equal rights, which equal law must protect, and to violate would be oppression.*
>
> THOMAS JEFFERSON
> 1801

immoral, and will not be tolerated by rich, poor, black, white, or anyone else? Wouldn't this allow for unity within diversity? Isn't this the basis of a saner, freer, yet safer society?

Because of our preoccupation with consensual crimes, we are raising a generation who believes anything is right as long as you get away with it.

Those who wish to sit smugly by, expecting police to ram the "proper" moral values down the throat of every "heathen, infidel, and low-life," may find that the heathens, infidels, and low-lifes are, to quote Paddy Chayefsky, "as mad as hell and not going to take it anymore." If for no other reason than to protect their own person and property, those currently in power should allow others to do whatever they please with their person and property.

If the arrests for consensual crimes were proportionately spread among the middle class and the rich, they wouldn't be crimes for long.

Women

Fewer than 6% of the prison population are women. At best, this means that women are more honest, peaceful, and law-abiding than men. At worst, it means that women are too smart to get caught. Whatever the reason, it's clear that men are, unquestionably, the criminal element in this country.

The crimes for which women are arrested, however, are more likely to be consensual crimes.

Almost 34% of the women in jail are there for drug offenses (compared with 22% of the men). In fact, there were more drug arrests of women than arrests of women for murder, manslaughter, rape, robbery, aggravated assault, burglary, motor vehicle theft, and arson combined. More than 20% of the arrests for that catch-all consensual crime, "disorderly conduct," are women.

And, not surprisingly, more than twice as many women are arrested for prostitution than men (the only crime in which women outnumber the men.)*

Women not only commit fewer crimes; the crimes they commit tend to be crimes without victims. Consequently, enforcement of laws against consensual activities strikes more heavily against women than against men. Perhaps this is why the song, "T'aint Nobody's Biz-ness If I Do," has been recorded more by women than men.

> *How wonderful it is that nobody need wait a single moment before starting to improve the world.*
>
> ANNE FRANK

Meanwhile, women are more likely to be the victims of real crime (rape, obviously, and crimes such as purse-snatching, for which there is no male equivalent) than are men, and the police—diverted to catching consensual criminals—leave women unnecessarily unprotected.

If plainclothes police officers went to high-crime areas and protected women rather than high-vice areas and arrested women, we'd all be a lot better off.

---

*Although prostitution is obviously an activity that requires two people—a buyer and a seller—and although both are considered equally wrong in the eyes of the law, when the female seller is arrested, the male buyer is often let go. Another reason more women than men are arrested is that prostitution arrests are often made by male undercover vice cops, who arrest but are not arrested themselves.

Problems Sometimes Associated with Consensual Activities Cannot Be Solved While They Are Crimes

NO ONE WILL DENY that the reason some people take part in consensual crimes is personal problems. No one will deny that, for some, taking part in consensual crimes can also create or exacerbate problems.

As long as certain consensual activities remain illegal, it is difficult for people who take part in those activities to know whether or not they have a problem (that is, a bad relationship) with any of those activities.

It wasn't until after Prohibition was repealed that people began to face up to their drinking problems. Total abolition automatically creates its opposite: total abandon. When both extremes were removed from consuming alcohol, people could see clearly where they fell on the spectrum of "normal" alcohol consumption. Prohibition ended in 1933; the first chapter of Alcoholics Anonymous was founded a few years later. Had the cultural stereotype that everyone who drinks is a hopeless drunk and the counter-cultural stereotype of hard-drinking hero not been eliminated by Prohibition's repeal, it's doubtful that Alcoholics Anonymous would have gotten off the ground.

As long as drugs, for example, are illegal, it's hard to say to a friend, "You might have a problem," without sounding like a bad drug-education commercial. People taking drugs have become immune to criticism: there's so much criticism, and so much of it is nonsense. (Please see the chapter, "Education, Not Legislation.") "Drug education" seems to be developed by people who know nothing about drugs. It's propaganda and justification, not education. People taking drugs eventually stop listening—even to their friends.

> *When we remember*
> *we are all mad,*
> *the mysteries disappear*
> *and life stands explained.*
>
> MARK TWAIN

This is not the case with, say, alcohol. Yes, alcoholics tend to deny they have a problem (denial is a symptom of addiction), but alcoholics cannot wrap themselves in the garb of the social martyr: *"My* only problem is that drugs are *illegal."*

Among social groups where most drugs are equally available and equally acceptable, more people can see that they have a problem. This has led to the growth of Cocaine Anonymous, Drugs Anonymous, Potsmokers Anonymous, Narcotics Anonymous, the Betty Ford Clinic, and the many other drug treatment centers.

Some people don't know why they take part in illegal consensual activities, other than they're not going to let any damn busybodies tell them what to do. As St. Augustine wrote in his *Confessions* (circa A.D. 398),

> Near our vineyard there was a pear tree laden with fruit that was not attractive in either flavor or form. One night, when I [at the age of sixteen] had played until dark on the sandlot with some other juvenile delinquents, we went to shake that tree and carry off its fruit. From it we carried off huge loads, not to feast on, but to throw to the pigs, although we did eat a few ourselves. We did it just because it was forbidden.

If the "forbidden fruit" temptation were removed, people

> *Appeasers believe that if you keep on throwing steaks to a tiger, the tiger will turn vegetarian.*
>
> HEYWOOD BROWN

could choose to take part in a consensual activity or not—as they do now with alcohol—based on the risks and merits of the activity itself. When consensual activities are illegal, it's hard to tell if the motivating factor is (a) simple rebellion, (b) the natural desire for recreation, or (c) a deep-seated personal difficulty.

Problems are caused when the balance is off, when the relationship with something (often ourselves) is not good. When activities are prohibited, it's difficult to explore that balance; it's hard to evaluate the relationship. The laws against consensual activities tend to hide the potential problems from the people who need to know about them most: the people taking part in the activities.

If one doesn't realize he or she has a problem, one will not seek effective treatment. (Being sentenced by a court to a treatment center does very little good except, possibly, to keep someone out of jail.) Solving a problem takes personal commitment, and that commitment comes through recognition. Keeping consensual crimes crimes, blocks that recognition.

In the words of Shakespeare, ". . . all are punish'd."

Laws against Consensual Activities Create a Society of Fear, Hatred, Bigotry, Oppression, and Conformity; a Culture Opposed to Personal Expression, Diversity, Freedom, Choice, and Growth

> *Idiot, n. A member of a large and powerful tribe whose influence in human affairs has always been dominant and controlling.*
>
> AMBROSE BIERCE

HUMAN BEINGS TEND to fear change. For most people, dislike of the new, the different, the out-of-the-ordinary seems to be instinctual. This makes sense: prehistoric humans found that a new animal might try to eat them, a strange vegetable might poison them, or a differently dressed human might try to kill them. Survival lay in sameness, predictability, the status quo.

This view led to demand for conformity within the group. It started with children who—for their own survival—were taught to eat certain foods and to avoid others, play with certain animals but stay away from others, walk in certain areas but avoid others. As children grew, they learned more cultural taboos: what to wear and what not to wear, what to say and what not to say, what to do and what not to do.

A watering hole may have been off limits simply because an elder saw a wild beast there generations before and declared it taboo. This taboo continued even though the wild beast hadn't been there in decades. An important source of water was lost to the entire tribe just because a wise elder suggested one day, long

> *The soft-minded man*
> *always fears change.*
> *He feels security in the status quo,*
> *and he has an almost morbid*
> *fear of the new.*
> *For him, the greatest pain*
> *is the pain of a new idea.*
>
> MARTIN LUTHER KING, JR.

ago, "Stay away from that watering hole."

Enter the nonconformists. There has always been a small percentage of humans who found sameness, predictability, and the status quo dull. They balked at conformity. They wanted newness, information, risk. What most of the tribe called danger, they called adventure. What most found fearful, they found exciting. They were the explorers, the experimenters, the eccentrics.

These nonconformists had a mixed reputation in the tribe. Some discovered new territories, techniques, and modes of behavior beneficial to the entire tribe. Others put the tribe in danger by their stubborn refusal to cooperate. The former became heroes; the latter became villains. Before the heroes became heroes, however, they went through a phase of seeming to be villains: they took part in—and later advocated—change, and (as the majority would say) we all know instinctively that change is not a good thing.

The minority favoring change has led the majority, kicking and screaming, into the future.

And this is as it should be. Society needs the majority of people to maintain the status quo; consistency is necessary to grow things, build things, and raise children. An adventurer might plow a field and plant a seed, then become hopelessly restless a week later. So the adventurer is off to a new field, planting a new seed. The conformist who stays by the planted seed for a season has the benefit of the harvest.

Will and Ariel Durant, in their *History of Civilization,* compare history to a fast-moving river, ever changing, bringing along the new, moment by moment. Civilization, however, happens on the banks of the river where the vast majority of humanity lives, watching the river go by, building their houses, planting

AIN'T NOBODY'S BUSINESS IF YOU DO

their crops, raising their children.

A healthy society needs a balance between the new and the old, between change and the status quo, between trying something different and maintaining tradition. If change happens too quickly, there's no time to see if the previous change is working. If change doesn't happen quickly enough, a society stagnates and begins persecuting the very adventurers who could have led it to a new and better place.

> *We are all full of weakness and errors,*
> *let us mutually pardon each other our follies—*
> *it is the first law of nature.*
>
> VOLTAIRE

A perfect example of too much change too soon was the aftermath of the French Revolution. From 1793 until 1800, France was ruled by *government du jour*. As Peter Weiss described it, "Years of peace, years of war, each one different than the year before." That was the trouble: before a new form of government had a chance to work, it was toppled, its leaders beheaded, and a whole new government put in its place. After a dozen or so attempts at "democracy," the French welcomed the dictator Napoleon with open arms. Although a despot, he brought with him what France desperately needed: law, order, and a sense of continuity.

⚖ ⚖ ⚖

How can we tell, as a society, which side of the balance point we are on—whether we're permitting too much or persecuting too much, whether we've gone too far in the direction of change or gone too far in the direction of conformity?

An excellent indicator is a society's attitude toward consensual crimes. Let's take a look at two proposals, both considered "different" based on our current cultural norms. One is "The best way to receive is to take—by force if necessary"; the other, "The best way to receive is to give—even if it means giving everything

> *Now the 21st century approaches and with it the inevitability of change. We must wonder if the American people will find renewal and rejuvenation within themselves, will discover again their capacity for innovation and adaptation. If not, alas, the nation's future will be shaped by sightless forces of history over which Americans will have no control.*
>
> JOHN CHANCELLOR

you own." Neither of these positions will have the majority of our society flocking to them. And yet, in a healthy society, the practice of one of these philosophies should be illegal and the practice of the other should not.

Let's say that each philosophy has a particularly charismatic leader. Two new groups find their way onto the American scene: the Takers and the Givers. The adherents of each group believe what they believe with fanatical devotion. *Newsweek* and *Time* do cover stories. *60 Minutes* does a special two-hour episode *(120 Minutes).*

The leader of the Takers says that Americans have gotten too soft, that the basic natural principle of survival of the fittest has been eliminated. Our gene pool is polluted. We will die as a society if we don't do something soon. We must put survival of the fittest back into our daily lives. The solution? If you want something, take it. If the people who own it can successfully defend it, they get to keep it. If the people taking it successfully take it, it's theirs—until they are defeated by another Taker. This would take the fat off of humanity fast. We would become strong, lean, and powerful once again.

The leader of the Givers maintains that energy is a flow, and the more you give, the more will flow back to you. If you feel you don't have enough, it's not because you need to take; it's because you need to give. Humanity is in trouble because we have not accepted the natural principle of giving practiced by the sun which gives us light, the trees which give us fruit, and all plant life which gives us oxygen. We have taken too much; it's time to give. And the more we want, the more we should give. If we want it all, we should give all that we have away.

As an example, the leader of the Takers takes a car, takes a house ("If you can't defend your house, you don't deserve to live there"), and takes—against their will—two or three attractive women as "his own." ("If their husbands want them, they can come and get them.")

The leader of the Givers, by way of example, gives away everything he owns and, whenever he is given something, immediately gives that away, too. Even when given food, he eats only a few bites and gives the rest away.

> *Arnold Schwarzenegger was paid $15 million for his role in Terminator 2, and spoke 700 words. That's $21,429 per word. Such classic lines and their monetary value: "Hasta la vista, baby," $85,716; "I insist," $42,858; and "Stay here, I'll be back," $107,145.*
>
> ENTERTAINMENT WEEKLY

From the point of view of the government, who should be put in jail? One? Both? Neither?

The actions of the Givers' leader are potentially only harming himself and those who choose to follow his example. He may give everything away, his philosophy may be flawed, and he may get little or nothing in return. His followers who likewise give everything away are also potentially hurting no one but themselves. If the philosophy fails, there will be sufficient examples of failure, and the vast majority of society will not follow suit.

The Takers, however, can do a great deal of harm to nonconsenting others before their philosophy is proven unworkable. Long before people learn it's inconvenient and expensive to go to the grocery store in a tank (and to make sure your tank is bigger than everyone else's tank), society has a right to defend itself from a minority of people involved in an experiment that hurts unwilling others.

Two radical points of view, and yet it's appropriate for the government to move in and stop—by force—one, and to practice tolerance with the other. We have the right to defend ourselves from theft, rape, and violence; we do not have the right to defend ourselves—by force of criminal law—from mental or emotional discomfort.

Further, from an enforcement point of view, it's easy to tell when the Takers have crossed the line: when they take some-

> *When we got into office,*
> *the thing that surprised me most*
> *was to find that things*
> *were just as bad*
> *as we'd been saying they were.*
>
> JOHN F. KENNEDY

thing without the owner's permission. But how does one set laws against the Givers? Pass a law saying that no one is allowed to give anything away? That you cannot give away more than 25 percent of your net worth? That before you give something away you must prove to an official of the state that giving it away will not negatively affect your well-being? (These suggestions may sound absurd, but take a look at the wording of some of the consensual-crime laws.)

Further still, who's going to complain? "She gave me five dollars, officer! Put her in jail!" Without a victim, it's highly unlikely that most of the "crimes" committed by Givers would ever be brought to justice. In order to catch them, the police would have to go undercover, pretending to be people in need, waiting for some gullible Giver to give them something. Then the whole question of entrapment arises. Is a Giver guilty of a crime only when the Giver gives unsolicited, or is the Giver also guilty when the receiver has asked? And are those who receive from a "known Giver" guilty as well? These are fine legal points—precisely the ones that come up every day in apprehending consensual criminals.

Meanwhile, all those Takers out there are taking, and the police are so busy entrapping the Givers that there is no time to arrest many Takers. The police are so busy protecting the Givers "from themselves" that the genuine victims of the Takers get taken.

⚖️ ⚖️ ⚖️

When a country protects itself from change too enthusiastically, it robs itself of the new information, ideas, and behaviors

that might make for a better country. When most
people's natural fear of the
new is supported by law,
the law justifies the fear,
thus institutionalizing
prejudice against anything
new and different. ("It's
against the law; it must be
wrong; my fear is right.")
When religious leaders
rummage about the Bible
for "scriptural proof" that

> *Let us forget such words,*
> *and all they mean,*
> *as Hatred, Bitterness and Rancor,*
> *Greed, Intolerance, Bigotry.*
> *Let us renew our faith*
> *and pledge to Man,*
> *his right to be Himself,*
> *and free.*
>
> EDNA ST. VINCENT MILLAY

the prejudice is justified (and you can prove anything by selec-
tively quoting the Bible), then the prejudice is enshrined. "The
law says it's bad; God says it's bad; I feel it's bad; therefore, it's
bad."

An attitude such as this demands conformity. "How dare you
go against what the government, God, and I know to be true?" In
our country, we've been asked to walk an increasingly narrow
line which shows us what we can and cannot put in our bodies,
whom we can and cannot love, what kind of sex we can and
cannot have, how we can and cannot heal ourselves, the recreational activities we can and cannot take part in, and how we can
and cannot worship.

The message clearly is "Morality—our way, *or else!*"

We create a culture in which people are incapable of free
choice because the culture doesn't allow an individual to gather
enough information to make a choice. Experiments in and discovery of viable lifestyle alternatives are replaced by a list of
should's, must's, have-to's, you'd-better's, and don't-you-dare's.
Some people have the feeling their choices in life are as limited
as that of a child being asked, "Do you want to go to bed now, or
five minutes from now?" Sure, there's a choice, but it's a narrow
one.

We are not permitted to grow up. America has become a
Never-Never Land in which the citizens are promising to be good
little boys and girls in exchange for the government, like good

> *The voice of protest, of warning, of appeal is never more needed than when the clamor of fife and drum, echoed by the press and too often by the pulpit, is bidding all men fall in and keep step and obey in silence the tyrannous word of command. Then, more than ever, it is the duty of the good citizen not to be silent.*
>
> CHARLES ELIOT NORTON

parents, protecting them from every evil and fulfilling every need. And the government-authorized religious beliefs (authorized by the laws the government chooses to enact or refuses to enact) tell us what to do while we're here and how to insure a happy hereafter.

The repression created by suppressing consensual activities has a trickle-down effect: "If these activities can get us put in jail, what about this much longer list of behaviors that are also disapproved of by the people who hold the jail keys?"

We have become a nation of individuals afraid to explore, afraid to try new things, afraid to be different. Consequently, we never fully discover—much less fulfill—our individual dreams, our heart's desires. Our individual strengths, talents, and abilities are never developed; we sacrifice the better part of ourselves in order to be the way we "should" be. We and the country as a whole suffer.

We deprive ourselves of the best political leaders because we maintain the pretense that our leaders should be "perfect"—perfect as defined by the keepers of conformity. Thank heavens this narrow-mindedness is loosening up. Kennedy was a Catholic; Carter had "lust in his heart"; Reagan was divorced; and Clinton smoked pot.* Yes, the times, they are a-changing. If it had been Kennedy who admitted to smoking pot—even being in the same room as pot—in 1960, Nixon would have been "the one" to have had the affair with Marilyn Monroe.

---

*Shortly after the famous "I smoked pot but I didn't inhale" statement, Clinton admitted that he was "as dumb as a mule-post" to make such a foolish remark. Yes, he inhaled. Dave Barry parodied this in his run for president on Larry King's show: "Yes, I injected the needle into my vein, but I never pushed the plunger!" Paul Krassner remarked in *The Realist*, that the official presidential song could become "Inhale to the Chief."

Alas, the times (that is, we) are not changing quickly enough. The fishbowl world in which everything a candidate ever did is fully exposed has run ahead of our acceptance for things people do that do not physically harm the person or property of another. The press's ability to tell us what's so has outstripped the American public's ability to say, "So what?"

> *James Bryce wrote his classic study of the United States,* The American Commonwealth, *in the 1880s.*
> *One of the chapters is titled, "The Best Men Do Not Go Into Politics."*
>
> JOHN CHANCELLOR

Gary Hart had a tryst on a boat called *Monkey Business,* apparently with his wife's permission. So what? Jimmy Swaggart enjoys entertaining prostitutes (or vice versa) in cheap motel rooms. So what? Jerry Brown practices eastern religions and is rumored to practice bisexuality as well. So what? Hugh Grant hires a hooker on the eve of the opening of his first Walt Disney movie. That's not a scandal. That's funny.

We have, then, people who are afraid to take leadership positions because some incidents from their pasts are sure to be judged by the moralists. Or we get leaders who are so dull—or so good at covering their tracks—that no taint of nonconformity is possible; example: George Bush. We may be getting the leaders we deserve, but not the best available.

⚖️ ⚖️ ⚖️

Ironically, our insistence on conformity hurts the very institutions it is designed to protect. When we attempt to force everyone into a certain set of behaviors, beliefs, or activities, those very behaviors, beliefs, and activities become eroded and diluted by the people who don't truly want to behave, believe, or act in that way—they are merely doing so out of fear that doing otherwise would "cost them."

If people do not freely choose to take part in something

> *Prejudice*
> *rarely survives experience.*
>
> EVE ZIBART
> *The Washington Post*

based on an inner need, desire, or, at the very least, curiosity, the power of the institution is diluted, its purpose diffused, and its future in question. For the good of the institutions we want to preserve, we must stop coercing people into them by force of law.

⚖ ⚖ ⚖

A country that punishes people simply for being different, for exploring the rich diversity of human experience, or for experimenting with alternate lifestyles is a country condemned to pettiness, vindictiveness, crushing conformity, oppression, decay, and ultimately death. A nation that tolerates or, preferably, celebrates diversity, exploration, and experimentation—is strong, dynamic, creative, alive; its citizenry mature, responsible, and able to make rational choices.

PART III

A CLOSER LOOK
AT THE
CONSENSUAL CRIMES

A Closer Look at
the Consensual Crimes

ENTIRE BOOKS CAN BE (and have been) written on each of the consensual activities currently prohibited by law. While the books already written have pretended to present "balanced views," almost all have reflected the bias of the writer, the publisher, or, in some cases, the sponsoring organization.

In this section of the book, I make no such pretense. This is not a "balanced look." The child who said, "The emperor wears no clothes," did not make a balanced statement. A balanced statement might have been, "The emperor is a fine and noble person who in almost all instances exercises great wisdom in his choices and is known for his fine taste in clothing which has revealed itself over the years in a display of tasteful, elegant, and sometimes spectacular attire. It is fair to say that our emperor is among the best dressed emperors in history. I wonder, then, why on this particular day the emperor, in all his wisdom, has chosen not to wear any clothing." That statement, of course, went beyond balance, passed swiftly through diplomacy, and came perilously close to elephant droppings before arriving at the truth of the matter. In this section of the book, I will spare you the preamble.

In order to put people in prison for something, it is essential for the ordinary citizen to believe that the activity the person is being put in jail for is particularly odious. If it does not harm the person or property of another, the general population must believe that the action is so vile and so inherently evil that merely

> *I can't stand to sing*
> *the same song the same way*
> *two nights in succession.*
> *If you can, then it ain't music,*
> *it's close order drill, or exercise*
> *or yodeling or something,*
> *not music.*
>
> BILLIE HOLIDAY

allowing it to take place in a country corrupts that country irreparably.

Those who want to keep something illegal, then, must (a) keep their hands in the political pie so that laws can be passed, enforced, and not repealed, and (b) use everything that is known about psychology, advertising, and public relations to make the population think that "a menace" is being kept at bay, and that the moralists—far from being seen in their true light as dismantlers of freedom and individual choice—are superheroes in the never-ending battle for truth, justice, and the American way.

This section of the book, then, is designed to counter those false negative impressions about specific consensual activities in the small way that limited space allows. As with all human activities, the activities currently set aside as illegal have built-in pros and cons, benefits and dangers, rewards and risks. For the most part, we have been told only about the cons, dangers, and risks. The average person, then, has a distorted view. My purpose here is to mention a few of the pros, benefits, and rewards so that, when combined with the programming we already have, the reader may be left with a more balanced view.

Because of this, it may seem as though I am endorsing one, another, or all of the consensual crimes. I am not. I am endorsing the *freedom* for each person to take part in any or all of them without fear of being jailed. Exploring any new activity is fearful enough without the fear of jail being added to it. Exploring is a matter of free choice.

A free country of free individuals must, of necessity, have free choice. The moralists in their paternalistic splendor want us to believe that, yes, we can handle certain choices (such as whom we can marry), but we cannot handle others (such as the gender of the person we marry, the number of people we can be married to at the same time, and who gets to wear the wedding dress).

The moralists attempt at every turn to convert us to their own sense of superiority. They want us to join the ranks of their paternalism. "You and I, of course, can take part in our simple pleasures without overdoing it," they tell us, "but whereas *we* use it to amuse ourselves, *they* use it to abuse themselves." When we get to the top of the power structure, then we will have total freedom.

> *We must learn to distinguish morality from moralizing.*
>
> HENRY KISSINGER

Such nonsense. It's nothing more than the elitism of the pecking order.

In fact, people who want to take part in the currently illegal consensual activities already do. Following the repeal of Prohibition, for example, after a minor burst of curiosity, alcohol consumption actually went down. Some people discovered they had problems with alcohol, and stopped drinking altogether. Others found that, when drinking stopped being clandestine, it wasn't as much fun. Still others found that one or two drinks a couple times a week were all they wanted. With alcohol readily available, they stopped overindulging because they no longer had to compensate for scarcity. As we shall see in the discussion between William F. Buckley, Jr., and Professor Gazzaniga in the chapter, "Drugs," the percentage of people who *abuse* rather than *use* a substance or activity will be roughly the same whether that substance or activity is illegal or not.

Which brings me to a few general points I would like to make or reiterate:

1. Use is not abuse.

2. You need not personally support or take part in any activity in order to support another person's freedom to take part in it.

3. One person's meat is another person's poison; one person's poison is another person's insight.

4. While we can control our *actions*, we cannot control our needs, desires, orientations, or preferences.

5. Although a society must have certain mores, rules, and codes of behavior, putting these mores, rules, and codes of behavior into the hands of the criminal justice system is the least effective method to bring about compliance.

6. Your freedom of choice is paid for by giving others their freedom of choice.

> *So little time,*
> *so little to do.*
>
> OSCAR LEVANT

Gambling

THERE SEEMS TO BE something in human nature that likes to (a) predict the future, and (b) be rewarded when right. The destinies of individuals, peoples, and entire nations have rested on someone saying, "I think it will go this way." If this tendency is not inborn, it is ingrained early on. One of the most frequent interchanges between even young children is, "Wanna bet?" "Yeah! How much?"

The leaders of big business—who already have more than enough money to live ostentatiously for the rest of their lives—often say, "I'm in business because I enjoy it. It's a game." Part of the excitement of the game is that it's a gamble; people evaluate data, make conclusions, and place their bets. (In business, it's known as taking risks.)

Gambling is as American as 1776. Guess how the fledgling colonies raised money to pay the Continental Army and fight the revolutionary war? A lottery. Gambling was perfectly legal in this country until the 1820s when, guess what? Yes, our old friends the evangelicals had their revivals and declared gambling—along with drinking, promiscuity, and all the rest—a sin against God. By 1830, most forms of gambling were outlawed. (It's a good thing for Liberty that the evangelicals held less influence in France—the French paid for the Statue of Liberty with a series of lotteries.)

The Civil War and the expansion of the West re-established legalized gambling, but by the early 1900s the evangelicals held sway again and, as they were doing with alcohol, re-established

> *The gambling known as business looks with austere disfavor upon the business known as gambling.*
>
> AMBROSE BIERCE

the prohibitions on gambling. (By 1910, even Nevada had outlawed it.)

Today, we see increasing acceptance of gambling. The fund-raising through raffles, Bingo, and even Las Vegas Nights keeps many churches from openly opposing gambling, and the government can hardly call gambling a social menace: most states run lotteries. (Having the full force of criminal law enforcement to eliminate competition makes gambling not just a monopoly, but a monopoly at gunpoint.)

The major objection people seem to have to gambling these days is not so much that it's wrong, but that their towns would start looking like Las Vegas: gaudy casinos, ostrich plumes, Wayne Newton, and red velour everywhere. People don't fear gambling; they fear bad taste.

That legalized gambling would cause no threat to community standards is evident from observing the evolution of betting on race horses in New York City. The police once spent heaven knows how much money and time raiding bookie joints. Then the city opened Off Track Betting (OTB) outlets in storefronts all over the city—near schools, churches, day-care centers, you name it. The OTB outlets have hardly become magnets for crime and corruption. In fact, there's hardly a better example than OTB to illustrate that addiction to gambling is no fun. The men and women who populate the storefronts appear to be *numb*. When the results of a race are announced, there is no cheering. Most silently drop their tickets to the floor (ripping up losing tickets is a movie cliché), and a few unenthusiastically shuffle over to the payoff window. It appears to be no fun at all. If you don't want to visit an Off Track Betting storefront, you can call your bet in, charging it to your Visa or MasterCard. Has this led to the downfall of civilization in the Big Apple? Nah.

⚖️ ⚖️ ⚖️

When it comes to people throwing away their money by gambling, nothing could be worse than the state-run lotteries. Here we have robbery by bureaucracy. The state-run gambling odds are so bad that wherever organized crime competes with state-run gambling, organized crime is not just winning but flourishing. This is because state governments spend hundreds of millions of advertising dollars to entice new gamblers into the arena. Most people find that, after buying a few lottery tickets, they're no longer interested in that form of gambling. The government, then, needs to encourage more people who have never gambled before to begin gambling. As law professor and expert on gambling I. Nelson Rose wrote in the *Los Angeles Times*,

> Lottery tickets are the only consumer products actively promoted and sold by the state. The state does not sell toothpaste, or even promote brushing your teeth. But it tells people they should gamble. The main marketing concern is how to attract new players, who otherwise wouldn't gamble.

Those who decide gambling is for them soon begin shopping around for better odds. They're not hard to find. Most people, however, spend their money on other pastimes. Lottery commercials are clearly targeted toward the poor. (Stockbrokers pitch their ads toward the rich.*) Even if one wins a million-dollar lottery, is one really a millionaire? Hardly. Although the payoff rules vary from state to state, large jackpots are usually paid off over, say, twenty years. That's $50,000 a year. Not bad, of course,

*I was once told by a senior editor of the *Wall Street Journal* that the paper was merely "the most elaborate scratch sheet in the world."

Gambling in a big city is like cancer. Clap a lid on this thing before it spreads.

DRAGNET

> *I don't know much
> about being a millionaire,
> but I bet I'd be
> just <u>darling</u> at it.*
>
> DOROTHY PARKER

but then taxes are taken off the top. That's up to 40% of $50,000, or about $20,000. Which means an income of $30,000 per year. Still very good, but not exactly enough to buy all those things you planned to buy when you became "a millionaire," and certainly not enough to live up to the expectations of all your friends who now want to be lavishly entertained by "a millionaire." After twenty years, your money's gone. (Those who live off lotteries get neither retirement nor health benefits.) More than one "instant millionaire" regretted ever winning in the first place.

One would think the government, just out of shame, would allow other forms of betting. Shame, however, is not something governments are famous for. With gambling available in many churches, every supermarket in many states, and a phone call away to any stockbroker or OTB, should it really matter whether one wants to gamble on the turn of a wheel, the turn of a card, or the turn of events on Wall Street?

AIN'T NOBODY'S BUSINESS IF YOU DO

Drugs

CONSUMERS UNION—the highly respected, scrupulously impartial organization responsible for *Consumer Reports*—studied the drug problem in this nation long and hard. Its conclusions—yet unpublished—are:

This nation's drug laws and policies have not been working well; on that simple statement almost all Americans seem agreed. . . . They are the result of mistaken laws and policies, of mistaken attitudes toward drugs, and of futile, however well-intentioned, efforts to "stamp out the drug menace." [What we have in this country is] aptly called the "*drug problem* problem"— the damage that results from the ways in which society has approached the drug problem.

The Consumers Union report made six recommendations. I quote:

1. Stop emphasizing measures designed to keep drugs away from people.

2. Stop publicizing the horrors of the "drug menace."

3. Stop increasing the damage done by drugs. (Current drug laws and policies make drugs more rather than less damaging in many ways.)

4. Stop misclassifying drugs. (Most official and unofficial classifications of drugs are illogical and capricious; they, therefore, make a mockery of drug law enforcement and bring drug education into disrepute. A major error of the current drug classification system is that it treats alcohol

and nicotine—two of the most harmful drugs—essentially as non-drugs.)

5. Stop viewing the drug problem as primarily a national problem, to be solved on a national scale. (In fact, as work- ers in the drug scene confirm, the "drug pro- blem" is a collection of local problems.)

6. Stop pursuing the goal of stamping out illicit drug use.

The report, which is nearly six hundred pages long, concludes,

These, then, are the major mistakes in drug policy as we see them. This Consumers Union Report contains no panaceas for resolving them. But getting to work at cor- recting these six errors, promptly and ungrudgingly, would surely be a major step in the right direction.

⚖ ⚖ ⚖

I'm sorry. I lied. The previous excerpts were *not* from a "yet unpublished" report. The report was published in 1972. It was published by Consumers Union in book form, *Licit and Illicit Drugs.** It asked for its proposed changes to be made "promptly and ungrudgingly." Instead in 1972, President Nixon began our most recent war on drugs. How successful has prohibition been? To give but one example: since 1972, according to the office of National Drug Control Policy, annual cocaine use in this country has risen from 50 metric tons to 300 metric tons.

How and Why Drugs Became Illegal

*This book is, alas, out of print. It is one of the finest I've seen on the subject.

One might wonder after reading the United States Constitution how Congress can justify making laws against drug sale, use, and possession. As we have seen, the enumerated powers given Congress by the Constitution have to do with keeping the national borders strong, keeping the business environment healthy, and collecting taxes. It would take the legal word-bending ability of a lawyer to stretch the enumerated powers enough to include making drugs illegal. Alas, one thing Congress has plenty of is lawyers.

> *It seems as if the Department [of Justice] sees the value of the Bill of Rights as no more than obstacles to be overcome.*
>
> PROFESSOR SANFORD H. KADISH

Here, then, is the abbreviated story of how and why drugs became illegal in the United States. It is filled with more abuses, horrors, deceptions, and possible harm than any illegal drug has ever done.

Prior to 1883, there were no federal laws against the manufacture, sale, use, or possession of drugs. As drugs had been available since before the Pilgrims arrived, the United States seemed to survive—even thrive—with no drug restrictions whatsoever. The primary "drug problem" was alcohol—not marijuana, morphine, or cocaine. Even state laws against drugs did not begin to appear until the late nineteenth century.

In California in 1875, a blatantly racist law against opium was passed. Prejudice against the Chinese was high. The city of San Francisco prohibited establishments where opium was smoked. The law—like all drug laws that followed—failed. The large, well-run opium houses closed, but were immediately replaced by smaller, less reputable opium dens. A similar law was passed in Virginia City, Nevada, and similarly failed to work. Rather than realizing that such laws don't work, the Nevada state legislature made even more stringent laws. The state laws didn't work any better than the city laws, but that didn't stop other cities and

> *A prohibition law strikes a blow
> at the very principles upon which
> our government was founded.*
>
> ABRAHAM LINCOLN

states from passing laws. When all these laws failed, the United States Congress got involved. (Sound familiar?)

In 1883, Congress used its constitutional power to "lay and collect taxes, duties, imposts, and excises" to heavily tax imported smoking opium.* That abuse of the tax provision of the Constitution was the foot in the door. What followed was a wedge of misuses and abuses of power that not only tore the door off the hinge, it ripped away the entire front of the house. Once taxation was used to act on a popular but inaccurate belief (in this case that the Chinese were debauching the youth of America by enticing the innocent young into their opium dens), the die was cast. The power to tax, then, was no longer what the founding fathers had intended—a way to raise money—but had become a way to legislate "morality" as well.

Making matters even worse, as this was a prohibition act pretending to be a tax bill, its enforcement fell under the Department of the Treasury. From 1883 until 1968, the Secretary of the Treasury had the dual duty as not only Collector of the Tax, but Keeper of the Public Good. Even if the United States needed a Keeper of the Public Good, putting it in the same department as the tax collectors and money counters was probably the worst choice.**

---

*Real Americans were opium eaters or injectors, not smokers, as were the Chinese, so the racism in regulating drug use reached all the way to Washington.

**The Secretary of the Treasury is still the Keeper of the Public Good in—among other areas—cult control. The Bureau of Alcohol, Tobacco, and Firearms (ATF) masterminded the 1993 raid on the Branch Davidians in Waco, Texas. (It was only after the ATF had thoroughly botched it up that

Once the precedent that the federal government could legislate morality was established, no one gave a second thought to the law passed five years later prohibiting altogether the importation of certain kinds of opium and preventing the Chinese in America from importing opium at all. The United States Treasury was now

> *The country's first drug ban explicitly targeted the opium of "the heathen Chinee." Cocaine was first banned in the south to prevent an uprising of hopped-up "cocainized Negroes."*
>
> DAN BAUM
> The Nation

giving up revenue (the tariff on the opium imported by the Chinese into America) in exchange for regulating consensual personal behavior. The anti-Chinese prejudice was such that the United States Treasury was permitted to abandon its primary job—collecting and spending money—in exchange for this new mission. Over the next thirty years, taxes on smoking opium went up, went down; smoking opium was banned altogether; the ban was lifted and reinstated again. During this time, the tax ranged from $6 per pound to $300 per pound.

All that these regulatory and restrictive efforts accomplished, however, was to build the Chinese underworld (the "tongs"), corrupt the Treasury Department, and increase the nation's opium smoking at least nine fold. The Secretary of the Treasury wrote the Speaker of the House of Representatives on January 12, 1888, "Although all possible efforts have been made by this Department to suppress the traffic, it has found it practically impossible to do so." The United States government, of course, responded with more laws and more law enforcement officers.

As this onslaught only affected "the heathen Chinee" [sic] and not "Americans," no one much cared. All other forms of opium—the types preferred by most white Americans—were perfectly

the FBI was called in to blow it up.) The ATF is under the Department of the Treasury, using the power to tax as the reason to control. The Secretary of the Treasury gave the go-ahead to make the raid. Why wasn't he watching the national debt instead?

> *I don't like principles.*
> *I prefer prejudices.*
>
> OSCAR WILDE

legal and modestly taxed. Why should anyone worry about defending the rights of the Chinese? If they wanted to smoke opium, it was said, they could go back to China. A legal precedent, however, was set by the racist opium restrictions.

The next major step in federal drug enforcement was the 1906 Pure Food and Drug Act. This act said that all patent medicines containing drugs had to say so on the label and, with later amendments, had to state the amount of the drug. This requirement was a positive step in that it allowed people to regulate the kind and amount of drugs they took. It was only later that this act became yet another weapon in the arsenal used for the federal attack on individual choice. (More on the Pure Food and Drug Act in the chapter, "Regenerative Use of Drugs and Other Unorthodox Medical Practices.")

The next major move by the federal government—and the great-granddaddy of all federal drug restrictions—was the Harrison Narcotics Act of 1914. The bill's chief proponent was then–Secretary of State William Jennings Bryan, a staunch fundamentalist, Prohibitionist, and famed orator. His oratory on behalf of Woodrow Wilson won Wilson the presidential nomination, and Wilson appointed him Secretary of State in appreciation. Eleven years later, Bryan would lead the prosecution in the Scopes Monkey Trial, winning a conviction against the schoolteacher who had the audacity to teach Darwin's "unbiblical" theory of evolution in the public schools.

The Harrison Act, in fact, did not prohibit drugs. The act only regulated and taxed the importation and distribution of "opium or coca leaves, their salts, derivatives, or preparations, and for other purposes." It seemed reasonable to regulate, not prohibit, opium, cocaine, and their derivatives. "It is unlikely that a single

wanted to be a hero in the Hearst papers, as Hearst was suddenly printing provocative anti-hemp stories. Perhaps he was on the take from DuPont. Perhaps it was some combination of these.

Dupont? Hearst? What did two business magnates have to do with marijuana prohibition? Plenty.

In the mid-1930s, ma-

> *Many people never grow up.*
> *They stay all their lives*
> *with a passionate need for*
> *external authority and guidance,*
> *pretending not to trust*
> *their own judgment.*
>
> ALAN WATTS

chinery was perfected that would allow the hemp fiber to be more easily and economically separated from the plant. This meant paper, clothing, and other manufactured articles could be produced from hemp at prices far more competitive than ever before. This did not sit well with two American giants: William Randolph Hearst and the DuPont Corporation. Hearst not only printed newspapers; he made the paper on which to print them. If hemp became the primary source of paper, not only would much of Hearst's paper-making machinery become obsolete, but all those forests he purchased could only be used as backdrops for Marion Davies movies. Hearst began attacking hemp at every opportunity.

Earlier, Hearst had successfully turned public opinion against Hispanics. Many believe he and fellow yellow-journalism baron Joseph Pulitzer started the unnecessary Spanish-American War. Hearst used the Mexican term for hemp, *marijuana,* in his many salacious anti-hemp stories. Most Americans never associated marijuana with the hemp their grandfathers grew, or the extract of cannabis their grandmothers took. Hearst's headlines included such joys as

NEW DOPE LURE, MARIJUANA, HAS MANY VICTIMS

MARIJUANA MAKES FIENDS OF BOYS IN 30 DAYS

HOTEL CLERK IDENTIFIES MARIJUANA SMOKER AS
"WILD GUNMAN" ARRESTED FOR SHOOTINGS

And guess who was quoted in Hearst's papers as saying, "If the hideous monster Frankenstein came face to face with the monster marijuana he would drop dead of fright"? Yes, none other than "H. J. Anslinger, head of the Federal Narcotics Bureau." Hearst's paper went on to "report,"

> *The propagandist's purpose is to make one set of people forget that certain other sets of people are human.*
>
> ALDOUS HUXLEY

This is not overstatement. Users of the marijuana weed are committing a large percentage of the atrocious crimes blotting the daily picture of American life.

It is reducing thousands of boys to CRIMINAL INSANITY.

And ONLY TWO STATES have effective laws to protect their people against it.

The marijuana weed, according to Mr. Anslinger, is grown, sold, and USED in every State in the Union. He charges, and rightly, that this is not a responsibility of one State, but OF ALL—and of the federal government.

DuPont, meanwhile, had just patented a process for making paper from wood pulp (which Hearst would use extensively in the years to come). The process, which relied heavily on DuPont chemicals, was not necessary in manufacturing paper from hemp. Additionally, DuPont had recently taken German patents and perfected the "miracle fiber" *nylon,* to be manufactured from coal tar and petroleum products. Inexpensive, readily grown hemp fibers would put a damper on two of DuPont's future money makers, paper production and textiles.

Make of these facts what you will. One thing is certain: Hearst and DuPont made a fortune thanks to the prohibition of hemp.*

---

*Anslinger was appointed head of the Federal Bureau of Narcotics by his

Anslinger used his position of authority to encourage states and cities to ban marijuana. In 1935, Anslinger announced,

> In the absence of Federal legislation on the subject, the States and cities should rightfully assume the responsibility for providing vigorous measures for the extinction of this lethal weed, and it is therefore hoped that all public-spirited citizens will earnestly enlist in the movement urged by the Treasury Department to adjure intensified enforcement of marijuana laws.

The shepherd always tries to persuade the sheep that their interests and his own are the same.

STENDHAL

By 1937, forty-six of the forty-eight states, as well as the District of Columbia, had laws against marijuana. At Anslinger's urging, marijuana was labeled a narcotic and had the same strict penalties as morphine and heroin.

The wild reports continued in Hearst newspapers and magazines. Commissioner Anslinger took quill in hand himself on occasion—his prose as bad as his prohibitions. This, for example, from Hearst's *American Magazine* of July 1937:

> An entire family was murdered by a youthful [marijuana] addict in Florida. When officers arrived at the home they found the youth staggering about in a human slaughterhouse. With an ax he had killed his father, mother, two brothers, and a sister.
>
> He seemed to be in a daze. . . . He had no recollection of having committed the multiple crime. The officers

uncle-in-law, Andrew Mellon, Secretary of the Treasury under Herbert Hoover. Mellon was the largest stockholder in Mellon Bank, one of two banks with which DuPont exclusively did business. This is, of course, entirely coincidental and has absolutely nothing to do with the discussion at hand.

> *I can't understand
> why people are frightened
> of new ideas.
> I'm frightened of the old ones.*
>
> JOHN CAGE

knew him ordinarily as a sane, rather quiet young man; now he was pitifully crazed. They sought the reason. The boy said he had been in the habit of smoking something which youthful friends called "muggles," a childish name for marijuana.

I don't know about you, but I've never met a pothead that ambitious.

In Hollywood, in his famous Production Code, Mr. Hayes prohibited any positive mention of drugs. (Cigarettes, of course, were just fine.) Hollywood joined in the propaganda madness (at Hearst's encouragement?) and made the now-classic *Reefer Madness.*

In 1937, Anslinger rushed through Congress the Marijuana Tax Act. Anslinger had waited because the question of whether or not it was acceptable to use the tax provisions of the Constitution to justify prohibitions was before the Supreme Court. On March 29, 1937, the Supreme Court decided that machine guns could be prohibited by first passing an act taxing them, then using the tax-law to ban them altogether.

On April 14, 1937, the Marijuana Tax Act was introduced to Congress.

The testimony before the congressional committee was, for the most part, provided by Anslinger, Anslinger employees, and Anslinger reading Hearst newspaper articles, some of which he had written. The hearings were reminiscent of the scene from John Huston's film, *The Bible,* in which John Huston, playing Noah, has a conversation with God, also played by John Huston. The film was produced and directed by John Huston. The narrator: John Huston.

Curiously, neither Hearst, DuPont, nor Anslinger had by 1937 created the myth that marijuana use leads to heroin addiction.

During the House hearings, a representative remarked, "I am wondering whether the marijuana addict graduates into heroin, and opium, or a cocaine user." Commissioner Anslinger replied,

> No, sir; I have not heard of a case of that kind. The marijuana addict does not go in that direction.*

> *But each day brings its petty dust*
> *Our soon-chok'd souls to fill,*
> *And we forget because we must,*
> *And not because we will.*
>
> MATTHEW ARNOLD

And how many doctors were heard in the congressional hearings in 1937? Precisely one. He represented the American Medical Association. The AMA opposed the bill. At least twenty-eight medicinal products containing marijuana were on the market in 1937, the doctor pointed out; drugs containing marijuana were manufactured and distributed by the leading pharmaceutical firms; and marijuana was recognized as a medicine in good standing by the AMA. From an editorial in the *Journal of the American Medical Association* (May 1, 1937):

> After more than 20 years of federal effort and the expenditure of millions of dollars, the opium and cocaine habits are still widespread. The best efforts of an efficient Bureau of Narcotics, supplemented by the efforts of an equally efficient Bureau of Customs, have failed to stop the unlawful flow of opium and coca leaves and their components and derivatives, on which the continuance and spread of narcotic addiction depends.

Like the Harrison Narcotics Act before it, the Marijuana Tax Act claimed—even in the title of the bill—only to tax marijuana. It was yet another deception perpetrated on Congress and the

---

*With another eighteen years to prepare, however, Anslinger got it right. Still commissioner, Anslinger testified before a Senate committee in 1955 that "Eventually if used over a long period of time [marijuana] does lead to heroin addiction."

> *The great masses of the people . . .*
> *will more easily fall victims*
> *to a big lie than*
> *to a small one.*
>
> ADOLF HITLER
>
> *Mein Kampf*
> 1933

American people: the intent of the bill was never to tax, but to prohibit. Beyond mere deception, however, the Big Lie to Congress was yet to come.

In testifying before the congressional committee, the doctor sent by the AMA said the AMA had only realized "two days before" the hearings that the "killer weed from Mexico" was indeed cannabis, the benign drug used and prescribed by the medical profession for more than a hundred years. Said Dr. Woodward,

> We cannot understand, yet, Mr. Chairman, why this bill should have been prepared in secret for two years without any intimation, even to the [medical] profession, that it was being prepared.

Anslinger and the committee chairman, Robert L. Doughton,* denounced and curtly excused Dr. Woodward. When the marijuana tax bill came before Congress, one pertinent question was asked from the floor: "Did anyone consult with the AMA and get their opinion?"

Representative Vinson answered for the committee, "Yes, we have . . . and they are in complete agreement."

The Big Lie. The bill passed, and became law in September 1937.

Anslinger was furious with the AMA for opposing him before the congressional committee. As the commissioner of the Federal Bureau of Narcotics, he could prosecute any doctors who prescribed narcotics for "illegal purposes." Which purposes were "illegal" was pretty much Anslinger's call. From mid-1937 through 1939, more than 3,000 doctors were prosecuted. In

*According to Jerry Colby, author of the book, *DuPont Dynasties,* Robert Doughton was a key DuPont supporter in Congress.

1939, the AMA made peace with Anslinger and came out in opposition to marijuana. From 1939 to 1949, only three doctors were prosecuted by the FBN for drug activity of any kind.

In 1944, Mayor Fiorello La Guardia and the New York Academy of Medicine released the La Guardia Marijuana Report, which, after seven years of re-search, claimed that marijuana caused no violence and had certain positive medical benefits. In a rage, Anslinger banned all marijuana research in the United States. He attacked La Guardia vehemently.

> *Stop judging by mere appearances, and make a right judgment.*
>
> JESUS OF NAZARETH
> John 7:24

In 1948, however, Anslinger dropped the "marijuana causes violence" argument. He made, in fact, a complete about-face when he testified before Congress in 1948 that marijuana made one *so* tranquil and *so* pacifistic that the communists were making abundant supplies available to the military, government employees, and key citizens. Marijuana was now part of a Communist Plot aimed at weakening America's will to fight.

That this statement was a complete reversal of his congressional testimony only eleven years before went unnoticed. Anti-communism put Anslinger back in the public eye, along with his good friend Senator Joseph McCarthy. It was later revealed by Anslinger in his book, *The Murderers,* and also by Dean Latimer in his book, *Flowers in the Blood,* that Anslinger supplied morphine to McCarthy on a regular basis for years. Anslinger's justification? To prevent the communists from blackmailing such a fine American just because he had a "minor drug problem."

In 1970, in passing the Controlled Substances Act, the federal government shifted its constitutional loophole for jailing drug users and providers from taxation to the federal government's obligation to regulate interstate traffic. This is as dramatic a violation of the Constitution as the taxation excuse, but it fit the

> *Prohibition goes beyond
> the bounds of reason
> in that it attempts to control
> a man's appetite by legislation,
> and makes a crime out of things
> that are not crimes.*
>
> ABRAHAM LINCOLN

government's plan better. Under this law a bureau-crat—usually not elected—decides whether or not a substance is dangerous and how dangerous that substance is. There's no more messing around with legislatures, presidents, or other bothersome formalities. When MDMA (ecstasy) was made illegal in 1986, no elected official voted on that. It was done "in house." People are now in jail because they did something that an administrator declared was wrong.

The Controlled Substances Act was circulated to the states where it was enthusiastically received; most states have modeled their programs on the federal plan. There is no longer a need, then, to deceive legislators: the agency heads and their minions simply decide what the law is, and that's that.

Today, the Federal Bureau of Narcotics is, like its former director Anslinger, no more. How's this for a bureaucratic shuffle: In 1968, the Federal Bureau of Narcotics (FBN) was transferred from the Treasury Department to the Justice Department, where it was merged with the Bureau of Drug Abuse Control (BDAC) to form the Bureau of Narcotics and Dangerous Drugs (BNDD). In 1973, during the early skirmishes of the war against drugs, the Bureau of Narcotics and Dangerous Drugs (BNDD), the Office for Drug Abuse Law Enforcement (ODALE), and the Office of National Narcotics Intelligence (ONNI) all combined to form the Drug Enforcement Administration (DEA). (I hope you're paying attention: there will be a quiz.) As the war against drugs escalated, one agency was not enough. In 1988, the National Drug Enforcement Policy Board (NDEPB) and the Office of National Drug Control Policy (ONDCP) were formed. The director of ONDCP—now a cabinet-level position—was given the title that Mr. Anslinger (anti-communist sentiments notwithstanding) would have killed for: The Drug Czar.

Who would have thought we'd have a czar in the same Washington that gave us Joseph McCarthy, the Bay of Pigs, and the cold war?

⚖ ⚖ ⚖

It's amazing how little Americans know about drugs. Considering that we spend $40 billion per year

to make 1,350,000 arrests and have sacrificed a good number of our personal freedoms and physical safety to the war on drugs, it might be valuable to take a look at the "enemy."

Because it is the consensual crime on which the greatest prohibitions are placed, we'll go into drug myths and facts in a fair amount of detail.

Opiates

The opiates are opium, morphine, and heroin. All three come from the opium poppy. They are generally known as *narcotics*.

At first, opium was smoked. It wasn't smoked, actually; it was heated until it gave off vapors—but did not yet "smoke"—and the vapors were inhaled. The active ingredient of opium, morphine, went directly into the bloodstream and to the brain. This was the method favored in China and by the Chinese immigrants brought to the U.S. to build the transcontinental railroads.

Morphine was first separated from opium in 1806. Any oral ingestion was referred to as "eating." Opium eating was usually drinking some concoction made with morphine. These included any number of patent medicines such as *laudanum*, an alcohol-morphine mixture. In addition to pain killing, morphine was known for its tranquilizing and relaxing effects. Many of the patent medicines were marketed to women to cure anxiety, nervousness, and menstrual cramps. By the 1890s, men went to the saloons to drink alcohol and women stayed home and "ate

> *Creation is a drug*
> *I can't do without.*
>
> CECIL B. DeMILLE

opium." Eugene O'Neill wrote eloquently and touchingly about his mother's morphine addiction, his brother's alcoholism, and his father's disapproval of both, in his play, *Long Day's Journey into Night.*

Physicians referred to morphine as G.O.M. or "God's Own Medicine." With the introduction of the hypodermic syringe in the mid-1800s, the effects of injecting morphine were discovered. The Civil War was an ideal laboratory to experiment with morphine's injectable anesthetic and painkilling qualities. The doctors went a little overboard: many soldiers returned from the war addicted to morphine. For quite some time, morphine addiction was known as the "soldier's disease."

Nevertheless, by 1880, physicians recommended G.O.M. for fifty-four "diseases" including anemia, insanity, and nymphomania. The addictive quality of morphine, however, did not concern doctors. Although many people needed the drug daily, as long as they were able to get the drug, morphine addicts functioned normally in society. Most addictions are only troublesome when the addictive substance is taken away. As a culture today, we are addicted to—among many other things—electricity, packaged foods, television, and automobiles. As long as these are readily available, we don't notice our addiction. If one—or all—were taken away, we would immediately exhibit the classic symptoms of addictive withdrawal.

Dr. William Stewart Halsted is widely recognized as "the father of modern surgery" and was one of the four founders of Johns Hopkins Medical Center. Dr. Halsted died at the age of 70, having revolutionized surgery (the sterile operating room was one of his many contributions). He enjoyed a thirty-two-year marriage, good health, and the admiration of his peers. However, Sir William Osler's "Secret History" of the medical center, made public in 1969, revealed that Dr. Halsted had been addicted to morphine until the end of his life. Dr. Osler, another of the founders of Johns Hopkins, wrote,

> He had never been able to reduce the amount to less than three grains [180 milligrams] daily; on this he could do his work comfortably, and maintain his excellent physical vigor.

> *Just say know.*
>
> MARY MATHREY, R.N.

A daily injection of morphine is certainly not recommended operating room procedure, but the history of Dr. Halsted is hardly the stereotype of narcotic addiction that we have come to believe.

In 1898, heroin was synthesized from morphine by the Bayer company, the folks who gave us aspirin. They were looking for a better painkiller than aspirin, and they found it. Heroin is four to eight times more potent than morphine. Unfortunately, it had this minor drawback: it was almost as addictive as tobacco. Knowing this, why would anyone risk addiction? The answer may be found in this description:

> Heroin's most valued effect is the ecstatic reaction that it gives after being intravenously injected; within seconds, a warm, glowing sensation spreads over the body. This brief but intense rush is then followed by a deep, drowsy state of relaxation [that] lasts two to four hours and then gradually wears off.

That was not an enticement from an illicit drug catalog or some pusher, but the description from the *Encyclopedia Britannica*. No matter how addictive heroin may be, however, most ill effects and almost all heroin fatalities are due to the laws against the drug, not the drug itself.

> *Of course drugs were fun.*
> *And that's what's so stupid about*
> *anti-drug campaigns:*
> *they don't admit that.*
> *I can't say I feel particularly*
> *scarred or lessened by my*
> *experimentation with drugs.*
> *They've gotten a very bad name.*
>
> ANJELICA HUSTON

It is impossible to accurately determine the strength and purity of heroin purchased on the street. Practically all overdoses occur because users cannot accurately determine a dosage level. In addition, most of the negative effects people associate with heroin addiction (premature aging, ill health, and what Roseanne Roseannadanna might describe as "You look *awful!*") come not from the heroin, but from the impure substances used to cut the heroin.

Heroin is cut—that is, diluted—at least six times by six different individuals (or organizations) on its way to market. When drug dealers cut heroin, anything that's white and dissolves in water will do—laxatives, powdered milk, baking soda, quinine. By the time the heroin reaches the end user, often more than 70% of the "white powder" is something other than heroin. All these "additives" may be perfectly fine for the stomach, but can play havoc on the body when directly injected into the bloodstream. When a heroin addict refers to being ill by "bad dope," he or she is referring not to the quality of the heroin, but the content of the contaminants.

Although heroin is the opiate most effective for killing pain, it is not available by prescription. What is readily available on street corners cannot be used in hospital wards. People are suffering needlessly at this very moment because the moralists of our time are concerned that heroin manufactured for medical use will be used "recreationally." Because of an ineffective attempt to control the personal habits of would-be heroin users, innocent hospital patients in advanced stages of degenerative diseases must suffer.

All of the opiates have the same active ingredient, morphine, in different degrees of concentration. While the most addictive of all illegal substances, it is seldom deadly, and the primary harm opiates cause is due to their illegality.

Cocaine, Crack, Amphetamines

Cocaine is simply a stimulant, an energizer. That's all. Its close chemical cousin is caffeine. In the early 1500s when the Spanish conquistadors con-

> *I always wanted to blunt and blur what was painful.*
> *My idea [in taking drugs] was pain reduction and mind expansion,*
> *but I ended up with mind reduction and pain expansion.*
>
> CARRIE FISHER

quered the Incas, they discovered the coca leaf was a gift more prized than silver or gold. "Priests and supplicants were allowed to approach the Altar of the Inca only if they had coca leaf in their mouths," writes Edward M. Brecher in *Licit and Illicit Drugs*. For religious and superstitious reasons, the conquistadors themselves did not chew the coca leaves, but did use it to encourage the Incas to work harder and produce more.

Although coca-leaf chewing never caught on in Europe or North America, wine drinks prepared with coca were very popular. They were first marketed in 1886 as a "remarkable therapeutic agent." Gounod, who wrote "Ave Maria," and Pope Leo XIII were regular imbibers of "Mariani's wine," a popular cocaine-wine concoction. Coca-Cola, also originated in 1886, contained cocaine from the coca plant and caffeine from the kola nut.

Cocaine, first synthesized from the coca leaf in 1844, was used as a local anesthetic, to fight fatigue, and as an antidepressant. Here's how one doctor described it in 1884:

> I take very small doses of it regularly against depression and against indigestion, and with the most brilliant success. . . . In short it is only now that I feel I am a doctor, since I have helped one patient and hope to help more.

This same doctor wrote to his fiancée:

> If you are forward you shall see who is the stronger, a gentle little girl who doesn't eat enough or a big wild

> *Cocaine habit forming?*
> *Of course not.*
> *I ought to know,*
> *I've been using it for years.*
>
> TALLULAH BANKHEAD

man *who has cocaine in his body.* [Italics in original.] In my last severe depression I took coca again and a small dose lifted me to the heights in a wonderful fashion. I am just now busy collecting the literature for a song of praise to this magical substance.

The interestingly titled "Song of Praise" to cocaine and its therapeutic benefits was published in a medical journal in July 1884. The doctor's name was Sigmund Freud.

Amphetamines were first synthesized in 1887, but their effect as a cocaine-like stimulant was not noted until 1927. In 1932, an amphetamine marketed under the trade name Benzedrine replaced cocaine as the "power drug" of choice. Several film historians report that *Gone With the Wind* never would have been made without producer David O. Selznick's twenty-two-hour Benzedrine-inspired work days. World War II has been called the Benzedrine War—the American, British, German, Italian, Russian, and Japanese armed forces were given amphetamines to counteract fatigue, elevate mood, and heighten endurance. After World War II, "pep pills" replaced caffeine for many students, cross-country truck drivers, and athletes.

A small minority of users were not content with the increased well-being and productivity cocaine and amphetamines supplied, so they began injecting themselves with amphetamines (the "speed freaks") and, later, smoking cocaine in preparations known as "freebase," "ice," or "crack."

As long as people regulate their use of these more concentrated and directly ingested forms to avoid "burnout," there is nothing intrinsically more addictive or harmful about mainlining amphetamines or smoking crack than there is in cocaine or amphetamines themselves. This is not to say that they are not addictive—cocaine and amphetamines are, although less addictive than tobacco or opiates—but to single out "crack" as though it were some newly discovered instant addicter and destroyer of humanity is a serious misrepresentation. In fact, if cocaine were legal, most people who chose to use it would drink it or take it in pill form.

> *Brownie pledge,*
> *I swear I've never,*
> *never, ever tried drugs.*
>
> BROOKE SHIELDS

The most popular drug in the Cocaine, Crack, and Amphetamines category is caffeine. It is the most popular drug in the world. I must caution you, however, that the National Institute on Drug Abuse has the following to say about caffeine:

> **Dependence:** A form of physical dependence may result with regular consumption. In such cases, withdrawal symptoms may occur if caffeine use is stopped or interrupted. These symptoms include headache, irritability, and fatigue. Tolerance may develop with the use of six to eight cups [of coffee] or more a day. A regular user of caffeine who has developed a tolerance may also develop a craving for the drug's effects.

> **Dangers:** Poisonous doses of caffeine have occurred occasionally and have resulted in convulsions, breathing failure, and even death.

These are roughly the same dependence and dangers of the illegal stimulants cocaine (crack) and amphetamines.

Narcotic means "inducing sleep or stupor"—or at least that's what it once meant. While this does describe the opiates, precisely the reverse is true of the stimulants cocaine and amphetamines. To lump these two types of drugs—opiates and stimulants—into a category (narcotics) which only applies to the opiates, is an unnecessary attack on the perfectly good word *narcotic*. The reason for this languagecide is that once the American public believed narcotics were bad, the easiest thing to do was lump every other drug the government wanted to control into that category.*

Psychedelics

The psychedelics include peyote, mescaline, psilocybin, and that relative newcomer, LSD. We will explore peyote and LSD in the chapter, "Religious and Psychologically Therapeutic Use of Drugs."

Marijuana
(Hemp, Cannabis)

Marijuana was among the first plants cultivated by humans. Approximately 10,000 years ago, at the same time humans began making pottery and working metal, they began weaving hemp fiber.**

As Jack Herer points out in his book, *The Emperor Wears No Clothes,*

> From at least the 27th to 7th century B.C. up until this century, cannabis was incorporated into virtually all the cultures of the Middle East, Asia Minor, India, China, Japan, Europe, and Africa for its superior fiber, medicines, oils, food, and for its meditative, euphoric, and relaxational uses. Hemp was one of our ancestors' most impor-

---

Narcotics has been shortened to simply *drugs* to fit limited headline space and television newscast time. At least *drugs* is more accurate.

**As we shall see in the chapter, "Hemp for Victory," in addition to its medicinal and recreational uses—which we will explore in this chapter—the hemp plant is and has been an excellent source of cloth, rope, canvas (which was named after *cannabis*), paper (early drafts of the Declaration of Independence were written on hemp paper), fuel, and even food.

tant overall industries, along with tool making, animal husbandry and farming.

Homer refers to a drug brought by Helen to Troy that sounds remarkably like marijuana. Dr. Robert P. Walton, an American physician, found passages from Pliny, *The Arabian Nights,* Herodotus, Marco Polo, and others clearly indicating that marijuana was used in the ancient world for purposes other than making rope.

> *There's been no top authority saying what marijuana does to you. I tried it once but it didn't do anything to me.*
>
> JOHN WAYNE

Although the Greek and Roman civilizations certainly had access to the ingestible forms of hemp, wine was the intoxicant of choice. The early Christians inherited this preference. The pagans, however, supplemented wine with various "herbs," one of which was hemp. The use of any intoxicant other than alcohol, then, became associated with paganism, and the Christian world turned its back (and eventually its wrath) on such practices. The use of any plant product other than grapes for consciousness-altering was considered a form of witchcraft. It was banned by the Church, and later enforced by the Inquisition. In 1430, for example, Joan of Arc was accused of using "witch" herbs to hear her "voices" and burned at the stake. The most popular "witch" herb at the time was cannabis. In 1484, Pope Innocent VIII proclaimed that cannabis, among other herbs, was central to satanic worship. Until the end of the Inquisition, lighting up could have led to burning at the stake.

Hemp continued to be grown, of course, as raw material for manufacture. The sails and ropes on Columbus's ships were made of hemp, as were the sails and ropes on the Mayflower. When the Mayflower arrived in 1620, marijuana had been grown on the American continent for almost a decade: the Jamestown settlers brought it to Virginia in 1611 and cultivated it for its fiber. As Edward M. Brecher wrote,

> *Any formal attack on ignorance*
> *is bound to fail*
> *because the masses are always*
> *ready to defend*
> *their most precious possession*
> *—their ignorance.*
>
> HENDRIK VAN LOON

From then until after the Civil War, the marijuana plant was a major crop in North America, and played an important role in both colonial and national economic policy. In 1762, Virginia awarded bounties for hemp culture and manufacture, and imposed penalties upon those who did not produce it.

It was common knowledge that smoking the flowering tops of the hemp plant caused intoxication. As tobacco at that time was smoked primarily for its high and usually in a pipe, the paraphernalia and the practice for pot smoking—as well as the cannabis plant itself—were readily available.

Marijuana was one of the few painkillers in colonial America. George Washington, who had dental problems his entire life, was obviously concerned about the medicinal uses of marijuana. His journal for August 7, 1765, states "—began to seperate [sic] the Male from the Female Hemp at Do—rather too late." It was the belief then that the unfertilized female plants produced the best resin for making hashish. Washington's comment that he was "rather too late" indicates that he wanted unpollinated female plants. Other than medicinal or recreational use, there is no reason to concern oneself with whether or not the male plants had fertilized the female plants.*

Throughout the nineteenth century, cannabis was prescribed for a number of conditions. It was listed in the *United States Pharmacopoeia* as *extractum cannabis* or *Extract of hemp,* and was so listed until 1942. In 1851, the United States *Dispensatory* reported of extract of hemp:

*The hemp plant is botanically quite advanced: some plants are male, some are female, and some are androgynous. Most species in the plant kingdom are merely androgynous.

AIN'T NOBODY'S BUSINESS IF YOU DO

The complaints in which it has been specially recommended are neuralgia, gout, rheumatism, tetanus, hydrophobia, epidemic cholera, convulsions, chorea, hysteria, mental depression, delirium tremens, insanity, and uterine hemorrhage.

> *The greatest service which can be rendered any country is to add a useful plant to its culture.*
>
> THOMAS JEFFERSON

By the second half of the 1800s, fluid extracts of hemp were marketed by Parke Davis, Squibb, Lilly, and Burroughs Wellcome. Grimault and Sons manufactured cannabis cigarettes as an asthma relief. All these products were sold at modest prices without a prescription at neighborhood pharmacies.

Recreationally, hemp was generally eaten or smoked in the form of hashish, a concentration of the THC*-containing portions of the hemp plant. Hashish was freely imported, and World's Fairs and International Expositions from the 1860s onward often featured the Turkish Hashish Smoking Exposition. At the 1876 Centennial Exposition in Philadelphia, for example, the Turkish Hashish Exposition was most popular, and fairgoers were encouraged to return again and again to "enhance" their enjoyment of the fair.

For the most part, however, Americans in the mid- to late 1800s either drank extracts of cannabis or ate hash. From the Civil War onward, for example, the Ganjah Wallah Hasheesh Candy Company sold a popular intoxicating hash candy. A typical ad read:

> **Hasheesh Candy.**—The Arabian "Gunje" of Enchantment confectionized.—A most pleasurable and harmless stimulant.—Cures Nervousness, Weakness, Melancholy, &c. Inspires all classes with new life and energy. A complete

---

*THC is tetrahydrocannabinol, the psychoactive chemical in marijuana.

> *Every form of addiction is bad,*
> *no matter whether*
> *the narcotic be alcohol*
> *or morphine*
> *or idealism.*
>
> CARL JUNG

mental and physical invigorator. Send for circular. Beware of imitations. 25 cents and $1 per box. Imported only by the Gunjah Wallah Co., 476 Broadway, N.Y.

And then there were Alice B. Toklas's favorite, "hash brownies"—actually called Haschich Fudge. Here, from her 1954 *Alice B. Toklas Cook Book,* is the recipe (which is presented here solely for its historical, gastronomical, and literary illumination):

HASCHICH FUDGE
(which anyone could whip up on a rainy day)

This is the food of Paradise—of Baudelaire's Artificial Paradises: it might provide an entertaining refreshment for a Ladies' Bridge Club or a chapter meeting of the DAR. In Morocco it is thought to be good for warding off the common cold in damp winter weather and is, indeed, more effective if taken with large quantities of hot mint tea. Euphoria and brilliant storms of laughter; ecstatic reveries and extensions of one's personality on several simultaneous planes are to be complacently expected. Almost anything Saint Theresa did, you can do better if you can bear to be ravished by *"un évanouissement reveillé."*

Take 1 teaspoon black peppercorns, 1 whole nutmeg, 4 average sticks of cinnamon, 1 teaspoon coriander. These should all be pulverized in a mortar. About a handful each of stoned dates, dried figs, shelled almonds and peanuts: chop these and mix them together. A bunch of canibus sativa can be pulverized. This along with the spices should be dusted over the mixed fruit and nuts, kneaded together. About a cup of sugar dissolved in a big pat of butter. Rolled into a cake and cut into pieces or made into balls about the size of a walnut, it should be eaten with care. Two pieces are quite sufficient.

Obtaining the *canibus* may present certain difficulties, but the variety known as *canibus sativa* grows as a common weed, often unrecognized, everywhere in Europe, Asia and parts of Africa; besides being cultivated as a crop for the manufacture of rope. In the Americas, while often discouraged, its cousin, called *canibus indica,* has been observed even in city window boxes. It should be picked and dried as soon as it has gone to seed while the plant is still green.

> *Seurat's eyes then began to tremble at what his eyes were seeing.*
>
> GERTRUDE STEIN

Only the poor and lower classes smoked (or ate) the hemp plant. Liquid extract of cannabis, hashish candy, and hashish itself were readily and inexpensively available. Why bother with the plant?

Marijuana is not a narcotic. Like alcohol, it is not sleep-inducing unless taken in large quantities. Unlike tobacco or opiates, it is nonaddictive. To quote from the Consumers Union Report, "the lethal dose is not known; no human fatalities have been documented."

⚖ ⚖ ⚖

As we're in the midst of a drug war, each day we are inundated with news—some heartening, some discouraging. For example, in *Newsweek,* June 14, 1993,

Fed up with mandatory sentences, about 50 senior federal judges have refused to hear any more drug cases. Others have disobeyed sentencing rules and a few have resigned in protest. "You get a kid who makes a mistake.

> *It's gotten to where
> defense attorneys
> in federal drug cases
> can do their clients
> about as much good
> as Dr. Kevorkian can do his—
> quietly shepherd them through
> to the least painful end.*
>
> DAN BAUM

If he's involved with enough drugs then it's a 10-year minimum mandatory sentence and he has to do 8-1/2 years. To me, that's ludicrous," says J. Lawrence Irving, who quit the federal bench in San Diego in 1990.

Fifty federal judges refusing to hear drug cases is unprecedented. Heartening. But then, on the same page,

> An 18-year-old Alabama high-school senior [was] sentenced to 10 years for federal drug conspiracy because she told an undercover agent where to meet her boyfriend to buy LSD.

Allow me to end this section on recreational drug use in an unusual way: by quoting at length from the *National Review*.

One might think if I wanted a supporting point of view, I would quote at length from *The Nation*, *The New Republic*, or maybe *High Times*. But no. The sanest words I've read in a while on drugs come from a discussion between William F. Buckley, Jr., and Michael S. Gazzaniga, Professor of Neuroscience at Dartmouth Medical School. I would like to thank Mr. Buckley for his permission to quote from this discussion at length.* So, this from the February 5, 1990, issue of the *National Review*. First, the magazine gives Professor Gazzaniga's credentials:

Professor Gazzaniga is the Andrew W. Thompson Jr. Professor of Psychiatry (Neuroscience) at Dartmouth Medical School. He is editor-in-

---

*In fairness, I should point out that Mr. Buckley is not a fan of my assertion that all laws against consensual activities should be repealed. He was kind enough to read the "An Overview" chapter of this book prior to publication and give me his comments. After reading his opinion, I began my reply with the punch line of an old joke: "Other than that, Mrs. Lincoln, how did you like the play?"

chief of the *Journal of Cognitive Neuroscience* (MIT Press) and his most recent book is *Mind Matters* (Houghton Mifflin, 1988).

BUCKLEY: It is said that the drug crack is substantively different from its parent drug, cocaine, in that it is, to use the term of Professor van den Haag, "crimogenic." In other words a certain (unspecified) percentage of those who take crack are prompted to—well, to go out and commit mayhem of some kind. Is that correct?

> *Our laws are telling people,*
> *"If you're concerned*
> *about getting caught,*
> *don't use marijuana,*
> *use cocaine."*
> *Well, that is not necessarily*
> *what people want to do.*
>
> JUDGE JAMES GRAY

GAZZANIGA: No, not in the way you put it. What you are asking is: Is there something about how crack acts on the brain that makes people who take it likelier to commit crime?

Let's begin by making it clear what crack is. It is simply cocaine that has been mixed with baking soda, water, and then boiled. What this procedure does is to permit cocaine to be smoked. Now any drug ingested in that way—i.e., absorbed by the lungs—goes more efficiently to the brain, and the result is a quicker, more intense experience. That is what crack gives the consumer. But its impact on the brain is the same as with plain cocaine and, as a matter of fact, amphetamines. No one has ever maintained that these drugs are "crimogenic."

The only study I know about that inquires into the question of crack breeding crime reports that most homicides involving crack were the result not of the use of crack, but of dealer disputes. Crack did not induce users to commit crimes. Do some crack users commit crimes? Of course. After all, involvement in proscribed drug traffic is dangerous. Moreover, people who commit crimes tend to use drugs at a high rate, though which drug they prefer varies from one year to the next.

BUCKLEY: You are telling us that an increase in the use of crack would not mean an increase in crime?

GAZZANIGA: I am saying that what increase there would be in crime would not be simply the result of the pharmacology of that drug. Look, let's say there are 200,000 users/abusers of crack in New York City—a number that reflects one of the current estimates. If so, and if the drug produced violent tendencies in all crack users, the health-care system would have to come to a screeching halt. It hasn't. In fact, in 1988 the hospitals in New York City (the crack capital of the world) averaged only seven crack-related admissions, city-wide, a day. The perception of crack-based misbehavior is ex-aggerated because it is the cases that show up in the emergency rooms that receive public notice, and the whole picture begins to look very bleak. All of this is to say: when considering any aspect of the drug problem, keep in mind the matter of selection of the evidence.

It is prudent to recall that, in the past, dangerous and criminal behavior has been said to have been generated by other drugs, for instance marijuana (you remember *Reefer Madness?*). And bear it in mind that since cocaine is available everywhere, so is crack available everywhere, since the means of converting the one into the other are easy, and easily learned. It is important to note that only a small percentage of cocaine users actually convert their stuff to crack. Roughly one in six.

BUCKLEY: Then would it follow that even if there were an increase in the use of crack, the legalization of it would actually result in a de-crease in crime?

GAZZANIGA: That is correct.

BUCKLEY: Isn't crack a drug whose addictive power exceeds that of many other drugs? If that is the case, one assumes that people who opt to take crack do so because it yields the faster and more exhilarating satisfactions to which you make reference.

GAZZANIGA: That is certainly the current understanding, but there are no solid data on the question. Current observations are confounded by certain economic variables. Crack is cheap—

BUCKLEY: Why? If cocaine is expensive, how can crack be cheap?

GAZZANIGA: Cocaine costs $1,000 per ounce if bought in quantity. One ounce can produce one thousand vials of crack, each of which sells for

$5. The drug abuser is able to experience more drug episodes. Crack being cheap, the next high can come a lot more quickly and since there is a down to every up, or high, the cycle can become intense.

So yes, crack is addictive. So is cocaine. So are amphetamines. The special punch of crack, as the result of going quickly via the lungs to the brain, may prompt some abusers to want more. By the way, it is the public knowledge that crack acts in this way that, as several studies document, causes most regular cocaine users to be cautious about crack. The casual-to-moderate user very clearly wants to stay in that category. So, all you can say is that there is a *perception,* widely shared, that crack is more addictive. Whether it is, isn't really known. One thing we do know is that crack does not begin to approach tobacco as a nationwide health hazard. For every crack-related death, there are three hundred tobacco-related deaths.

> *The number of teenagers "huffing" or inhaling household products is reportedly higher than the number abusing cocaine.*
>
> NATIONAL INSTITUTE ON DRUG ABUSE

Another example of hyperbole is the recent claim that there were 375,000 "crack babies" born last year; how could that possibly be, when the government (the National Institutes on Drug Abuse) informs us that there were only 500,000 crack *users* last year? Exaggeration and misinformation run rampant on this subject.

BUCKLEY: Well, if crack were legally available alongside cocaine and, say, marijuana, what would be the reason for a consumer to take crack?

GAZZANIGA: You need to keep your drug classifications straight. If your goal were, pure and simple, to get high, you might try crack or cocaine, or some amphetamine. You wouldn't go for marijuana, which is a mild hallucinogen and tranquilizer. So, if you wanted to be up and you didn't have much time, you might go to crack. But then if it were absolutely established that there was a higher addiction rate with crack, legalization could, paradoxically, diminish its use. This is so because if cocaine were reduced to the same price as crack, the abuser, acknowledging the higher rate of addiction, might forgo the more intensive high of crack, opting for the slower high of cocaine. Crack was introduced years ago as offering an alluring new psycho active experience. But its special hold on the ghetto is the result of its price. Remember that—on another front—we know that 120-proof alcohol doesn't sell as readily as 86 proof, not by a long shot, even though the higher the proof, the faster the psychological effect that alcohol users are seeking.

BUCKLEY: Is there evidence that the current consumption of drugs is restrained by their illegality? We have read that ninety million Americans have experimented, at one time or another, with illegal drugs. Would more than ninety million have experimented with them if drugs had been legal?

GAZZANIGA: I think illegality has little if anything to do with drug consumption—and, incidentally, I am certain that far more than ninety million Americans have at some point or other experimented with an illegal drug.

This gets to the issue of actual availability. Drugs are everywhere, simply everywhere. In terms of availability, drugs might just as well be legal as illegal. Now it has been argued that legalization will create a different social climate, a more permissive, more indulgent climate. It is certainly conceivable, primarily for that reason, that there would be greater initial use—the result of curiosity. But the central point is that human beings in all cultures tend to seek out means of altering their mental state, and that although some will shop around and lose the powers of self-discipline, most will settle down to a base rate of use, and a much smaller rate of abuse, and those rates are pretty much what we have in the United States right now.

BUCKLEY: Then the factor of illegality, in your opinion, does not weigh heavily? But, we come to the critical question, if ninety million (or more) Americans have experimented with the use of drugs, why is drug abuse at such a (relatively) low level?

GAZZANIGA: If you exclude tobacco, in the whole nation less than 10 per cent of the adult population abuses drugs. That is, 9 to 12 million adult Americans abuse drugs. That figure includes alcohol, by the way, and the figure remains fairly constant.

Consider alcohol. In our culture alone, 70 to 80 per cent of us use alcohol, and the abuse rate is now estimated at 5 to 6 per cent. We see at work here a major feature of the human response to drug availability, namely, the inclination to moderation. Most people are adjusted and are intent on living productive lives. While most of us, pursuing that goal, enjoy the sensations of euphoria, or anxiety reduction, or (at times) social dis-inhibition or even anesthesia, we don't let the desire for these sensations dominate our behavior. Alcohol fills these needs for many people and its use is managed intelligently.

> *We're in a war.*
> *People who blast some pot*
> *on a casual basis*
> *are guilty of treason.*
>
> DARYL GATES
> Los Angeles Police Chief

It is worth noting that the largest proportion of this drug is sold to the social drinker, not the drunk, just as most cocaine is sold to the casual user, not the addict. Now, early exposure to alcohol is common and inevitable, and youthful drinking can be extreme. Yet studies have shown that it is difficult to determine which drunk at the college party will evolve into a serious alcoholic. What is known is that the vast majority of early drinkers stop excessive drinking all by themselves. In fact, drug use of all types drops off radically with age.

BUCKLEY: Wait a minute. Are you telling us that there is only a 10 per cent chance that any user will become addicted to a drug, having experimented with it?

GAZZANIGA: The 10 per cent figure includes all drugs except tobacco. The actual risk for abuse of some drugs is much lower. Consider last year's National Household Survey (NHS) which was carried out by the National Institutes on Drug Abuse. It is estimated that some 21 million people tried cocaine in 1988. But according to the NHS only three million defined themselves as having used the drug at least once during the month preceding their interview. Most of the three million were casual users. Now think about it. *All* the cocaine users make up 2 per cent of the adult population, and the addicts make up less than one-

> *No major American decision was ever made without the influence of alcohol, nicotine, caffeine— often all three.*
>
> NOTE ON BULLETIN BOARD

quarter of 1 per cent of the total population. These are the government's own figures. Does that sound like an epidemic to you?

BUCKLEY: But surely an epidemic has to do with the rate at which an undesirable occurrence is increasing. How many more cocaine users were there than the year before? Or the year before that?

GAZZANIGA: The real question is whether or not more and more Americans are becoming addicted to something. Is the rate of addiction to psycho active substances going up? The answer to that is a flat no. Are there fads during which one drug becomes more popular than another as the drug of abuse? Sure. But, when one drug goes up in consumption, others go down. Heroin use is down, and so is marijuana use. That is why the opiate and marijuana pushers are trying to prove their purity—so they can grab back some of their market share, which apparently they have done for heroin in New York City.

But having said that, you should know that the actual use of cocaine and all other illicit drugs is on the decline, according to the NHS. The just-published National High School Survey carried out by the University of Michigan reports that the same is true among high-school students. Crack is used at such a low rate throughout the country that its use can hardly be measured in most areas.

BUCKLEY: Well, if a low addiction rate is the rule, how do we come to terms with the assertion, which has been made in reputable circles, that over 40 per cent of Americans fighting in Vietnam were using heroin and 80 per cent marijuana?

GAZZANIGA: Stressful situations provoke a greater use of drugs. Vietnam was one of them. But what happens when the soldiers come home?

That point was examined in a large study by Dr. Lee Robbins at Washington University. During the Vietnam War, President Nixon ordered a study on the returning vets who seemed to have a drug problem.

(Nixon didn't know what he was looking for, but he was getting a lot of flak on the point that the war was producing a generation of drug addicts.) Dr. Robbins chose to study those soldiers returning to the United States in 1971. Of the 13,760 Army enlisted men who returned and were included in her sample, 1,400 had a positive urine test for drugs (narcotics, amphetamines, or barbiturates). She was able to re-test 495 men from this sample a few months later. The results were crystal clear: Only 8 per cent of the men who had been drug positive in their first urine test remained so. In short, over 90 per cent of them, now that they were back home, walked away from drug use. And all of them knew how to get hold of drugs, if they had wanted them. Incidentally, Dr. Robbins did a follow-up study a couple of years later on the same soldiers. She reported there had not been an increase in drug use.

> *As a first-time drug law offender, I was sentenced to 27 non-parolable years in prison. The amount of time was based on liquid waste found in the garage and unprocessed chemicals. There were no drugs.*
>
> DAVID A. NICHOLS
> May 29, 1993

BUCKLEY: Aha! You are saying that under special circumstances, the use of drugs increases. Well, granted there was stress in Vietnam. Isn't there stress also in American ghettos?

GAZZANIGA: If you live in poverty and frustration, and see few rewards available to you, you are likelier than your better-satisfied counterpart to seek the escape of drugs, although the higher rate of consumption does not result in a higher rate of addiction. Virtually every study finds this to be the case with one possibly interesting twist. A recent Department of Defense study showed that drug use in the military was lower for blacks than for whites, the reverse of civilian life. (It is generally agreed that the military is the only institution in our country that is successfully integrated.) In short, environmental factors play an important role in the incidence of drug use.

BUCKLEY: So you are saying that there are social circumstances that will raise the rate of consumption, but that raising the rate of consumption doesn't in fact raise the rate of addiction. In other words, if 50 per cent of the troops in Vietnam had been using crack, this would not have affected the rate at which, on returning to the United States, they became addicted. They would have kicked the habit on reaching home?

GAZZANIGA: That's the idea. Drug consumption can go up in a particular population, fueled by stress, but the rate of addiction doesn't go up no matter what the degree of stress. Most people can walk away from high drug use if their lives become more normal. Of course, the stress of the ghetto isn't the only situation that fuels high drug consumption. Plenty of affluent people who for some reason or another do not find their lives rewarding also escape into drugs.

BUCKLEY: If it is true, then, that only a small percentage of those who take crack will end up addicted, and that that is no different from the small percentage who, taking one beer every Saturday night, will become alcoholics, what is the correct way in which to describe the relative intensity of the addictive element in a particular drug?

GAZZANIGA: That is an interesting question and one that can't satisfactorily be answered until much more research is done. There are conundrums. Again, it is estimated that 21 million people tried cocaine in 1988. Yet, of those, only 3 million currently use it, and only a small percentage are addicted. As for crack, it is estimated that 2.5 million have used it, while only a half million say they still do, and *that* figure includes the addicted and the casual user. Some reports claim that as many as one half of crack users are addicted. As I have said, crack is cheap, and for that reason may be especially attractive to the poor. That is a non-pharmacological, non-biological factor, the weight of which we have not come to any conclusions about. We don't even have reliable data to tell us that crack creates a greater rate of addiction than, say, cocaine. My own guess is it doesn't. Remember that the drug acts on the same brain systems that cocaine and amphetamines do.

BUCKLEY: To what extent is the addictive factor affected by education? Here is what I mean by this: Taking a drug, say heroin or cocaine or crack—or, for that matter, alcohol—is a form of Russian roulette, using a ten-cartridge revolver. Now, presumably, an educated person, concerned for his livelihood, wouldn't take a revolver with nine empty cartridges and one full cartridge, aim it at his head, and pull the trigger. But granted, decisions of that kind are based on ratiocinative skills. And we have to assume these skills don't exist even among college students. If they did, there would be no drinking in college, let alone drug taking. Comments?

> *Nothing will ever be attempted
> if all possible objections
> must be first overcome.*
>
> DR. SAMUEL JOHNSON

GAZZANIGA: Most people perceive themselves as in control of their destiny. They do not think the initial exposure will ruin their lives, because of their perceived self-control, and they are right. Take the most difficult case, tobacco—the most highly addictive substance around. In a now classic study, Stanley Schachter of Columbia University formally surveyed his highly educated colleagues at Columbia. At the same time, he polled the working residents of Amagansett, a community on Long Island where he summered. He first determined who were ongoing smokers, and who had been smokers. He took into account how long they had smoked, what they had smoked, and all other variables he could think of.

It wasn't long before the picture began to crystallize. Inform a normally intelligent group of people about the tangible hazards of using a particular substance and the vast majority of them simply stop. It wasn't easy for some, but in general they stopped, and they didn't need treatment programs, support programs, and all the rest. Dr. Schachter concluded, after this study, that it is only the thorny cases that show up at the treatment centers, people who have developed a true addiction. For those people, psychological prophylactics, including education, are of little or no value. Yet it is these people that are held up as examples of what happens when one uses drugs. This is misleading. It creates an unworkable framework for thinking about the problem. Most people can voluntarily stop using a psycho active substance, and those people who do continue to use it can moderate their intake to reduce the possibility of health hazards. This is true, as I say, for most substances, but I repeat, less true for tobacco because of its distinctively addictive nature. The people who unwisely continue to use tobacco tend to smoke themselves into major illness even though they are amply warned that this is likely to happen.

BUCKLEY: So no matter how widely you spread the message, it is in fact going to be ignored, both by Ph.D.s and by illiterates?

GAZZANIGA: If they are real abusers, yes. That is the reason for the high recidivism rate among graduates of drug treatment centers. Here we are talking about the true addicts. Education appears not to help the recalcitrant abusers, who are the ones that keep showing up at health centers.

Yet, manifestly, education contributes to keeping the abuse rate as low as it is. I think the message gets to the ghetto, but where there are other problems—the need for an artificial reward—drugs are going to be taken by many people because the excruciating pain of a current condition overrides long-term reason. In short, the ghetto citizen or the psychologically isolated person might well decide that the probability of living a better life is low, so grab some rewards while you can.

BUCKLEY: In that case, education, even in the popular media, is likely to influence primarily the educated classes. That has to mean that the uneducated class will suffer more addiction than the educated class.

GAZZANIGA: Well, again, people in the lowest socio-economic status will continue to consume more drugs, but that doesn't change the addiction rate. Still, legalization shouldn't change the current figures, since drugs are literally available everywhere in the ghetto. They are also available on every college campus. They are available in prisons! I suppose if one wants to conjure up fresh problems brought on by legalization, they will center on the folks living on Park Avenue, where drugs are less easily secured, not the ghetto. Legalization of drugs would reduce crime in the ghetto, and much that is positive would follow. The vast majority of the crime network ought to crumble. The importance of that cannot be underestimated.

BUCKLEY: What would be your prediction, as a scientist, of what the advent of [drugs sold legally and without prescription to adults in a kind of] Federal Drugstore, combined with a program of intensified education, would accomplish in the next ten years?

> *Adulation is all right if you don't inhale.*
>
> ADLAI STEVENSON

GAZZANIGA: Drug-consumption rates will bounce around, related as they are to environmental factors, fads, and a host of other factors. Drug-abuse rates will not change much, if at all. Yet many of the negative social consequences of keeping drugs illegal will be neutralized. The health costs of drug abuse will always be with us. We should try to focus on those problems with more serious neurobiologic and neurobehavioral research and help where we can to reduce the percentage that fall victim. I am an experimental scientist, and like most people can see that the present system doesn't work. We need to try another approach. If, for whatever reason, legalization doesn't improve the situation, it would take five minutes to reverse it.

Thank you, Mr. B. and Professor G. Good conversation: what a drug.

I close this chapter with this quote from the National Institute of Justice, from a program sponsored by the Police Foundation:

> The goal of legalizing drugs is to bring them under effective legal control. If it were legal to produce and distribute drugs, legitimate businessmen would enter the business. There would be less need for violence and corruption since the industry would have access to the courts. And, instead of absorbing tax dollars as targets of expensive enforcement efforts, the drug sellers might be-

gin to pay taxes. So, legalization might well solve the organized crime aspects of the drug trafficking problem.

On average, drug use under legalization might not be as destructive to users and to society as under the current prohibition, because drugs would be less expensive, purer, and more conveniently available.

> *The trouble with most folks isn't so much their ignorance, as knowing so many things that ain't so.*
>
> JOSH BILLINGS

Religious and Psychologically Therapeutic Use of Drugs

*I have sworn upon the altar of God
eternal hostility
against every form of tyranny
over the mind of man.*

THOMAS JEFFERSON

LONG, LONG BEFORE the white man traveled on hempen sails to find religious freedom in a New World, the natives on a land now called North America used sacramental plants to commune with nature, the universal brotherhood, and the Great Spirit.

The Incas chewed coca leaves, but only for spiritual purposes and only with the permission of their spiritual leader, the Inca. The conquistadors from Spain turned what was once a sacrament into a reward for work and, later, a stimulant for the energy to do more work. Changing the purpose and use of coca leaves was but one part of the European destruction of a great civilization.

Indigenous tribes throughout North America ate the buds of the peyote cactus as an expression of thanksgiving, a request for guidance, or in support of a brother who wanted to give thanks or seek direction. Peyote was always used in a formal, ceremonial way, and "recreational" use was considered a sacrilege. It took the white man—who knew or cared so little about the Native American way—until 1899 to find out what was going on and, of course, make it illegal. Oklahoma passed a law against peyote in 1899; New Mexico outlawed it in 1929. Not until the 1960s, when a sufficient number of white people began seeking mystical experience, was peyote considered "a menace" that had to be controlled nationally.

⚖ ⚖ ⚖

> *We are not clear as to*
> *the role in life of these chemicals;*
> *nor are we clear as to*
> *the role of the physician.*
> *You know, of course,*
> *that in ancient times there was*
> *no clear distinction between*
> *priest and physician.*
>
> ALAN WATTS

Humans have always sought ways to alter everyday consciousness. This is usually achieved either through changes in normal behavior, or by ingesting a consciousness-altering substance.

We "civilized" types—descendants of the primitive Native Americans' conquerors—have a strong bias that religious experiences should be obtained through *altered action* rather than *sacramental ingestion*. Prayer, fasting, penance, and personal sacrifice are all acceptable forms of achieving greater connection with God and Spirit. Ingesting chemicals, sacramental plants, or other consciousness-altering substances is not.

What we are aware of and that we are aware at all is due to a complex biochemical-electrical process in the human nervous system. A slight alteration creates a shift in consciousness. Any number of stimuli can trigger the chemical-electrical shift that leads to the change in consciousness.

All the "acceptable" techniques for achieving religious experiences involve chemical change. Prayer is changing one's focus—altering what one is thinking. Fasting causes a significant biochemical change. Even the "born again" experience as practiced by many churches is based on psychological pressure ("You are a sinner and you will spend all eternity in hell") and release ("Accept Jesus and you will spend all eternity in paradise"), which produces profound biochemical change.

When we have a shift in consciousness, our belief determines whether or not the shift is perceived as a religious experience. If we connect a certain positive feeling with God, each time we have that feeling we think of God. If we attach that same pleasant feeling to our spouse, each time we feel that feeling, we will think of our spouse. If we attach the same feeling to our favorite television program, each time we feel that feeling, we will think of our favorite television program, and so on.

A change of consciousness is an experience. If we choose to give that experience religious meaning, it becomes a religious experience. If we choose to associate it with someone we are in love with, it becomes a romantic experience. If we choose to associate it with our favorite television show, it becomes a video experience. We could even choose to associate it with something wicked and evil ("This is the devil tempting me" or "I'm having a psychotic episode"), and the same experience becomes a negative one.

> It is well for people who think
> to change their minds occasionally
> in order to keep them clean.
> For those who do not think,
> it is best at least to rearrange
> their prejudices once in a while.
>
> LUTHER BURBANK

⚖ ⚖ ⚖

It takes very little chemical change to bring about a profound shift in consciousness. LSD, for example, is not measured in *milligrams,* or thousandths of a gram, but in *micrograms*—millionths of a gram. As few as 25 micrograms—that is, twenty-five millionths of a gram—can bring about a profound change in consciousness that lasts many hours. After Dr. Albert Hofmann accidentally ingested LSD on April 16, 1943, he described his experiences :

> I was seized with a feeling of great restlessness and mild dizziness. At home, I lay down and sank into a not unpleasant delirium, which was characterized by extremely excited fantasies. In a semiconscious state, with my eyes closed (I felt the daylight to be unpleasantly dazzling), fantastic visions of extraordinary realness and with an intense kaleidoscopic play of colors. After about two hours this condition disappeared.

> *Every happening,*
> *great and small,*
> *is a parable*
> *whereby God speaks to us,*
> *and the art of life*
> *is to get the message.*
>
> MALCOLM MUGGERIDGE

Note that there's not much talk about God in there. In fact, at first psychiatrists thought the LSD experience closely resembled the delirium of extreme schizophrenia and explained, perhaps, the paintings of Vincent van Gogh. He was not interpreting those swirling sunflowers and "turbulent indigo" (Joni Mitchell's phrase) skies—he was painting what he saw. LSD, it was thought, should be taken by therapists to better understand the working of the schizophrenic mind, or by architects so that they might better design mental institutions to be healing and comforting places from an "insane" person's point of view.

Others thought LSD would be useful in therapy because it produced such a pronounced shift from ordinary consciousness. If insane people could be sufficiently jarred from their insanity—even for a brief period of time—perhaps their reality could be restructured, through therapy, into a healthier pattern.

Still others—such as author Aldous Huxley and Harvard professors Timothy Leary and Richard Alpert—thought that LSD opened the "doors of perception" (as Huxley called it) through which human consciousness could glimpse mystical visions. They maintain that LSD opened the consciousness through which all the great spiritual teachers—Moses, Buddha, Zoroaster, Krishna, Jesus, Mohammed, and others—had their insights and revelations.

Some thought LSD produced psychoses; others thought it produced enlightenment. How people approached the experience significantly influenced the results of the experience.

Those who took LSD thinking it was going to simulate schizophrenia left the LSD experience thinking, "Oh, that's what it's like to be crazy." Many who took LSD expecting mystical revelation got mystical revelation.

In the 1960s and early 1970s, hundreds of thousands—perhaps millions—accepted the Huxley-Leary-Alpert interpretation of LSD and, for the most part, had experiences they would describe as spiritual.

The "set and setting" was vitally important. The *set* was the mind-set: One had to ask oneself, "Am I taking part in this experience for kicks or for illumination?" The latter was recommended. The *setting* was the environment in which you took LSD, whom you were taking it with, what physical activities were planned: music, silence, readings aloud from the New Testament or the *Tibetan Book of the Dead.* In properly planned sessions one had a *guide* who had had the experience before, to provide safety, support, and encouragement.

Less than ten years later, by the mid-1970s, people were "dropping acid" on the way to the disco. "The Bee Gees! Jesus!" the psychedelic old-timers would lament. "What happened to the *Beatles?* And why are they going to a *disco?* If they want to go out, why don't they go to a *real* religious experience—like seeing *2001: A Space Odyssey* in Cinerama?"

Soon "acid" became synonymous with any orally ingested consciousness-altering substance: tranquilizers, strychnine, it didn't matter. People were looking for a "trip," not a journey; a "high," not a higher state of consciousness.

Some of the original "mystical" LSD takers went on to explore God in more traditional ways: LSD was advertised as only one door to the house of perception; how you moved in was up to you. Richard Alpert took an ancient route, went to India, and became Ram Dass. Timothy Leary took the techno route and became fascinated with space travel, computers, and cyberspace. Whatever the outcome, LSD was a bright flash between the black

> *Not a shred of evidence exists in favor of the idea that life is serious.*
>
> BRENDAN GILL

> WOMAN:
> *Thank you for saving the world!*
>
> HENRY KISSINGER:
> *You're welcome.*

and white '50s and the technicolor '70s. What people did with that flash was and is entirely up to them.

⚖ ⚖ ⚖

Throughout history, humans have sought the tree of life. People have tried to "return to the garden" by ingesting substances from the plant, mineral, and animal kingdoms. Some worked; most didn't.*

Alas, in our country today sincere seekers cannot seek in this way. They are entitled to use the traditional methods as much as they please—but only those tried and accepted by "our Judeo-Christian forefathers." People can pray, fast, join a monastery or convent, become missionaries, and that's okay. Changing consciousness through external actions that produce internal chemical reactions is acceptable. Ingesting chemicals is not. If you do, you are not taking part in a sacrament, but committing a sacrilege. You will be punished for it not only in the hereafter, but here.

We'll explore further the absurdity of jailing people for religious beliefs in the chapter, "Unconventional Religious Practices." The point of this chapter is: although ingesting chemicals may not be part of the Judeo-Christian tradition, it certainly has a long and dignified history in the human tradition. To deny Americans—native or immigrant—the right to explore chemical sacraments is not only an interference with our religious freedom, but yet another example of imposing Judeo-Christian religious beliefs on others by force of law.

⚖ ⚖ ⚖

*Many of these worldwide explorations—past and present—are described in Terence McKenna's book, *Food of the Gods*. (Not to be confused with a Greek cookbook by the same name.)

An understandably quiet movement of sincere, well-educated ("they have more degrees than a protractor," comments the *Los Angeles Times*) individuals is exploring anew the value of psychedelics. Today the "mind expanding" chemicals are often referred to as *empathogens* (empathy producing) or *entheogens* (become one with *theos,* God).

> *If you surveyed a hundred typical middle-aged Americans, I bet you'd find that only two of them could tell you their blood types, but every last one of them would know the theme song from "The Beverly Hillbillies."*
>
> DAVE BARRY

And—shock and joy—the FDA is giving begrudging approval to limited research.

"We're like early man who says fire is too dangerous," says Rick Doblin, Harvard-trained social scientist and spokesperson for the Multidisciplinary Association for Psychedelic Studies. "We're not even at the stage where we've figured out that fire can keep you warm in winter." MAPS is a nonprofit group that tracks the handful of approved psychedelic research projects throughout the United States.

The preliminary research has been encouraging, especially when empathetic chemicals are used in conjunction with the therapeutic process. "Psychotherapy is enhanced by an altered-state experience," said Charles S. Grob, M.D., one of the lead researchers of MDMA ("ecstasy") use in therapy. In other studies, using chemicals such as MDMA, MDA, and LSD has resulted in significant progress treating recidivism, sexual dysfunction, depression, and addiction, among many others.

Of course, even these token research programs are under fire and, by the time you read this, may have been halted altogether by ignorance and misplaced grief. One of the primary organizations challenging any research is Drug Watch International. This was formed by Dr. William Bennett (not the former Drug Czar turned bestselling pontiff on morality, but another one—how many can we take?) and his wife, Sandra, after "losing our son to cocaine in 1986."

> *They hated me without reason.*
>
> JESUS OF NAZARETH
> John 15:25

This sort of kill-the-messenger response was echoed by actor Carrol O'Connor, who, in his grief following the suicide of his son, blamed it all on his son's drug dealer, who was promptly arrested. The fact that O'Connor's son killed himself after being out of work for a year and after spending his third wedding anniversary alone was not mentioned. (The dealer was sentenced to a year in prison.)

How does one explain to a parent grieving for a lost child that putting other parents' children in prison is not the solution? No one, apparently, has found the way to communicate this to the Bennetts. "Illicit drugs are illicit because they're harmful," they claim in circular, ignorance-perpetuating logic.

In fact, research has shown drugs in general and psychedelics in particular to be far less harmful than formerly feared. In 1995, UCLA's Ronald K. Siegel, one of the few researchers permitted to perform scientific studies on LSD after the blanket governmental ban in 1970, reported,

> Dangers [of psychedelics] are not as great as the public was led to believe in the '60's. Risks of brain damage and schizophrenia have been discounted. Most psychedelics are stimulants, and like any stimulant, they can be harmful to those with high blood pressure and heart conditions.

Meanwhile, a much larger group of individualists—just as sincere but lacking governmental sanction—explore their psyches, their world, their loved ones, their lives, and their God with entheogens. For many, LSD, due to its sometimes tedious "electric" qualities, has been replaced with psilocybin ("mushrooms"), MDMA, and MDA.

MDMA was first synthesized in 1912. In the early 1980s, it was rediscovered and named ecstasy. "I wanted to call it *empathy*," its rediscoverer said, "but I thought *ecstasy* would sell better." It did—perhaps too much better. It was banned in 1986, when after enthusiastic articles in (among other publications) *The Wall Street Journal, Time,* and *Newsweek*—a bureaucrat in Washington decided it should be banned.

> *Instant gratification takes too long.*
>
> CARRIE FISHER

MDA, a naturally occurring chemical with empathetic effects similar to MDMA, is found in more than seventy plants as well the human brain. When the chemicals the body produces to suppress the effects of MDA are suppressed, small doses of MDA can produce powerful results. "The heart opens," one psychiatrist explained in nonpsychiatric terms.

While MDMA is still illegal, the plants containing MDA are not. (Think they'll ever get around to banning nutmeg, green tea, or the kola nut?) These plants are sold by various companies* working entirely within the law.

For the most part, these enthogens are taken not as a high, but as a sacrament—a sacrament not to meant placate a venge-

---

*One sells a combination of herbs and such in capsule form and calls it Ecstasy. Considering its product, the company is oddly called Global World Media Corporation (800–940–9292). Another company, Of The Jungle, has a catalog featuring "exotic ethnobotanical products, extracts, rare medicinal herbs, oils, tropical plants & seeds." The catalog is $2 and available from P.O. Box 1801, Sebastopol, CA 95473. For everything you wanted to know about entheogenic plants—including chemical content, drawings, and other elaborate details—read *Ayahuasca Analogues* by Jonathon Ott, from Jonathan Ott Books, P.O. Box 1251, Occidental, CA 95465. Ott's *Pharmacotheon* is a brilliant compendium of knowledge, as is the Psychedelics Encyclopedia, Ronin Publishing, Box 1035, Berkeley, CA 94701.

ful God "out there," but to celebrate the essence of God within us all. From the standpoint of some Christians, who believe this life is to be suffered through and pleasure should only be found in paradise, it seems the pagans have returned again, their "Devil's Mass" in tow.

For the Glory of God, they must be forbidden to practice such hedonistic sacrileges so. If they do, they must be punished. Severely. Here on earth. Now.

> *The big thieves*
> *hang the little ones.*
>
> CZECH PROVERB

Regenerative Use of Drugs and Other Unorthodox Medical Practices

HOW CAN SOMETHING start out so good and become so bad? That's the question I ask myself each time I think about the Food and Drug Administration (FDA). It began as a good idea, designed to educate and protect the citizens of the United States. Now it regularly raids alternative healers, keeps healing and rejuvenative drugs away from those who might benefit from them, dictates what is and is not proper healing, and wants to severely limit our ability to buy vitamins, minerals, and other nutritional supplements. The FDA has, like Dr. Frankenstein's experiment, gone awry.

In the early 1900s, prepared foods and packaged medicines were a mess. As Upton Sinclair described in *The Jungle,* his 1906 exposé of the meatpacking industry, meatpackers would pack anything into skins—sawdust, rat droppings, the digestive tracts of animals and all that they contained—and sell it as "pure beef sausage." One could never be sure if a quart of beef stew contained an entire quart of beef stew—or even if it contained beef. Over-the-counter "patent" medicines did not list ingredients or strength of concentration on the label. Or they might claim to contain medicines and be nothing but sugar-water in an imposing bottle.

Normally, it would be left to the states to regulate food and drugs through local health codes, honest-weight restrictions, and other regulatory laws. With improvements in packaging, trans-

> *Sailing round the world*
> *in a dirty gondola*
> *Oh, to be back in the land*
> *of Coca-Cola!*
>
> BOB DYLAN

portation, and marketing, however, by the turn of the century many products were traveling across state lines. This brought them under the jurisdiction of the federal government: regulation of interstate commerce was one of the powers enumerated to Congress.

In 1906, Congress passed the Pure Food and Drug Act, which established that foods and drugs should be "unadulterated," and that their contents be clearly labeled. This was a much-needed regulation. The act, however, had this little loophole: What is "adulterated" and who decides what is adulterated?

Ironically, according to the book, *The Big Drink: The Story of Coca-Cola* by E. J. Kahn, Coca-Cola was taken to court by the government for marketing a "mislabled" product. In 1903, Coca-Cola had replaced "the real thing," cocaine, with caffeine (it was cheaper). Coca-Cola was in trouble not because it contained cocaine, but because it *didn't*. The case continued in court for nine years, and Coca-Cola eventually agreed to make changes in its manufacturing process and to list its ingredients—which included neither coca nor kola.

In 1927, the enforcement of the law moved from the Bureau of Chemistry (a division of the Department of Agriculture) into its own bureaucratic structure: the Food, Drug, and Insecticide Administration—a formidable, respectable name if there ever was one. Not surprisingly, in 1931 it dropped the Insecticide from its title and became the Food and Drug Administration.

The FDA was then given the power to ban "harmful" additives. By what criteria do we define "harmful"? If a chemical has a known lethal dose, should it be prohibited? If that were the case, salt could never be used as an additive. For the most part, whatever the FDA decided was harmful was harmful. The deci-

AIN'T NOBODY'S BUSINESS IF YOU DO

sions were (and are) capricious at best.

Over time, the FDA also grew to encompass regulation over all medical techniques, practices, and devices. The original Pure Food and Drug Act (also known as the "Wiley Act") only required that food not be "adulterated" or "misbranded" when shipped across state lines. In 1912,

> *Despite the belief that handwashing is the most important measure to prevent the spread of infection in hospitals, less than one third of physicians wash their hands between patients.*
>
> THE AMERICAN HOSPITAL ASSOCIATION
> 1992

the act was amended to prohibit false therapeutic claims. The problem with that is the same as determining what is "harmful": Who is to say what is and is not therapeutic?

For example, the placebo effect is a scientifically proven fact: if people take an absolutely worthless substance and believe it's going to make them better, it tends to make about a third of the people better. Bona fide, licensed, reputable physicians use placebos every day—with the approval of both the Food and Drug Administration and the American Medical Association. The doctor will charge the full amount for an office visit, write a prescription, send the patient to a pharmacy to pay a large amount of money for sugar pills. And insurance companies knowingly and willingly pay the bills. Whether it's belief in the doctor, in the pills, in getting out of the house and paying some money, or a combination of all those factors, one thing is certain: many people who take the sugar pills get better faster than people who are told by the doctor, "There's nothing I can do about this; it will have to run its course."

And so it was with the patent medicines. If advertising copy (and patent medicines were the largest advertisers in the country at the turn of the century) could convince you that Mother's Soothing Syrup would cure your cold, for a certain number of people, the cold got cured sooner than it would absent Mother's Soothing Syrup. If the medicine didn't work, the most the government could do was require that the manufacturer issue a refund.*

The 1912 law put the burden of proof on the government: a manufacturer had to be clearly defrauding the public. This was not stringent enough, however, and in 1938 the federal Food, Drug, and Cosmetic Act was passed. Since then it has been up to the manufacturer to prove—scientifically—that its drugs are effective. Good-bye placebo effect. (For patent medicines, at least. For the AMA and "legitimate" pharmaceutical companies—*fine!*)

> *Bureaucracy,*
> *the rule of no one*
> *has become*
> *the modern form*
> *of despotism.*
>
> MARY McCARTHY

While the spirit behind strengthening the FDA was certainly a good one, the results have been anything but. Yes, we can buy foods relatively free of rat droppings (FDA guidelines restrict the *amount* of animal droppings and insect parts permitted in foods, but do not prohibit them altogether), and while it's good to know that hemorrhoid cream has actually shrunk a "hemorrhoidal tissue" here or there, much of the FDA's current activity amounts to dictating what does and does not heal people and prohibiting the latter.

Just as people should have the freedom to find and worship God as they choose, so too should they have the freedom to maintain and enhance their own health as they choose.

The FDA neither believes nor supports this contention. Only medicine as the FDA and the AMA (it's hard to tell them apart most of the time) define medicine is medicine. Everything else is *quackery.* Quackery, according to the FDA, is not just misguided medical practices that American consumers need to be educated about; quackery is fundamentally evil, and those who traffic in it—both suppliers and consumers—must be punished.

**Can you imagine what our health care system would be like if it worked on this simple principle? If you went to the doctor and didn't get cured, you wouldn't have to pay.

In some cases, the quackery of yesteryear is the sound medical practice of today; the sound medical practice of yesteryear is utter foolishness today.

George Washington, for example, was literally bled to death. It was the medical belief in Washington's day that, when ill, "pressure" had to be relieved and the "evil humors" had

> *Taking vitamin E supplements daily for at least two years appears to dramatically reduce the risk of heart disease.*
> *Separate studies of men and women who took daily vitamin E supplements had about a 40 percent lower risk of heart disease.*
>
> NEW ENGLAND JOURNAL OF MEDICINE
> May 1993

to be bled away. There's hardly a practice or procedure that was considered sound medical science 200 years ago that someone wouldn't be arrested for attempting today—and with good reason. As Thurman Arnold observed,

> The principles of Washington's farewell address are still sources of wisdom when cures for social ills are sought. The methods of Washington's physicians, however, are no longer studied.

Conversely, to suggest fifty years ago that diet, exercise, or vitamins would help prevent or cure heart disease would have been considered blatant quackery. According to medical doctors, bed rest was needed if you had a weak heart, and lots of red meat. People were arrested for suggesting that exercise, reduced meat diets, and vitamin supplements would help the heart. Now these techniques are part of standard medical practice.

All this restriction came about because the FDA took a leap that defies logic. This from the official FDA history:

> It was recognized that no drug is truly safe unless it is also effective, and effectiveness was required to be established before marketing—one of the major advances of medical history.

How can one equate *safety* with *effectiveness?* A safe drug is one I can put in my body and know that, as long as I take it in recommended doses, will not cause me to shrivel up and die. An

> *The Puritan*
> *through Life's sweet garden goes*
> *To pluck the thorn*
> *and cast away the rose.*
>
> KENNETH HARE

effective drug is something else again. Yes, if one takes an ineffective drug when one could, instead, be taking an effective drug, the illness may become worse, and this is not good. To say, however, that the ineffective drug is not safe is confusing the issue and torturing the language. Saying a drug cures something that it does not makes the manufacturer guilty of false advertising, not of marketing unsafe substances.

The most the government should be able to do is warn the consumer of the potential risks—which include the risk that the drug or medical procedure may not be effective at all. Instead of giving certain products the "FDA seal of approval," the FDA wants to remove all products that it has not approved. The FDA also wants to arrest those products' manufacturers. I shouldn't say the FDA wants to do this—it's doing it right now.

⚖ ⚖ ⚖

According to *Science* magazine, it costs, on average, $231,000,000 and takes twelve years to do the necessary testing on a drug to receive FDA approval. If difficulties arise in the testing stage, the cost can be considerably more. This sheer financial burden keeps any number of useful drugs off the market. Pharmaceutical companies often don't bother with the necessary testing on promising drugs because they doesn't feel they will make back their investments. Even if a pharmaceutical company moves full speed ahead, cures are still, for the most part, twelve years from market. The FDA guidelines are known to be so strict and so all-pervasive that clothing manufacturer Lees can say of its Relaxed Riders jeans: "If they were any more relaxing, we'd need FDA approval."

Even worse than suppressing newly discovered drugs is the fact that drugs discovered years ago will never receive FDA approval and therefore can never be marketed. Who is going to spend twelve years and $231,000,000 proving the safety and effectiveness of a drug that anyone can then manufacture? No pharmaceutical company in the known world, that's for sure.

> *In the scheme of things I'm not as important as Dr. Jonas Salk.*
>
> TOM SELLECK

These many hurdles are keeping essential drugs and treatments from the American public. Jane S. Smith observes in her 1990 book, *Patenting the Sun: Polio and the Salk Vaccine,*

> As Jonas Salk has often remarked, it would be impossible to repeat his polio work today, when such ventures need to be passed by human-subject review boards and peer review boards and various other qualifying agencies. In 1952 you got the permission of the people involved and went out and did it, and then wrote up your results in a scientific journal. If something terrible happened, the blame would be on your head and the blood on your hands, and of course your career would be over—but in the planning stages, at least, life was a great deal easier for the medical experimenter than it has since become.

By today's standards, the Salk vaccine (which was used widely starting in 1953) would not have been available until the mid-1960s—providing that Dr. Salk could have found a pharmaceutical company willing to gamble $231,000,000 on his vaccine. With current FDA guidelines, polio might be a common disease even today.

⚖ ⚖ ⚖

Imagine what the FDA would have to say about these unorthodox medical practices:

> If we are not our brother's keeper, at least let us not be his executioner.
>
> MARLON BRANDO

They came to Bethsaida, and some people brought a blind man and begged Jesus to touch him. He took the blind man by the hand and led him outside the village. When he had spit on the man's eyes and put his hands on him, Jesus asked, "Do you see anything?"

He looked up and said, "I see people; they look like trees walking around."

Once more Jesus put his hands on the man's eyes. Then his eyes were opened, his sight was restored, and he saw everything clearly. (Mark 8:22–25)

There some people brought a man to him who was deaf and could hardly talk, and they begged him to place his hand on the man.

After he took him aside, away from the crowd, Jesus put his fingers into the man's ears. Then he spit and touched the man's tongue. He looked up to heaven and with a deep sigh said to him, "Ephphatha!" (which means, "Be opened!"). At this, the man's ears were opened, his tongue was loosened and he began to speak plainly. (Mark 7:32–35)

Spitting! Can you imagine!

⚖️ ⚖️ ⚖️

As Julian Whitaker, M.D., points out:

> In medical school I was taught that the *only* tools that work to help people are drugs and surgery. In the twenty years

since then, I have seen that much of what I was taught is just plain *wrong.*

The medical establishment has been *wrong* about the big killers and cripplers like heart disease, stroke, cancer, diabetes, high blood pressure, obesity, and arthritis. *Wrong* about the origins of these diseases. And wrong about how to remedy them. Their record is shameful.

As young doctors we all take a solemn oath to uphold human life and well-being above all else. Sadly, it seems today's physicians care more about their *profession* than their *patients.*

> *Half of the modern drugs could well be thrown out of the window, except that the birds might eat them.*
>
> DR. MARTIN HENRY FISCHER

Traditional Western medicine is known as *symptomatic* medicine. It diagnoses and treats *symptoms.* This is fine—and for the elimination of certain symptoms there is nothing like symptomatic medicine. To pretend, however, that symptomatic medicine represents the full range of healing and health enhancements available is a severely limited view. In fact, the two reasons (neither of them medical) the human life span has tripled in the past 400 years are *plumbing,* which took septic waste away from homes, streets, and cities; and *transportation,* which made fresh fruits and vegetables available year-round. The majority of lives saved by modern medical science can be summed up by the Three A's: Anesthesia (which permits surgery), Antiseptics, and Antibiotics.

While symptomatic medicine is marvelous, it does not justify our current attitude, which was summed up by George Bernard Shaw: "We have not lost faith, but we have transferred it from God to the medical profession." Many of the alternative methods of obtaining, maintaining, and enhancing health should be, if not encouraged, at least not forbidden by the FDA.

⚖ ⚖ ⚖

> The first time
> I met and embraced
> Judy Garland,
> it made pharmaceutical history.
>
> OSCAR LEVANT

Not that genuine, bonafide, certified quacks don't exist. They do. But these charlatans would best be put out of business by a few civil lawsuits from disgruntled patients than from the meddling of the government, which is generally too slow to act and then overreacts.

The Food and Drug Administration is intimately connected with the American Medical Association as well as the handful of pharmaceutical companies which create and manufacture the majority of prescription drugs. Working at the FDA, being on the board of the AMA, and working for any of the large pharmaceutical companies is like playing musical chairs. The high-paying jobs—the gold ring on the merry-go-round—are at pharmaceutical companies. The best way to get a raise is to become a "public servant" for a couple of years and spend some time at the FDA or AMA.

Politicians frequently own pharmaceutical stocks. For example, when George Bush became vice-president, the *New York Times* reported, "The Vice President still owned the Eli Lilly stock upon taking office. It was his most valuable stock holding." Dan Quayle's family owns an enormous amount of stock in Eli Lilly. When Bush left the CIA in 1977, he was made the director of Eli Lilly (appointed by Dan Quayle's father), a post he held until 1979 when he began running for vice-president (with a generous campaign contribution from guess who).

While vice-president, Bush made what the *New York Times* called "an unusual move" when he "intervened with the Treasury Department in March in connection with proposed rules that would have forced pharmaceutical companies to pay significantly

AIN'T NOBODY'S BUSINESS IF YOU DO

more taxes" (*New York Times,* May 19, 1982).

Alternative healing methods directly threaten the profitable prescription drug business. Here—as with the banning of marijuana—we see not just old-time religion, but good old corporate greed as a motivating factor. To quote Dr. Whitaker again:

> *Upjohn Co., which makes Halcion, the most widely prescribed sleeping pill in America, has confirmed that it submitted incomplete data on the side effects of the controversial drug to the Food and Drug Administration when it sought approval to sell the drug here.*
>
> *THE WASHINGTON POST*

The U.S. government's recommended daily allowances (RDA) for vitamins and minerals are insufficient. Powerful food lobbies work overtime to keep these figures low. A nutrition label may proudly state it contains 100% of the RDA for Vitamin C. And since the RDA for Vitamin C is only 60 mg per day, the product looks good. But consider that some medical research puts the optimal intake of Vitamin C at 3,000 mg per day. Now, the manufacturer's claim seems ridiculous, as it contains only 2% of the optimal intake.

And now the FDA wants to limit vitamin supplements to the recommended daily allowance. Larger doses would require a doctor's prescription. This means (a) doctors will be paid to write the prescriptions and (b) only certain authorized pharmaceutical companies will be able to manufacture the pills. Is the FDA really concerned that some of us are taking too much vitamin C?

⚖ ⚖ ⚖

The FDA does not, by the way, sit quietly in Washington rubber-stamping its approval or disapproval on various proposals. It has its own army of armed agents who—augmented by state and local law enforcement authorities—make raids. For example, here is how Saul Kant, director of the Life Extension Institute, described a typical FDA raid:

> *We must free science and medicine from the grasp of politics.*
>
> PRESIDENT BILL CLINTON

On February 26, 1987, an armed force of about 25 FDA agents, U.S. marshals, and members of the Hollywood, Florida, police department smashed down the glass doors of our store at 2835 Hollywood Boulevard, and stormed into our nearby warehouse with guns drawn. As Bill Feloon, the vice president of the Foundation, was trying to leave the warehouse to find out what was going on at the building, he suddenly found himself staring down the barrel of a .45 caliber pistol, which belonged to a member of a second group of FDA agents, U.S. marshals, and police officers, who were simultaneously attacking the warehouse.

The FDA can, overnight, put a nutritional supplement manufacturer out of business.*

⚖ ⚖ ⚖

To say that the FDA sometimes overreacts is an understatement. When some truly despicable person laced Tylenol with cyanide in 1982, resulting in seven deaths, what did the FDA do? The answer you'll discover every time you open a bottle or a package of practically anything—tamper-resistant packaging. Notice it's called tamper-*resistant* packaging and not tamper-*proof* packaging. *That's because no packaging is truly tamper-proof. Any deranged person with a hypodermic needle can poison any product wrapped in plastic, paper, or cellophane. To make the food and drug supply truly tamper-proof would require metal and glass packaging for everything from candy bars to loaves of bread to boxes of cereal.*

*The Life Extension Institute is fortunately still in business. A catalog of their nutritional supplements is available by calling 214–484–7000.

Nonetheless, the FDA requires certain tamper-resistant packaging on certain consumable products. How much time do you spend each day removing tamper-resistant packaging? If it's only a minute a day, over 70 years of package opening, you will have wasted 425 hours thanks to FDA overreaction. More than 17 days (and these are

> *Allen Ginsberg said he saw the best minds of his generation destroyed by madness. I have seen the best minds of my generation go at a bottle of Anacin with a ball-peen hammer.*
>
> P. J. O'ROURKE

24-hour days) of your life will be spent complying with an FDA regulation which fails to solve a problem we no longer have.

Fortunately, whoever was insane enough to poison Tylenol in the first place stopped doing it. Voluntarily. And, thankfully, there have been few "copycat" occurrences. But this had nothing to do with tamper-resistant packaging. If some nut wants to randomly poison innocent people, he or she still can.

⚖️ ⚖️ ⚖️

It is our right to seek the health care we choose. Whether it's taking drugs not yet approved by the FDA, visiting "unorthodox" healers (from chiropractors to acupuncturists to witch doctors to faith healers to prayer therapists), purchasing health machinery (did you know you can't buy oxygen—or even plastic tubing used to transport oxygen—without a prescription?), or anything else that does not physically harm the person or property of a non-consenting other, it ain't the FDA's business if we do. (But, FDA, please keep the rat droppings and insect parts in my frozen pizzas down to an absolute minimum.)

Prostitution

LET'S FACE IT: WE'RE ALL whores. We've all done something with our bodies we wouldn't have done if we hadn't gotten paid for it. We've all worshiped at the shrine labeled "In God We Trust."

We do things every day that we wouldn't do if we had a billion dollars. When we reach the point of having so much money we no longer have to put out, we start buying. We become the procurer, the customer, the john. But please don't be upset—we're in good company:

> I'm a whore. All actors are whores. We sell our bodies to the highest bidder. —*William Holden*

> I do everything for a reason. Most of the time the reason is money.—*Suzy Parker*

> People think I sit here and push buttons and get things accomplished. Well, I spent today kissing behinds.— *Harry S. Truman*

> I did it for the loot, honey, always the loot.—*Ava Gardner*

> I went into the business for the money, and the art grew out of it. If people are disillusioned by that remark, I can't help it. It's the truth.—*Charlie Chaplin*

> I've been in trouble most of my life; I've done the most unutterable rubbish, all because of money. I didn't need it . . . the lure of the zeros was simply too great.—*Richard Burton*

> Sometimes I feel like an old hooker.—*Cher*

Sometimes at the end of the day when I'm smiling and shaking hands, I want to kick them.—*Richard Nixon*

I am never quite sure if I am one of the cinema's elder statesmen or just the oldest whore on the block.—*Joseph L. Mankiewicz*

The only reason I'm in Hollywood is that I don't have the moral courage to refuse the money.—*Marlon Brando*

I made appearances at cocktail parties in Florida for $500 a pop, pretending to be an old friend of the host.—*Mickey Rooney*

I'd love to sell out completely. It's just that nobody has been willing to buy.—*John Waters*

> *Losing my virginity was a career move.*
>
> MADONNA

I view prostitution as a purely economic exchange, inherently no more or less degrading for either buyer or seller than any other professional relationship. The same arguments against prostitution—buying or selling—could be made against any professional service: psychologist, psychiatrist, doctor, lawyer, priest, minister—you name it.

"You mean you *sell* your knowledge of God?"

"Well, not exactly, I, well . . ."

"Do you get paid for it?"

"Well, I do get a salary, yes. A small stipend."

"Do you have to do any manual labor; I mean, do you have to landscape the grounds or sweep out the church or anything?"

"No, but I do have other duties."

"Such as?"

"I counsel people, I have administrative duties in the church, I perform marriage ceremonies . . ."

"You get *paid* to officiate in the spiritual union of two human

> *After I die,*
> *I shall return to earth*
> *as a gatekeeper of a bordello*
> *and I won't let any of you enter.*
>
> ARTURO TOSCANINI
> to the NBC Orchestra

beings? Do you do anything in your job in which you are not the representative of God?"

"Well, there is the administrative work."

"Do you have training in administration?"

"No. Among my pastoral duties is running the church."

"But you don't have a degree in administration."

"No, my degree is in divinity."

"So, you sell divinity."

"Well, if you put it that way—you know, you're really distorting this whole thing."

Yes, it is a distorted way of looking at it. It is, however, the same distortion people apply to prostitution. Some people become prostitutes because they like it; others become prostitutes because they feel they are providing a service; many become prostitutes because—all things considered—it's the best job they can get.

But isn't prostitution degrading?

Other than the unjustified cultural taboos against it, prostitution is no more degrading than any other job, and, in talking with prostitutes, one discovers that many find prostitution less degrading than other jobs.

"I make good money. That's why I do it," commented one prostitute; "if I worked at McDonald's for minimum wage, then I'd feel degraded."

One of the myths about prostitution is that it is full of drugged-out, washed-out, otherwise worthless men and women. This is not the case. "I find that the women, generally, are ambitious, clever, intelligent, gregarious, and usually like people," says Margo St. James, founder of C.O.Y.O.T.E., the organization for prostitutes' rights. C.O.Y.O.T.E. stands for Call Off Your Old Tired Ethics. "The profession itself is not abusive; it's the illegality; it's the humiliation and degradation that is dealt to them at the hands of the police."

Norma Jean Almodovar agrees, and she knows whereof she speaks: Ms. Almodovar was a Los Angeles police officer for ten years and, tired of police corruption and genuinely immoral acts she was asked to condone daily, she quit and became a prostitute. If a prostitute went on to become a police officer, her prostitute friends would probably throw her a party. When a police officer became a prostitute, however, the police considered it a personal insult and felt they had to do something about it. They did. She was targeted, entrapped, and jailed. Ms. Almodovar's story is told in her 1993 book, *Cop to Call Girl: Why I Left the LAPD to Make an Honest Living as a Beverly Hills Prostitute.* In her book, she gives her views on whether or not prostitution is degrading:

> From a simple beginnin',
> just see how her sinnin' has paid.
> She's the picture of happiness
> now that she's mastered a trade.
>
> SHELDON HARNICK

> That really depends on the individual involved or how one views sex. It was not degrading to me because I think that sex is a positive, nurturing act, and whether it is given out of love or rendered as a service, as long as it is consensual it is still positive.

> On a scale of the pain or pleasure human beings can inflict on each other, if murder, rape, and torture are the worst, certainly giving another person an orgasm must be among the best. I cannot fathom how one could think that making another human being feel good for a fee could be degrading or demeaning unless it is degrading to make other people feel good.

> If the reason society continues to arrest men and women who engage in prostitution is that it is degrading, then perhaps someone could explain how going to jail, being strip-searched, checked for lice, and asked to undress in

> *Prisons are built*
> *with stones of Law,*
> *Brothels with bricks of Religion.*
>
> WILLIAM BLAKE

front of dozens of insensitive guards and inmates somehow resolves this problem. Jail and prison were degrading to me, not prostitution.

When asked if prostitution is immoral, Ms. Almodovar replied,

Morality is the belief of the person. I don't consider it immoral. Everyone who works "sells" one or more parts of his or her body. Athletes, actors, actresses, and construction workers "sell" their body. The body is what is needed to engage in physical work. It would be difficult to engage in any profession without the use and therefore "sale" of one's body.

Perhaps because the genitalia are involved, people object to prostitution. In a free country people should be able to engage in behavior that others find immoral or objectionable as long as no force or fraud is involved. As an adult I feel confident that I can make my own moral judgments. For me it is not immoral to make other people feel good in a sexual way and receive payment for providing the service.

People are often surprised to learn that many prostitutes actually enjoy their work. Like all professionals who feel they are filling a need, prostitutes can feel a profound psychological satisfaction. Here is what Barbara, a Los Angeles prostitute, had to say:

I derive a great deal of satisfaction knowing that I'm turning some guy on, more than he's ever been turned on in his life. And I know I'm turning him on more than his wife. That's not that difficult to do, because the average American housewife, from what I've been able to tell through the husband, most definitely is not very adept. Most of them have this typical Anglo-Saxon–American guilt complex, and use sex as a tool against their husbands. They definitely don't know how to give pleasure to their husband.*

> *It is a silly question to ask a prostitute why she does it. These are the highest-paid "professional" women in America.*
>
> GAIL SHEEHY

Which brings us to the question, "Why do people visit prostitutes?" First, we must accept that sex and the desire to be touched in a nurturing way are human needs, like eating. (If not a need, after enough time they're certainly high on the list of wants.)

Sex always involves some sort of exchange. Those who are attractive enough exchange their attractiveness with other people—their attractiveness is the coin with which they pay for sex. Some people have a good personality; they trade charm for sex. Others spend time with and do things for the people (or person) they have sex with. Some people exchange the exclusivity of their emotional affection, tenderness, and care. The list of what people "spend" in order to have sexual and sensual needs fulfilled goes on and on.

Those who are too busy, not very attractive, too shy, or who simply don't want to be bothered with the dating game sometimes visit prostitutes. People also visit prostitutes because they want a walk on the wild side; some have a specific sexual fantasy they would like fulfilled. (Here, I am not necessarily talking about outrageously kinky things: many men, for example, visit prostitutes simply to receive oral sex—The Hugh Grant Syndrome, Part IV.)

There is no more need to pity or censure someone who visits prostitutes than there is to pity someone who doesn't always get

---

*The same can certainly be said about men by women, which, perhaps, is the reason the number of male prostitutes is growing.

> *Remove prostitutes from human affairs, and you will destroy everything with lust.*
>
> SAINT AUGUSTINE

home-cooked meals. Perhaps the person doesn't want all that comes with home-cooked meals. Perhaps the person hasn't found someone who wants to stay home and cook his or her meals. Or perhaps the person is simply tired of home-cooked meals and wants a little variety. As Sophie Tucker explained, "All men like a little piece of mutton on the side." And a good many women, too.

Some people are hypocritical about their purchase of sex: they know their interest in another is primarily sexual and will "buy" that person with candy, flowers, dinners, shows, concerts, gifts, and, perhaps, a few words of affection. They might even pay for sex by using the magic word that flings open the portals of sexual pleasure—*love*.

People on the receiving end of this are sometimes deceived, but often they're just playing the game, too. They want the attention, flattery, companionship, presents, and experiences ("I haven't been to that new restaurant, have you?") and are willing to trade sex for those.

⚖️ ⚖️ ⚖️

There are two reasons prostitution is so despised in our culture: hatred of women and the taboos against paganism. In ancient times (pre-1985) women were valued for either domestic abilities (having children, raising children, keeping house, making clothes, cooking food) or entertainment (sex, pleasant talk, sex, dancing, sex, and sex). As women were not viewed as human beings but as necessary (and often burdensome) means to an end, a split developed—what we now call the "madonna/whore complex." A woman is either put on a pedestal, protected, taken care of, seen as "the mother of my children and the light of my life"; or she is used for sex, emotionally and perhaps physically abused, and seen as nothing more than "a slut." In the minds of many men, women must fall into one of these two categories. One seldom goes from the whore category to the madonna category, but the slide from madonna to whore (at least in the eyes of the man) is fairly common.

> *I'm a marvelous housekeeper.*
> *Every time I leave a man,*
> *I keep his house.*
>
> ZSA ZSA GABOR

In the ancient Judaic culture, for example, the only woman with independence was the prostitute. All professions were filled by men. Everything was owned by men. The only valuable commodity a woman was allowed to own was her body and her charm. Women became whores because they didn't want to prostitute themselves to one man in marriage.

What men really resented about prostitution was the woman's independence.

In pagan cultures, however, women could aspire to a parallel but very different profession: temple (or sacred) prostitute. Pagans believed that physical pleasure signified the presence of the gods. Sexual pleasure—among the greatest of physical pleasures—was one of the gods' greatest gifts. Not only was sex pleasurable, it was essential to fertility, and fertility was life. The fertile ground gave its crops; the fertile livestock gave their young; the fertile trees gave their fruit. Human fertility was necessary for the propagation of the species. Everything was viewed in sexual terms: the rain falling on the receptive earth, the seed planted in the receptive ground, the net thrown into the receptive sea.

In this system, the feminine (receptive) quality was not just appreciated; it was worshiped. The temple prostitute—whether female or male*—developed this quality to an art.

---

*As we shall see in the "Homosexuality" chapter, the ancient world was not

> *My ancestors wandered
> lost in the wilderness
> for forty years
> because even in biblical times,
> men would not stop
> to ask for directions.*
>
> ELAYNE BOOSLER

The temple prostitute performed many functions. She was the High Priestess (or he was the High Priest) of the temple. She or he would make offerings to the goddess or god of the temple, explore erotic visual delights through dance, play music, write and recite poetry, prepare sumptuous food, and concoct potions of love. The temple prostitute was, of course, also well trained in the arts of massage, touch, and erotic stimulation.

Sex was a sacrament; orgasm, a religious experience. The community respected and revered the sacred prostitute as much as any other priest or priestess. Prostitution was a high calling, an honorable and exalted position.

In Judaism and, later, Christianity, paganism did not fit. In the Old Testament, God demanded obedience, not orgasm. The temple prostitute was a sign of civilization, of refinement. For the Jews to wander in the desert for forty years and be successful warriors, all this pagan frivolity had to go. Among the most popular of the pagan frivolities—not surprisingly—was the temple prostitute.*

In the New Testament, Paul (in particular) denounced pagan practices at every opportunity.** Paul speaks specifically against

divided into homosexuals and heterosexuals, but active and passive. Men could be temple prostitutes as easily as women, and often were.

*When the nation of Israel finally settled down, civilization and its frivolities returned—up to a point. Some of the songs of David (Psalms) and the song of Solomon (Song of Songs) could have been written to, by, or about sacred prostitutes. These songs were certainly more pagan than puritan in content.

**Some pagan practices, however, did survive: the actual date of Christmas has nothing to do with the birthdate of Jesus, but was the pagan celebra-

346   AIN'T NOBODY'S BUSINESS IF YOU DO

the temple prostitutes, not prostitution in general. Paul is condemning all pagan practices—the work of the temple prostitute being just one of them.

⚖️ ⚖️ ⚖️

Sex being their profession, prostitutes are better versed in the prevention of sexually transmitted dis-

> *Women were in such short supply in Louisiana in 1721 that the government of France shipped twenty-five prostitutes to the colony. By this action the government hoped to lure Canadian settlers away from Indian mistresses.*
>
> *ONE NIGHT STANDS WITH AMERICAN HISTORY*

eases than the average "amateur." Just as doctors, dentists, and other healthcare workers routinely put on rubber gloves for standard medical procedures, so too do prostitutes routinely insist customers wear condoms. Most prostitutes, in fact, have techniques for applying condoms that are nonobtrusive and erotic.

Where prostitution is legal, prostitutes are professionals. They know how to protect themselves and their clients. For example, a study of 535 prostitutes working in legal Nevada brothels showed that none of them was infected with HIV. Prostitutes also show a lower incidence than the general public of all other sexually transmitted diseases. Prostitutes know how to (discreetly) examine a client for signs of sexually transmitted diseases. They know what herpes sores look like, for example, and are not going to fall for the I-just-caught-it-in-my-zipper deception. Prostitutes also know how to satisfy their clients in safe ways even if the client does have a sexually transmitted disease. (Masturbation, for example, can be erotic and safe.)

In study after study, prostitutes who are not intravenous drug users have a lower rate of HIV infection than the general population. Prostitutes do not spread AIDS any more than drug use spreads AIDS. What spreads AIDS is unsafe sex and the use

tion of the winter solstice. The pagans-turned-Christians simply refused to give up the celebration, so the Christian fathers, wisely, declared it Jesus' birthday celebration, and the festivities continue annually to this day.

> *The big difference*
> *between sex for money*
> *and sex for free*
> *is that sex for money*
> *usually costs*
> *a lot less.*
>
> BRENDAN BEHAN

of contaminated needles. When the purchase of sex is legalized and the use of drugs is legalized, both of these transmission routes will be almost completely eliminated.

It is unsafe sex that spreads AIDS and other sexually transmitted diseases, and unsafe sex can only be eliminated through education, not by prohibition.

⚖ ⚖ ⚖

Prostitution is not disgusting, but what's happening today in connection with prostitution is. In several cities, the names of men arrested for soliciting prostitutes are published in the newspaper. These men have not been convicted, mind you—just arrested. Some cities send letters to wives and employers. Spurred by the laws, vigilante groups of moralists have formed. One group writes down license numbers of cars driving in areas known for prostitution, gets the owner's address from the department of motor vehicles (which cooperates in this "effort"), and calls the wives and employers telling them drivers were seen "looking for prostitutes." Some cities use the assets forfeiture laws and confiscate cars—permanently—even for a first offense.

It's obscene.

The police are thoroughly corrupted by the techniques they must use in order to enforce the laws against prostitution. According to *The Washington Post,*

> The police engage in substantial perjury to avoid the charge of entrapment and to obtain sufficient evidence for conviction "beyond a reasonable doubt." And perhaps even more upsetting, the police often must suppress their best evidence because they cannot admit having sex with the prostitute before the arrest.

AIN'T NOBODY'S BUSINESS IF YOU DO

The illegality of prostitution also creates an unsafe environment for the prostitutes. Those who object to prostitution because they find that it "degrades women" should realize that the women who take part in prostitution may or may not be degraded by the job, but are certainly degraded by the rape and other violence that can take place because prostitutes must ply their trade in clandestine ways and clandestine places. Further, these rapes and other acts of violence against prostitutes are seldom if ever reported to the police. If they are, the police dismiss them with, "That's part of the game. If you don't want it, don't be a hooker," or simply respond, "You can't rape a whore."

> *Lawyers and tarts are the two oldest professions in the world. And we always aim to please.*
>
> HORACE RUMPOLE

As with all consensual crimes, arresting women for prostitution sets them on a life of crime. As Margo St. James describes,

> 70% of all women who are in jail today were first arrested for prostitution. When a woman is charged for a sex crime, it's a stigma that lasts her lifetime, and it makes her unemployable.

Like entering any other profession, becoming a prostitute is a choice. Exercising free choice of professions is certainly guaranteed to us by the Constitution and the Bill of Rights. We may not treat "sex workers" (as some prostitutes prefer to be called) with the reverence that once was given the sacred prostitute, but sexual professionals are entitled to the respect, protection against violence, and freedom to make a living anyone else has.

Pornography, Obscenity, Etc.

CENSORSHIP APPLIES TO basically three subjects: (1) Sex, (2) Violence, and (3) Ideas. Of the three, censorship of ideas is by far the most serious. It is also the most subtle.

A major motivation behind censorship is paternalism. "You are not able to handle this information," the censor says; "therefore—for your own protection—we will keep it from you." The variation on that, of course, is *"You and I* will not be corrupted by this, but *they*—those poor uneducated, unsophisticated, unwashed masses—will not be able to handle it, so for their own good and the good of the country, we'll ban it."

The other major motivation—far more pernicious—is to protect power. Here, someone or some group with power decides, "If this information got out, it might prove damaging to my (our) power, so I'd (we'd) better suppress it."

All censorship is a violation of the First Amendment:

> Congress shall make no law respecting an establishment of religion, or prohibiting the free exercise thereof; or abridging the freedom of speech, or of the press; or the right of the people peaceably to assemble, and to petition the Government for a redress of grievances.

It was a brilliant move for the founding fathers to put all of these guarantees together in one amendment. Almost all censorship is based on the religious and/or political beliefs of those in power. The bottom-line justification for censorship is invariably (a) "It's immoral!" (meaning, of course, against their religious beliefs), and/or (b) "It's un-American!" (which means it doesn't agree with their view about the kind of government America should have and the way that government should be run). In addition to the obvious free speech and free press guarantees, most censorship violates our First Amendment rights to freedom of and from religion.

> *It is the function of speech to free men from the bondage of irrational fears.*
>
> JUSTICE LOUIS BRANDEIS

Even if the "freedom of speech, or of the press" clause were not there, applying the remainder of the First Amendment would eliminate almost all censorship as we know it.

But just in case the primary justification for all censorship—that is, religious and political suppression—was missed, the founding fathers added the freedom of speech and press clause: "Congress shall make no law . . . abridging the freedom of speech, or of the press." As I've asked before, what could be clearer than that? The only limitation on this freedom is, as always, harming the person or property of nonconsenting others. Supreme Court Justice Oliver Wendell Holmes expressed this in his famous example from 1919:

> The most stringent protection of free speech would not protect a man in falsely shouting fire in a theatre and causing a panic. [The] question in every case is whether the words used are used in such circumstances and are of such a nature as to create a clear and present danger that they will bring about the substantive evils that Congress has a right to prevent.

One could not, then, in supervising the demolition of a building, give the order, "Blow it up," knowing that there still were people inside. The willful murder of those people cannot be protected by saying, "Well, I was just exercising my right of free speech." Unfortunately, over the years, the "clear and present

> *If the First Amendment means anything, it means that a state has no business telling a man, sitting alone in his own house, what books he may read or what films he may watch.*
>
> JUSTICE THURGOOD MARSHALL
> from a unanimous
> Supreme Court decision, 1969

danger" of "substantive evils" that Justice Holmes gave as the exception to the First Amendment rights has been interpreted beyond his obvious physical example of starting a panic by falsely yelling "Fire!" More and more, the "clear and present danger" has been interpreted as a potential danger to our national *morality*—and we've already established the source of most "morality."

In 1991, for example, the Supreme Court ruled that nude dancing by women in a Las Vegas bar was not protected by the First Amendment. This dancing, the Court held, was on the level of shouting "Fire!" in a crowded theater. How retrograde we have gone from '19 to '91. This is considered a landmark decision. As Stanford University law professor Gerald Gunther explained,

> The court is saying that public morality trumps legitimate rights of expression. That's never happened before.

In the past, one had to define the "clear and present danger" by comparing whether or not the censored material would potentially cause the same physical harm as shouting, "Fire!" in a crowded theater. Now, the "clear and present danger" need only be as potentially harmful as consenting adults dancing nude in front of other consenting adults, in a bar—*in Las Vegas*. What a wonderful gift the Supreme Court gave us in 1991 to celebrate the 200th anniversary of the passage of the Bill of Rights.

⚖️ ⚖️ ⚖️

I'll explore the censorship of political ideas more fully in the chapter, "Unpopular Political Views." For now, let me turn to the two other favorites of censorship: sex and violence.

With censorship, we find another conservative-liberal division. Conservatives usually want to censor the sexual; liberals generally want to censor violence. Neither camp uses the word *censor*—they use words such as *curb, protect, control, modify,* and *limit.*

The Problem with Pornography

The problem with pornography is that it is done so poorly. "There is no such thing as a moral or an immoral book," said Oscar Wilde more than one hundred years ago. "Books are well written, or badly written. That is all." Nothing much has changed since then. In 1993, Calvin Tomkins wrote in the *New Yorker:*

> Of all the minor art forms, pornography has remained the least developed. Certified pornographic masterworks, from Sappho to Nabokov, can be counted on the fingers of one hand. The best-known critical theorists of the form, from Anthony Comstock to Jesse Helms, have had the disadvantage of being morons. The National Endowment for the Arts supports pornographic experiment unwillingly, at best, and our popular culture contents itself with unimaginative increases in the gross annual depiction of bare skin and earnest copulation.

"I don't think pornography is very harmful," Sir Noël Coward summed it up in 1972, "but it is terribly, terribly boring."

Violence has its artists—Sam Peckinpah, Francis Ford Coppola, Ridley Scott. Where are pornography's artists? Twenty years ago, *Deep Throat* got publicity just because it had *a plot.* What have we got today? Mapplethorpe and Madonna?

Once upon a time, some of our best artists gave us our erotica. Today the Bible is used as a reason to censor. Not long ago, the Bible was used as a method to *avoid* the censor.

> *God forbid that any book should be banned. The practice is as indefensible as infanticide.*
>
> REBECCA WEST

Michelangelo was able to do a magnificent male nude statue by calling it *David* (the model's real name was probably something closer to Tadzio). Michelangelo was also able to place a reclining male nude in the very center of the ceiling of the Sistine Chapel (the pope's personal chapel, for heaven's sake) by calling it Adam.

Gustave Doré (1832–1883), who had a taste for subjects not acceptable in his own time (although his obvious love for sex and violence would be right at home in our time), was able to create some of the most bizarre art of the nineteenth century simply by illustrating Bible stories. Because he had the good sense to call his etchings *The Deluge* and *Jehu's Companions Finding the Remains of Jezebel,* his work was welcomed in the same Victorian parlors and praised by the same Victorian social leaders who probably would have put him in jail if he had accurately entitled his etchings *Naked Man, Naked Woman, and Four Naked Children Writhing in the Water and on a Wet Rock* and *Selected Body Parts of an Attractive Young Woman Being Examined by Four Men prior to Her Being Eaten by Dogs.* Because he was clever, however, *Doré's Bible* became so popular many people assumed that he wrote the text, too.

In 1967, Congress established and funded a National Commission on Pornography. Its report, published in 1970, found that it was not pornography, but the puritanical attitudes toward pornography that cause problems in America. The report said the problems stemmed "from the inability or reluctance of people in our society to be open and direct in dealing with sexual matters." In surveys, the commission found that only 2 percent of Americans thought sexually explicit material was a significant social problem. The report recommended that all legislation interfering with the right of adults to read, obtain, or view explicit sexual material be repealed.

The findings of this exhaustive study did not happen to fit the personal morals of Washington's power structure—from President Nixon on down. Nothing was done about repealing the laws.

When President Reagan put together another commission to study pornography, he did it right—*extreme* right. Attorney General Edwin Meese carefully selected eleven God-fearing (and, apparently, sex-fearing) Americans. One of the Meese Commission members was James C. Dobson, who wrote:

> *That is what the pornographers are doing to my country. They are hammering down the supporting columns and blasting away the foundations. We must stop the devastation before the entire superstructure crashes to the earth!* With the diligent prayers and personal involvement of God-fearing people, we can save the great edifice called America. But there is not a minute to lose. "But each one is tempted when he is carried away and enticed by his own lust. Then when lust has conceived, it gives birth to sin; and when sin is accomplished, it brings forth death." (James 1:14–16, NASB) [italics in original]

Is there any doubt where his personal sense of morality comes from? And does the rhetoric sound familiar? This from Donna A. Demac in her book, *Liberty Denied: The Current Rise of Censorship in America:*

> The antipornography movement of the 1980s represents yet another attempt by certain groups to impose their morals on the rest of society. What makes these efforts more threatening than those of the past is the extent to which they have been abetted by federal, state, and local authorities. The climate engendered by

> *We must never forget that if the war in Vietnam is lost the right of free speech will be extinguished throughout the world.*
>
> RICHARD M. NIXON
> October 27, 1965

> *Whenever they burn books,*
> *they will also,*
> *in the end,*
> *burn people.*
>
> HEINRICH HEINE

initiatives such as the Meese Commission has been described with only a bit of hyperbole by Hugh Hefner as "sexual McCarthyism."

The Problem with Violence

The problem with violence is that it is not violent enough. According to the National Coalition on Television Violence, by the age of eighteen the average American will have seen 250,000 acts of violence and 40,000 attempted murders on television. And yet, how realistic will they be? Not very. When people are shot on TV, they grab the part of their body that is shot, fall over (if they are severely hurt), and continue with the written dialog. The dialog usually includes an obligatory "Ow" or "Ouch" or "Ahh" and then adds such stellar commentary (which must be a holdover from radio) as, "Why did you shoot me?" "My arm! [leg! chest! head!]" and the classic "I've been shot!" No matter how much dialog the victims have or how long it takes for the paramedics to arrive, we see very little blood. We seldom even see holes in clothing, and almost never see holes in flesh.

In real life, when someone is shot, blood is—to put it mildly—abundant. The victim goes into shock. Shock is not pretty: pasty face, severe trembling, eyes rolling toward the back of the head. Coherent dialog seldom passes the lips, but dinner frequently does—on the way out.

> [CAUTION: The next two paragraphs are going to get a little graphic. Skip them if you want to avoid explicit descriptions of violence. Now that I have your complete attention, I'll continue.]

Even movies famous for violence are not allowed to go as far as real life. In *The Godfather, Part III,* for example, one of the villains is killed by being stabbed in the throat with his own eyeglasses. As originally filmed, the character sprayed large quantities of blood from his mouth. In order to avoid an X rating, however, the scene had to be re-shot, sans spraying.

In *The Godfather, Part II,* when the Godfather (played by Robert DeNiro) becomes the Godfather by committing his first murder, he sticks the revolver in the mouth of his victim and, bang. In the movie, we see a little bit of brain and blood splatter on the door behind him. (The scene was shot for television sans even that little splattering.) In fact, even the movie version was incredibly tame. The *AMOK Assault Video* contains a news clip that was too graphic even for the evening news (if you can imagine that). It showed a politician who had been caught with his hand in the cookie jar. He called a press conference. There he proclaimed his innocence, protested the unfairness of his persecution, pulled out a .357 Magnum, put it in his mouth, and pulled the trigger. What the camera captured is certainly enough to convince anyone not to play with firearms—or enter into politics. After his head exploded (a look at the Zapruder film in the movie *JFK* will give you an idea), blood *poured* from his nose and mouth. Although he was clearly dead, the blood kept gushing. We didn't see this in *The Godfather, Part II.**

The other myth perpetrated in television and movies is how little people bruise and how quickly they heal. The day after a severe beating, the hero has a few red marks, wears a little white tape, and that's about it. In real life, he'd look terrible. Two days

> *People want to know why I do this,*
> *why I write such gross stuff.*
> *I like to tell them*
> *I have the heart of a small boy—*
> *and I keep it in a jar on my desk.*
>
> STEPHEN KING

---

*A friend told me that, when he was a boy, his father committed suicide with a shotgun. "What did you do?" I asked. "What could we do?" my friend replied. "We painted the room and we moved."

> *After seeing <u>Rambo</u> last night*
> *I know what to do*
> *next time this happens.*
>
> PRESIDENT RONALD REAGAN
> following the hijack of an airplane
> carrying American passengers
> 1985

after a beating, in the movie, he's fine. In real life, two days after a beating you look worse than you did the day after the beating.

All of this sanitized violence only makes real violence a more acceptable solution to problems. It's not that violence is shown, and that causes violence; it's that violence is shown as the solution to problems; that causes violence. "A single death is a tragedy, a million deaths is a statistic," said Joseph Stalin (who knew). If, however, the way in which each of those million died and the suffering each went through had to be viewed one at a time in great detail, perhaps it would no longer be a statistic, and perhaps such tragedies would happen less often.

Portraying violence in all its gory would probably have these positive effects:

1. Far fewer people would watch violent programs. In television, people vote with their remotes. In magazines, movies, and newspapers, they vote with their purchase. If enough people vote no, fewer violent acts would be depicted.

2. People would be less likely to take part in violence. In your own home, you'd be less likely to shoot someone because you wouldn't want all that blood, vomit, and other internal fluids on your floor (wall, ceiling, couch, fish tank, etc.). You would also assiduously avoid situations where violent harm to your own person was remotely possible. One California judge sentences teenage drunk driving offenders to witness an autopsy of a traffic fatality caused by a drunk driver. It's been remarkably effective. Such a cold, forensic reality of violence would remove any sense of glamour from either hurting or being hurt. It's the human equivalent of the idea, "If each person had to kill his or her own dinner, there would be a lot more vegetarians."

⚖️ ⚖️ ⚖️

The Problem with Censorship

The problem with censorship can be summed up in two words: *who decides?*

If someone other than the end consumers—voting with their purchases, attendance, or remote controls—decides what should or should not, can or cannot, must or must not be said, depicted, or offered for sale, who should *that* person be? And who decides who that person should be? And who decides if those people are doing a good job deciding?

Ultimately, censorship comes down to taste. What offends me may enlighten you. Do you want me deciding—based on my taste—what you should or should not be exposed to?

Most censors don't stop at what offends them, of course: their overheated imaginations begin conjuring up what might offend this person or that group, and pretty soon almost everything is "pornographic." Many start sounding like Mervyn Griffiths-Jones, the prosecuting attorney in the 1960 trial to keep *Lady Chatterly's Lover* banned:

> You may think one of the ways in which you can test this book is to ask yourself the question: would you approve of your own son and daughter, because girls can read as well as boys, reading this book? Is it a book you could have lying in your own house? Is it a book you would wish your wife or your servant to read?

So much of what we'd want to censor depends on where we stand, what we're standing on, and whom we're standing with. Shelley Winters, tongue well in cheek, pointed out,

> I think nudity on the stage is disgusting, shameful and unpatriotic. But if I were twenty-two with a great body,

> *I am mortified to be told that, in the United States of America, the sale of a book can become a subject of inquiry, and of criminal inquiry too.*
>
> THOMAS JEFFERSON

> *Without censorship,*
> *things can get terribly confused*
> *in the public mind.*
>
> GENERAL WILLIAM WESTMORELAND

it would be artistic, tasteful, patriotic and a progressive, religious experience.

In addition, besides deciding what's good and what's bad, who decides what the punishment should be for violating these standards? For example, consider this comment from a young artist:

> Anybody who sees and paints a sky green and pastures blue ought to be sterilized.

This may seem to be a trivial, even silly, comment for a young artist to make, but what if this young artist sets aside his art and turns to the art of politics? What if he gains enough power to fulfill not only his censorship dreams, but to inflict the punishments he finds appropriate? Well, that's precisely what happened. The artist-turned-politician who detested green skies and blue pastures had tens of thousands sterilized, and presided over the most sterile artistic period in the history of Europe—and these were the least of his crimes. As I'm sure you've guessed, the censor was Adolph Hitler. Which brings us to the F-WORD.

The F-WORD

In our use of language, we go beyond the hypocritical directly to the silly. When I say, "F-WORD," you know precisely which word I mean. Isn't it silly, though, that if I actually use that word, I would be unnecessarily giving ammunition to those who want to attack this book not for its ideas, but for the use of a single word. (Or who do want to attack the ideas, but would use the F-WORD as an excuse.)

As a writer, I don't mind that the F-WORD is taboo. Being taboo gives it extra power. It's good that certain words have the power that only prohibition can provide.

In the film *Mommy Dearest*, Joan Crawford meets with the Board of Pepsi Cola, who think they have the better of her. She drops the demure and dignified act long enough to deliver the line, "Don't [F-WORD] with me, fellas! This ain't my first time at the rodeo." The line is most effective.

> *Loretta Young, a devout Catholic (despite having an illegitimate daughter sired by Clark Gable) would fine actors for using coarse language on the movie set— 25 cents for "hell," 50 cents for "damn." One actor tossed her ten dollars, "Here Loretta: go F-WORD yourself!"*

When Walt Disney Productions decided to make non-children's films (I can't say "adult films," because that has other connotations), they started Touchstone Pictures. Touchstone had a rule: only two F-WORDS per picture. That was fine. The creators carefully selected the two points in the film where the F-WORD would have the most impact.

Having a few words forbidden allows creative people to be even more delightfully creative. Woody Allen, for example:

> Some guy hit my fender the other day, and I said unto him, "Be fruitful, and multiply." But not in those words.

Or, Dorothy Parker:

> Ducking for apples—change one letter and it's the story of my life.

When all words are accepted—even expected—language deteriorates. As the British journalist Sir William Connor described,

> All were swearing steadily and quietly and all were using the same time-dishonoured Army oaths with such lavishness that made it necessary to split words open in the middle in order to cram all the obscenities in.

Alexander Woollcott replied to a critic about the unnecessary use of "God damn," which was the F-WORD of his day:

> When you speak of "three unnecessary 'God damns'" you imply that there is such a thing as a *necessary* God damn.

This, of course, is nonsense. A God damn is never a necessity. It is always a luxury.

"I was arrested for using a ten-letter word that began with 'c,'" said Lenny Bruce, "and I would marry no woman who was not one."

From the standpoint of consensual crimes and freedom of speech, (if I may paraphrase Lenny Bruce) we must use that marvelous ten-letter word that begins with "t" (and certainly no one would marry me who didn't have a great deal of it): *toleration*. If I don't want Jerry Falwell editing my books, I must forgo the luxury of editing his sermons. (But I can dream, can't I?) To have a freedom ourselves, we must pick up the banner of that great light of the Enlightenment, Voltaire, and declare: "I disapprove of what you say, but I will defend to the death your right to say it."*

As long as we keep censoring, we are lost in the symptoms of our society's problems, thus ignoring the problems themselves. Pornography, for example, doesn't degrade women; women are degraded by our culture, and certain forms of pornography reflect that. Yes, we have a serious problem with the way women are treated in our culture, and pornography is a symptom, but let's not kill the messenger. Let's get the message and do something about it.

Similarly, violence is a messenger. The idea that problems can be solved through violence causes violence. We have a problem with drugs? Let's declare a war on drugs! We have a problem with crime? Let's declare war on crime! We have a problem with

> *The press,*
> *confined to truth,*
> *needs no other*
> *legal restraint.*
>
> THOMAS JEFFERSON
> Second Inaugural Address

---

*In fact, he never said that. What he said was the less quotable, "I never approved either the errors of his book, or the trivial truths he so vigorously laid down. I have, however, stoutly taken his side when absurd men have condemned him for these same truths."

AIN'T NOBODY'S BUSINESS IF YOU DO

violence? Let's declare war on violence! The deeply ingrained American attitude that we can solve any problem with enough force creates, feeds, and rewards the epidemic of violence we are currently experiencing.

The actual depiction of violence in TV, movies, and song, in fact, has little effect. As Jon Stewart observed:

> *Seeing a murder on television can help work off one's antagonisms. And if you haven't any antagonisms, the commercials will give you some.*
>
> ALFRED HITCHCOCK

The song "Cop Killer" doesn't make me want to murder a policeman any more than Julie Andrews singing "Climb Ev'ry Mountain" makes me want to go hiking.

Violations of Marriage:
Adultery, Fornication, Cohabitation, Bigamy, and Polygamy

> DR. CHASUBLE:
> *Your brother was, I believe
> unmarried, was he not?*
>
> JACK:
> *Oh yes.*
>
> MISS PRISM [Bitterly]:
> *People who live entirely for pleasure
> usually are.*
>
> OSCAR WILDE
> *The Importance of Being Earnest*

IS MARRIAGE SUCH A fragile institution that it must be defended by putting all dissenters in jail?

The obvious answer: "No—there will always be a fairly large percentage of people who *want* a lifelong, monogamous, formal, committed relationship with a partner of the opposite sex to keep the $32 billion bridal industry humming." Then why, I wonder (just as I wonder why it's called the *bridal* industry and not the *bridal and groomal* industry or simply the *wedding* industry), why must there be so many laws to encourage, support, and protect marriage?

When it comes to *professional* relationships, the law recognizes just about every kind. In business, there are sole proprietorships, limited partnerships, corporations, and any number of other government (and, more important, IRS) recognized relationships. The laws and customs are neatly in place for mergers, takeovers, creating, and dissolving professional relationships of all shapes, sizes, and durations.

Why is it, then, when it comes to *personal* relationships, there is only one legally recognized, community approved, IRS sanctioned relationship: one man and one woman promising fidelity until one of them dies? Only in this relationship—known as marriage—do people get the tax breaks, bank loans, realtor acceptance, and Welcome Wagon visits.

AIN'T NOBODY'S BUSINESS IF YOU DO

Further, consenting adults entering into personal, romantic, or erotic relationships other than marriage might find themselves in jail. If you're sixty-three and a twenty-two-year-old fashion model finds your charm, sex appeal, and $500 million net worth absolutely irresistible, and this model, as Stephen Sondheim put it, "marries you a little," there may be a few raised eyebrows. Although eventually you'll probably be raising alimony payments, one thing you won't have to raise is bail. If, however, the same financial relationship were offered in more straightforward terms, in all fifty states (with the exception of a few counties in Nevada) you'd be arrested for solicitation, prostitution, or pandering.

> *It doesn't matter what you do in the bedroom as long as you don't do it in the street and frighten the horses.*
>
> MRS. PATRICK CAMPBELL

Even if you firmly believe in, staunchly support, and passionately desire a one-on-one, monogamous, committed, lifelong partnership, if you happen to want that with a member of your own sex, that's illegal in all fifty states.* Let's say you're heterosexual, then—so heterosexual, in fact, that you want to marry two members of the opposite sex. Sorry, that's a little too heterosexual: just one to a customer, please. To paraphrase Oscar Wilde, bigamy is having one spouse too many; monogamy is the same.

Generally, polygamy is thought of as one man with several wives. As the King in *The King and I* explains it:

A woman is like a blossom with honey for just one man.
The man must be like the honey bee, and gather all he
can. To fly from blossom to blossom, the honey bee must
be free. But blossom must not ever fly From bee to bee
to bee.

*As this is being written, Hawaii is teetering on the brink of legalizing same-sex marriages. California, however, has already said, "Nyet!"

Anna, the Welsh school-teacher tutoring the children of the King of Siam's "favorite" wives, has an alternate view:

In your pursuit of pleasure, you have mistresses who treasure you.
They have no ken of other men, beside whom they can measure you.
A flock of sheep, and you the only ram.
No wonder you're the wonder of Siam!

> *The plural of spouse*
> *is spice.*
>
> CHRISTOPHER MORLEY

There is no reason, of course, why a woman cannot have many husbands. The word *polygamy*, in fact, is not attached to gender. A man with several wives technically practices *polygyny;* a woman with several husbands practices *polyandry.*

We know Cleopatra, for example, was not exactly the queen of denial, and only World War II went through more Russians than Catherine the Great. Mae West, in her play *Catherine Was Great,* played the Russian empress on Broadway. In her curtain speech, West told the audience,

> I'm glad you like my Catherine. I like her too. She ruled thirty million people and had three thousand lovers. I do the best I can in two hours.

In a few parts of the country—particularly among Mormons—polygamy (or, more accurately, polygyny) is quietly accepted. Some Mormons, in fact, consider polygamy their religious right. It is certainly true that polygamy, as a religious tenet of Mormonism, was driven out by this country's traditional religious intolerance and the government's willingness to give such intolerance full force of law. Professor Robert Allen Rutland tells the story:

> From 1831 onward the Mormons, whose religion embraced the practice of polygamy, had been hounded from

settlement to settlement, and in 1844 their leader, Joseph Smith, and his brother were lynched by an Illinois mob; the surviving believers then trekked from the Mississippi to their New Zion in present-day Utah. After Congress outlawed bigamy in 1862 Mormons challenged the law, claiming that it violated their guarantee to worship freely. The high court decision upheld the law and kept Utah out of the Union until 1896.

> *I was thrown out of NYU for cheating— with the Dean's wife.*
>
> WOODY ALLEN

Brigham Young, who led the Mormons from Illinois to Utah, had at least twenty wives and fathered forty-seven children. "He is dreadfully married," wrote Artemus Ward. "He's the most married man I ever saw in my life."

⚖ ⚖ ⚖

As of early 1996, adultery (sex with someone who is married, or sex with anyone other than your spouse if you are married) is illegal in twenty-seven states. Oral sex (called *sodomy* in some states)—either giving or receiving—is illegal for consenting heterosexual adults in fourteen states. Even missionary style, conventional, heterosexual sex between unmarried consenting adults is illegal in nine states. Cohabitation (living as married with someone you're not married to) is illegal in ten states.*

And let's not forget local ordinances. There are any number of laws—such as this one from Long Beach, California—which sound more like a passage from a Sidney Sheldon novel than a legal statute:

No person shall indulge in caresses, hugging, fondling,

---

*In seven states you can have sex if you're not married, but you can't live together. What sort of morality is *that* set of laws teaching?

> *You can point to any item in the Sears catalog and somebody wants to sleep with it.*
>
> DETECTIVE STANLEY WOJOHOWICZ
> *Barney Miller*

embracing, spooning, kissing, or wrestling with any person or persons of the opposite sex . . . and no person shall sit or lie with his or her head, or any other portion of his or her person, upon any portion of a person or persons, upon or near any of the said public places in the city of Long Beach.

⚖️ ⚖️ ⚖️

Any guess where all these restrictions come from? Almost invariably they are religious in origin. In their attempt to protect "the American family," fundamentalists are, in fact, destroying the institution of marriage. Lifelong, monogamous marriage is a relationship that many people are naturally drawn to. But when society programs those not drawn to that particular relationship to believe that they should or even must be married, people who have no business being in a marriage muck it up for those who want to be.

It's like visiting Disneyland. Some people naturally love the place. As long as only those who are drawn to Disneyland visit Disneyland, it is "the happiest place on earth." If, however, everyone were forced by law to visit Disneyland, then those who were not congenitally suited for Disneyland would—with their noticeable displeasure, rebellious acts, and disparaging comments—ruin it for those who wanted to be there.

That's the state of marriage in America today. When people who really want to be married marry people who only think they should get married, both end up suffering. If people who want to get married, get married to other people who want to get married, the likelihood of success is fairly high. Meanwhile, if the people who don't want to get married but think they should get married are no longer told they should get married, they are free to explore and enter into whatever sort of relationships they do want. (On a purely physical level, psychiatrists say that 20 percent of the American public has no appreciable sex drive whatsoever.)

If business law had an equivalent to the laws concerning personal relation-

> *This may sound terribly selfish,*
> *but I love the freedom I have.*
> *I don't have to worry*
> *about a man's wardrobe,*
> *or his relatives,*
> *or his schedule,*
> *or his menu,*
> *or his allergies.*
> *I would not be married again.*
>
> ANN LANDERS

ships, it would say, "If you're in business, you must have one partner, and only one partner, and keep that partner, until one of you dies." If this were the law, can you imagine the state of business in America? The same is true of the state of personal relationships.

If we allow people to follow their hearts (and what else should they primarily follow in romantic relationships?) and allow relationships the freedom to grow, dissolve, merge, and interact with the same legal freedoms and protections we give business, then everyone—including (and perhaps especially) those who want a traditional marriage—would be a lot better off.

This topic, of course, is the subject of its own book, which I have no intention of writing someday. From a legal point of view, to sanction (reward, in fact) only one kind of relationship and punish other relationships is simply not the law's business.

Homosexuality

> Homosexuality is Satan's
> diabolical attack upon the family
> that will not only have
> a corrupting influence
> upon our next generation,
> but it will also bring down
> the wrath of God upon America.
>
> JERRY FALWELL

CALL ME DIM-WITTED, thickheaded, or just plain insensitive, but the consensual crime laws that seem the silliest to me are the ones directed against homosexuality. Why should criminal law care about whom other people love, feel affection for, date, live with, marry, or have sex with? I just don't get it.

I also don't understand the astonishing prejudice against gay people.* The *New York Times* reported findings of the (New York) Governor's Task Force on Bias-Related Violence:

> In one of the most alarming findings, the report found that while teenagers surveyed were reluctant to advocate open bias against racial and ethnic groups, they were emphatic about disliking homosexual men and women. They are perceived "as legitimate targets that can be openly attacked," the report said. . . . The feelings were as strong among twelve-year-olds as among seventeen-year-olds. Many students added gratuitous vicious comments about homosexuals; that was not the case with other groups.

Gays seem to be at the bottom of the pecking order: no matter how far down the pecking order another group is, its

---

*As you may have noticed, I use the terms *homosexual* and *gay* almost interchangeably. Some gays prefer *gay,* some prefer *homosexual.* One group (a minority, as of this writing) likes the word *queer.* When I use *gay* or *homosexual,* I automatically mean both men and women; so, if I say "gays" or "homosexuals," I mean "lesbians and homosexual men." If I offend anyone with my selection of words, I apologize. No disrespect is intended.

members still feel superior to and have no problem picking on gays.

It also seems that groups that hate each other and disagree on absolutely everything else find one common point of agreement: homosexuality is bad, wrong, evil, wicked, and all the rest. Take, for example, L. Ron Hubbard and Jerry Falwell. One

> *Few people can be happy unless they hate some other person, nation, or creed.*
>
> BERTRAND RUSSELL

would think these two individuals were about as far apart as possible on every known spectrum. The fact that one is dead and the other is not quite dead is the least of their differences. Falwell dismisses Hubbard's creation, the Church of Scientology, as a "satanic cult." On the subject of homosexuality, however, Falwell and Hubbard seem to find some common ground.

In the chapter, "His Master's Voice?" we'll explore how Falwell feels about "perverts." Here are some excerpts from L. Ron Hubbard's *Dianetics,* the "15 million copy bestseller":

> The sexual pervert (and by this term Dianetics, to be brief, includes any and all forms of deviation . . . such as homosexuality, lesbianism . . .) is actually quite ill physically. . . . He is also so far from normal and so extremely dangerous to society that the tolerance of perversion is as thoroughly bad for society as punishment for it.

> To make a pervert is, rather, something on the order of kicking a baby's head in, running over him with a steamroller, cutting him in half with a rusty knife, boiling him in Lysol, and all the while with crazy people screaming the most horrifying and unprintable things at him.

⚖️ ⚖️ ⚖️

As Dr. Edward W. Bauman, United Methodist pastor who for more than twenty years conducted a Bible class on television in

> [Even though gay teens amount
> to less than ten percent
> of the teen-age population,]
> one-third of all
> teenage suicides
> are gays and lesbians.
>
> U.S. DEPARTMENT OF HEALTH

the Washington, D.C., area, observed,

The thing that impressed me most, however, and moved me deeply was the discovery of the incredible amount of suffering experienced by homosexuals. For centuries the church refused to serve them Holy Communion. They were often stripped, castrated, marched through the streets, and executed. In Hitler's Germany they were exterminated by the thousands in the furnaces and gas chambers.

In our own country, gay persons are disowned by their families, ridiculed and rejected by society, made the object of cruel jokes, and forced to laugh at the jokes lest their "secret" be revealed.

They are barred from jobs and housing, often living in loneliness, seeking companionship in sordid places and in devious (and dangerous) ways. They have become the "lepers" of our society. How many young people are there who lie awake at night, terrified by these "feelings," with no one to talk to?

Quite a number it seems, as the suicide rate among teen-aged gays is several times that of heterosexual teens.

What causes such deep and unreasonable hatred?

Prior to the late 1800s, the concept of homosexuality did not exist. The idea that one would exclusively feel romantically and sexually drawn to a member of the same sex was not considered. Yes, there was certainly homosexual *activity*, but this had always existed. The Hebrews, for example, did not have a word for homosexuality. When they wanted to describe the forbidden activity, they had to say, "Do not lie with a man as one lies with a

AIN'T NOBODY'S BUSINESS IF YOU DO

woman; that is detestable"
(Leviticus 18:22). Similarly,
the Greeks had no word for
homosexual. Paul had to
explain: "Even their women
exchanged natural relations
for unnatural ones. In the
same way the men also
abandoned natural rela-
tions with women and
were inflamed with lust for
one another" (Romans
1:26–27). There was no

> *Can it matter where or*
> *in whom you put it?*
>
> MARK ANTONY
> 81–30 B.C.

word, then, for a man who went to bed only with men or a
woman who went to bed only with women.

To even ask the question would be as unusual as asking
today, "Are you a hot dog eater or a hamburger eater?" The idea
that one preference would exclude the other made no sense.
Even if one has not eaten a hot dog in twenty years, one would
never think of defining oneself as a *hamburgerist*. Likewise, a
person who had never had a hamburger in his or her life but
adored hot dogs, would not be labeled "a hotdogger."

In societies of ancient Greece and Rome, sexual activity with
either gender was perfectly acceptable. To exclusively go to bed
with one sex or the other, in fact, was considered a bit odd—just
as eating only raw vegetables might be considered a bit unusual
today. In the ancient world, the distinction was: "Were you the
dominant or the *passive* partner in the sex act?" In relationships
between men, the dominant partner was praised, and the passive
partner was condemned. Why? Because to play the passive partner meant a man *voluntarily played the part of a woman.*

It's the ancient anti-woman prejudice that permeates what
we call Western Civilizations. Why would a *man* want to play the
part of a *woman?* To do so was considered unnatural, self-depre-
cating, and perverse. If slaves or captives did it with their owners, that was acceptable: they had to. But for a man who had a
choice to take the passive role in sex was considered degrading.

And therein lies the seed of the prejudice. It wasn't that

> *Athenians attributed the establishment of their democracy to a pair of gay lovers.*
>
> **JOHN BOSWELL**
> *Christianity, Social Tolerance, and Homosexuality*

homosexual activity was wrong; it was a man playing the woman's role in homosexual activity that was considered perverted.

Alexander the Great—whose masculinity was never in doubt—had as a primary sexual partner a castrated Persian boy. Alexander also had a wife. No one questioned the arrangement. Alexander played the dominant role in both relationships. He was a "man." Both Alexander's wife and the Persian boy were treated with the respect due the ruler's favorites, but with little admiration.

As we shall see, any number of prohibitions in both the Old and New Testaments were abandoned long ago. And yet, the one against homosexuality remained because the bias against women remained. That's the first reason homosexuality has continued to be viewed in a negative light long after the practical reason (it doesn't propagate the species) no longer mattered.

The second reason homosexuality is so feared and despised is that *homosexuality is too close to home.* It's fairly easy for, say, white people to become tolerant of black people because white people are not black. White people seldom think, "I think I'll have black skin for the next two hours." White people and black people are so fundamentally different—in terms of skin color—that white people almost never think, "I wonder if I'm really black?"

This sense of security is not found with homosexuality. On a purely biological level, the human animal responds sexually to lubricated friction. It doesn't much matter whether this lubricated friction is being applied by a man, a woman, a machine, or a well-trained dog; human sexual response on the biological level is automatic.

It is also true that human beings can feel affection—even love—for members of their own sex. Affection is not a tidy emotion. It tends to lap into mental, emotional, physical, sensual, and even sexual expression.

When one first realizes that he or she is actually capable of some kind of sexual and/or emotional response with a member of the same sex, panic ensues. Before children are even aware of their sexuality, they know that homosexuality is bad. Very bad. Among boys eight years or older, the most pejorative name they can call each other is "faggot!" Later, when they become aware of their sexuality and find—even for a moment—that it flashes in the direction of the same sex, there's trouble in River City.

At this point, one has the choice to (a) confront one of the greatest and most pervasive taboos in our culture or (b) deny the inner reaction vehemently by supporting the taboo all the more enthusiastically. Invariably, (b) is the choice. It's an old psychological truism: the more you want to taste of the forbidden fruit, the more you condemn it. Shakespeare realized this, and assumed his audience understood the concept so well that he made it a joke: "The lady doth protest too much, methinks."* That line has been met by the laughter of recognition for almost four hundred years.

By soundly condemning homosexuality outwardly, one avoids facing even the possibility that one might—just maybe—feel love for or be capable of responding sexually to a member of one's own sex.

⚖ ⚖ ⚖

Hating gays seems to be the only fashionable prejudice left. Maybe that's why it's dying so hard—some people just can't

> *In my very rare
> homosexual moments
> I often glance through
> the pages of Vogue,
> where the other day
> I saw a picture of you.*
>
> ALFRED HITCHCOCK
> in a letter to Joan Crawford

---

*Hamlet, Act III, Scene 2, Line 242.

> *People should not be surprised when a morally offensive lifestyle is physically attacked.*
>
> THE VATICAN

stand to be without at least one unjustifiable hatred. Some stores sell t-shirts with sayings such as "Homophobic and Proud of It" and "Club Faggots, Not Seals." Or the bumper sticker sold at the 1995 National Federation of Republican Women Convention: "THE MIRACLE OF AIDS TURNED FRUITS INTO VEGETABLES." What other minority is subjected to such unchallenged, cruel, and violent hatred?

As with most prejudices, the hatred of gays is based on a series of misconceptions. Our culture seems to have more myths about gays than most. Let's see if we can shine a little light on a few of them.

Myth #1: *Homosexuality is unnatural.* In order to see what *is* natural, we must look to nature. In nature, every mammal has been observed taking part in same-sex activities, affection, and bonding. In some animals, homosexuality increases during times of overpopulation—sort of nature's birth control.

In nature, by the way, what is decidedly not natural is monogamy—especially for life. The only mammals who even sometimes mate for life are foxes, wolves, gibbons, beavers, dik-diks, coyotes, elephant shrews, and geese. Some animals mate for a season; most animals mate and move on.

I stuck to mammals for this example because the lower forms of life—while natural—are positively *inhuman.* You could say, for example, that the praying mantis "mates for life" only because, while the male shudders in orgasm, the female bites his head off. Then she eats him. The male praying mantis is an animal that comes and goes at the same time. Maybe that's why he's always praying. We all know how the black widow spider becomes a widow and why there is no such thing as a black widower (some animals get so *hungry* after sex).

Here's how Phyllis Lindstrom explained the birds and the

bees—well, at least the bees—on *The Mary Tyler Moore Show*: "Did you know the male bee is nothing but the slave of the queen? And once the male bee has, how should I say, *serviced* the queen, the male dies. All in all, not a bad system."

> *Homosexual activity occurs under some circumstances in probably all known human cultures and all mammalian species for which it has been studied.*
>
> WARREN J. GADPAILLE, M.D.
> *Comprehensive Textbook of Psychiatry*

Earthworms have male sexual organs on one end and female sexual organs on the other. They cannot, however, fertilize themselves. To mate, earthworms lie next to each other—how can I say this without becoming numerical?—head-to-toe and simultaneously play both male and female. Amoebas seem to have the best idea—the simplest, anyway: when they've had enough of themselves, they just divide. When one discusses what's natural, then, one has quite a range of behaviors to choose from.

From a purely human point of view, homosexual behavior has been recorded in every culture that kept detailed enough records. Sociologists and anthropologists have documented homosexual behavior in every country on earth—including in tribes that had no contact with outside human beings until the arrival of the anthropologists. Any behavior observed among all races, all peoples, all cultures, and in all countries throughout all recorded time must certainly be considered natural for humans.

Myth #2: *People are either homosexual or heterosexual.* Not true. People do tend to specialize—partially because people are conditioned to think they should specialize. (We are addicted to "either/or" in our culture.) Sexual behavior is a continuum with exclusive heterosexuality on one end and exclusive homosexuality on the other. People, however, can be found at any point along that spectrum. A corollary to Myth #2 is:

Myth #3: *Homosexuality is contagious.* The myth goes something like this: If you try a homosexual experience and find it even marginally enjoyable, a seed (more like a virus) has been

> *It is a great injustice*
> *to persecute homosexuality*
> *as a crime,*
> *and cruelty too.*
>
> SIGMUND FREUD

planted, and, eventually, you will wind up a full-fledged, card-carrying, flag-waving homosexual. This is simply not the case. You can't "catch" homosexuality any more than you can "catch" heterosexuality (although the latter myth is supported by the concept that "the love of a good woman" will "cure" a gay man). In either case, even a successful liaison with the gender one is not normally drawn to will have little, if any, lasting effect.

I'm amazed at the power those who propound the you-can-catch-homosexuality theory give to homosexuality—with only a small dose, it suddenly takes over an otherwise robust hetero-sexual? This myth probably springs from observing some individuals who severely suppressed their homosexuality, but once they got one foot out the closet door there was no stopping them. ("I am not just out of the closet," a greeting card reads, "I am sitting in the living room with my feet propped up watching television.") We pretty much are what we are, and neither homosexuality nor heterosexuality can be "caught." The next myth seems to contradict this myth but, like different aspects of a used-car salesman's pitch, myths don't have to support each other for people to believe them. "The American public," said Pat Robertson, "has a very short memory." And this is a man who knows.

Myth #4: *Homosexuality is a choice.* It has been established for some time that one's sexual orientation is part of the basic personality structure and formed before the age of two. The most recent studies, however, both behavioral and biological, indicate one's sexual orientation is genetic—something determined at conception. Whether it happens before birth or it happens by age two, the determination of sexual orientation can hardly be considered a choice. One can, of course, choose not to follow one's natural orientation, but this is not the sort of choice the proponents of this myth mean. They mean that gay people choose to be gay in the same way that they might sit down and choose which program to watch on television, which team to bet on in the Super Bowl, or whether or not they want pepperoni on their pizza.

> We need laws that protect everyone.
> Men and women,
> straights and gays,
> regardless of sexual perversion
> . . . ah, persuasion.
>
> BELLA ABZUG

The idea behind this myth is: a perfectly normal, well-adjusted heterosexual is sitting around one day and just *decides* to go gay, as one might decide to move to Antarctica or try to flush hockey pucks down the toilet. It is truly aberrant behavior, but it is his or her choice. Implied in this choice, of course, is a certain hostility to God, parents, society, and the American way. It's as though being gay is a pathological act of rebellion.

Gays don't choose to be gay; they *discover* they're gay. Like heterosexuals, they find themselves increasingly attracted (romantically as well as sexually) to a particular gender. The bisexuals find themselves attracted to both. (Even though, as Woody Allen says, "Bisexuality immediately doubles your chances for a date on Saturday night," discovering one's bisexuality must be more confusing than discovering one is primarily gay or straight.)

Like being left- or right-handed, there is no "choice" to one's sexual orientation. Allow me to give you an example. Clasp your hands together by interlocking your fingers. Is your right thumb on top or your left? Now switch your clasp, so that the other thumb is on top. Feel unnatural? Well, for half the population, this way is natural—it's the way they formed their clasp when first asked. Although one feels "normal" to you and one does not, when did you choose which was which? At what age? Who offered you the choice? The answer to these questions is also the answer to the question, "When do gays choose to be gay?"

Considering the many cultural prejudices, to discover one is

> *As a mother,*
> *I know that homosexuals*
> *cannot biologically reproduce*
> *children; therefore, they must*
> *recruit our children.*
>
> ANITA BRYANT

(or might be) gay can be traumatic; one can be in denial for some time. With society screaming, "Stay in the closet!" and nature pleading, "Get out! Get out!" one does have the choice of which voice one listens to. Does one choose to use the courage to be oneself? In this way—and in this way only—is homosexuality a choice.

Myth #5: *Homosexuals recruit others.* This is a myth that grew out of the evangelical camp where proselytizing, testifying, missionaryizing, and converting are basic tenets of the faith. Evangelicals somehow feel that gays have the same zeal to spread a gay-spell that they have to spread a God-spell. It's a simple matter of evangelicals projecting their recruitment tactics on gays. As with most projections, the image is distorted—and very wrong.

Gays have no desire to "recruit" heterosexuals into becoming homosexual. A gay person may, individually, want to have sex with a heterosexual of the same sex whom he or she finds attractive; the gay person may even make a pass. The gay person is making a personal statement of desire, not fulfilling a recruitment quota. ("If you recruit ten heterosexuals this month, you get this beautiful 26-piece set of Tupperware!") Additionally, gays who are out of the closet may offer support and encouragement to gays who are miserably in the closet, but that's about as far as it goes. Besides, the whole idea of recruitment rests on the concept that homosexuality is a choice, and every homosexual knows that just ain't so.

Myth #6: *You can spot a gay a mile away.* In 1985, when Rock Hudson publicly admitted his homosexuality, I was visiting two gay friends in Maine. Both men were in their eighties and had been lovers in 1925. In this rather remote region of Maine (is there any other kind of region in Maine?) the people did not

AIN'T NOBODY'S BUSINESS IF YOU DO

have what you would call a cosmopolitan view of life. They had somehow heard about Rock Hudson's sexual proclivities (an issue of *People* must have washed ashore in a bottle). They were stunned, numb. Not since the news of Kennedy's assassination (which they found out about in 1971) had the people of this town been so bereft.

> VICTIM'S GRIEVING WIDOW:
> *Do you know what it's like to be married to a wonderful man for fourteen years?*
>
> DETECTIVE DREBIN:
> *No, I can't say that I do. I did . . . uh . . . live with a guy once, though, but that was just for a couple of years. The usual slurs, rumors, innuendoes— people didn't understand.*
>
> POLICE SQUAD!

"Rock Hudson?" "No." "He couldn't be." "He doesn't look . . ." "Rock Hudson was such a *man*." My two friends and I were visiting the general store (yes, it was called the general store); it was all anyone could talk about. I wondered what this group of shoppers would say if I told them that the dear, sweet, elderly men to whom they were expressing their astonishment had been lovers sixty years earlier. But I figured, no, one Rock crumbling that week was enough.

Some gay men are effeminate; most are not. Some straight men are effeminate; most are not. Some lesbians are masculine; most are not. Some heterosexual women are masculine; most are not. According to the organization that considers itself an expert on homosexuality, the Pentagon, "feminized males make up only a small proportion of homosexuals, perhaps 10 percent. Thus 90 percent . . . display no overt behavioral stigmata." Regarding effeminacy in men, remember the most notorious ladies' man in history, Casanova, could probably not walk into a pool hall today and order a *creme de menthe* without being beaten silly with pool cues. Casanova was—like many men of his era—foppish. It was something men strived for. It indicated refinement, discernment, taste. All those King Louises of France wore wigs that even Dolly Parton would find too elaborate. And let's not forget our own founding fathers: satin pants, powdered wigs, make-up and all.

Linking effeminacy with homosexuality is primarily an American assumption. In the 1880s, Oscar Wilde toured America and

> Humor is
> a prelude to faith and
> Laughter is
> the beginning of prayer.
>
> REINHOLD NIEBUHR

lectured widely on *aesthetics*. He carried a lily on stage and was as much an aesthete as an Irishman could possibly be. The press ridiculed him, he ridiculed America, his lectures sold out, and everybody loved it. "A man in Leadville, Colorado," Wilde would say, "sued the railroad company because the reproduction of the Venus deMilo he ordered arrived without arms." Wilde would pause for dramatic effect while breathing in the fragrance of his lily. "The man collected on his claim." At the time he was touring the United States, Wilde was a married man with two children. No one linked his studied effeminacy with sexual orientation any more than they linked it to Ireland, lecturers, or playwrights. In 1895, however, when Wilde was found guilty of being a "sodomite" and, in 1897, when Havelock Ellis coined the word *homosexuality* in his *Studies in the Psychology of Sex,* Americans linked the two: "There are homosexuals; Oscar Wilde is a homosexual; so *that's* what they're like." Ironically, had America used as a stereotype one of its homegrown homosexuals of that era—such as the rough and rugged Walt Whitman—we might all have a very different view of how to "spot" homosexuals. (Could Gabby Hayes have lived down the stigma?) The stereotype would be just as inaccurate, but different.

Myth #7: *There aren't enough gays to really worry about.* The percentage of primarily homosexual people in this country is estimated at from one to ten percent. One percent seems low— if it were one percent, that would mean roughly half the nation's gay population traveled to the capital for the 1993 March on Washington. This is unlikely. But the number of gays is unimportant. As the *Los Angeles Times* editorialized on April 25, 1993,

What does all this mean in regard to current debates

about the place of homosexuals in American society? It means exactly nothing.

Whether homosexuals are 1% of the population or 10% or some figure in between, they are beyond any argument or cavil 100% entitled to the same protection under the law and the enjoyment of

> *The grounds for this membership revocation are the standards for leadership established by the Boy Scouts of America, which specifically forbid membership to homosexuals.*
>
> LETTER TO EAGLE SCOUT
> JAMES DALE
> August 10, 1991

the same rights that everyone else is guaranteed. That specifically includes the right to be free from discrimination and intimidation in employment, housing and schooling. It means the right to be protected from hate-inspired physical assaults. It means the right to privacy as that right applies to everyone else.

Gays have been—and continue to be—hidden from view in the media, except in the form of (a) psychotic killers, or (b) effeminate jokes. The first time the word *homosexual* was uttered in a film was 1961. When plays and novels featuring gay characters were made into movies, those characters turned into heterosexuals who were simply "sensitive." Film biographies completely expunged any mention of a gay hero's true sexual preference. For example, when the story of Lorenz Hart's life was filmed, the movie had him overcoming people's prejudice against him for "being too short." The oddest example was probably *Night and Day,* in which Cary Grant, a bisexual, played Cole Porter, a homosexual, as a heterosexual. Even today, "sophisticated" films tend to avoid homosexuality. Peter Biskind reported in *Premiere* that in the novel, *Fried Green Tomatoes at the Whistle Stop Café,* "the two main characters engage in a robust lesbian relationship. Where was the lesbianism when the novel was adapted for the screen?"

Myth #8: *God is opposed to homosexuality.* There are basically two Biblical prohibitions cited repeatedly and forcefully by those claiming homosexuality is condemned by God, hence should remain illegal. These two are Leviticus, chapter 20, verse 13 and Romans chapter 1, verses 26 and 27. Let's take a look at each.

Taken out of context, Leviticus 20:13 would certainly seem to prohibit homosexuality:

> *Both read the Bible day and night,*
> *But thou read'st black*
> *while I read white.*
>
> WILLIAM BLAKE

> If a man lies with a man as one lies with a woman, both of them have done what is detestable. They must be put to death; their blood will be on their own heads.

A quick look at the violations punishable by death in the same chapter of Leviticus, however, tells a very different story:

> If anyone curses his father or mother, he must be put to death. (Leviticus 20:9)

I wouldn't even have a chance to get to verse 13; I'd be dead by verse 9.

> If a man commits adultery with another man's wife—with the wife of his neighbor—both the adulterer and the adulteress must be put to death. (Leviticus 20:10)

Bye bye Jimmy Swaggart and Jim Bakker.

> If a man sleeps with his father's wife, he has dishonored his father. Both the man and the woman must be put to death; their blood will be on their own heads. (Leviticus 20:11)

Poor papa!

> If a man sleeps with his daughter-in-law, both of them must be put to death. What they have done is a perversion; their blood will be on their own heads. (Leviticus 20:12)

Poor son!

If a man has sexual relations with an animal, he must be put to death, and you must kill the animal. (Leviticus 20:15)

Poor livestock!

If a woman approaches an animal to have sexual relations with it, kill both the woman and the animal. (Leviticus 20:16)

> *After a couple was seen simulating sex inside a helicopter hovering outside the windows of the Club Hotel in Tiberias, Israel, the city's chief rabbi revoked the hotel's kosher license.*
>
> NEWS ITEM

Note the man has to do it, but the woman need only approach.

A man or woman who is a medium or spiritist among you must be put to death. (Leviticus 20:27)

O, the carnage at the Psychic Hotline!

It's easy to see that, in context, the always-quoted-out-of-context admonition against homosexuality is hardly God singling out gays for special punishment.

It was, in fact, one of the laws of Leviticus that was responsible for the death of Jesus:

[A]nyone who blasphemes the name of the LORD must be put to death. (Leviticus 24:16)

Jesus was tried by Sanhedren, the ruling religious body of Jerusalem, and found guilty of blasphemy. According to the religious powers that were, to claim he was the son of God was blasphemous. The charge of sedition was added so the Romans would approve of and carry out the death sentence.

Speaking of Romans, let's move on to the New Testament. Paul, in his epistle to the Romans, chapter 1, verses 26–27, describes the fate of Christians who reverted to paganism:

They exchanged the truth of God for a lie and worshiped and served created things . . . . Because of this, God gave them over to shameful lusts. Even their women ex-

> *The New Testament takes no demonstrable position on homosexuality. To suggest that Paul's references to excesses of sexual indulgence involving homosexual behavior are indicative of a general position in opposition to same-sex eroticism is as unfounded as arguing that his condemnation of drunkenness implies opposition to the drinking of wine.*
>
> JOHN BOSWELL

changed natural relations for unnatural ones. In the same way the men also abandoned natural relations with women and were inflamed with lust for one another. Men committed indecent acts with other men, and received in themselves the due penalty for their perversion.

This seems to condemn homosexuality. But it wasn't just a loss of proper gender infatuation that these non-truthsayers wrought . . .

> Furthermore, since they did not think it worthwhile to retain the knowledge of God, he gave them over to a depraved mind, to do what ought not to be done. They have become filled with every kind of wickedness, evil, greed and depravity. They are full of envy, murder, strife, deceit and malice. They are gossips, slanderers, God-haters, insolent, arrogant and boastful; they invent ways of doing evil; they disobey their parents; they are senseless, faithless, heartless, ruthless. Although they know God's righteous decree that those who do such things deserve death, they not only continue to do these very things but also approve of those who practice them. (Romans 1:28–32)

Glancing at the list reminds me of some of the characteristics of certain "Christian" leaders when they discuss homosexuality: deceit (quoting the Bible out of context), malice, slander, insolence, arrogance, boastfulness, heartlessness, ruthlessness. Paul's clear message to these people, echoing Jesus most accurately:

> You, therefore, have no excuse, you who pass judgment on someone else, for at whatever point you judge the other, you are condemning yourself, because you who

pass judgment do the same things. (Romans 2:1)

Amen.

If we look more carefully into Paul's comments concerning homosexual behavior, however, he does not condemn homosexual behavior itself but "unnatural relations." As an example, he mentions heterosexuals taking part in homosexual behavior. As a regular practice, this would be unnatural. (Curiosity and experimentation, however, are perfectly natural.)

> *They brought to the Pharisees the man who had been blind. Now the day on which Jesus had made the mud and opened the man's eyes was a Sabbath. Some of the Pharisees said, "This man is not from God, for he does not keep the Sabbath."*
>
> JOHN 9:13–14, 16

In this light, people who are naturally homosexual would have "abandoned natural relations" if they committed firmly to a life of other-gender joys. This is precisely what many Christian "ministries," such as Exodus, tell gays to do. (By the way, the two men who started Exodus fell in love with each other, were instantly exiled by their brethren, and later married.)

The "indecent acts with other men" most likely were pagan acts that *were* indecent: human sacrifice springs to mind. Paul was giving the Christians in Rome a laundry list, which included the various examples of unnatural behavior. His message was "Once you know God and you turn from God, woe unto you"— not "Homosexuality is bad."

No doubt Paul could have been more clear. Even Peter, who contributed precious few words to the New Testament, had to defend Paul:

> [Paul's] letters contain some things that are hard to understand, which ignorant and unstable people distort, as they do the other Scriptures, to their own destruction. (2 Peter 3:16)

If I wanted to join the Let's-Misinterpret-the-Bible Club (hardly an exclusive membership), I could quote this from Paul:

> *My lesbianism is an act*
> *of Christian charity.*
> *All those women out there*
> *are praying for a man,*
> *and I'm giving them my share.*
>
> RITA MAE BROWN

Are you unmarried? Then do not look for a wife . . . From now on, those who have wives should live as if they have none. (1 Corinthians 7:27, 29)

Couldn't that be twisted into an admonition to have only gay relations? Sure. A literal interpretation would cause an end to all Christian marriage. Paul was, in fact, encouraging a focus on spiritual matters rather than worldly ones, such as marriage and family.

Let's move on to the preachers who don't even quote the Bible but prefer Bible stories. They like to go on and on about "the sin of Sodom and Gomorra," which they incorrectly conclude was sodomy. Hence the sodomites of the world, incorrectly viewed as only homosexuals, must have caused God's wrath to fall upon the city. Let's go to the Bible for the real story.

Sodomy, in fact, is a grab-bag legal term that encompasses anything the legislative moral fathers of a given state find personally disgusting. It can include anal sex between men or between men and women (including married couples); oral sex between men, between women, men and women (including married couples); and sex between humans and animals.

In August 1982, a Mr. Hardwick was in his bedroom engaging in an act of sodomy with another consenting adult male. Sodomy is defined in Georgia (the state where this took place) as when one "performs or submits to any sexual act involving the sex organs of one person and the mouth or anus of another." In this case, it was Mr. Hardwick's mouth and the other man's sex organ. A police officer came in and, without a warrant, arrested them both. Mr. Hardwick took the case as far as the Supreme Court. What did the Supreme Court have to say? "The Constitution does not confer a fundamental right upon homosexuals to engage in sodomy."

One wants to play the Supremes to the Supremes: "Stop! In the Name of Love."

But, Biblically speaking, what *is* the sin of sodomy? (And what ever happened to Gomorrahy?)

> Now the men of Sodom were wicked and were sinning greatly against the Lord. (Genesis 13:13)

> *When Pat Buchanan thundered, and I quote, "We stand with George Bush against the amoral idea that gay and lesbian couples should have the same standing in law as married men and women," I wondered: Who is Pat Buchanan to pronounce anybody's love invalid?*
>
> BARBRA STREISAND

We gather they must have been doing something not very nice. But what was it? Five chapters later we find:

> Then the Lord said, "The outcry against Sodom and Gomorrah is so great and their sin so grievous that I will go down and see if what they have done is as bad as the outcry that has reached me. If not, I will know." (Genesis 18:20–21)

But what is the sin? We still have not been told. In the next chapter, we finally get to the meat of the story:

> The two angels arrived at Sodom in the evening, and Lot was sitting in the gateway of the city. When he saw them, he got up to meet them and bowed down with his face to the ground. "My lords," he said, "please turn aside to your servant's house. You can wash your feet and spend the night and then go on your way early in the morning."

> "No," they answered, "we will spend the night in the square." But he insisted so strongly that they did go with him and entered his house. He prepared a meal for them, baking bread without yeast, and they ate.

> Before they had gone to bed, all the men from every part of the city of Sodom—both young and old—surrounded the house. They called to Lot, "Where are the men who came to you tonight? Bring them out to us so that we can

> The Bible is clear about hate:
> Hate is wrong.
>
> BRUCE HILTON

have sex with them."
(Genesis 19:1–5)

Obviously, the sin here about to be attempted is *rape,* not consensual sex. Further, the sin is *inhospitality.* In desert regions, not being hospitable—that is, denying a traveler food and water; or, worse, taking advantage of a traveler in a violent way—was a sin second only to murder. Certainly, if travelers come out of the desert looking for water and get raped instead, that's pretty sinful—whether the travelers are men, women, or, in this case, angels. We'll get to other comments made about what the sin of Sodom was in a moment, but let's continue with our story. These are the parts the televangelists never get around to reading on television:

> Lot went outside to meet them and shut the door behind him and said, "No, my friends. Don't do this wicked thing. Look, I have two daughters who have never slept with a man. Let me bring them out to you, and you can do what you like with them. But don't do anything to these men, for they have come under the protection of my roof." (Genesis 19:6–8)

I don't want to sound like a prude, but isn't Lot supposed to be the hero of this piece? Here he is offering this rowdy crowd his two virgin daughters so that the crowd might "do what you like with them." If Lot had offered himself, that might have been noble. "Take me, but leave my guests and daughters alone." Frankly, in comparing the sins of raping two strangers and offering your two virgin daughters to an unruly mob, I think the latter is worse. Maybe I'm just too old-fashioned for the Old Testament.

When the assembled throng continue to demand divine flesh, the angels blind the nasty mob, pull Lot into the house, send Lot and his family on their way, and destroy Sodom and Gomorrah. After Lot's wife disobeys the angels' instructions and turns to look back at the city and becomes a pillar of salt, the story gets exciting again: Lot's daughters show that kinkiness runs in the family:

> *As a child my family's menu consisted of two choices: take it or leave it.*
>
> BUDDY HACKETT

> He and his two daughters lived in a cave. One day the older daughter said to the younger, "Our father is old, and there is no man around here to lie with us, as is the custom all over the earth. Let's get our father to drink wine and then lie with him and preserve our family line through our father."
>
> That night they got their father to drink wine, and the older daughter went in and lay with him. He was not aware of it when she lay down or when she got up. (Genesis 19:30–33)

That must have been some wine.

> The next day the older daughter said to the younger, "Last night I lay with my father. Let's get him to drink wine again tonight, and you go in and lie with him so we can preserve our family line through our father." So they got their father to drink wine that night also, and the younger daughter went and lay with him. Again he was not aware of it when she lay down or when she got up. So both of Lot's daughters became pregnant by their father. (Genesis 19:34–36)

Okay, enough peeking into the caves of the morally upright. Let's return to defining the sin of Sodom. Nowhere in the remainder of the Bible—Old or New Testament—is the sin of Sodom defined as sex between consenting male adults. Here are the sins of Sodom (this is God speaking, by the way):

> *I believe in God,*
> *only I spell it Nature.*
>
> FRANK LLOYD WRIGHT

> Hear the word of the Lord, you rulers of Sodom; listen to the law of our God, you people of Gomorrah!
>
> Learn to do right! Seek justice, encourage the oppressed. Defend the cause of the fatherless, plead the case of the widow.
>
> See how the faithful city has become a harlot! She was once full of justice; righteousness used to dwell in her—but now murderers! Your silver has become dross, your choice wine is diluted with water. Your rulers are rebels, companions of thieves; they all love bribes and chase after gifts. They do not defend the cause of the fatherless; the widow's case does not come before them. (Isaiah 1:10, 17, 21–23)

This sounds more like Washington, D.C., than West Hollywood to me.

> Now this was the sin of your sister Sodom: She and her daughters were arrogant, overfed and unconcerned; they did not help the poor and needy. They were haughty and did detestable things before me. Therefore I did away with them as you have seen. (Ezekiel 16:49–50)

"Arrogant, overfed and unconcerned; they did not help the poor and needy. They were haughty. . . ." Sounds more like some televangelists I could name. Note, there is still no specific mention of same-sex activities.

Each time Jesus mentions Sodom and Gomorrah he does so in connection with inhospitality:

> If anyone will not welcome you or listen to your words, shake the dust off your feet when you leave that home or town. I tell you the truth, it will be more bearable for Sodom and Gomorrah on the day of judgment than for

that town. (Matthew 10:14–15)

Or, perhaps, when he encountered ingratitude (or just plain stupidity):

> And you, Capernaum, will you be lifted up to the skies? No, you will go down to the depths. If the miracles that were performed in you had been performed in Sodom, it would have remained to this day. But I tell you that it will be more bearable for Sodom on the day of judgment than for you. (Matthew 11:23–24)

The only biblical passage that even mentions sexual behavior that might apply to homosexuality is this from Jude:

> In a similar way, Sodom and Gomorrah and the surrounding towns gave themselves up to sexual immorality and perversion. They serve as an example of those who suffer the punishment of eternal fire. In the very same way, these dreamers pollute their own bodies, reject authority and slander celestial beings. (Jude 7–8)

"Sexual immorality" and "perversion" refer to violent pagan practices of idolatry—including human sacrifice—and not what goes on between consenting adults in their own bedrooms. According to Methodist pastor Dr. Edward Bauman,

> The real irony is that homosexuals have been the victim of inhospitality for thousands of years in the Christian nations of the world. Condemned by the church and the state, they have been ridiculed, rejected, persecuted, and even executed. In the name of an erroneous interpretation of the crime of Sodom, the true crime of Sodom has been continuously perpetrated to our own day.

In his book, *Can Homophobia Be Cured?*, Bruce Hilton presents

---

We must be on guard against giving interpretations of scripture that are far-fetched or opposed to science, and so exposing the word of God to the ridicule of unbelievers.

SAINT AUGUSTINE
(354–430)

---

an amusing reversal on the role of gays in the church:

> We have read the Navy report on Tailhook yet we have concluded that it would be wrong
> —fundamentally wrong—
> to ban heterosexuals from serving in the military.
>
> REPRESENTATIVE GERRY STUDDS

WHY HETEROSEXUAL MEN SHOULD NOT BE ORDAINED

1. According to divorce statistics, fewer than half of them are able to maintain a long-term relationship.

2. The literature is full of tales of clergymen becoming sexually involved with women of the congregation.

3. Three out of four straight males in the United States admit to being unfaithful to their long-term partners.

4. Thousands of straight men are in jail for molesting little girls. A shocking percentage of these victims were their own daughters.

5. Straight males are the driving force behind the declaration of wars—the only other activity described in the Social Principles as "incompatible with Christian teaching."

6. Jesus saved his harshest words for the self-righteousness of groups like the Pharisees and Sadducees—which, if they lived according to the code they promoted, were made up of straight males.

⚖ ⚖ ⚖

On the other hand, the Bible does give some positive images of male affection. These from the Old Testament:

> After David had finished talking with Saul, Jonathan became one in spirit with David, and he loved him as himself. From that day Saul kept David with him and did not let him return to his father's house. And Jonathan made a

covenant with David because he loved him as himself. Jonathan took off the robe he was wearing and gave it to David, along with his tunic, and even his sword, his bow and his belt. (1 Samuel 18:1–4)

> *Among the ancient Chinese the most popular literary expression for gay love was "the love of the cut sleeve," referring to the selfless devotion of the last emperor of the Han dynasty, Ai-Ti, who cut off his sleeve when called to an audience rather than wake his lover, Tung Hsien, who had fallen asleep across it.*
>
> JOHN BOSWELL

After the boy had gone, David got up from the south side of the stone and bowed down before Jonathan three times, with his face to the ground. Then they kissed each other and wept together—but David wept the most. Jonathan said to David, "Go in peace, for we have sworn friendship with each other in the name of the Lord, saying, 'The Lord is witness between you and me, and between your descendants and my descendants forever.'" (1 Samuel 20:41–42)

"Saul and Jonathan—in life they were loved and gracious, and in death they were not parted. They were swifter than eagles, they were stronger than lions." (2 Samuel 1:23)

"I grieve for you, Jonathan my brother; you were very dear to me. Your love for me was wonderful, more wonderful than that of women." (2 Samuel 1:26)

As to Jesus' relationship with those who vary from today's sexual norms, the incident of Jesus and the centurion is telling:

> When Jesus had entered Capernaum, a centurion came to him, asking for help, "Lord," he said, "my servant lies at home paralyzed and in terrible suffering."
>
> Jesus said to him, "I will go and heal him." (Matthew 8:5–7)

Matthew uses the Greek word *pais*, which means "boy," and Luke (7:1–10) uses *Doulas*, or "slave." That a Roman officer would seek out a Jewish healer for his servant shows a deeper relationship than simply master-servant. We also know the depth of the relationship was not based on the amount of time the servant had spent with him: being a "boy," he would not be, say, the slave who raised the centurion from birth.

The boy-slave was what was often referred to as a *body slave*, a young man who would wash, groom, and take care of the personal needs of his master—including sexual ones. Body slaves were common among Roman officers—especially while on a campaign or stationed outside Rome. Only the highest officers were allowed to bring their wife (or wives), and, even then, many found a male body slave a more practical traveling companion. Bisexuality was commonplace in Rome, as it had been in Greece. Even Julius Caesar was said to be "every man's wife and every women's husband" by Curio the Elder. He was not being pejorative, but merely mentioning one of Caesar's many accomplishments.

When the centurion arrived (or, in Luke's account, sent emissaries) and expressed concern over the slave-boy, the centurion's relationship with the boy was obvious. It made no difference to Jesus. He agreed to heal the boy. This was remarkable in that Jesus was addressing his teachings to the Jews, not the Gentiles, and the centurion and the boy would clearly be of the Gentile/pagan category. According to Luke, the centurion had helped build a synagogue and was a friend of the Jewish people, but it's doubtful that would have influenced Jesus very much. Jesus was a pushover for *faith*.

> The centurion replied, "Lord, I do not deserve to have you come under my roof. But just say the word, and my servant will be healed. For I myself am a man under authority, with soldiers under me. I tell this one, 'Go' and he goes; and that one, 'Come', and he comes. I say to my servant, 'Do this,' and he does it."

When Jesus heard this, he was astonished and said to those following him, "I tell you the truth, I have not found anyone in Israel with such great faith." Then Jesus said to the centurion, "Go! It will be done just as you believed it would." And his servant was healed at that very hour. (Matthew 8:8–10, 13)

> *Plato argued that pairs of homosexual lovers would make the best soldiers and the Thebans actually formed an army of such pairs in what turned out to be an extraordinarily successful experiment.*
>
> JOHN BOSWELL

Similarly, Jesus had no condemnation for effeminate men or eunuchs. After all, he described himself metaphorically as a eunuch when referring to his own sexuality. Within the Jewish culture, however, eunuchs and effeminate men were outcasts.

> So he sent two of his disciples, telling them, "Go into the city, and a man carrying a jar of water will meet you. Follow him." (Mark 14:13)

Carrying water in Israel was "woman's work." Telling his disciples to look for "a man carrying a jar of water" would be the same as saying today, "Look for a man in a dress, high heels, and a bouffant hairdo." That Jesus would have either a eunuch or an effeminate male lead his disciples to the upper room where the Last Supper would be held is one of Jesus' many statements of acceptance, inclusion, and compassion.

Myth #9: *God made Adam and Eve, not Adam and Steve.* Yes, God *did* make Adam and Steve, as well as Adam and Eve, and Eve and Genevieve—some people just don't like it that way.

Myth #10: *Homosexuals are promiscuous.* Some are; most are not. The same can be said of heterosexuals. In fact, almost anything—good or bad—that can be said about homosexuals can also be said of heterosexuals. Homosexuals are indistinguishable from heterosexuals except in whom they love and with whom they go to bed.

Myth #11: *Homosexuals can't control their sex drives.* When you consider how well most homosexuals have controlled not just their sex drives but their conversations, their innuendoes, and even their inferences for so many years, it seems as though homosexuals have remarkable control. If closeted gays have been able to keep their homosexuality secret from friends and co-workers, obviously, should they happen to stumble out of the closet, they can keep their sexual urges under control.

> *Viscount Waldorf Astor owned Britain's two most influential newspapers, The Times and the Observer, but his American wife, Nancy, had a wider circulation than both papers put together.*
>
> EMERY KELLEN

Myth #12: *Gays are not fit for military service.* All the reasons why gays shouldn't serve in the military boil down to one: the excessive prejudice of the heterosexuals against homosexuality would make the heterosexuals unfit for combat. The pro-prejudice group argues, "Wouldn't *you* be uncomfortable if some gay guy kept trying to hit on *you?*"

What the heterosexuals in the military are afraid of is that the gays in the military—should they be allowed to come out—would start hitting on the heterosexuals with the same levels of determination and deception that the heterosexual men hit on women. The heterosexual men, then, are afraid to be treated the way they treat women. Well, who can blame them? That gay men will behave as disreputably as straight men is an unfair projection on the part of straight men. Give the gays a chance. If some gays treat the straights the way the straights treat women, one can only quote: "What goes around, comes around."

As to gay women in the military, here's this herstorical tidbit from the June 21, 1993, issue of *Newsweek:*

> General Dwight D. Eisenhower received some unsettling news while he was in occupied Germany after World War II. There were, he was told, a significant number of lesbians in his Women's Army Corps (WAC) command. He called in Sgt.

Johnnie Phelps and ordered her to get a list of all the lesbians in the battalion. "We've got to get rid of them," he barked. Phelps said she'd check into it. But, she told the general, "when you get the list back, my name's going to be first." Eisenhower's secretary then interrupted. "Sir, if the

> *Belief in a cruel God makes a cruel man.*
>
> THOMAS PAINE

general pleases, Sergeant Phelps will have to be second on the list, because mine will be first." Dumbfounded, Ike realized he'd lose many of his key personnel if he persisted. "Forget that order," he told Phelps.

Myth #13: *Homosexuals spread AIDS.* AIDS is a disease spread by unsafe sexual contact (primarily to the passive partner in intercourse), dirty hypodermic needles, contaminated blood transfusions, and from mother to child before birth. Gays have taken great care to educate their community, practice safe sex, and minister (in the true sense of the word) to those unfortunate enough to have caught the disease. Because most gays have changed their sexual activities and are now practicing safe sex, new infections in the gay community have leveled off. Meanwhile, infections are on the rise in the heterosexual community. The myth, "If you don't go to bed with someone gay you won't get AIDS," is hurting the heterosexual community more severely than it's hurting the homosexual community.

Worldwide, AIDS is primarily a heterosexual, not homosexual, disease. It is a sexually transmitted disease that—for whatever reason—entered the gay community in the United States and stayed fairly contained there for a number of years. It is now spreading through the heterosexual community, and will continue to do so until heterosexuals realize that AIDS is not a "gay disease." Any sexually active person—male, female, gay, straight—can get it. *If you have intercourse, use a condom.* There's hardly a gay person in the country who does not know this rule of safe sex. Can the same

> *Leaving behind books*
> *is even more beautiful—*
> *there are far too many children.*
>
> MARGUERITE YOURCENAR

be said of heterosexuals?

Further, 25 percent of the AIDS cases—including almost all cases involving heterosexuals and children—were spread by or directly connected to dirty needles. If heroin or morphine were inexpensive, readily available, and sold in use-once syringes, do you think these 25 percent of AIDS cases would be suffering today?

Myth #14: *AIDS is God's curse upon homosexuals.* Crises bring out the best in people—and the worst. They also bring out the best people—and the worst. What can one say about ignorant, arrogant, politically active people who say things like, "AIDS is God's curse upon homosexuals"? I can remember the words of Jesus: "Forgive them, Father, for they know not what they do," but then I remember Jesus said that moments after he was nailed to the cross.

Unconventional
Religious Practices

> *I believe there is
> something out there
> watching over us.
> Unfortunately,
> it's the government.*
>
> WOODY ALLEN

WE ARE SHOCKED and saddened by the events in Waco, Texas. We grieve with the families on both sides who lost loved ones.

The federal government is conducting investigations to find out what happened at the Branch Davidian compound in Waco to prevent similar occurrences in the future. While we think such an investigation is appropriate, we oppose any attempt to define what is a valid religion or set the parameters of a proper church.

Under the religious liberty provisions of the First Amendment, government has no business declaring what is orthodox or heretical, or what is a true or false religion. It should steer clear of inflammatory and misleading labels. History teaches that today's "cults" may become tomorrow's mainstream religions.

The United States is a religiously diverse country. We treasure its religious pluralism. Such diversity is a natural and expected result of our constitutionally protected religious liberty and is a source of strength, not weakness. These religious contours add to the American landscape, they do not detract from it. In the midst of our national mourning, we must fend off any inclination to shrink from our commitment to religious pluralism or to seek security at the expense of liberty.

This heady freedom is not absolute. It should be exercised responsibly. Religion is no excuse for violent or criminal conduct that harms other people or threatens public safety or welfare.

> *A way of life
> that is odd or even erratic
> but interferes with no rights
> or interests of others
> is not to be condemned
> because it is different.*
>
> CHIEF JUSTICE WARREN E. BURGER

Absent some compelling justification, however, government should not restrict religious exercise. And force—if ever appropriate—must be employed as a last resort.

Public discourse should be conducted with integrity. The nation's leaders ought to measure their words carefully and temper their passion with reason. Government must resist any temptation to retreat from our "first freedom." To deny religious liberty to any is to diminish religious liberty for all.

⚖️ ⚖️ ⚖️

I didn't write the opening of this chapter. It was taken, verbatim, from a document released just after the events in Waco, entitled "Religious Liberty at Risk," and signed by American Baptist Churches in the U.S.A.; American Civil Liberties Union, Washington Office; American Conference on Religious Movements; Americans United for Separation of Church & State; Association of Christian Schools International; Baptist Joint Committee on Public Affairs; Church of Scientology International; Center for Theology/Public Policy; Episcopal Church; First Liberty Institute; General Conference of Seventh-Day Adventists; Greater Grace World Outreach; National Association of Evangelicals; National Council of Churches of Christ; Presbyterian Church (U.S.A.), Washington Office; Union of American Hebrew Congregations.

Quite a diverse list. I have very little to add to their comments.

As much as I may personally dislike the political meddlings of church groups or the thought control that seems to be a central activity of cults, the answer is not to be found in more, new, and better laws.

If a religious group is gathering money under false pretenses (telling its followers the cash is going to feed the poor while it really goes to the campaign fund of conservative candidates, or collecting money to build a "retreat center" for the use of all members while the money goes to support the cult leader's forty-some horses with

> *Who says I am not under the special protection of God?*
>
> ADOLF HITLER

nary a retreat in sight), it may be appropriate for the government to step in. Certainly, religious groups should be subject to the same laws as any other organization or corporation. For the most part, however, facts—not government acts—will keep at bay those who use the name of God to support their own personal mammon.

Organizations such as the Cult Awareness Network (CAN) provide an invaluable service by maintaining open files on thousands of cults and cult-like groups around the world. These files are available to anyone wanting to research the background and methods of any cult.

I owe CAN an apology. In the hardcover edition of *Ain't Nobody's Business If You Do*, I'm afraid I trashed CAN. This was because (guess why?) I was under the influence of a cult (John-Roger's Movement of Spiritual Inner Awareness or MSIA). Had I only read CAN's files on John-Roger and MSIA *first*.*

But as much as I personally dislike cults, I despise any organization or individual that robs people of their individuality. I still feel the entire Waco incident was the result of an overfed federal bureaucracy gone mad, not an example of "the danger of cults." (William Sessions, the director of the FBI, told Congress, "Were

---

*For the complete story of my adventures in Cultland, please see my book *LIFE 102: What to Do When Your Guru Sues You*. On the World Wide Web free at http://www.mcwilliams.com.

> *What kind of government is this? It's getting more like California all the time.*
>
> WOODY ALLEN

we supposed to stand by and suck our thumbs?") And then we saw what many consider the (admittedly insane) backlash in the Oklahoma City bombing.

Ultimately, cults ain't the law's business. If adults want to destroy their lives by believing a cult leader is God, that is their unfortunate choice. Retribution must come through civil litigation. It is not the government's business to bring Armageddon to their door—even if our government *does* have God on its side.

Unpopular Political Views

> *If our democracy is to flourish*
> *it must have criticism,*
> *if our government is to function*
> *it must have dissent.*
> *Only totalitarian governments*
> *insist upon conformity and they—*
> *as we know—do so at their peril.*
>
> HENRY STEELE COMMAGER
> 1947

THE UNITED STATES constitution is a fascinating document. It has within itself the rules by which it can be changed, modified, or eliminated altogether. This flexibility allows the United States to have one of the oldest continuing governments in the world.

Some people, however, believe that the Constitution needs to be "protected" from even the *idea* of another system of government. Ironically, those who, in order to "defend the Constitution," suspend people's constitutional right to advocate another form of government are the ones who destroy the Constitution. That the people may someday vote out our current form of government and replace it with another is a risk inherent in our form of government. Those who try to eliminate the risk are, simultaneously, destroying the present system.

It has always amazed me that the people who claim the greatest allegiance to the Constitution and our form of government should trust either so little. Why do people seem to think our system of government is so fragile that it can't stand on its own among other ideas of government? Why do they assume a system of government that's been able to flourish for more than 200 years is some fragile butterfly? It is, in fact, an iron butterfly, a system that becomes stronger by being challenged, just as we become stronger through exercise. When not challenged, our government—like our bodies or our minds—becomes flabby, self-indulgent, and complacent.

⚖ ⚖ ⚖

> *Their point of departure*
> *is different and their paths diverse;*
> *nevertheless, each seems called*
> *by some secret design of Providence*
> *one day to hold in its hands*
> *the destinies of half the world.*
>
> ALEX DE TOCQUEVILLE
>
> on Russia and America
> 1835

Now that the "communist menace" has been safely laid to rest, I trust I can make a few frank observations about communism, the United States' reaction to the "communist threat," and how great a menace or threat there really was. Prior to 1989, as someone accurately observed, the only state-sponsored religion in the United States was anti-communism. One of the tenets of this religion was that if you did anything but denounce communism in the most virulent terms, you were a communist. Now that it's all over, however, and we can use the word *communist* without prefacing it with *dirty* or *goddamn,* let's take a look at the growth of anti-communism—and thus the growth of state-enforced political conformity—in the United States.

We never really hated communism as much as we hated the way communism was practiced in the Soviet Union, which was *totalitarianism.* Understandably, we especially hated Stalin's brand of totalitarianism.

It was hard not to hate Joseph Stalin. Of few people in history can one say, "He was personally responsible for the death of millions." Countries have been responsible for the death of millions, but individuals who can claim this distinction are few. Stalin's politics in a nutshell: Kill those who oppose you; terrorize those who support you. Using this method, Stalin succeeded, by 1924, in gaining total control of Russia. He rounded up millions of dissidents, put them in prison camps (the *Gulags)* and, essentially, starved them to death.

That Stalin was a monster may not have been good for the Russian people, but historically, it was good for the United States. If Stalin had been a weaker leader (like Mussolini), he probably would have joined ranks with Hitler in the 1930s (like Mussolini) and Hitler would have won World War II.

AIN'T NOBODY'S BUSINESS IF YOU DO

⚖️ ⚖️ ⚖️

Although *communal* societies have existed throughout history, what we now call *communism* was first proposed by Karl Marx and Friedrich Engels in the mid-1800s. Suggesting that everything be owned *in common* was, naturally, a threat to those

> *A reactionary is someone with a clear and comprehensive vision of an ideal world we have lost.*
>
> KENNETH MINOGUE

who already owned everything. Marx and Engels's book, *The Communist Manifesto,* published in 1848, began:

> A specter is haunting Europe—the specter of Communism. All the powers of old Europe have entered into a holy alliance to exorcise this specter: Pope and Czar, Metternich and Guizot, French Radicals and German police spies.

For the next seventy years, communism made for stimulating political discussion. In 1918, however, the communists won the Russian Revolution—under the leadership of Vladimir Lenin—and the world's first communist state was established.

In the United States by 1918, communism, socialism, anarchism, or any *ism* other than Americanism was soundly denounced. In early 1920, for example, a national "Red Scare" resulted in the arrests of 2,700 "communists," "anarchists," and other "radicals." The most famous case during this time was that of Sacco and Vanzetti. They were arrested in Massachusetts in 1920, found guilty in 1921, and executed in 1927, primarily because of their unpopular political beliefs. (They were vindicated on July 19, 1977, in a proclamation by the governor of Massachusetts.)

Prior to his execution, Nicola Sacco wrote in a letter to his son Dante:

> Help the weak ones that cry for help, help the prosecuted and the victim . . . they are the comrades that fight

> *If Karl,*
> *instead of writing a lot*
> *about capital,*
> *had made a lot of it*
> *it would have been much better.*
>
> KARL MARX'S MOTHER

and fall . . . for the conquest of the joy of freedom for all the poor workers. In this struggle for life you will find more love and you will be loved.

Meanwhile, in Germany, Hitler won the support of the powerful bankers and the industrialists with his virulent anti-communist stance.

In Russia, along came Stalin. After three years in a seminary, Stalin saw the light and became a politician. By 1922, Stalin was the general secretary of the Communist Party. Even though shortly before his death in 1924 Lenin had written a "testament" urging that Stalin be removed from his post for inappropriate and arbitrary conduct, Stalin succeeded Lenin as leader of the Soviet Union in 1924.

Throughout the remainder of the 1920s and the 1930s, Stalin repeatedly sought European and American support in forming an alliance against Adolf Hitler. England, France, and America, however, were not interested in dealing with a "communist," forcing Stalin to enter into a nonaggression pact with Hitler in 1939. While this did not make Hitler and Stalin allies, each agreed not to interfere with the military aggression of the other. This gave Hitler the green light to attack Poland, which he promptly did. World War II was underway.

⚖ ⚖ ⚖

In 1911, at the age of twenty-nine, Franklin Delano Roosevelt said, "There is nothing I love as much as a good fight." Roosevelt got what he loved: he was assistant secretary of the Navy during World War I; ran a losing vice-presidential race in 1920; was stricken with polio in 1921, leaving him permanently disabled; successfully ran for president in 1932; battled the depression during the 1930s; and led the Allies to victory in World War II.

In the 1930s, while enacting and administering some of the most sweeping socialistic programs in American history (the New Deal), Roosevelt remained, in speeches, violently anti-communist. While running for presidential re-election in 1936, for example, he made this speech:

> *We must especially beware of that small group of selfish men who would clip the wings of the American Eagle in order to feather their own nests.*
>
> FRANKLIN D. ROOSEVELT

> I have not sought, I do not seek, I repudiate the support of any advocate of Communism or of any other alien "ism" which would by fair means or foul change our American democracy.

Note "by fair means or foul." What Mr. Roosevelt was saying—and as practiced by American politicians before and since—is that communism should not be tolerated even if it were introduced by "fair means."

In other words, even if the communists were legally voted into office, it would be unacceptable to President Roosevelt. That the successful 1936 presidential candidate (and the liberal candidate at that) could make such hostile statements, indicated the tenor of the times—a tenor which became increasingly shrill as the years went by.

When the discussion turned to Stalin, Roosevelt applied the nastiest word one could use in 1940, *dictatorship:*

> The Soviet Union, as everybody who has the courage to face the fact knows, is run by a dictatorship as absolute as any other dictatorship in the world.

Roosevelt was saying Stalin was another Hitler. Roosevelt even had trouble with the Russian people:

> I don't know a good Russian from a bad Russian. I can tell

> *The Marxist analysis
> has got nothing to do
> with what happened
> in Stalin's Russia:
> it's like blaming Jesus Christ
> for the Inquisition in Spain.*
>
> TONY BENN

a good Frenchman from a bad Frenchman. I can tell a good Italian from a bad Italian. I know a good Greek when I see one. But I don't understand the Russians.

In a radio broadcast on October 1, 1939, Churchill shared Roosevelt's uncertainty of Russia:

I cannot forecast to you the action of Russia. It is a riddle wrapped in a mystery inside an enigma.

In addition to being the leader of the Soviet communists, financing communist movements in America, murdering millions, and other distastefulness, the former seminary student had also become an outspoken enemy of all religion. When it was suggested he might want to make a political alliance with the pope, Stalin replied, "The pope? How many divisions has *he* got?" Stalin was responsible for the adjective *godless* being grafted onto *communism,* a phrase which did not help Stalin's—or communism's—standing in American popularity polls.

Anti-communism may have been a national religion in the United States before World War II, but it became a national hysteria after the war. During the cold war, the general public labeled Russia, who had been our vital ally only a few years earlier, our vilest enemy. If the American people had remembered some details about World War II and its peace settlement, we might have seen the "communist menace" in a more realistic perspective, and we might not have spent as much money and destroyed as many lives fighting communism.

⚖️ ⚖️ ⚖️

In the 1930s, the mood of America was isolationist. We had fought the first world war "to keep the world safe for democracy," and here it was, less than twenty years later, and those quarrelsome Europeans were about to go at it again. The conflict was referred to as the coming "European war" and Americans wanted none of it. With the depression, Americans had enough troubles of their own. In 1937, we were about as likely to return to fight in

> *I have been forced to the conclusion that we cannot win this war for England, regardless of how much assistance we extend.*
>
> CHARLES A. LINDBERGH
> 1941

Europe as we would return to Vietnam today. Various politicians attempted to tell the American people that this war was *different*—there was this man named *Hitler,* but the American people, for the most part, were not buying.

In a campaign speech on October 30, 1940, President Roosevelt, campaigning for an unprecedented third term, said:

> And while I am talking to you mothers and fathers, I give you one more assurance. I have said this before, but I shall say it again and again and again: Your boys are not going to be sent into any foreign wars.

No less an American hero than Charles Lindbergh visited Germany and returned to inform the American people that there was no comparison between the air power of England and the air power of Germany: Germany would win the European war. Unless we wanted to go over and fight for ourselves, Lindbergh suggested the path of strict neutrality. His voice was persuasive. He was a realist, but did not take into consideration two factors: first, the tenacity of the British people; and, second, their good sense in making in 1940 Winston Churchill their prime minister.

Far from being neutral in the European conflict, Roosevelt leaned heavily toward England. Churchill said, "Give us the tools," and Roosevelt did. Through a program known as lend-lease, the United States supplied Great Britain with ships, airplanes, and armaments. The resulting surge in industrial output,

> *Mistreatment of Jews
> in Germany may be considered
> virtually eliminated.*
>
> CORDELL HULL
>
> U.S. Secretary of State
> April 3, 1933

more than any other single factor, helped bring America out of its depression. Although America was not sending fighting men into the European conflict, the United States was no longer officially neutral.

Throughout the 1930s, Winston Churchill, though not holding a public office, had made repeated warnings to England about Nazi Germany. The warnings were ignored. In Churchill's 1936 book, *While England Slept,* he wrote:

> I have watched this famous island descending incontinently, fecklessly, the stairway which leads to a dark gulf.

Once Hitler's tanks rolled into Poland, then captured Paris, England saw Churchill had been right all along. They made him prime minister, and he sailed to America where he charmed the armaments out of the United States.

The only alliance that could possibly beat Hitler would be one between Roosevelt, Churchill, and Stalin. As much as these three differed, they enthusiastically agreed on one crucial subject: their loathing for Herr Hitler.

From a radio broadcast on September 11, 1940, Churchill purred:

> This wicked man Hitler, the repository and embodiment
> of many forms of soul-destroying hatred, this monstrous
> product of former wrongs and shame.

When Hitler without warning broke the nonaggression pact and attacked Russia in June of 1941, Churchill found himself defending Russia.

> Hitler is a monster of wickedness, insatiable in his lust for
> blood and plunder. Not content with having all Europe
> under his heel, or else terrorized into various forms of

abject submission, he must now carry his work of butchery and desolation among the vast multitudes of Russia and of Asia. The terrible military machine, which we and the rest of the civilized world so foolishly, so supinely, so insensately allowed the Nazi gangsters to build up year by year from almost nothing, cannot stand idle lest it rust or fall to pieces. . . . So now this bloodthirsty guttersnipe must launch his mechanized armies upon new fields of slaughter, pillage and devastation.

> *No matter what happens, the U.S. Navy is not going to be caught napping.*
>
> FRANK KNOX
>
> U.S. Secretary of the Navy
> December 4, 1941

Secretly, of course, Churchill was thrilled. He knew Hitler's invasion of Russia would take the pressure off England and provide additional proof to the United States that Hitler respected no treaty, territory, or bounds of decency. Hitler would not take over Europe and leave America alone: Hitler's goal was world domination. The attack on Russia made it no longer a European war, but a world war. On July 14, 1941, Churchill said,

> We will have no truce or parley with you [Hitler], or the grisly gang who work your wicked will. You do your worst—and we will do our best.

In December 1941, Pearl Harbor was attacked and the United States was officially in the war. This achieved, Churchill paused for a moment of self-congratulation with a touch of British wit:

> When I warned [the French] that Britain would fight on alone whatever they did, their generals told their prime minister and his divided cabinet, "In three weeks England will have her neck wrung like a chicken." Some chicken; some neck.

Like Churchill, Stalin was vindicated in his warnings of Hitler's danger. On November 6, 1942, with Hitler's army only

> *If Stalin had learned
> to play cricket
> the world might now be
> a better place to live in.*
>
> ARCHBISHOP R. DOWNEY

fifty miles from Moscow, Stalin did not flinch:

> The Hitlerite black-guards . . . have turned Europe into a prison of nations, and this they call the new order in Europe.

In late 1943, Roosevelt, Churchill, and Stalin met in Teheran. Although still holding the weakest hand, Stalin was in a better negotiating position than anyone had previously thought possible: he had received a gift from Mother Russia. As she had done with Napoleon in 1812, the worst Russian winter in recent memory attacked Hitler's finest army with a fierceness Hitler had not anticipated. Although the newsreels sent back to Berlin showed naked German soldiers rollicking in the snow and having a jolly good time, the reality was far more somber. The snows of winter and the mud of spring made either advance or retreat impossible. Tens of thousands died, the army was demoralized, and Hitler was faced with his first defeat in the war. Roosevelt, Churchill, and Stalin became, if not comrades, certainly allies.

In his 1943 Christmas Eve Fireside Chat, President Roosevelt assured the people of the United States:

> I believe that we are going to get along very well with [Stalin] and the Russian people—very well indeed.

⚖️ ⚖️ ⚖️

By early 1945, as an allied victory was in sight, all was not so rosy. In February, the "Big Three" gathered in Yalta in the U.S.S.R. Roosevelt had been elected to a fourth term of office. He was very ill. Stalin found Roosevelt's weakened condition disgusting: born rich, well-educated, a lawyer, disabled in adulthood by a disease that struck mostly children, and now in perpetual ill health. That Americans would elect this man as their leader only four months before indicated the pathetic condition of capitalism and the West. Stalin, three years older than Roosevelt, was still robust. A leader, Stalin felt, must be strong, and strength begins with physical power. The very name *Stalin*—which he chose for himself when he became a revolutionary—meant "man of steel."

> *You can no more win a war than you can win an earthquake.*
>
> JEANNETTE RANKIN

Stalin was feeling strong politically, too. What he brought to the conference table was not insignificant: Stalin had lost 20 million people in the war, compared to Roosevelt's 407,000, and Churchill's 378,000. There was no doubt that had Stalin given in to Hitler in 1941, the war would be over and Hitler would be the winner. Stalin considered himself, then, a full partner in the war and, as an equal victor, was entitled to a full share of the spoils.

Roosevelt and Churchill had other ideas.

It wasn't that Churchill and Roosevelt wanted to take more of the spoils than Stalin; Churchill and Roosevelt wanted to *give them back to the Germans.* Stalin was incensed. When you lose a war, you lose your land: that's what wars were about. If you win a war, you win the land—*especially* when you are the one attacked. Stalin had not lost 20 million Russians for nothing: he had every intention of expanding the Soviet empire, and that was going to include his fair share of Germany and the lands conquered by Germany earlier in the war.

Roosevelt and Churchill had no designs on Europe—particularly Germany. Germany, they felt, still belonged to the German *people:* had they not been taken over by Hitler and his SS, they would never have gone to war. Besides, argued Roosevelt and Churchill, Stalin was playing by the *old* rules of war: Stalin wanted material booty; Roosevelt and Churchill were fighting for *ideology,* not land.

> *The arts of power and its minions*
> *are the same in all countries*
> *and in all ages.*
> *It marks its victim; denounces it;*
> *and excites the public odium*
> *and the public hatred,*
> *to conceal its own abuses*
> *and encroachments.*
>
> HENRY CLAY
> 1834

Stalin had never heard such nonsense. He maintained that all Germans seriously opposed to Hitler had left Germany, been eliminated, or were in concentration camps. The vast majority of the people Roosevelt and Churchill wanted to give Germany back to were firmly behind Adolf Hitler, and had been since at least the first military victories. Besides, this is what happened at the end of World War I: Germany was given back to the German people, who, within two decades, had rearmed and started another world war.

Stalin thought Roosevelt and Churchill's claim that the United States and England fought wars for ideological reasons was particularly ironic: America had declared war on millions of Native Americans, taken their land, and built a country using the forced labor of African Americans who were savagely taken from their homeland. Less than a hundred years before the Yalta Conference, the United States had still been actively involved in the "relocation" of millions of Native Americans and the "migration" of millions more Africans. How, wondered Stalin, could Roosevelt—less than fifty years after the last Indian surrender, which happened not just within Roosevelt's lifetime but within Roosevelt's memory (he would have been sixteen at the time)—have the nerve to tell Stalin that the rules of war had now been "civilized"? Only three months before the Yalta Conference, on November 4, 1944, while campaigning in Boston, Roosevelt acknowledged:

> All of our people all over the country—except the pure-blooded Indians—are immigrants or descendants of immigrants, including even those who came over here on the Mayflower.

And how dare Roosevelt criticize Stalin's prison camps (the

Gulags)? Didn't Roosevelt have more than 110,000 American citizens of Japanese descent rounded up and, without trial, sent to prison camps in the United States? And, speaking of Japan, why was Japan in this war?

Until the mid-1800s, Japan was a fiercely isolationist "floating kingdom." It was content to be completely uninvolved with the rest of the world and remain "floating in the middle of the sea." In 1853, Commander Perry arrived with his gunboat diplomacy. He was intent not on conquering, but on opening trade routes. (Much more civilized than war.) If, however, the United States had left Japan in its 1853 feudal, shogun-dominated state, it would have been about as formidable in the 1940s as, say, Guam. Only eighty-eight years after the American gunboats forced Japan to become a trading partner, who was surprised that Japan would take its revenge by dropping bombs on the modern-day American gunboats at Pearl Harbor?

In a speech to the United States Congress nineteen days after Pearl Harbor, Winston Churchill asked indignantly, "What kind of people do [the Japanese] think we are?" They think, Sir Winston, that we are a pushy people who used gunboats to open up trade with a country that wanted nothing more from the world than to be left alone. "They want to be left alone, do they? FIRE!"

And as for England, although Churchill gave speeches which included lines such as, "We do not covet anything from any nation except their respect," Britain was still, in fact, an imperialist nation: England dominated several countries and had absolutely no intention of giving up control of them after World War II. Although by 1945 the sun occasionally set upon the British empire, it was not sundown for long. India was the perfect example. England had occupied and exploited the country for hun-

> *Politics is the art
> of looking for trouble,
> finding it whether it exists or not,
> diagnosing it incorrectly,
> and applying the wrong remedy.*
>
> ERNEST BENN

> *I can retain neither respect
> nor affection for a Government
> which has been moving
> from wrong to wrong
> in order to defend
> its immorality.*
>
> MOHANDAS K. GANDHI
> on Britain

dreds of years, and it was not about to stop. Let us not forget Winston Churchill's words about the man who would eventually force England to leave: Mahatma Gandhi.

It is . . . nauseating to see Mr. Gandhi, a seditious Middle Temple lawyer now posing as a fakir of a type well known in the East, striding half-naked up the steps of the Vice-regal Palace, while he is still organizing and conducting a defiant campaign of civil disobedience, to parley on equal terms with the representative of the King . . .*

So, perhaps Germany would be Russia's India, or, perhaps it would be Russia's Africa, supplying slave labor for Russian agriculture, or, perhaps Russia would populate Germany and "relocate" the Germans as the United States had the Native Americans.

Stalin maintained, whatever he planned to do with his portion of Germany after the war was *his* business, and it was not that of either England or the United States.

To add insult to injury, Roosevelt and Churchill wanted to bring France in as a full partner in the postwar division of Germany. France! Its "impregnable" Maginot line was a joke: Germany simply took Belgium and went around it. France fell in six weeks. France had refused an alliance with the Soviet Union when Stalin offered it in the 1930s. Why should Stalin give away any of Germany to them? By rights, France should be part of the spoils to be divided: it had lost to Germany, and now Germany was about to lose to the Allies. In Stalin's view, France had sur-

---

*On a visit to England, Gandhi was asked, "What do you think of Western Civilization?" He thought for a moment and replied, "That would be a good idea."

rendered its sovereignty in 1940.

Roosevelt, Churchill, and Stalin reached a compromise: Russia would agree to remain in the war until the victory in Japan was won; Germany would be occupied by four countries, including France; Russia would have full control of the countries east of Germany, but Poland would be guaranteed a representative form of government; and a United Nations would be formed as soon as the war was over.

And so, back to war.

> *Religion may in most of its forms be defined as the belief that the gods are on the side of the Government.*
>
> BERTRAND RUSSELL

⚖ ⚖ ⚖

President Roosevelt died on April 12, 1945, the victory of the largest battle in his career—World War II—clearly in sight: Germany surrendered less than a month later. Vice-president Truman took over as president and the nation simultaneously mourned the loss of Roosevelt and celebrated the victory in Europe. Harry S. Truman was, if nothing else, a realist.

> My choice early in life was either to be a piano-player in a whorehouse or a politician. And to tell the truth there's hardly any difference.

In his first message to Congress on April 16, 1945, he gave his view of the post-war world:

> The responsibility of the great states is to serve and not to dominate the world.

This concept was directly counter to Stalin's, who believed that three powers had won the war and three powers should divide the world. When Truman, Churchill, and Stalin gathered at Potsdam in mid-summer 1945, the chill of the coming cold war was in the air. As at Yalta, Stalin brought the same trump card:

war casualties. In terms of the dead, Stalin paid a higher price than all the Allied countries combined. (Roughly half of all World War II casualties were Russian.)

To the Potsdam Conference, however, Truman (whose favorite game was poker) came to the table holding a wild card that would guarantee him the winning hand again and again: the day before the conference began, on July 16, the first atomic bomb was successfully exploded at Alamogordo, New Mexico.

Although Roosevelt may not have been strong physically, he was smart. When Roosevelt took office in 1932, he organized what was called the Brain Trust. He sought the power of intellect, ideas, and creativity to help solve the formidable problems facing the country. World War II was won because, at the beginning of the war, the West, inferior in armaments, had a slight *technological* advantage. Although Britain did not have the air power (brute force) of Hitler's Luftwaffe, England had radar, giving it *information.* Before a British plane left the ground, Air Command knew where the German planes had entered English airspace, how many there were, and at what speed they were flying. Without radar, England would have lost the war.

Another example of brain over brawn was the British mathematical genius who, early in the war, broke the Nazi code. By intercepting radio communications, Britain knew of German ship and submarine movements, as well as other vital military information. Germany was quite certain it was protected by its "unbreakable" code. One brain unlocked the information without which England would have fallen.*

---

*The man who broke the code, Alan Turing, was a homosexual. After the war, rather than being treated as a war hero, he was persecuted for his

Hitler appreciated brains and technology, too. His "flying bombs" brought untold destruction to British cities. When his rocket bomb, the V-1, was first dropped on England toward the end of the war, the devastation was so great and the potential devastation so awesome that the news was kept from the British people.

> *Do you mean to tell me you are actually going to eat that corpse soup?*
>
> ADOLF HITLER
>
> A frequent chide to dinner guests about to eat soup containing meat. Hitler was a devout vegetarian.

What cost Hitler some of his best technology—and the war—was his pathological antisemitism. The finest Jewish scientists, mathematicians, and inventors either died in Hitler's concentration camps or fled the country. One was Albert Einstein. On August 2, 1939, relocated to America, he wrote a letter to President Roosevelt discussing the wartime possibilities of $E=mc^2$:

> This new phenomenon [atomic energy] would also lead to the construction of bombs. . . . A single bomb of this type, carried by boat and exploded in a port, might very well destroy the whole port, together with some of the surrounding territory.

Stalin, in direct contrast to the technological West, fought the war in the time-honored tradition of "throw more troops at the enemy." In creating the love of country and fear of retribution necessary for whole towns and regiments to fight to the bitter end, Stalin was unmatched. When it came to ideas, well, let's just say that Stalin would never have been part of Roosevelt's Brain Trust.*

sexual orientation. He was arrested in 1952 for "gross indecency" and placed on probation with the condition that he submit to "treatment" for his homosexuality. Two years of "treatments" failed to "cure" him of his homosexuality. On June 7, 1954, he dipped an apple in cyanide, ate it, and died.

> We have grasped
> the mystery of the atom
> and rejected
> the Sermon on the Mount.
>
> GENERAL OMAR BRADLEY

And so the hot war, for all practical purposes, ended with the hottest-ever manmade flash in the New Mexico desert on July 16, and the cold war began on July 17 as Truman and Stalin sat down at the poker table in Potsdam.

"Deal," Truman said coolly.

With the atomic bomb, the United States no longer needed Russia's support in the invasion of Japan. The atomic bomb also neutralized Stalin's implied threats concerning Europe that "There are 20 million more Russians where those came from." Stalin knew that England and the United States were not willing to risk high casualties in order to have their way on post-war Germany. England and the United States had this funny quirk: they actually cared about how many troops they lost. Stalin found this a weakness in war: as a general, he only cared if there were more troops available. Stalin mercilessly exploited what he saw as the West's weakness. At Yalta it had worked. At Potsdam it did not. The West now had the power to, with one bomb, succeed where both Napoleon and Hitler had failed: to destroy Moscow.

With the bomb, the West did not just have the winning hand: it owned the casino. Stalin backed off, licked his wounds, and began making other plans. Some say we should have continued the war until Stalin was eliminated; others say Stalin should have

---

**In the brain versus brawn department, Stalin wanted Russian troops to be the first to enter Berlin: they were. The taking of Berlin was a great show of force and a display of power. The Americans, meanwhile, were busy scurrying off the German scientists—led by Wernher von Braun—who had developed the V-1 rocket. Stalin wanted the brawn; America wanted von Braun. Herr von Braun became the head of the U.S. space program. When the first rocket to the moon was about to be launched, a reporter asked von Braun, "How do we know this won't land on London?"

been given the Germany he wanted. One side said destroy him; another side said make him a friend. The United States did neither. Stalin left Potsdam humiliated but not weakened.

The cold war had begun.

⚖ ⚖ ⚖

> *A really good diplomat does not go in for victories, even when he wins them.*
>
> WALTER LIPPMANN

Publicly, the Potsdam Conference was labeled a success. U.S. Undersecretary of State Dean Acheson issued the following statement:

> Never in the past has there been any place on the globe where the vital interests of American and Russian people have clashed or even been antagonistic . . . and there is no reason to suppose there should be now or in the future ever such a place.

Truman immediately began a plan to rebuild Europe and give it back to the Europeans—including the Germans. Congress approved the spending of—in today's dollars—the equivalent of $100 billion. This rebuilding of Europe has usually been couched in humanitarian terms and, from one point of view, it was a humanitarian venture. Stalin, however, saw it as a military action against Russia and an insult to him personally. The rebuilding of Europe was even administered by a U.S. general and named after him: the Marshall Plan.

Here was the West, returning German control to Germany. Russia shared a border with Germany. England was across the English Channel, and America was across the Atlantic. Just as Hitler had not invaded England or the United States, Stalin reasoned, so, too, Germany's next leader would invade Russia first.

On a more immediate level, Stalin perceived the United States as "buying" the favor of the European people. These were the *enemies*. Where was the money for the *allies?* The United States would have a strong presence in Europe—perhaps strong

> *When the tyrant has disposed*
> *of foreign enemies by conquest*
> *or treaty, and there is nothing*
> *to fear from them,*
> *then he is always stirring up*
> *some war or other,*
> *in order that the people*
> *may require a leader.*
>
> PLATO

enough in a few years to take over Russia. Stalin began rebuilding Russia, but always with a cautious eye on the West.

The United States had dictated that Japan, only 25 sea miles from the Soviet Union across the LaPerouse Strait, would not be included—even in part—in the Soviet spoils of war. And if you're not happy with this ultimatum, Comrade Stalin, allow us to show you the photographs of Hiroshima. (Some say Truman dropped the bombs as much to intimidate Stalin as to win in Japan.)

Soon, practically all contact between the East and the West was cut off. This rapid deterioration was, officially, kept from the American people, but rumors abounded. After meeting with President Truman at the White House on February 12, 1946, Churchill joked with the reporters,

> I think "No Comment" is a splendid expression. I am using it again and again.

By the time Churchill addressed Westminster College in Fulton, Missouri, on March 5, 1946, however, the lines of the cold war were drawn—and given a name:

> From Stettin in the Baltic to Trieste in the Adriatic an iron curtain has descended across the Continent.

At Nuremberg, only a handful of Nazis were punished; in Japan, the emperor not only got to live, but got to continue as emperor. Germany and Japan were now our friends. Russia, on the other hand, was the new enemy. Anti-communism grew into a frenzy.

In 1949, Stalin exploded a bomb: the same bomb Truman had exploded at Potsdam. Russia now had The Bomb.

Russia's atomic bomb lit a fire under the already overheated Senator Joseph McCarthy. The McCarthy witch hunts began.

Had this era not produced so much tragedy, it would be a good theme for a comedy. Looking back, Joseph McCarthy was absolutely ridiculous. Take, for example, three statements made by him on February 9, 10, and 20, 1950. From these statements, can you answer the question, "How many communists are there in the State Department?":

> *The greatest dangers to liberty lurk in insidious encroachment by men of zeal, well-meaning but without understanding.*
>
> JUSTICE LOUIS D. BRANDEIS

> I have here in my hand a list of 205 that were known to the Secretary of State as being members of the Communist Party and who, nevertheless, are still working and shaping policy in the State Department.

> Last night I discussed Communists in the State Department. I stated that I had the names of 57 card-carrying members of the Communist Party. Now, I want to tell the Secretary this: If he wants to call me tonight at the Utah Hotel, I will be glad to give him the names of those 57 card-carrying members.

> There is a serious question whether I should disclose names to the Senate. I frankly feel, in view of the number of cases—there are 81 cases—that it would be a mistake to disclose the names on the floor. I should be willing, happy and eager to go before any committee and give the names and all the information available.

McCarthy made statements that were so illogical any child should have been able to see through them. In 1951, for example:

> The Communists within our borders have been more responsible for the success of Communism abroad than Soviet Russia.

McCarthy was, in fact, a raving paranoid. Consider this quote

> They'll nail anyone
> who ever scratched his ass
> during the national anthem.
>
> HUMPHREY BOGART

from Richard Hofstadter's book, *The Paranoid Style in American Politics,* taken from a speech given by McCarthy on the Senate floor, June 14, 1951:

How can we account for our present situation unless we believe that men high in this government are concerting to deliver us to disaster? This must be the product of a great conspiracy, a conspiracy on a scale so immense as to dwarf any previous venture in the history of man. A conspiracy of infamy so black that, when it is finally exposed, its principals shall be forever deserving of the maledictions of all honest men.

Although Truman later claimed, "I've said many a time that I think the Un-American Activities Committee in the House of Representatives was the most un-American thing in America!" he was remarkably silent about it while he was president and while it was happening. Dwight D. Eisenhower, who took over the presidency on January 20, 1953, gave speeches (such as this at Columbia University on May 31, 1954):

Here in America we are descended in blood and in spirit from revolutionaries and rebels—men and women who dared to dissent from accepted doctrine. As their heirs, may we never confuse honest dissent with disloyal subversion.

Nevertheless, Eisenhower did little to interfere with the House Un-American Activities Committee. It took individual citizens, refusing to cooperate with the committee, to slow the committee from the Stalinesque purge it so desperately wanted. On May 16, 1953, Albert Einstein wrote:

Every intellectual who is called before one of the committees ought to refuse to testify, i.e., he must be prepared . . . for the sacrifice of his personal welfare in the interest of the cultural welfare of his country . . . . This kind of inquisition violates the spirit of the Constitution.

If enough people are ready to take this grave step they will be successful. If not, then the intellectuals of this country deserve nothing better than the slavery which is intended for them.

> *The highest proof of virtue is to possess boundless power without abusing it.*
>
> LORD MACAULAY
> 1843

Those who failed to cooperate by "naming names of known communists" were fired, blacklisted, and jailed. To give you an idea of the sort of power the committee thought it had, consider this from Representative J. Parnell Thomas during a House Un-American Activities Committee hearing to a witness who claimed a constitutional right:

> The rights you have are the rights given to you by Committee. We will determine what rights you have and what rights you have not got.

The United States was so caught up with its own internal anti-communist witch hunt that it failed to notice the most important event of 1953: the death of its enemy. With Stalin's passing in 1953, the cold war could have been over. All this witch hunting was, apparently, too much fun (and there were darker motives, which we shall get to shortly), so it continued. In 1956, when the Soviet Communist Party denounced Stalin's "policies and personality" (and there's not much more about a political leader you can denounce than that), once again the door was wide open for a warmer relationship with Russia: we could blame the cold war on Stalin, declare the hostilities over, and get on with our lives. Although Stalin's replacement, Nikita Khrushchev, pursued a policy of "peaceful coexistence" and even toured the

> *If we maintain our faith in God,*
> *our love of freedom,*
> *and superior global air power,*
> *I think we can look to the future*
> *with confidence.*
>
> GENERAL CURTIS LEMAY
> February 1956

United States in 1959 (visiting Disneyland and the set of the film *Can-Can),* h e canceled a 1960 Paris Summit Conference when a United States reconnaissance plane was shot down over Russia. The flying of illegal spy planes over Russia was hardly a gesture that would help end the cold war.

To prove that Khrushchev was another Stalin with world domination on his mind, one phrase was repeated over and over: "We will bury you." Khrushchev said this at the end of a longer speech given at the Polish Embassy in Moscow on November 18, 1956. The speech ended:

> About the capitalist states, it doesn't depend on you whether or not we exist. If you don't like us, don't accept our invitations, and don't invite us to come and see you. Whether you like it or not, history is on our side. We will bury you.

The last two sentences, however, do not appear in either *Pravda* or the *New York Times,* both of which printed the complete text of the speech. How did these lines get added? And why? Even the translation, "We will bury you," is inaccurate: a better translation would be, "We will walk on your graves," which only implies disrespect; "We will bury you" implies aggression.

In the artificially heated American environment, FBI Director J. Edgar Hoover became a bestselling self-help author. In his 1958 book, *Masters of Deceit: The Story of Communism and How to Fight It,* Hoover tells us how to spot a communist—and why communists are so difficult to spot:

> The communist official will probably live in a modest neighborhood. His wife will attend the corner grocery store, his children attend the local school. If a shoe store or butcher shop is operated by a Party member, the offi-

cial will probably get a discount on his purchases.

Most Party officials drive cars, usually older models. They are generally out late at night, attending meetings. Except for special affairs, communist activity is slight early in the morning. The organizer, coming in around midnight or one o'clock, will sleep late. But that doesn't mean all day. One Southern official was severely censured for sleeping too late; to solve the problem the Party bought him an electric alarm clock.

> *Once lead this people into war and they will forget there ever was such a thing as tolerance.*
>
> PRESIDENT WOODROW WILSON

The questions, "Who perpetuated the U.S. religion of anti-communism?" and "Why?" were answered by President Dwight David Eisenhower on January 17, 1961. During his televised farewell address to the American people, three days before turning over the presidential reins to John F. Kennedy, he said:

> This conjunction of an immense military establishment and a large arms industry is new in the American experience. The total influence—economic, political, even spiritual—is felt in every city, every statehouse, every office of the federal government. . . .We must not fail to comprehend its grave implications.

> In the councils of government, we must guard against the acquisition of unwarranted influence, whether sought or unsought, by the military-industrial complex. The potential for the disastrous rise of misplaced power exists and will persist.

Eisenhower spilled the beans—and then went off to play golf. Ike slipped the truth into his speech and slipped out of town. His warning went right over the heads of the American public, where, for the most part, it dangles even today.

> *All through history
> it's the nations that have given
> most to the generals
> and the least to the people
> that have been the first to fall.*
>
> HARRY S. TRUMAN

Without the threat of communist aggression, the cold-war build-up of the military—with its blank-check policy with industry—would have been entirely unnecessary. If Russia was our friend, who would be our enemy? There was none. A wartime economy, however, is terrific for industry. In a wartime economy, industry makes guaranteed profits with no fear of competition or need for efficiency. The typical defense contract reads: "Spend what you need, deliver it when you can, pay the executives of your company whatever you like, and add a 15 percent profit." What industry wouldn't want that kind of contract rather than competing for profits in a free marketplace? Capitalism is work. Defense Department contracts are play.

Just as a wartime economy does not require industry to follow the precepts of capitalism, so, too, in time of war, the military is not required to follow democratic principles. The military structure, of course, is precisely the opposite of a democracy; the will of the people is not communicated from below: orders are passed down from above. For those who love power, democracy is inconvenient. The military is the power seeker's paradise.

So, the profit-hungry industrialists and the power-hungry militarists were busy destroying capitalism and democracy in the name of defending capitalism and democracy.

John F. Kennedy knew of the military-industrial complex's power—his father made quite a lot of money with a more primitive form of this economic system. President Kennedy did what he could to work within it. He attempted, for example, to switch from war production to space production. The "space race" was not sold to the American public as a way of advancing humanity's scientific knowledge, but as a way to "beat the Russians to the moon." Kennedy hoped to redirect the anti-communist sentiment into a peacetime activity that would keep the military-industrial complex happy. Alas, a race to the moon was not enough. The military-industrial complex needed a war. The military-industrial complex thought Vietnam held all the delicious possibilities of Korea. Kennedy resisted. Many assassination buffs maintain that this resistance is what got Kennedy killed.*

> *If the United States gives up [in Vietnam] the Pacific Ocean will become a Red Sea.*
>
> RICHARD M. NIXON
> October 15, 1965

Within weeks of the assassination, according to Stanley Karnow's book, *Vietnam: A History,* at a 1963 Christmas party, President Lyndon Baines Johnson told some military-industrial complex types, "Just get me elected and you can have your damn war."

Poor Johnson. Here was a man who passed more civil rights legislation than any president in history, and the people he thought would praise him for his agenda of social change were the very ones who attacked him for Vietnam. By 1968, Johnson was fed up and chose not to run again. By this time, however, as one commentator noted, "Our fear that communism might someday take over most of the world blinds us to the fact that anti-communism already has."

The perfect military-industrial presidential candidate? Richard Milhous Nixon. Here's the man who had, as vice-president, successfully defended American industry against none other than Nikita Khrushchev in Moscow in the Kitchen Debates. He was also prone to making such statements as, "What are schools for if not indoctrination against communism?" (Not that his opponent, Hubert Horatio Humphrey, could for a moment be consid-

---

*Conversely, in his 1995 memoirs, *Palimpsest,* Gore Vidal claims Kennedy was looking for a war. Vidal quotes Kennedy as saying, "Where would Lincoln be without the Civil War?"

> *The belief in the possibility*
> *of a short decisive war*
> *appears to be one*
> *of the most ancient and dangerous*
> *of human illusions.*
>
> ROBERT LYND

ered soft on communism. Humphrey said, "The greatest risk is communist aggression, communist conquest, and communist advance.")

As a staunch pro-capitalist Republican with strong anti-communist credentials, Nixon could do some things that no liberal democrat would dare to do. For example, as Gore Vidal described it, "Nixon sort of *wandered over* to Communist China one day in 1972 and made friends with them all." Well, at least that was a billion fewer communists to worry about. But those Russians. We still had to worry about the Russians.

After the Vietnam War was lost in 1973, the domino theory fell, too. One country after another in Southeast Asia did not fall to communist aggression. U.S.-Soviet relations entered into a period of *detente*, which is Russian for, "We're both really tired; why don't we rest for a while?" Presidents Ford and Carter were happy with this policy. So, apparently, were most of the American people. Ronald Reagan was not.* He found pockets of subversive communism in South America, Central America, and, of course, North America. The cold war heated up.

But Russia was not ready for another round. It was bankrupt. As the Iron Curtain came crashing down in the late 1980s and early 1990s, what we found was not a political superpower, but a near-third-world country without roads, industry, communications, or a viable economy. If Russia hadn't been Russia, we would have been giving it foreign aid for decades. As it turns out, Russia was just "putting on a show." (Even the film of Russia's first space walk was later proven to be shot in a film studio.)

---

*When I say "Ronald Reagan" I mean, of course, the people who were behind him. We know he was—literally—only an actor. To say he was the star player in the Military-Industrial-Complex Playhouse is probably not unfair.

AIN'T NOBODY'S BUSINESS IF YOU DO

Commentators differ as to when the cold war could have ended. Some say Stalin could have been made a friend in 1945. Others say it could have ended after Stalin's death in 1953. Others say after Stalin's denouncement by even Russia in 1956. John Chancellor's theory, as reported in his book, *Peril and Promise: A Commentary on America:*

> HELEN THOMAS:
> *Mr. President, would your view of Communism have been different if you had gone to Russia twenty years ago and saw how they laughed, cried, and were human?*
>
> PRESIDENT REAGAN:
> *No. They've changed.*

> The cold war was a necessity when it began, when the Soviet regime posed a genuine threat to democratic governments. It was a necessity at least until Khrushchev put missiles in Cuba in 1962. After that, its own momentum kept the cold war going until it was stopped by the internal contradictions of the communist system. But while it lasted, life in the U.S. was shaped by it.

If Chancellor's analysis is correct, the Vietnam War was completely unnecessary. Some commentators say after the fall of Vietnam and the failure of communism to spread throughout the Mideast, there was no need for the massive nuclear and military build-up that continued taking place. Looking back, few except the extreme right accept the necessity for the multi-trillion dollar military build-up during the Reagan-Bush years.

Who (or what) kept the fact that Russia was bankrupt from the American people for so long? It wasn't Russia—U.S. intelligence knew it well. Why weren't we told? Do you suppose the initials M-I-C had something to do with it?

⚖️ ⚖️ ⚖️

What did the cold war cost us? We can start with the 118,000 American military deaths and 256,000 injuries suffered since 1945—most of which resulted from various anti-communist military conflicts. We can add to that a good portion of the

> *The tendency to claim God as an ally for our partisan values and ends is the source of all religious fanaticism.*
>
> REINHOLD NIEBUHR

accumulated Defense Department budget from 1945 to 1993: a mere $20 trillion. If we hadn't wasted much of this amount in unnecessary defense, the national debt—currently dragging us down—would be a national surplus. In this country alone, the Defense Department has left behind 11,000 sites which are contaminated either by radioactive materials or toxic chemicals. And then there are the all-but-forgotten Vietnam veterans, a disproportionate number of whom fill the ranks of the homeless.

One more thing: these military-industrial people are still in charge. Maybe not the same people, but the same organizations. The Military-Industrial-Complex Playhouse plays on. They're just having a little trouble finding a new leading player: Bush failed. Casting, however, continues in earnest. The religious right keeps the campfires burning, and liberals who worry more about stomping out drug use and gun ownership than preventing others from stomping on the Constitution throw napalm on those campfires.

Meanwhile, the war on drugs is being sold to the American public with the same techniques and even the same terminology as the war on communism. "What's next?" one wonders.

What may be next is any political thought that doesn't fit into the conservative Democrat/Republican range. Libertarians, for example—even though their basic philosophy seems completely in tune with the Constitution—are routinely characterized as kooks who want to let vicious criminals run free, machine guns in hand.

⚖ ⚖ ⚖

The solution to the cold war—or any other war against unpopular political views, including the war against selected consensual activities—was given in 1961 by George F. Kennan in his book, *Russia and the West under Lenin and Stalin:*

> If we are to regard ourselves as a grown-up nation—and anything else will henceforth be mortally dangerous—then we must, as the Biblical phrase goes, put away childish things; and among these childish things the first to go, in my opinion, should be self-idealization and the search for absolutes in world affairs: for absolute security, absolute amity, absolute harmony.

> *I think one of the by-products of the communications explosion is a sort of "corruption fatigue." We've lost our ability to be shocked or enraged by the machinations of politicians. We've been battered with such frequency that we've become indifferent. We're punch drunk with scandal.*
>
> LARRY GELBART

John Chancellor talks about the end of the cold war:

> The cold war was won by the west, but there were no victory celebrations, no ticker-tape parades. For Americans, the cold war didn't have a real ending. It just stopped, like a movie projector that had run out of film.

There's a lot more film available for that projector, however, and we must be careful to know a movie when we see one. A consensual crime—drug use—currently monopolizes that projector. Other reels are being edited and, if sufficiently menacing political enemies cannot be found, consensual criminals will have to do. Note the horror films the Pentagon (not to mention Jerry Falwell) had ready when it was suggested the military acknowledge the gays already in its ranks. Films are available for all the other consensual crimes, as well. For them to surface, all it takes is someone in power—or a sufficient number of the American people—to seriously suggest legalization.

For a preview, call your favorite bigoted person and suggest that your favorite consensual activity be legalized. Before you can say "the United States Constitution and its Bill of Rights," the projector will be threaded, the house lights dimmed, and the next show begun at the Military-Industrial-Complex-Cineplex. Let the good times roll.

⚖ ⚖ ⚖

> Tyranny is always better organised than freedom.
>
> CHARLES PÉGUY
> (1873–1914)

Concerning the question of our current military spending—several hundred billion borrowed dollars just to keep this behemoth in place—one fact should by now be obvious: Future American wars will be fought against terrorists, not armies. The battles will be fought over which organization seeking dominion over the United States can assemble an atomic bomb in America first—and whether we find out about it in time. Impeccable intelligence, not brute force, is what will be necessary to defend our sovereignty in the twenty-first century.

And what are our intelligence-gathering forces doing? Tracking down drug runners, drug users, pot growers.

As Joni Mitchell wrote in her song, "Marching Toward Bethlehem," based on a poem by W. B. Yeats:

> Turning and turning within the widening gyre.
> The falcon cannot hear the falconer.
> Things fall apart.
> The center cannot hold.
> And a blood-dimmed tide
> is loosed upon the world . . .
> The best lack conviction,
> given some time to think,
> and the worst are full of
> passion without mercy.

Suicide and
Assisted Suicide

> *Beware!*
> *To touch these wires*
> *is instant death.*
> *Anyone found doing so*
> *will be prosecuted.*
>
> SIGN AT A RAILROAD STATION

THERE CAN BE NO MORE fundamental statement concerning individual freedom and responsibility than this: *Our bodies and our lives belong to ourselves.* Our bodies do not belong to the state, to our relatives, or to our friends.

The laws against suicide and assisted suicide run directly counter to this concept. These laws spring from our cultural unwillingness to face the reality of death, and the religious belief that "only God can take a life."[*]

The laws against suicide are obviously the silliest laws in the world: if one is successful, who gets punished? If one does not succeed at suicide, then are we to assume that arresting and locking that person up is somehow going to help? "Where am I?" "You're in a jail cell. You attempted suicide. You're going to spend the next ten years of your life here." Terrific.

When Derek Humphrey's book on suicide, *Final Exit,* was published, it caused an absolute scandal. You would think he had divulged some great mystical secret; as though we didn't know that the means to our own end is in our hands, and is always at hand. That we can commit suicide at any time is a given. The only thing that laws against suicide force one to do when committing suicide is use techniques that are either messy, painful,

---

[*]It is ironic that those who are the most ardent supporters of laws against suicide and assisted suicide based on religious grounds are precisely the ones who support capital punishment. Could we at least have a little consistency here, please?

dangerous to others—or all three.

In attempting suicide, there's always the chance that one will wind up not dead, but a vegetable. It is this fear that causes people to use fail-safe (that is, absolutely guaranteed) methods of suicide that either hurt (hanging, slitting wrists in a warm bathtub), are messy (bullets in the head), or could potentially harm others (jumping off buildings, high-speed car crashes). The standard technique of "taking a bottle of sleeping pills" is uncertain at best. If one takes too few, one may wind up a vegetable. If one takes too many, one may vomit before sufficient medication is absorbed through the stomach and one may wind up a vegetable.

> To save a man's life
> against his will
> is the same as killing him.
>
> HORACE
> B.C. 65–8

All of this is so unnecessary because, with the proper number of pills, a simple injection, or inhaling carbon monoxide or nitrous oxide, one can peacefully and painlessly die.

When one chooses to die, shouldn't one have the right to do so in the presence of friends and loved ones? In more than half the states (and the number is growing), the law says no. If you invite friends or loved ones to be there, you put them at risk of being charged with "assisted suicide," "accessory to suicide," or even murder (first degree murder in at least two states). So many suicide notes contain messages such as, "I'm so sorry we couldn't be together at the end, but I did not want to endanger you. I thought this way was best."

Note that I haven't said a word about motivation. One's motivation to commit suicide is not the issue here. What is at issue is the fundamental right to make decisions about one's own life. Without government intervention.

Suicidal thoughts are a symptom of emotional depression. Our culture's taboo against suicide often keeps people who are thinking about suicide from talking about it. By talking about it, people can often get the emotional and psychological support they need to see them through a rough time. When people are afraid to talk about it, the pressures can increase to the point that they actually do something about it. If suicide itself were not forced to be—by law— such a lonely activity, we might have fewer suicides. Even if we did not, however, there is no reason for laws that make one's last moments painful and lonely.

> *Razors pain you;*
> *Rivers are damp;*
> *Acids stain you*
> *And drugs cause cramp;*
> *Guns aren't lawful;*
> *Nooses give;*
> *Gas smells awful;*
> *You might as well live.*
>
> DOROTHY PARKER

⚖ ⚖ ⚖

Nowhere is the concept of assisted suicide and the cruelty of making it illegal more pronounced than when individuals are unable to take their own lives. People in advanced stages of life-threatening illness, for example, sometimes either don't have the use of their limbs or are unable to gather the proper drugs or paraphernalia by which they might deliver themselves. Here, suicide is only available through assistance. By filling out the proper legal documents ahead of time, people can clearly indicate the point of deterioration after which they choose to no longer live. When this point is reached, death then becomes a medical procedure.

We accept the fact that if one makes a living will, his or her life will not be artificially extended through the use of life support systems. Once the life support systems are removed (an accepted medical procedure), have you considered what death might be like for that person? To find out, exhale completely and do not take your next breath while you continue reading. (Please try this.) If one is taken off artificial respiration, he or she no longer has the ability to inhale. Death may come "within a matter of minutes," but what are those minutes like? "Well, they'll

> *Give strong drink*
> *unto him*
> *that is ready*
> *to perish.*
>
> PROVERBS 31:6

be given painkilling medications, won't they?" To the degree prescribed by law, yes. These are, however, sometimes woefully inadequate. To take a breath (as you probably notice if you are attempting the experiment) is a powerful biologic imperative. The lack of oxygen can sometimes rouse one from the effects of limited legal dosages of medication. This torture may go on for days. One might be able to rouse oneself to, say, two breaths per minute. Or, one's lungs may be filling up with fluids in what the doctors acknowledge will be the inevitable form of death. Here, one is permitted to slowly drown. If intravenous feeding tubes (medically considered a form of life support) are removed, one dies of dehydration; this while one is starving to death.

People who take part in the "death watch," in hospitals when the end is near, often ask the doctors, "Isn't there something you can give [him or her]?" The answer: no. Certainly not by law. That some hospital personnel quietly give larger doses of painkilling medication than legally permitted is a well-known and generally accepted medical fact. The administration of these drugs, of course, must be kept absolutely confidential. The family, then, cannot know the moment of death. (In fact, such medical mercies are usually performed when no one is present.)

The desire to be with loved ones when they die is a strong one. Once a person who is clearly dying has indicated his or her desire to die after a certain point of deterioration, why should being with that person for the final moments be a matter of chance? The days—sometimes weeks—of waiting around hospitals twenty-four hours a day, being afraid to leave even for a moment because that might be when the loved one dies, are an unnecessary torture on friends and relatives.

As Charlotte Perkins Gilman wrote in her suicide note:

Human life consists in mutual service. No grief, pain, misfortune or "broken heart" is excuse for cutting off one's life while any power of service remains. But when all usefulness is over, when one is assured of an unavoidable and imminent death, it is the simplest of human rights to choose a quick and easy death in place of a slow and horrible one.

> Who knows?
> Maybe my life belongs to God.
> Maybe it belongs to me.
> But I do know one thing:
> I'm damned if it belongs
> to the government.
>
> ARTHUR HOPPE

⚖ ⚖ ⚖

Again, I am not discussing the ethics of when *others* decide your life is over, but the rights you yourself have to determine when you no longer want to live. If individuals—for spiritual, religious, or any other reasons—choose to hang on until God or nature determines their last breath, they certainly have that right. What I am speaking of here is abolishing laws that prohibit people from taking their own lives, either with or without the assistance of others.

Life is a precious possession. As with all of our possessions, how we use, manage, and eventually say good-bye to life is our own business, not the law's.

The Titanic Laws:
Public Drunkenness,
Loitering, Vagrancy,
Seat Belts, Motorcycle Helmets,
Public Nudity, Transvestism

> *If you have
> ten thousand regulations
> you destroy all respect for the law.*
>
> SIR WINSTON CHURCHILL

IN THIS CHAPTER WE explore a variety of consensual crimes. Each one demonstrates yet again (a) the government does not trust its citizens to take care of themselves; (b) the moralists of our time don't believe in the ancient wisdom, "live and let live"; (c) if we put a bunch of lawyers together, call them "lawmakers," give them a hefty salary, and provide them with nearly unlimited power, they will make laws.

I named this chapter "The Titanic Laws" not because these laws are so gargantuan (they are, in fact, only large in their pettiness). No, this chapter was named after an actual law, passed by the Congress of the United States after extended and expensive debate, and signed into law by President Ronald Reagan on October 21, 1986—just in time for Halloween.

The *Titanic* Maritime Memorial Act of 1985 makes it illegal for any U.S. citizen to buy, sell, or own anything that went down with the *Titanic*. This flies in the face of international maritime salvage laws written long before the formation of the United States. The *Titanic* Maritime Memorial Act is yet another unnecessary hindrance to free enterprise and our rights as citizens to

AIN'T NOBODY'S BUSINESS IF YOU DO

buy, sell, or own whatever we choose. The lawmakers wanted to allow the *Titanic* to rest "undisturbed" on the ocean floor and discourage salvage operations by eliminating the American market. I don't know about you, but ever since hearing about this law I have *desperately* wanted to own a piece of the *Titanic*. Call me a rebel without a pause, but anything will do: a rusty bolt, a broken tea cup, an ice cube.

> *Reader, suppose you were an idiot.*
> *And suppose you were a member of Congress.*
> *But I repeat myself.*
>
> MARK TWAIN

In order for such a nonsensical law to pass, the bill had to discuss such concepts as not disturbing the graves of those brave passengers who sank in mid-Atlantic in 1912. Well, a great many of the bodies were recovered and properly buried. The rest were eaten by fishes long ago. (Perhaps we should pass a law saying that no fishing can take place within 300 miles of the *Titanic* to make sure we don't eat any of those fish who might be descendants of fish who nibbled on one of those "brave" passengers.)

⚖️ ⚖️ ⚖️

Speaking of federal laws, death, and the ocean, did you know that "burial of cremated remains shall take place no closer than three nautical miles from land"? This is to make sure that the remains "will have minimal adverse environmental impact." And, did you know that you have to report all such burials "within 30 days to the (EPA) Regional Administrator of the Region from which the vessel carrying the remains departed"?

When a body is cremated, it is exposed to 1800- to 2000-degree heat for $1\frac{1}{2}$ to 3 hours. Nothing is left but some brittle bones, which are ground up—one's ashes are not really ashes; they are ground calcium—and placed in a container. What remains is about two quarts of, well, *remains*.

> *The trouble with this country*
> *is that there are too many*
> *politicians who believe,*
> *with a conviction based on*
> *experience, that you can fool*
> *all of the people*
> *all of the time.*
>
> FRANKLIN PIERCE ADAMS

The Environmental Protection Agency (EPA) permits raw sewage, toxic waste, and poisons of various kinds (within certain limits) to be dumped into lakes, streams, and directly offshore. Outrageously sanitized calcium, however, must go outside the three-mile limit. One also wonders, "What does the Regional Administrator *do* with all those reports? What does he or she need them for? Is it possible that there could be so much ash dumping in a certain section of ocean outside the three-mile limit that the Regional Administrator would be forced to cordon off a segment of the ocean? Give people a job administrating, and they'll create things to administer.

⚖ ⚖ ⚖

Granted, disturbing the "International Maritime Memorial to the men, women, and children who perished aboard" the *Titanic* (I was quoting from the law there) and dumping Uncle Nathan's ashes only 2½ miles and not 3 miles from shore do not exactly fill the police blotters or jail cells, but let's consider a crime that does: *public drunkenness.* More than 6% of all arrests in 1994— 713,200—were for public drunkenness. This is, simply, being drunk in public—not operating a motor vehicle, trespassing, or disturbing the peace (they each have their own arrest categories). Public drunkenness is someone staggering down the street or leaning against the proverbial lamp post. Like loitering (another 128,400 arrests) or vagrancy (25,300 arrests), public drunkenness is generally considered one of those "discretionary laws": the police make the arrest or not based on their own discretion. Police are not supposed to arrest everyone who appears drunk in public (imagine the jail load on New Year's Eve if that were the case), but those who are, well . . . what?

Here's the problem with discretionary laws: what are the criteria of discretion? Not having specific criteria allows law enforcement officers to write the law, try the case, and enforce it on the spot. Ultimately (and inevitably), this leads to a police state. To protect our freedom, we keep those who make the laws, those who arrest people for breaking the laws, and those who decide whether the suspects are guilty or not in three distinct groups. Any breach of that system invites trouble.

> *The natural progress of things is for liberty to yield and governments to gain ground.*
>
> THOMAS JEFFERSON

As it is, the public drunkenness, loitering, and vagrancy laws can be used as excuses by unethical law enforcement officers to arrest people they happen not to like. "I smell alcohol on your breath. I'm taking you in for public drunkenness." You won't be convicted, generally, but a night in jail is punishment enough. Sue the officer for false arrest? Right. That means hiring a lawyer. Out of the jail cell and into the fire.

Please keep in mind that if public drunkenness, loitering, or vagrancy become trespassing, disturbing the peace, vandalism, or obstructing traffic, then arrests are in order. Yes, it may be uncomfortable seeing drunks, loiterers, and vagrants staggering, loitering, and being vague on public streets, but that's the price we pay for keeping them *public* streets and not "Official Police Property."

⚖ ⚖ ⚖

Seat belt laws and helmet laws are perfect examples of the government's not trusting us to make our own decisions about our own lives. But—with seat belt laws in particular—there's a lot more than mere paternalism in the works. Here politics,

> *So long as a man rides his*
> *hobbyhorse peaceably and quietly*
> *along the King's highway,*
> *and neither compels you or me*
> *to get up behind him*
> *—pray, Sir, what have either*
> *you or I to do with it?*
>
> LAURENCE STERNE
> 1759

power, and simple greed enter trap door, center. This from *Consumer Reports,* April 1993:

The single most significant safety improvement is the air bag, an improvement that auto manufacturers fought every step of the way.

The first air-bag regulations were promulgated by the National Highway Traffic Safety Administration in 1970. But when auto makers complained that air bags were too expensive, the Nixon administration quashed the rule.

An air bag standard was reissued in 1977, under Jimmy Carter, but was revoked again, in 1981, when the Reagan Administration caved in to auto makers' complaints.

After the Supreme Court ruled that the Administration unlawfully rescinded the rule, a new air-bag standard was issued in 1984. But the auto makers again succeeded in watering it down, so that it required only "passive restraints." Those could be air bags or "automatic" safety belts, or a combination—at the carmaker's discretion.

This is where the seat belt laws came from. The federal government forced states to enact mandatory seat belt laws. (If the states wanted to continue receiving federal highway funding, they had to pass seat-belt laws.) Yes, this was a major intrusion on the rights of drivers—especially drivers who believed they were safer without seat belts. (A minority, but certainly entitled to risk their own lives on their opinion.) The reason for these seat belt laws is that Detroit did not want to include the air bags—which automatically protect the driver and passenger better than seat belts do—and the Nixon and Reagan administrations cooperated with the major-political-campaign-donor auto makers.

Instead of telling the American public the truth, however, Detroit and the federal regulators regaled us with one story after another about how many lives would be saved, how many injuries prevented, and how kind the federal government was to force the states to enact seat belt laws. However, to continue from the *Consumer Reports* article:

> *There ought to be one day —just one—when there is open season on senators.*
>
> WILL ROGERS

> A driver's-side air bag increases the driver's chance of surviving a crash by 29 percent. That's on top of the margin afforded by wearing lap-and-shoulder belts. Had all cars on the road in 1971 been equipped with a driver's-side air bag, some 4,000 people killed that year would have survived.

That's 100,000 people over the past twenty-five years—*without* the mandatory seat belt law. So, really: does the federal government care about us? Not unless we're a major lobby. What's especially galling is the sanctimonious attitude with which the government takes away our personal freedoms and convinces us it's for our own good, while, in reality, the government is allowing people to die unnecessarily every day because it caved in to political and economic pressure from a powerful lobby. To quote again from *Consumer Reports:*

> Now that safety has become a major selling point, no carmaker wants to mention that air-bag technology was developed in Detroit more than 20 years ago and left unexploited for nearly as long. Neither do the ads touting safety mention the years of delay and lives lost through auto maker opposition.

And through inappropriate government action.

⚖ ⚖ ⚖

> *I do not participate in any sport*
> *with ambulances*
> *at the bottom of a hill.*
>
> ERMA BOMBECK

Laws that require motorcycle riders to wear helmets were passed not due to the lobbying of the motorcycle industry (no motorcycle air bag has yet been perfected), but due to a general public dislike (shared by many law enforcement officers) of motorcyclists. It's not the argument, "Helmet laws will save motorcyclists' lives," that convinces people to favor such laws, but the argument, "People are more severely injured in motorcycle accidents if they aren't wearing a helmet, so insurance rates and the potential financial burdens to society go up." No one seems to worry much about the "cost to society" of cigarettes, alcohol, prescription drugs, or any of the other lethal legal activities. Motorcyclists opposed to helmets claim their vision, hearing, and the mobility of their head are impaired by the helmet; therefore, they feel they are more likely to get into an accident. Further, they claim, if you're going to be killed in a motorcycle accident, you're going to be killed: helmets probably won't help that much. According to the General Accounting Office, of the more than 3,000 motorcycle deaths in the United States in 1990, 45% of the riders were wearing helmets.

But safety is not the issue: personal choice is. The motorcycle rider who is more seriously injured or even killed because he or she is not wearing a helmet hurts himself or herself only. If insurance companies and states want to require special insurance coverage for those who choose to ride without helmets, that's fine: those who take risks should see to it that they are not a financial burden on society. Health insurance companies that offer better rates to nonsmokers are, in effect, charging smokers higher rates. That's fair. Charging motorcyclists a premium to not wear a helmet is also fair.* Insisting that a cyclist wear a helmet *or else* is not fair.

AIN'T NOBODY'S BUSINESS IF YOU DO

People obviously don't want helmet laws. In 1967, the federal government issued another of its financial ultimatums: if a state didn't enact a helmet law, it ran the risk of losing highway funding. By 1975, all but three states (as diverse as California, Illinois, and Utah) had complied (succumbed?). In 1976, when Congress rescinded the ruling, twenty-nine states repealed their laws. Now the federal government is back with a let's-do-helmet-laws-again attitude.

> *You may be sure*
> *that the Americans*
> *will commit all the stupidities*
> *they can think of,*
> *plus some*
> *that are beyond imagination.*
>
> CHARLES DeGAULLE

Allow me for a moment to view with the cold eye of an insurance actuary a motorcyclist's potential for hurting others. A motorcyclist involved in a serious accident becomes a projectile: the rider's motorcycle stops, the rider does not, and we have a human rocket flying through space. If this human rocket hits something or someone, the human rocket is more dangerous wearing a heavy, hard helmet than not. To reduce potential injury to nonconsenting others, then, the law should *prohibit* motorcycle helmets. Okay. Enough actuarial thinking. Let's return to the question: "Why helmet laws?"

When the California helmet law was passed in 1991,* the

**Ironically, that premium would probably not be very high, as death costs insurance companies far less than serious injury. If it's true that people not wearing helmets die more often, then it must mean that those wearing helmets, rather than dying, sustain serious injuries. A serious injury could cost an insurance company hundreds of thousands, perhaps millions of dollars. Death is a one-time payment to the survivors. From the cold-hearted view of insurance companies, in fact, those not wearing helmets might be entitled to a rate reduction.

*Yes, as soon as most of the other states repealed their laws, California had to get one. The Marine Corps motto is *Semper fidelis,* always faithful. The California motto is *Semper differens,* always different. By the way, do you know what George Washington's family motto was? *Exitus acta probat:*

> *Politics, n. Strife of
> interests masquerading as
> a contest of principles.*
>
> AMBROSE BIERCE

California Highway Patrol "lobbied heavily," according to the *Los Angeles Times,* for the law's passage. Why? What possible business is it of the California Highway Patrol to force its concept of personal safety on motorcycle riders? Wouldn't the California Highway Patrol's precious lobbying time be better spent getting more highway patrol officers, better equipment, or making sure Ted Turner doesn't colorize old episodes of *Highway Patrol?* Yes, it may be that the Highway Patrol thought it was saving lives, or could it be—as some pro-choice motorcycle helmetists claim—that the Highway Patrol wanted to separate the "bad" cyclists from the "good" cyclists? (The "bad" cyclists don't want to wear motorcycle helmets; the "good" cyclists may or may not want to, but will because "it's the law.") Now the Highway Patrol knows a "bad" cyclist on sight: no helmet.

There's also the matter of fines: a first offense is $100, second offense $200, third offense $250. With enough offenses, "bad" motorcycle riders will lose their licenses. If they ride anyway, they'll go to jail. Just where "bad" motorcycle riders belong. In the first year of California's helmet law, close to $1 million worth of tickets were written. If enough laws like this are enacted on relatively powerless, marginally unpopular groups, the rich, powerful people won't have to pay any tax at all. (Do they anyway?) Well, before I get too cynical about this one, let's move on to a much more exciting topic: public nudity.

⚖ ⚖ ⚖

By public nudity, I'm not referring to flashers or other aggressive, pseudo-sexual behavior. I'm referring to people who want

the end justifies the means. Really.

certain beaches set aside on which clothing is optional. Frankly, I don't think nudity in public should be a major concern for the same reason I don't think we need to concern ourselves about people wearing fried eggs on their foreheads or people heavily rouging their nostrils and skipping down the street singing "Rudolph the Red-Nosed Reindeer." I mean, how many people actually want to do it?

> *I'm a bit of a prude myself.*
>
> GYPSY ROSE LEE

Even if something is illegal, if people really want to do it, a certain number of them do it. How many people have you actually seen shopping nude in the supermarket? How many people have confessed to you how satisfying it was to walk in the nude amongst the nude paintings at the Metropolitan Museum of Art? In the many lists of "secret fantasies" I have read, "walking around Sears Roebuck nude"—or doing anything else nude that didn't involve Tom Cruise or Sharon Stone—did not make the list.

The laws against nudity make no sense. The idea that Jerry Falwell can go topless while Cindy Crawford cannot is an absolute affront to logic, common sense, and the 5,000-year human struggle for aesthetic taste. The reason that women should wear more clothing than men goes back to the old possession concept: "This is my *property,*" sayeth the man, "and you can't even *look* at it." In the 1890s, for a woman to show an ankle in public was scandalous. By 1910, it was the calf. By the 1920s, it was the knees. By the 1950s, two-piece bathing suits were all the rage (and scandal). Today, in England, women appear topless regularly in magazines, newspapers, and even on television. It's been going on for years. England has not exactly fallen into complete moral collapse because of it.

Other than a spate of streaking in the early 1970s (which was more about playful shock than nudity), the only real social nudity we've been confronted with in our country is at beaches. Some people like more of their fun exposed to the sun than others. The police in Pinellas County, Florida, began locking up nudists who frequented an isolated beach. "Come on, deputies," Don Addis chided them in the *St. Petersburg Times,* "If that's all you've got to do with your time, go join a Big Brother program or something." Mr. Addis continued,

> A member of the sheriff's marine unit, it says here, came jogging along the beach posing as an average, everyday gawker then pulled a badge. That undercover technique will have to do for now, until the rubber naked-person suits arrive.

> At first the deputies approached the beach from the open sea in their official boats in hopes of catching skinny-baskers unaware. I wonder how long it took them to figure out why that wasn't working. (You'd think they would have learned something from the Normandy invasion. By the time the Allied forces came ashore, the Germans all had their clothes on.)

> Meanwhile, down at the Addis-Holtz Behavioral Research Institute and Sub Shop, laboratory rats are being used extensively in the study of nudity, with the aim of helping humans afflicted with the dread condition. One group of rats was dressed in tiny little polyester suits, complete with shirts, ties, hats, two-tone wingtip shoes, socks and colorfully patterned boxer undershorts. Another group of rats was left unclothed.

> It was found that the rats without clothes mated more readily than those trussed up to the incisors in off-the-

rack ratwear. Conclu-
sion: Nudity causes lust
in rats.

The findings have been
challenged in some
scientific circles on
the grounds that re-
searchers failed to take
into account the possi-
ble effects of (1) em-
barrassment on the
part of rats whose un-
dershorts had trom-

> *Football combines
> the two worst features
> of American life:
> violence and committee meetings.*
>
> GEORGE WILL

bones printed on them, (2) fear of criticism from Mr.
Blackwell and (3) chafing.

With 2,000 beaches closed in 1992 due to unacceptable levels of water pollution, don't we have more important things to
concern ourselves with than whether or not some mammals are
exposing their mammary glands on beaches?

"And what about the children?" some ask. In 1920, it was
considered scandalous for a man to appear in any public arena
other than prize-fighting (with its all-male audience) with his
shirt off. Children raised not seeing men with their shirts off
were naturally a bit giggly and curious as the first daring shirtless
men began appearing on beaches, in magazines, and in movies.
Today, because it's what children are raised with, no one thinks
of a topless male as a threat to the morality of children. After a
similar period with topless women (or even fully nude adults),
the children will adjust (a lot faster than their parents, probably),
life will go on, and police can go catch real criminals. Remember:
children are born naked. They seem to like nothing better than
getting naked. It's adults who teach them what parts of their
bodies are and are not shameful to expose. A child has no natural
guilt about this at all.

The most publicized nudity case of the past several years is
the man who padded around the University of California,
Berkeley, campus wearing sandals, a bookbag, and nothing else.
This went on for months; his fanny appeared in every publication

> *Men become civilized,*
> *not in proportion to*
> *their willingness to believe,*
> *but in their readiness*
> *to doubt.*
>
> H. L. MENCKEN

but *Christian World* (where it might have appeared: I must admit I'm not a regular reader), and the campus did not seem to either disintegrate or lose its academic credentials—although it did lose a bit of its radical chic when it finally banned nude students.

⚖ ⚖ ⚖

Okay, so you think women's clothing is important. You think it should be worn. Well, some men would agree with you: they love wearing women's clothing. While some men want to come out of the closet, other men want to go into the closet: Madonna's.

Now why on earth should transvestism be illegal? As a Frenchman accurately observed in the 1930s, "Mae West is the greatest female impersonator in the world!" Somehow in this country, as long as a female impersonator has been a female, it's been okay: Jayne Mansfield, Marilyn Monroe, Zsa Zsa Gabor.* Just as Charlie Chaplin used to refer to his Tramp character as "the little fellow," so Bette Midler referred to her outrageous stage persona when honoring a male female impersonator who impersonated her: "He did a better Bette than I."

The closest we've come to accepting a male female impersonator is Liberace. Of course, it's hard to tell exactly what he was impersonating. Was he impersonating a Rockette? A Las Vegas showgirl? Wayne Newton? A piano player? Whatever it was, it made him famous, rich ("I cried all the way to the bank"), and adored.

Liberace followed Quentin Crisp's advice, detailed in

---

*Paul Krassner wrote in *The Realist* that gays were planning to boycott Zsa Zsa Gabor because she'd made some derogatory comments about lesbians, but the gays couldn't figure out what to boycott.

Quentin's book, *How to Become a Virgin:* if what you're doing causes people to cross the street to avoid you, confess every detail of what you're doing on television. This is the act of national cleansing. All your sins are forgiven. You become a virgin again. More importantly, you become a *celebrity* virgin. People will now cross the street—at great peril to their lives—in order to shake your hand and say, "I saw you last night on the *telly!*"

> *Of course, the last thing*
> *my parents wanted*
> *was a son who wears*
> *a cocktail dress that glitters,*
> *but they've come around to it.*
>
> DIVINE

While Quentin never hovered over audiences at Caesar's Palace suspended by piano wire (the best use of a piano part Liberace made in his entire career), Quentin made his daring—and personally more dangerous—statement that if boys will be girls, well, *c'est la vie.* In the 1930s in England, he wore make-up, scarves, and reddened his hair with henna. He was beaten up fairly regularly for his independence, but he persisted.

His flamboyance also made him highly unemployable, so he took a job as a nude model for state-run art schools. His manner of dress did not concern them, for obvious reasons. As all models worked for the government, the title of Quentin's autobiography is *The Naked Civil Servant.* When the rationing at the beginning of World War II was announced, he went out and bought two pounds of henna.

Sting immortalized Quentin Crisp's courage to be himself against the most impossible odds in his song, "Englishman In New York."

> *Takes more than combat gear to make a man,*
> *Takes more than a license for a gun.*
> *Confront your enemies, avoid them when you can—*
> *A gentleman will walk but never run*
>
> *If "manners maketh man" as someone said,*

> *I'm the Connie Francis*
> *of rock 'n' roll.*
>
> ELTON JOHN

Then he's the hero of the day.
It takes a man to suffer ignorance and smile:
Be yourself no matter what they say.

In his liner notes for his album, . . . *Nothing Like the Sun*, Sting explains,

I wrote "Englishman In New York" for a friend of mine who moved from London to New York in his early seventies to a small rented apartment in the Bowery at a time in his life when most people have settled down forever. He once told me over dinner that he looked forward to receiving his naturalization papers so that he could commit a crime and not be deported. "What kind of crime?" I asked anxiously. "Oh, something glamorous, non-violent, with a dash of style" he replied. "Crime is so rarely glamorous these days."

"To me," Quentin said, "a movie star has to be something you couldn't have invented for yourself if you sat up all night." He speaks of Evita Perón with only half-veiled envy:

The crowning moment of her entire career was when she stood up in her box in the opera house in Buenos Aires and made a speech. She lifted her hands to the crowd, and as she did so, with a sound like railway trucks in a siding, the diamond bracelets slid down from her wrists. When the expensive clatter had died away, her speech began, "We, the shirtless . . .!"

You may not believe in Mrs. Perón, but the Argentinians did. So much so that when she died they petitioned the Pope to make her a saint. His Holiness declined; but if he'd consented, what a triumph for style that would have been! A double fox stole, ankle-strap shoes, and eternal life. Nobody's ever had that.

Of course, most transvestites are not as flamboyant as Evita. Chuck Shepherd, John J. Kohut, and Roland Sweet, in their *More News of the Weird*, report,

> In 1989 jazz musician Billy Tipton died of a bleeding ulcer, leaving an ex-wife and three adopted sons. While the funeral director was preparing the body for burial, he discovered the 74-year-old saxophonist-pianist was really a woman. "He'll always be Dad," said one of Tipton's boys.

Contrary to popular misbelief, a good number of transvestites—both male and female—are also heterosexual. Just because they want to get dressed up like the opposite sex does not necessarily mean they want to go to bed with the same sex. Some have successful heterosexual marriages and enjoy the most delightful shopping expeditions with their spouses. It must be reminiscent of the scene on an episode of *Soap* in which the Billy Crystal character is discovered by his mother in one of her dresses. "What are you doing wearing my dress?" she yells, taking a hard look at him. She takes a closer look. "Oh! You wear it with a *belt*."

Laws against transvestism, obviously, spring from the hatred of women: "Why would a man want to get dressed up like a woman?" The fear of homosexuality that grew out of that same irrational disgust has kept the laws against cross-dressing on the books: "normal" heterosexual men don't want to be "tricked" into falling for a "woman" who's really a man. What a waste of testosterone! And what an embarrassment. Who wants to feel like the Charles Durning character in *Tootsie? Falling for Dustin Hoffman in drag. How demeaning. And then he winds up your son-in-law no less! No, there's gotta be a law against this.*

PART IV

SIX CHAPTERS
IN SEARCH OF
A SHORTER BOOK

I'd call this section a collection of essays, but no one seems to write essays any-more—nonfiction authors write feature articles, op-ed pieces, pitch-letters to *Hard Copy,* and grant applications. So I re-fer to this as a section of chapters which might abandon ship if they ever find a skinny book in need of plumping up.

The Enlightenment
or
We Were So Much Older Then;
We're Younger Than That Now

> *My people and I*
> *have come to an agreement*
> *which satisfies us both.*
> *They are to say*
> *what they please,*
> *and I am to do*
> *what I please.*
>
> FREDERICK THE GREAT
> (1712–1786)

IT WAS KNOWN AS THE Enlightenment. Remarkable human beings shined the light of reason on areas of human endeavor that, for centuries, were kept in the darkness of dogma, fear, and prejudice. Philosophy, anatomy, medicine, astronomy, music, physics, and even the most taboo subjects of all—religion and government—were explored anew. It was the time of Bacon, Locke, Descartes, Spinoza, Voltaire, Rousseau, Franklin, Jefferson, Swift, Kant, Sir Isaac Newton, Mozart, and Beethoven. The death of Beethoven—punctuated by lightning—marked the end of the Enlightenment.

Nothing would ever be the same again.

One of the Age of Enlightenment's great creations—an experiment that continues to this day—is the government of the United States. No less than Voltaire's *Candide* or the Beethoven symphonies, the Declaration of Independence and the United States Constitution with its Bill of Rights are masterpieces of the Enlightenment.

Helping to lay the foundation of the Enlightenment (also known as the Age of Reason) was John Locke (1632–1704). Locke was an Englishman who, thanks to his "treasonous" thoughts, spent a good deal of time outside England. When he began to explore government, he—like all good thinkers—started at the

> *It is not only vain, but wicked,*
> *in a legislator to frame laws*
> *in opposition to the laws of nature,*
> *and to arm them*
> *with the terrors of death.*
> *This is truly creating crimes*
> *in order to punish them.*
>
> THOMAS JEFFERSON
> 1779

beginning. He asked, "Why should there be a government? What is the purpose of government?" These questions, *in themselves,* were considered treasonous. At that time, everyone knew there was a government because God wanted it that way. If God didn't want it that way, there wouldn't be a government. Anyone who questioned further was guilty not only of treason, but heresy. The church and the state ruled together, by Divine Right. Anyone who questioned this arrangement questioned the authority of God. For such blasphemy, the law declared, one should be put to death. Many were. Nonetheless, John Locke asked his question, "What is the purpose of government?"

First, Locke concluded that all human beings are endowed with what he called *natural rights.* Human beings, individually, belonged to *themselves.* This notion directly countered the prevailing belief that one's body belonged to the state and that one's soul belonged to the church. One could be granted *privileges* from the state and purchase *indulgences* from the church, but the "rights of man," both here and hereafter, belonged to the state and the church.

The idea that humans owned their own lives and had certain freedoms simply because they *existed* was central to the Enlightenment. The great minds of the period saw the logic and the fundamental reasonableness of individual liberty and natural rights.

If we are free, then, and if we have natural rights, why should we give some of these rights over to a government? The only reason for doing so, Locke explained in his *Two Treatises of Government* (1690), was that people get more from the government by surrendering some rights than they would by keeping them. Individuals form communities because *it serves the individual.*

For example, a community might agree that, if bandits come, everyone will join to fight off the bandits. Even if only one person in the community is attacked by bandits, the entire community agrees to rise up and protect that one member. In this way, each member of the community is giving away a natural right (the right not to risk your life to save someone else) for a benefit (protection from invaders).

> *Every tyrant who has lived has believed in freedom—for himself.*
>
> ELBERT HUBBARD

Another example: Within the community, everyone might agree that what one grows or makes is one's own and cannot be taken away without the owner's permission. Being part of this community, then, means giving up a certain right (taking all you can) in exchange for a benefit (keeping what you've got). You agree not to take things from people weaker than yourself in exchange for knowing that you will not have your things taken by people stronger than you. For Locke, government was

> for the regulating and preserving of property and of employing the force of the community in the execution of such laws, and in the defense of the commonwealth from foreign injury, and all this only for the public good.

Noticeably absent from this plan is religion. Prior to Locke, religion was used—sometimes for good and sometimes for ill—as the fundamental moral principle behind government. During the 1600s, the Catholic and Protestant monarchs played musical thrones in England, which only led to suffering and waste. Locke saw firsthand the inequity, impracticality, and downright unreasonableness of the state based on the ruler's religion. In his *A Letter Concerning Toleration*, Locke began the process of separating church and state. A trained physician, he knew this would be a delicate but necessary operation. The letter was first published

> *Civil laws against adultery and fornication have been on the books forever, in every country. That's not the law's business; that's God's business. He can handle it.*
>
> JUSTICE THOMAS G. KAVANAGH

in 1689 and revised by him several times prior to his death in 1704.

Locke, who trained for the clergy, did not attack religion. He used the arguments *of* religion to show that both church and state would, in fact, be better off apart. The state has its job; the church has its job; and, when both are left to do their jobs, everything is fine. When the government tries to do the church's job and the church tries to do the government's job, all sorts of mischief arise.

Just as he argued in *Two Treatises on Government* that an individual's body and property belong to the individual, in *A Letter Concerning Toleration* Locke argued that the individual's soul belongs to the individual, not the church. "The care, therefore, of every man's soul belongs unto himself and is to be left unto himself." Thus the basis for freedom of religion was established.

But what if a person is clearly off the path and headed for unhappiness in this lifetime and hellfire in the next? Shouldn't we do something to make that person change course? No, argues Locke, if we are compelled to help another, that help must be limited to *persuasion.* "It is one thing to persuade, another to command," wrote Locke; "one thing to press with arguments, another with penalties." If these wayward souls fail to heed our arguments and continue to harm themselves, placing their afterlife in danger, then should we not physically alter their course? Absolutely not, Locke maintains:

> If any man err from the right way, it is his own misfortune, no injury to thee; nor therefore art thou to punish him in the things of this life because thou supposest he will be miserable in that which is to come.

The government, Locke explains, must have the power of

physical force to protect people and their property from the physical violations of others. Using the government's physical power, however, to enforce a religious belief is wrong:

> Let them not supply their want of reasons with the instruments of force, which belong to another jurisdiction and do ill become a Churchman's hands.

> *In a civilized society, all crimes are likely to be sins, but most sins are not and ought not to be treated as crimes. Man's ultimate responsibility is to God alone.*
>
> GEOFFREY FISHER
> Archbishop of Canterbury

If we can't win people over to our belief in God by reason, we shouldn't ask the government to back up our failure with physical force. This is unseemly, Locke maintains, both in the eyes of reason and in the eyes of God.

But what if we don't insist that people do things to save their souls? What if we only ask them to do things which are good for them in this lifetime? Don't we have the right to make people take good care of themselves in this world? No, says Locke. "No man can be forced to be rich or healthful whether he will or no." To which Locke makes a significant addition: "Nay, God Himself will not save men against their wills." Obviously, God *can* keep people from doing things that harm themselves in this life but, for whatever reason, does not do so. How dare we, as humans, presume to know more than God? By what arrogance do we interfere with other people's lives by force, when God chooses not to do so? In other words, far from helping God's work by using the force of government to enforce "His laws," government interference may be hindering that work.

Locke's thoughts on the separation of church and state and the purpose of government influenced the minds that shaped the government of the United States. In 1825, while creating the University of Virginia, Jefferson acknowledged the authors who most influenced the American experiment:

> *For why should
> my freedom
> be judged
> by another's conscience?*
>
> PAUL
> 1 Corinthians 10:29

. . . that as to the general principles of liberty and the rights of man, in nature and in society, the doctrines of Locke in his essay concerning the true original extent and end of civil government and of Sydney in his discourses on government may be considered as those generally approved by our fellow citizens of Virginia and the United States.

⚖ ⚖ ⚖

The next significant year in the history of consensual crime was 1859. "It was the best of times, it was the worst of times." Charles Dickens first published that in 1859, the opening line of *A Tale of Two Cities.* (He forgot to complete the thought, however: It is the best of times and the worst of times *all* the time.) Among 1859's "worst of times," the Supreme Court upheld the Fugitive Slave Act, which said that slaves who escaped to free states had to be returned to their "owners." (In 1857, the Supreme Court had declared that slaves were property and not human beings.) Georgia passed a law in 1859 stating that slaves freed in wills were not free, and that legitimately freed slaves who went into debt would be sold again to satisfy the debt. Nevertheless, the hit song of the year was "I Wish I Was in Dixie's Land." (Away! Away!) Fundamentalists were infuriated by the publication of Charles Darwin's *On the Origin of Species,* but were comforted by the introduction of "Nearer My God to Thee."

In England, the House of Commons finally seated its first Jewish member, Lionel Rothschild. Although elected two years before, he had been unable to take his seat because the oath of office insisted he proclaim his "true faith of a Christian." In 1859,

AIN'T NOBODY'S BUSINESS IF YOU DO

Parliament reluctantly altered the oath. In Manchester, England, some were outraged at the opening of the world's first playground. Swings and horizontal bars, they determined, were far too dangerous for children, and should not be permitted. On the drug front, cocaine was first isolated from coca leaves, and the Great American Tea Company began selling extra-potent Chinese and Japanese tea at one-third the going rate. The latter venture was such a success, it became the Great Atlantic and Pacific Tea Company, and later simply A&P. Fortunately, no one attempted to protect circus performers from themselves. Gravelet successfully crossed Niagara Falls on a tightrope, and, in Paris, Jules Lèotard demonstrated his discovery: the trapeze act. "The Man on the Flying Trapeze" was written about him, and the shockingly tight tights he wore were named after him. That women came to see more than his act shocked even Paris.

> *History repeats itself;*
> *that's one of the things*
> *that's wrong with history.*
>
> CLARENCE DARROW

In 1859, while the United States was about to be "engaged in a great civil war," a major event in the history of personal freedom took place in England: John Stuart Mill (1806–1873) published *On Liberty*.

On Liberty was the first major writing since the Bill of Rights (almost seventy years before) to delineate clearly the relationship between the individual and the enormous powers of the state.

"That so few now dare to be eccentric," he wrote, "marks the chief danger of the time." People's fear of punishment for consensual crimes stifled personal growth, thus stifling the advancement of the culture:

> It is not by wearing down into uniformity all that is individual in themselves, but by cultivating it, and calling it forth, within the limits imposed by the rights and interests of others, that human beings become a noble and

beautiful object of contemplation. . . .

Where, not the person's own character, but the traditions or customs of other people are the rule of conduct, there is wanting one of the principal ingredients of human happiness, and quite the chief ingredient of individual and social progress. . . .

> *We are all tolerant enough of those who do not agree with us, provided only they are sufficiently miserable.*
>
> DAVID GRAYSON

In proportion to the development of his individuality, each person becomes more valuable to himself, and is therefore capable of being more valuable to others . . .

The worth of a State, in the long run, is the worth of the individuals composing it. . . . A State which dwarfs its men, in order that they may be more docile instruments in its hands even for beneficial purposes—will find that with small men no great thing can really be accomplished.

Mill argues, then, that the real victims of repressive laws are not just the people caught and punished for violating those laws, but everyone—individually and collectively:

The peculiar evil of silencing the expression of an opinion is that it is robbing the human race; posterity as well as the existing generation. . . . If the opinion is right, they are deprived of the opportunity of exchanging error for truth: if wrong, they lose, what is almost as great a benefit, the clearer perception and livelier impression of truth, produced by its collision with error.

The solution? Discover your "own character"; become involved in "cultivating" and the "development" of your "individuality." Mill wrote:

Liberty consists in doing what one desires. . . .

So long as we do not harm others we should be free to think, speak, act, and live as we see fit, without molestation from individuals, law, or government. . . .

The only freedom which deserves the name, is that of pursuing our own good in our own way, so long as we do not attempt to deprive others of theirs, or impede their efforts to obtain it.

> *Republic.*
> *I like the sound of the word.*
> *It means people can live free,*
> *talk free, go or come,*
> *buy or sell, be drunk or sober,*
> *however they choose.*
>
> JOHN WAYNE

Is society responsible for the moral good of an individual? No, says Mill. "Each is the proper guardian of his own health, whether bodily, or mental and spiritual." Mill writes that one's independence over anything that "merely concerns himself" is "absolute. Over himself, over his own body and mind, the individual is sovereign." Mill writes, "Neither one person, nor any number of persons, is warranted in saying to another human creature of ripe years, that he shall not do with his life for his own benefit what he chooses to do with it."

What are the limits to all this free expression? "The liberty of the individual must be thus far limited; he must not make himself a nuisance to other people." Is this the loophole through which government can determine that any number of consensual activities are crimes? No, says Mill; there must be genuine "harm," "injury to others."

> That the only purpose for which power can be rightfully exercised over any member of a civilized community against his will is to prevent harm to others. His own good, either physical or moral, is not a sufficient warrant. . . .
>
> There should be different experiments of living, that free scope should be given to varieties of character, short of

> *A government
> is the only known vessel
> that leaks from the top.*
>
> JAMES RESTON

injury to others; and that the worth of different modes of life should be proved practically, when any one thinks fit to try them.

What can society do to individuals who practice behaviors that society finds distasteful, but do not physically harm the person or property of another? "Advice, instruction, persuasion, and avoidance by other people if thought necessary by them for their own good, are the only measures by which society can justifiably express its dislike or disapprobation of his conduct."

And what should be the individual's response to excessive advice, instruction, persuasion, dislike, and disapprobation? Mill suggests that "intrusively pious members of society" be told "to mind their own business." And he adds, "This is precisely what should be said to every government and every public, who have the pretension that no person shall enjoy any pleasure which they think wrong."

> There is a limit to the legitimate interference of collective opinion with individual independence: and to find that limit, and maintain it against encroachment, is as indispensable to a good condition of human affairs, as protection against political despotism. . . .
>
> If all mankind minus one were of one opinion, and only one person were of the contrary opinion, mankind would be no more justified in silencing that one person, than he, if he had the power, would be justified in silencing mankind.

"Most people don't like it" is, thus, insufficient ground for stifling unpopular thought or behavior. Protecting the minority's freedom is the purpose of government, not oppressing the mi-

AIN'T NOBODY'S BUSINESS IF YOU DO

nority for the comfort of the majority.

> The will of the people, moreover, practically means the will of the most numerous or the most active part of the people; the majority, or those who succeed in making themselves accepted as the majority; the people, consequently may desire to oppress a part of their number; and precautions are as much needed against this as against any other abuse of power.

> *No democracy can long survive which does not accept as fundamental to its very existence the recognition of the rights of minorities.*
>
> FRANKLIN D. ROOSEVELT

As examples of the majority using force to control an unpopular minority, Mill cites no less than the lives of Socrates and Jesus.

> Mankind can hardly be too often reminded that there was once a man named Socrates, between whom and the legal authorities and public opinion of his time there took place a memorable collision. . . . This acknowledged master . . . was put to death by his countrymen, after a judicial conviction, for impiety and immorality.

As to Jesus being sentenced to death for "blasphemy," and the men who took such an action, Mill says:

> The high-priest who rent his garments when the words were pronounced, which, according to all the ideas of his country constituted the blackest guilt, was in all probability quite as sincere in his horror and indignation as the generality of respectable and pious men now are in the religious and moral sentiments they profess.

For the pious who are unwilling to change their minds and who dismiss Mill's examples as ones that could not possibly apply to themselves, Mill makes this comment:

Orthodox Christians who are tempted to think that those who stoned to death the first martyrs must have been worse men than they themselves are, ought to remember that one of those persecutors was Saint Paul.*

> *The policy of the American government is to leave its citizens free, neither restraining nor aiding them in their pursuits.*
>
> THOMAS JEFFERSON

Mill rejects the idea that individual expression will lead to uncontrolled atheism, hedonism, and other ism's. Those who want us to be other than ourselves are the same people who think that "trees are a much finer thing when clipped . . . into the figures of animals than as nature made them." To the contrary, Mill claims that it is only by following our inner nature—the desires and instincts that God gave us—that we discover ourselves and truly begin to fulfill our divine purpose.

> If it be any part of religion to believe that man was made by a good Being, it is more consistent with that faith to believe that this Being gave all human faculties that they might be cultivated and unfolded, not rooted out and consumed, and that he takes delight in every nearer approach made by his creatures to the ideal conception embodied in them, every increase in any of their capabilities of comprehension, of action, or of enjoyment.

Amen.

*Paul, before his conversion, was a Jewish Pharisee and Roman citizen named Saul who executed early Christians with the same zeal he later used to spread Christianity (Acts 8:3, 9:1–2).

AIN'T NOBODY'S BUSINESS IF YOU DO

Prohibition: A Lesson
in the Futility (and Danger)
of Prohibiting

> *Prohibition is a great*
> *social and economic experiment—*
> *noble in motive*
> *and far-reaching in purpose.*
>
> HERBERT HOOVER

PROHIBITION (1920–1933 R.I.P.) was known as The Noble Experiment. The results of the experiment are clear: innocent people suffered; organized crime grew into an empire; the police, courts, and politicians became increasingly corrupt; disrespect for the law grew; and the per capita consumption of the prohibited substance—alcohol—increased dramatically, year by year, for the thirteen years of this Noble Experiment, never to return to the pre-1920 levels.

You would think that an experiment with such clear results would not need to be repeated; but the experiment is being repeated; it's going on today. Only the prohibited substances have changed. The results remain the same. They are more devastating now than they were then.

Let's take a look into that not-too-distant-mirror.

Prohibition did not strike suddenly; *zap*—one day you could get a drink and the next day you could not. It settled on the country gradually, county by county, state by state, for the better part of a century. National Prohibition in 1920 was simply the final turn of the spigot.

Alcohol was consumed in all the colonial settlements in America. No one was particularly against drinking—even the Puritans enjoyed it. What they frowned on was drinking to excess: generally known as drunkenness. This was of practical concern in

> *There are more old drunkards than old doctors.*
>
> BENJAMIN FRANKLIN

the smaller communities: there were crops to plant, fish to catch, animals to trap, and a wilderness to be tamed. If one's excessive drinking got in the way of these activities, the community as a whole might suffer; thus, drunkeness was frowned on and this frowning found its way into some early laws.

The first of them, in Virginia in 1619, through New Hampshire's law of 1719 were against drunkenness, not against drinking. The first law limiting liquor sales with a religious base was passed in New York in 1697; it ordered that all public drinking establishments be closed on Sunday because, on the Lord's day, people should be worshiping the Bible not the bottle. In 1735, the religious had a prohibition law enacted for the entire state of Georgia. The law was a complete failure and was abandoned in 1742.

For the most part, however, during the 1700s and early 1800s, those opposing liquor on religious grounds used sermons and persuasion rather than politics and laws to make their point. These persuasive efforts were known as the Temperance Movement, and its goal was to get everyone to voluntarily temper use of spirits.

By 1820, complete abstinence from all alcoholic beverages was a basic rule of most evangelical churches. The intense revivalism of the 1820s and 1830s preached that alcohol was a tool of the devil and that Satan himself was in every drop. Moral campaigns to spread the truth about "demon rum" and other Lucifer Liquids raised huge amounts of money.

Never mind that Jesus' first miracle was turning water into wine at the wedding feast at Cana. Never mind that Jesus and his apostles drank wine at the Last Supper. Never mind that Jesus promised to drink wine again with his disciples in Paradise.

For anyone who had the impertinence to actually *read* the

New Testament and question why wine (which was obviously not condemned by Jesus) should suddenly become such a wicked, evil thing, the preachers explained that the word for *wine* in the language Jesus spoke could also mean "grape juice" or "grape jelly." Jesus trafficked only in these, the preachers would say, not in wine. Those who doubted that Jesus turned water into grape juice at the wedding feast or that grape jelly was served at the Last Supper were condemned to the fires of eternal perdition.

> *The first clergyman was the first rascal who met the first fool.*
>
> VOLTAIRE

The rhetoric about drinking heated and became increasingly sentimental in the 1840s as former drunkards "saw the light," telling in pamphlet—and speech and at financial profit—the harm alcohol did to themselves and to the innocent members of their families. Booklets such as *The Reformed Drunkard's Daughter* told the heart-rending story of a man who had not seen a sober moment in fifteen years. He perceived the error of his ways when, one cold, wintry day, his little daughter Hannah pleaded, "Papa, please don't send me for whiskey today." Yes, drinking was a crime, not just a crime against God and a crime against decency, but a crime against innocent wives and children.

By the late 1840s, everyone who was going to be convinced by persuasion or fear of hell fire had already signed a temperance pledge. Some fanatics decided that this was not enough: everyone had to be sober all the time for their own good and the good of all. Temperance turned to prohibition and prohibition meant politics.

For some, alcohol was a problem. Some found the solution to their drinking through God, others through reason, others through medicine (Dr. Benjamin Rush, the Surgeon General of Washington's Continental Army, prescribed complete abstinence).

> *The objection to Puritans
> is not that they try
> to make us think as they do,
> but that they try to make us
> do as they think.*
>
> H. L. MENCKEN

But how to keep alcohol away from the rest? The answer: make it illegal to all. Put the full force of law behind it. Those who did not have a problem with drink, who could take it or leave it, were asked to leave it—permanently—for the glory of God and the greater good of all.

Maine went completely dry in 1851 and, by 1855, so had New Hampshire, Vermont, Delaware, Michigan, Indiana, Iowa, Minnesota, Nebraska, Connecticut, Rhode Island, Massachusetts, and New York. In some states, prohibition was declared unconstitutional; in others, it went virtually unenforced, but the primary setback to prohibition after 1855 was the Civil War.

It's hard to keep alcohol away from troops in time of war. Thanks to the prohibitionists, whiskey in the U.S. Army was eliminated in 1830, but field commanders, at their discretion, could issue a "ration" of whiskey to each man—about four ounces. Private purchase and consumption of alcohol by military personnel, even in dry states, was condoned, and only drinking while on guard duty, on maneuvers, or just prior to battle was punished.

Then there was the aspect of alcohol that, due to its later abuses, we usually laugh about today: its "medicinal value." At the time of the Civil War, alcohol was one of the most frequently prescribed—and most effective—medicines known to doctors. (The Native Americans had some useful herbal concoctions, but the natives were not consulted.) No one quite knew why whiskey worked; they just knew it did. It was poured on external wounds to prevent infection. It cured any number of internal maladies, including one that swept throughout the Northern troops dubbed "the Tennessee Quick Step" (later called "Montezuma's Revenge" by visitors to Mexico and "the Pharaoh's Curse" by visitors to Egypt). Eventually, the germ theory would scientifically

AIN'T NOBODY'S BUSINESS IF YOU DO

explain the antibacterial, antiviral, and antiparasitic nature of alcohol.

During the Civil War, the use of anesthesia was in its infancy. At makeshift battlefield hospitals, ether and chloroform were in short supply. Alcohol was not. Many an operation was performed—and a life saved—while the patient was heavily under the influ-

> *I once shook hands with Pat Boone and my whole right side sobered up.*
>
> DEAN MARTIN
>
> *There's something about me that makes a lot of people want to throw up.*
>
> PAT BOONE

ence. Then there was the basic, overall good feeling produced by spirits, and the healing effect they could have on what we now call psychosomatic illness. If nothing else, in some cases alcohol eased the pain while nature did the healing.

Soldiers returning from the Civil War, many of whom were exposed to alcohol either recreationally or medicinally for the first time during the war, wanted none of this talk about temperance. They had lived through hell and didn't want some "Bible thumper" telling them what they could and could not drink. There were also far more important issues to deal with in both the North and the South than who drank what where. Prohibition was put on the back burner.

The cause came back to life in the 1880s. Women joined the fight, becoming politically active for the first time. A broad range of social reforms was demanded—banning tobacco, closing all theaters, labor laws, women's suffrage, and even socialism—but the only one that caught on was the proposal to close the saloons.

Saloons were seen as hotbeds of corruption, contagion, and vice. These male-only (except for "dance-hall girls") establishments were, to the pious, positive hell holes. Drinking, gambling, prostitution, tobacco smoking, tobacco chewing (and its natural by-product, spitting), dancing, card playing, and criminal activity of all kinds were all traced to the saloon. Saloons were irresistible temptations to the otherwise righteous and virtuous

> *I envy people who drink—*
> *at least they know*
> *what to blame everything on.*
>
> OSCAR LEVANT

men of the community. Invited there for a social drink by the "recruiters of Satan," the young men of the community found themselves hopelessly caught in a spider's web of immorality, lust, and depravity. Alcohol (a.k.a. the devil) was the spider at its very center. The Anti-Saloon League was formed, "an army of the Lord to wipe away the curse of drink."

One of the anti-saloon monthly magazines—very popular with evangelical churches—offered the following:

> "Come in and take a drop." The first drop led to other drops. He dropped his position; he dropped his respectability; he dropped his fortune; he dropped his friends; he dropped finally all prospects in this life, and his hopes for eternity; and then came the last drop on the gallows. BEWARE OF THE FIRST DROP.

If people were not afraid for their own lives and the eternal damnation of their immortal souls, they should at least fear for the children. "In this age of cities, temptations about our youth increase, such as foul pictures, corrupt literature, leprous shows, gambling, slot machines, saloons, and Sabbath breaking. *We are trying to raise saints in hell.*" To these bulwarks of Prohibition ("Satan is drink" and "save the children"), the evangelical reformers added two familiar fears: racism and fear of "foreigners."

Stories of newly freed slaves drinking their first alcohol and raping white women were repeated again and again. Meanwhile, prohibitionists exploited the fear and hatred of immigrants felt by many "Americans." The millions of "wretched refuse" and "huddled masses yearning to breathe free" brought with them the drinking habits of their homelands. Irish loved whiskey; Germans loved beer; Italians loved wine. That they were primarily

Catholics in this primarily Protestant country only made the prejudice worse. If one could just get the bottle (or the beer stein or the wine glass) out of their hands, the immigrants would have a spiritual awakening, see God's true purpose for them, become Protestants and, *ipso facto,* good citizens.

My dad was the town drunk. Usually that's not so bad, but New York City?

HENNY YOUNGMAN

As Paul Sann pointed out in his book, *The Lawless Decade,* "The Drys invariably found a way, however slick, to air the view that it was the immigrant much more than the 100% American who needed the splendid discipline of Prohibition."

By the 1890s, prohibitionists were prominent on school boards. Anti-alcohol material flooded the school house. Young children were asked to memorize this pledge:

I promise not to buy, sell, or give
Alcoholic liquors while I live;
From all tobacco I'll abstain
And never take God's name in vain.

High school biology books showed the physiological ruin a single drink caused the human body. Most of these children grew into staunch Prohibitionists. A few needed a drink.

By the turn of the century, more than half the state legislatures—dominated by rural Protestants—had declared their states "dry." The wet people within the dry states did not complain too much, however—there were loopholes. The primary loophole was this: since interstate commerce was regulated by the federal government and not by the individual states, one could order liquor by mail. As state after state became dry, the parcel post wagon jingled, jangled, clinked, and sloshed with increasing wetness.

This infuriated the Drys and in 1913, the Interstate Liquor

> *Hell hath no fury*
> *like a bureaucrat scorned.*
>
> MILTON FRIEDMAN

Act, prohibiting the shipment of alcohol into dry states, was passed over President Taft's veto. This was a major coup for the Drys. Still not content, they used the anti-German feelings surrounding World War I and the association of Germans with beer ("the Kaiser's mightiest ally") to press for all-out national prohibition. In 1917, the Eighteenth Amendment to the Constitution was proposed.

The Prohibitionists got an unexpected boost from a strange quarter: disease. The influenza epidemic of 1918 killed 20 million people worldwide. This was more than twice the number of people killed worldwide during the four years of World War I; 548,000 died of the flu in the United States, the equivalent today of 1,500,000 people dying in a single year. Guess what the preachers blamed for this disaster? Sin, of course. God was punishing a wicked nation for straying from the path of righteousness. Only a great moral crusade could save the nation. Alcohol, as usual, was high on the hit list.

If the evangelicals had simply tempered their intemperance, they might have, over time, gotten more of what they wanted. By 1920, thirty-three states encompassing 63% of the country had already voted themselves dry. The Prohibitionists probably could have closed every saloon outside big cities and, by continuing to control the curriculum in the schools, might have created generation upon generation of teetotalers and moderate drinkers. If they had allowed people their mail-order hooch, beer, and wine, the Prohibitionists would have come closer to controlling alcohol use. But they got greedy.

As with all reformers who are aiming for "the perfection of mankind," one success is only the foundation for another campaign designed to perfect humans even further. That success leads to yet another campaign, and a series of unbroken successes leads inevitably to excess. Prohibition was one such excess. The Eighteenth Amendment to the Constitution of the United States was ratified by the necessary number of states on January 29, 1919; and, on January 29, 1920, Prohibition became the law of the land. The final turn of the screw came with the Volstead Act.

> *Although man is already ninety per cent water, the Prohibitionists are not yet satisfied.*
>
> JOHN KENDRICK BANGS

The Eighteenth Amendment only prohibited "manufacture, sale, or transportation of intoxicating liquors . . . for beverage purposes." Although this was the "supreme law of the land," it still required an Act of Congress to make it enforceable. Enter the super-dry, ultra-religious congressman from Minnesota, Andrew J. Volstead.

Many who supported the Eighteenth Amendment took the term "intoxicating liquors" to mean *liquor:* whiskey, rum, and other distilled spirits. Most liquors were at least 40% alcohol ("eighty proof"); some, particularly of the "greased lightning" variety, were as much as 90% alcohol. Surely beer, with its three to seven percent alcohol content, and wine, with its less-than-fifteen percent alcohol content, would be permitted—with certain restrictions and regulations, of course.

Much to people's surprise, Volstead, backed by the triumphant evangelicals, defined "intoxicating liquors" as any beverage containing more than one-half of one percent alcohol. Using the momentum of the anti-German, anti-beer bias, Volstead was able to pass his National Prohibition Act over President Wilson's veto. Understandably, many supporters of the Eighteenth Amendment felt betrayed.

Also feeling betrayed were many of the veterans returning home from World War I. Like the Civil War veterans, they had fought a brutal and bloody war. In Europe, particularly in France, they had seen that moderate daily alcohol consumption and ordinary life could co-exist. Many learned that what they had been taught about the inherent dangers of alcohol was simply not true. Although expressed light-heartedly in songs such as "How Ya Gonna Keep 'Em Down on the Farm after They've Seen Paree," the disillusionment over what they had been taught versus what they had experienced ran deep. Coming home to find that the evangelicals, reformers, prudes, and blue noses had won a total victory embittered the veterans even more.

> *Prohibition only drives drunkenness behind doors and into dark places, and does not cure or even diminish it.*
>
> MARK TWAIN

Oblivious to the discontent of many (or simply chalking it up to "the devil's last grumblings" on the issue), the Drys celebrated. "Hell will be forever for rent," declared evangelist Billy Sunday, who looked forward to an America "so dry, she can't spit." The Anti-Saloon League claimed, "Now for an era of clear thinking and clean living." A Long Island church leaflet crowed, "An enemy has been overthrown and victory crowns the forces of righteousness."

A religious belief had become the law of the land. Never mind that if Jesus tried turning water into wine in the United States, he could have been arrested for bootlegging, or that the Last Supper might have been raided by federal Prohibition agents. In exchange for giving up one of their basic freedoms, the people of the United States were promised great things by the reformers. The great things never came. As Herbert Asbury described in his book, *The Great Illusion:*

> The American people had expected to be greeted, when the great day came, by a covey of angels bearing gifts of peace, happiness, prosperity and salvation, which they had been assured would be theirs when the rum demon had been scotched. Instead they were met by a horde of bootleggers, moonshiners, rum-runners, hijackers, gang-

sters, racketeers, trig-
germen, venal judges,
corrupt police, crooked
politicians, and speak-
easy operators, all
bearing the twin sym-
bols of the eighteenth
a m e n d m e n t — t h e
Tommy gun and the
poisoned cup.

⚖️ ⚖️ ⚖️

They can never repeal it.

SENATOR ANDREW J. VOLSTEAD

Prohibition began easily enough: the people who drank
stocked up on liquor before it was illegal; those who planned to
give up drinking treated January 28, 1920 as though it were New
Year's Eve, and the following day their New Year's resolutions
began. The poor, who couldn't afford to stock up, were catered
to by saloon keepers who, rather than closing voluntarily, stayed
open until they were shut down. It would take months to close
them all down, and, after they were closed, many bought new
booze and opened again. In an attempt to keep them from re-
opening, the federal authorities began destroying not just the
liquor, but bars, fixtures and furnishings.

After a year or so, the reserves (and resolves) were depleted,
and people got thirsty again—including some people who had
never been thirsty before. The fact that alcohol was now prohibited made it somehow irresistible. There's always something tantalizing about forbidden fruit—in this case, the fruit of the vine.

Once people wanted to drink, nothing could stop them.
Good old American ingenuity came to the fore. By 1923, finding
ways to "beat the feds" had surpassed even baseball as the national pastime.

- The saloons went underground and became speakeasies. There were lots of them. The 16,000 saloons in
  New York City, for example, became (depending on
  whose estimate you believe) from 32,000 to more than
  100,000 "speaks." Unlike the saloons, which were

propaganda—much of it grossly exaggerated or downright dishonest—disseminated by the evangelicals tainted the entire alcoholic beverage industry and everyone who worked in it. It was hard for these people to find jobs in other industries. Saying, "I worked in a brewery" or "I worked in a liquor store" had a tinge of disrespectability.

> *There should be asylums for habitual teetotalers, but they would probably relapse into teetotalism as soon as they got out.*
>
> SAMUEL BUTLER

Many of these people, out of economic necessity, were forced into a life of crime, doing precisely what they did before it became a crime.

Then there were the tens of thousands of people who worked in bars, restaurants, beer gardens, hotels, resorts, and related businesses that went out of business as a direct result of Prohibition. Yes, the speakeasies could hire some of these people—if they became criminals. Others, in order to keep their jobs, had to look the other way. Although hotels, for example, had sternly worded signs warning that drinking alcohol in hotel rooms was a federal crime and that violators would be prosecuted, the sight of a bellman carrying a tray with nothing but glasses, ice, and a bottle or two of ginger ale was common. The bellman in this instance, in order to keep his job, had to become an accessory to a federal crime. Such difficult choices corrupted the morals of millions.[*]

7. Prohibition caused physical harm. When "safe" alcoholic beverages were no longer available (that is, beverages in

---

[*]In Geroge Bernard Shaw's *Pygmalion*, Henry Higgins asks Alfred P. Doolittle, "Have you no morals, man?" to which Doolitle calmly replies, "Can't afford 'em." A lot of people, some of whom may have favored Prohibition, found themselves in similar situations: the farmer selling grain or grapes to a known bootlegger, the landlord renting a basement knowing it might become a speakeasy, the entertainer or musician offered a job playing in a speakeasy.

> *Every major horror*
> *of history*
> *was committed*
> *in the name of*
> *an altruistic motive.*
>
> AYN RAND

which the purity and alcoholic content were regulated by law), people began assembling all sorts of concoctions, either for their own use or for sale. Some worked; some didn't. Some killed. Alcohol made from fruits, vegetables, or grains—either fermented or distilled—tends to be safe. Alcohol distilled from wood products ("wood alcohol") is not. Wood alcohol, nonetheless, smells like alcohol, tastes like alcohol, and gets you high.

Some desperate people tried to find ways of making wood alcohol safe to drink; some despicable people repackaged it and sold it as "the real thing." Some used the less expensive wood alcohol to cut the more expensive grain alcohol to make it go further. During the Noble Experiment, more than 10,000 people died from wood-alcohol poisoning, 1,565 in 1928 alone.

With "cutting" becoming a common practice in bootlegging and tens of millions of people drinking each day, the only reason this figure wasn't higher was because of a peculiar characteristic of wood alcohol: before you died from it, you would go blind—permanently, irreversibly, blind. While drinking, if one's vision began to go, the drill was clear: stop drinking and upchuck as much as you could, as fast as you could. If people acted quickly enough, sometimes they would not end up with complete blindness, but with impaired vision—plus permanent kidney, liver, and brain damage.

Rather than having a little "Christian charity" for these people who, if alcohol had been legal, would have had nothing more than a hangover, the evangelicals proclaimed that people harmed by drinking wood alcohol "had it coming" for breaking both God's law and the law of the land.

In addition, there were the various beatings, stabbings, shootings, and killings between the bootleggers and the feds, the feds and the bootleggers, and the bootleggers amongst themselves. Along the way, any number of innocent people were caught in the crossfire, saw something they shouldn't have seen and were eliminated, or were rubbed out due to "mistaken identity."

8. Prohibition changed the drinking habits of a country—for the worse.

> *In a generation,*
> *those who are now children*
> *will have lost their taste for alcohol.*
>
> JOHN FULLER
> 1925

Prior to Prohibition, almost all drinking took place outside the home. Some—mostly recent immigrants—had beer or wine with meals; some of the rich had a little brandy or port after dinner; but, for the most part, alcohol consumption in the home was "for medicinal purposes only." Because the public drinking places closed, people (especially the poor: speakeasies tended to be expensive) began drinking at home more and more. With liquor now conveniently stored at home, people could drink more often.

Another phenomenon was drinking to get drunk. Prior to Prohibition, alcohol consumption was secondary to eating or socializing. With Prohibition, people gathered with the primary intention of getting drunk. ("I got a new bottle, just off the boat. Come over tonight and we'll drink it.") Although some speakeasies served food, people didn't go to the speakeasies to eat; they went to drink.

Prohibition also forced people to drink more than they usually would: if caught with a bottle, one could be arrested, so, before traveling, one tended to finish it. This got people into the habit of drinking more. If it was illegal to carry a bottle with you and you weren't sure there would be liquid refreshment at your destination, you might drink enough for the entire evening prior to leaving home. This got Americans in the habit of driving drunk.

The open and increasingly fashionable flouting of Prohibition

> *Robert Benchley's list of infallible symptoms of intoxication in drivers:*
> • *When the driver is sitting with his back against the instrument panel and his feet on the driver's seat.* • *When the people in the back seat are crouched down on the floor with their arms over their heads.* • *When the driver goes into the rest-room and doesn't come out.*

caused drinking to become a public occurrence. The hip flask became a symbol of rebellion. It was used everywhere: football games, theaters, at work. People carried booze in hollow canes, hot water bottles, even garden hoses wrapped around their waists.

Prior to Prohibition, women drank very little and almost never drank distilled spirits. Some women had a little elderberry wine, some a little sherry. That immigrant women drank beer or wine was considered an outrage to the guardians of (Protestant) morality, and keeping this evil habit from spreading to the pure womanhood of (Protestant) America was one of the Prohibitionists' most persuasive arguments. Prohibition, in fact, had just the opposite effect. Saloons, which were all-male preserves (except for bar maids, entertainers, and ladies of the evening), gave way to the speakeasies, which were decidedly coeducational. Outside the speakeasy, the passing of the flask included women as well as men. At home, men included their wives (and sometimes wives included themselves) in imbibing. Now that alcohol had to be stored at home—an uncommon practice prior to Prohibition—women decided to take a taste and find out what all the fuss was about. They found out.

Another necessary invention of Prohibition made alcohol far more popular: the cocktail. People turned to hard liquors during Prohibition because, drink for drink, it was cheaper to produce and easier to transport than beer or wine. In the same amount of space it took to transport eight ounces of beer, one could transport eight ounces of alcohol, which became the basis for eight drinks. In addition, the quality of unaged distilled alcohol was, to say the least, harsh. ("Sippin' whiskey," brandies, and other liquors designed for direct consumption are aged for years to mellow the flavor and take the edge off.)

The solution? Simple. The cocktail. Prior to Prohibition there were few mixed drinks. Gin and tonic began as a medicinal preparation during the British colonization of India. To protect against malaria, the British consumed a small amount of quinine mixed in water each day and, to take the bitterness from the quinine, they would add some sugar. To this, gin was added, initially for medicinal purposes. Long after returning to England, and with malaria no longer a concern, the Englishman continued consuming gin and tonics recreationally. Scotch mixed with a little soda or water was acceptable, but not terribly popular. And that was about it. The mixing of alcohol with every known sugar-water combination, soft drink, and fruit juice grew directly out of Prohibition's attempt to make bootleg liquor palatable. Millions of people who didn't like the taste of beer, wine, or hard liquors found cocktails irresistible.

> *The aim of the law*
> *is not to punish sins.*
>
> JUSTICE OLIVER WENDELL HOLMES

9. **Prohibition made cigarette smoking a national habit.** High on the evangelicals' hit list, second only to alcohol as a substance that had to be prohibited, was tobacco. In 1921, cigarettes were illegal in fourteen states, and anti-cigarette bills were pending in twenty-eight others. The prohibition of cigarettes, promoted by the very people who gave us the prohibition of alcohol, made cigarette smoking almost irresistible. As the experiment of Prohibition failed, the anti-cigarette laws fell. By 1930, they were legal almost everywhere; during Prohibition, the consumption had nearly tripled. Hollywood used cigarettes to indicate independence, sophistication, and glamour.

10. **Prohibition prevented the treatment of drinking problems.** It was stylish, fashionable, trendy, and daring to be drunk. No one had a drinking problem. ("I drink; I get drunk; I fall down. Where's the problem?") With alcohol illegal, there were no social

> *No nation is drunken where wine is cheap.*
>
> THOMAS JEFFERSON
> 1818

norms for reasonable, moderate alcohol consumption against which to compare one's own drinking. The official social sanction (enforced by law) was complete sobriety. Anything less—from one drink per month to ten per day—made one a Wet. Anyone who suggested to a friend, "You may have a little problem here," sounded like one of the preachy blue noses whose moralizing started all the trouble in the first place.

With the clearly immoderate act of Prohibition, all moderation was abandoned. The only "therapy" recommended by the Drys was jail and prayer. And how could people go for pastoral counseling for a possible drinking problem? People were thrown out of congregations for drinking only once. Imagine what might happen if one admitted to drinking enough times to cause a problem. Alcoholism, unrecognized and untreated, became an epidemic during Prohibition due to Prohibition.

Within a few years after Prohibition, some people began to realize that they had personal problems that involved drinking and, by the end of the 1930s, Alcoholics Anonymous was formed—the first of many organizations to point out that drinking for some people is the symptom of an illness, an illness that can be successfully treated.

11. Prohibition caused "immorality." Far from Prohibition leading to Great Moments in Morality, as the evangelicals had promised, it led directly to an unparalleled explosion of immorality—as immorality was defined by them. As speakeasies were unregulated, outlawed, underground, and co-educational, they tended to breed unregulated, outlawed, underground, and co-educational activities. Because the sexes mingled freely, the sexes tended to mingle freely. A great deal of the increase in unmarried sexual activity during the 1920s can be directly linked to the potent combination of alcohol and an atmosphere of illicit activity and abandon.

Prostitution also flourished—although professionals complained that some of these newly liberated women were destroying the business by giving it away. Drugs other than alcohol were used by people who never would have

> *I have taken more out of alcohol than alcohol has taken out of me.*
>
> SIR WINSTON CHURCHILL

come into contact with them were it not for the permissive atmosphere of the speakeasies.

College, traditionally a center for higher learning, became, for some, the center for learning how to get higher. Alcohol paved the way for seeking "kicks" in other formerly forbidden activities. "Anything goes" became the slogan of an entire generation. Prohibition made the twenties roar.

All these developments, of course, were soundly denounced in lurid terms by the keepers of morality—but then, those were the things they said about alcohol, too.

12. Prohibition was phenomenally expensive. The exact cost of this thirteen-year experiment is difficult to estimate. Between law enforcement, courts, the operation of jails, and all the rest, some estimates top a billion dollars (and this is a billion dollars when a Ford factory worker—among the highest paid unskilled laborers—made only $5 a day*). In addition to this cost, let's not forget the taxes on alcohol the government lost because of Prohibition, and the profit denied honest business people and diverted into the pockets of organized crime. The artificially increased price of alcohol hit the poor and working classes hardest of all. It was a very expensive experiment.

*Some Ford workers made more. Henry Ford, for example, made $264,000 per day in 1921, about $8.4 million in today's dollars.

⚖ ⚖ ⚖

> *We learn from history that we do not learn from history.*
>
> GEORG WILHELM HEGEL

Prohibition had a handful of good effects: Fewer people listened to the ranting of self-appointed moralists; women took an important (albeit wobbly) step toward personal freedom; and lawmakers became slightly more hesitant to prohibit things—for a while.

The effects were, however, mostly negative. For good or for ill, there's hardly an American alive today whose life was not touched by Prohibition.

George Santayana warned, "Those who cannot remember the past are condemned to repeat it." If only we would remember the past as often as we remember to quote Santayana.

Alas, we have forgotten our recent past and are repeating it even now.

AIN'T NOBODY'S BUSINESS IF YOU DO

What Jesus and the Bible Really Said about Consensual Crimes

> *If only God would give me some clear sign! Like making a large deposit in my name at a Swiss bank.*
>
> WOODY ALLEN

W.C. FIELDS LAY ON his deathbed, reading the Bible. An old friend came in and said, "Bill! You don't believe in God. Why are you reading the Bible?" Fields responded in his familiar cadence, "Looking for loopholes."

Anyone interested in social change—regardless of religious beliefs or lack of them—should read the Bible for no other reason than it is the book quoted most often to relieve us of our personal freedoms.

I must admit that I initially turned to the Bible "looking for loopholes." I knew I could pull quotations out of context to support my point of view. In planning this, I thought of myself in an adversarial relationship: the religious right has presented its out-of-context quotations, and has done a good job popularizing them. I could do the same, and make my out-of-context quotations support my beliefs. Somewhere between the extremes, perhaps people would discover something approaching the truth.

Along the way, however, I made an astonishing discovery: There was no need to pull quotations out of context. There was no need for me to ignore certain passages and highlight others. The "scriptural basis" for the religious right's claim to righteousness *simply did not exist*. In order to support my opinion I didn't have to—with a certain degree of guilt—leave out "incriminating" passages: *the passages were not there*.

Certain quotations were there, of course, but considering the *context* they were in, no sane human being would take them

> *Get your facts first,*
> *and then you can distort them*
> *as much as you please.*
>
> MARK TWAIN

seriously. (All of the admonitions against "sexual immorality" fall into this category.) Other concepts—promoted loudly by the Bible-quoting moralists of our day—were entirely absent.[*]

The Bible can be used to praise or condemn practically any human activity, thought, belief, or practice. As with the works of Shakespeare, if one looks carefully, one can find a quotation, incident, or story to support or undermine anything.

Alas, this practice has been used by many people to justify their own prejudices (by proving that "God thinks this way, too"), as a justification for grabbing and holding power ("It's not what *I* want, it's what *God* wants!"), or as the perfect excuse for not taking a fearless look at themselves and making necessary—although admittedly uncomfortable—personal changes in attitude and behavior.

It's not the Bible itself that condemns most consensual crimes, but the misuse of the Bible by petty, fearful, manipulative, or misguided individuals who deceptively quote from the Bible not as an illumination of truth, but as a justification of their own limited point of view.

Allow me to quote Alan Watts at length. He says all I want to say here, and says it much better than I.[**]

---

[*]Although it's not the point of this book, the intolerant interpretation of the Bible by the fundamentalists also keeps sincere seekers from a potential source of inspiration and wisdom. For more on this, please read *Rescuing the Bible from Fundamentalism*, by Bishop John Shelby Spong.

[**]Some readers may be asking, "Who is Alan Watts?" Alas, Alan Watts does not have the wide audience, readership, or reputation he deserves. In my estimation, he was one of the finest philosophers of this century. Although

[The Bible is] an anthology of ancient literature that contains sublime wisdom along with barbaric histories and the war songs of tribes on the rampage. All this is taken as the literal Word and counsel of God, as it is by fundamentalist sects, which—by and large— know nothing of the history of the Bible, of how it was edited and put together. So we have with us the social menace of a huge population of intellectually and morally irresponsible people.

> The Bible is the inerrant word of the living God. It is absolutely infallible, without error in all matters pertaining to faith and practice, as well as in areas such as geography, science, history, etc.
>
> JERRY FALWELL

[The Bible is a] translation of Hebrew and Greek documents composed between 900 B.C. and A.D. 120. There is no manuscript of the Old Testament; that is, of the Hebrew Scriptures, written in Hebrew, earlier than the Ninth Century B.C. But we know that these documents were first put together and recognized as the Holy Scriptures by a convention of rabbis held at Jamnia (Yavne) in Palestine shortly before A.D. 100. On *their* say-so. Likewise, the composition of the Christian Bible, which documents to include and which to drop, was decided by a council of the Catholic Church held in Carthage in the latter part of the Fourth Century.

The point is that the books translated in the . . . Bible were declared canonical and divinely inspired by the

he had a master's in theology and a doctorate in divinity, he seldom had the pretension of calling himself "Dr. Watts" (although, while an Episcopal priest, he probably tolerated the obligatory "Father Watts"). As fine as his writing is, I find his recorded lectures even more delightful. (His tapes and several books are available from his son, Mark Watts, P.O. Box 938, Point Reyes Station, CA 94956.) Although Watts died in 1973, his writings and his lectures are as contemporary, witty, and penetrating as ever.

> *I could not believe that anyone who had read this book would be so foolish as to proclaim that the Bible in every literal word was the divinely inspired, inerrant word of God. Have these people simply not read the text? Are they hopelessly uninformed? Is there a different Bible? Are they blinded by a combination of ego needs and naivete?*
>
> BISHOP JOHN SHELBY SPONG

authority (A) of the Synod of Jamnia and (B) of the Catholic Church, meeting in Carthage more than 300 years after the time of Jesus. It is thus that fundamentalist Protestants get the authority of their Bible from Jews who had rejected Jesus and from Catholics whom they abominate as the Scarlet Woman mentioned in *Revelation*.

As Archbishop Desmond Tutu explained,

> When the missionaries came to Africa they had the Bible and we had the land. They said, "Let us pray." We closed our eyes. When we opened them we had the Bible and they had the land.

⚖️ ⚖️ ⚖️

In exploring the Bible, I chose the New International Version (NIV). This is the translation favored by most of the evangelical churches. (I don't want them accusing me of using some "heathen translation.")* Some evangelicals still use the King James Version because the New International Version is entirely (and dangerously) too clear.

The Bible is divided into two sections, the Old Testament and the New Testament. Each Testament is a collection of "books" (although the word *bible* itself means book). Each book has a series of chapters, and each chapter is divided into verses. These

---

*The preface of the New International Version shows the fundamentalist influence: "That [the translation scholars] were from many denominations—including Anglican, Assemblies of God, Baptist, Brethren, Christian Reformed, Church of Christ, Evangelical Free, Lutheran, Mennonite, Methodist, Nazarene, Presbyterian, Wesleyan and other churches—helped to safeguard the translation from sectarian bias."

AIN'T NOBODY'S BUSINESS IF YOU DO

chapter and verse citations are uniform throughout all translations of the Bible and are written: BOOK CHAPTER: VERSE. So, "Genesis 24:1–3 and 9" means the book of Genesis, chapter 24, verses 1 through 3, also verse 9.

> *Man is an exception,*
> *whatever else he is.*
> *If it is not true that*
> *a divine being fell,*
> *then we can only say*
> *that one of the animals*
> *went entirely off its head.*
>
> G. K. CHESTERTON

Old Testament Admonitions

The Old Testament presents long lists of forbidden activities, some of which most of us do regularly (shaving, getting a haircut, wearing clothing woven of two kinds of material, eating rare meat). These books also present a series of acceptable or even required practices that we wouldn't dream of doing (animal sacrifices, keeping slaves, stoning people to death for infractions such as cursing their parents).

Please understand that, in this examination, I in no way intend to ridicule, question, or even minimize any of the wisdom to be found in the Bible. I simply mean to show that no one follows all the teachings of the Bible. Certainly not a single fundamentalist Christian—*not one.* Even the most devout Jew has abandoned burnt offerings, keeping slaves, stoning, and a great many other activities which are permitted or required by the biblical Laws of Moses.

The first seventeen chapters of the book of Leviticus, for example, go into great detail as to which animals are to be sacrificed for what sins or celebrations, which skin irritations are diseases and which are sins, and which animals cannot be eaten—or even touched. These animals include rabbit, lizard, pig, shrimp, lobster, clam, scallop, eel, octopus, or squid. You may, however, eat "any kind of locust, katydid, cricket or grasshopper" (Leviticus 11:22–23).

Chapter 18 of Leviticus contains sexual activities that are not acceptable. It's a long list; here's the *Reader's Digest* version: don't have sex with your stepmother, stepsister, "the daughter of your father's wife," your aunt, "a woman and her daughter," a woman and "her son's daughter or her daughter's daughter"; with any woman while she's having her period; with your neighbor's wife. As verse 29 explains, "Everyone who does any of these detestable things— such persons must be cut off from their people" (18:29).

Chapter 19 is a grab bag of laws:

Verse 19: "Do not mate different kinds of animals. Do not plant your fields with two kinds of seed. Do not wear clothing woven of two kinds of material."

Verse 27: "Do not cut the hair at the sides of your head or clip off the edges of your beard."

Verse 28: "Do not . . . put tattoo marks on yourselves."

Verse 32: "Rise in the presence of the aged, show respect for the elderly. . . ."

Similarly, chapter 20 offers a variety of sins and punishments. Among them:

Verse 6: "I will set my face against the person who turns to mediums and spiritists to prostitute himself by following them, and I will cut him off from his people."

Verse 9: "If anyone curses his father or mother, he must be put to death. He has cursed his father or mother, and his blood will be on his own head."

Verse 10: "If a man commits adultery with another man's wife—with the wife of his neighbor—both the adulterer and the adulteress must be put to death."

Verse 11: "If a man sleeps with his father's wife, he has dishonored his father. Both the man and the woman must be put to death; their blood will be on their own heads."

Verse 13 (Falwell's Favorite): "If a man lies with a man as one lies with a woman, both of them have done what is detestable. They must be put to death; their blood will be on their own heads."

Verse 14: "If a man marries both a woman and her mother, it is wicked. Both he and they must be burned in the fire, so that no wickedness will be among you."

Verse 15: "If a man has

> *The Old Testament is responsible for more atheism, agnosticism, disbelief— call it what you will— than any book ever written.*
>
> A. A. MILNE

sexual relations with an animal, he must be put to death, and you must kill the animal."*

Verse 16: "If a woman approaches an animal to have sexual relations with it, kill both the woman and the animal. They must be put to death; their blood will be on their own heads."

Verse 27: "A man or woman who is a medium or spiritist among you must be put to death. You are to stone them; their blood will be on their own heads."

---

*If this seems an extreme punishment—whether your compassion is for the man or the animal—and if you think it could never be a law, allow me to quote from William Bradford, governor of Plymouth, Massachusetts (1642): "Ther was a youth whose name was Thomas Granger; he was servant to an honest man of Duxbery, being aboute 16 or 17. years of age. (His father & mother lived at the same time at Sityate.) He was this year detected of buggery (and indicted for the same) with a mare, a cowe, two goats, five sheep, 2. calves, and a turkey. Horrible it is to mention, but the truth of the historie requires it. He was first discovered by one that accidentally saw his lewd practise towards the mare. (I forbear perticulers.) Being upon it examined and committed, in the end he not only confest the fact with that beast at that time, but sundrie times before, and at severall times with all the rest of the forenamed in his indictmente. And accordingly he was cast by the jury, and condemned, and after executed the 8. of September, 1642. A very sade spectakle it was; for first the mare, and then the cowe, and the rest of the lesser catle, were kild before his face, according to the law, Levit: 20:15, and then he him selfe was executed."

> *Scrutamini scripturas*
> [Let us look at the scriptures].
> These two words
> have undone the world.
>
> JOHN SELDEN
> 1689

In Chapter 24 someone has "blasphemed the Name with a curse" (24:11).

Then the Lord said to Moses: "Take the blasphemer outside the camp. All those who heard him are to lay their hands on his head, and the entire assembly is to stone him. Say to the Israelites: 'If anyone curses his God, he will be held responsible; anyone who blasphe-mes the name of the Lord must be put to death. The entire assembly must stone him. Whether an alien or native-born, when he blasphemes the Name, he must be put to death. . . .' " Then Moses spoke to the Israelites, and they took the blasphemer outside the camp and stoned him. (24:13–16,23)

Chapter 25 introduces the Year of Jubilee. Every seven years—Leviticus instructs—the land is to go fallow. Whatever grows there is to be harvested by the poor. This is the Sabbath for the land. Every seventh Sabbath for the land—seven times seven years—becomes the Year of Jubilee. In the Year of Jubilee, all slaves purchased are to be set free, all houses purchased (except houses within walled cities) are to return to their original owner ("Quick! There's only three months until the Year of Jubilee. Let's build a wall."), and all land sold is to return to its original holder. Nothing, it seems, is sold permanently; it is sold only until the Year of Jubilee; all contracts are good for a maximum of forty-nine years.

In Chapter 27, the last chapter of Leviticus, the price is set for slaves of various ages. A male between the ages of twenty and sixty is worth fifty shekels, and a female between twenty and sixty is worth thirty shekels. "If it is a person between the ages of five and twenty, set the value of a male at twenty shekels and of a female at ten shekels. If it is a person between one month and five years, set the value of a male at five shekels of silver and that of a female at three shekels of silver (27:5–6).

Thus ends Leviticus, just one of Moses' four "lawgiving" books of the Old Testament. Here are selected laws from the other three, Exodus, Numbers, and Deuteronomy:

> *I never had any doubt about it [the Bible] being of divine origin— point out to me any similar collection of writings that has lasted for as many thousands of years and is still a best-seller, world wide. It had to be of divine origin.*
>
> PRESIDENT RONALD REAGAN

Laws from Exodus

If a man sells his daughter as a servant, she is not to go free as menservants do. If she does not please the master who has selected her for himself, he must let her be redeemed. He has no right to sell her to foreigners, because he has broken faith with her. (21:7–8)

If a man beats his male or female slave with a rod and the slave dies as a direct result, he must be punished, but he is not to be punished if the slave gets up after a day or two, since the slave is his property. (21:20–21)

If a man seduces a virgin who is not pledged to be married and sleeps with her, he must pay the bride-price, and she shall be his wife. If her father absolutely refuses to give her to him, he must still pay the bride-price for virgins. (22:16–17)

Whoever sacrifices to any god other than the Lord must be destroyed. (22:20)

If you lend money to one of my people among you who is needy, do not be like a moneylender; charge him no interest. (22:25)

You must give me the firstborn of your sons. (22:29)

Whoever does any work on the Sabbath day must be put to death. (31:15)

Do not light a fire in any of your dwellings on the Sabbath day. (35:3)

> *When you eat fish,*
> *you don't eat the bones.*
> *You eat the flesh.*
> *Take the Bible like that.*
>
> ROBERT R. MOTON

Laws from Numbers

While the Israelites were in the desert, a man was found gathering wood on the Sabbath day. Those who found him gathering wood brought him to Moses and Aaron and the whole assembly, and they kept him in custody, because it was not clear what should be done to him. Then the Lord said to Moses, "The man must die. The whole assembly must stone him outside the camp." So the assembly took him outside the camp and stoned him to death, as the Lord commanded Moses. (15:32–36)

So Moses said to Israel's judges, "Each of you must put to death those of your men who have joined in worshiping the Baal of Peor." (25:5)

Laws from Deuteronomy

If your very own brother, or your son or daughter, or the wife you love, or your closest friend secretly entices you, saying, "Let us go and worship other gods" . . . do not yield to him or listen to him. Show him no pity. Do not spare him or shield him. You must certainly put him to death. Your hand must be the first in putting him to death, and then the hands of all the people. Stone him to death, because he tried to turn you away from the Lord your God. . . . (13:6, 8–10)

Do not eat anything you find already dead. You may give it to an alien living in any of your towns, and he may eat it, or you may sell it to a foreigner. (14:21)

There should be no poor among you. (15:4)

You will lend to many nations but will borrow from none. (15:6)

The man who shows contempt for the judge or for the priest who stands ministering there to the Lord your God must be put to death. (17:12)

Show no pity: life for life, eye for eye, tooth for tooth, hand for hand, foot for foot. (19:21)

I stand fearlessly for small dogs, the American Flag, motherhood and the Bible. That's why people love me.

ART LINKLETTER

A woman must not wear men's clothing, nor a man wear women's clothing, for the Lord your God detests anyone who does this. (22:5)

Do not plow with an ox and a donkey yoked together. (22:10)

If a man happens to meet in a town a virgin pledged to be married and he sleeps with her, you shall take both of them to the gate of that town and stone them to death. (22:23–24)

You must not bring the earnings of a female prostitute or of a male prostitute into the house of the Lord your God to pay any vow, because the Lord your God detests them both. (23:18)

If you enter your neighbor's vineyard, you may eat all the grapes you want, but do not put any in your basket. (23:24)

If you enter your neighbor's grainfield, you may pick kernels with your hands, but you must not put a sickle to his standing grain. (23:25)

If brothers are living together and one of them dies without a son, his widow must not marry outside the family.

> *The Chinese said*
> *they would bury me*
> *by the Western Lake*
> *and build a shrine to my memory.*
> *I might have become a god,*
> *which would have been very chic*
> *for an atheist.*
>
> BERTRAND RUSSELL

Her husband's brother shall take her and marry her and fulfill the duty of a brother-in-law to her. (25:5)

If two men are fighting and the wife of one of them comes to rescue her husband from his assailant, and she reaches out and seizes him by his private parts, you shall cut off her hand. Show her no pity. (25:11–12)

Those were just some of the laws from four of the thirty-nine books of the Old Testament. A few obvious observations:

1. Aren't you glad the police aren't out enforcing more of these laws than they already are?

2. The laws of the Bible (the ones we've just reviewed are more than 3,500 years old) make a poor basis for the laws of the United States today.

3. The religious right has decided to disregard most of the Old Testament laws as no longer applicable. Yet these same people cling to a select few Old Testament restrictions as a basis for judging other people's morality and criminality.

4. What justification is there for almost everyone to ignore one biblical law and make another biblical law the basis for imprisonment, persecution, and discrimination?

5. The next time a televangelist (or senator) quotes Exodus, Leviticus, Numbers, Deuteronomy, or any other Old Testament book of the Bible as a justification for locking people up, remember the context from which their interpretation of "God's law" comes.

⚖ ⚖ ⚖

Jesus of Nazareth and Consensual Crime

More evil and injustice have been done (and continue to be done) "in the name of Jesus" than one could possibly document. Those who have not taken the time to read what Jesus actually said may—mistakenly—blame Jesus for this evil and injustice. Those who take the time to read the first four books of the New Testament will probably be surprised to discover what Jesus himself actually said. Once you've read those books, the next time someone says he or she is doing something "in the name of Jesus," you can say "But he never said that!" or "That's not what he meant at all!"

> *No man ever believes that the Bible means what it says:*
> *he is always convinced that it says what he means.*
>
> GEORGE BERNARD SHAW

The first four books of the New Testament—Matthew, Mark, Luke, and John—tell the story of Jesus' life and teachings. For the most part, they are the only books in the Bible that report what Jesus said while he lived. The remainder of the New Testament contains Luke's account of the early church (Acts); letters (Epistles) written by James and Jude (Jesus' brothers), Peter, John, and Paul to various Christian communities, to set forth doctrine and guidelines for living. The New Testament culminates with the apocalyptic vision for the end of the world (Revelation), which the evangelicals believe is due any day now—just as fervently hopeful believers have predicted for 2,000 years. About half of the New Testament consists of Paul's Epistles.

The first three Gospels—Matthew, Mark, and Luke—are known as the *synoptic Gospels. Synoptic* means a general view or summary; to give an account from the same point of view. These were written from twenty to fifty years after Jesus' death. The synoptic Gospels seem to rely on each other—the authors of the later two perhaps having read the first—or, at the very least, they relied on similar source material. This material was most

> Christian:
> one who believes that
> the New Testament is a divinely
> inspired book admirably suited
> to the spiritual needs
> of his neighbors.
>
> AMBROSE BIERCE

likely the written collections of "sayings" circulated, perhaps even while Jesus lived. These "quote books" (scrolls, actually) were quite popular and allowed the essence of a teacher's message to be conveyed in those pre–printing press days. Using these scrolls as a basis, and adding what they knew, remembered, or could discover, Matthew, Mark, and Luke wrote their Gospels (a word which simply means "good news").

John wrote his Gospel some time after Matthew, Mark, and Luke. Although it's fair to assume that he read the first three, he did not rely on them, nor the underlying "quote books," as heavily. John accepted the events in the first three Gospels as "given," and added new information. He also wanted to "set the record straight" on a few events—and he does. He was the only disciple at the Crucifixion, and was part of Jesus' "inner circle" (which included John's brother James and Peter). John gives accounts and insights Matthew, Mark, and Luke do not.

The four Gospels give us the same life and the same teachings seen from four different viewpoints. If you think that personal agendas did not affect the Gospels, consider what Mark had to say about a woman: "She had suffered a great deal under the care of many doctors and had spent all she had, yet instead of getting better she grew worse" (Mark 5:26). Compare that with what Luke, the physician, had to say about the same woman: "And a woman was there who had been subject to bleeding for twelve years, but no one could heal her" (Luke 8:43). Whether Luke was protecting his profession or Mark had a bias against physicians—or both—is hard to say. Personal filtering—conscious or unconscious—is inevitable when people write about events, especially events that happened decades earlier.

And yet, with all these differences—sometimes in interpretation and sometimes with the facts themselves— there emerges a pattern of a man who, fundamentally, taught love, acceptance, and tolerance. That is the essence of Jesus' teaching. He said it himself, quoting the "heart" of the Jewish faith: "'Love the Lord your God with all your heart and with all your soul and with all your mind'" (Matthew 22:37) and he summed up the rest of the Old Testament—the Law of the Prophets—as "Love your neighbor as yourself" (Matthew 22:39). To this, at the very end of his teaching (at the Last Supper), he gave those closest to him a final command. "A new command I give you: Love one another. As I have loved you, so you must love one another. By this all men will know that you are my disciples, if you love one another" (John 13:34–35).

> *The world is equally shocked at hearing Christianity criticised and seeing it practised.*
>
> DR. ELTON TRUEBLOOD

And how did Jesus love?

1. He healed the sick.

2. He taught love, compassion, and tolerance.

3. He attacked hypocrisy, especially among those in power.

4. He taught grace rather than law, acceptance rather than judgment, and forgiveness rather than punishment.

And then Jesus made one of the most brilliant moves in the history of human thought. He gave a series of examples that illustrated a being so loving, so giving, and so trusting in God that it was absolutely impossible for a human being to achieve the ideal. He then *specifically prohibited* any attempts to improve others until you, yourself, were entirely loving, giving, and trusting.

According to Jesus' plan, everyone would be so busy loving, giving, and trusting (or learning to be that way) that there would simply be no time to judge others. If one, however, were tempted to judge others, giving in to the temptation was specifically prohibited by the teachings of Jesus.

When Anita Bryant was at the height of her campaign against homosexuals and had the backing of most fundamentalist Christian organizations and celebrities, Dale Evans—a popular Christian lecturer and author—was asked what she thought about homosexuals. Expected to give the knee-jerk reaction ("The Bible says it's an abomination and unnatural, and I'll take God's word for it"), Dale surprised everyone by, instead, stating the essence of Christ's teaching: "I'm too busy loving *everybody* to have any time to hate *anybody.*"

It's a marvelous system. Too bad the people who ask for consensual criminals to be punished in the name of Jesus aren't following his teaching.

Jesus' lack of Old Testament wrath irritated his disciples: they wanted to see some of those vengeful-God pyrotechnics. In that, alas, Jesus was a disappointment.

> When the disciples James and John saw this, they asked, "Lord, do you want us to call fire down from heaven to destroy them?" But Jesus turned and rebuked them, and they went to another village. (Luke 9:54–56)

Jesus taught, instead, that if you're perfect, you can judge others; otherwise, keep working on yourself.

> "Why do you look at the speck of sawdust in your brother's eye and pay no attention to the plank in your own eye? How can you say to your brother, 'Let me take the speck out of your eye,' when all the time there is a plank in your own eye? You hypocrite, first take the plank out of your own eye, and then you will see clearly to re-

move the speck from your brother's eye." (Matthew 7:3–5)

But we never reach perfection, so by Jesus' teachings, we never have the right to judge another. In fact, we don't even have the right to judge ourselves. That, quite simply, is God's job.

> *The trouble with some of us is that we have been inoculated with small doses of Christianity which keep us from catching the real thing.*
>
> LESLIE DIXON WEATHERHEAD

Jesus and Traditional Family Values

One of the most absurd claims made by the religious right is that their interpretation of "traditional family values" is supported by Jesus. It is not. In fact, nothing could be further from the truth.

Jesus never married. Within the Jewish tradition in the time of Jesus, not marrying was nearly a sacrilege. Jewish males were considered men at thirteen. It was then a boy had his bar mitzvah; he declared to the community, "Today I am a man," and the responsibilities of manhood were upon him. By this time, he knew a trade (which he entered into), and he married. (Marriages, like the son's profession, were almost always arranged by the parents.) The first child was expected within the year.

By not marrying and fulfilling his obligation to God, his family, and his ancestors, Jesus blatantly defied tradition. The pressure on him could hardly have been more intense, and yet he resisted.

When Jesus was twelve, his parents took him to Jerusalem for their annual celebration of the Passover.

> After the Feast was over, while his parents were returning home, the boy Jesus stayed behind in Jerusalem, but they were unaware of it. (Luke 2:43)

Here they are, leaving Jerusalem for Nazareth—quite a

trek—and Mary and Joseph must have assumed he was with the caravan. (Caravans were the jumbo jets of their day.) Besides, Mary and Joseph had at least six other children—four of them boys. Jesus, the eldest, was expected to be responsible.

Thinking he was in their company, they traveled on for a day. Then they began looking for him among their relatives and friends. When they did not find him, they went back to Jerusalem to look for him. After three days they found him in the temple courts, sitting among the teachers, listening to them and asking them questions. Everyone who heard him was amazed at his understanding and his answers. When his parents saw him, they were astonished. His mother said to him, "Son, why have you treated us like this? Your father and I have been anxiously searching for you." (Luke 2:44–48)

Jesus is hardly the apologetic child:

"Why were you searching for me?" he asked. "Didn't you know I had to be in my Father's house?" But they did not understand what he was saying to them. (Luke 2:49–51)

Given his druthers, it's obvious he would rather stay in the house of his Father, where he "had to be." It also indicates, that Mary and Joseph did not realize the significance of Jesus' mission on earth. That it took them three days to figure out Jesus would be in the temple indicates that they hardly saw Jesus as the Messiah.

The Bible is entirely silent about Jesus for his next eighteen years. When we fade back in, we find Jesus performing his first public miracle—thanks to his mother:

On the third day a wedding took place at Cana in Galilee.

Jesus' mother was there, and Jesus and his disciples had also been invited to the wedding. When the wine was gone, Jesus' mother said to him, "They have no more wine."

"Dear woman, why do you involve me?" Jesus replied. "My time has not yet come." (John 2:1–4)

> *I want to have children and I know my time is running out: I want to have them while my parents are still young enough to take care of them.*
>
> RITA RUDNER

Not exactly the anything-you-say devotion we have been led to believe Jesus had for his mother.

Jesus is saying, in essence, that he is not yet ready to perform a public miracle, that his mother knows this, and why is she bothering him with this problem of the wine? What does his mother do? Like most mothers, *she completely ignores him:*

> His mother said to the servants, "Do whatever he tells you." (John 2:5)

Mary starts involving other people. One can almost hear her saying, "My son will take care of the wine problem. Servants! Come over here! Help my son make some more wine. Do whatever he tells you." Jesus performed the miracle, and, according to John, "thus revealed his glory." Imagine: being spiritually outed by your own mother.

One of the most important passages indicating Jesus' relationship with his family is found in the third chapter of Mark and also in Matthew (12:46–50) and Luke (8:19–21). Concerning "traditional family values," here is one of the most significant—and least quoted—passages in the entire Bible:

> When his family heard about this [healing the sick and teaching], they went to take charge of him, for they said, "He is out of his mind." (Mark 3:21)

If you were teaching and your mother and brothers thought

you were out of your mind and came "to take charge of" you, what would you do? That's just what Jesus did: he didn't go near them. He stayed in the house where he was protected by his followers and sent to his mother and brothers his true message concerning "family values":

> Then Jesus' mother and brothers arrived. Standing outside, they sent someone in to call him. A crowd was sitting around him, and they told him, "Your mother and brothers are outside looking for you."
>
> "Who are my mother and my brothers?" he asked.
>
> Then he looked at those seated in a circle around him and said, "Here are my mother and my brothers! Whoever does God's will is my brother and sister and mother." (Mark 3:31–35)

Considering Jesus' relationship with his brothers, this incident from the book of John is telling:

> But when the Jewish Feast of Tabernacles was near, Jesus' brothers said to him, "You ought to leave here and go to Judea, so that your disciples may see the miracles you do. No one who wants to become a public figure acts in secret. Since you are doing these things, show yourself to the world." For even his own brothers did not believe in him. (John 7:2–5)

If it wasn't for John's comment, "For even his own brothers did not believe in him," it might sound as though his brothers were encouraging him to make his teachings more widely known. In fact, with the information John provides us, we know that they are, at best, encouraging him to "go public" so he'll get this whole savior thing out of his system, or, at worst, they are taunting him with some sibling, "We dare you! We double dare you!" Jesus handles them as any typical misunderstood sibling might: he deceives them.

> "You go to the Feast. I am not yet going up to this Feast, because for me the right time has not yet come." Having said this, he stayed in Galilee. However, after his brothers had left for the Feast, he went also, not publicly, but in secret. (John 7:8–10)

> *We never talked, my family.*
> *We communicated*
> *by putting Ann Landers articles*
> *on the refrigerator.*
>
> JUDY GOLD

In his hometown of Nazareth, Jesus was not exactly remembered as "Little Jesus, Boy Messiah":

> Jesus left there and went to his hometown, accompanied by his disciples. When the Sabbath came, he began to teach in the synagogue, and many who heard him were amazed. "Where did this man get these things?" they asked. "What's this wisdom that has been given him, that he even does miracles! Isn't this the carpenter? Isn't this Mary's son and the brother of James, Joseph, Judas and Simon? Aren't his sisters here with us?" And they took offense at him.

> Jesus said to them, "Only in his home town, among his relatives and in his own house is a prophet without honor." (Mark 6:1–4)

Like many before and since, Jesus found it difficult to "be himself" "among his relatives."

On another occasion, Jesus was preaching and a woman interrupted his teaching.

> As Jesus was saying these things, a woman in the crowd called out, "Blessed is the mother who gave you birth and nursed you."

> *It was no great tragedy being Judy Garland's daughter. I had tremendously interesting childhood years— except they had little to do with being a child.*
>
> LIZA MINNELLI

He replied, "Blessed rather are those who hear the word of God and obey it." (Luke 11:27–28)

Jesus did not say, "Yes, and. . . ." He said, "Blessed rather. . . ." Jesus somehow felt the need to correct the impression that his mother was especially "blessed."

After Jesus' childhood, Mary is conspicuous in her absence, except for sometimes being mentioned as one of the women who followed Jesus. Except for the Nativity, practically every incident involving Jesus' mother in the books of Matthew, Mark, Luke, and John has been detailed here. There is no record of Jesus returning to her after his resurrection, and in the remainder of the New Testament, she is mentioned only once.

None of this is intended to denigrate Mary. It is merely intended to show that Jesus' relationship with his blood relatives— including his mother—was far closer to normal than we have been led to believe.

When it came time to gather his chosen family (his disciples), Jesus concerned himself not at all with what their "traditional" families (that is, their blood relatives) might think, say, be, or feel.

> As Jesus was walking beside the Sea of Galilee, he saw two brothers, Simon called Peter and his brother Andrew. They were casting a net into the lake, for they were fishermen. "Come, follow me," Jesus said, "and I will make you fishers of men." At once they left their nets and followed him. Going on from there, he saw two other brothers, James son of Zebedee and his brother John. They were in a boat with their father Zebedee, preparing their nets. Jesus called them, and immediately they left the boat and their father and followed him. (Matthew 4:18–22)

Peter said to him, "We have left all we had to follow you!"

"I tell you the truth," Jesus said to them, "no one who has left home or wife or brothers or parents or children for the sake of the king-dom of God will fail to receive many times as much in this age and, in the age to come, eternal life." (Luke 18:28–30)

> *"Family" this and "family" that. If I had a family I'd be furious that moral busybodies are taking the perfectly good word <u>family</u> and using it as a code for censorship the same way "states' rights" was used to disguise racism in the mid-sixties.*
>
> JOHN WATERS

Still another said, "I will follow you, Lord; but first let me go back and say good-by to my family." Jesus replied, "No one who puts his hand to the plow and looks back is fit for service in the kingdom of God." (Luke 9:61–62)

Another disciple said to him, "Lord, first let me go and bury my father." But Jesus told him, "Follow me, and let the dead bury their own dead." (Matthew 8:21–22)

"If anyone comes to me and does not hate his father and mother, his wife and children, his brothers and sisters—yes, even his own life—he cannot be my disciple." (Luke 14:26)

"For I have come to turn 'a man against his father, a daughter against her mother, a daughter-in-law against her mother-in-law—a man's enemies will be the members of his own household.' " (Matthew 10:35–36)

"From now on there will be five in one family divided against each other, three against two and two against three. They will be divided, father against son and son against father, mother against daughter and daughter against mother, mother-in-law against daughter-in-law and daughter-in-law against mother-in-law." (Luke 12:52–53)

"Brother will betray brother to death, and a father his

> "For this cause shall a man
> leave his mother and
> father and cleave to his flesh"—
> I mean, "cleave to his wife."
>
> PAT ROBERTSON
>
> *Larry King Live!*
> August 17, 1992

child. Children will rebel against their parents and have them put to death. All men will hate you because of me, but he who stands firm to the end will be saved." (Mark 13:12–13)

Not exactly *Leave It to Beaver,* is it? But what did Jesus have to say about other relationships, like marriage and sex? If he didn't teach traditional family values, surely he taught morality with regard to sex.

Oh, yes—far stricter than most Christians care to know.

Jesus on Sex and Marriage

How did Jesus really feel about sex? It's a hard question to answer because (a) he almost never talked about it, and (b) the one time he did, his answer did not prove very palatable. "It is better," religious leaders throughout the centuries have decided, "to assume that Jesus was a good man, that we are good men, so the way we feel about sex must be the way he felt about sex."

Here, however, is what Jesus had to say:

> When they were in the house again, the disciples asked Jesus about this. He answered, "Anyone who divorces his wife and marries another woman commits adultery against her. And if she divorces her husband and marries another man, she commits adultery." (Mark 10:10–12)

A hard teaching this, but it leads directly to Jesus' true feelings about sex:

> The disciples said to him, "If this is the situation between a husband and wife, it is better not to marry."
>
> Jesus replied, "Not everyone can accept this word, but only those to whom it has been given. For some are

eunuchs because they were born that way; others were made that way by men; and others have renounced marriage because of the kingdom of heaven. The one who can accept this should accept it." (Matthew 19:10–12)

For Jesus himself, then, marriage was out of the question—the ideal was celibacy.

> *Adultery is in your heart*
> *not only when you look*
> *with excessive sexual zeal*
> *at a woman who is not your wife,*
> *but also if you look*
> *in the same manner at your wife.*
>
> POPE JOHN PAUL II

The word *eunuch* in Greek is *eunouchos*, which means "a castrated person," or "an impotent or unmarried man." It's doubtful that Jesus is recommending all males become castrated. His suggestion for those who "can accept this word" is to abstain from marriage and sexual activity.

Does Jesus expect perfection in the pursuit of celibacy? Hardly. That's why marriage poses a problem. If one is single and "slips," no one is harmed other than the person slipping. If married, however, slipping means breaking one's word with another, and that's not good. Jesus invokes the larger sense of *adultery:* not keeping one's word; not being faithful to one's promise; adulterating one's integrity. Jesus' message, then, was, "fornication is a lesser sin than adultery, so before you get married be absolutely sure that this is the only person you plan to have sex with for the rest of your life."

How did Jesus treat those who had a sexual orientation or practice different from his own? Without exception, his response was tolerance and acceptance.

No incident from the Gospels more clearly shows how Jesus wants his followers to behave toward those who have "sinned" sexually than the one in which he saves the adulteress from being stoned.

The teachers of the law and the Pharisees brought in

> *Mr. Mercaptan went on
> to preach a brilliant sermon
> on that melancholy
> sexual perversion
> known as continence.*
>
> ALDOUS HUXLEY

a woman caught in adultery. They made her stand before the group and said to Jesus, "Teacher, this woman was caught in the act of adultery. In the Law Moses commanded us to stone such women. Now what do you say?" They were using this question as a trap, in order to have a basis for accusing him. (John 8:3–6)

If Jesus said, "Don't stone her," he would—according to the law—be as guilty as she. The Pharisees would then have grounds for stoning him, too. On the other hand, if he said, "Go ahead and stone her," he would be betraying his central teaching of love, tolerance, and forgiveness. From a consensual-crimes perspective, it's important to note that adultery was a sexual transgression which Jesus personally and spiritually frowned on. Nevertheless...

> But Jesus bent down and started to write on the ground with his finger. When they kept on questioning him, he straightened up and said to them, "If any one of you is without sin, let him be the first to throw a stone at her." Again he stooped down and wrote on the ground. (John 8:6–8)

Brilliant. Jesus took the responsibility from a faceless crowd self-righteously fulfilling "God's law" and placed it in the hands of each individual, saying, "If you've never made a mistake, go ahead: throw the first stone." It was restating his fundamental teaching: "First, take the plank out of your own eye, and then you will see clearly to remove the speck from your brother's eye" (Matthew 7:5). He was saying, yet again, "Unless you're perfect, don't judge." Here, in fact, he was taking it a step further: "If you *ever* have sinned, don't judge." So much for judgment. So much for throwing stones. So much for Jesus' supposed endorsement of laws against consensual activities.

> Jesus straightened up and asked her, "Woman, where are they? Has no one condemned you?"
>
> "No one, sir," she said.
>
> "Then neither do I condemn you," Jesus declared. "Go now and leave your life of sin." (John 8:10–11)

> *Who are you*
> *to condemn another's sin?*
> *He who condemns sin*
> *becomes part of it,*
> *espouses it.*
>
> GEORGES BERNANOS
>
> *The Diary of a Country Priest*
> 1936

He does not demand prayer, fasting, or atonement—he simply tells her to leave her life of sin.*

If each elected official, before voting on the next law to take away yet another consensual freedom, would reflect on his or her own personal transgressions, unpopular preferences, and unsuccessful experiments, maybe we'd have a Christian nation after all.

Jesus and the Separation of Church and State

Jesus of Nazareth was clearly in favor of separation of church and state. Few things in the Bible are more certain. His teaching was spiritual: he had no interest in this world. His disinterest in the governments of this world—and the world itself—is profound.

> "My kingdom is not of this world." (John 18:36)

> "You are from below; I am from above. You are of this world; I am not of this world." (John 8:23)

The only organization he left behind was twelve men with Peter as their leader. That was it. When turning over his authority to his apostles, he even warned against political involvement:

---

*Sin in the original Greek meant "mistake"—not "transgression against God."

> *Christianity neither is,*
> *nor ever was*
> *a part of the common law.*
>
> THOMAS JEFFERSON
> February 10, 1814

"The kings of the Gentiles lord it over them; and those who exercise authority over them call themselves Benefactors. But you are not to be like that. And I confer on you a kingdom, just as my Father conferred one on me." (Luke 22:25–26, 29)

Even when he was offered absolute political power on earth, he turned it down.

The devil led him up to a high place and showed him in an instant all the kingdoms of the world. And he said to him, "I will give you all their authority and splendor, for it has been given to me, and I can give it to anyone I want to. So if you worship me, it will all be yours." Jesus answered, "It is written: 'Worship the Lord your God and serve him only.'" (Luke 4:5–8)

Even when Jesus was offered a kingdom on earth by the will of the people, he rejected it:

After the people saw the miraculous sign that Jesus did, they began to say, "Surely this is the Prophet who is to come into the world." Jesus, knowing that they intended to come and make him king by force, withdrew again into the hills by himself. (John 6:14–15)

Not only was Jesus disinterested in political matters; he was disinterested in civil matters as well.

Someone in the crowd said to him, "Teacher, tell my brother to divide the inheritance with me." Jesus replied, "Man, who appointed me a judge or an arbiter between you?" (Luke 12:13–14)

Two of the most famous incidents of the New Testament show Jesus' attitude toward church and state. He was as opposed to state intervention by the church as he was to church intervention by the state.

> When it was almost time for the Jewish Passover, Jesus went up to Jerusalem. In the temple courts he found men selling cattle, sheep and doves, and others sitting at tables exchanging money. So he made a whip out of cords, and drove all from the temple area, both sheep and cattle; he scattered the coins of the money changers and overturned their tables. To those who sold doves he said, "Get these out of here! How dare you turn my Father's house into a market!" (John 2:13–16)

> *The wages of sin are death,*
> *but by the time*
> *taxes are taken out,*
> *it's just sort of a tired feeling.*
>
> PAULA POUNDSTONE

Jesus felt so strongly that the temple should be used as "a house of prayer" and not be involved in material matters at all (even though the livestock was being sold for religious sacrifice and the money changers were there so foreigners could pay the temple tax), he resorted to physical violence. This is the only recorded incident of Jesus using physical violence.

There is nothing more intimate to the function of government than taxes. No taxes, no government. Among the Jews in Palestine at the time of Jesus, many (including some of his disciples) believed that if the Jews stopped paying taxes, the Romans would find it no longer profitable to stay in Judea and would leave. Israel would then be restored. Paying taxes, then, was far more controversial than it is even today. Nonetheless, Jesus' stand was firm. When asked whether Caesar's tax should be paid, Jesus answered,

> "Show me the coin used for paying the tax." They brought him a denarius, and he asked them, "Whose portrait is this? And whose inscription?" "Caesar's," they replied. Then he said to them, "Give to Caesar what is Cae-

> *And what of the curious resemblances between Protestant churches and courts of law? The minister and the judge wear the same black robe and "throw the book" at those assembled in pews and various kinds of boxes, and both ministers and judges have chairs of estate that are still, in effect, thrones.*
>
> ALAN WATTS

sar's, and to God what is God's." When they heard this, they were amazed. So they left him and went away. (Matthew 22:19–22)

That is the essence of the separation of church and state. It is one powerful group saying to another: You do what you do best, we'll do what we do best; and we'll leave each other alone.

For more than thirty years, the most heated issue surrounding the separation of church and state has been prayer in schools. The evangelicals would have us believe (as they do) that not allowing prayer in publicly funded schools is "anti-Christian." The religious right is demanding that prayer in schools be reinstated by a constitutional amendment. As a matter of fact, praying in public *at all* is against the teachings of Jesus:

> "And when you pray, do not be like the hypocrites, for they love to pray standing in the synagogues and on the street corners to be seen by men. I tell you the truth, they have received their reward in full. But when you pray, go into your room, close the door and pray to your Father, who is unseen. Then your Father, who sees what is done in secret, will reward you." (Matthew 6:5–6)

Jesus was opposed to public prayer of any kind. He prayed in public on very few occasions: his baptism, the Last Supper, and on the cross. Even when he prayed just prior to his arrest and Crucifixion, he did so in private:

> Then Jesus went with his disciples to a place called Gethsemane, and he said to them, "Sit here while I go over there and pray." (Matthew 26:36)

When he prayed the Lord's Prayer, he did it as instruction on how to pray, not as a prayer itself. Of the more than sixty times in the Bible the words *pray,* *prayer,* or *prayed* are said by or descriptive of Jesus, only three relate to *praying in public.*

Certainly public schools are among the least private places on earth, and Jesus is firmly on the side of the "infidels" when it comes to prayers not belonging in school.

It's also interesting to note that "so help me God" got tacked onto the presidential oath of office, even though the Constitution specifically does not include it. Surely Jesus would be happy that most civil courts, swearing-in ceremonies, and even the presidential oath of office include an acknowledgment of God and a request of his help. Not so.

> To justify Christian morality
> because it provides
> a foundation of morality,
> instead of showing
> the necessity of Christian morality
> from the truth of Christianity,
> is a very dangerous inversion.
>
> T. S. ELIOT

> "But I tell you, Do not swear at all. Simply let your 'Yes' be 'Yes,' and your 'No,' 'No'; anything beyond this comes from the evil one." (Matthew 5:34, 37)

If, however, someone recommended that the next presidential inauguration eliminate the phrase, "so help me God," guess who the fundamentalists would say was in league with "the evil one"?

Our founding fathers had the good sense to follow the teachings of Jesus when it came to the separation of church and state. Would that we continue in the faith of our fathers.

⚖ ⚖ ⚖

His Master's Voice?

The group Jesus attacked most often (almost exclusively, in fact), were the Pharisees. Being political, the Pharisees cared more how they appeared than what they did. They knew how to posture, thus appearing more righteous and, therefore, more worthy to lead than others. They took advantage of every photo opportunity. They were in the right place at the right time doing the piously right thing.

The Pharisees controlled Jerusalem's ruling body, t h e Sanhedrin. Although Rome's occupation of Jerusalem kept them from having complete power, the Pharisees appointed themselves to maintain "traditional Jewish values" in a time of social upheaval. One of their self-appointed tasks was to separate true prophets from false prophets. They "investigated" all reports of prophets, but it was merely show; the Pharisees knew that a prophet could only rise from within the ranks of the righteous: the Pharisees. Anyone not raised as a Pharisee didn't have the proper credentials for prophecy. The punishment for being a false prophet was death. One holy person after another fell before the judgment of the Pharisees. Said Jesus:

> "Woe to you, teachers of the law and Pharisees, you hypocrites! You are like whitewashed tombs, which look beautiful on the outside but on the inside are full of dead men's bones and everything unclean. In the same way, on the outside you appear to people as righteous but on the inside you are full of hypocrisy and wickedness." (Matthew 23:27–28)

The Pharisees were well versed in Scripture. They could quote chapter and verse to justify whatever behavior they found expedient.

The most dangerous part about the Pharisees, however, was that they believed what they were doing was right. They didn't see themselves as hypocrites; they saw themselves as exemplary spiritual leaders. They didn't see themselves as murdering people for expressing new religious points of view; they saw themselves as keeping the people safe from false prophets. While they certainly felt themselves spiritually superior to "ordinary" men, they were willing to share the benefit of their superior learning and discipline by sacrificing their personal time to take leadership roles in the synagogues. They did what they did because they honestly believed they were the chosen among God's chosen people.

> *Moralizing and morals*
> *are two entirely different things*
> *and are always found*
> *in entirely different people.*
>
> DON HEROLD

While ordinary people were moved by the miracles of Jesus, the Pharisees denounced them as sorcery—punishable by death. While the people found the teachings of Jesus liberating, the Pharisees found them blasphemous. On the other hand, while the people found the Pharisees ideal role models for achieving righteousness and godliness, Jesus found them "hypocritical vipers."

The Pharisees, then, (a) represented strict adherence to the letter of the law, while violating the spirit of the law; (b) inflicted harsh punishments for violation of the law (such violations as determined by the Pharisees); (c) knew everything and *knew* they knew everything, therefore could not be taught anything; and (d) were hypocritical in their holier-than-thou attitudes. It wasn't the Pharisees themselves whom Jesus opposed; it was this set of values and behavior.

⚖️ ⚖️ ⚖️

Let's take a look at the religious right in this country and compare what they do and teach with what Jesus said about the Pharisees. This is not an exhaustive look—that's a book in itself. This discussion limits itself to those hypocrisies that directly affect the laws against consensual activities and the enforcement of those laws today.

> *Let's leave religion to the televangelists. After all, they're the professionals.*
>
> CHEVIOT
> Max Headroom

"Thus you nullify the word of God for the sake of your tradition. You hypocrites! Isaiah was right when he prophesied about you: 'These people honor me with their lips, but their hearts are far from me.'" (Matthew 15:6–8)

"They worship me in vain; their teachings are but rules taught by men." (Matthew 15:9)

The religious right relies on concepts such as "traditional American values," "family values," and "the American way." With great piety, they discuss the "faith of our fathers," "the pride of the pilgrims," and the "Christian nation." They misquote and misrepresent the American founding fathers mercilessly. And all to justify their hatred of anyone who is "different." They use the Bible to justify prejudice, exclusion, and persecution. They contradict Jesus' fundamental message, which is love everyone, not just those who believe what you believe or do what you do.

> "Woe to you, teachers of the law and Pharisees, you hypocrites! You have neglected the more important matters of the law—justice, mercy and faithfulness." (Matthew 23:23)

Since the Civil War, the churches that make up the religious right have not taken a leadership stand on any positive social change. Quite the contrary, they have opposed social change. Whether it be the treatment of blacks, Jews, immigrants, homosexuals, or any minority (including women), the religious right has quoted chapter and verse to prove that one group or another doesn't even deserve the "privileges" it already has.

> "I tell you the truth, the tax collectors and the prostitutes are entering the kingdom of God ahead of you." (Matthew 21:31)

The leaders of the religious right have the love of power, righteousness (read: intolerance), fame, and money in their hearts. They pray—loudly and often—but only for effect.

> *I am patient with stupidity, but not with those who are proud of it.*
>
> EDITH SITWELL

> "You Pharisees clean the outside of the cup and dish, but inside you are full of greed and wickedness." (Luke 11:39)

The lack of love, tolerance, and compassion in religious right leaders is evident to all but their most devout followers.

> "But I know you. I know that you do not have the love of God in your hearts." (John 5:42)

> "Be on your guard against the yeast of the Pharisees, which is hypocrisy." (Luke 12:1)

> "Beware of the teachers of the law. They like to walk around in flowing robes and love to be greeted in the marketplaces and have the most important seats in the synagogues and the places of honor at banquets. They devour widows' houses and for a show make lengthy prayers." (Luke 20:46–47)

The leaders of the religious right love to be photographed with presidents, governors, and dignitaries of all kind. They dress well (by their standards, anyway), travel first class, and seem to want for nothing. Meanwhile, all this luxury is financed primarily by widows, unemployed people, and the working poor, who send $5 and $10 donations, genuinely believing they are doing something for Jesus.

> "No servant can serve two masters. Either he will hate the one and love the other, or he will be devoted to the one and despise the other. You cannot serve both God

> *Moral indignation
> permits envy or hate
> to be acted out
> under the guise of virtue.*
>
> ERICH FROMM

and Money." The Pharisees, who loved money, heard all this and were sneering at Jesus. (Luke 16:13–14)

The other effective money-raiser is fear. The religious right's ministries fight one "conspiracy" after another. They see every minority with "an agenda" and the agenda invariably is "recruiting your children" and "destroying the principles on which this great nation was founded." So, to save our way of life, our children, and the country itself, *send money.* ("There's an 800 number on your screen right now . . .")

> "Woe to you experts in the law, because you have taken away the key to knowledge. You yourselves have not entered, and you have hindered those who were entering." When Jesus left there, the Pharisees and the teachers of the law began to oppose him fiercely. (Luke 11:52–53)

The key to knowledge, as taught by Jesus, was prayer, nonjudgment, and forgiveness. All three—although they do get occasional lip service—are not part of what the religious right teaches.

The idea of nonjudgment and acceptance does not clog the televangelist airwaves. Sermons, speeches, and teachings of the religious right are full of one hellfire-and-damnation judgment after another. Only those who accept Jesus, and practice that acceptance of Jesus *the right way,* are acceptable. Everything else is "abominable."

These spiritual leaders seldom discuss forgiveness, but rely on "repentance." To them this means, "Change your ways to our ways and then you will be forgiven."

> "And you experts in the law, woe to you, because you load people down with burdens they can hardly carry,

AIN'T NOBODY'S BUSINESS IF YOU DO

and you yourselves will not lift one finger to help them." (Luke 11:46)

Because the religious right teaches guilt, but not forgiveness, it heaps on its followers responsibilities (blame) for situations they cannot effectively deal with themselves. For example, the religious right teaches that God will hold each

> *Among life's perpetually charming questions is whether the truly evil do more harm than the self-righteous and wrong.*
>
> JON MARGOLIS

person in this country personally responsible for the 30 million abortions (which they categorize as "the murder of innocent little babies") performed since 1972. "If there's anything you could have done you didn't do, then God will hold *you* responsible." Never mind the 30 million illegal abortions that took place from 1952 to 1972 (and the women who died from them)—as long as it's legal now, *you* are responsible. That's why anti-abortion protesters are so frantic, why one can shoot and kill a doctor outside an abortion clinic and sincerely believe he is doing "God's work," and why Jerry Falwell can excuse the shooting by saying, "Let's not forget the doctor was a mass murderer."*

> "Woe to you, teachers of the law and Pharisees, you hypocrites! You travel over land and sea to win a single convert, and when he becomes one, you make him twice as much a son of hell as you are." (Matthew 23:15)

The religious right points with great pride to its "overseas rescue missions," in which the "rescuing" that's going on is not so much feeding hungry mouths (although a little of that goes on because it makes good video) as it is "rescuing" human souls. In America we are supposed to keep our "traditional values," but around the world people are supposed to "cast off" their traditional values in favor of the Americanized version of "Christianity." These converts are then supposed to preach "Christianity,"

*The Old Time Gospel Hour, May 2, 1993.

WHAT JESUS AND THE BIBLE REALLY SAID

> *God bless you
> and keep you safe from anything
> as dangerous as knowledge.*
>
> ALEXANDER WOOLLCOTT

which is, of course, nothing but the religious right's own political conservatism. People in foreign countries are encouraged to become politically active, not for social change and justice within that country, but for policies that will favor the right-wing conservative causes the religious right preaches are one and the same with Christianity. The communists in their heyday never had a group of infiltrators as numerous, organized, and well-financed (by people who think they're feeding the poor of the world) as the standard-bearers of the American political-religious right.

With the religious right, there are no discussions any more. If you don't agree with them on everything, you hate Jesus. Pure and simple. No matter what position you take, if it's not the position they take, your reasoning will be knocked down by one pseudo-scriptural argument after another. That these arguments often contradict each other doesn't seem to matter.

> Then they hurled insults at [a blind man healed by Jesus]
> and said, "You are this fellow's disciple! We are disciples
> of Moses!" (John 9:28)

If you do anything that's not "in the name of Jesus," it doesn't count. You can heal the sick, feed the poor, and shelter the homeless, but if you don't do it in the name of Jesus, you're just part of the devil's work. The "secular humanists" (as the evangelicals call them) are some of Satan's greatest warriors. Those humanists go out and do good *for the sake of humanity* and not for the sake of Jesus. Can you imagine? Sacrilege! The religious right teaches that suffering is good because it leads one to Jesus, and anything that alleviates suffering except in the name of Jesus is bad because it postpones the sufferer's ultimate conversion. So, people who do good without doing it for Jesus are bad. The more effective one is at making positive change, the more one is seen as the agent of the devil.

> All the people were astonished and said, "Could this be the Son of David?" But when the Pharisees heard this, they said, "It is only by Beelzebub, the prince of demons, that this fellow drives out demons." (Matthew 12:23–24)

> *A religion that requires persecution to sustain it is of the devil's propagation.*
>
> HOSEA BALLOU
> (1771–1852)

And, of course, the religious right demand more laws against consensual acts—and the strict enforcement of the laws already on the books—in the name of Jesus.

> "A time is coming when anyone who kills you will think he is offering a service to God." (John 16:2)

Jerry & Pat

For Christians, Easter is a day of celebration second only to Christmas. For many Christians, in fact, Easter is a greater day of celebration than Christmas: on Christmas the Christ Child was born; on Easter, Jesus, the man, was resurrected, proving he was not just a prophet or a martyr, but the Christ.

What, however, was the theme for the 1993 Easter Sunday sermon on Jerry Falwell's *The Old Time Gospel Hour?* The resurrection was never mentioned: there was not one word about Jesus conquering death so that we may all have eternal life. Nor was there a mention of the Crucifixion. I don't know why I was expecting some mention of Jesus on Easter. Perhaps I'm just too old fashioned for *The Old Time Gospel Hour.*

Falwell's sermon was exclusively about what has been his pet subject for the past thirty-seven years: What is *politically* wrong with America? If Falwell dislikes something politically, it is, automatically and without further discussion, both immoral and un-

> He's all buttoned up
> in an impenetrable
> little coat of complacency.
>
> ILKA CHASE

christian. (No, more than *un*christian: *anti*-Christian.) *We are under attack.* ("We" being "all good Christians," and "all good Americans" [those two being synonymous].)

The show opens with Falwell not preaching, but peddling: he looks directly and sincerely into the camera from what is supposed to be his office (but is obviously a television set) and pitches four of his sermons: "a $100 value!" for "only $35." The set of four sermons is collected under the general title, "Who Killed America?" One of the sermons was today's sermon. If Falwell mentioned Easter in his sermon, you see, it would date the entire video package and make it less salable in the future. All good marketers know not to mention a holiday on a show that you want to sell year 'round, and Falwell is a good marketer.

The Old Time Gospel Hour is not a religious show, but an infomercial for the religious right.

Jerry Falwell, of course, inspired the Moral Majority, which inspired the bumper sticker, "The Moral Majority Is Neither." The Moral Majority did well by Falwell: it made him famous, rich, and fat. In the late 1980s, he declared "victory," and disbanded the organization. What really happened was that the Moral Majority had stopped making money because Falwell had run out of things to hate. Oh, there was still plenty to hate (from Falwell's perspective); hating just wasn't raising enough money any more. Even the war on drugs didn't raise much money: everyone had declared war on drugs. So Jerry shut down the Moral Majority.

What brought Falwell back out of the closet? Homosexuality, of course.

In the fall of 1992, an obscure fundamentalist church in the California desert began selling a videotape taken at a Gay Pride parade. It was carefully edited by the church to show only what

AIN'T NOBODY'S BUSINESS IF YOU DO

the congregation would find as the most salacious homosexual activity: men kissing, men wearing dresses, lesbians walking about with their hooters out—and all of them not going to church on Sunday. You could get nearly the same footage of heterosexuals by going to Fort Lauderdale during spring break, a Shriner's conven-

> *The partisan,*
> *when he is engaged in a dispute,*
> *cares nothing about*
> *the rights of the question,*
> *but is anxious only*
> *to convince his hearers*
> *of his own assertions.*
>
> PLATO

tion, or any fraternity beer bash. Nonetheless, it was presented as an example of what every town in America would look like twenty-four hours a day if the "Gay Agenda" came to pass. The tape was outrageously successful. It put a struggling church located in the California desert on the map, making it rich, famous, and powerful. Tens of thousands of copies of the tape were sold. Political commentators said it tipped the scales in the Colorado referendum in which voters narrowly decided that gays were not entitled to civil rights, and it was shown to the Joint Chiefs of Staff before they came out against gays in the military.

Falwell must have watched this phenomenon from his church in Lynchburg, Virginia, and chewed his nails (and everything else that wasn't nailed down). He had been against the *homa-sex-ya'alls* for years. He thought that vein of hatred had been fully mined. He was wrong. There was still gold in that thar homophobia, and *damn* if some other fundamentalist preacher hadn't struck the Mother Lode! Like the phoenix of old, Jerry girded his loins, put on his girdle, and set out again for the gold rush.

Falwell sent *his* camera crews to cover the Clinton inauguration. Of the many inaugural balls, it seemed that the gays and lesbians had one of their own (Gasp!). Jerry's crew videotaped hours and hours of men in tuxedos dancing with men in tuxedos, women in formals dancing with women in formals, men in tuxedos dancing with men in formals, women in tuxedos dancing with women in formals, men in formals dancing with men in

> *Distrust all men in whom*
> *the impulse to punish is powerful.*
>
> FRIEDRICH NIETZSCHE

formals, women in tuxedos dancing with women in tuxedos, women in tuxedos dancing with men in formals, and even (can't these perverts get anything straight?) men in tuxedos dancing with women in formals. It's what *Arthur Murray's Dance Party* would have been like if Liberace had been the guest host.

Yes, Jerry put together a video of this, and, over images of men kissing men and women kissing women (which you can buy for "only $35, and charge it to your Visa or MasterCard, so call toll-free now, and it's all tax deductible"), Falwell tells us that President Clinton "is considering" legislation to make homosexuals "a minority." Does this imply gays are currently a majority? No, Falwell explains, once gays are recognized as a minority, they are entitled to *equal rights!* They would be protected from job discrimination (Horrors!), entitled to equal housing (Terrors!), and might even be permitted to get married (No!) to each other (No! No!).

Then Falwell crosses even his own line between reality and illusion. If we didn't know Falwell better, it might seem like simple paranoia, but, knowing Falwell as we do, we know it's nothing but a good fund-raising technique, one of Falwell's favorites: If he can scare the be-Jesus out of people with dishonest and outrageous statements, he can scare the money out of them too. Falwell explains that the federal government could require a certain number of homosexuals to be hired by private churches. Over videos carefully selected to show gays to be as salacious as possible, Falwell asks, "Do you want gays working in *your* church, preaching *your* Sunday sermons, educating *your* children?" The idea that the federal government is going to shove homosexuality down our throats and down the throats of our children *in church* is enough to open pocketbooks, purses, and checkbooks all across the country.

But buying a video is not enough—one must also *vote*. Falwell, you see, has discovered the 900 number. Legitimate network current affairs programs have used 900 numbers to have their audiences vote on controversial subjects for some time. The charge is nominal, usually 50 cents, and any profits are donated to charity. Fal-

> *A fanatic is a man that does what he thinks the Lord would do if he knew the facts of the case.*
>
> FINLEY PETER DUNNE

well, too, has 900 numbers; one to call if you support protecting our children from federally imposed homosexuality, the other to call if you're in favor of perverts, perverts everywhere. Either call costs you $1.95 per minute. The money—after the phone company takes its cut—goes to Jerry Falwell. If you oppose homosexual rights, Falwell will send your name to the White House stating your position (which Falwell has kindly worded for you, including biblical citations). Falwell will also be kind enough to add your name to his mailing list, as you are obviously a right-thinking, all-American Christian. (Besides, you might want to buy some of his tapes, books, sermons, or even send your children to his university.) If you support gay rights, Falwell does nothing. No petition to the White House, no mailing list, no solicitations for videos, books, sermons, and your children are *not* welcome at his university. He keeps your $1.95 per minute anyway.

Speaking of education, Falwell also regularly gives an extended pitch for Liberty University. There—over images of Falwell roughhousing with the guys, talking respectfully to the girls, roughhousing with the guys, talking respectfully to the girls, and roughhousing with the guys—we are told that this institute of higher learning has no co-educational dorms; no drugs; no alcohol; no secular, humanistic, atheistic teachings (such as evolution); no Marxist, Leninist, communist propaganda (the kind you might find at, say, the Democratic National Headquarters); no Godless liberalism; and—most important of all—"no sex outside

> *I never saw a contradiction between the ideas that sustain me and the ideas of that symbol, of that extraordinary figure [Jesus Christ].*
>
> FIDEL CASTRO

of marriage." With all these restrictions, it's no wonder that the pitch is directed toward "parents and grandparents" and not at the potential students themselves.

One thing there's obviously plenty of at Liberty University, however, is white people. Of the dozens, perhaps hundreds of students shown in the promotional video, I spotted precisely two students who were darker than Debby Boone. One must suspect from this footage that—at Liberty University—either (a) the term *racial minority* is given new and vibrantly literal meaning, or (b) Falwell wants the parents and grandparents to *think* the term *racial minority* is given new and vibrantly literal meaning.

The whole idea is that your children or grandchildren will be *safe* at Liberty University—safe from drugs, safe from alcohol, safe from radical politics, safe from homosexuals and other minorities. Your child or grandchild will even be safe from his or her own lust. One assumes the school motto is *"Non libertas Libertaum"* ("No liberties are taken at Liberty").

As the weeks passed, I continued watching *The Old Time Gospel Hour* (it's like a traffic accident—can't look at it; can't look away). The videos taken at the gay inaugural ball (under the title "Exposé of the Clinton Inaugural Gala") must have been a hit. Falwell sent a camera crew to the 1993 Gay March on Washington, and brought back even more "shocking and disgusting" video of men kissing men, women kissing women, and (prepare yourself) men marrying men and women marrying women.

If Falwell was the Pharisee I believed him to be, I wondered how long it would take me to discover hypocrisy. The rules of my little game were: it had to be *his* hypocrisy and he had to be hypocritical on *his own* terms. It didn't take long. In fact, I had my choice. On his show of May 2, 1993, Falwell said *seventeen times* that this was the absolute last and final week to get a copy of the "Exposé of the Clinton Inaugural Gala." Two weeks later, he offered it again. I faxed a letter to Jerry, pointing out his, shall we say, discrepancy, just in case his misrepresentation was inadvertent. No: he meant it. The next week he offered the "Exposé of the Clinton Inaugural Gala"

> *A lie will easily get you*
> *out of a scrape,*
> *and yet,*
> *strangely and beautifully,*
> *rapture possesses you when*
> *you have taken the scrape*
> *and left out the lie.*
>
> C. E. MONTAGUE

again. Again, he said it was the last week. The following week, guess what? Yes, more Clinton Inaugural Galas. But this time, he actually *admitted* that he had previously said, "this is the last week," on two other broadcasts, and sure enough, he was offering them again. He freely admitted that he was going to, in his own words, "renege," "change my mind," and "go back on my word." Isn't this commonly known as *lying?* Well, what had Falwell said about lying and its consequences on recent shows? He had quoted,

> But the fearful, and unbelieving, and the abominable, and murderers, and whoremongers, and sorcerers, and idolaters, and all liars, shall have their part in the lake which burneth with fire and brimstone: which is the second death. (Revelation 21:8)

According to God (according to Falwell), "all liars" fall into the same category as "the fearful, and unbelieving, the abominable, and murderers, and whoremongers, and sorcerers, and idolaters." All are *abominable*.

The reason we should all join God in hating homosexuals, Falwell claims, is because God condemns it. He cites (over and over) this passage:

> Thou shalt not lie with mankind, as with womankind: it is abomination. (Leviticus 18:22)

So, lying is in the same biblical category as to "lie with

> *His studie was but litel*
> *on the Bible.*
>
> GEOFFREY CHAUCER
> *The Canterbury Tales*
> 1387

mankind, as with woman-kind" (both are abomina-ble). And what does Rever-end Falwell say about ministers who are not mor-ally up to snuff? This from his Easter Sunday sermon, April 11, 1993:

> But I do not believe that when a preacher's ever guilty of moral de-fault, he should ever be allowed in the pul-

pit again. Period.

By his own standards, by his own Bible verse, and by his own admission, Falwell was no longer fit to preach. I wrote and asked him for his resignation. Do you think he resigned? Do you think he even wrote back? Do you think Falwell would say no to a Hostess Twinkie?*

I purchased the "Exposé of the Clinton Inaugural Gala" and "The March on Washington" videos, and guess what I got in the mail? A letter from Jerry, *begging* for more money to help save America from the homosexuals. If I sent $49, he'd send me even *more* "uncensored" videos! How many hours of gay video can one Christian take?

Jerry knows he's got to mine this prejudice as quickly as he can. Science has fairly well proven that most homosexuality is not a choice, but something people are born with. This being the case, homosexuality must then be God's will, and if it's God's will, good Christians must accept it—no matter how much it may hurt.

On March 21, 1993, Falwell said,

> We must evangelize America beyond any past efforts . . .
> With more than 200 television stations now carrying *The*

---

*Falwell is amazingly cooperative: I was watching *The Old Time Gospel Hour* one day, and wondered, "How overweight *is* he, anyway?" Within five min-utes he told me. (He said he was 59 years old, 6'1" and 282 pounds. That makes him 89 pounds overweight.) Interactive television!

AIN'T NOBODY'S BUSINESS IF YOU DO

Old Time Gospel Hour worldwide, I am re-committed to giving the pure Gospel of Jesus Christ to a lost world.

In the twenty or so shows broadcast since then, I have not seen Falwell spend more than one minute per hour "giving the pure Gospel of Jesus Christ" to anyone. It's poli-

> *You must believe in God,*
> *in spite of*
> *what the clergy say.*
>
> BENJAMIN JOWETT

tics, politics, politics, hate, hate, hate, fear, fear, fear. It's the same anti-gay, anti-women (one of the tapes he sells is "Why True Christian Women Do Not Participate in the Feminist Movement"*), anti-Clinton (to the sins of communism and onanism, Falwell apparently wants to add Clintonism), anti-choice, and anti-ACLU (which he calls the "American Communist Lawyers Union").

At first, I thought that by this lack of focus on Jesus, Falwell was just breaking yet another promise. Then it dawned on me: This *is* what he considers "giving the pure Gospel of Jesus Christ to a lost world." He has so thoroughly left behind the separation of church and state that he actually believes his $99\frac{44}{100}\%$ political *Old Time Intolerance Hour* is *The Old Time Gospel Hour*. "We must again learn to view governmental action from God's viewpoint," he explains. He then goes on to say,

A great American, Pat Robertson, recently said: "Man's

---

*A typical quote: "Calling a woman a 'Christian feminist' is a contradiction in terms. It is much like saying, 'Christian prostitute.' If a woman takes the Bible seriously, she cannot be a committed Christian and a feminist at the same time." Or, "In the event, young lady, you are being persuaded by some feminist to join the movement, you have to make a major choice in your life. You must reject the Bible if you do it." Or, "I have difficulty understanding why Norman Lear [founder of People for the American Way] so aggressively promotes feminism since his last divorce settlement cost him $125 million. One would think he would be angry with women."

law is important, but it must reflect God's law to be truly valid. . . .

What a gift our forefathers have given us. By their example we learn that it is our right and duty as citizens to judge the laws and the lawmakers of this nation by the laws of God in the created order and in God's Word, and then to act."

Although Jerry Falwell and Pat Robertson think of themselves as the prima donnas of rival opera companies (they kiss in public but bitch about each other in private), they will quote even each other when desperate to prove a point.

⚖ ⚖ ⚖

Pat Robertson hosts the daily *700 Club* (named after his first 700 devoted donors), is the founder of the Christian Broadcasting Network (CBN), writes bestselling books on what God would do if He only had control of Washington, is the ringleader of the Christian Coalition, and runs for president whenever he is "forced" to. Between Falwell and Robertson, from the standpoint of consensual crimes, Robertson is far more dangerous.

In 1989, Robertson formed the Christian Coalition, a tax-exempt "social welfare organization" which gathers money from Christians and puts it into political campaigns. Not directly, mind you, but in the form of "voter information pamphlets" which supposedly tell where candidates stand on particular issues in a supposedly fair and balanced way. Of course, the pamphlets are neither fair nor balanced. The conservative candidate (almost always a Republican) is the knight in shining armor for God's righteous forces while his or her opponent is, at best, anti-Christian and, most likely, in league with the devil. The Christian

Coalition sent out 40 million such "voter information pamphlets" in support of George Bush during the 1992 presidential campaign. That didn't bring a victory, but sometimes it does. In 1990, the Christian Coalition sent out 350,000 pieces of literature at the last minute to help Jesse Helms win what many thought was a lost senatorial campaign.

> KING: *God told you to be for George Bush. Is that true? Did you say that?*
>
> ROBERTSON: *I'm not sure if I did . . .*
>
> KING: *Pat—Did you, Pat?*
>
> ROBERTSON: *I may have, to some of my close friends . . .*
>
> KING: *Pat!*
>
> ROBERTSON: *Yes! I think he's going to win.*
>
> *LARRY KING LIVE!*
> August 17, 1992

The Christian Coalition campaigned heavily in the 1993 Los Angeles mayoral race, sending out 450,000 pamphlets, and its candidate, Richard Riordan, won. The next morning on the *700 Club*, Pat Robertson gloated that "Christian-bashing politics and anti-Christian campaign tactics" were no longer going to work. He showed the "Christian-bashing," "anti-Christian" commercial prepared by Riordan's opponent. The commercial was *only* anti–Pat Robertson. Christ and Christianity were never mentioned. If one criticizes Pat Robertson's role in the political process, then, one is *of course* bashing Christianity and is anti-Christian. Or so Pat Robertson wants his followers to believe.

That same morning on the *700 Club*, Robertson interviewed, via satellite, the gushingly grateful new senator from Texas, also backed by the Christian Coalition. One by one, election by election, Robertson is pocketing elected officials at all levels of government, right up to and including the United States Senate. They owe Robertson political favors, and the political favor Robertson wants is for God's law to become man's law. More accurately, it is for Pat Robertson's interpretation of God's law to become man's law.

The goose laying all these political golden eggs is the *700 Club*. It's an hour-long Monday-through-Friday right-wing Christian infomercial modeled after *Good Morning, America (Good Morning, Religious Right)*. Other *700 Club* golden eggs include Regent

> *It is a curious thing
> that every creed promises
> a paradise which will be
> absolutely uninhabitable
> for anyone of civilized taste.*
>
> EVELYN WAUGH

University, of which Robertson is chancellor; the Christian Broadcasting Network, run by Robertson's son; the Family Channel (which purchased with God's money all the old *Mary Tyler Moore Show* episodes—couldn't ya' die?); and "a lavish faux-eighteenth-century motel called the Founders Inn, whose walls are adorned with gigantic oil portraits of George Washington, Thomas Jefferson and . . . Pat Robertson,"* as Joe Conason described it in the April 27, 1992, issue of *The Nation*.

The *700 Club* has a set format. Robertson chats amiably with Ben, Robertson's obsequious sidekick, who is as devoted to Robertson as he supposedly is to Jesus. Then we go to "CBN News" which, in network-reporting style (on-air reporter, stock footage, interviews, sound bites, and lots of graphics), a news story is told from an unabashedly politically conservative point of view. We then go back to Pat and Ben, who chat about it. In case anyone missed the point (liberals are Godless heathens and conservatives are America's only hope), Robertson calmly lets us know God's point of view on every political and social issue, while Ben leads him on with question after question, as though Robertson were somehow shy—even reluctant—to share his personal point of view. "Ah, shucks, Ben, I don't know. But if I had to take a guess . . ." and then he moves in with an obviously well-prepared kill. After a report on Hurricane Andrew, for example, Robertson revealed its true cause: the fact that God had removed "his blessing" from America. "If we're not a Christian nation," Robertson said, "why should God give us his blessing?" Why indeed? Next news item.

Then it's time for guests. These are either celebrities paying

---

*Can you spot the one "Christian" in this trio?

homage, authors of Christian books, experts pontificating on current events, politicians looking for votes, or entertainers looking for a little PR—typical morning talk-show fare. The only difference is everyone must acknowledge Pat Robertson's form of Christianity at least once during the interview.

> *How could the Pat Robertsons and the Pat Buchanans, presuming to be the spokespeople for God, spew such doctrines of divisiveness, intolerance and inhumanity? Who is that God?*
>
> BARBRA STREISAND

And then there are the Geraldo-like guests designed to keep viewers glued to their sets with personal stories involving tantalizing, even scandalous, twists of fate. An example: "This Christian mother and father of three children have AIDS. Their story later in our show. But now. . . ." It makes for good sound bites. The husband and wife, as it turns out, don't have AIDS, but are infected with "the AIDS virus." They got it through "heterosexual promiscuity" prior to their conversion to Christ. Two and a half years after being "rooted in the Lord" they discovered their condition, but, "praise the Lord," none of their children is HIV-positive. That the *700 Club* is telling its viewers AIDS is also transmitted by heterosexuals is good news. The bad news? On the *700 Club* Christians are not encouraged to use condoms; children should not be instructed in condom use; and condoms should not be passed out in public schools. The only answer to stop the spread of AIDS is complete and total abstinence until marriage. Period.

This facade of journalistic integrity is reminiscent (and why shouldn't it be?) of Robertson's 1990 book, *The New Millennium*. In his book, Robertson rattles along just fine outlining, with proper statistical background, some real problems in America (the national debt, violent crime, and so on) and then, suddenly, he makes a sharp turn to the right, another sharp turn to the right, another sharp turn to the right, another sharp turn to the right, and then retraces his ground. Like most commentators who only turn right or only turn left, he winds up going in

> *Watch out*
> *that you are not deceived.*
> *For many will come in my name,*
> *claiming, "I am he,"*
> *and, "The time is near."*
> *Do not follow them.*
>
> JESUS OF NAZARETH
> Luke 21:8

circles. Violent crime, he claims, is caused by feminists (by destroying the American family, which erodes society, which raises immoral children, who go out and commit violence). The national debt was caused by homosexuals. (I won't torture you with the logic of *that* one.) The rhetoric harkens back to Hitler, who blamed everything on (a) the International Jewish Conspiracy, (b) communism, (c) the impurity of the Aryan race, (d) homosexuality, or, (e) all of the above.

The *700 Club* spends at least two minutes of each hour praying. Good. One can only take so much politics. And then there's fund-raising. That gets a lot more than two minutes each hour, but not as much as politics—except during fund-raising periods. Yes, Robertson loves saving souls. He also loves getting conservative Christian voters on his mailing lists. In 1992, Robertson declared his Christian Coalition's goal:

> We want to see a working majority of the Republican
> Party in the hands of pro-family Christians by 1996 or
> sooner.

If that comes to pass—and there's not much reason why it should not—by the new millennium, I'll be able to publish a book the size of this one just listing the consensual crimes. But, of course, that book would be banned.

⚖️ ⚖️ ⚖️

I'm not against Falwell and Robertson because they are politically conservative; I'm against them because they are against fundamental freedoms. They don't believe we, as adults, have the right to do with our person and property as we see fit, as long as we do not physically harm the person or property of another.

Why? "Because it's against God's law." Who says? "God does!" Where? "Just read the Bible!" I did, and as this chapter has gone to great lengths to show, "It's not there." Alan Watts offers his perspective:

> Why don't you judge
> for yourselves
> what is right?
>
> JESUS OF NAZARETH
> Luke 12:57

Fundamentalists veer to the extreme right wing in politics, being of the personality type that demands strong external and paternalistic authority. Their "rugged individualism" and their racism are founded on the conviction that they are the elect of God the Father, and their forebears took possession of America as the armies of Joshua took possession of Canaan, treating the Indians as Joshua and Gideon treated the Bedouin of Palestine. In the same spirit the Protestant British, Dutch and Germans took possession of Africa, India and Indonesia, and the rigid Catholics of Spain and Portugal colonized Latin America. Such territorial expansion may or may not be practical politics, but to do it in the name of Jesus of Nazareth is an outrage.

Amen.

Traditional Family Values

THOSE OF US WHO grew up in the 1950s got an image of the American family that was not, shall we say, accurate. We were told, *Father Knows Best, Leave It to Beaver,* and *Ozzie and Harriet* were not just the way things were supposed to be—but the way things were.

Things were not that way.

It's probably good that life wasn't like the television shows in the '50s—we wouldn't have many women now. Take a look at the ratio of boys to girls on the most popular family shows. *Ozzie and Harriet* had two boys, no girls. *Leave It to Beaver* had two boys, no girls. *Rifleman* had one boy, one rifle, no girls. *Lassie* had one boy, one dog (supposedly a girl, but played by a boy), and no girls. *My Three Sons* had—well, that one's obvious. *Bonanza* had three grown-up boys. Although Lucille Ball and Desi Arnaz in real life had one boy and one girl, on *I Love Lucy* they had one boy. The only shows with daughters were *The Donna Reed Show* (one boy, one girl) and that lighthouse to womanhood—despite its title—*Father Knows Best* (one boy, *two* girls). Grown to maturity, that's a late-1960s dating population of fifteen men to three women.

Almost all the households were mama-papa-kiddies: the nuclear family. (The exceptions were *My Three Sons* and *Bonanza*: Steve Douglas [Fred MacMurray] and Ben Cartwright were widowers.) There were no prior marriages, no children from prior relationships, no threat or even thought of divorce, and the closest thing we saw to physical abuse was Ralph Kramden's, "One of these days, Alice, one of these days . . . to the moon!" There were no infidelities, no drinking problems, no drugs (not even prescription tranquilizers), no racism (How could there be? With the exception of Hop Sing and Ricky Ricardo, there was only one race; even the Hispanic gardener on *Father Knows Best* was named Frank Smith). There was no dropping out of school, no political discus-

> *Whatever trouble he's in,*
> *his family has the right*
> *to share it with him.*
> *It's our duty to help him if we can*
> *and it's his duty to let us*
> *and he doesn't have*
> *the privilege to change that.*
>
> JARROD BARKLEY
> *The Big Valley*

sion (much less political differences), no unemployment (except for Ozzie's early retirement), no severe economic problem (except for a crop failure on *Lassie*, when they had to sell all the livestock, including Lassie; but just before being carted off, Lassie pawed the ground and struck oil, and everything was okay again. Except for Lassie, who looked as though the Exxon Valdez had dumped its forward holding tanks on her). The father was the breadwinner; the mother was the bread maker (the only mother who came close to working was Lucy, becoming the spokeswoman for Vitavita-Vegimen or that afternoon at the candy factory). There was no fear of the bomb (which is what we kids were *terrified* about in the '50s), and no severe disobedience (although white lies, mischief, and misunderstandings were needed for laughs). Life was wholesome, wholesome, wholesome.*

That life doesn't exist anymore. But then, it never did.

In her book, *The Way We Never Were,* Stephanie Coontz explains,

---

*As much as the religious right likes to point to 1950s sitcom wholesomeness as the Ideal American Family, these shows, in fact, had a remarkable lack of religion. What religion *were* these people? They certainly weren't Jewish. And, other than possibly Ricky Ricardo, none of them was Catholic. They were probably safely mainline Presbyterians. But that was the name of the game: play it safe. In playing it safe, there was less mention of God and religion on these shows than actually took place in American families in the '50s.

> *When I was a boy, my family took*
> *great care with our snapshots.*
> *We really planned them.*
> *We posed in front of expensive cars,*
> *homes that weren't ours.*
> *We borrowed dogs.*
> *Almost every family picture taken*
> *of us when I was young*
> *had a different borrowed dog in it.*
>
> RICHARD AVEDON

Pessimists argue that the family is collapsing; optimists counter that it is merely diversifying. Too often, both camps begin with an ahistorical, static notion of what "the" family was like before the contemporary period. Thus we have one set of best sellers urging us to reaffirm traditional family values in an era of "family collapse" and another promising to set us free from traditional family traps if we can only turn off "old tapes" and break out of old ruts. . . . The actual complexity of our history—even of our own personal experience—gets buried under the weight of an idealized image.

Families have always been in flux and often in crisis; they have never lived up to nostalgic notions about "the way things used to be."

Here are some facts about "the good old days":

- In 1960, one in three children lived in poverty.

- Fewer than half the students who entered high school in the late 1940s ever finished.

- The United States has had the highest homicide rate in the industrial world for almost 150 years.

- From 1950 to 1959, 257,455 cases of polio were reported, mostly in children; 11,957 died of it.

- In 1940, one American child in ten did not live with either birth parent. Today the figure is one in twenty-five.

- More couples reported their marriage "happy" in 1977 than did in 1957. (The "happy marriage" index dropped slightly by the late 1980s, but still remained

AIN'T NOBODY'S BUSINESS IF YOU DO

higher than it was in 1957.)

- A woman over thirty-five has a better chance of marrying today than she did in the 1950s.

- In the mid-1950s, 25% of the population lived below the poverty line.

> *So four men and four women*
> *have sealed themselves off*
> *inside Biosphere 2.*
> *No contraceptives are allowed*
> *and if a woman*
> *gets pregnant she's expelled.*
> *This is progress?*
> *Sounds more like high school*
> *in the 1950s.*
>
> CHRISTOPHER BLINDEN

- In 1958, 60% of the population over sixty-five had incomes below $1,000.

- In the 1950s, one-third of the white, native-born families could not get by with the income of only one working parent.

- In the 1950s, racism was deeply institutionalized. 50% of black families lived below the poverty line; migrant workers suffered appalling working and living conditions; people of color were not permitted to take part in the American dream.

- In 1952, there were 2,000,000 more wives working outside the home than there were at the peak of wartime production.

- Women who failed to conform to the June Cleaver/Margaret Anderson role of housewife and mother were severely criticized. A 1947 bestselling book, The Modern Woman, called feminism a "deep illness," labeled the idea of an independent woman a "contradiction in terms," and explained that women who wanted equal pay and equal educational opportunities were engaged in a "ritualistic castration" of men.

- Women were often denied the right to serve on juries, convey property, make contracts (including leases on apartments), and establish credit in their own names (including mortgages and credit cards).

- Men who failed to marry were considered immature, selfish, or homosexual. A man without a wife found it difficult finding work or getting promoted.

- Unmarried men and women were routinely paid less than married men and women because, it was explained, their needs were less.

- The witch hunts against communists extended to homosexuals and other political and social "deviants." During the 1950s, 2,611 civil servants were fired as "security risks"; 4,315 resigned while being "investigated."

- In her book, *Private Lives: Men and Women of the '50s,* Benita Eisler quotes film producer Joel Schumacher: "No one told the truth. People pretended they weren't unfaithful. They pretended they weren't homosexual. They pretended they weren't horrible." The uniformity we sense about the '50s, with everyone happily "fitting in," was, in fact, a great number of frightened people pretending to fit in—and pretending to enjoy it.

- A "sure cure" for homosexuality for either men or women was marriage. This myth was propagated not just by popular culture, but by psychologists and psychiatrists as well. When marriage failed to be the "cure," as it always did, having a child would surely take care of the problem. When that didn't work, a second child was "prescribed." When that didn't work, well, the least you could do is pretend to be heterosexual and do your duty—for your children's sake.

- Congress discussed nearly two hundred bills to deal with the problem of "juvenile delinquency" in 1955—the year *Rebel Without a Cause* was released.

- Marilyn Van Derbur, Miss America of 1958, revealed in 1991 that her wealthy, respect-able father had sexually violated her from age five until eighteen.

> *10,000 Negroes work at the Ford plant in nearby Dearborn, [but] not one Negro can live in Dearborn itself.*
>
> *LIFE MAGAZINE*
> 1957

- Alcoholism soared in the 1950s.

- Wife-beating was not really considered a crime. Many psychologists explained that battered wives were masochists who provoked their husbands into beating them.

- A husband raping his wife was not a crime at all, but a sign that the woman was deficient in fulfilling her marital obligations.

- One half of the marriages that began in the 1950s ended in divorce.

- During the 1950s, more than 2,000,000 legally married people lived separately.

- Staying together "for the children" surpassed baseball as the national pastime.

- Far from Beaver and Wally telling Ward and June care-fully edited versions of their daily adventures over the dinner table, more often the evening meal was a TV dinner on a TV tray in front of the TV.

- What the TV couldn't numb, tranquilizers could. A *New Yorker* cartoon illustrated a 1950s couple, floating

> *I was a loner as a child.*
> *I had an imaginary*
> *friend—*
> *I didn't bother with him.*
>
> GEORGE CARLIN

down the river in a gondola, surrounded by beautiful flowers, singing birds, and playful butterflies. The husband asks the wife, "What was the name of that tranquilizer we took?" In 1958, 462,000 pounds of tranquilizers were consumed in the United States. A year later, consumption had more than tripled to 1.5 million pounds.

- By the end of the 1950s, when *Redbook* asked readers to supply examples for an upcoming article, "Why Young Mothers Feel Trapped," they received 24,000 replies.

- The number of pregnant brides more than doubled in the 1950s.

- In 1957, there were more than twice as many births to girls aged fifteen to nineteen than in 1983.

- The number of illegitimate babies put up for adoption rose 80% from 1944 to 1955.

Ms. Coontz concludes, "The historical record is clear on one point: Although there are many things to draw on in our past, there is no one family form that has ever protected people from poverty or social disruption, and no traditional arrangement that provides a workable model for how we might organize family relations in the modern world."

⚖️ ⚖️ ⚖️

Depending on whose statistics you read, today the traditional nuclear family represents anywhere from 6% to less than

50% of the American population. One can fiddle with the statistics endlessly. Should the household have only the male as the breadwinner? Should there be no one living in the household except the mother, father, and children? Should the household be in a single-family house, or will an apartment do? Does a couple living alone without children count? However we look at it, the point is clear: even taking the most generous estimate, today more than half the country lives outside a nuclear family.

> *What really causes marital abuse is small families.*
> *If all women had a lot of brothers, this would never take place.*
>
> REPRESENTATIVE CHARLES PONCY

Are those who want to return to traditional family values saying half of America is doomed to lives of quiet desperation? It's obviously not true, but that is what the rhetoric proclaims.

We must understand that the family is not the basic building block of society, the individual is.

The people who want us to return to traditional family values are the ones who had it good in the 1950s: white, male, married, Christian heterosexuals. The '50s were a bad time for women, minorities, homosexuals, political dissidents, and anyone who was in any way "different." Naturally these groups have been demanding what they are rightfully due as citizens of the United States.

Take, for example, this rather simple statement: "Equality of rights under the law shall not be denied or abridged by the United States or by any State on account of sex."*

Straightforward. Clear. Fair. And yet, here's what Pat Robertson had to say about it:

> It is about a socialist, anti-family political movement
> that encourages women to leave their husbands, kill

---

*The Equal Rights Amendment fell three states short of the thirty-eight it needed for ratification.

> *Human beings are not animals, and I do not want to see sex and sexual differences treated as casually and amorally as dogs and other beasts treat them. I believe this could happen under the ERA.*
>
> RONALD REAGAN

their children, practice witchcraft, destroy capitalism and become lesbians.

The prejudice is obvious, but do we also detect a little fear? Pat Robertson wants to marry June Cleaver, not Murphy Brown. He finds it more comfortable that way.

An unprecedented economic boom hit the United States in the 1950s that had never happened before and, almost certainly, will never happen again. The United States was almost the only industrial country untouched by World War II. The international competition lay in ruins; the United States was ready to switch from wartime production to peacetime production. It didn't matter what we made—it sold. The gas-guzzler—one of the most inefficient objects assembled by humans—is an icon of that era. (By the late 1950s, Germany was already challenging the American automotive vise-hold with its Volkswagen. Japan made a sneak attack with its transistor radio. American industry would never be as fat and sassy again.)

We will never have the economic domination of the world we had in the 1950s, nor will the white, male, Christian heterosexual be able again to dominate the women, blacks, Jews, Hispanics, gays, and the rest. There's no going back—nor should there be a going back. It never should have happened in the first place.

⚖️ ⚖️ ⚖️

Families are important because human infants require three years of care before they can manage without the help of an adult. (If three years seems young to be without parental care, it is far from unheard of in third world countries, or in countries torn by war or natural disaster.) But who says the child needs more than one adult? And who says the adult needs to be a birth parent? Only tradition. Long before the nuclear family, tribes raised children collectively—a system that continues in many parts of the world to this day.

Our modern concept of two people raising their children under one roof grew out of feudal necessity. The absolute minimum number of people necessary to maintain a plot of land during the Middle Ages was two. As the lord of the land wanted his serfs to "be fruitful and multiply" (thus multiplying the wealth of the lord), it was necessary that one of the two people be a man and the other a woman. Serfs were paired until death did them part. Love had nothing to do with it. (The only people who had time for such luxuries as love were those in the royal court—hence the term *courtship*.) The man tended the land all his waking hours, and the woman tended the house, livestock, and children. Even if a husband and wife hated each other, all they had to do was wait a little while: what with disease, war, childbirth, and an average life span of about thirty-five years, most marriages lasted less than five years. The departed partner was immediately replaced, and the system continued—not because the serfs liked it, but because it was economically viable for the aristocracy.

The system worked so well and the aristocracy was so pleased, they got the church involved. A marvelous theology developed (marvelously useful to the landowners): work hard in this life (which is but a blink in the eye of eternity), serve your lord (who represented the Lord), and you will have paradise for all eternity—and that's a long, long, time Mr. and Mrs. Serf. Rebel against the lord (Lord), and you will spend all eternity (which is a long, etc.) in hell. Be true to your spouse (not being true to your spouse would take valuable time away from essential serf stuff), work hard, and eternal paradise will be yours.

> *The knowledge of the world is only to be acquired in the world, and not in a closet.*
>
> EARL OF CHESTERFIELD
> letter to his son
> 1746

> *What is a family?*
> *They're just people*
> *who make you feel less alone*
> *and really loved.*
>
> MARY TYLER MOORE

Today, of course, the idea that two people are the minimum to make one economic unit is no longer true. With labor-saving devices, reduced work hours, and prepackaged everything, one person can make a living and raise a child perfectly well. So can twenty.

So what are these "family values" we want to maintain?

In a 1989 *Newsweek* survey, only 22% of the respondents believed that family was directly tied to blood lines, marriage, children, and adoption. More than 74% said a family is any group whose members love and care for one another. It's too bad former Vice-President Quayle didn't read this poll before he accused Murphy Brown of destroying traditional family values by having a child without the formality of marriage.

As Diane English said when accepting her Emmy for creating *Murphy Brown,*

> To all you mothers out there who are raising your children alone either by choice or necessity, don't let anyone
> tell you you're not a family.

America's "traditional family values" are love, support, tolerance, caring, nurturing, and—if you don't mind my adding my favorite—a sense of humor.

Isn't that what the situation comedy is all about? We find ourselves in a situation (life) and are faced with the fundamental question: do we laugh or do we cry? The choice is up to us—choice being a traditional American value, too.

Putting the "Problem" in Perspective

> *Drugs are murdering our children.*
>
> PRESIDENT GEORGE BUSH
> 1989

EVER SINCE THE UNITED States declared war on drugs (poor drugs), "the drug problem" has scored in opinion polls as one of the top five concerns of the American public. During the decade preceding the official declaration of war in 1982, however, America's concern about drug use hovered around #20.* Interestingly, it was not that public concern grew and a war was declared; rather, a war was declared, wartime propaganda grew (at an alarming rate), and the public concern rose. It's like William Randolph Hearst's reply to the newspaper illustrator who cabled, "NO WAR IN CUBA." Hearst cabled back, "GIVE ME THE PICTURES; I'LL GIVE YOU THE WAR."

It's as though someone looked at the deterioration of Soviet communism (a perennial top-five concern) and said, "We need a new war here; let's find a problem." In fact, many of the anti-drug warriors are the same people who were, just a decade ago, fervent anti-communists. They attack drugs with the same rhetoric they used attacking communism.

On another front, gays have served in the United States military ever since General Von Steuben arrived at Valley Forge in

---

*For example, in 1974, Dr. Peter Bourne, who later became President Carter's drug policy advisor, called cocaine "the most benign of illicit drugs currently in widespread use." Today it is widely believed that if you come within even a three-mile radius of cocaine, it will do such immediate and irreparable harm to your mental functioning that you will become one of those people who actually believe that those little buttons you push to change the light at a crosswalk are connected to something.

> *AIDS is not just
> God's punishment
> for homosexuals;
> it is God's punishment
> for the society that
> <u>tolerates</u> homosexuals.*
>
> JERRY FALWELL
> 1993

February 1778. He was rec-ommended to General Washington by Benjamin Franklin. Von Steuben turned the rag-tag troops into a fighting army by spring; Burke Davis pointed out in his book, *George Washington and the American Revolution,* "the value of Von Steuben's service could hardly be overesti-mated." Von Steuben was gay. More than two hundred years later, President Clinton took office and, of all the problems facing the country and its new president, what got most press (and, therefore, seemed most pressing)? Would Clinton honor his campaign pledge to stop throwing people out of the military simply for being gay? You would think he was trying to give Maine to Canada—oh, the furor, the furor.

And so it continues down the list of consensual crimes: Los Angeles seems more concerned about fighting prostitution than pollution; the Bureau of Alcohol, Tobacco, and Firearms ignores the 22,000 alcohol-related traffic deaths, the 500,000 cigarette-related deaths, and the 10,000 handgun deaths in 1993, and instead waged war on 100 Branch Davidians in Waco, Texas; authorized medical practitioners overbill insurance companies to the tune of $80 billion per year while the Food and Drug Administration (the federal agency assigned to watch over the medical community) sees to it that dying people cannot have the most effective painkilling medications, launches armed raids on healers doing anything "unorthodox," and wants to require a prescription for doses of vitamin C larger than 60 milligrams.

We have lost our perspective.

This chapter is a list of our dirty laundry. We have a lot more pressing concerns than putting people in jail for activities that do not physically harm the person or property of another.

When I say "we," I do not refer to the governmental we, but

"we the people" when "they the government" stop taking our money in taxes and then wasting it. But, that's another book.

This chapter is not designed to support the predictions of doomsday theorists. It also does not purport to offer solutions to any of these problems— this book offers a solution to only one problem, the

> *All casual drug users*
> *should be taken out*
> *and shot.*
>
> DARYL GATES
> Los Angeles Police Chief

problem of consensual crimes. Solving the problems in this chapter is going to take commitment, creativity, money, and a lot of work—precisely the resources currently squandered in the futile attempt to regulate individual morality.

In this chapter, we will use two words that have become increasingly popular in recent years, *billion* and *trillion*. Because *million*, *billion*, and *trillion* rhyme, we often think of them as roughly the same amount of money: "Oh, a billion is more than a million, but not a whole lot more."

A billion is a whole lot more.

> If a million dollars in hundred dollar bills were laid end to end,* they would stretch approximately 97 miles— roughly the distance from New York to Philadelphia.
>
> One billion dollars laid end to end would circle the globe at the equator nearly four times; alternatively, they could go two-fifths of the distance to the moon.
>
> One trillion dollars in one hundred dollar bills, laid end to end, would circle the equator 3,900 times. Or, if you

---

*Every time I hear these end-to-end analogies, I think of Dorothy Parker's remark, "If all the debutantes in New York were laid end to end, I wouldn't be surprised." Or, as Will Durst asked, "Did you know that if you took all the veins and arteries out of a man's body and laid them end to end, that man would die?" More to the point of this book, Arthur Baer said, "If you laid all our laws end to end, there would be no end."

> *Any company executive
> who overcharges the government
> more than $5,000,000
> will be fined $50
> or have to go to
> traffic school
> three nights a week.*
>
> ART BUCHWALD

don't want to go around the world that many times, one trillion dollars in hundred dollar bills, laid end to end, would extend from the earth to the sun, and, once there, you would still have $41 billion to burn.

If you had a million dollars, and spent $1,000 per day, you would run out of money in two years and nine months. Sad.

If, however, you had a billion dollars and spent $1,000 per day, it would take you 2,737 years, 10 months and 1 week to run out of money.

If you had a trillion dollars and spent $1,000 a day, you would be destitute in 2,739,726 years.

Speaking of trillion, let's begin our list with the national debt.

The National Debt. Forty-five years of fighting the cold war had devastating economic effects on both the Soviet Union and the United States; the only difference is, the United States had better credit than the Soviet Union—the Soviet Union is bankrupt; the United States is merely in receivership. As a nation, we (as of 1996) owe more than $5 trillion ($5,000,000,000,000.00); that's $19,200 for each man, woman, and child in the United States. The average American family owes more to "the company store" than they do on their house. (The share of the national debt for a family of five is $96,000. If they have a cat, it's $98,000. If they have a dog, it's $99,000. If they have a large dog, it's an even $100,000.) The interest alone on the national debt is somewhere between $240 billion and $355 billion per year (depending upon whom you listen to—the government [$240 billion] or balanced-budget advocates [$355 billion]). More than 40% of personal income taxes go just to pay the *interest* on the national debt.*

It's too bad that we didn't take Cicero's advice, given around 63 B.C.:

> The budget should be balanced, the Treasury should be refilled, public debt should be reduced, the arrogance of officialdom should be tempered and controlled . . . lest Rome become bankrupt.

> *I am concerned about the national debt. I am concerned about international terrorism. But, I'm scared to death about drugs.*
>
> **WILLIAM VON RAAB**
> Commissioner,
> U.S. Customs Service

We also didn't take the suggestion of Thomas Jefferson when in 1789 he warned the electorate: "The principle of spending money to be paid by posterity, under the name of funding, is but swindling futurity on a large scale." Well, futurity, do you feel swindled? *(Futurity.* Sounds like one of those prototype automobiles from the 1950s. "Drive into the '60s with the new Ford Futurity.") As Sid Taylor, research director for the National Taxpayers Union, put it, "Deficit spending is bankruptcy pending." But not all world leaders believed that a large national debt was a bad thing. One of the most famous national leaders in this century said, "No country has ever been ruined on account of its debts." The year was 1940. The economic expert: Adolf Hitler.

The Savings and Loan Debacle. It cost the federal government (that is, *us)* more than $100 billion dollars to bail out the savings and loans. That's an amount equal to all federal, state, and local government spending on education for the next year. Dave Barry calls the S&L bailout the "964.3 hillion jillion bazillion dollar" scandal. Where were the regulatory agencies?

---

*Although I said I wouldn't offer any solutions, here's a fairly obvious one: between the money we spend every year prosecuting consensual crimes and the revenue lost by not taxing consensual activities, if we did nothing else, the elimination of consensual crimes would wipe out the national debt in twenty years. As it is, our current policy on consensual crimes will add a trillion dollars to the national debt in the next five years, which will cost us about $6 trillion in interest over the following 20 years.

> *I hate mankind,*
> *for I think myself*
> *one of the best of them,*
> *and I know how bad I am.*
>
> SAMUEL JOHNSON

Rather than regulating private lives, shouldn't the government spend its time regulating the institutions it is charged to regulate? (Or at least let us know it is no longer regulating them so we'll read our *Consumers Reports* more carefully?) As Linda Winer pointed out in New York *Newsday,* August 9, 1991,

Texans have the U.S. Justice Department task force on obscenity to thank for its 18-month sting operation, which included setting up cloak-and-dagger agents in a phony video business called "Good Vibrations," reportedly with the intention of making an example of the porno devils. Nice work. We certainly could have used some of that federal enterprise when the S & L executives were stealing the country away.

And where are the crooks who committed the *real* crime of "misappropriating" all that money (an average of $400 for every man, woman, and child in the United States)? We go to Panama to drag "drug lords" to "justice"; where are the indictments against the "S&L lords"? As Senator Richard C. Shelby complained, "The taxpayers are on the hook for hundreds of billions of dollars, and yet, criminals are still playing golf at the country club."

Other Supposedly Regulated Delights. The same federal regulatory agencies that let the S&Ls get away with financial murder apparently let another endearing financial organization get away with genuine murder. I am referring to that billionaires' social club, the Bank of Credit and Commerce International, or BCCI. This multinational "bank" was, in reality, a clearing house for crooks. Here's an excerpt from Senator John D. Kerry's congressional testimony on August 8, 1991:

You need a Mirage jet to go to Saddam Hussein? BCCI could facilitate it. If you wanted weapons in the Mideast, and possibly even atomic weapons? Who do you call? BCCI. You want drug money to move from cartel to safe haven? BCCI. It gave new meaning to the term *full service bank*. . . .

> JON WINOKUR:
> *How did you react
> to winning a Pulitzer?*
>
> DAVE BARRY:
> *I figured it was just
> one more indication
> of the nation's drug problem.*

What strikes me particularly is the degree to which this bank thought it could steamroll any obstacles that lay in its path. Certain laws and standards were no barrier. Why? Because BCCI thought it could buy everything. Buy lawyers, buy accountants, buy regulators, buy access, buy loyalty, buy governments, buy safety, buy protection, and even buy silence. . . .

With purchased endorsements from more elected officials than you could wave a laundered checkbook at, BCCI was able to illegally take over several American banks with hardly an investigation. What about murder? It is said that murder (under the more corporately acceptable title, *assassination*) was part of BCCI's stock in trade. Whereas most banks have departments such as Trust, Savings, Money Orders, New Accounts, Safety Deposit Boxes, and Loans, BCCI had Assassinations, *Coups d'État*, Money Laundering, Arms Trafficking, Nuclear Weapons, and Political Destabilization. The BCCI. Lovely people to be in business with; and, while the federal regulators were out regulating consensual crimes, it made American banks part of its empire.* And

---

*This scandal involved so many people in Washington, and was such a truly bipartisan effort, that we don't hear anything about it anymore—or about all the people running it, who have no doubt set up shop under another name. When Washington as a whole wants to cover up something, they usually (a) find a scapegoat and (b) step up the "war" on some consensual

what is the next scandal in a supposedly government-regulated industry? I nominate . . .

Health Care Fraud. Insurance fraud is the biggest white-collar crime in the nation, second only to income-tax evasion. Each year, $80 billion is stolen from health insurance companies, Medicaid, and Medicare by the medical establishment. It uses cute terms like "overbilling," but it's really stealing. And much of it is done by doctors and hospitals, the very people and institutions we are supposed to trust with our lives. Overbilling also jacks up medical insurance premiums so that millions of people who otherwise would have health insurance, can't afford it. The average American's share of this real crime last year: $320. However, according to the House Subcommittee on Human Resources, "In some jurisdictions, federal prosecutors may not accept criminal health-care cases involving less than $100,000 because of limited resources. . . . Prosecutorial and judicial resources are limited, necessarily restricting the number of cases that can be legally pursued." With well over half the prosecutor case load made up of drug offenses, it's not hard to guess what's limiting those resources. (From 1982 to 1990, drug-related cases in federal courts increased by almost 400%.) The congressional report goes on to say, "The deterrent and financial benefits of pursuing fraud must be weighed against the

activity (now that we don't have Russia to kick around anymore). The scapegoat was Clark Clifford, who arranged poker games for Truman and Vietnam for Johnson. For his influence peddling, his law firm over an 18-month period received $33 million from BCCI. Congress (mostly lawyers) can only respond with horror—and envy. Meanwhile, the American public knew more about David Koresh's cult of 100 than how (and who in) the federal government looked the other way while BCCI illegally bought up American banks. Nice spin control.

considerable legal and administrative costs of doing so." If only the government would use on consensual crimes the logic it applies to the real crime of fraud.

Automobile Insurance Fraud. More than $17.5 billion a year is paid in inflated auto insurance claims. Who pays? Everyone who buys auto insurance—and everyone who

can't afford to. Car insurance fraud adds 10 to 30% to every car insurance bill. And what is the government doing to end this crime? Not much. According to a journal of the insurance industry, *Insurance Review*,

> With law enforcement officials mired in murder and drug cases,* and industry investigators focused on costlier and more sophisticated scams, the odds that an otherwise law-abiding citizen will be caught, much less prosecuted, for his misdeeds are minuscule. The Florida study concluded that as long as policy holders are knowledgeable, and not too greedy, they can "commit fraud with impunity."

Real Crime. In addition to paying more than you need to for

---

*While I certainly don't think that law enforcement time should be taken away from murder investigations to track down insurance fraud, more law enforcement time is spent on drugs than murders—a frightening thought in itself. Here's one example of the ratio between "murder" and "drug cases" in the United States: In 1991, there were fewer than 25,000 arrests for murder and more than 1,000,000 arrests for drug violations. Of these more-than-1,000,000 arrests, 672,666 were for simple possession. Here's an even more frightening statistic: In 1990, the average sentence at U.S. District Courts for first-degree murder was 12.8 years; for "other drug-related statutes," 20.4 years. The drug terms are usually mandatory; by law they must be served. Murderers, on the other hand, can be paroled at any time.

> *Patience, n. A minor form of despair,*
> *disguised as a virtue.*
>
> AMBROSE BIERCE

insurance due to fraud, or watching your tax money (which you must pay) bail out savings and loan mismanagement and embezzlement, there are other real crimes to worry about. On the average, every four years you or someone in your household will be robbed, raped, or physically assaulted. (That once-every-four-years statistic does not include murder, manslaughter by drunk drivers, kidnaping, child abuse, or other violent crimes.) Five out of six people living in the United States will be the victims of violent crimes during their lifetimes. For every 133 people you meet, one of them will be murdered. (If you live in a household of five, the chances are 1 in 27 that one of you will be murdered.) Then there are embezzlers, shoplifters, and other "white-collar criminals" who add to the price of everything we buy; a dramatic increase in "hate crimes" (that is, violent crimes against people just because they happen to belong to an ethnic, national, religious, or sexual minority); and so many others. And where are the police? Crimes with real victims (us) are out of control, yet roughly half the law enforcement time is spent investigating consensual crimes. Eliminating consensual crimes would effectively double law enforcement personnel and easily halve the number of real crimes almost overnight. (There I go again: offering solutions.)

Abducted Children. According to the United States Department of Justice, 400,000 children are abducted every year. There are currently 1.4 million missing children in this country. Of the 1.4 million, some of them are runaways, some were abducted by family members, some are simply "missing" (the "lost, injured, or otherwise missing" category lists 440,000). Some children are kidnaped—primarily for rape and torture. When they are no longer young enough to be interesting, they are killed.

AIN'T NOBODY'S BUSINESS IF YOU DO

Although there is a central clearing house to report all missing children, there is no federal law instructing local law enforcement personnel to send information to this clearing house. Many law enforcement officials don't even know the National Center for Missing and Exploited Children exists. The FBI does not get involved in kidnapings unless a ransom is demanded (which almost never happens anymore) or unless the parents can prove that, after abduction, the child was transported across a state line (good luck proving that). When Project Alert was formed in 1992 to help locate missing children, it had a whopping initial budget of $200,000. This is .0015% of the federal drug enforcement budget, or .0004% of what is spent prosecuting consensual crimes in this country each year.

> *The Department of Justice estimates that there are over 400,000 children abducted every year. Add to this 450,000 runaways and over 100,000 lost, injured, or otherwise missing.*
>
> NICHOLAS BRADY
> Secretary of the Treasury

Those who say that consensual crimes really do have victims—that consensual crimes are a bad influence on children—might want to consider whether the time, money, and effort spent keeping children safe from "bad examples" might be better spent reuniting abducted children with their parents and putting behind bars some of the worst imaginable criminals—people who abduct small children for rape, torture, and murder. Perhaps the people who want to make the entire world as wholesome as Disneyland should consider the anguish of hundreds of thousands of parents who are not only physically separated from their children, but are also tortured by thoughts of the horrors their children are being subjected to.

Terrorism. We don't hear much about terrorism in this country because if we really knew what was going on, we'd all be, well, terrorized. The car bomb (or, more accurately, the mini-van bomb) explosion at the base of the World Trade Center in March 1993 was not only an act of terrorism—it was a warning. "Imag-

> *Patriotism is your conviction that this country is superior to all other countries because you were born in it.*
>
> GEORGE BERNARD SHAW

ine if this were a nuclear device . . ." If it had been a nuclear bomb, there would be no more Manhattan (an irony, since the code name for the invention of the atom bomb was the Manhattan Project). With Manhattan goes the financial center of the world, the communications center of the United States, and the corporate headquarters of more major U.S. companies than you can rattle off in the time it takes a physics professor to explain $E=mc^2$. One atom bomb in Los Angeles would wipe out the movie industry, what was left of the television industry (much of which went with Manhattan), and could create enough seismic vibrations to set off The Big One. Another atom bomb in Washington, D.C., would wipe out the federal government. And one in Chicago would eliminate the idea that the Midwest was somehow immune to attack. Four atom bombs, and the United States as we know it would cease to be. (I haven't even discussed the lasting effects of radiation, especially if they happen to be "dirty" bombs—which terrorists' bombs almost certainly would be.) The remainder of the country would, however, have 24-hour news coverage of the death of the United States: CNN is located in Atlanta.

The international underground originally set up to sell drugs has decided—with typical big-business logic—to sell anything the customer wants to buy. One of these organizations, the previously mentioned BCCI, has come to light. Many have not. Underground organizations are perfectly willing to sell the parts necessary to make atomic bombs. As Senator John D. Kerry reported during a Senate investigation of the Bank of Credit and Commerce International,

> The spread of nuclear weapons, needless to say, creates even greater risks for confrontation and of destruction.

AIN'T NOBODY'S BUSINESS IF YOU DO

When a bank like BCCI moves drug money and big-dollar weapons money and helps terrorists acquire the material to make nuclear bombs . . . while political leaders who are supposed to be protecting them move aside, then governments themselves wind up becoming partners in the enterprise of those criminals.

> *Trying to determine what is going on in the world by reading newspapers is like trying to tell the time by watching the second hand on a clock.*
>
> BEN HECHT

The only thing Russia had that, for example, Saddam Hussein or the Ayatollah Khomeini did not was a delivery system for its atom bombs. Russia had missiles. With the World Trade Center bombing, however, terrorists proved that, although they don't have missiles, they can rent mini-vans.

The 1995 Oklahoma City bombing proved that terrorists don't need an atomic bomb to make their deadly point, and that the terrorism we need fear is not only foreign inspired. All it takes is someone with a grudge, some fertilizer, some fuel oil, and some way to ignite it.

Meanwhile, what are the FBI, CIA, and United States Customs—our only realistic defense against terrorism—up to? You guessed it: defending us against consensual crimes. Drugs, of course, head the list. Terrorism is a footnote.

And what are customs officials trained to find? Drugs, of course. Do you think one in a thousand customs officials knows what the components of a nuclear bomb look like? But how many know what cocaine looks like or how marijuana smells? And then there are all those drug-sniffing dogs. How about a few plutonium-sniffing dogs? (Some 9,600 pounds of plutonium and highly enriched uranium are missing from U.S. inventories. It takes only 15 pounds of plutonium to make an atomic bomb.)

And where are J. Edgar's best? After an investigation that lasted several years, on June 30, 1992, more than 1,000 FBI

> *It's time to stop living*
> *with the paranoia of "what if"*
> *and start facing*
> *the reality of "what is."*
> *"What is" is a real crisis in education,*
> *in health care, in the economy.*
> *"What is" the real national security,*
> *is the need for a nation*
> *to feel secure.*
>
> BARBRA STREISAND

agents simultaneously swooped down on doctors and pharmacies in fifty cities, making arrests and confiscating everything in sight, in an attempt to stop prescription drugs from ending up "on the black market." It was called Operation Gold Pill.

The FBI, however, does not just protect us from purloined prescription drugs. On June 23, 1991, after extensive investigation, 150 FBI agents invaded the bankrupt mining town of Wallace, Idaho, and confiscated every video poker machine from every bar in town. It wasn't that these video poker machines accepted bets, like the Las Vegas versions, but that people would bet each other and sometimes the bar owner on who could get more points. Horrors! According to a *New York Times,* August 20, 1991,

> Federal lawyers are moving in court to take control of the places that were raided, a move that would make the Government owner of every bar in Wallace.
>
> To a community that considers itself on its knees, racked by a series of economic and environmental calamities, the raid has provoked protests and stirred old animosities.
>
> In an age when banking scandals have cost the nation's taxpayers billions of dollars, many residents here say the Government has spent far too much time and money on video poker machines in a crippled mining town.

Meanwhile, on September 28, 1992, the Office of the Attorney General and the Office of the Drug Enforcement Administration revealed "a truly unique joint effort involving the participation of law enforcement agencies on three continents." Was this "truly unique" two-year international effort designed to track down and uncover terrorism? No. Known as Operation Green Ice, its purpose was to terrorize drug dealers. "Operation Green Ice has a message for drug dealers everywhere: the world is mobilized against you. U.S. law enforcement will continue with our colleagues around the world to defeat these purveyors of human misery."

Couldn't all of this intelligence be used more intelligently?

> *The current environment is so polluted with hysteria that nothing rational can happen to solve the drug problem. Until we're able to get the facts into perspective and debunk the myths, we're just not going to make progress and effectively deal with these issues.*
>
> GEORGETTE BENNETT

Environmental Disasters. One might expect the flashing electronic billboard above L.A.'s trendy Hard Rock Cafe to provide information about either music or food. Instead, it has two rows of numbers. One is labeled POPULATION OF THE WORLD and the other, ACRES OF RAIN FOREST REMAINING. At a rate of roughly one-per-second, the population number grows, while the rain forest number shrinks. It's a graphic illustration of the collision course we are on: both population growth and the destruction of the rain forest are out of control. The population of the world surpasses six billion. By early in the next century, it will double. Overpopulation is the basis of most environmental problems. The rain forests are not only the lungs of the earth—producing oxygen and removing impurities*—they are also the medicine chest. Eighty percent of all pharmaceutical drugs come from plant products. Less than three percent of the plants in the rain forest have been identified. Whole species of plants that might contain the cure for current and future diseases are being destroyed forever. Yet, instead of tying U.S. foreign aid to reasonable population growth or preservation of the rain forests, to what do we tie it? The elimination of drug production and traf-

---

*More than 40% of the earth's oxygen is produced by the Amazonian rain forests. Each year, an area of rain forest the size of Ohio is destroyed. Eighty percent of Amazonian deforestation has taken place since 1980.

ficking. We are far more concerned about destroying poppy fields in Thailand or cocaine farms in Colombia than preserving the rain forests in Brazil.

Then there's the ozone. In his 1993 Pulitzer Prize–winning play, *Angels in America,* Tony Kushner describes the ozone layer:

> When you look at the ozone layer, from outside, from a spaceship, it looks like a pale blue halo, a gentle, shimmering aureole encircling the atmosphere encircling the earth. Thirty miles above our heads, a thin layer of three-atom oxygen molecules. . . . It's a kind of gift, from God, the crowning touch to the creation of the world: guardian angels, hands linked, make a spherical net, a blue-green nesting orb, a shell of safety for life itself.

The ozone layer filters out the harmful rays of the sun. If the ozone layer ceased to be, so would we.

A few random environmental disasters: ¶ During the summer of 1992, 2,000 U.S. beaches were closed due to toxic levels of water pollution. ¶ In the fifteen major urban metropolitan areas, from 1987 to 1990, there were 1,484 "unhealthy" air days (more than half of them were in Los Angeles). ¶ Acid rain—precipitation containing sulfuric and nitric acids—continues to reign, destroying lakes, forests, and crops. ¶ Global warming—caused, in part, by burning fossil fuels—may melt the ice caps, raising ocean levels and flooding coastal areas. More than 53% of the U.S. population live in coastal areas. ¶ Our planet loses three species per day. By the year 2000, 20% of all species could be lost forever. ¶ An Environmental Protection Agency review of the 1,000 worst hazardous waste dumps revealed that 80% were leaking toxins into ground water. ¶ Due to lead plumbing, one in six Americans drinks water with excessive amounts of lead. ¶ We are running out of landfills. The average American disposes of four pounds of solid waste every day. In a lifetime, the average American will produce 600 times his or her adult body weight in garbage. In 1988, Americans disposed of 14 million tons of plastic, 31.6 million tons

> *We shall never understand*
> *the natural environment*
> *until we see it*
> *as a living organism.*
> *Land can be healthy or sick,*
> *fertile or barren, rich or poor,*
> *lovingly nurtured or bled white.*
>
> PAUL BROOKS

of yard wastes, and 180 million tons of other wastes. In addition, there are also tons of nuclear waste, which remains deadly for centuries. How do we dispose of this? Where do we put it? What kind of containers can we store it in? These questions have not been adequately answered, and yet we continue to produce nuclear waste.

The United States is the pollution capital of the world. We are 6% of the world's population, but consume 70% of the world's resources. We also produce far more than our share of the pollutants. The world is not happy with us about this.* Alan Watts once said that, from the earth's point of view, the human race could be considered nothing more than a bad case of lice. If that's an accurate analogy, the United States is the breeding ground. There is simply no way the entire world can support the lifestyle of even an impoverished American. If every family in China wanted nothing more than a refrigerator, the escaping fluorocarbons just to manufacture them would destroy the ozone. The American dream, infinitely exported, would be a nightmare. Our 6% of the world's population pollutes more than the other 94% put together. Americans, for the most part, are benignly unaware of this, but the rest of the world is not. In the world view, the Ugly American of the 1960s has been replaced by the Arrogant

*This is an understatement comparable to that of the NASA spokesman who deemed the Challenger explosion, "Obviously a major malfunction."

American of the 1990s.

Oil Addiction. America is, quite simply, addicted to foreign oil. Although Nixon, while president, declared that the United States should be energy independent by the end of the decade (which decade *was* the Nixon decade?), and although Carter gave an executive order stating that the average fuel efficiency

> *God has a strange sense of humor. He guided the Chosen People to the only spot in the Middle East without oil.*
>
> GOLDA MEIR

of automobiles sold in 1990 should be 40 mpg, Reagan—succumbing to the pressures of the petroleum and automobile lobbies—progressively reduced that minimum standard each year he was in office. Today we have, on average, 27.5 mpg cars. If we had gotten to 40 mpg in 1990, there would be no need to import oil today. We could, in fact, become an oil-*exporting* nation. The direct result of Reagan's policy came to visit his successor, Bush; it was called, appropriately, the Gulf War. Although Bush was properly outraged when he spoke of one small sovereign nation being overrun by an imperialist, nasty, larger nation, everyone knew the war was about oil. In the words of tell-it-like-it-is Ross Perot: "Does he *really* want us to believe that we're going in to defend a nation [Kuwait] whose leader has a Minister of Sex, whose job it is to get him a new virgin to deflower each Thursday night?" Although the Gulf War cost us "only" 390 American lives, it could have been far worse; and the anxiety suffered by the troops and their families in the early days of deployment, with rumors of poison gases and prolonged desert fighting, was torture enough. Unnecessary torture.

Our dependence on foreign oil and the hundreds of billions of dollars paid to the Middle East have given enormous power to a group of people who are profoundly anti-American and politically unstable. If it weren't for our dependence on foreign oil, could an Ayatollah afford to casually put a $2 million price tag on the head of Salman Rushdie? Would Israel need $3 billion of U.S.

foreign aid per year in order to play keep-up-with-the-Joneses-in-military-equipment with its neighbors? We are also burning a limited resource—petroleum—which we would be better off using to make certain plastics, synthetics, lubricants, and solvents that are derived best or exclusively from oil. The irony is that America is rich in

energy resources—both natural in the form of wind, water, and sunlight, and renewable through plant-based ethanol, methane, and diesel-grade vegetable oils. (See the chapter, "Hemp for Victory.") Our oil addiction is unnecessary.

Illiteracy. What on earth is going on in our schools? More than 100,000 high school students take guns to class every day; 5% of the population cannot fill out a job application; 13% are considered "illiterate"; 20% are considered "functionally incompetent"; 34% are considered "marginally competent"; and 80% cannot look at a bus schedule and determine what time the next bus arrives. (Based on some of the bus schedules I've seen, I may be among that 80%.)

Any number of other practical matters aren't directly taught in twelve years of schooling: how to sew on a button, how to diagnose basic automobile problems, how to set goals and achieve them, how to budget money, how to budget time, what the police will and will not do to protect you, how to file a case in small claims court, how to find an apartment, how to fill out a credit application, how to do one's personal income tax. Junior high school and high school are designed to prepare one for college—which is good for those going on to college; but those who aren't would benefit more by learning a trade. The school system's inability to teach the basics of life and how to make a living leads directly to . . .

Poverty. We have somehow numbed ourselves to one of the

> *German soldiers were*
> *victims of the Nazis*
> *just as surely as the victims*
> *in the concentration camps.*
>
> PRESIDENT RONALD REAGAN
> 1985

greatest tragedies in our midst. There are 49.2 million people living below the poverty level in the United States. That's 19.4% of the total population. More than 20 million of them are children. From 1978 to 1990, 20% more Americans fell below the poverty level. (I guess trickle-down economics just didn't trickle down far enough.) Meanwhile, the ratio of the average CEO's salary to that of a blue collar worker in 1980 was 25 to 1; in 1992, it was 91 to 1.

AIDS. There is a myth that AIDS is limited to homosexuals, intravenous drug users, and prostitutes. This myth may end up killing millions of heterosexual, drug-free men and women who wouldn't dream of visiting or becoming a prostitute. The fact is, worldwide, there are more heterosexually transmitted cases of AIDS than all other cases combined. The World Health Organization estimates that, by the year 2000, more heterosexual women in the United States will be newly infected with the AIDS virus than any other group. The Center for Disease Control reports that, in the United States, "the percentage of AIDS cases attributed to heterosexual contact has increased 21% from 1990 to 1991." And yet many continue to believe that, if they avoid sex with homosexuals, intravenous drug users, and prostitutes, they will be safe. The spread of this disease into the heterosexual world in the United States is a direct result of the centuries-old prejudices held against homosexuals, drug users, and prostitutes. It will be a sad irony to watch this prejudice turn, bite, and perhaps devour its keepers. The disease is being spread through the heterosexual world due to the belief, "it can't happen here." Heterosexuals still seem to think the simple advice, "Use a condom when you have intercourse," only applies to "them."

Other Problems. In case you're interested, the Union of International Associations has published a 2,133-page book entitled *Encyclopedia of World Problems.* In eight million words—enough for 80 to 100 normal-sized books— the *Encyclopedia* describes 13,167 problems. This is up from 10,233 problems in 1986 and a considerable jump from the 2,560 problems listed in 1976. This may be the beginning of a new science—*problemology.*

> *On May 31, 1987, President Ronald Reagan made his first speech on AIDS after a six-year public silence on the issue.*
>
> TONY KUSHNER

⚖️ ⚖️ ⚖️

Please understand I am not a great believer in throwing problems at the government, sending in my income tax, and crossing my fingers.

Again, this is not a chapter of solutions or even an indication of which direction solutions may lie.

This chapter simply asks the question: don't we have more important things to worry about than legislating individual morality?

Hypocrites

THROUGHOUT HISTORY, few behaviors have been condemned more often and more soundly than hypocrisy. Almost 3,000 years ago, Homer wrote, "I detest that man, who hides one thing in the depths of his heart, and speaks forth another." In the sixth century B.C., Lao-tzu said, "To pretend to know when you do not know is a disease." In the fifth century B.C., Confucius said, "Hold faithfulness and sincerity as first principles," and "[The superior man] speaks according to his actions."

There seems to be little Jesus of Nazareth hated as much as hypocrisy; he condemned it more than anything else.

Jesus also claims that hypocrites "have neglected the more important matters of the law—justice, mercy and faithfulness" (Matthew 23:23). Peter advised, "Therefore, rid yourselves of all malice and all deceit, hypocrisy, envy, and slander of every kind" (1 Peter 2:1).

In the fourteenth century, Geoffrey Chaucer called a hypocrite, "The smyler with the knife under the cloke." Shakespeare: "With devotion's visage and pious action we do sugar o'er the devil himself." Molière noticed an interesting consequence of hypocrisy, which is as true today as it was then: "Hypocrisy is a fashionable vice, and all fashionable vices pass for virtue."

During the Revolutionary War, Thomas Jefferson gave some insight into the underpinnings and history of hypocrisy:

> Is uniformity attainable? Millions of innocent men, women, and children, since the introduction of Christianity, have been burnt, tortured, fined, imprisoned; yet we

have not advanced one inch towards uniformity. What has been the effect of coercion? To make one half the world fools, and the other half hypocrites.

Less than a hundred years later, Abraham Lincoln wrote:

> Our progress in degeneracy appears to me to be pretty rapid. As a nation we began by declaring that "all men are created equal." When the Know-Nothings get control, it will read "all men are created equal, except Negroes and foreigners and Catholics." When it comes to this, I shall prefer emigrating to some country where they make no pretense of loving liberty—to Russia, for instance, where despotism can be taken pure, and without the base alloy hypocrisy.

*The prohibition law,
written for weaklings and derelicts,
has divided the nation,
like Gaul, into three parts—
wets, drys, and hypocrites.*

FLORENCE SABIN
1931

Leo Tolstoy (one of the people Lincoln might have met had he gone to Russia) observed:

> Hypocrisy is anything whatever may deceive the cleverest and most penetrating man, but the least wide-awake of children recognizes it, and is revolted by it, however ingeniously it may be disguised.

One of the most perceptive observers of hypocrisy in our country, Mark Twain, was once told by a blustering tycoon, "Before I die, I mean to make a pilgrimage to the top of Mt. Sinai in the Holy Land and read the Ten Commandments aloud." "Why don't you stay right home in Boston," suggested Twain, "and keep them?"

Which leads us to the problem observed by André Gide, "The true hypocrite is the one who ceases to perceive his deception, the one who lies with sincerity." People actually start to believe they are not being hypocritical; they say one thing and do an-

> *The only vice
> that can not be forgiven
> is hypocrisy.*
>
> WILLIAM HAZLITT

other with impunity—with pride, in fact. They have told themselves so many rational lies about their deception, they deceive even themselves. Those who have lost track of their hypocrisy—especially those who begin to consider it virtuous—are the most dangerous hypocrites of all. Alas, when it comes to consensual crimes, they're the most prevalent form.

As Don Marquis pointed out, "A hypocrite is a person who—but who isn't?"

⚖ ⚖ ⚖

With respect to consensual crimes, *hypocrisy* is often spelled C-I-G-A-R-E-T-T-E-S.

More than 500,000 deaths each year in the United States are related to cigarette smoking. According to the American Council on Science and Health, cigarette smoking is the #1 cause of preventable death in the United States. Four of the five leading causes of death are related to cigarette smoking. One in six deaths in this country, 87% of all lung cancer deaths, and 30% of all other cancer deaths are tobacco related. Cigarettes are the #1 cause of heart disease, and heart disease is the #1 cause of death in the United States. Out of 100 regular smokers in the United States, one will be murdered, two will die in traffic accidents, and 25 will be killed by tobacco use.

And yet, not only are cigarettes perfectly legal and available everywhere, tobacco growers are subsidized by the federal government,* and cigarettes are advertised using beautiful young

---

*One of the most virulent supporters of consensual crime prosecution, Senator Jesse Helms of North Carolina, is also one of the most outspoken supporters of the tobacco industry and the federal government's tobacco-

people and with such words as *enjoy, refresh,* and that perennial favorite, *satisfaction.*

Cigarettes are our country's most serious drug problem. Three thousand teenagers start smoking each day—more than 1,000,000 each year. "A teenager who smokes more than one cigarette," says Andrew Weil, M.D., "has only a 15% chance of remaining a nonsmoker." More than 50% of all smokers start before they are eighteen. According to the American Cancer Society, "The pharmacologic and behavioral processes that determine addiction [to tobacco] are similar to those that determine addiction to drugs such as heroin and cocaine."

If you're wondering whether tobacco harms truly innocent victims, the answer is "Yes." More than 53,000 deaths each year are attributed to secondhand cigarette smoke—the smoke breathed by people near a smoker. A study of nonsmoking women whose husbands smoked a pack or more a day found that these women were twice as likely to develop lung cancer as women married to nonsmokers. Environmental tobacco smoke is the #3 preventable cause of death in the United States (just behind regular smoking and alcohol abuse).

"Well, she can leave the room when he smokes. She's still

> *It is now clear that disease risk due to inhalation of tobacco smoke is not limited to the individual who is smoking.*
>
> C. EVERETT KOOP
> Former U.S. Surgeon General

---

grower subsidies. This comes as no shock: North Carolina is the #1 tobacco-producing state in the nation. With towns such as Winston-Salem and Raleigh, who's surprised? In fact, North Carolina produces nearly 40% of the tobacco grown in this country. In his book about the tobacco industry, *Merchants of Death,* Larry C. White tells about a 1986 incident involving government subsidies to tobacco growers in which "it is only the taxpayers who are being shortchanged—for about $1 billion . . . . Jesse Helms is responsible for this boondoggle." Has anyone explained to Senator Helms how much more his state could make growing hemp?

> *Sentimentality is a superstructure covering brutality.*
>
> C. G. JUNG

responsible," some might argue. All right. What about children? This from the American Cancer Society:

Environmental tobacco smoke (ETS) poses additional health hazards for unborn and young children. Children exposed to secondhand smoke have increased risks of respiratory illnesses and infections, impaired development of lung function, and [a higher incidence of] middle ear infections. If a woman smokes while she's pregnant, her baby may be born with low birth weight, birth defects, chronic breathing difficulties and learning disabilities. Women who smoke a pack or more a day suffer about a 50% greater risk of infant mortality. Infants born to women who smoked during pregnancy are more likely to die from Sudden Infant Death syndrome.

According to the American Academy of Pediatrics, more than 9,000,000 children under the age of five are exposed daily to environmental tobacco smoke. People who justify enforcing laws against consensual activities because they may "set a bad example" for children need to look no further than this actual physical harm to which millions of parents expose their children—unborn and born—every day. (At least drug addicts don't keep giving their babies drugs after they're born.)

And then there's the cost. Cigarettes cost the economy $65 billion annually—to treat smoking-related diseases and in lost productivity. That's $2.17 per pack of cigarettes sold.

Meanwhile, we are exporting death. Cigarette exports have increased 200% since 1985. (In the same period, exports to Japan have increased 700%.) The world wants to visit Marlboro Country. Have we bothered to warn them that Marlboro Country is Boot Hill? Worldwide, cigarettes kill 2,500,000 each year.

AIN'T NOBODY'S BUSINESS IF YOU DO

In addition to causing cancer, the cigarette industry itself is a cancer. Cigarettes are extremely profitable (drug dealing usually is). Cigarette companies take in about $28 billion in cigarette sales each year, and on that make a profit of more than $6 billion. That's a profit margin of 23%. Most companies are thrilled with a profit margin of 10%. (The national corporate average in 1991 was 6.9%.) *Forbes* magazine commented, "Only the Mint makes money more easily than cigarette companies." Ironically, it's because cigarettes are deadly that competition is low: other companies simply don't want to be involved in peddling death. (Addictions they don't mind; death, they do. Call them old-fashioned.) Six tobacco giants make practically every brand of cigarette sold in the United States. How do they avoid anti-trust or price-fixing proceedings? They simply argue that the more cigarettes cost, the better: fewer people will buy them; therefore, fewer people will smoke. As hypocrites often do, they play both sides of every coin—and they have a lot of coins. Once people are hooked, they're hooked, and they'll pay whatever is necessary for their next fix.

> *This very night*
> *I am going to leave off tobacco!*
> *Surely there must be*
> *some other world*
> *in which this*
> *unconquerable purpose*
> *shall be realized.*
>
> CHARLES LAMB
> 1815

With this money, the cigarette industry hides from the public the simple fact that tobacco is the most addictive substance known (more addictive than even heroin), and that cigarettes kill. Cigarette companies spend a fortune each year on advertising, and they use that clout to eliminate or soften media stories that might be hazardous to the health of the tobacco industry. In the past, only the media accepting cigarette advertisements were vulnerable to this pressure. Over the years, however, the cigarette companies have bought just about every wholesome brand in America.* Now they can use their advertising clout to control almost all media—even television, where cigarette ads have been banned for years. When cigarette advertising was allowed on television, the cigarette companies put enormous pressure on all shows to include smoking as one of the "good guy" activities and eliminate smoking as a "bad guy" activity. In other words, they wanted the heroes to smoke and the villains to do something else—playing pool was okay, taking other drugs was fine, arrogantly driving expensive cars purchased with ill-gotten gains was terrific.

Gene Roddenberry told me that while he was creating *Star Trek,* the network (NBC) and the production company (Paramount) put enormous pressure on him to include cigarettes on the starship *Enterprise.* Roddenberry pointed out that, considering the health risks known about cigarettes even in 1966, no one would be smoking by stardate 1513.1 (circa A.D. 2264).

The network and studio executives used both pressure and persuasion. They tried to get Roddenberry enthused about how cigarettes might look in the twenty-third century. Maybe they would be square instead of round; perhaps they would come in colors; perhaps cigarettes would *light themselves!* Roddenberry's

---

**Nabisco, General Foods, Oreo Cookies, Jell-o, Ritz Crackers, Planters Peanuts, Triscuits, Miller Beer, Jim Beam Bourbon, Kool-Aid, Log Cabin Syrup, Oscar Mayer Wieners, Maxwell House Coffee, Entenmann's Cakes, Post Grape-Nuts (Euell Gibbons is rolling in his grave), Fleischmann's Margarine, Kraft (yes, something as American as Kraft Macaroni & Cheese is owned by a tobacco company), Carefree Sugarless Gum, Lifesavers, Fig Newtons, Cool-Whip, Velveeta, Pinkerton Guards, and Franklin (Ben is rolling in *his* grave) Life Insurance (a company that gives lower rates to nonsmokers) and, heaven help us, Animal Crackers. This list is subject to change. Cigarette companies buy and sell other businesses as easily as you or I might pick up a box of Triscuits, a six-pack of Miller Genuine Draft, or a roll of Lifesavers—they just throw them in their shopping carts and head for the check-out counter (the stock market).

creative juices were not stimulated. Finally, the executives gave him an ultimatum: either the starship *Enterprise* would officially be declared a Smoking Zone, or Roddenberry's other radical idea—to have a woman as an officer of the *Enterprise* crew—would be abandoned. The executives were clever in offering this choice: Roddenberry's

> *BEAM ME UP, SCOTTY!*
> *THERE IS NO INTELLIGENT*
> *LIFE ON EARTH!*
>
> SLOGAN ON T-SHIRT

wife was already cast to play the female officer. After quite a bit of soul-searching, Roddenberry came to the only conclusion he could: both cigarettes and his wife did not get an intergalactic boarding pass. The irony was that, in later years, when smoking was less fashionable, Paramount pointed with pride to *Star Trek* as one of the few shows in syndication that had none of those "distasteful" cigarettes.

The cigarette companies' control extends beyond elected officials and much of the media. In early 1984 (that ominous year), Greg Louganis, a former smoker, was asked by the American Cancer Society to be national chairman of its annual Great American Smokeout. Louganis was excited. He had smoked from junior high until he was twenty-three. One day he saw a twelve-year-old smoking, asked the boy why, and was told, "I want to be just like you!" Louganis stopped cold. He later said, "After I quit, I wanted to tell every twelve-year-old that I had quit." His story, told at the peak of his Olympic fame, could have inspired tens of thousands to quit smoking—or avoid starting in the first place. Alas, it was not to be.

Louganis trained in California at the Mission Viejo pool. His coach, the best in the world, was employed by Mission Viejo. Philip Morris essentially owns the town of Mission Viejo. Philip Morris made it clear: if Louganis became chairman of the Great American Smokeout, he would lose his pool and his coach. Philip Morris also threatened to fire other Mission Viejo employees

> *Laws do not persuade*
> *just because they threaten.*
>
> SENECA
> A.D. 65

close to Louganis. Louganis had no choice. He declined the American Cancer Society's invitation, without comment. As Larry C. White pointed out in *The Merchants of Death,* "The threat of Louganis's being sent away from Mission Viejo, away from his coach, was the sports world's equivalent of saying, 'I'll kill your mother.'" The California Department of Health said it best: "Smokers are addicts. Cigarette companies are pushers."

Is all this an argument for banning cigarettes? No. It's education, not prohibition, that makes constructive change. Remember when cigarettes were considered glamorous, sophisticated, and even healthy? No one believes that now. Through education alone, more than 40,000,000 Americans have quit smoking.

This chapter is meant to show that we have a deeply ingrained hypocrisy in our culture. It allows cigarette companies to knowingly kill 500,000 people each year and make a profit on it, while we insist that our government arrest consensual "criminals" whose harm, either to themselves or to others, if combined, doesn't even begin to approach the damage done by cigarettes.

In terms of addiction, prescription and over-the-counter drugs run a close second (some say, first) to cigarettes. Tens of millions of Americans can't get through the day without (that is, they are addicted to) tranquilizers or amphetamines, or can't make it through the night without sleeping pills. Each year 125,000 deaths are linked to prescription drugs. In 1989, Tom Kelly, then–Deputy Administrator of the Drug Enforcement Administration, said on C-SPAN,

> I think it's very obvious that, on the legitimate side of
> drug use, we have become a totally drug dependent soci-

ety in this country. That's strictly on the legitimate side. That's what we teach our children in this country today. How bad is it? . . . We have about 30 million people who are regular users of stimulants. We have approximately 20 million who are regular users of sedatives. And

> *While the collateral consequences of drugs such as cocaine are indisputably severe, they are not unlike those which flow from the misuse of other, legal, substances.*
>
> JUSTICE BYRON R. WHITE

we have about 8 million who are chronic users of tranquilizers. And that's all on the legitimate side. Thinking of those numbers, are we not drug-dependent on the legitimate side?

And let's not forget America's Favorite Drug, *caffeine*. According to a research report published in the *Archives of General Psychiatry* in 1992:

> Our results indicate that some coffee drinkers exhibit common signs of drug dependence, i.e., they self-administer coffee for the effects of caffeine, have withdrawal symptoms on cessation of caffeine and experience adverse effects from caffeine intake.

The most widely used recreational drug in this country is, of course, alcohol. A 1990 study by the U.S. Department of Health asked participants which drugs they had used in the past thirty days. It was found that 51% had used alcohol, while only 5% had used marijuana, and less than 1% had used cocaine. A 1991 U.S. Department of Health study asked young people, ages eighteen to thirty, the same question. Almost 71% had used alcohol within the past thirty days; 28% had used cigarettes; 13% had used marijuana; 2% had used cocaine; less than 2% had used stimulants; about 1% had used tranquilizers; and less than 1% had used LSD, inhalants, and steroids. None of the study participants had used heroin and only 0.5% had used other opiates. Of high school students, 2% said they currently used cocaine, 14% said they cur-

> *If you are young*
> *and you drink a great deal*
> *it will spoil your health,*
> *slow your mind,*
> *make you fat—*
> *in other words,*
> *turn you into an adult.*
>
> P. J. O'ROURKE

rently used marijuana, while 59% said they currently used alcohol. (Of high school seniors, 28% smoked cigarettes.)

Alcohol is also the recreational drug most likely to be abused: 43% of college students, 35% of high school seniors, and 26% of eighth grade students (thirteen-year-olds!) said that they had had five or more drinks *in a row* at some point during the last *two weeks*. In 1990, more than half of the fatal car accidents in this country were related to alcohol, killing 22,083 people.* This is the equivalent of a fully loaded 747 crashing. Three times a week. Every week. An additional 469,000 nonfatal car crashes involved alcohol. Half of all teenage fatalities are alcohol-related. In a confidential survey of high school seniors who had received a traffic ticket in the

---

*The old saying, "Statistics don't lie, but liars use statistics" describes perfectly the people and organizations trying to overestimate the "drug problem." I have seen this figure of 22,083 listed as "drug and alcohol-related traffic fatalities." They were, almost entirely, alcohol-related. Another of my favorites is the statistic officially labeled, "Drug Abuse–Related Emergency Room Episodes." It says that 371,208 people were admitted to emergency rooms in 1990 for drug abuse–related reasons. I have seen this figure bandied about as proof that drugs are not safe, and are a horrendous problem ("Almost 400,000 people wind up in emergency rooms every year due to the drug epidemic!"). Further examination, however, shows that 172,815 of the cases—46%—were attempted suicides. To call attempted suicide "drug abuse–related" is absurd. Drugs were the method, not the problem. Just because 1,000 people commit suicide by jumping off tall buildings, does not make tall buildings dangerous. Only 29,817 of the 371,208 total emergency room episodes resulted from "recreational use" of drugs (only 8% of the total) and 74% of those patients were treated and released without being admitted to the hospital. (The figure 29,817 certainly indicates a problem, but compare it with the 500,000 smoking *deaths*. There are approximately 6,000 "illicit"-drug-related deaths each year—1.2% of the tobacco deaths.)

last twelve months, 10% of them admitted being under the influence of alcohol at the time they received the ticket. Only 3% were under the influence of marijuana or hashish, and 1% under the influence of any other drugs. More than 11 million Americans have witnessed a family member killed or seriously injured by a drunk driver in the last nine years. Society's loss in wages, productivity, medical and legal costs caused by death and injuries in drunk-driving crashes exceeds $24 billion each year. On an average Friday or Saturday night, one of every ten drivers on the road is drunk. In 1991, 13% of all male arrests were for drunk driving.

Alcohol is involved in 80% of fire deaths, 77% of falls, 65% of drownings, 65% of murders, 60% of child abuse cases, 35% of rapes, and 55% of all arrests. According to a 1992 study by the National Center for Health Statistics, "10,500,000 Americans are alcoholics; 76,000,000 more are affected by alcohol abuse, having been married to an alcoholic or problem drinker or having grown up with one."

Is this a call for a new Prohibition? No. As with cigarettes, the key to helping people from hurting themselves is education. There is, however, a great deal more we could do to protect nonconsenting victims of alcohol abuse—such as sober drivers and pedestrians. (Please see the chapter, "Protective Technology.")

⚖️ ⚖️ ⚖️

There are only two possible actions we, as a nation, can take to remove this deeply ingrained hypocrisy: ban cigarettes, alcohol, and caffeine, then have all drugs—including those currently sold over-the-counter—require a prescription from at least two

> *Tobacco is a culture productive of infinite wretchedness.*
>
> THOMAS JEFFERSON
> 1782

> *The ultimate result*
> *of shielding men*
> *from the effects of folly*
> *is to fill the world with fools.*
>
> HERBERT SPENCER

doctors. Or we can repeal the laws against currently illegal consensual activities. We can no longer afford to maintain the pretense that we really care whether or not people harm their own person and property. If we really cared and if prohibition worked (two of the larger if's in the known cosmos), we'd outlaw all legal evils.

Does removing laws against consensual activities make us an uncaring nation? Not at all. It makes us a mature nation; one that realizes you cannot legislate morality, prevent people from hurting themselves, or protect people from the consequences of their own behaviors. If we accept this mature stance, then we must legalize all consensual activities. Or continue being hypocrites.

Part V

WHAT TO DO?

My kind of loyalty was to one's country, not to its institutions or its officeholders. The country is the real thing, the substantial thing, the eternal thing; it is the thing to watch over, and care for, and be loyal to; institutions are extraneous, they are its mere clothing, and clothing can wear out, become ragged, cease to be comfortable, cease to protect the body from winter, disease, and death.

MARK TWAIN

Education,
Not Legislation

> *The only fence against the world is a thorough knowledge of it.*
>
> JOHN LOCKE
> 1693

I N ORDER TO MAKE intelligent choices, we must have accurate information about the potential consequences of our choices. Learning about those potential consequences—how to maximize the positive ones and how to minimize the negative ones—is the essence of education. True education is not deciding what is right or wrong and then convincing the student of the wisdom of the decision. That's propaganda. True education says, "Here are the possible rewards; here are the potential risks; here's how to maximize the rewards and minimize the risks; you make the choice."

Nowhere do we need true education more than in the area of consensual crimes: it seems as though all we've had for the longest time is propaganda—both negative and positive. Society teaches us that committing consensual crimes is always bad, wrong, dangerous, and deadly. The indulgers, on the other hand, teach that society is entirely wrong, that there are no risks, no dangers, no down sides. Neither of these polarized points is valid; neither is true education.

Much of what passes for drug education, for example, is not education at all, but simply scare tactics; terrors for children. The idea (as one popular billboard depicts) that snorting cocaine is the same as sticking a pistol in your nose and pulling the trigger is absurd. One famous television commercial shows an egg being dropped into a frying pan heated to at least 3,000 degrees; as

> *There is no slavery but ignorance.*
> *Liberty is the child of intelligence.*
>
> ROBERT G. INGERSOLL

the egg fries and burns, a voice-over says, "This is your brain. This is your brain on drugs." Come on. This is not only untrue and misleading; it's a waste of good food.

All this propaganda is as transparently silly as the supposed documentary films from the '30s: *Sex Madness*, *Cocaine Madness*, and the ever-popular *Reefer Madness*. In these films, ordinary, healthy (but, one must admit, terribly boring), young men and women are driven insane by, respectively, sex, cocaine, and marijuana.

One television commercial sponsored by the Partnership for a Drug Free America shows a wholesome young ghetto child having to jump over fences, run down alleys, and hide behind trees in order to make the journey from school to home without being caught by the drug dealers and forced to take drugs.

Another shows photographs of Janice Joplin, John Belushi, and River Phoenix. The announcer pipes in: "We were told celebrity endorsements help sell things." Then the title "Partnership for a Drug-Free America" flashes on the screen. This is an especially irritating commercial because if drugs weren't illegal, these people would not have died of accidental overdoses.

This modern-day misinformation can cause a person to conclude about all education efforts, "I know what they're saying about this is wrong; therefore everything they say is wrong."

A government that lies to its people divides itself: some people believe everything they're told and others believe nothing they're told. Both attitudes are dangerous to the health and well-being of a nation. The misinfomercials from the Partnership for a Drug Free America only show those already ignorant of drug use how right their righteous position is, while further alienating those who know that eggs in frying pans and children hiding behind trees have nothing to do with drugs.

Who pays for all this propaganda? Who finances the Partnership for a Drug Free America? Some of its contributors could be said to have vested interests in not making additional drugs legal.

According to *The Nation*,

> The Partnership for a Drug Free America received $150,000 each from Philip Morris (Miller beer and Marlboro cigarettes), Anheuser-Busch (Budweiser) and R. J. Reynolds (Camel) over 1988–91. Other contributors: American Brands (Jim Beam and Lucky Strike), Pepsico, and Coca-Cola. Contributing pharmaceutical companies included Bristol-Meyers Squibb, CIBA-Geigy, Dow, DuPont, Glaxo, Hoffman-La Roche, Johnson & Johnson, Merck, Pfizer, Schering-Plough, Smith-Kline and Warner-Lambert.

> *The highest result of education is tolerance.*
>
> HELEN KELLER

It's not just the Partnership for a Drug Free America propagandizing; media over the years have thought they were somehow helping by spreading scare stories as fact, or by dramatizing extreme cases of abuse as though they were everyday occurrences.

Two 1967 *Dragnet* episodes are a perfect example. (These weren't the gritty *film noir* episodes of the 1950s, but the technicolor episodes of the '60s. *Film noir* was better.) Jack Webb, the producer, director, star, etc., must have considered himself a one-person war on drugs. In one episode, Detective Sergeant Joe Friday takes a night-school class in "sensitivity training." No one in the class knows he's a cop. One of the participants admits to having taken drugs. Friday thinks he sees marijuana in the man's notebook. He arrests his classmate. The man is sent up the river. Meanwhile, the teacher of the class is outraged. People were encouraged to open up, to share, to be vulnerable and honest,

> MOTHER: *People just don't understand the boy.*
>
> SGT. JOE FRIDAY: *San Quentin is full of people hard to understand.*
>
> *DRAGNET*

and along comes an unannounced policeman who arrests a class member for doing just that. The professor wants to throw Friday out of the class. Friday asks for the class to decide: he'll give his point of view, and then they can vote. What follows is an impassioned speech (well, as impassioned as Jack Webb could get) about the dreadful things that he, as a Los Angeles cop, has seen drugs do to people. The speech goes on and on, one horror story after another. The class, initially hostile, sees the light, and votes to let Friday stay. If this were high school, they probably would have elected him class president.

An even more amazing *Dragnet* episode tackled another drug. A young man has his head stuck in the sand, one side of his face painted blue, the other side painted yellow. He is carrying a pocketful of sugar cubes. He is babbling about seeing the "pilot light" at the center of the earth and then believes he is becoming a tree. Guess what drug he is on? Based on the cubes in his pocket, it is either a sugar rush or LSD.

Yes, the scientist in the lab confirms it is LSD. The scientist in the lab seems to know a great deal about LSD, although his specialty is forensics. (According to *Dragnet,* there is precisely one scientist in the entire Los Angeles Police Department. He was played by the same actor, week after week.* This scientist could answer every question, from "What kind of gun could make a hole that size in a man?" to "We found this goldfish on the floor of the victim's apartment. Can you check it for fingerprints?")

---

*That this same actor occasionally played a judge on *Dragnet* might have caused some audience confusion, except when he played a scientist he always wore white and when he played a judge he always wore black.

AIN'T NOBODY'S BUSINESS IF YOU DO

The scientist, as it turns out, doesn't know that much about LSD after all. Although he looks very authoritative in his white science-coat and is surrounded by the paraphernalia of scientific investigation, not one of the "facts" he reveals in his five-minute lecture on the horrors of LSD is known to medical science. Although we, the audience, now know LSD is a Truly Bad Thing, the boy cannot be arrested: alas, there is no law against LSD. "I sure hope they give you boys something to fight with out there real soon," the scientist says. Friday nods grimly.

> CRIMINAL: *You made a mistake and I'm not going to pay for it.*
>
> SGT. JOE FRIDAY: *You going to use a credit card?*
>
> *DRAGNET*

The boy is now back to his normal self. He wipes the blue and yellow greasepaint off with his mother's handkerchief. His parents want to take him home. Not so fast: Friday wants to book 'em. "I happen to know there is no law against LSD," says the father. Friday looks frantically at his captain with a look that says, "I want to book him. I already *said,* 'I want to book him.' Please, help me find some way to book him!" The captain, an old hand at all this, says, "Book him on a 601." While the boy is taken to juvenile hall, Friday's voice-over explains a 601. It has something to do with suspicion of intent to commit conspiracy to corrupt your own morals in a way that is particularly disagreeable to Los Angeles police sergeants.

When the boy is released from juvenile hall, he commits the worst sin in Joe Friday's book: disrespect for Joe Friday. The boy has the nerve to call Friday "Sherlock." From his look, it's obvious that Friday doesn't know what the boy is talking about, but Friday knows it's not good.

Meanwhile, two teenaged girls are at police headquarters. They apparently spent the day "tripping." One of them describes how she watched Los Angeles melt; either that, or she stumbled into a movie theater showing *The House of Wax*. The girls show us

> HUSBAND: *[About wife]*
> *Lousy, sloppy drunk.*
>
> SGT. JOE FRIDAY:
> *Don't knock her. She had a*
> *good reason to drink.*
>
> HUSBAND: *Yeah, what was that?*
>
> SGT. JOE FRIDAY:
> *She was married to you.*
>
> DRAGNET

what it's like to "come down" from an LSD trip. It looks like a combination of nausea and bad menstrual cramps. Not at all appealing. Oh, by the way, they purchased their LSD from the boy.

Six months pass. The captain comes in and hands Joe Friday a booklet. It is a new law declaring LSD a "dangerous substance." Joe Friday is like a kid at Christmas. The captain is Santa Claus. "When does this law go into effect?" Friday asks, eyes ablaze. "Forty-eight hours," the captain tells him. These men are high, truly high. They've just gotten a fix of the drug they love most: control. Forty-eight hours. Just enough time to roll out the (dum-da-dum-dum) dragnet.

In search of the boy, they visit an LSD party. It looks something like *Laugh In's* cocktail party, but much slower and without jokes. Friday calls some uniformed police. They arrive within thirty seconds. (Ah, the good old days.) Everyone at the party is arrested. Talk about a bad trip. The boy, unfortunately, is not there. Fortunately, however, a pharmacy calls in: they have just sold 1,000 empty gelatin capsules to a young man fitting the description of the boy. (What happened to his sugar-cube method of distribution? And here Friday has been asking supermarket managers all over Los Angeles to report excessive sugar cube purchases.) Friday goes to the pharmacy. Yes, after being shown mug shots, the pharmacist (who has precisely one shelf with about twelve bottles of pills on it) gives Friday the address of where the capsules were delivered. (Which means the boy came in, ordered 1,000 empty gelatin capsules, which must weigh about five ounces, and then said, "Here, deliver these." Yes, this boy was *clearly* on drugs—or the scriptwriter was.)

The landlady happily provides Detective Friday with a passkey. Friday enters (apparently having no use for that seven-letter

AIN'T NOBODY'S BUSINESS IF YOU DO

four-letter word: *warrant)* and finds a friend of the boy, who says of the boy, "He kept taking more and more pills. He kept wanting to go far out, far out, far out . . ." "He made it;" intones Friday, "he's dead."

Dum-da-dum-dum.

After the commercial, we are told that a coroner's inquest found the boy died of an LSD overdose. (Barbiturates are mentioned somewhere in there, parenthetically.) Yes, ladies and gentlemen, for the first and only time in history, LSD kills.

> *You got to know the rules before you can break 'em. Otherwise, it's no fun.*
>
> SONNY CROCKETT
> *MIAMI VICE*

Dragnet was famous, of course, for Joe Friday's sardonic and ironic comment just before the final dum-da-dum-dum. In keeping with that tradition, here is my sardonic and ironic comment: Detective Sergeant Joe Friday stoically acknowledged defeat and celebrated victory in precisely the same way. He lit a cigarette. According to the American Heart Association, cigarette smoking is the #1 cause of heart disease. Jack Webb, a life-long smoker, died of a heart attack on December 23, 1982.

Dum-da-dum-dum.

A hipper, trendier show for the hipper, trendier '80s was *Miami Vice.* It was *so cool* to catch drug dealers. The only burning question, however, was: how did Crockett afford thousands of dollars in new designer clothes and other hip paraphernalia each week on a Miami detective's salary? Yes, it was cool to put the bad guys away, but never forget the most essential American lesson: There is nothing cooler than money.

Films such as *The Gene Krupa Story* perpetuated the myth that, if you even tried marijuana, within six months you would be hopelessly addicted to heroin, which, as everyone knew, meant an agonizing death in the gutter three months later—but only after pulling everything and everyone you ever loved into the gutter with you.

> *I've over-educated myself*
> *in all the things*
> *I shouldn't have known.*
>
> NOËL COWARD

As millions of Americans learned, that domino theory, like the one about Southeast Asia, isn't true.

⚖ ⚖ ⚖

The purpose of education is to make the choices clear to people, not to make the choices for people.

Cigarettes are readily available, seductively advertised, and you may even be offered one from time to time, and yet, the vast majority of the American public simply chooses to say no. Only the most unbalanced person would respond to the friendly offer of a cigarette with, "What? Are you trying to get me hooked? Are you a recruiting agent for one of the tobacco companies? You should be put in jail!" The answer is simply: "No, thank you," and people go about their business.

Cigarette consumption has dropped dramatically in this country during the past two decades, and it's not due to government restrictions or prohibitions. The kingpins of the tobacco industry were not rounded up. A tobacco czar was not appointed to arrest and prosecute all the tobacco lords. A person caught selling a cigarette to another did not have his or her home confiscated and was not sent to jail for tobacco trafficking. Habitual cigarette users ("nickies") were sentenced neither to jail nor to mandatory rehabilitation programs.

No. Cigarette consumption in this country has dropped thanks to one thing: education.

Education has caused people to think of cigarettes as hazardous, not glamorous. The federal government played only a small part in this educational process (in the person of former Surgeon General C. Everett Koop. Dr. Koop was to cigarettes what Ralph Nader was to Corvairs). The educators were, for the most part, nonprofit organizations funded by voluntary donations—the

American Cancer Society, the American Lung Association, the American Heart Association, and several others. Their factual information was picked up by the media, and the attitude of an entire nation changed in a short time.

> *Education's purpose
> is to replace an empty mind
> with an open one.*
>
> MALCOLM S. FORBES

(The tobacco industry, of course, continues to claim that cigarette smoking is good for you. The Tobacco Institute claims that all this smoking-is-harmful nonsense is merely a conspiracy engineered and paid for by the people who make those "Thank You for Not Smoking" signs. My favorite no-smoking sign is, "If you're smoking in here, you'd better be on fire.")

Calling unreasonable scare tactics *education* only produces some people who are unreasonably scared and other people who are unreasonable. Trying to wipe out drug abuse with the commercials from the Partnership for a Drug Free America is, as Alan Watts put it, "Like trying to kill mosquitoes with a machine gun." As Maria Montessori wrote in *The Montessori Method,*

> Discipline must come through liberty. . . . We do not consider an individual disciplined when he has been rendered as artificially silent as a mute and as immovable as a paralytic. He is an individual *annihilated,* not *disciplined.*

As Franklin Delano Roosevelt pointed out,

> Knowledge—that is, education in its true sense—is our best protection against unreasoning prejudice and panic-making fear, whether engendered by special interest, illiberal minorities, or panic-stricken leaders.

Or all three.

A Call to My Media Brethren

> *Hastiness and superficiality*
> *are the psychic diseases*
> *of the twentieth century,*
> *and more than anywhere else*
> *this disease*
> *is reflected in the press.*
>
> ALEXANDER SOLZHENITSYN

AND NOW I TURN MY criticism to my own profession, journalism. I consider myself a journalist who happens to write chapters more often than articles. Alas, I am afraid that my media colleagues have been guilty of reporting the party line on consensual crimes rather than investigating and revealing the facts. Nowhere is this more evident than in covering the war on drugs.

To win the war for personal freedoms, however, we must hold the media to its task: to discover and report the facts accurately. To these ends, I have occasionally dropped a line to my fellow scribblers—with no perceivable results whatsoever. Nonetheless, I press on.

Here, for example, is a letter I spent moments slaving over which the *Los Angeles Times* failed to acknowledge, much less print. It pretty much sums up what I think the media must do to free itself from the inaccuracies perpetrated by the drug war propaganda machine.

November 15, 1993

Dear Editor:

Your headline of 11–13–93, "PHOENIX: Drugs Killed Actor, 23," was as misleading as, say, a report of James Dean's death headlined: "DEAN: Porsche Killed Actor, 24." Both brilliant actors died in unfortunate accidents.

But River Phoenix was killed not by drugs, *but by the fact that drugs are illegal*. When the government gets on its moral high horse and declares something completely prohibited, the government turns all control over to unregulated manufacturers, possibly disreputable distributors, and organized crime. The purity and strength of the banned substance cannot be monitored. The consumer has no protection. Prohibition returns us to the law of the jungle.

> *The most important service rendered by the press and the magazines is that of educating people to approach printed matter with distrust.*
>
> SAMUEL BUTLER

According to the DEA, the white powder sold on the streets as "heroin" can be anywhere from 32% to 90% pure heroin. The other famous white powder, cocaine, has a similar potency range. That's quite a range, a deadly range, the range which caused the deaths of River Phoenix, John Belushi, and more than 50,000 other Americans since the war on drugs was declared in 1982. If heroin and cocaine were legal, their potency would be clearly labeled, and most of these people would still be alive.

Let's face it: the war on drugs is over. This year, the federal government admitted that the war has achieved nothing. In the past eleven years, after spending more than three hundred billion dollars; diverting unknown trillions of dollars into international organized crime; arresting more than ten million Americans; overburdening police, courts, and prisons; alienating minorities; creating a rise in crime and a disrespect for the law unseen since Prohibition; the availability, street price, and use of prohibited drugs remains virtually unchanged.

More than fifty federal judges refuse to hear drug cases. There are more people in federal prisons today for drug charges than the total federal prison population in 1982. The Drug Czar, Attorney General Reno, and knowledgeable observers in and out of government state frankly that what we're doing isn't working.

It will be a long time before the war on drugs—like its parallel atrocity, the Vietnam War—will be officially declared over.

> *The rising power of the United States in world affairs . . . requires, not a more compliant press, but a relentless barrage of facts and criticism . . . . Our job in this age, as I see it, is not to serve as cheerleaders for our side . . . but to help the largest possible number of people to see the realities.*
>
> JAMES RESTON
> *The Artillery of the Press*

(We Americans so dislike admitting defeat, and bureaucracies absolutely abhor being dismantled.) The least we can do as journalists, however, is put an end to the wartime rhetoric. In war, the first casualty is truth. Truth, accuracy, balance, fairness, and all the other qualities we worship in our "freedom of the press" were abandoned by the mainstream media as soon as the war began.

Here are my suggestions for eliminating the now-obsolete wartime propaganda from our nation's media:

1. **Stop using phrases such as "drugs kill."** To paraphrase the NRA: Drugs don't kill people; people kill themselves with drugs. To perpetuate the myth that "people are powerless over drugs" only adds to the level of personal irresponsibility that has already grown to fatal proportions in this country.

2. **Stop pretending that illegal drugs do more harm than legal ones.** More than 500,000 Americans die prematurely each year due to cigarette smoking and more than 200,000 from alcohol abuse. Meanwhile, all the illegal drugs combined cause approximately 6,000 deaths (mostly accidental overdoes due to the unknown strength and purity of prohibited substances). Growing marijuana—which in 10,000 years of recorded human use has never caused *one* death—can get you a life sentence without possibility of parole. Growing tobacco can get you a government subsidy.

3. **Stop calling recreational drugs "dangerous."** There are no "bad" drugs; there are only bad *relationships* with drugs. It is the relationship the human being forms with a drug that makes the drug harmful, harmless, or beneficial. The same drug can be good for one person and bad for another, based on the relationship each has established with that drug. Yes, some drugs (generally the ones that are physically addictive) are easier to form bad

relationships with than others. Reporting this is both legitimate and necessary. By these standards, the most "dangerous" (physically addictive) recreational drugs are morphine (often consumed as heroin) and cigarettes.

4. **Stop referring to recreational drugs as "poison."** That's only true about always-lethal substances, which, for the most part, are perfectly legal. For example, no one uses Drāno recreationally (although a few desperate people *do* use Lysol, heaven help them). Drāno is so consistently deadly that the only law controlling its sale says it must be labeled "poison." There are no reports of a "Drāno problem." Drāno smuggling is, I would wager (if wagering weren't illegal), not rampant. Airports have no Drāno-sniffing dogs. An Omnibus Drāno Bill was never proposed to Congress. "DEA" does not stand for "Drāno Enforcement Agency."

5. **Stop perpetuating the myth that "the only way to use drugs safely is not to use them at all."** Instead, give the rules for using the drugs with maximum safety. For example, your 11-3-93 article implicating GHB in the death of River Phoenix ("Designer Drug Enters Hollywood's Fast Lane") never told the simple rules for using GHB safely (or as safely as one can use any drug—legal or illegal). The primary rule: never take GHB with any other drug. When people take more than a proper dose of GHB, they fall asleep. If GHB is consumed in higher levels, the person vomits. As long as GHB is not interacting with another drug, not taken with a drug that suppresses nausea, and used in moderation, GHB is relatively harmless. In fact, your article on 11-13-93 stated that the corner's final report listed an overdose of morphine (probably ingested as heroin) and cocaine as the cause of Phoenix's death. Although you are careful to point out, "No alcohol was detected," you fail to mention that no GHB was detected,

> You cannot hope to bribe or twist (thank God!) the British journalist. But, seeing what the man will do unbribed, there's no occasion to.
>
> HUMBERT WOLFE

> *Report me and my cause aright.*
>
> WILLIAM SHAKESPEARE
> *Hamlet*

either. Why not correct your earlier indictment of GHB—and apologize for any inaccurate or exaggerated reporting? If drugs had lawyers and PR agencies, the nation's press would be heavy with retractions and lawsuits.

All of this comes down to the simple idea: tell us the truth about drugs. Almost anything can be harmful if abused. Tell us what causes abuse and how to avoid it. Educate us as to the possible negative reactions when using a drug, what percentage of users experience these reactions, and what to do if one happens. Children are taught early the potential dangers of and safe use of knives, matches, and yes, even Drāno. Please show your readers at least as much respect and have as much confidence in us as parents show their children.

Sincerely,

Peter McWilliams
Los Angeles, CA

Protective Technology

> *For a list of all the ways
> technology has failed
> to improve the quality of life,
> please press 3.*
>
> ALICE KAHN

TECHNOLOGY HAS moved ahead at a rapid pace. At the turn of the century, the consensus in the medical community was that the human body could not withstand traveling at the inconceivable rate of a mile a minute. Today, even though many of us travel daily at speeds once considered humanly impossible, the technology for devices to prevent these mile-a-minute missiles (automobiles) from being operated by incapable drivers is no further along than it was when the first carriage moved without a horse in 1885.

In that same year, 1885, mass communication consisted of newspapers, phonograph cylinders, and illustrated monthlies. Our view of the world came from paintings, etchings, and stereopticon slides. Communication took place by letter or the quaint old custom of visiting people and talking with them. In an emergency, one could send a telegram (by going to a Western Union office), and a handful of people had telephones. The business world gravitated around the ticker tape, and the carrier pigeon was still in use. That was about it.

Today we have radios, telephones, VCRs, computers, mobile telephones, fax machines, movies, televisions (with hundreds of cable channels), Walkmen, boomboxes, home stereos, car stereos, the Internet, as well as all the other communication devices of the earlier days. And yet, those who don't want to be exposed, or their children to be exposed, to certain material must rely on minor variations of the censorship practiced in Victorian times.

It's time technology better served the nonconsenting.

⚖ ⚖ ⚖

> *The ordinary*
> *"horseless carriage"*
> *is at present a luxury for the*
> *wealthy; and although its price*
> *will probably fall in the future,*
> *it will never, of course, come*
> *into as common use as the bicycle.*
>
> *THE LITERARY DIGEST*
> October 14, 1899

It's hard to imagine the kind of damage a 3,000-pound metal and glass object traveling a mile a minute can do. Hard, that is, until you see a traffic accident. Then we look and look away at the same time. We like to think that degree of devastation is a fluke of nature. (It's not.) We like to think it won't happen to us. (You have a two percent chance of dying in a traffic accident.) Most of these accidents are caused by a driver's *not being capable of operating a motor vehicle at the time of the crash.*

At the risk of stating the obvious, people who are not capable of operating a motor vehicle—for whatever reason—have no business operating it; not because they may harm themselves, but because there is a very good chance they may harm nonconsenting others. Of this country's 44,000 annual traffic deaths, 22,000 are alcohol related. Of the 22,000 that are not alcohol related, a good many happen because the drivers are too stoned (on drugs other than alcohol), emotionally upset, physically impaired, senile, exhausted, or in some way physically, mentally, or emotionally incapable of driving.

A simple device, installed in each car, could prevent the majority of deaths caused by these impairments.

Let's call this device, for lack of a better name, the "Tester." Imagine a panel on the dashboard with a numeric keypad, like those on touch-tone telephones. Above the keypad is a screen to display numbers and brief messages. There is also a slot, about the size of a credit card. The Tester works like this:

When you want to use the car, first insert your driver's license, which would act and look like a credit card. The Tester reads your driver's license as an automated teller machine reads your credit card, and then asks for your four-digit personal identification number (PIN), much as a teller machine would. Your PIN is known only to you, but is encoded in your license. After your four-digit personal identification number is successfully given, the screen displays seven random numbers—the number of digits in a phone number. You must then, within a certain period of time and with a certain degree of accuracy, enter those numbers on the key-pad. Once you complete this procedure, which should take less than a minute, the car is ready to operate normally.

> *The last-ditch stand against "accidents" will be the car. After seat belts, after air bags, after drunken driving and speed, there will be changes in the car.*
>
> JOHN BARBOUR
> *Chicago Tribune*

That extra minute will keep a good many unlicensed and incapable drivers off the road.

Driving is not an inalienable right. We must meet certain standards of knowledge, ability, and competence before we receive a license to drive. A great many car accidents are caused by people whose licenses have been revoked or suspended, or people who don't have licenses at all. Without a license, people have no business—and certainly no right—to drive a car. If, potentially, they could only hurt themselves, they would have the right. (They can drive around on their own property, for example, all they want.) The potential for hurting innocent others, however, moves driving into the realm of licensing. Hang gliding, for example, should require no license. The chances of harming anyone but yourself are extremely slim. On the other hand, the chances of an incompetent person hurting someone with a car are very high.

The Tester assures that only licensed drivers are using automobiles. Your PIN means that your license can't be used if it's stolen. Because it's encoded in your driver's license, however, the PIN works in any car. Yes, sophisticated license thieves will have machinery to read PINs, but the average would-be license-and-car thief would find the lack of a PIN a sufficient deterrent.

The Tester can be programmed so that each car will accept

> *The means by which we live*
> *have outdistanced*
> *the ends for which we live.*
> *Our scientific power has outrun*
> *our spiritual power.*
> *We have guided missiles*
> *and misguided men.*
>
> MARTIN LUTHER KING, JR.

only certain licenses. This deters theft and keeps unauthorized family members from "accidentally" using the wrong car. Or, a car can accept any license except those specifically excluded (very handy in recent divorces).

After one has been authorized by the state (through licensing) and by the owner of the car (who has selected which licenses can and cannot operate the car), the randomly generated seven-digit number appears. If one cannot see, read, comprehend, or summon the hand-eye coordination necessary to enter seven randomly generated digits into a keypad within a certain period of time, that person has no right (based on his or her demonstrated lack of ability) to operate a motor vehicle.

If one fails to accurately enter the number, a new number is generated. If the second attempt is not successful, the person gets one more try, and a third randomly generated number appears. As with baseball, three strikes and you're out—at least for the inning. The Tester then displays the message, "TRY AGAIN IN 15 MINUTES," and then keeps track of the time ("TRY AGAIN IN 14 MINUTES," "TRY AGAIN IN 13 MINUTES," and so on). During this mandatory waiting period, one can chill out, warm up, breathe deeply, or do whatever one must do to meet the minimum mental and physical standards for operating an automobile. After a driver fails three consecutive tests (nine times in a row failing to enter a seven-digit number correctly), the Tester shuts the car down for two hours and suggests, "CALL A CAB." (The Tester would, however, allow a different license to be entered and the car to be driven by a competent driver.)

The Tester controls the link between the engine and the transmission. The car cannot be put in gear unless the Tester signals its okay. This allows you to start the car and use the heater, air conditioner, radio, tape player, telephone, or any car function other than moving it.

There is, of course, an emergency button, which overrides the Tester entirely and allows one to start the car and drive it immediately. Pushing the emergency button, however, automatically activates the emergency flashers and beeps the horn once every two seconds. This alerts law enforcement officers that you need aid, and they will be happy to supply it. It also alerts other motorists on the road that you have an emergency and, perhaps, they might want to get out of your way.

Traffic signals in New York are just rough guidelines.

DAVID LETTERMAN

As with all fail-safe devices, this one has built-in drawbacks, the primary one being that someone else can enter the code for an inebriated, stoned, or otherwise incompetent friend. Yes, this could be made illegal. But, again, the solution lies in education and creating the cultural belief that overriding the fail-safe system for another is neither an act of kindness, friendship, or love. In fact, it could be seen as an act of indifference and dismissal. A true friend would offer a ride, call a cab, or walk the person around the block a few times.

No, this system will not get every incompetent driver off the road.* It's designed to keep some of the most blatant offenders off the road. We must handle the problem of incompetent drivers *at its source:* not banning the alcohol or drugs that contribute to the incompetency, but stopping the problem at the point it becomes a problem—when an incapable driver gets behind a steering wheel.

---

*Accountants would probably have no trouble entering randomly generated numbers in their sleep, much less when drunk. But then, how often do accountants get drunk? "You don't want to see me drunk," one accountant said. "When I get drunk, all I do is talk about stock options."

> *What we are seeing is a sea change in the way people view driving. We are getting away from the word "accident," which is sort of a luck-fate-magic approach and into the word "crashes," where people understand what specific things they can do to reduce their risk.*
>
> CHARLES HURLEY
> Insurance Institute for Highway Safety

Just to show you how quickly technological changes can take place (an idea whose time has come and all that), in the original hardcover edition of *Ain't Nobody's Business If You Do*, in a chapter called "Fail-Safe Safety Devices," I proposed something called the Sensor, which would monitor television broadcasts and eliminate those aspects selected as objectionable by the viewer. This was in late 1993. Of all the people I talked to, only one of them had ever heard of such a thing. Most people thought it was a fine idea that had a snowball's chance in a sauna.

Less than three years later, however, the V-Chip is law, all signed, sealed, and legal-like. Astonishingly, it was the broadcasters (short-sighted little money grubbers) who put up the biggest stink. Yes, it may make a little more bureaucratic work to encode all those programs, but what broadcasters gain in exchange is freedom. Don't they remember how the multiple ratings system in the movies (rather than the Hayes Office "approved" or "not approved") gave freedom to the motion picture industry? Both Disney and *Deep Throat* thrived. Now the same can happen with broadcast television.

There's no reason the Tester shouldn't be installed at once in the cars of each person caught driving under the influence (at the guilty party's expense, of course), and mandated for all new cars within a year. (Cost per new car? Maybe ten bucks.) Traffic accidents and deaths should go down by 50%. And please keep in mind such a device is not to protect the incapacitated driver, but the rest of us.

⚖ ⚖ ⚖

The ideas behind these fail-safe devices are just an indication of what technology can do to make everyone physically safer—and free people from being exposed to some of the objectionable aspects of other people's freedom. The possibility for using technology—rather than unenforceable, unworkable, unjust laws—to regulate potentially harmful behavior is vast and largely untapped.

> *There should be some schools called deformatories to which people are sent if they are too good to be practical.*
>
> SAMUEL BUTLER

Hemp for Victory

YOU MAY FIND THE information in this chapter astonishing, unlikely, fascinating, unbelievable, amazing, and too good to be true. That, at least, was my first reaction. What amazed me even more was that I first heard this information not from an underground newspaper, but on the ABC Radio Network, presented by someone who ranks right up there with Walter Cronkite as a trustworthy journalist, Hugh Downs:*

> The reasons the pro-marijuana lobby wants marijuana legal have little to do with getting high, and a great deal to do with fighting oil giants like Saddam Hussein, Exxon and Iran. The pro-marijuana groups claim that hemp is such a versatile raw material that its products not only compete with petroleum, but with coal, natural gas, nuclear energy, pharmaceutical, timber and textile companies. It is estimated that methane and methanol production alone from hemp grown as bio-mass could replace 90% of the world's energy needs. If they're right, this is not good news for oil interests, and could account for the continuation of marijuana prohibition.

As we explored, marijuana is the hemp plant *(Cannabis sativa)*, and was one of the primary agricultural products in this country for more than 250 years. We saw how the DuPont Corporation and William Randolph Hearst, working with Federal Bureau of

*A similar report was printed in his excellent 1995 book *Perspectives,* and recorded by him on the audio version of the book.

Narcotics Director Harry Anslinger, succeeded in having marijuana prohibited nationally in 1937. On his ABC Radio broadcast, Hugh Downs explored possible reasons why marijuana is still illegal today:

> They've outlawed
> the number one vegetable
> on the planet.
>
> TIMOTHY LEARY

When Rudolph Diesel produced his famous engine in 1896, he assumed that the diesel engine would be powered by a variety of fuels, especially vegetable and seed oils. Rudolph Diesel, like most engineers then, believed vegetable fuels were superior to petroleum. Hemp is the most efficient vegetable.

In the 1930s, the Ford Motor Company also saw a future in biomass fuels. Ford operated a successful biomass conversion plant that included hemp at their Iron Mountain facility in Michigan. Ford engineers extracted methanol, charcoal fuel, tar, pitch, ethyl acetate, and creosote—all fundamental ingredients for modern industry, and now supplied by oil-related industries.

The difference is that the vegetable source is renewable, cheap and clean, and the petroleum or coal sources are limited, expensive and dirty. By volume, 30% of the hemp seed contains oil suitable for high-grade diesel fuel, as well as aircraft engine and precision machine oil. Henry Ford's experiments with methanol promised cheap, readily-renewable fuel. And, if you think methanol means compromise, you should know that many modern race cars run on methanol.

Jack Herer's book, *The Emperor Wears No Clothes,* is the bible on industrial uses for marijuana. The subtitle of the book is *The Authoritative Historical Record of the Cannabis Plant, Marijuana Prohibition, and How Hemp Can Still Save the World.* This is an ambitious

> *It takes an entire forest—*
> *over 500,000 trees—*
> *to supply Americans with their*
> *Sunday newspapers every week.*
>
> *Over one billion trees*
> *are used to make*
> *disposable diapers every year.*

subtitle—especially for a book that looks more like the *Whole Earth Catalog* than a scholarly tome. For the most part, however, Herer succeeds. He may become a little too enthusiastic about the industrial uses of hemp at times, but even if 10% of his information is accurate (and certainly more than that is), marijuana could prove a major boon to the economy, the environment, and humanity.

In addition to oil and fuel, here are some of the industrial uses for the hemp plant:

- **Paper.** Whereas trees—currently our primary source of paper—take twenty years to grow, hemp reaches full maturity in a single growing season. Warm climates can produce three hemp harvests per year. This makes hemp a far more efficient plant for producing paper than trees. In addition, making paper from hemp—unlike wood pulp—doesn't require acid, so all hemp paper is "acid free," thus lasting for hundreds of years. Hemp could supply virtually all of our paper, cardboard, and other packaging needs. (Half the paper used in America is for packaging.) And if you're wondering why books, newspapers, and magazines are costing more and more, it's probably because the worldwide shortage of pulp caused paper prices to double in 1995.

- **Textiles and Fabrics.** The hemp fiber is very similar to flax—in fact, much of the linen produced prior to the 1930s (including fine Irish linen) was made from hemp, not flax. The hemp plant, then, is an excellent source for textiles. Prior to the invention of the cotton gin, most clothing in the United States was made from the hemp plant. The hemp fiber is stronger, softer, warmer, and more durable than cotton.

- **Food**. The hemp seed is an excellent source of protein. It can be ground, baked into breads, sprouted, and turned into a tofu-like food. In addition, hemp seed makes an excellent oil similar to flaxseed

> *It doesn't matter*
> *whether you're right or not,*
> *you're never going to be able*
> *to use hemp.*
> *A lot of people*
> *have heavy feelings about marijuana*
> *and they're not going*
> *to allow you to grow it.*
>
> DR. STEPHEN EVANS
> U.S. Department of Agriculture

oil. You cannot "get high" eating marijuana seeds or their oil. ("Hash oil," which is highly intoxicating, does not come from the seeds.)

- **Medicine**. Marijuana (yes, the part that gets you high) is the best medicine for reducing nausea in people being treated with chemotherapy or other medications.[*] Marijuana is also an excellent treatment for glaucoma, which is responsible for 14% of all blindness in America and affects 2.5 million people.[**] Marijuana has also been proven effective in treating asthma, epilepsy, MS, back pain and muscle spasms, arthritis, cystic fibrosis, rheumatism, emphysema, migraines, in reducing tumors, and—as should come as no surprise to anyone who has ever smoked marijuana—in enhancing one's appetite. And yet, as of early 1996, precisely

---

[*]Some states allow the psychoactive chemical, THC, to be sold in pill form as a treatment for nausea. These states, however, do not allow the smokeable form of marijuana to be sold, even to cancer or AIDS patients. The absurdity of this is immediately evident: if one is nauseated, he or she would be unable to keep down the pill form of THC long enough for it to be absorbed into the system. The smokeable form of marijuana, however, acts much more quickly than the pill form and can be inhaled—even on an upset stomach.

[**]Some doctors hint strongly that glaucoma patients obtain marijuana illicitly to use in their glaucoma treatment.

eight people in the United States can legally use marijuana as medicine.

- **Building Materials.** The hemp plant can be pressed into fiberboard which is fire resistant and has excellent thermal- and sound-insulating qualities.

- **Other Products.** The hemp plant is rich in cellulose. Cellulose can be used for making more than 150,000 plastic products, many of which are made from petroleum today. Hemp can also be used to make paint, varnish, and even dynamite.

⚖ ⚖ ⚖

Here are some fascinating hemp facts, taken directly from *The Emperor Wears No Clothes:*

> HEMPstead, Long Island; HEMPstead County, Arkansas; HEMPstead, Texas; HEMPhill, North Carolina; HEMPfield, Pennsylvania; among others, were named after cannabis growing regions, or after family names derived from hemp growing.

> Cannabis hemp was legal tender (money) in most of the Americas from 1631 until the early 1800s. You could pay your taxes with cannabis hemp throughout America for over 200 years.

> You could even be jailed in America for not growing cannabis during several periods of shortage, e.g., in Virginia between 1763 and 1767.

> George Washington and Thomas Jefferson grew cannabis on their plantations. Jefferson, while envoy to France,

went to great expense—and considerable risk to himself and his secret agents—to procure particularly good hemp seeds smuggled illegally into Turkey from China. The Chinese Mandarins (political rulers) so valued their hemp seeds that they made their exportation a capital offense.

> *Cultivators of the earth are the most valuable citizens.*
>
> THOMAS JEFFERSON
> 1785

Benjamin Franklin started one of America's first paper mills with cannabis. This allowed America to have a free colonial press without having to beg or justify paper and books from England.

The United States Census of 1850 counted 8,327 hemp "plantations" (minimum 2,000 acre farms) growing cannabis hemp for cloth, canvas and even the cordage used for baling cotton. (This figure does not include the tens of thousands of smaller farms growing cannabis, nor the hundreds of thousands—if not millions—of family hemp patches in America.)

In 1942, after the Japanese invasion of the Philippines cut off the supply of manila (Abaca) hemp, the U.S. government distributed 400,000 pounds of cannabis seeds to American farmers from Wisconsin to Kentucky, who produced 42,000 tons of hemp fiber annually for the war effort until 1946. In 1942–43 farmers were made to attend showings of the USDA film *Hemp for Victory*, sign that they had seen the film and read a hemp cultivation booklet. Farmers from 1942 through 1945 who agreed to grow hemp were waived from serving in the military, along with their sons; that's how vitally important hemp was to America during World War II.

The paintings of Rembrandt, Van Gogh, Gainsborough, etc.,

were primarily painted on hemp canvas, as were practically all canvas paintings.

One of the most beneficial aspects of using hemp (or other plants) for fuel is that, as plants grow, the plants take carbon dioxide out of the atmosphere and replace it with oxygen. This helps solve one of our primary environmental problems: too much carbon dioxide. When a portion of the hemp plant is burned for fuel, it has already "earned" the oxygen it uses by having placed that oxygen in the atmosphere while it grew. Fossil fuels (oil, gas, or coal), on the other hand, come from plant and animal sources that died millions of years ago—whatever carbon dioxide they took or oxygen they left happened millions of years ago. Burning fossil fuels, then, only adds to carbon dioxide and reduces the amount of oxygen in the atmosphere.

The hemp plant has remarkable potential for agriculture, manufacturing, energy, and the environment. And yet, cultivating, using, or even possessing hemp can get you mandatory life imprisonment. If you possess enough of it and the government determines you are a big time pot seller, you could be put to death.

As with most consensual crimes, this prohibition of hemp is both silly and sinister. As Dr. Fred Oerther asked,

> Should we believe self-serving, ever-growing drug enforcement/drug treatment bureaucrats, whose pay and advancement depends on finding more and more people to arrest and "treat"?

> More Americans die in just one day in prisons, penitentiaries, jails and stockades than have ever died from marijuana throughout history. Who are they protecting? From what?

A State-by-State Look at Consensual Crime

> *Rebellion to tyrants*
> *is obedience to God.*
>
> THOMAS JEFFERSON
> chosen as the motto for his seal
> 1776

IT HAS ALWAYS STRUCK me as odd that a consensual act should be legal in one state and illegal in another. What is it about stepping over the imaginary line dividing state from state that converts you from a criminal to a noncriminal?

Imagine a bed in a motel room. The state line divides the bed: on one side of the bed you are in one state, on the other side of the bed you're in another. You and your consenting adult partner, lying on either side of the bed, could be committing the same activity, but one of you would be a criminal and the other would not.

If you were on the Connecticut–Rhode Island border, for example, you could be involved in an act of oral sex (either heterosexual or homosexual) and the partner on the Rhode Island side would be breaking the law while the partner on the Connecticut side would not.

On the New York–New Jersey border, if one of you happens to be married to another, you are guilty of adultery on the New York side of the bed, but not guilty of adultery (in the legal sense) on the New Jersey side.

Perhaps the most stunning example of this would be anal sex (again, either homosexual or heterosexual) if you were on the Idaho-Wyoming border. The partner on the Wyoming side of the bed would be committing no crime at all; the partner on the Idaho side would be subject to life imprisonment.

Drug use and unconventional medical practices, thanks to the

> *I believe we are on
> an irreversible trend toward
> more freedom and democracy.
> But that will change.*
>
> VICE-PRESIDENT DAN QUAYLE

Drug Enforcement Agency and the Food and Drug Administration, are illegal everywhere.

Full-scale gambling is legal only in Nevada and Atlantic City. Limited forms of gambling (race tracks, card clubs, off-track betting) are usually determined at the local (not state) level, thus too ambitious for our humble chart. If your state has a state-run lottery, you'll know: lotteries tend to advertise more than Coca-Cola.

This leaves us with a state-by-state chart that deals mostly with sex and assisted suicide. What a combination. The "Age of Consent" column applies to sex only, not alcohol—due to federal pressure, alcohol is limited to persons twenty-one and older.

The chart is as accurate as we could make it as of early 1996. The fastest growing category, in terms of illegality, seems to be assisted suicide. This chart is provided as a starting point for political change. Before you take part in any activity within any state, please check with local authorities. End of disclaimer; let's move on to the chart. (Information provided by Thomas Coleman, Spectrum Institute, P.O. Box 65756, Los Angeles, California 90065.)

	HETERO ORAL SEX	HETERO ANAL SEX	GAY ORAL SEX	GAY ANAL SEX	ADULTERY	PROSTITUTION	FORNICATION	COHABITATION	PORNOGRAPHY	AGE OF CONSENT	ASSISTED SUICIDE
ALABAMA	☹	☹	☹	☹	☹	☹				16	
ALASKA						☹				18	☹
ARIZONA	☹	☹	☹	☹	☹	☹		☹		18	☹
ARKANSAS			☹	☹		☹			☹	16	☹
CALIFORNIA						☹				18	☹
COLORADO					☹	☹			☹	18	☹
CONNECTICUT						☹			☹	15	☹
DELAWARE						☹				16	☹
D.C.						☹	☹			16	
FLORIDA	☹	☹	☹	☹	☹	☹		☹		18	☹
GEORGIA	☹	☹	☹	☹	☹	☹	☹		☹	16	
HAWAII						☹			☹	14	
IDAHO	☹	☹	☹	☹	☹	☹	☹	☹	☹	16	
ILLINOIS					☹	☹	☹			16	
INDIANA						☹				16	☹
IOWA						☹			☹	14	
KANSAS			☹	☹	☹	☹				16	☹
KENTUCKY						☹				16	
LOUISIANA	☹	☹	☹	☹		☹			☹	17	
MAINE						☹			☹	14	☹
MARYLAND		☹	☹	☹	☹	☹				16	

☹ = INDICATES LAWS PASSED
(or severe constipation, or both)

A STATE-BY-STATE LOOK AT CONSENSUAL CRIME

	HETERO ORAL SEX	HETERO ANAL SEX	GAY ORAL SEX	GAY ANAL SEX	ADULTERY	PROSTITUTION	FORNICATION	COHABITATION	PORNOGRAPHY	AGE OF CONSENT	ASSISTED SUICIDE
MASSACHUSETTS		☹		☹	☹	☹	☹			16	
MICHIGAN	☹	☹	☹	☹	☹	☹		☹	☹	16	☹
MINNESOTA	☹	☹	☹	☹	☹	☹	☹		☹	16	☹
MISSISSIPPI	☹	☹	☹	☹	☹	☹		☹		14	☹
MISSOURI			☹	☹		☹			☹	17	☹
MONTANA			☹	☹		☹			☹	16	☹
NEBRASKA					☹	☹			☹	17	☹
NEVADA						☹			☹	16	
NEW HAMPSHIRE					☹	☹				18	☹
NEW JERSEY						☹			☹	18	☹
NEW MEXICO						☹		☹		13	☹
NEW YORK					☹	☹				17	☹
NORTH CAROLINA	☹	☹	☹	☹	☹	☹		☹		16	
NORTH DAKOTA					☹	☹		☹	☹	16	☹
OHIO						☹			☹	16	
OKLAHOMA			☹	☹	☹	☹			☹	16	☹
OREGON						☹			☹	18	
PENNSYLVANIA						☹				16	☹
RHODE ISLAND	☹	☹	☹	☹	☹	☹			☹	16	
SOUTH CAROLINA	☹	☹	☹	☹	☹	☹	☹			16	
SOUTH DAKOTA						☹			☹	16	☹
TENNESSEE			☹	☹	☹	☹				18	☹
TEXAS						☹			☹	17	☹
UTAH	☹	☹	☹	☹	☹	☹	☹			18	
VERMONT						☹				16	
VIRGINIA	☹	☹	☹	☹	☹	☹	☹	☹	☹	15	
WASHINGTON						☹			☹	18	☹
WEST VIRGINIA					☹	☹	☹	☹	☹	16	
WISCONSIN					☹	☹			☹	18	☹
WYOMING						☹			☹	19	

AIN'T NOBODY'S BUSINESS IF YOU DO

We Must All Hang Together

When bad men combine,
the good must associate;
else they fall, one by one,
an unpitied sacrifice
in a contemptible struggle.

EDMUND BURKE

SIGNING THE DECLARA-TION of Independence was a dangerous act. To call the king of England a ty-rant—especially in such a public and eloquent way—was high treason, punish-able by death. Although the signers of the Declaration of Independence had differ-ent reasons for doing so, were very different indi-viduals, and had radically different political points of view, the executioner's rope could be equally effective for one and all. John Hancock was bold. He signed his name first and large. "There," he said; "King George should be able to read that without his spectacles." When Ben-jamin Franklin signed, he was expected to say something witty, pithy, and to the point; he was, after all, the greatest aphorist of his day. Franklin did not disappoint. "We must all hang together," he said, "or, most assuredly, we shall all hang separately."

The most popular American flag (prior to Betsy Ross's getting her hands on it) showed a snake divided in parts representing the thirteen colonies. The slogan was: UNITE OR DIE. All of us consensual criminals find ourselves in a similar situation today: we must unite or continue to have our rights denied by our own government. Another popular early flag showed the snake united, with the warning:

DON'T TREAD ON ME.

Another way of stressing the need for unity came from Mar-tin Niemoeller:

> *He that would make*
> *his own liberty secure*
> *must guard even his enemy*
> *from oppression.*
>
> — THOMAS PAINE
> 1795

In Germany they came first for the Communists, and I didn't speak up because I wasn't a Communist. Then they came for the Jews, and I didn't speak up because I wasn't a Jew. Then they came for the trade unionists, and I didn't speak up because I wasn't a trade unionist. Then they came for the Catholics, and I didn't speak up because I was a Protestant. Then they came for me, and by that time no one was left to speak up.

The people who oppose recreational drug use for health reasons must realize that the same people who outlaw recreational drugs now are working on outlawing certain vitamins, too. Prostitutes, gays, adulterers, sodomites, and heterosexuals who have sex outside of marriage all violate the same sexual taboo. (If you live in a state where sex outside of marriage, adultery, oral intercourse, or homosexual acts are legal, be assured that there are forces of the religious right who are working diligently right now to correct that legal and moral oversight.) The law that makes adults wear seat belts springs from the same paternalism—and political compromise—that would if it could (and apparently it can) regulate every other aspect of your life; for your own good, of course.

We are all chickens in the same farmer's yard. What would happen if the chickens all got mad at the farmer instead of pecking each other? Remember Alfred Hitchcock's *The Birds*? There is a reason falcons, lions, and tigers are not raised for their eggs, milk, and meat: chickens, cows, and sheep are far more docile; they don't complain when their eggs are taken, readily cooperate when being milked, and are easily led to slaughter.

There is, of course, the rare animal that does act up. It's branded a renegade, and quickly eliminated. If, however, the

AIN'T NOBODY'S BUSINESS IF YOU DO

entire group of animals—
that is, the entire *species*—
is known for acting up
when trod upon, these animals are, for the most part,
left alone. If consensual
criminals stood up not only
for their own rights, but
the rights of each other, we
would have the power to
keep the government from
treading upon us.

> *To preserve the freedom*
> *of the human mind then*
> *and freedom of the press,*
> *every spirit should be ready*
> *to devote itself to martyrdom.*
>
> THOMAS JEFFERSON
> June 18, 1799

The Politics of Change

> *To knock a thing down,*
> *especially if it is cocked*
> *at an arrogant angle,*
> *is a deep delight*
> *of the blood.*
>
> GEORGE SANTAYANA

THIS IS A CHAPTER ON what to do if you'd like to see the laws against consensual activities changed.

The single most effective form of change is one-on-one interaction with the people you come into contact with day-by-day. The next time someone condemns a consensual activity in your presence, you can ask the simple question, "Well, isn't that their own business?" Asking this, of course, may be like hitting a beehive with a baseball bat, and it may seem—after the commotion (and emotion) has died down—that attitudes have not changed. If, however, a beehive is hit often enough, the bees move somewhere else. Of course, you don't have to hit the same hive every time. If all the people who agree that the laws against consensual crimes should be repealed post haste would go around whacking (or at least firmly tapping) every beehive that presented itself, the bees would buzz less often.

Also, some people actually start to think when they are asked a question such as, "Shouldn't people be allowed to do with their own person and property whatever they choose as long as they do not physically harm the person or property of another?" Granted, these thinking people are few and far between, but they do exist and, perhaps, some of the people you know or meet may have never been asked that question. It is not a very popular one.

A good follow-up question: "Is it worth putting people in jail for doing these things?" Other possibilities: "Isn't it up to God to punish violations of God's laws?" "Who decides what is and is not 'right'?" "Don't we have more important things to worry about?" "Have *you* ever committed a consensual crime?" If "yes": "Do you think you might feel differently about laws against consensual activities if you had gone to jail for your crime?"

Although it may not seem so, asking such questions and challenging people's misconceptions is a political act. This personal contact is, in fact, the essence of politics. Change begins with individuals, and individuals communicating with individuals is the way attitudes are most often changed. If any of your thoughts or beliefs changed as you read this book, that's because we've been communicating one-on-one. When I write a book, I write to one person. I think of a book as a long letter I might write a friend.

In television, radio, and lectures, the most effective communicators are those who speak directly to individuals, not to a group. People like Larry King and Oprah Winfrey, and even Ross Perot, are effective communicators because they speak to people, not masses.

Changing one mind by talking to one person is more valuable than lecturing at one million people who walk away indifferent. You can make a change; you can make a difference in the thinking of the people with whom you naturally come into contact.

Another effective influence is through the media. Here, too, we can make personal statements. Writing letters to the editor, calling talk shows, asking questions from a studio audience gets your message out to thousands, even millions of people. A certain percentage of those people are going to personally relate to you, what you have to say, and the way you say it. You will probably never know who these people are, but—even if you seem to lose the argument with the host or guest on the show or even if the editor of the newspaper prints your letter with the

> *The only thing necessary*
> *for the triumph of evil*
> *is for good men to do nothing.*
>
> EDMUND BURKE
> 1770

> *Washington is a city*
> *of Southern efficiency*
> *and Northern charm.*
>
> JOHN F. KENNEDY

comment, "Get a load of what the kooks are writing these days!"—a certain number of people will accept what you have to say, and a change will be put in motion.

And then there's traditional politics.

Government is organized at three levels: local, state, and national (or federal). Any action you take on any of these levels counts. The simplest action is to write a letter or make a phone call. Here, of course, one must know whom to call or write.

At the national level, the four most important people to contact are (a) your two senators (every state has two), (b) the member of the House of Representatives who represents your congressional district (we each have one of those), and (c) the president of the United States. While technically senators are there to serve all the people of the United States, their special interest group is the citizens (more particularly the voters) of their home state. Similarly, every member of the House of Representatives is there to serve all the people of the United States, but representatives have a special interest in the needs and opinions of the voters in their congressional districts.

When the mail comes in to a congressional office, it is sorted into two piles: "Constituents" and "Everybody Else." The "Constituent" pile gets preferential treatment. This is not unfair—in fact, it's the way the system was designed: each citizen of the United States has the same number of representatives in Congress (two senators and one member of the House) who consider that citizen a constituent.* Members of the House of Representatives usually divide the "Everybody Else" pile into "My

---

*Of course if you have a vacation home in another state, that automatically doubles your list of potential political correspondents.

AIN'T NOBODY'S BUSINESS IF YOU DO

State" and "Those Other States." A member of Congress, then, will pay attention to, in order, (1) the voters within his or her own congressional district, (2) the rest of the citizens of his or her home state (he or she may run for statewide office one day), and (3) everyone else (he or she may run for president one day). The next group of

> *You should never wear your best trousers when you go out to fight for freedom and truth.*
>
> HENRIK IBSEN

people to write to, then, on the national level, are all the members of the House of Representatives from your state.

State governments are set up with variations, but generally there is a house of representatives (or an assembly) and a senate. Here, you also have elected representatives who consider you their constituents, and these are the people to write first (in addition, of course, to the governor). Start with the state senator and representative from your own senatorial and house (or assembly) districts.

Local government is a hodge-podge of city and county elected and appointed officials. To make change on a local level, however, it's worth your time to find out who runs the show. You might not be able to fight city hall, but you can sometimes influence it, and a call to city hall will get you the names and addresses of those in power.

When writing a public servant, there's no need to be elaborate or eloquent. Usually, your letter will not be read carefully—it will be scanned and summarized. If you're writing about a particular issue in the public debate, your letter will become part of a statistic. ("Today's mail: 673 letters in favor of [the topic]; 2,476 letters opposed.") The same is true of phone calls, post cards, telegrams, and e-mail. Even though you're just a number, you are an important number.

The religious right is well organized and can produce massive mailings (millions of pieces) on key issues within a few days.

> *One man can completely change*
> *the character of a country,*
> *and the industry of its people,*
> *by dropping a single seed*
> *in fertile soil.*
>
> JOHN C. GIFFORD

You can bet that, for the most part, they are going to favor enacting more laws against consensual activities, strict enforcement of the laws we already have, and, in the name of the Prince of Peace, violently oppose repealing or eliminating any oppressive law. No similar network exists for those who favor eliminating laws against consensual activities, and the legislators know this. Each letter, then, that comes in supporting a position *not* endorsed by the religious right is given special attention—and extra weight—by most legislators. As the religious right can "out-letter" its opposition by a ratio that is sometimes 10 to 1, one letter in favor of our freedom can count for as many as ten letters written by those who think our laws should be dictated by their moral code.

A copy of this book was sent to all members of the United States Senate and House of Representatives, as well as to the legislators and governors of all fifty states, and to the mayors of the top 100 cities (those who held office as of April 1996). If you generally agree with the idea of this book, please write your elected representatives: "Have you read the book, *Ain't Nobody's Business If You Do?* If not, I certainly recommend it. After you read the book, I would appreciate your thoughts on it."

An amazing number of consensual crimes can be repealed on the local level. In fact, most consensual crimes are enforced on the state and local, not the federal, level. People working at the state and local levels to dismantle the laws against consensual activities—and to keep new ones from being put on the books— could give us a free country in a short time.

⚖️ ⚖️ ⚖️

At the other end of the spectrum, perhaps the thing to do is to propose a constitutional amendment that restates what is already in the Constitution. The amendment might read:

> No citizen of the United States, or the several States, shall be subject to criminal prosecution unless he or she physically harms the person or property of a nonconsenting other.

The hottest places in hell are reserved for those who in a period of moral crisis maintain their neutrality.

DANTE

That would lay it out clearly, I think. The "or the several States" insures that state governments don't pass restrictive codes in the name of "states' rights."

Proposing a constitutional amendment would stir a national debate, as well as directly counter the religious right's desire to introduce a constitutional amendment declaring the United States a "Christian nation."

⚖ ⚖ ⚖

Obviously, a lot of work needs to be done. The religious right is well financed, well organized, and *big*. It is involved in politics as an *act of religious faith*. Those who do not believe that religion and politics should be one and the same don't seem to have the same fervor when it comes to political action. The religious right has also co-opted every phrase and symbol that those who fought religious oppression once rallied around. *Freedom, liberty* (Jerry Falwell's institute of higher political learning is called Liberty University), the American flag, the Liberty Bell—even the word *American.**

---

*That the religious right completely took over the word *Christian* is a given. At one time, phrases such as *Christian charity* and *Christian tolerance* were used to denote kindness and compassion. To perform a "Christian" act meant an act of giving, of acceptance, of toleration. Now, *Christian* is in-

> *What we have now is democracy*
> *without citizens.*
> *No one is on the public's side.*
> *All the buyers*
> *are on the corporation's side.*
> *And the bureaucrats*
> *in the administration*
> *don't think the government*
> *belongs to the people.*
>
> RALPH NADER

Because there is such formidable opposition, those of us who believe that the laws against consensual activities should be repealed have our work cut out for us. Saying that people should be permitted to do with their person and property what they choose as long as they don't physically harm the person or property of another is not perceived by the religious right as a political statement, but as *an attack on God.* Those who are not willing to take the heat of the emotional outburst that will inevitably follow will soon leave the kitchen.

Then there are those who want to keep the laws against consensual activities in place due to greed. Lots of people are making lots of money because certain consensual activities are illegal. Naturally, they do not want to lose any meal tickets.

Those who want personal freedom in this country, then, have such interesting and diverse opponents as organized crime on one hand, and law enforcement on the other. Organized crime would practically go out of business if all consensual activities were legal. The politicians and media that organized crime already owns (or has a few favors coming from) will be opposed to legalizing consensual activities—but will oppose it with the highest moral, legal, social, and even scientific justifications. Law enforcement would (a) lose funding (the tens of billions being thrown at it to fight the war on drugs plus all that assets forfeiture money), and (b) have to catch real criminals (who have *guns).* The big businesses that currently make a fortune on legal (including prescription) drugs don't want any of the currently illegal drugs cluttering up the marketplace. This is a spectrum that has

variably linked to right-wing conservative political thought—*Christian nation, Christian morality, Christian values, Christian family.*

tobacco and alcohol companies at one end and the AMA and pharmaceutical companies at the other.

Yes, consensual crimes make strange bedfellows: organized crime and law enforcement; cigarette companies and the AMA. Not surprisingly, none of them wants to get out of bed. People can be as passionate about money as they can about God (if not more so).

> *"Do you pray for the Senators, Dr. Hale?"* someone asked the chaplain.
>
> *No, I look at the Senators and pray for the country.*
>
> EDWARD EVERETT HALE

⚖ ⚖ ⚖

I cannot point to the Democratic or Republican party and say, "Here, join this party; they support this cause." Neither political party supports this cause; nor do, necessarily, either liberals or conservatives. Take a guess, for example, at the political orientation of the author of the following piece, published in a letters to the editor column of *American Heritage* magazine, May/June 1993:

> Would you want your son or daughter or spouse to spend their [sic] days smoking crack, or injecting heroin, or hallucinating on LSD? . . .
>
> I remain convinced that the drugs we outlaw today must remain illegal, because I have personally witnessed the effects of drugs too often and too painfully. I have seen crack babies, trembling, their minds and bodies damaged by their mothers' drug abuse. . . . I have seen innocent victims maimed and murdered by drug addicts. . . .
>
> Candidly, no society has ever or will ever succeed in abolishing the use of all mind-altering drugs, just as no society in the foreseeable future will succeed in abolishing all cancer. But that doesn't mean we can simply throw up our hands and say we won't even defend ourselves against these plagues. While the cost of prohibit-

ing drugs is high, the cost of legalizing them would be much, much higher.

Drugs are cancer. Trembling crack babies. Sound like some of George Bush's comments? Pat Robertson's? Pat Buchanan's? Rush Limbaugh's? No, these words come from a person some consider to be the prototypical liberal, Governor Mario Cuomo of New York. There is no guarantee that a liberal's bleeding heart is going to bleed for the cause of repealing the laws against consensual activities. (What about all the prisoners, Mario? What about the prisoners' families?)

Dave Barry made these astute observations:

> The Democrats seem to be basically nicer people, but they have demonstrated time and time again that they have the management skills of celery. They're the kind of people who'd stop to help you change a flat, but would somehow manage to set your car on fire. I would be reluctant to entrust them with a Cuisinart, let alone the economy. The Republicans, on the other hand, would know how to fix your tire, but they wouldn't bother to stop because they'd want to be on time for Ugly Pants Night at the country club.

Removing the prohibitions from consensual activities will probably take place due to popular opinion within both political parties. When Prohibition was enacted in 1920, both parties strongly favored it. By 1924, the Republicans still strongly favored it, and the Democrats were vacillating. By 1928, the Democrats opposed it, but the Republicans still favored it. By the election of 1932, both parties opposed Prohibition. That's the politics of change.

In the 1992 election, Ross Perot introduced the urgency of

reducing the national debt and, due to the immediate popular support of this idea, it was quickly adopted by both parties. The idea of eliminating the laws against consensual activities will probably gain acceptance along the same lines. (And, I pray, as quickly.)

The political party that supports this concept—in

> *When you hear a man speak of his love for his country, it is a sign that he expects to be paid for it.*
>
> H. L. MENCKEN

fact, seems to be based on it—is the Libertarian party. Although its political philosophy is interesting and its information educational, I doubt if the majority of the American people are going to switch party affiliations in order to support this one issue. When the idea of eliminating consensual crimes becomes popular enough, one of the major political parties will adopt it, thus removing whatever wind the Libertarian sails might have captured. People, however, may be so fed up with both the Democratic and the Republican parties that they'll switch to Libertarianism just for the hell of it.*

The people most motivated to change the laws against consensual activities, of course, are those who have been arrested for them, and the "criminals'" friends and families. That includes the 750,000 people currently in jail, the 3,000,000 currently on parole or probation, the 4,000,000 arrested each year, as well as their loved ones. These are people who know, from personal experience, the absurdity of laws against consensual activities. They also know the arbitrary and often cruel ways in which these laws are enforced.

One can only quote Woody Guthrie's advice to union organizers: "Take it easy, but take it." So often, people trapped in the legal system alternate between rage and resignation. Neither emotion will help repeal the laws against consensual activities. A

*You can contact the Libertarian Party at 1–800–637–1776.

> *Under democracy one party
> always devotes its chief energies
> to trying to prove that
> the other party is unfit to rule—
> and both commonly succeed,
> and are right.*
>
> H. L. MENCKEN

middle ground in which the rage is channeled into constructive action not only provides an effective outlet for one's justifiable frustration; it gives one the satisfaction of, day by day, doing his or her part to change an unjust system.

⚖️ ⚖️ ⚖️

And let's not forget the value of *money.* Donate some to organizations that defend personal freedom. If you have no money to send, write a note of encouragement to a group whose work you admire.

Here is a criminally incomplete list of organizations and publications currently fighting for freedom. I will be happy to correct my omissions in future editions and on my web site (http://www.mcwilliams.com/consent).

The Libertarian Party
2600 Virginia Avenue N.W. - Suite 100
Washington, DC 20037
800 / 637-1776
(http://www.lp.org/lp) *[those are lower case L's not numeral 1's]*

The political party that believes government should stay out of individual lives. Not as powerful as it might be (yet), the Libertarian Party certainly offers a refreshing alternative to the Democrats and Republicans, who both— for vastly different reasons—think it's just fine to meddle in our lives and tax the bejesus out of us to pay for all that costly interference.

American Civil Liberties Union (ACLU)
132 West 43rd Street
New York, NY 10036
212 / 944-9800
(http://www.aclu.org)

Since 1920 (that ominous year of National Prohibition), the ACLU has been at the forefront of defending rights guaranteed us by the Constitution. The ACLU has been so successful in bringing test cases before the Supreme Court that Pat Buchanan, unable to eliminate the ACLU, now wants to eliminate the Supreme Court.

"The ACLU believes that unless they do harm to others, people should not be punished—even if they do harm to themselves." My, that has a familiar ring to it.

People for the American Way
200 M Street N.W. - Suite 400
Washington, DC 20036
202 / 467-4999
(http://www.pfaw.org)

While occasionally more liberal than libertarian, People for the American Way performs the essential service of directly countering the work of the Christian Coalition, Pat Robertson's well-financed and painfully effective religious right political group. The People for the American Way, founded by Norman Lear, works to keep creationism out of textbooks and repressive religious-based legislation out of law books.

Cato Institute
1000 Massachusetts Avenue N.W.
Washington, DC 20001
202 / 842-0200
(http://www.cato.org)

Cato's web page boldly proclaims: "Promoting public policy based on limited government, free markets, individual liberty, and peace." Cato publishes some great books on ending consensual crimes. Its web page has links to other liberty and freedom web sites, including local organizations (such as Oregon's stellar Cascade Institute) and student groups.

The Drug Policy Institute
4455 Connecticut Avenue N.W. - Suite B-500
Washington, DC 20008
202 / 537-5005

A think-tank warring against the war on drugs. Dignified, distinguished, factual. The board of directors includes the mayor of Baltimore, a U.S. District Judge, a New Haven Chief of Police, professors and lawyers galore. A fascinating quarterly newsletter (magazine) comes with membership.

National Drug Strategy Network
1899 L Street N.W. - Suite 500
Washington, DC 20036
202 / 835-9075

A division of the Criminal Justice Policy Foundation, the National Drug Strategy Network publishes a monthly *News Briefs* which reports major milestones in drug prohibition.

National Organization for the
Repeal of Marijuana Laws (NORML)
1001 Connecticut Avenue N.W. - Suite 1010
Washington, DC 20036
202 / 483-5500
(http://www.norml.org)

The laws against marijuana are the most illogical of all drug laws: in 10,000 years of known human use, not one death has been caused by a "marijuana overdose." When you consider that hundreds of thousands of glaucoma suffers, chemotherapy patients, people with AIDS, and others could benefit from the medicinal uses of marijuana, the laws against marijuana are criminal. NORML focuses on overturning these absurd laws. It publishes a quarterly newspaper, *Active Resistance*.

Families Against Mandatory Minimums Foundation (FAMM)
1001 Pennsylvania Avenue N.W. - Suite 200 South
Washington, DC 20004
202 / 457-5790
(http://famm.org)

Due to mandatory minimum sentencing, drug possessors (not even dealers) often spend more time in prison than murders, rapists, and people who produce infomercials (crimes which do not have mandatory minimums).

How mandatory are the mandatory minimums? In 1995, U.S. District Court Judge Lyle E. Storm tried to give two crack cocaine defendants a break and sentence them to "only" 20 years each. The U.S. Court of Appeals ordered Judge Storm to resentence the defendants to the mandatory minimum: 30 years each.

"I know it's no justification or solace to you, but I am saying to you there is no justification to this sentence," Judge Storm told the defendants at the sentencing. "I apologize to you on behalf of the United States government." Families Against Mandatory Minimums fight atrocities within absurdities such as this.

The Fully Informed Jury Association
P. O. Box 59
Helmville, MT 59843
406 / 793-5550

Here's a grass-roots way of ending consensual crime prosecution, one juror at a time. The Fully Informed Jury Association promotes a fact that is as true as it is potentially powerful: once twelve jurors go into the deliberation room, when they decide to acquit *for whatever reason,* the "criminal" walks free. If the jury believes the defendant did take part in a prohibited consensual activity but the activity shouldn't be a crime, it can acquit. In most states, even if one juror feels this way, the worst that would happen is a hung jury, and the state has to start all over again. (With minor consensual crimes, the state sometimes doesn't bother.) Read all about it in *FIJActivist*, the newsletter of the Fully Informed Jury Association.

Laissez Faire Books
938 Howard Street - #202
San Francisco, CA 94103
415 / 541-9780
(http://www.lf.org) *[that's a lower case L in "lf," not the numeral 1]*

Laissez Faire has the largest catalog of books from all publishers on the subjects of liberty, freedom, and the government leaving us blessedly alone. Laissez Faire Books defines *laissez faire* as "Leave the people alone, let them be, in their economic activities, in their religious affairs, in thought and culture, in the pursuit of fulfillment in their own lives."

Council for Democratic and Secular Humanism
(Free Inquiry Magazine and *Secular Humanist Bulletin)*
3965 Amherst
New York, NY 14228
716 / 636-7571
(http://codesh.org)

The term *secular humanism* has been so thoroughly trashed by the religious right (it's essentially the religious right's replacement for the F-WORD—with none of the F-WORD's more pleasant meanings), it might be interesting to see what secular humanists really believe. This list of principles taken from the web page of Council for Democratic and Secular Humanism, publishers of *Free Inquiry Magazine* and *Secular Humanist Bulletin*:

- We are committed to the application of reason and science to the understanding of the universe and to the solving of human problems.

- We deplore efforts to denigrate human intelligence, to

seek to explain the world in supernatural terms, and to look outside nature for salvation.

- We believe that scientific discovery and technology can contribute to the betterment of human life.

- We believe in an open and pluralistic society and that democracy is the best guarantee of protecting human rights from authoritarian elites and repressive majorities.

- We are committed to the principle of the separation of church and state.

- We cultivate the arts of negotiation and compromise as a means of resolving differences and achieving mutual understanding.

- We are concerned with securing justice and fairness in society and with eliminating discrimination and intolerance.

- We believe in supporting the disadvantaged and the handicapped so that they will be able to help themselves.

- We attempt to transcend divisive parochial loyalties based on race, religion, gender, nationality, creed, class, sexual orientation, or ethnicity, and strive to work together for the common good of humanity.

- We want to protect and enhance the earth, to preserve it for future generations, and to avoid inflicting needless suffering on other species.

- We believe in enjoying life here and now and in developing our creative talents to their fullest.

- We believe in the cultivation of moral excellence.

- We respect the right to privacy. Mature adults should be allowed to fulfill their aspirations, to express their sexual preferences, to exercise reproductive freedom, to have access to comprehensive and informed healthcare, and to die with dignity.

- We believe in the common moral decencies: altruism, integrity, honesty, truthfulness, responsibility. Humanist ethics is amendable to critical, rational guidance. There are normative standards that we discover together. Moral principles are tested by their consequences.

- We are deeply concerned with the moral education of our children. We want to nourish reason and compassion.

- We are engaged by the arts no less than by the sciences.

- We are citizens of the universe and are excited by discoveries still to be made in the cosmos.

- We are skeptical of untested claims of knowledge, and we are open to novel ideas and seek new departures in our thinking.

- We affirm humanism as a realistic alternative to the theologies of violence and as a source of rich personal significance and genuine satisfaction in the service to others.

- We believe in optimism rather than pessimism, hope rather than despair, learning in the place of dogma, truth instead of ignorance, joy rather than guilt or sin, tolerance in the place of fear, love instead of hatred, compassion over selfishness, beauty instead of ugliness, and reason rather than blind faith or irrationality.

- We believe in the fullest realization of the best and noblest that we are capable of as human beings.

High Times Magazine
235 Park Avenue South - Fifth Floor
New York, NY 10003
212 / 387-0500
(http://hightimes.com)

This magazine is both fun and informative. It's hard to determine which is more interesting, the articles or the advertisements. The *High Times* web begins with this warning, which certainly applies to the magazine as well:

> Warning! This HIGH TIMES web site contains information about hemp, marijuana and psychedelic drugs (such as LSD and ecstasy). Some of the subjects covered include cannabis cultivation, drug laws, pot humor, high art, drug tests, legal highs, industrial uses of hemp such as paper, hemp clothing, hemp foods, hemp oil and other hemp products, the legalization of marijuana, the

recreational use of marijuana, the medical uses of marijuana, and the worldwide uses of hemp and marijuana . . .

The information you are about to read is for informational purposes only and is designed for adults only. HIGH TIMES does not promote the use of marijuana or other recreational or illicit drugs, including alcohol or tobacco, by minors. For this reason, we must request that you verify that you are 21 years or older.

Once the minors are removed and it's just the Haight Ashbury survivors left, the *High Times* web site lightens up: "Finally! Somewhere you can relax, light a phattie, and enjoy the atmosphere." Phattie? By the context I'm pretty sure I know what that means, but I didn't know before. I'm not even sure how to pronounce it. God, I'm getting old. It reminds me of a Firesign Theater routine in which the police go about arresting all the old farts like me who are no longer cool. "Check out his body paint," says one cop. His partner replies, voice mixed with pity and contempt: "Faded San Francisco art nouveau."

These are interesting times. The idea that the government should leave people alone unless they are physically harming the person or property of others is catching on quickly, and from many directions. Simultaneously, the forces that want more government intervention in our lives are gathering political momentum. Yes, these are interesting times. The Chinese have an ancient saying, "May you live in interesting times."

Unfortunately, the Chinese use it as a curse.

ABOUT THE AUTHOR

PETER McWILLIAMS has been writing about his passions since 1967. In that year, he became passionate about what most seventeen-year-olds are passionate about—love—and wrote *Come Love With Me & Be My Life.* This began a series of poetry books which have sold nearly four million copies.

Along with love, of course, comes loss, so Peter became passionate about emotional survival. In 1971 he wrote *Surviving the Loss of a Love,* which was expanded in 1976 and again in 1991 (with co-authors Melba Colgrove, Ph.D., and Harold Bloomfield, M.D.) into *How to Survive the Loss of a Love.* It has sold more than two million copies.

He also became interested in meditation, and a book he wrote on meditation was a *New York Times* bestseller, knocking the impregnable *Joy of Sex* off the #1 spot. As one newspaper headline proclaimed, MEDITATION MORE POPULAR THAN SEX AT THE *NEW YORK TIMES.*

His passion for computers (or more accurately, for what computers could do) led to *The Personal Computer Book,* which *Time* proclaimed "a beacon of simplicity, sanity and humor," and the *Wall Street Journal* called "genuinely funny." (Now, really, how many people has the *Wall Street Journal* called "genuinely funny"?)

His passion for personal growth continues in the ongoing LIFE 101 Series. Thus far, the books in this series include *You Can't Afford the Luxury of a Negative Thought: A Book for People with Any Life-Threatening Illness—Including Life*; *LIFE 101: Everything We Wish We Had Learned About Life In School—But Didn't* (a *New York Times* bestseller in both hardcover and paperback); *DO IT! Let's Get Off Our Buts* (a #1 *New York Times* hardcover bestseller); and *WEALTH 101: Wealth Is Much More Than Money.*

His passion for visual beauty led him to publish, in 1992, his first book of photography, *PORTRAITS,* a twenty-two-year anthology of his photographic work.

In 1994, after successfully being treated for depression, he wrote with Harold Bloomfield, M.D., *How to Heal Depression.*

His fifteen-year sojourn through John-Roger's destructive cult, the Church of the Movement of Spiritual Inner Awareness (MSIA), is documented (with a surprising degree of humor) in *LIFE 102: What to Do When Your Guru Sues You.*

All of the above-mentioned books were self-published and are still in print.

Peter McWilliams has appeared on *The Oprah Winfrey Show, Larry King* (both radio and television), *Donahue, Sally Jessy Raphael,* and, a long time ago, the *Regis Philbin Show* (before Regis met Kathie Lee—probably before Kathie Lee was *born).*

Personal freedom, individual expression, and the right to live one's own life, as long as one does not harm the person or property of another, have long been his passions. Now, he writes about them.

The complete text
of most of Peter McWilliams' books,
including an elaborately indexed
version of this book,
are available free on the Internet:

http://www.mcwilliams.com

I have only made
this [letter] longer
because I have not
had the time
to make it shorter.

BLAISE PASCAL
1657

Bibliography

Adams, Abby, comp. *An Uncommon Scold.* New York: Simon & Schuster, 1989.

Adams, Edie, and Robert Windeler. *Sing A Pretty Song. . . : The "Offbeat" Life of Edie Adams, Including the Ernie Kovacs Years.* New York: Morrow, 1990.

Alley, Robert S., ed. *James Madison on Religious Liberty.* Buffalo: Prometheus Books, 1985.

Almodovar, Norma Jean. *Cop to Call Girl: Why I Left the LAPD to Make an Honest Living as a Beverly Hills Prostitute.* New York: Simon & Schuster, 1993.

Anderson, Patrick. *High in America: The True Story Behind NORML and the Politics of Marijuana.* New York: Viking, 1981.

Andrew, Christopher. *The First World War: Causes and Consequences.* New York: Paul Hamlyn, 1969.

Andrist, Ralph K., ed. *The American Heritage History of the 20's & 30's.* New York: American Heritage Publishing Co., 1970.

Appleby, Amy, ed. *Quentin Crisp's Book of Quotations.* New York: MacMillan, 1989.

Bailyn, Bernard. *The Ideological Origins of the American Revolution.* Enlarged Edition. Cambridge, MA: Harvard University, Belknap Press, 1992.

Barrett, Marvin. *A Dramatic View of the Twenties and Thirties.* Boston: Little, Brown and Company, 1962.

Barry, Dave. *Dave Barry's Greatest Hits.* New York: Fawcett Columbine, 1988.

_____. *Dave Barry Slept Here: A Sort of History of the United States.* New York: Fawcett Columbine, 1989.

Barth, Alan. *The Rights of Free Men: An Essential Guide to Civil Liberties.* New York: Knopf, 1984.

Bazelon, David L. *Questioning Authority: Justice and Criminal Law.* New York: Knopf, 1988.

Bergland, David. *Libertarianism In One Lesson.* Costa Mesa, CA: Orpheus Publications, 1984.

Blumenfeld, Warren J., ed. *Homophobia: How We All Pay the Price.* Boston: Beacon, 1992.

Boatner, Mark M. III. *The Encyclopedia of the American Revolution.* New York: McKay, 1966.

Booth, Father Leo. *When God Becomes a Drug: Breaking the Chains of Religious Addiction & Abuse.* Los Angeles: Tarcher, 1991.

Boswell, John. *Christianity, Social Tolerance, and Homosexuality: Gay People in Western Europe from the Beginning of the Christian Era to the Fourteenth Century.* Chicago: University of Chicago Press, 1980.

Bowen, Catherine Drinker. *The Most Dangerous Man in America: Scenes from the Life of Benjamin Franklin.* Boston: Little, Brown and Company, Atlantic Monthly Press, 1974.

Bowen, Ezra, ed. *This Fabulous Century, Sixty Years of American Life.* Volume II: 1910-1920. New York: TimeLife Books, 1969.

_____, ed. *This Fabulous Century.* Volume III: 1920-1930. New York: TimeLife Books, 1969.

Brecher, Edward M. *Licit and Illicit Drugs: The Consumers Union Report on Narcotics, Stimulants, Depressants, Inhalants, Hallucinogens, and Marijuana Including Caffeine, Nicotine, and Alcohol.* Boston: Little, Brown and Company, 1972.

Buckley, William F., Jr. *Right Reason.* "A Collection Selected by Richard Brookhiser." Garden City, NY: Doubleday, 1985.

Calkins, Carrol C., ed. *The Story of America.* Pleasantville, NY: The Reader's Digest Association, Inc., 1975.

Carmen, Arlene, and Howard Moody. *Working Women: The Subterranean World of Street Prostitution.* New York: Harper & Row, 1985.

Carson, Gerald. *The Social History of Bourbon: An Unhurried Account of Our Star Spangled American Drink.* New York: Dodd, Mead, 1963.

Cerf, Christopher, and Victor Navasky. *The Experts Speak: The Definitive Compendium of Authoritative Misinformation.* New York: Pantheon Books, 1984.

Chancellor, John. *Peril and Promise: A Commentary on America.* New York: Harper & Row, 1990.

Church, F. Forrester. *God and Other Famous Liberals: Reclaiming the Politics of America.* New York: Simon & Schuster, 1991.

Coontz, Stephanie. *The Way We Never Were: American Families and the Nostalgia Trap.* New York: HarperCollins, Basic Books, 1992.

Coote, Colin, and Denzil Batchelor. *Winston S. Churchill's Maxims and Reflections.* New York: Barnes & Noble, 1992.

Cowan, Thomas. *Gay Men & Women Who Enriched the World.* New Canaan, CT: Mulvey, 1988.

Currie, Elliott. *Reckoning: Drugs, the Cities, and the American Future.* New York: Farrar, Straus and Giroux, Hill and Wang, 1993.

Davis, Burke. *George Washington and the American Revolution.* New York: Random House, 1975.

Dover, K. J. *Greek Homosexuality.* New York: Random House, Vintage, 1978.

Duster, Troy. *The Legislation of Morality: Law, Drugs, and Moral Judgement.* New York: The Free Press, 1970.

Dynes, Wayne R., ed. *Encyclopedia of Homosexuality,* Vols. 1 and 2. New York: Garland, 1990.

Earley, Pete. *The Hot House: Life Inside Leavenworth Prison.* New York: Bantam, 1992.

Earth Works Group. *50 Simple Things You Can Do To Save the Earth.* Berkeley: Earthworks Press, 1989.

Ellman, Richard. *Oscar Wilde.* New York: Knopf, 1988.

Federal Bureau of Investigation. *Uniform Crime Reports for the United States 1991.*

Feinberg, Joel. *The Moral Limits of the Criminal Law: Vol. 3, Harm to Self.* New York: Oxford, 1986.

_____. *The Moral Limits of the Criminal Law: Vol. 4, Harmless Wrongdoing.* New York: Oxford, 1988.

Ferris, Robert G., ed. *Signers of the Constitution.* Washington: U.S. Department of the Interior, 1976.

_____, ed. *Signers of the Declaration.* Washington: U.S. Department of the Interior, 1975.

Flanagan, Timothy J., and Kathleen Maguire, eds. *Bureau of Justice Statistics Sourcebook of Criminal Justice Statistics.* Washington: U.S. Government Printing Office.

Foner, Eric, and John A. Garraty, eds. *The Reader's Companion to American History.* Boston: Houghton Mifflin Company, 1991.

Friedman, Milton. *Capitalism and Freedom.* Chicago: University of Chicago Press, 1962.

Fromm, Erich. *Escape from Freedom.* New York: Avon Books, 1969.

Geis, Gilbert. *Not the Law's Business? An Examination of Homosexuality, Abortion, Prostitution, Narcotics and Gambling in the United States.* Rockville, MD: National Institute of Mental Health, 1972.

Gerberg, Mort. *The U.S. Constitution for Everyone.* New York: Putnam, Perigee Books, 1987.

Gilfoyle, Timothy J. *City of Eros: New York City, Prostitution, and the Commercialization of Sex, 1790-1920.* New York: Norton, 1992.

Green, Mark, ed. *Changing America: Blueprints for the New Administration.* "A Citizens Transition Project." New York: Newmarket Press, 1992.

Grinspoon, Lester. *Marihuana Reconsidered.* Cambridge: Harvard University Press, 1971.

Gross, K. Hawkeye. *Drug Smuggling: The Forbidden Book.* Boulder: Paladin Press, 1992.

Grun, Bernard. *The Timetables of History of People and Events.* New, Updated Edition. "Based on Werner Stein's *Kulturfahrplan.*" New York: Simon & Schuster, 1979.

Hadden, Briton, and Henry R. Luce, eds. *Time Capsule/1923: A History of the Year Condensed From the Pages of Time.* New York: Time Incorporated, 1967.

Hamowy, Ronald, ed. *Dealing With Drugs: Consequences of Government Control.* San Francisco: Pacific Research Institute for Public Policy, 1987.

Harris, Richard. *The Fear of Crime.* New York: Praeger, 1969.

Herer, Jack. *The Emperor Wears No Clothes: Hemp & The Marijuana Conspiracy.* Revised Edition. Van Nuys, CA: HEMP Publishing, 1992.

Heward, Edward Vincent. *St. Nicotine of the Peace Pipe.* London: George Routledge & Sons, 1909.

Higginbotham, Don. *The War of American Independence.* New York: Macmillan, 1971.

Hilton, Bruce. *Can Homophobia Be Cured? Wrestling with Questions That Challenge the Church.* Nashville: Abingdon Press, 1992.

Hodges, Andrew. *Alan Turing: The Enigma.* New York: Simon & Schuster, 1983.

Hoffman, Frederick J. *The Twenties: American Writing in the Postwar Decade.* Rev. Ed. New York: Macmillan, The Free Press, 1962.

Hoffman, Mark S., ed. *The World Almanac and Book of Facts 1993*. New York: Pharos Books, 1992.

Hofstadter, Richard. *The Paranoid Style and American Politics*. New York: Knopf, 1965.

Hoover, J. Edgar. *Masters of Deceit: The Story of Communism and How to Fight It*. New York: Henry Holt, 1958.

Hunter, Nan D., Sherryl E. Michaelson, and Thomas B. Stoddard. *The Rights of Lesbians and Gay Men: The Basic ACLU Guide to a Gay Person's Rights*. Carbondale, IL: Southern Illinois University Press, 1992.

Hutchens, John K., ed. *The American Twenties: A Literary Panorama*. Philadelphia: J.B. Lippincott Company, 1952.

International Association of Chiefs of Police. *Building Integrity and Reducing Drug Corruption in Police Departments*. Monograph NJC 120652, September 1989. Washington: U.S. Department of Justice, 1992.

Janus, Samuel S., and Cynthia L. Janus. *The Janus Report on Sexual Behavior*. New York: John Wiley & Sons, 1993.

Jensen, Merrill. *The Making of the American Constitution*. Malabar, FL: Robert E. Krieger, 1958. Reprint 1979.

Johnson, Otto, ed. *Information Please Almanac Atlas & Yearbook 1993*. Boston: Houghton Mifflin, 1993.

Johnson, Paul. *A History of Christianity*. New York: Atheneum, 1976.

Kaltenborn, H. V. *It Seems Like Yesterday*. New York: G.P. Putnam's Sons, 1956.

Karnow, Stanley. *Vietnam: A History*. New York: Viking, 1983.

Katz, Jonathan Ned. *Gay American History*. New York: Harper & Row, 1985.

_____. *Gay/Lesbian Almanac: A New Documentary*. New York: Harper & Row, 1983.

Kettelhack, Guy, comp. *The Wit and Wisdom of Quentin Crisp*. New York: Harper & Row, 1984.

King, Coretta Scott, ed. *The Martin Luther King, Jr., Companion: Quotations from the Speeches, Essays, and Books of Martin Luther King, Jr.* New York: St. Martin's Press, 1993.

Krassner, Paul, ed. *Best of The Realist*. Philadelphia: Running Press, 1984.

Larzelere, Bob. *The Harmony of Love*. San Francisco: Context Publications, 1982.

Leary, Timothy. *High Priest*. New York: World Publishing Company, 1968.

Lett, AlexSandra. *Natural Living: From Stress to Rest*. Raleigh, NC: ALL Communications, 1984.

Levy, Leonard W. *The Establishment Clause: Religion and the First Amendment*. New York: MacMillan, 1986.

Leyland, Winston, ed. *Gay Sunshine Interviews, Vol. 1*. San Francisco: Gay Sunshine Press, 1978.

Locke, John. *A Letter Concerning Toleration*. Edited by Charles L. Sherman. Chicago: *Encyclopedia Britannica*, 1952.

Logan, Joshua. *Movie Stars, Real People, and Me*. New York: Delacorte Press, 1978.

Ludlam, Charles. *The Complete Plays of Charles Ludlam*. New York: Harper & Row, 1989.

Maggio, Rosalie, comp. *The Beacon Book of Quotations by Women*. Boston: Beacon, 1992.

Mannix, Daniel P. *The History of Torture*. New York: Dorset, 1986.

Marsh, Dave. *50 Ways to Fight Censorship and Important Facts to Know About the Censors*. New York: Thunder's Mouth Press, 1991.

McKenna, George, and Stanley Feingold, eds. *Taking Sides: Clashing Views on Controversial Political Issues*, 7th Edition. Guilford, CT: Dushkin Publishing Group, 1991.

McKenna, Terence. *Food of the Gods: The Search for the Original Tree of Knowledge: A Radical History of Plants, Drugs, and Human Evolution*. New York: Bantam, 1992.

Mitford, Jessica. *Kind and Usual Punishment: The Prison Business*. New York: Knopf, 1973.

Montgomery Ward & Co. *Catalogue and Buyer's Guide No. 57, Spring and Summer 1895.* "An unabridged reprint of the original edition with a new introduction by Boris Emmet." New York: Dover Publications, Inc., 1969.

National Narcotics Intelligence Consumers Committee. *The NNICC Report 1991: The Supply of Illicit Drugs to the United States.* Washington: Drug Enforcement Administration, 1992.

New York Public Library. *The New York Public Library Desk Reference.* "A Stonesong Press Book." New York: Webster's New World, 1989.

Noble, William. *Bookbanning In America: Who Bans Books? And Why.* Middlebury, VT: Eriksson, 1990.

Office of National Drug Control Policy. *National Drug Control Strategy: A Nation Responds to Drug Use: Budget Summary,.* Washington: The White House.

Osborne, David, and Ted Gaebler. *Reinventing Government: How the Entrepreneurial Spirit is Transforming the Public Sector.* New York: Penguin, 1993.

Packer, Herbert L. *The Limits of the Criminal Sanction.* Stanford: Stanford University Press, 1968.

Paine, Thomas. *Common Sense.* Audiotape version. Nashville: Knowledge Products

Paxton, John, and Sheila Fairfield. *Calendar of Creative Man.* New York: Facts on File, 1979.

Petras, Ross, and Kathryn Petras. *The 776 Stupidest Things Ever Said.* New York: Doubleday, 1993.

QuallsCorbett, Nancy. *The Sacred Prostitute: Eternal Aspect of the Feminine.* Toronto: Inner City Books, 1988.

QuickVerse for Windows Version 1.0G. Hiawatha, IA: Parsons Technology, Inc.

Radcliff, Peter, ed. *Limits of Liberty: Studies of Mill's "On Liberty."* Belmont, CA: Wadsworth Publishing Company, 1966.

Reiterman, Tim, with John Jacobs. *Raven: The Untold Story of the Rev. Jim Jones and His People.* New York: Dutton, 1982.

Robertson, Pat. *The New Millennium: 10 Trends That Will Impact You and Your Family by the Year 2000.* Dallas: Word Publishing, 1990.

Rogers, Agnes, comp. *I Remember Distinctly: A Family Album of the American People 1918–1941.* New York: Harper & Brothers, 1947.

Sann, Paul. *The Lawless Decade: A Pictorial History of a Great American Transition: From the World War I Armistice and Prohibition to Repeal and the New Deal.* New York: Crown, 1957.

Scanzoni, Letha, and Virginia Ramey Mollenkott. *Is the Homosexual My Neighbor? Another Christian View.* San Francisco: Harper San Francisco, 1978.

Schur, Edwin M. *The Americanization of Sex.* Philadelphia: Temple University Press, 1988.

_____. *Crimes Without Victims: Deviant Behavior and Public Policy.* Englewood Cliffs, NJ: PrenticeHall, 1965.

_____, and Hugo Adam Bedau.*Victimless Crimes: Two Sides of a Controversy.* Englewood Cliffs, NJ: PrenticeHall, 1974.

Scott, George Ryley. *Curious Customs of Sex and Marriage.* London: Torchstream Books, 1953.

Scott, Peter Dale, and Jonathan Marshall. *Cocaine Politics: Drugs, Armies, and the CIA in Central America.* Berkeley: University of California Press, 1991.

Shaw, George Bernard. *Plays by George Bernard Shaw.* New York: Penguin, Signet Classic, 1960.

Sheehy, Gail. *Hustling: Prostitution in Our Wide Open Society.* New York: Delacorte Press, 1973.

Shenkman, Richard. *"I Love Paul Revere, Whether He Rode or Not."* New York: HarperCollins, HarperPerennial, 1992.

_____. *Legends, Lies & Cherished Myths of American History.* New York: Harper & Row, 1988.

Shepherd, Chuck, John J. Kohut, and Roland Sweet. *More News of the Weird.* New York: Penguin, Plume, 1990.

Shipley, Joseph T. *Dictionary of Word Origins.* New York: The Philosophical Library, 1945.

Silberman, Charles E. *Criminal Violence, Criminal Justice.* New York: Random, 1978.

Sloan, Irving J. *Our Violent Past: An American Chronicle.* New York: Random House, 1970.

Smith, Jane S. *Patenting the Sun: Polio and the Salk Vaccine.* New York: William Morrow, 1990.

Smith, Malcolm E. *With Love, From Dad: Why Haven't Marijuana Smokers Been Told These Facts?* Smithtown, NY: Suffolk House, n.d.

Sowle, Claude R., ed. *Police Power and Individual Freedom.* Chicago: Aldine, 1962.

Spiegelman, Art, and Bob Schneider, eds. *Whole Grains: A Book of Quotations.* New York: Douglas Links, 1973.

Spong, John Shelby. *Rescuing the Bible from Fundamentalism: A Bishop Rethinks the Meaning of Scripture.* San Francisco: Harper San Francisco, 1991.

Spoto, Donald. *Lawrence Olivier: A Biography.* New York: HarperCollins, 1992.

Stevenson, Elizabeth. *Babbitts and Bohemians: The American 1920s.* New York: Macmillan, 1967.

Stone, Oliver, and Zachary Sklar. *JFK: The Book of the Film.* "The Documented Screenplay." New York: Applause Books, 1992.

Swezey, Stuart, and Brian King, eds. *AMOK: Fourth Dispatch.* Los Angeles: AMOK, 1991.

Sykes, Charles J. *A Nation of Victims: The Decay of the American Character.* New York: St. Martin's Press, 1992.

Szasz, Thomas. *Ceremonial Chemistry: The Ritual Persecution of Drugs, Addicts, and Pushers.* Revised edition. Holmes Beach, FL: Learning Publications, 1985.

_____. *Our Right to Drugs: The Case for a Free Market.* New York: Praeger, 1992.

Toklas, Alice B. *The Alice B. Toklas Cook Book.* New York: Harper & Row, 1954.

Trager, James. *The People's Chronology: A Year by Year Record of Human Events from Prehistory to the Present.* Rev. Ed. New York: Henry Holt and Co., 1992.

Trebach, Arnold S. *The Heroin Solution.* New Haven: Yale University Press, 1982.

U.S. Department of Commerce. *Historical Statistics of the United States: Colonial Times to 1970,* Part 1. Bicentennial Edition. Washington, 1975.

U.S. Department of Commerce. *Historical Statistics of the United States: Colonial Times to 1970,* Part 2. White Plains, NY: Kraus International Publications, 1989.

U.S. Department of Commerce. *Statistical Abstract of the United States 1992.* 112th Edition. Washington, 1992.

U.S. Department of Justice. *Bureau of Justice Statistics, National Corrections Reporting Program, 1988.* Washington, 1989.

U.S. Department of Justice. *Census of Local Jails, 1988.* Vol. I. Selected Findings; Methodology and Summary Tables. Washington, 1989.

U.S. Department of Justice. *Correctional Populations in the United States, 1988.* Washington, 1989.

U.S. Department of Justice. *Data Collections Available From the National Archive of Criminal Justice Data.* Update: Summer 1992. Washington: National Archive of Criminal Justice Data, 1992.

U.S. Department of Justice. *Drugs and Crime Facts, 1991.* Washington, 1992.

U.S. Department of Justice. *Drugs, Crime, and the Justice System: A National Report from the Bureau of Justice Statistics,* December 1992, NJC133652. Washington, 1992.

U.S. Department of State. *International Narcotics Control Strategy Report, March, 1992.* Washington, 1992.

U.S. Department of the Treasury. *Protecting America: The Effectiveness of the Federal Armed Career Criminal Statute. An Assessment Conducted by the Bureau of Alcohol, Tobacco and Firearms, March, 1992.* Washington, 1992.

U.S. Sentencing Commission. *Annual Report 1991.* Washington, 1992.

Vergon, Vertner. *Abuse of Privilege: How to Deal with Lawyers.* Los Angeles: Exeter, 1986.

Vidal, Gore. *United States: Essays 1952-1992.* New York: Random House, 1993.

Wasserman, Harvey. *America Born & Reborn.* New York: Macmillan, Collier, 1983.

Watts, Alan. *The Book on the Taboo Against Knowing Who You Are.* New York: Random House, Vintage Books, 1989.

White, Larry C. *Merchants of Death: The American Tobacco Industry.* New York: William Morrow, Beech Tree Books, 1988.

Winokur, Jon, ed. *A Curmudgeon's Garden of Love.* New York: Penguin, New American Library, 1989.

_____, ed. *The Portable Curmudgeon.* New York: Penguin, New American Library, 1987.

_____, ed. *The Portable Curmudgion Redux.* New York: Penguin, Dutton, 1992.

_____, ed.*True Confessions.* New York: Penguin, Dutton, 1992.

Wright, John W., ed. *The Universal Almanac 1993.* Kansas City: Andrews and McMeel, 1992.

Wyly, James. *The Phallic Quest: Priapus and Masculine Inflation.* Toronto: Inner City Books, 1989.

Zahniser, J. D., comp. *And Then She Said . . . Quotations by Women for Every Occasion.* Second Ed. St. Paul, MN: Caillech Press, 1990.

_____, comp. *And Then She Said . . . More Quotations by Women for Every Occasion.* St. Paul, MN: Caillech Press, 1990.

Zall, P. M., ed. *Ben Franklin Laughing: Anecdotes from Original Sources by and about Benjamin Franklin.* Berkeley: University of California Press, 1980.

INDEX

A

A&P 467
ABC Radio Network 623
Abzug, Bella 379
Acheson, Dean 423
Adam 132, 230, 397
Adams, Edie 42
Adams, Franklin Pierce 444
Adams, John 60-61, 65, 79, 103, 111, 117
Adams, Samuel 117
Addams Family 211-212
Addiction........................... 300
  10% chance 307-308
  amphetamines 295
  caffeine 39, 295
  cocaine 295
  crack 304-305
  effect of education to prevent 311-313
  falling in love 39
  morphine 290
  myth that marijuana leads to heroin 285
  rate not rising...................... 308
  religion 40
  transference of 47
  work 40
Addis, Don 452
Adler, Polly......................... 158
Adorno, Eli 185
Adultery 525-526
  illegal in twenty-seven states 367
  in Laws of Moses 506
  of U.S. Presidents 41-42
Agnosticism......................... 507
AIDS............................. 14, 186
  growth in heterosexual population 584
  not God's curse upon homosexuals 400
Alcohol
  abuse in '50s 559
  abuse rate 307
  and Jesus.......................... 474
  and Satan 474, 477-478, 482, 487
  consumption by women.............. 496
  consumption in colonies 473
  early religious opposition
    in U.S. 474-475, 477
  grain 485
  home brewing during Prohibition 485
  importing during Prohibition.......... 484
  medicinal value......... 476-477, 486, 495
  poisoning during Prohibition.......... 494
  popularized by cocktail 496

  related traffic deaths................. 566
  use compared to drug use
    and abuse 595, 597
Alcoholics Anonymous 248
Alcoholism
  epidemic during Prohibition........... 498
Alexander the Great 374
Allen, Woody 115, 361, 367,
                379, 401, 404, 501
Almodovar, Norma Jean............ 341-342
Alpert, Richard.................... 318-319
Amendment
  Fifth 87
  First 99, 122
  Fourth 88
  Third 89
American Academy of Pediatrics......... 590
American Association for
  Public Health...................... 151
American Baptist Churches............. 402
American Brands..................... 604
American Cancer Society 589,
                 593-594, 610
American Civil Liberties Union
  (ACLU) 91, 93, 402, 547, 645
American Conference on Religious
  Movements 402
American Council on Science
  and Health........................ 588
American dream 9
American Heart Association 608, 610
American Heritage..................... 642
American Hospital Association 327
American Lung Association............. 610
American Magazine.................... 283
American Medical
  Association 285-286, 327, 334
American Medicine..................... 277
Americanism 51
AMOK Assault Video 357
Amphetamines
  addiction 295
  early use 294
  effects 294
  injecting.......................... 295
Anacin 337
Andrew 522
Andrews, Julie 363
Angels in America 580
Anheuser-Busch...................... 604
Anslinger, Harry.......... 279-280, 282-285,
                 287-289, 624

C

AIN'T NOBODY'S BUSINESS IF YOU DO

M

AIN'T NOBODY'S BUSINESS IF YOU DO

P

AIN'T NOBODY'S BUSINESS IF YOU DO

I have suffered
from being misunderstood
but I would have suffered
a hell of a lot more
if I had been understood.

CLARENCE DARROW